MW00450419

THE JOSEPH SMITH PAPERS

Dean C. Jessee

Ronald K. Esplin

Richard Lyman Bushman

GENERAL EDITORS

PREVIOUSLY PUBLISHED

Journals, Volume 1: 1832–1839

FACSIMILE EDITION

THE
JOSEPH SMITH PAPERS

REVELATIONS AND TRANSLATIONS

&

MANUSCRIPT REVELATION BOOKS

Robin Scott Jensen
Robert J. Woodford
Steven C. Harper

VOLUME EDITORS

THE CHURCH
HISTORIAN'S
PRESS

Copyright © 2009 by Intellectual Reserve, Inc. All rights reserved.

THE CHURCH HISTORIAN'S PRESS is an imprint of the Church History Department
of The Church of Jesus Christ of Latter-day Saints, Salt Lake City, Utah,
and a trademark of Intellectual Reserve, Inc.

www.josephsmithpapers.org

The Joseph Smith Papers Project is endorsed by
the National Historical Publications and Records Commission.

Library of Congress Cataloging-in-Publication Data

Smith, Joseph, 1805–1844.
Revelations and translations / Dean C. Jessee, Ronald K. Esplin, Richard Lyman Bushman, general editors;
Robin Scott Jensen, Robert J. Woodford, Steven C. Harper, volume editors. — Facsimile ed.
p. cm. — (The Joseph Smith papers)
Includes bibliographical references.
ISBN 978-1-57008-850-6 (v. 1: hardbound: alk. paper)
1. The Church of Jesus Christ of Latter-day Saints—Sacred books. 2. Mormon Church—Sacred books.
3. The Church of Jesus Christ of Latter-day Saints—Doctrines. 4. Mormon Church—Doctrines.
I. Jessee, Dean C. II. Esplin, Ronald K. III. Bushman, Richard L.
IV. Title. V. Series: Smith, Joseph, 1805–1844. Joseph Smith papers.

BX8621.S52 2009   289.3'2—dc22   2009018416

Printed in the United States of America on acid-free paper.
10 9 8 7 6 5 4 3 2 1

Preface

The Joseph Smith Papers are being prepared under the auspices of the office of the historian of The Church of Jesus Christ of Latter-day Saints and published by The Church Historian's Press. Before its completion, the project will involve numerous staff members and many years of scholarly labor. The motivation to engage in this vast project comes from the great respect in which Latter-day Saints hold Joseph Smith as the church's founder and a modern prophet. We believe Joseph Smith will be better understood and appreciated if the documents he produced are available for all to examine.

In that spirit, the editorial staff has sought to present Smith's papers as accurately and completely as possible. We have gathered every known Joseph Smith document, verified each transcript at least three times, and provided extensive annotation on the historical context. The documents shed light on many dimensions of Joseph Smith's life and personality, his strengths and weaknesses, and the successes and failures of the movement he led.

Of the thousands of items in the Joseph Smith papers, his revelations are among the most significant and contested. According to his own account, the revelations came in a number of forms: visions, inspired words in the voice of God, what he called "translations," and impressions of the Holy Ghost. Although the revelations have religious meaning to us as Latter-day Saints, we present them in these volumes without comment on their ultimate source. In the tradition of documentary editing, our aim is simply to reproduce the documents and their historical setting so far as we can reconstruct it.

To assure balance and rigorous scholarly standards, we have consulted a national advisory board of distinguished scholars. With their guidance, we have sought to produce volumes on which scholars and Latter-day Saints can rely for accurate information.

The General Editors

The Joseph Smith Papers

EXECUTIVE COMMITTEE
Marlin K. Jensen
Paul K. Sybrowsky

EDITORIAL BOARD
Richard E. Turley Jr.
Steven L. Olsen
Max J. Evans

NATIONAL ADVISORY BOARD
Stephen J. Stein
Harry S. Stout
Mary-Jo Kline
Terryl L. Givens

MANAGING EDITOR
Ronald K. Esplin

PROGRAM MANAGER
David L. Willden

PROJECT ARCHIVIST
Jeffery O. Johnson

SENIOR RESEARCH AND REVIEW EDITOR
Richard L. Jensen

SENIOR PRODUCTION EDITOR
R. Eric Smith

EDITORS CONTRIBUTING TO THIS VOLUME

DOCUMENT SPECIALISTS
Dean C. Jessee
Christy Best
Glenn N. Rowe

RESEARCH AND REVIEW EDITOR
Richard Lloyd Anderson

PRODUCTION EDITORS
Sarah Gibby Peris
Riley M. Lorimer
Nathan N. Waite
Rachel Osborne

In Memory of
Larry H. Miller
Friend, Counselor, Benefactor
1944–2009

Contents

Detailed Contents of Revelation Books

The following table lists all documents that were inscribed in Revelation Books 1 and 2 in the order in which they appear in the manuscript books. The table also includes two documents that were later inserted into the manuscript books, thereby becoming associated with the books though not physically part of them. These documents are presented herein as appendixes. The first column gives the standard date of each item, based on careful study of original sources. The "standard date" is the date a revelation or other item was originally dictated or recorded. If that date is ambiguous or unknown, the standard date is the best approximation of that date, based on existing evidence. These standard dates do not always correspond to the dates written in the manuscript books. In cases in which two or more items bear the same date, such as April 1829, a letter of the alphabet has been appended, providing each item a unique editorial title—for example, April 1829–A or April 1829–B. A bracketed "D&C" reference to the 1981 edition of the Doctrine and Covenants is included for each item that was later canonized by The Church of Jesus Christ of Latter-day Saints.

The second column identifies the scribe or scribes who originally inscribed each document in these manuscript books. When more than one scribe inscribed an item, the scribe who wrote the most text in that item is listed first. These scribes are Oliver Cowdery, Orson Hyde, Sidney Rigdon, Joseph Smith, John Whitmer, and Frederick G. Williams (Thomas Bullock, William W. Phelps, and Willard Richards also inscribed historical notes in Revelation Book 2 in the 1840s). Because Revelation Book 1 is missing multiple leaves, several revelations originally inscribed in the manuscript book are no longer extant therein and are therefore not printed in this volume. These revelations can be determined from an index written in the manuscript book and are identified below. When an entire revelation is missing from the manuscript book, the scribe for that revelation is listed as "unknown" in the table. When only a portion of a revelation is extant, the name of the scribe who inscribed that portion is marked with an asterisk (*), indicating that the scribe for the nonextant portion cannot be positively identified.

The page numbers in the third column correspond to page numbers in this published volume, not to manuscript page numbers. No page number is listed in the table for missing revelations. Readers wishing to locate a particular revelation or other item may also consult the table titled Correspondence of Items in Revelation Books 1 and 2 with Selected Published Versions (pages 690–694 herein), which lists the items in chronological order and includes manuscript page numbers.

REVELATION BOOK 1

REVELATION BOOK 2

Timeline of Joseph Smith's Life

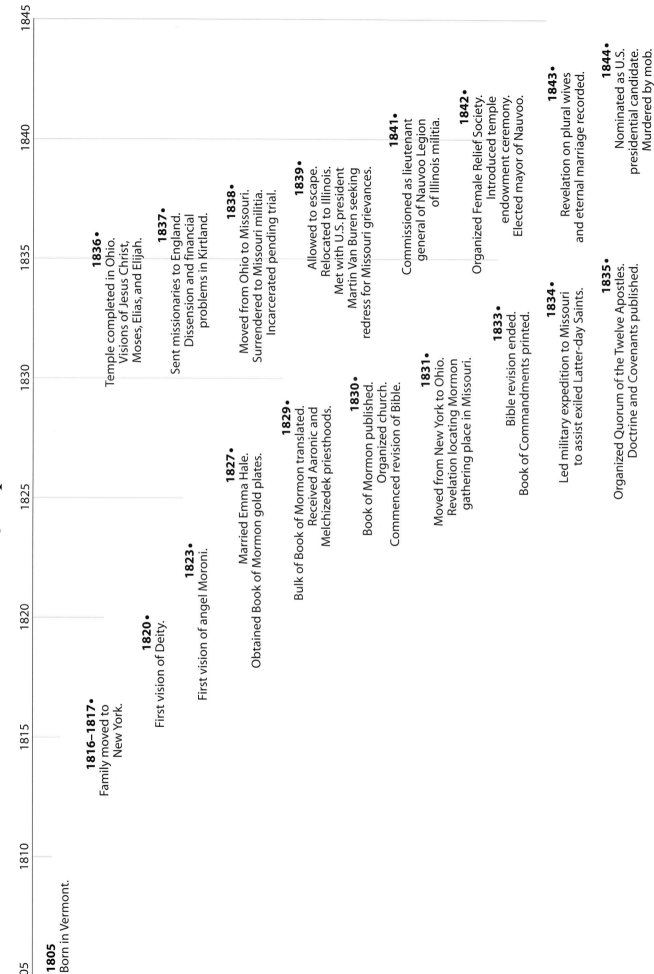

1805
Born in Vermont.

1816–1817
Family moved to New York.

1820
First vision of Deity.

1823
First vision of angel Moroni.

1827
Married Emma Hale.
Obtained Book of Mormon gold plates.

1829
Bulk of Book of Mormon translated.
Received Aaronic and
Melchizedek priesthoods.

1830
Book of Mormon published.
Organized church.
Commenced revision of Bible.

1831
Moved from New York to Ohio.
Revelation locating Mormon
gathering place in Missouri.

1833
Bible revision ended.
Book of Commandments printed.

1834
Led military expedition to Missouri
to assist exiled Latter-day Saints.

1835
Organized Quorum of the Twelve Apostles.
Doctrine and Covenants published.

1836
Temple completed in Ohio.
Visions of Jesus Christ,
Moses, Elias, and Elijah.

1837
Sent missionaries to England.
Dissension and financial
problems in Kirtland.

1838
Moved from Ohio to Missouri.
Surrendered to Missouri militia.
Incarcerated pending trial.

1839
Allowed to escape.
Relocated to Illinois.
Met with U.S. president
Martin Van Buren seeking
redress for Missouri grievances.

1841
Commissioned as lieutenant
general of Nauvoo Legion
of Illinois militia.

1842
Organized Female Relief Society.
Introduced temple
endowment ceremony.
Elected mayor of Nauvoo.

1843
Revelation on plural wives
and eternal marriage recorded.

1844
Nominated as U.S.
presidential candidate.
Murdered by mob.

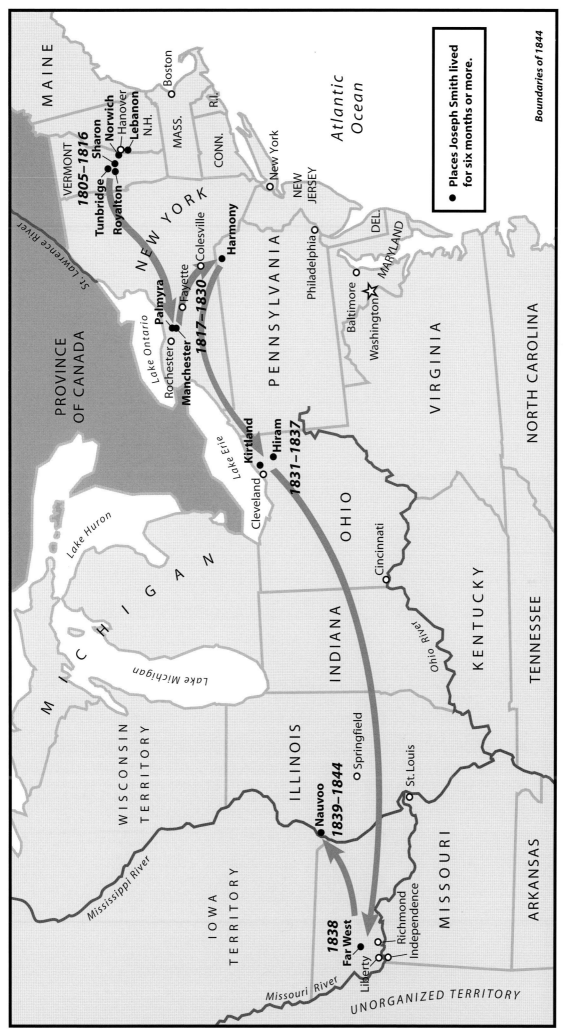

Joseph Smith's residences. Joseph Smith's major places of residence and the general direction of his migrations. (Design by John Hamer.)

Joseph Smith as Revelator and Translator

The Revelations and Translations series of *The Joseph Smith Papers* reproduces many of the earliest extant manuscripts of Joseph Smith's written revelations and translations, together with official editions of these documents published during his lifetime.[1] These publications include *The Book of Mormon: An Account Written by the Hand of Mormon, upon Plates Taken from the Plates of Nephi* (first edition, 1830); *A Book of Commandments, for the Government of the Church of Christ, Organized according to Law, on the 6th of April, 1830* (1833); and *Doctrine and Covenants of the Church of the Latter Day Saints: Carefully Selected from the Revelations of God* (first edition, 1835).[2] In early Latter-day Saint usage, the terms *revelation* and *translation* acquired specialized meaning. In this series, *revelation* generally refers to messages expressed in the first-person voice of Deity that Joseph Smith dictated to his scribes. The term may occasionally be applied to other texts Smith presented as being revealed or inspired. *Translation* refers to works such as the Book of Mormon that Joseph Smith said were based on sacred, ancient texts and translated "by the gift and power of God,"[3] that is, by a revelatory or inspired process and not by natural means. As used in this series, *translation* does not refer to conventional translations, such as Smith's exercises in the study of Hebrew.

A revelation to Joseph Smith dated 6 April 1830, the day he organized the Church of Christ, describes him as "a seer & Translator & Prop[h]et."[4] What did these titles

---

1. The earliest extant manuscripts of revelations not published in this series can be found elsewhere in *The Joseph Smith Papers.* Some of the revelations copied into Joseph Smith's journal, for example, are published only in the first volume of the Journals series because they do not exist as discrete manuscripts outside the journal. Similarly, reports of visions and visitations that exist only as part of other manuscript records will not appear in this series. For example, accounts of Joseph Smith's 1820 encounter with Deity will be found in other volumes, including the first volume of the Journals series and the first and second volumes of the History series.

2. In *The Joseph Smith Papers,* as in Latter-day Saint usage and in the field of Mormon studies, publication titles for Mormon scriptures are usually rendered in shortened form, without italics, consistent with widespread editorial treatment of the titles of scriptural works. Thus: Book of Mormon, Book of Commandments, Doctrine and Covenants (D&C). Some later editions of the Book of Mormon and the Doctrine and Covenants bear slightly different titles; for example, the 1844 edition of the Doctrine and Covenants is titled *The Doctrine and Covenants of the Church of Jesus Christ of Latter Day Saints; Carefully Selected from the Revelations of God.*

3. Preface to Book of Mormon, 1830 ed., iii; JS, Kirtland, OH, to N. C. Saxton, Rochester, NY, 4 Jan. 1833, in JS Letterbook 1, p. 17.

4. Revelation, 6 Apr. 1830, p. 27 herein [D&C 21:1]. The original name of the church is documented in the church's founding articles, dated four days after the church was organized. Other contemporary movements were similarly named, especially the newer restoration movements, such as those led by Barton Stone and Alexander Campbell. On 3 May 1834, Joseph Smith convened a conference that changed the church's name to the Church of the Latter Day Saints, reflecting emphasis on the restoration of the primitive gospel and anticipation of the millennial reign of Christ. This name remained until a revelation dated 26 April 1838 combined elements of both names into the Church of Jesus Christ of Latter Day Saints. (Articles and covenants, 10 Apr. 1830, p. 77 herein [D&C 20:1];

mean to him and his followers? His work in translating the Book of Mormon helped shape their understanding. The Book of Mormon tells of a king who asks Ammon, an emissary from another kingdom, if he can translate an ancient, indecipherable record in the king's possession. "I can assuredly tell thee, O king, of a man that can translate," Ammon replies, "for he hath wherewith that he can look, and translate all records that are of ancient date; and it is a gift from God." Such power constitutes a "seer," Ammon says, which he defines as "a revelator, and a prophet also." A seer by this definition possesses "great power given him from God" that enables him to know of things past, present, and future and to reveal what is otherwise unknowable. "Therefore," the Book of Mormon states, "he becometh a great benefit to his fellow beings."[5]

For early Latter-day Saints, Joseph Smith's roles as seer, translator, and prophet constituted such a gift from God. He and his followers considered his translation and the subsequent publication of the Book of Mormon a great benefit to humanity and regarded him as a servant of God who, like Moses, revealed God's commandments. "The fact is," Smith declared, "that by the power of God I translated the book of Mormon from hierogliphics; the knowledge of which was lost to the world. In which wonderful event, I stood alone, an unlearned youth, to combat the worldly wisdom and multiplied ignorance of eighteen centuries."[6] Such confidence in his calling characterized Smith's life.

Years before he published the Book of Mormon, young Joseph Smith had his first experience with Deity. Stirred by preachers and revivalists in upstate New York, by 1820 he became seriously concerned for what he called "the wellfare of my immortal Soul." Having come of age in an evangelical culture, he used the vocabulary of the revival preachers to describe how he became "convicted" of his sins and longed for an assurance of salvation. He turned to the Bible and found it reassuring but insufficient, and the denominations he observed did not seem to him to be "built upon the Gospel of Jesus Christ as recorded in the new testament."[7]

During this period of personal distress, Joseph Smith "cried unto the Lord for mercy." According to his account, his prayer was answered with a dramatic vision. "A pillar of light above the brightness of the sun at noon day come down from above and rested upon me," he wrote. "I was filled with the spirit of god and the Lord opened the heavens upon me and I saw the Lord and he spake unto me." Smith recounted that he "could find none that would believe" in his experience, and he apparently grew careful of how and to whom he recounted it. "Nevertheless," he said, "I pondered these things in my heart."[8] Though an 1830 statement apparently refers to the vision,[9] he waited a dozen years to write specifically about this experience.

Despite the intensely private nature of Joseph Smith's 1820 vision, his spiritual experiences gradually drew him into a public role. In September 1823, concerned about his standing before God, he again sought guidance through prayer. This time, Smith

---

Hatch, *Democratization of American Christianity,* 57, 71; "Communicated," *The Evening and the Morning Star,* May 1834, 160; Revelation, 26 Apr. 1838, in JS, Journal, 26 Apr. 1838, JS Collection, CHL [D&C 115:4].)

5. Book of Mormon, 1830 ed., 172–173 [Mosiah 8:13, 16, 18].

6. JS, Nauvoo, IL, to James Arlington Bennet, Arlington House, NY, 13 Nov. 1843, JS Collection, CHL.

7. JS History, ca. summer 1832, 2.

8. JS History, ca. summer 1832, 3.

9. Articles and covenants, 10 Apr. 1830, p. 77 herein [D&C 20:5].

later recounted, an angel calling himself Moroni appeared to him with a message that foretold his future roles as seer and translator. The angel spoke of a buried record "written upon gold plates, giving an account of the former inhabitants of this continent and the source from whence they sprang." The messenger said the record contained "the fullness of the everlasting Gospel . . . as delivered by the Saviour to the ancient inhabitants." The angel also spoke of "two stones in silver bows . . . deposited with the plates," saying "the possession and use of these stones was what constituted seers in ancient or former times."[10] Joseph Smith later used the Old Testament term "Urim and Thummim" to refer to such stones. In ancient Israel, certain stones were associated with the priestly or prophetic office and were considered a means of revelation.[11] By the early nineteenth century, however, Enlightenment rationalism had relegated such objects to the realm of superstition and magic. Smith rejected that judgment and may have seen a link between Old Testament revelatory practices and the folk religion of his region.[12]

Previous experience had prepared Joseph Smith to understand and believe the angel's words concerning the stones. Even before learning of the inscribed gold plates, he gained experience with a mysterious gift he had by which he could look into certain stones and, according to his mother's report, "discern things, that could not be seen by the natural eye."[13] Smith acknowledged that through this means he had occasionally sought buried treasure and frequently searched for lost property.[14] With his 1827 reception of the plates, the ancient seer stones (sometimes called interpreters), and a mandate from heaven, Joseph Smith embarked on a new path as a translator of ancient records.[15] He began translating the Book of Mormon in early 1828, and the translation, as he explained it, was made known to him through the stones or interpreters.[16] Whether using the interpreters or his own stone, he characterized as divine his power to look into seer stones and translate.[17]

In July 1828, Joseph Smith recorded a revelation for the first known time. In its earliest surviving manuscript form, the introduction to that revelation reads, "Given to Joseph the Seer after he had lost certan writings [of the Book of Mormon] which he had Translated by the gift & Power of God."[18] He had previously entrusted over a hundred pages of the dictated manuscript to a supporter named Martin Harris, who lost them. The loss devastated Smith, and he wept inconsolably upon learning the news.[19]

The revelation that resulted included both reproof and comfort. The text begins in the voice of a just God who rebukes Joseph Smith for boasting and repeatedly neglecting his counsel. The tone of the revelation turns midway, however, with the words "but remember God is merciful therefore repent of that which thou hast done & he will

---

10. JS History, vol. A-1, 5.

11. See Van Dam, *Urim and Thummim,* 216.

12. Bushman, *Believing History,* 241–242.

13. Lucy Mack Smith, History, 1845, 95.

14. Trial record, Bainbridge, NY, in "A Document Discovered," *Utah Christian Advocate,* Jan. 1886, 1.

15. JS History, vol. A-1, 8, 13; Bushman, *Believing History,* 240–242.

16. Oliver Cowdery, Norton, OH, to William W. Phelps, 7 Sept. 1834, *LDS Messenger and Advocate,* Oct. 1834, 1:14. Joseph Smith's followers, notably Brigham Young, subsequently used the term *seer stone* to describe the instrument he used to translate and receive revelations. ("History of Brigham Young," *Deseret News,* 10 Mar. 1858, 3.)

17. JS, "Church History," *Times and Seasons,* 1 Mar. 1842, 3:707; see also preface to Book of Mormon, 1830 ed., iii–iv.

18. Introduction to Revelation, July 1828, p. 9 herein [D&C 3].

19. Lucy Mack Smith, History, 1844–1845, bk. 7, [6]–[7].

only cause thee to be afflicted for a season." Smith is assured that he is "still chosen & will again be called to the work." Still, he is admonished, "except Thou do this thou shalt be delivered up & become as other men & have no more gift."[20] One historian has said that this revelation "gave the first inkling of how Joseph would speak in his prophetic voice. The speaker stands above and outside Joseph, sharply separated emotionally and intellectually. The rebuke of Joseph is as forthright as the denunciation of Martin Harris. There is no effort to conceal or rationalize, no sign of Joseph justifying himself to prospective followers."[21]

Joseph Smith dictated most of the Book of Mormon between April and June 1829.[22] When the manuscript was finished, he contracted with printer E. B. Grandin of Palmyra, New York, to print and bind five thousand copies. The book went on sale in March 1830. By that spring, dozens outside of Joseph Smith's family had accepted him as a divinely inspired revelator and translator, and the number soon grew. Such a group of believers was essential for his texts to function as scripture: "Texts without . . . an interactive group are mere texts," wrote historian Stephen Stein, "ancient texts perhaps, or even modern texts, but not scripture."[23] After the Book of Mormon was published and Smith organized a church, the number of converts continued to grow, beginning with many of the women and men who knew him best, who "accepted the voice in the revelations as the voice of God, investing in the revelations the highest authority, even above Joseph Smith's counsel. In the revelations, they believed, God himself spoke, not a man."[24]

Witnesses described how Joseph Smith captured the revealed words in written texts, giving them permanence. "The scribe seats himself at a desk or table, with pen, ink and paper," recounted one scribe. "The subject of enquiry being understood, the Prophet and Revelator enquires of God. He spiritually sees, hears and feels, and then speaks as he is moved upon by the Holy Ghost, the 'thus saith the Lord,' sentence after sentence, and waits for his amanuenses to write and then read aloud each sentence."[25] As with the 1820 theophany, the revelations preserved in his manuscripts are mostly dialogic. Smith posed questions to Deity, who answered directly. Pressing questions frequently catalyzed revelation, and the divine response contained specific answers. This form of revelation also pervades the Book of Mormon, where "prayer frequently and dramatically evokes an answer that is impossible to mistake as anything other than an individualized, dialogic response."[26]

Many of Joseph Smith's revelations share common threads. Pronounced themes in the first revelations—such as apostasy, fulfillment of biblical prophecy, and the imminent return of Christ—reappear frequently in many of the later revelations. The revelations

---

20. Revelation, July 1828, pp. 9–11 herein [D&C 3:10–11].

21. Bushman, *Rough Stone Rolling,* 69; see also Bushman, *Believing History,* 254.

22. See Givens, *By the Hand of Mormon,* 26–37.

23. Stein, "America's Bibles," 171.

24. Bushman, *Believing History,* 258–259.

25. William E. McLellin, "Revelations," *Ensign of Liberty,* Aug. 1849, 98–99; see also William E. McLellin, Independence, MO, to Joseph Smith III, [Plano, IL], July 1872, typescript, Letters and Documents Copied from Originals in the Office of the Church Historian, Reorganized Church, CHL. Another witness remembered: "Each sentence was uttered slowly and very distinctly, and with a pause between each, sufficiently long for it to be recorded, by an ordinary writer, in long hand." (Pratt, *Autobiography,* 65.)

26. Givens, *By the Hand of Mormon,* 217; see also 218–220.

also follow the New Testament pattern of quoting and paraphrasing earlier scripture; words, phrases, and ideas found in the Old and New Testaments and in the Book of Mormon are diffused throughout. Revelations addressed to numerous individual followers repeat a commission to proclaim to all humankind the message of the gospel as revealed to Joseph Smith.

His work on the Book of Mormon was not Joseph Smith's only activity as a translator. In April 1829, he envisioned, translated, and dictated the text of an ancient parchment that included an expanded version of John 21 that he said had been written and hidden by the apostle John.[27] Soon after organizing the church the following year, he turned his attention to what he called a "new Translation" of the Bible, perhaps best described as an inspired revision (and in some cases expansion) of biblical passages.[28] Unlike contemporaries who produced more accessible English Bibles from Greek, Hebrew, or Latin versions, he read the King James Version and "translated" it by adding glosses, rearranging clauses, and at times appending entire pages of revealed text. The most significant of these additions came between June and December 1830 when Smith dictated a text expanding on the book of Genesis. Though this translation of the Bible occupied much of his time from June 1830 to July 1833, he did not live to see the publication of the entire manuscript. The earliest manuscripts of this translation will be published in this Revelations and Translations series.

In 1835, Joseph Smith acquired manuscripts written on Egyptian scrolls, along with several smaller papyrus documents and four Egyptian mummies. He dictated a translation of some of this material to scribe Warren Parrish. As with the Book of Mormon, Smith claimed no knowledge of the ancient language but, as Parrish noted, "claimed to receive it by direct inspiration from Heaven."[29] As a result of these labors, he published a translation of "some ancient Records . . . purporting to be the writings of Abraham" in the church newspaper *Times and Seasons* in 1842, leaving the impression that more was forthcoming.[30]

Preserving his revelations and translations was among Joseph Smith's earliest priorities. Smith's letters from the 1820s did not survive and neither his journal nor his history predates 1832,[31] but from the beginning, he worked to preserve and publish his revelations and translations. He copyrighted the Book of Mormon in 1829 and closely monitored its publication, and he took care to preserve the manuscripts used for publication.[32] By summer 1830, he and convert John Whitmer "began to arrange and

27. Account of John, Apr. 1829–C, pp. 17–19 herein [D&C 7].

28. JS, Kirtland, OH, to "Dear Brethren," [Missouri], 15 June 1835, JS Collection, CHL.

29. Warren Parrish, Kirtland, OH, 5 Feb. 1838, letter to the editor, Painesville, OH, *Painesville Republican,* 15 Feb. 1838, [3].

30. "The Book of Abraham," *Times and Seasons,* 1 Mar. 1842, 3:703–706; 15 Mar. 1842, 3:719–722; 16 May 1842, 3:783–784 [Abraham 1–5]; "Notice," *Times and Seasons,* 1 Feb. 1843, 4:95.

31. Though some minutes survive from as early as 1830, the first minute book, the first letterbook, the first journal, and the first effort at writing a history all date from 1832.

32. Copyright, 11 June 1829, Copyright Registration Forms, 1829–1870, Copyright Office, Library of Congress, Washington DC; retained copy at CHL; see also Wadsworth, "Copyright Laws and the 1830 Book of Mormon," 77–99; and Bushman, *Rough Stone Rolling,* 80–83. Joseph Smith preserved both the original manuscript and the printer's manuscript, or second copy, well past the publication of the Book of Mormon in 1830. He placed the original manuscript in the cornerstone of the Nauvoo House in 1841, and it was removed in 1882. Though significantly damaged, about thirty percent of this manuscript is extant, most of which is held at the Church History Library. The printer's manuscript was in Oliver Cowdery's custody until his death in 1850, followed by David Whitmer's custody until his death in 1888. It was eventually sold to the Reorganized Church of Jesus Christ of Latter

copy the revelations" received to that point.[33] The receipt, transcription, entry into manuscript books, and publication of the revelations frequently occupied his attention. The book referred to herein as Revelation Book 1 is the earliest extant fruit of those labors, likely dating from early 1831, though possibly from 1830. This text was penned mainly by John Whitmer. He and Oliver Cowdery carried Revelation Book 1 to Missouri in November 1831, where the revelations were to be published. By early 1832, Smith and his scribes had procured another book, designated herein as Revelation Book 2, in which to record further words from heaven. Both manuscript books are published in this volume.

Though loose manuscript copies of some revelations also circulated, Revelation Book 1 became the principal basis for the Book of Commandments, and Revelation Books 1 and 2 became the basis for the 1835 edition of the Doctrine and Covenants. The revelations recorded in these two manuscript books date from 1828 to 1834, the period when Joseph Smith's written revelations were most frequent.[34] By introducing offices and defining roles for presidents, apostles, bishops, and priesthood quorums, these early revelations informed the creation of an institutional church. One of the last items in Revelation Book 1 is a heading intended for minutes of the February 1834 organization of a standing "high counsel" established to provide counsel and handle difficulties. Such councils were expected to administer church business according to revelations already received and to seek further revelation for themselves—always, however, within their particular purview, the bounds of which were set by the canonized revelations.[35]

The revelations and translations of Joseph Smith have made him known worldwide. Since the time these texts were recorded, they have been revered as God's word and dismissed as frauds, considered canonical and regarded as blasphemous. Reflecting in 1841 on Smith's production of such texts, one writer noted that "it is difficult to imagine a more difficult literary task than to write what may be termed a continuation of the Scriptures."[36] But producing scripture, Joseph Smith believed, was a fundamental component of his role as a revelator and translator, and this series will provide unprecedented access to the material that resulted from his efforts.

Day Saints and is held at the Community of Christ Library-Archives. (See Jessee, "Original Book of Mormon Manuscript," 264–265; Skousen, *Original Manuscript,* 6–7; and Skousen, *Printer's Manuscript,* 4.)

33. JS History, vol. A-1, 50.

34. Later revelations are sprinkled throughout Joseph Smith's journals and record books as well as the papers of bishops, apostles, and other followers. Although several revelations date from the last decade of Smith's life (1835–1844), the written texts from this period are relatively few. Sermons and temple rituals that he established in that decade hint at important unrecorded revelations beyond the revelatory foundation already in place by 1835 that largely established doctrine and church organization.

35. See Bushman, *Rough Stone Rolling,* 252–253.

36. Josephine, "The Book of Mormon," *Times and Seasons,* 1 Feb. 1841, 2:306.

Manuscript Revelation Books

Joseph Smith understood how important his revelations were to the work in which he was engaged. He marveled at them, defended them, and ensured that many were recorded, copied, edited, and published.[1] And he and his followers acted on them, often at great cost. When the revelations called for a new gathering place despite inadequate resources, they responded. When the revelations commanded a small community with little means to construct an impressive House of the Lord, they complied. Joseph Smith's revelations restored, organized, and built The Church of Jesus Christ of Latter-day Saints and oriented thousands who converted to it in his lifetime and millions since.

The earliest years of Mormon record keeping (1828–1831) consisted almost exclusively of recording revelatory texts. During that period Joseph Smith translated and published the 584-page Book of Mormon, began work on a revision of the Bible, and recorded many revelations. He dictated most of his written revelations between 1828 and 1834, and in summer 1830 he and John Whitmer began to arrange and copy them.[2] Joseph Smith and his associates continued this effort for the next several years, ultimately compiling the revelations, along with a few additional documents, in the two manuscript books that are featured in this volume of the Revelations and Translations series. In *The Joseph Smith Papers,* these manuscript books are given the editorial titles Revelation Book 1 and Revelation Book 2, consistent with the widespread documentary editing practice of referring to documents by generic titles.

Revelation Book 1, the spine of which is labeled "Book of Commandments and Revelations,"[3] was procured sometime during the first year after the church was founded in April 1830. The manuscript book, which was initially used to preserve revelation texts, was taken from Ohio to Missouri in November 1831 for use in publishing the revelations. Church leaders in Missouri continued to update the volume when they received copies of revelations sent by mail or in person from Ohio. Containing copies of more than one hundred revelations, Revelation Book 1 was the source text for multiple revelations published in the church's first newspaper, *The Evening and the Morning*

---

1. See Minute Book 2, entries for 1, 2, 8, and 12 Nov. 1831; JS, Kirtland, OH, to Edward Partridge et al., Clay Co., MO, 30 Mar. 1834, in Cowdery, Letterbook, 30–36.

2. JS History, vol. A-1, 50.

3. This title captures two terms that Joseph Smith and his followers used to refer to texts they viewed as divine communications. *Commandment* was used perhaps more frequently than *revelation* into the early 1830s; the latter term became standard in the mid-1830s. Usage patterns in Revelation Book 1 and some other early documents suggest that in the earliest years, Latter-day Saints may have seen subtle differences in the meaning of these terms. *Commandment* may have denoted communications that required action or obedience, whereas *revelation* may have referred to communications on doctrinal topics or "truth" more generally.

Star, in 1832 and 1833 and in the canonical compilation called the Book of Commandments (1833). After being returned to Ohio by May 1835, it also served as a supplemental source text for an expanded collection of revelations known as the Doctrine and Covenants, first published in 1835. Revelation Book 2, the cover of which is labeled "Book of Revelations" and which has often been referred to as the Kirtland Revelation Book, was obtained for use in Ohio shortly after Revelation Book 1 was taken from Ohio to Missouri. It too was used for preserving and later publishing revelation texts. Containing about fifty copied revelations, many of which were also copied into Revelation Book 1 in Missouri, this manuscript book was an important source text for the 1835 Doctrine and Covenants.

This volume presents Revelation Books 1 and 2 in their entirety. Revelations and other documents copied into them are presented as they appear in each book, and the books are published as a complete record with textual annotation only. In addition to contemporaneous emendations, later redactions made to the revelations are represented, allowing readers to analyze the process of their preparation for publication as well as their composition. In contrast, the Documents series of *The Joseph Smith Papers* will present each Joseph Smith revelation separately, placed in chronological order with other documents of various genres (correspondence, sermons, articles in periodicals, and so forth). It will present as precisely as possible the text as originally dictated and recorded, ignoring later redactions. That series will include the earliest and best extant version of each revelation, providing contextual annotation and a historical introduction for each. Volumes in the Documents series will also contain supplementary resources to aid in understanding the texts, including a detailed chronology, maps, a biographical directory, and an index. Users of the present volume should consult the Documents series for information about the setting and significance of individual revelations.

In most cases, the two manuscript books featured in this volume contain the earliest extant revelation texts. They also include texts for which there is no other known version, such as a revelation on securing a copyright for the Book of Mormon in Canada.[4] Most of the revelations in these two books were published as Latter-day Saint scripture during Smith's lifetime; others were later canonized by vote of the general membership of the church. Nine of the revelations in these two books have not been canonized by The Church of Jesus Christ of Latter-day Saints.

By late 1831, Joseph Smith was planning to publish the revelations. A dramatic expansion of print culture in America meant that a wide variety of religious and political groups were publishing newspapers and books, reaching wider audiences than ever before. Latter-day Saint missionaries valued the revelations and tried to use them in their ministry, but they had to rely on handwritten copies that they could obtain only at church headquarters or from other missionaries who had copies. As the number of converts increased, so did the need to publish the revelations. Already a revelation had assigned the experienced editor William W. Phelps to be a printer for the church.[5] Joseph Smith convened a conference on 1 November 1831 in Hiram, Ohio, to plan publication of the revelations in book form. At this conference, Oliver Cowdery asked "how many copies of the Book of commandments it was the will of the Lord should be

---

4. Revelation, ca. early 1830, pp. 31–33 herein.
5. Revelation, 20 July 1831, p. 161 herein [D&C 57:11].

published in the first edition of that work." The conference determined to publish ten thousand copies[6] and later voted that the revelations should "be prized by this Conference to be worth to the Church the riches of the whole Earth."[7]

The value placed on the revelations, and especially the plan to publish them, would enlarge a divide between Latter-day Saints and the mainstream Christian world for which the Bible was the complete and final word of God. The Book of Mormon, sometimes derided as "the Mormon Bible" because believers claimed it to be a companion volume of ancient scripture comparable to the Holy Bible, first opened the fissure. Reducing modern declarations of God to written words and then publishing them as "what may be termed a continuation of the Scriptures" must have seemed a presumptuous enterprise and further highlighted the Latter-day Saints' rejection of the notion of a closed canon and their belief that God could speak to man in any age.[8] While many of their Christian contemporaries believed that divine guidance was still possible, most believed that the Bible was the terminal formulation of scripture.

Preparing the revelation texts for publication—indeed the very act of capturing revelations in writing—also raised important issues for believers about the relationship between divine communication and human language.[9] At the November 1831 conference, Joseph Smith dictated a revelation, designated as a preface to the anticipated book, that declared, "I am God & have spoken it[.] these commandments are of me & were given unto my Servents in their weakness after the manner of their Language that they might come to understanding." Presented to the elders attending the conference, this revelation provided context for discussion of issues related to the authenticity and language of the revelations.[10]

The discussion apparently arose in response to Joseph Smith's solicitation of an endorsement for the proposed publication. Smith stated, "The Lord [has] bestowed a great blessing upon us in giving commandments and revelations." He asked the men present "what testimony they were willing to attach to these commandments which should shortly be sent to the world." After "a number of the brethren arose and said that they were willing to testify to the world that they knew that they were of the Lord," Smith oversaw the composition of a statement confirming that testimony. It stated that they had received divine inspiration assuring them that the revelations intended for publication were "given by inspiration of God & are profitable for all men & are verily true."[11] Smith's history notes that "some conversation was had concerning Revelation and language."[12] By the following morning, it was apparent that some of the elders lacked the divine confirmation that the written testimony required them to affirm. Seeking a solution to the impasse, Joseph Smith dictated an additional revelation. It noted the elders' disappointment and chided them for wishing to improve upon Smith's imperfect language: "Your eyes have been upon my Servent Joseph & his

6. Minute Book 2, 1 Nov. 1831.

7. Minute Book 2, 12 Nov. 1831.

8. Josephine, "The Book of Mormon," *Times and Seasons,* 1 Feb. 1841, 2:306; see also Givens, *By the Hand of Mormon,* chap. 7.

9. See Bushman, *Rough Stone Rolling,* 173–175.

10. Revelation, 1 Nov. 1831–B, p. 225 herein [D&C 1:24].

11. Minute Book 2, 1 Nov. 1831; Testimony, ca. 1 Nov. 1831, p. 215 herein.

12. JS History, vol. A-1, 161.

language you have known & his imperfections you have known & you have sought in your hearts knowlege that you might express beyond his language."[13]

This revelation also provided a novel way for them to test the divine origin of the revelations that were about to be published. It invited the wisest man present to produce a text on par with the "least" of the manuscript revelations. Failure to produce an equivalent text would be evidence that Joseph Smith's revelations were from God. The men who were present would then be responsible to testify of them: "if you cannot make one like unto it ye are under condemnation if ye do not bear [record] that it is true for ye know that there is no unrighteousness in it & that which is righteous cometh down from above."[14] Joseph Smith's later history tells that William E. McLellin, who the preceding week had served as scribe as Smith dictated, "endeavored to write a commandment like unto one of the least of the Lord's, but failed."[15] According to the history, the elders who observed the proceedings responded with renewed faith "in the truth of the commandments and revelations which the Lord had given to the Church through my instrumentality; and . . . signified a willingness to bear testimony of their truth to all the world."[16]

McLellin and four others signed the statement, and John Whitmer copied both the text and their names into Revelation Book 1, where thirteen additional men later signed it in support.[17] The men present at the conference "arose in turn and bore witness to the truth of the Book of Commandments. After which br. Joseph Smith jr arose & expressed his feelings & gratitude."[18]

Joseph Smith undoubtedly appreciated this demonstration of faith in his revelations. He stood in awe of the charge God had given him, calling it "an awful responsibility to write in the name of the Lord."[19] The revelation introducing the soon-to-be-published Book of Commandments affirmed that God "called upon [his] Servent Joseph & spake unto him from heaven & gave him commandment," and another revelation declared, "This generation shall have my word through you."[20] By testifying to the divine origin of the revelations and signing a formal statement of support, believers helped shoulder this "awful responsibility."

Preparing the revelation texts for publication was no simple matter. Joseph Smith dictated the words of these texts to a scribe, who committed them to paper. A scribe then copied them into the manuscript books, portions of which were eventually typeset and published as scripture. Sometimes the process was more complicated. For example, Joseph Smith dictated a revelation on 6 December 1832 as Sidney Rigdon wrote

---

13. Revelation, 2 Nov. 1831, p. 203 herein [D&C 67:5].

14. Revelation, 2 Nov. 1831, p. 203 herein [D&C 67:7–9].

15. JS History, vol. A-1, 162; see also McLellin, Journal, 29 Oct. 1831.

16. JS History, vol. A-1, 162.

17. No original of the statement is extant. In Revelation Book 1, the signatures of those who signed the statement at the Ohio conference (Sidney Rigdon, Orson Hyde, William E. McLellin, Luke Johnson, and Lyman Johnson) are all written in John Whitmer's handwriting. The individuals who signed the statement after it was copied into Revelation Book 1 are Reynolds Cahoon, John Corrill, Parley P. Pratt, Harvey Whitlock, Lyman Wight, John Murdock, Calvin Beebe, Zebedee Coltrin, Joshua Fairchild, Peter Dustin, Newel Knight, Levi Hancock, and Thomas B. Marsh. (Testimony, ca. 1 Nov. 1831, p. 215 herein.)

18. Minute Book 2, 1 and 2 Nov. 1831.

19. JS History, vol. A-1, 162.

20. Revelation, 1 Nov. 1831–B, p. 225 herein [D&C 1:17]; Revelation, Mar. 1829, in Doctrine and Covenants 32:3, 1835 ed. [D&C 5:10].

it. Frederick G. Williams then made a copy of the text, Orson Hyde copied that copy, and John Whitmer then recorded Hyde's copy into Revelation Book 1, from which it was edited for publication.[21] It is unknown how many of the revelations in Revelation Books 1 and 2 made such an arduous textual journey, but it appears that few, if any, of the revelations is an original in pristine form. Changes both intentional and inadvertent were made throughout the process.

Joseph Smith and his followers considered his revelations to be true in the sense that they communicated the mind and will of God, not infallible in an idealized sense of literary flawlessness. "The revelations were not God's diction, dialect, or native language," historian Richard Bushman has written. "They were couched in language suitable to Joseph's time."[22] Smith and others appointed by revelation (including Oliver Cowdery, Sidney Rigdon, John Whitmer, and William W. Phelps)[23] edited the revelations based on the same assumption that informed their original receipt: namely, that although Smith represented the voice of God condescending to speak to him, he was limited by a "crooked broken scattered and imperfect language."[24] The November 1831 conference resolved that he should "correct those errors or mistakes which he may discover by the holy Spirit."[25]

Although church leaders originally intended to print ten thousand copies of the Book of Commandments, limited resources forced a more modest plan of three thousand. But even that plan was upset, and only a few dozen incomplete copies of the Book of Commandments were actually produced. In July 1833, before William W. Phelps had finished the project, antagonistic citizens of Jackson County, Missouri, demanded that he cease printing what they called "pretended revelations from Heaven" and then destroyed the printing office and Phelps's home to ensure that printing stopped.[26] Most of the printed revelations were destroyed, but some uncut pages were preserved and later folded and bound. The manuscript book now known as Revelation Book 1, the primary source for the Book of Commandments, escaped the violence and was returned to Kirtland by May 1835. There, in September 1834, the high council had appointed and a general church council had approved a committee composed of Joseph Smith, Oliver Cowdery, Sidney Rigdon, and Frederick G. Williams to prepare the revelations for publication in a new compilation.[27] This endeavor resulted in the Doctrine and Covenants, which was first published in 1835.[28] Both Revelation Books 1 and 2 were used as sources for the 1835 Doctrine and Covenants.

---

21. Revelation, 6 Dec. 1832, p. 331 herein [D&C 86].

22. Bushman, *Rough Stone Rolling,* 174.

23. Revelation, 12 Nov. 1831, p. 221 herein [D&C 70:1–5].

24. JS, Kirtland, OH, to William W. Phelps, [Independence, MO], 27 Nov. 1832, in JS Letterbook 1, p. 4.

25. Minute Book 2, 8 Nov. 1831.

26. "Regulating the Mormonites," *Missouri Republican,* 9 Aug. 1833, [3]; see also "To His Excellency, Daniel Dunklin, Governor of the State of Missouri," *The Evening and the Morning Star,* Dec. 1833, 114; and John Whitmer, Independence, MO, to JS and Oliver Cowdery, [Kirtland, OH], 29 July 1833, in JS Letterbook 2, p. 52.

27. Minute Book 1, 24 Sept. 1834.

28. The change in name from the Book of Commandments to the Doctrine and Covenants reflects, in part, an expansion of content. The latter work added seven lectures or essays on the subject of faith delivered to the Elders School in Kirtland, Ohio, in the winter of 1834–1835. The lectures constitute part 1, or the "doctrine" portion, of the 1835 Doctrine and Covenants, which part bears the heading "Theology." The first essay in that part is titled "Lecture First On the doctrine of the church of the Latter Day Saints. Of Faith," and the other six essays are numbered in sequence. Part 2 of the 1835 Doctrine and Covenants is titled "Covenants and Commandments of the Lord, to his

Joseph Smith was absent on business in August 1835 when a general church assembly convened to approve the new collection of revelations as authoritative for the church. In the conference Oliver Cowdery held up an unbound copy of the Doctrine and Covenants and proceeded to take a vote of those present, beginning with the church leaders. William W. Phelps said that he had carefully examined the book of revelations and that it was "well arranged and calculated to govern the church in righteousness, [and] if followed would bring the members to see eye to eye." He further stated that he knew the revelations were true, "having received witness from Heaven & not from men." John Whitmer followed with a similar expression of certainty, testifying "that he was present when some of the revelations contained therein were given, and was satisfied they come from God."[29]

Expressions from representatives of each group of church officers present, from the presidency through the deacons, were followed by the votes of each group in support of the book. Levi Jackman, representing the high council of Missouri, said "he had examined as many of the revelations contained in the book as were printed in Zion, & as firmly believes them as he does the Book of Mormon or the Bible." William W. Phelps read a statement in behalf of the recently called Twelve Apostles, absent in the East on their first quorum assignment. Bishop Newel K. Whitney testified that he knew the revelations "were true, for God had testified to him by his holy Spirit, for many of them were given under his roof & in his presence through President Joseph Smith Junr." Thus continued the process by which Joseph Smith's followers formally consented to his revelations, giving them canonical status. The conference culminated with "all the members present, both male & female," giving "a decided voice in favor of it."[30]

Others besides Joseph Smith arose in the early American republic claiming heavenly visions, but his revelations were a class apart. He produced distinctive revelatory documents that explore, in the words of one historian, "realms of doctrine unimagined in traditional Christian theology."[31] Others wrote in terms that were comparatively more modest, even ambiguous.[32] As one scholar has noted, very few religious leaders "founded faiths based on new dispensations and discoveries [like] Joseph Smith's creation of Mormonism."[33] By committing his revelations to writing and then seeing them published and canonized, Smith provided his followers with new scripture based on biblical precedents. The manuscript books featured in this volume affirm his commitment to create and preserve sacred texts and constitute a fundamental part of his effort to document his dealings with God.

---

servants of the church of the Latter Day Saints" and comprises the revelations (that is, the "covenants" and "commandments") and other related items.

29. Minute Book 1, 17 Aug. 1835.

30. Minute Book 1, 17 Aug. 1835.

31. Holifield, *Theology in America,* 335.

32. Kirschner, "Tending to Edify, Astonish, and Instruct," 216, 229; see also Juster, *Doomsayers: Anglo-American Prophecy;* and Wallace, *Death and Rebirth of the Seneca.*

33. Abzug, *Cosmos Crumbling,* 6.

Editorial Method

The goal of the Joseph Smith Papers Project is to present verbatim transcripts of Joseph Smith's papers in their entirety, making available the most essential sources of his life and work and preserving the content of aging manuscripts from damage or loss. The papers include documents that were created by Joseph Smith, whether written or dictated by him or created by others under his direction, or that were owned by Smith, that is, received by him and kept in his office (as with incoming correspondence). Under these criteria—authorship and ownership—the project intends to publish, either in letterpress volumes or electronic form, every extant Joseph Smith document to which its editors can obtain access. Certain routine documents, such as some notes and certificates and some legal or business documents, will be calendared and published in their entirety online with only samples published in the letterpress edition. This volume—the first in the Revelations and Translations series and the first of a small number of volumes in *The Joseph Smith Papers* to be presented as a "facsimile edition"—presents photographic facsimiles and transcripts of two early manuscript revelation books. The manuscript revelation books are printed in a parallel format, with the facsimiles printed adjacent to transcripts of each inscribed page of the original books. These high-resolution color images and careful transcripts of the original documents allow unprecedented access to these founding documents.

Rules of Transcription

Because of aging and sometimes damaged texts and imprecise penmanship, not all handwriting is legible or can be fully deciphered. Hurried writers often rendered words carelessly, and even the best writers and spellers left out letters on occasion or formed them imperfectly or incompletely. Text transcription and verification is therefore an imperfect art more than a science. Judgments about capitalization, for example, are informed not only by looking at the specific case at hand but by understanding the usual characteristics of each particular writer. The same is true for deciphering spelling and punctuation. If a letter or other character is ambiguous, deference is given to the author's or scribe's usual spelling and punctuation. Where this is ambiguous, modern spelling and punctuation are favored. Even the best transcribers and verifiers will differ from one another in making such judgments.

Ink analysis aids in identifying the scribes of many emendations and redactions. Studying the sentence structure and ink flow of surrounding material often provides more clues about who inscribed small words, numbers, and punctuation than does studying the shapes of the characters themselves. Great care has been taken to accurately identify the scribes of all emendations and redactions, but improving technology may alter some of the identifications in this volume.

To better understand how the transcription rules described herein have been applied and to see elements of the document that cannot be conveyed by typography, readers can compare the transcripts herein with images of the original manuscripts, found on the left-hand page of each spread and at the Joseph Smith Papers website, josephsmithpapers.org.

To ensure accuracy in representing the texts, transcripts were verified three times, each time by a different set of eyes. The first two verifications were done using high-resolution scanned images. The first was a visual collation of these images with the transcripts, while the second was an independent and double-blind image-to-transcript tandem proofreading. The third and final verification of the transcripts was a visual collation with the original document. At this stage, the verifier employed magnification and ultraviolet light as needed to read badly faded text, recover heavily stricken material, untangle characters written over each other, and recover words canceled by messy "wipe erasures" made when the ink was still wet or removed by knife scraping after the ink had dried. The verified transcripts meet or exceed the transcription and verification requirements of the Modern Language Association's Committee on Scholarly Editions and the National Archives and Records Administration's National Historical Publications and Records Commission.

The approach to transcription employed in *The Joseph Smith Papers* is conservative by historical documentary editing standards, and this volume employs an even more rigorous approach than that guiding most *Papers* volumes. The transcripts render every word letter-by-letter, as accurately as possible, preserving the exact text of the original manuscript books. This includes incomplete words, variant spellings of personal names, repeated words, and idiosyncratic grammatical constructions. The transcripts also reproduce both emendations made when the text was originally inscribed and redactions made later, including labeling and other archival marking. For reader convenience, each scribe's redactions are shown in a different color, as indicated by a scribal key that appears on each transcription page. The scribal key remains consistent from page to page within a particular document, except that in Revelation Book 2, Orson Hyde and Sidney Rigdon made so few redactions that their names appear in the key only on the pages on which they made redactions. The original inscription is printed in black ink, and sidenotes indicate when the original scribe changes. The scribal key for each page also identifies the scribes who wrote the original inscription on each page. In this volume, when the original inscription is in the handwriting of Joseph Smith, the text is printed in roman (not boldface) type over a cream-colored background. Later redactions in Joseph Smith's handwriting are rendered in boldface type.

In order to match the adjacent photographic facsimiles line by line, the transcripts present line breaks and insertions where they occur in the manuscript. Incorrect dates, place names, and other errors of fact are left to stand. The intrusive *sic,* sometimes used to affirm original misspelling, is never employed, although where words or phrases are especially difficult to understand, editorial clarifications or corrections are inserted in brackets. Correct and complete spellings of personal names are supplied in brackets the first time each incorrect or incomplete name appears in each revelation or other item; if an incorrect or incomplete name is stricken in the transcript, the correction is found in a note. Place names that may be hard to identify are clarified or corrected within brackets.

All full-word write-overs are reproduced, as are most letter write-overs. (In cases when the original scribe immediately retraced a letter, the write-over is not reproduced in the transcript.) If a later scribe corrected a word by changing an existing letter to a different letter rather than inserting a new one, the transcript reproduces the later scribe's intent. For example, a scribe might have changed "the" to "thus" by adding an additional stroke after the "e" to form a "u" and then adding an "s." No complete cancellation or overwriting actually took place, but the "e" was effectively changed to a "u." In this case, the transcript would represent an "e" overwritten by a complete "u" and an "s." Partial cancellations are treated similarly. For instance, a scribe might have changed "by" to "be" by leaving the first stroke and canceling the second stroke of the "y." The transcript would represent a complete "e" written over the "y."

Blank spaces and blank lines in the manuscript are reproduced, and blank pages are noted in the transcripts but not reproduced. Documents later inserted into the manuscript books, thereby becoming associated with the books though not physically part of them, are reproduced as appendixes at the end of each manuscript book. Ink spills and tears, which are visible in the provided images, are not described in the transcripts. Horizontal rules and other devices inscribed between items to mark them off from each other are reproduced as a standardized line. An editorial symbol inserted in the left margin indicates where each new revelation or other item begins. End-of-line hyphens and double hyphens joining words or parts of the same word at line breaks are transcribed where they occur in the original.

Both manuscript books contain printer's marks that were made to prepare the revelations for publication. The transcripts reproduce these marks with standard typographic symbols when possible. When such a mark is difficult to portray, such as when a word is circled or an entire paragraph is crossed out with an X, a sidenote provides an explanation.

Certain elements of the original manuscript books are not reproduced in the transcripts. Dashes of various lengths are standardized to a consistent length. Insertions written in the left margin are transcribed at the beginning of the line into which they were inserted. The width of original paragraph indentions is standardized. Instances of four underlines (signifying an instruction to capitalize) are standardized to three underlines. The short vertical strokes commonly used in early American writing for abbreviation punctuation are transcribed as periods. Flourishes and other decorative inscriptions are noted with a standardized symbol. Without changing the characters, scribes often retraced letters, mended letters with incomplete strokes, or deleted extra strokes or overextensions of terminal characters; such corrections are not noted or transcribed. Words in the manuscript books that appear much larger than the surrounding text are standardized to one larger size. The locations of inscribed page numbers are standardized in the transcripts.

A version of the transcripts presenting only the text as it was originally written down—omitting later redactions and archival markings but including contemporaneous emendations—will be made available in the electronic edition of *The Joseph Smith Papers.* Standard documentary editing transcripts of many of the documents in this volume may also be found in the Documents series. There the emphasis is on recovering the earliest texts rather than presenting the manuscripts as they exist today, complete with later editorial marks. The Documents series will also provide historical context for each item, whereas this volume conveys textual history.

Transcription Symbols

The effort to render mistakes, canceled material, and later insertions sometimes complicates readability by putting Joseph Smith and his scribes behind the "barbed wire" of symbolic transcription. However, conveying such elements with transcription symbols can aid in understanding the text and the order and ways in which the words were inscribed. The following symbols are used to transcribe and expand the text:

/ⁿ	The slash mark indicates a change in handwriting in the original inscription. A sidenote identifies the previous and commencing scribes in all cases except those involving the handwriting of JS (whose handwriting, when in the original inscription, is noted by a cream-colored background). This symbol is used only when the original scribe changes; scribal redactions are identified by color.
[roman]	Brackets enclose editorial insertions that expand, correct, or clarify the text. This convention may be applied to the abbreviated or incorrect spelling of a personal name, such as Jerad [Jared] Carte[r], or of a place, such as Hyram [Hiram]. Obsolete or ambiguous abbreviations are expanded with br[acket]s. Bracketed editorial insertions also provide reasonable reconstructions of badly miss[p]elled worsd [words]. Missing or illegible words may be supplied within brackets in cases where the supplied word is based on textual or contextual evidence.
[*italic*]	Significant descriptions of the writing medium are italicized and enclosed in brackets: [*pages 99–102 blank*].
◊	An illegible character within a partially legible word is rendered with a hollow diamond. Repeated diamonds represent the approximate number of illegible characters: sto◊◊◊◊s.
✍	Flourishes or decorative inscriptions of any shape or size are indicated by a standardized symbol.
<u>underlined</u>	Underlining is typographically reproduced according to final intent. If underlining in the original misses the last letter within a word, the entire word is underlined. Likewise, if two letters are underlined in the original but only one letter was meant to be underlined, the single letter is underlined in the transcripts. <u>Individually</u> <u>underlined</u> <u>words</u> are distinguished from <u>passages underlined with one continuous line.</u> Double and triple underlining, which are used to indicate that the underlined material should be capitalized, are typographically reproduced. Quadruple underlining is standardized to triple underlining.
superscript	Superscription is typographically reproducᵉᵈ.
~~canceled~~	A single horizontal strikethrough bar is used to indicate any single method of cancellation: strikethrough and cross-out, wipe erasure and knife erasure, or other methods. ~~Individually~~ ~~canceled~~ ~~words~~ are distinguished from ~~passages eliminated with a single cancellation.~~ Characters individual~~ly~~ cancel~~ee~~d are distinguished from ~~words canceled in their entirety.~~ Cancellation is typographically reproduced according to final intent. A strikethrough bar over all but the final letter of a word, for example, is represented as a cancellation of the whole word. When two letters are canceled in the original but only one letter was meant to be canceled, the single letter is canceled in the transcripts. Sidenotes indicate most instances of multiple layers of cancellation (but a few such instances, such as where a word was wipe-erased and then written over, are not noted).

⟨inserted⟩   Intralinear insertions made at the time of original inscription are enclosed by angle brackets. Inserted letter⟨s⟩ and other c⟨h⟩aract⟨er⟩s are distinguished from ⟨words⟩ ⟨and phrases⟩ inserted in their entirety. Interlinear insertions appear without angle brackets either above or below the line in the color that corresponds to the scribe who made the correction. Insertions are also noted in instances of superimposition (see below). Intralinear insertions written in the left margin of the manuscript are flush at the beginning of the line into which they were inserted, surrounded by angle brackets only if inserted at the time of original inscription. Angle brackets are also employed to represent double interlinear emendations or redactions (for example, an insertion above an insertion above the original line).

{super-imposition}   Superimposed inscriptions, as well as the original inscriptions that they are written over, are enclosed within curly brackets. The {first\original} entry is printed first, followed by a backslash and the {final layer\correction}. Original inscriptions that were canceled prior to any overwriting, such as {~~crossed out~~\stricken} or {~~erased~~\wipe-erased} inscriptions, are distinguished from inscriptions that were merely canceled by {write-over\superimposition}. A superimposition made by a different scribe is rendered in that scribe's corresponding color. If, at the time of original inscription, a scribe went back and wrote over his own inscriptions, those superimpositions are shown within angle brackets in this {manner\⟨fashion⟩}. In contrast, if a scribe immediately superimposed new material before writing anything else, the superimposition is rendered like th{e\is}.

| A line break artificially imposed in the original manuscript is rendered as a vertical line in textual notes.

⏎   When a line of the original manuscript is too long to fit on a single line in the transcript, a line break is artificially imposed. The break is marked by a carriage return symbol at the end of the first line and by indention at the beginning of the next line.

♦   The beginning of each revelation or other item is indicated with a solid black diamond in the left margin.

Annotation Conventions

Annotation in this volume is designed to clarify and further explain the textual history of the manuscript books. Although the introductory essays place the manuscript books within their historical framework, this volume does not provide the historical background necessary to contextualize the individual revelations or other items. For extensive historical analysis and context, readers should consult the Documents series under the date of each individual item.

Certain conventions simplify the presentation of the annotation. Joseph Smith is usually referred to by the initials JS. The terms *Saint, Latter-day Saint,* and *Mormon*—all used by mid-1834 in reference to church members—are employed interchangeably here. Most sources are referred to by a shortened citation form, with a complete citation given in the Works Cited. Some documents are referred to by editorial titles rather than by their original titles or the titles given in the catalogs of their current repositories. These editorial titles are in some cases similar to informal names by which the documents have come to be known. The editorial titles are listed in the Works Cited along with the complete citations by which the documents can be found in repositories.

The annotation extensively cites Joseph Smith's revelations. In the 1830s, Smith and his followers used the terms *commandment* and *revelation* to refer to these dictations that they viewed as divine communications. Usage patterns in early documents suggest that in the earliest years, Latter-day Saints may have seen subtle differences in the meaning of these terms: *commandment* may have denoted communications that required action or obedience, whereas *revelation* may have referred to communications on doctrinal topics. During the mid-1830s, *revelation*—the term used throughout *The Joseph Smith Papers* to refer to these works—became standard. Many of these revelations were first collected and published in 1833, with numbered chapters and paragraphs (or verses), as the Book of Commandments. An expanded collection, organized into sections and with new versification, was published in 1835 as the Doctrine and Covenants. In 1844, at the time of his death, Joseph Smith was overseeing publication of a revised edition of the Doctrine and Covenants, which was published later that year. Since then, the Doctrine and Covenants has been published in several editions, some including newly canonized revelations or other items.

Source citations in this volume identify revelations by their original date and by a citation of the version most relevant to the particular instance of annotation (usually the version found in one of the two revelation books published in this volume). In cases in which two or more revelations bear the same date, such as April 1829, a letter of the alphabet is appended so that each revelation has a unique editorial title—for example, April 1829–A or April 1829–B. Revelation citations also include a bracketed "D&C" reference that provides the Doctrine and Covenants section and verse numbers that have been standard in The Church of Jesus Christ of Latter-day Saints since 1876. Bracketed D&C references are provided for the benefit of Latter-day Saints, who can easily access the revelations in their familiar canon of scriptural works, and other students of early Mormonism who may wish to access the most widely available editions of these revelations.

Redactions in the revelation texts herein were often incorporated into early published versions. Where there is a clear correlation between the redactions and a particular publication, sidenotes indicate in which publication the redactions first appeared, referring to the publications by shortened titles. Readers may also use the table on pages 690–694 herein to refer from the cited version of a revelation to other published versions of the same revelation.

This volume includes a Scribal Directory that contains brief biographies of the scribes who penned or corrected documents in Revelation Books 1 and 2 and an overview of their work for Joseph Smith. Following the entry for each scribe who penned substantial sections of the manuscript is a description of his most problematic handwriting characteristics. Ambiguous or unusual habits of the scribes are explained to help readers understand how certain characteristics have been transcribed. Other people whose names appear in this volume or who inscribed material not associated with the original purpose of the manuscript books are not identified in the directory. Readers seeking more information about such individuals should consult the biographical directories in the initial volumes of the Documents series, in volume 1 of the Journals series, or on the Joseph Smith Papers website, josephsmithpapers.org. Complete documentation for the reference material in the back of the volume will be made available at the Joseph Smith Papers website, as will other resources, including a complete calendar of Joseph Smith's papers.

Note on Photographic Facsimiles

No matter the care put into transcribing a text, a gap still remains between the reader and the physical document. The use of photographic facsimiles in this volume narrows that gap but does not eliminate it. This note explains how these photographs were created and prepared for publication and identifies some of their limitations.

Creating the Photographs

The textual photographs herein were created specifically for this publication and its web counterpart by Welden C. Andersen, a lead photographer for the Audiovisual Department of The Church of Jesus Christ of Latter-day Saints. Andersen used a Hasselblad H3DII-39 multishot camera equipped with a Hasselblad HC 120mm f4 macro lens. By taking a sequence of four photographs, each offset by an increment of one pixel, this camera captures red, green, and blue data for every pixel, whereas a single-shot camera records only one color per pixel. The four-shot technology therefore captures much more detail. The lens is optimized for extremely close focusing, allowing for images of documents that can resolve to the level of individual fibers of the paper. Each digital image produced by the camera comprises approximately 229 megabytes of information. Though the resolution of these images must be reduced significantly for print publication, the Joseph Smith Papers Project retains the original full-resolution files, which will allow textual researchers to view extremely detailed electronic images. Indeed, a primary purpose for creating these photographs was to minimize the need for researchers to consult the original documents.

As illustrated in figure 1, during photography the manuscript books were positioned on a low, leveled table. Studio lights diffused by a fabric screen were used to illuminate the subject, and a computer was attached to the camera to process and store the images. To avoid having to repeatedly reposition the camera and lighting, Andersen photographed recto pages first, followed by verso pages. Because of concern for the bindings of the books and in order to lay the pages as flat as possible, the books were positioned on the table with one cover flat on the surface and the other cover opened slightly more than ninety degrees and resting on a prop. The camera was positioned about four feet above the table on a camera stand (the camera was temporarily lowered for the photograph in figure 1, in which it can be seen in the upper right corner). Andersen hand-focused each photograph from a ladder and then remotely triggered the shutter. After ensuring the quality of the first image on the computer monitor, he made a second exposure to create a security backup copy for each image.

Andersen followed standard professional procedures to achieve the highest accuracy in color, tone, contrast, and exposure. Before photographing each book and any time he adjusted lighting, exposure, or document angle, he calibrated and corrected color using a color test card and color adjustment software. This eliminated any bias of

Fig. 1. Welden C. Andersen with the equipment he used to create the textual photographs in this volume. Revelation Book 1 is open on the table with a color test card on the page.

the camera sensor and the light source, meaning that the colors captured in the photographs are as close as possible to the colors of the documents as they exist today.

Because of tight binding within some of the gatherings in Revelation Book 1, manuscript pages 73, 91, 93, 95, 181, 183, 185, 187, and 189 would not lie sufficiently flat without assistance. An archivist used a microspatula to hold down these pages while they were being photographed (see figure 2). The spatula did not obscure any text, but in the images presented in this volume it has been digitally removed and the small area of paper underneath the spatula has been digitally cloned from the surrounding paper.

Preparing the Photographs for Print Publication

Charles M. Baird, a prepress specialist with the Materials Management Department of The Church of Jesus Christ of Latter-day Saints, prepared the images for printing. Following standard prepress methods, Baird reduced the images to fit the page size in this volume at a resolution of approximately 300 dpi and converted the images from

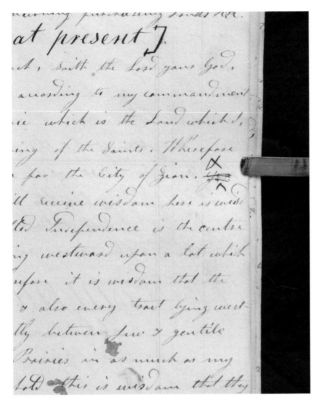

Fig. 2. Manuscript page 93 of Revelation Book 1 and eight other pages in that volume were held flat by a microspatula for photography. The spatula was digitally removed from the images published in this volume.

the color format stored by the camera (red, green, and blue) to the colors used in printing (cyan, magenta, yellow, and black). While converting color, Baird frequently consulted the original documents to ensure that the color proofs matched the original documents as closely as possible. The prepress proofs were later checked against official press proofs from the printer. Any differences in color between the original documents and the photographs herein result from the limitations inherent in printing.

As mentioned earlier in this note, the documents featured in this volume were photographed resting on a table. For aesthetic reasons, Baird used photo-editing software to digitally remove the table from the background and to add a thin shadow at the bottom of the images. Baird also used photo-editing software in two other cases. The first case—digitally removing the microspatula from nine images in Revelation Book 1—was described earlier. The other case relates to manuscript page 67 of Revelation Book 1. The text on that page is obscured by a slip of paper affixed to the original page (see figure 3). This slip can be partially lifted so that most of the underlying page and all of the text on the back of the slip can be seen and photographed, but the slip cannot be removed without damaging the adhesive wafer used to seal the slip to the page (see figure 4; see also 105n126 herein). To represent what the underlying page looks like, Baird created a composite image, digitally collating a photograph of the text above the slip with another photograph of the text underneath and below the slip. The composite image, which contains a triangular whited area to represent the portion of the page that cannot be uncovered because of the presence of the wafer, accompanies the transcript of that page in this volume. As for the slip itself, Baird cropped out the background from Andersen's photographs of the front and back of the slip. Those cropped photographs are shown along with their corresponding transcripts following manuscript page 67 of Revelation Book 1.

Except as described in this note, the textual photographs in this volume have not been altered.

Limitations of the Photographs

Even careful photographs can underplay important features of the original document. Two categories of such features are worth noting here.

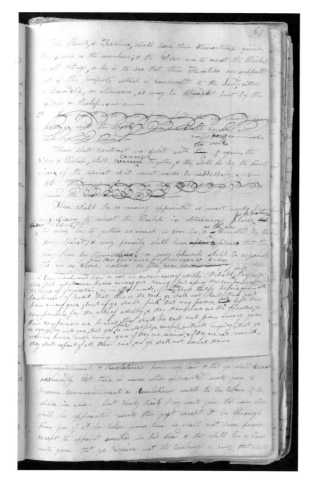

Figs. 3 and 4. A slip of paper is affixed to manuscript page 67 of Revelation Book 1. The slip was lifted so that the underlying page and the back of the slip could be photographed. The photograph accompanying the transcript of manuscript page 67 herein is a composite.

First, some details described in the annotation of this volume can be seen in the original documents and in the electronic images but are too small to be seen well, if at all, in the photographs printed herein. For example, some pages of Revelation Book 1 bear uninked vertical marks that correspond to line breaks in *The Evening and the Morning Star* (see figure 5), and various pages in both books contain pinholes that were created when slips of paper were pinned to the page (see figure 6).

Second, certain physical features obscure text of the original documents. For example, because of age, some pages have worn along the outer edges, resulting in curling

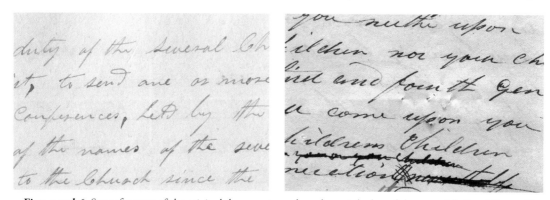

Figs. 5 and 6. Some features of the original documents, such as the uninked mark between "the" and "several" on the top line of manuscript page 58 of Revelation Book 1 (left) and pinholes on manuscript page 69 of Revelation Book 2 (right), are too small to be seen well in the photographs published herein.

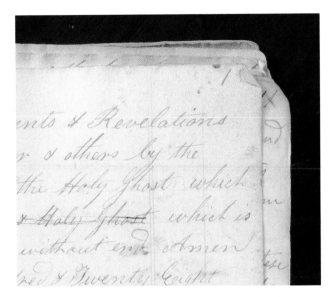

Fig. 7. Wear from aging and use can cause the edges of paper to curl and fold, obscuring text from the camera and sometimes from the transcriber. This fold, in the upper right corner of manuscript page 1 of Revelation Book 1, partially obscures "st.".

or inward folding of small portions of the page (see figure 7). Text may also be obscured by tight binding and unusual folds in pages. In cases such as these, the transcripts present more text than the photographs themselves because the transcribers could uncover text not visible to the camera's lens.

A few pages of the manuscript books have slips of paper attached to them that obscure text. The single instance of this that occurs in Revelation Book 1 was discussed earlier. Revelation Book 2 contains three slips of paper, one attached to the inside front cover, one placed between manuscript pages 60 and 61, and one attached to manuscript page 69. The slip attached to the inside front cover was lifted by an archivist during photography so that the back of the slip could be photographed (see figure 8). The text on the front and back of this slip is transcribed herein, but the brief notation on the underlying page (visible in figure 8) is not transcribed because it was likely written before the book was purchased. The slip at manuscript page 60 is not presently attached to the page itself (see figure 9). This slip was temporarily removed so its front and reverse sides and the underlying page could be photographed for this volume. The slip on manuscript page 69 of Revelation Book 2 was probably originally attached square with the page itself; later, the slip was moved and repinned in its present diagonal position (see figures 10 and 11; see also 553n109 and 555n111 herein). For production of this volume, an archivist temporarily unpinned the slip so the back of the slip and the underlying page could be photographed. Then the archivist repinned the slip using the same pin and pinholes. Photographs of the front and back of all these slips appear adjacent to their corresponding transcripts in this volume.

Techniques Used to Recover Canceled Text

Transcribers for this volume used multispectral imaging and photo-editing software to recover canceled text in two instances in Revelation Book 1. The first instance is a twentieth-century notation. On manuscript page 117, "DC | 108" was written in the upper left corner in graphite and then erased. This page is in the custody of the Community of Christ, and that institution's section number for the revelation thereon is section 108 (the equivalent in the Latter-day Saint canon is D&C 133; see 207n263 herein for further discussion of this notation). Multispectral imaging, a technology that uses different wavelengths of light to extract additional information that cannot be seen by the human eye, revealed this notation (see figure 12). On manuscript page 31, two words were heavily stricken. Analysis of both the original document and of a

Figs. 8, 9, 10, and 11. Revelation Book 2 contains three slips of paper that obscure text on the underlying pages. Top left: A slip of paper affixed to the inside front cover of the volume was lifted so the verso and the underlying page could be photographed. Top right: A slip inserted at manuscript page 60 but not currently attached to the book was temporarily removed during photography. Bottom left: A slip of paper was probably originally attached to manuscript page 69 in the position shown in this photograph. Bottom right: The slip was later moved and pinned in the position shown. The slip was temporarily removed during photography and then repinned in the same location.

digital image that was enhanced using photo-editing software (see figure 13) allowed a partial recovery of the original inscription.

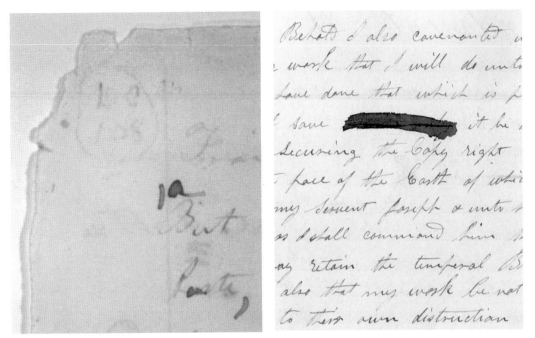

Figs. 12 and 13. Transcribers used different technologies to recover canceled text. Left: Multispectral imaging recovered the erased notation "DC | 108" in the upper left corner of manuscript page 117 of Revelation Book 1. Right: This enhanced digital image of manuscript page 31 of Revelation Book 1 was used along with the original document to partially reconstruct heavily stricken text. The stricken text reads "M◊◊tin [Martin] only."

MANUSCRIPT REVELATION BOOKS

Revelation Book 1. John Whitmer copied many of Joseph Smith's early revelations into this manuscript book, which was later used to prepare many of those revelations for publication. Items were recorded in the book from early 1831 to mid-1835. Remnants of the original binding can be seen in the image on the left. The brown paperboard cover pictured on the right was a later addition. Revelation Book 1, Church History Library, Salt Lake City.

REVELATION BOOK 1

Source Note

"A Book of Commandments & Revelations of the Lord given to Joseph the Seer & others by the Inspiration of God & gift & power of the Holy Ghost which Beareth Re[c]ord of the Father & Son & Holy Ghost which is one God Infinite & eternal World without end Amen," Revelation Book 1, [ca. Mar. 1831–July 1835]; handwriting of John Whitmer and Oliver Cowdery in both original inscription and later redactions; handwriting of William W. Phelps, Sidney Rigdon, JS, and an unknown number of unidentified scribes in later redactions only; 208 pages (18 pages missing) and four inserted leaves; volume at CHL and four loose leaves in Restoration Scriptures Collection at CCLA. Includes redactions and archival marking.

This volume likely contained nine gatherings of twelve leaves (twenty-four pages) each, measuring 12⅝ x 7¾ inches (32 x 20 cm), plus two pastedowns and an unknown number of flyleaves (one flyleaf is extant in the back of the volume). The existing sheets are ledger paper with thirty-six blue horizontal lines, most faint or completely faded, and four red vertical lines. The binding was disassembled, possibly for ease in printing the revelations, and the original cover was discarded or lost. Evidence suggests that the book was originally sewn all along over recessed cords, likely with a tight-back case with quarter-leather binding. A brown paperboard cover was placed around the pages, perhaps as soon as the early 1830s but certainly before the mid-1850s. With the current paperboard cover, the volume measures 13⅛ x 8½ inches (33 x 22 cm) and is ¾ inches (2 cm) thick. The front cover is labeled "S" in black ink that later turned light brown, and "can" or "cam" is written at the bottom in blue-green ink. The inside back cover has "2 | 1 | 1 | 1 | 75 | 55 | ◊◊ | wisdo" written vertically along the right margin in various shades of brown (formerly black) ink. A slip of blue paper pasted on the spine reads "Book of Commandments and Revelations". This notation was written by Leo Hawkins, a clerk for the Church Historian's Office, 1853–1856.

The current state of the volume makes it difficult to determine its original condition. Nine gatherings of the volume are currently accounted for, but additional gatherings may have existed. The volume bears remnants of the original glue and leather used for binding on the inside edges of the gatherings, and some of the gatherings are still attached to this original binding. In addition, some gatherings are completely uncut, meaning the original six sheets folded to make the twelve-leaf gatherings are attached and complete. Others are completely or partially cut and separated. The first gathering contains only four of its original leaves, and one leaf is missing from the second gathering. The leaves from the third and fourth gatherings are still mostly attached to the original binding. The fifth and sixth gatherings are mostly disconnected from the original binding. In the sixth gathering, the scribe mistakenly repeated the numbers "134" and "135" when numbering pages, leaving two pages numbered 134 and two numbered 135. As a result, the remaining page numbers are off by two and the gathering's last manuscript page is incorrectly numbered 142 (rather than 144). While the seventh gathering remains mostly attached to remnants of the original binding and the eighth gathering is completely intact, the ninth gathering is disconnected from the original binding altogether. If the ninth gathering originally contained twelve leaves, three are missing. There is also one flyleaf at the end of the volume.

Needle holes along the spine of the paperboard cover match up with needle holes on the edge of the fifth gathering, and one piece of thread remains at the center of that gathering. Because this rough sewing was evidently done when the fifth gathering was still an intact unit, it likely attached the makeshift cover to the text block until the cover was separated and the fifth gathering was disassembled.

The first 127 pages of the manuscript book contain seventy-six revelations and four other items. These eighty items were likely entered in the order in which they originated, the exceptions being Articles and covenants, 10 April 1830; Explanation of scripture, circa December 1830; and the revelations dated circa 8 March 1831–B and 1 November 1831–B (known as D&C 20, 74, 47, and 1, respectively, in the 1981 Latter-day Saint edition of the

Doctrine and Covenants). There are over thirty items in the remainder of the volume, about half of which appear out of chronological order.

The leaves for the following manuscript pages are missing from the volume and their whereabouts are not known: 3–10, 15–22, and 25–26. These pages were likely numbered, and it is not known when they were separated from the manuscript book. The leaves for manuscript pages 111–112, 117–120, and 139–140 are currently held at the Community of Christ Library-Archives. Markings on these loose pages indicate that they were likely separated from the manuscript book during work on the 1835 edition of the Doctrine and Covenants or sometime thereafter.

In 1902, the First Presidency of the Reorganized Church of Jesus Christ of Latter Day Saints approved purchase of the loose pages from George Schweich, David Whitmer's grandson.[1] The pages were likely separated by John Whitmer or Oliver Cowdery before Whitmer and Cowdery were excommunicated in 1838. A secondhand source states that David Whitmer received these pages from Oliver Cowdery in 1850.[2] However, at the time these leaves were acquired by the RLDS church, they were grouped with the John Whitmer copy of the JS Bible revision and the Book of John Whitmer, suggesting that the leaves were in John Whitmer's possession until his death in 1878.[3] Neither John Whitmer nor David Whitmer left known accounts of either man having possession of the leaves. The provenance of the leaves between 1835 and 1902, therefore, is uncertain.

The custodial history of the manuscript book itself is uncertain between the publication of the 1835 Doctrine and Covenants and the 1846 Latter-day Saint exodus from Nauvoo, Illinois, though the book likely remained in the possession of JS, his office staff, and subsequent leadership of the LDS church. The Church Historian's Office inventory from 1846 lists "Rough Book—Revelation History &c.," possibly referring to Revelation Book 1.[4] By the 1850s, the spine of Revelation Book 1 had been labeled "Book of Commandments and Revelations" by the Church Historian's Office staff, and it appeared with that title on subsequent Church Historian's Office inventories through 1878.[5] Evidence indicates that the manuscript book was part of the papers of church historian and recorder Joseph Fielding Smith, who held that office from 1921 to 1970. The manuscript book became part of the First Presidency's papers when he became president in 1970.[6]

Historical Introduction

Revelation Book 1, also known as "Book of Commandments and Revelations," is a manuscript book of revelations and other items that was begun less than a year after JS organized the Church of Christ in April 1830. John Whitmer was the principal scribe, although Oliver Cowdery also wrote a few pages. The book may have originated in New York in summer 1830 when JS and John Whitmer began to "arrange and copy the revelations" previously received.[7] More likely, however, Whitmer

---

1. "Minutes of First Presidency," 24 Apr. 1902, CCLA. The Reorganized Church of Jesus Christ of Latter Day Saints purchased from Schweich additional material that was passed down from David Whitmer, including the Book of Mormon printer's manuscript and parts of the manuscript from JS's Bible revision. (Walter Smith, Independence, MO, to S. A. Burgess, Independence, MO, 15 Apr. 1926, J. F. Curtis Papers, CCLA.)

2. Former RLDS church historian Walter Smith, who was present when these papers were turned over to the Reorganized Church of Jesus Christ of Latter Day Saints, heard from both George Schweich and David Whitmer's family that the leaves were "received by David Whitmer from Oliver Cowdery at his death in 1850" (Walter Smith, Independence, MO, to the RLDS First Presidency, Independence, MO, 14 Sept. 1925, Whitmer Papers, CCLA; see also Walter Smith, Independence, MO, to R. L. Fulk, Ogden, UT, 13 Dec. 1919, Subject Folder Collection, Book of Commandments, CCLA.)

3. Walter Smith noted on two different occasions that "these pages [of revelations] . . . were in the Whitmer manuscript book [Book of John Whitmer] and were the same that [George] Schweich turned over to the [RLDS] church." (W. Smith to S. A. Burgess, 15 Apr. 1926; see also W. Smith to the RLDS First Presidency, 14 Sept. 1925.)

4. Historian's Office, "Schedule of Church Records," [1], Catalogs and Inventories, 1846–1904, CHL.

5. Historian's Office, "Contents of the Historian and Recorder's Office," [5]; "Index Records and Journals in the Historian's Office 1878," [5], Catalogs and Inventories, 1846–1904, CHL.

6. In a 1909 article in which he discussed the history surrounding the securing of the Book of Mormon copyright in Canada, B. H. Roberts, an LDS assistant church historian, did not appear to know about the revelation found in Revelation Book 1 that deals with that topic. In a 1907 letter, Joseph Fielding Smith made an indirect reference to Revelation Book 1, indicating that he knew of its existence. Because Roberts apparently did not know about the manuscript volume and Smith did, it may be inferred that the volume was in Smith's possession as early as 1907. A 1970 inventory establishes the document was in the possession of Joseph Fielding Smith later in his life. (Revelation, ca. early 1830, pp. 31–33 herein; Roberts, "History of the Mormon Church"; Joseph Fielding Smith, Salt Lake City, UT, to John R. Haldeman, Independence, MO, 24 May 1907, Joseph Fielding Smith Papers, 1893–1973, CHL; "Inventory of President Joseph Fielding Smith's Safe," 23 May 1970, CHL.)

7. JS History, vol. A-1, 50.

began inscribing material in Revelation Book 1 in Ohio, circa March 1831, following his appointment to keep church records and history.[8] Textual evidence indicates that Whitmer and Cowdery copied revelations and other items into Revelation Book 1 from even earlier manuscripts that are no longer extant. All items in the manuscript book date from 1828 to 1834. Textual analysis suggests that the first half was copied mostly between spring 1831 and the end of that year, and the final item was copied in July 1835. Revelation Book 1 contains the earliest known copies of many revelations and, in some cases, the only surviving early manuscript copy. It also contains items not found anywhere else, including a revelation on securing a copyright in Canada for the Book of Mormon.[9]

In November 1831, church leaders meeting in a conference in Hiram, Ohio, authorized publication of a volume of revelations later known as the Book of Commandments and appointed Oliver Cowdery to take the revelations to Missouri for printing. Cowdery and John Whitmer, who was appointed by revelation to accompany him, departed from Hiram, Ohio, that same month, taking Revelation Book 1 and possibly other manuscript revelations with them. They arrived in Independence, Missouri, in January 1832 to work with William W. Phelps, who had been appointed church printer by revelation[10] and had already purchased a printing press. They published the first issue of the church newspaper *The Evening and the Morning Star* five months later, and twenty-four revelatory items eventually appeared in that publication. All but one of those items also appear in Revelation Book 1, which was likely their source for publication.[11]

The first eighty items in Revelation Book 1 appear on manuscript pages 1–127. Of these items, only four dated items are known to have been copied into the book out of chronological order. This portion of the manuscript book was likely inscribed in 1831 and includes items dated October–November 1831 that were copied shortly before John Whitmer and Oliver Cowdery left Ohio for Missouri (manuscript pages 108–127). Whitmer's access to the revelations dictated in Ohio after his departure to Missouri was, of course, limited to those delivered by mail or in person.

In the remainder of the manuscript book, about half of the revelations and other items are out of chronological order. Manuscript pages 128–148 contain fourteen items dated December 1831–April 1832 that were copied into the manuscript book after April 1832. The manuscript source of these revelations and other items is unknown, but JS and other church leaders possibly brought them to Missouri in April 1832. While these fourteen items are out of order chronologically, Whitmer copied more of them into Revelation Book 1 than other scribes copied into Revelation Book 2, which was begun in late February or early March 1832 and kept by JS and his scribes at church headquarters in Ohio.[12] This suggests that Revelation Book 1 was a more complete record of revelations than Revelation Book 2, even though Revelation Book 1 was being updated outside of church headquarters.

Manuscript pages 148–170 contain seven entries that appear in chronological order. Whitmer likely copied the next three revelations, on manuscript pages 171–177, from a letter to Missouri leaders dated 6 August 1833. This letter contains all three revelations, and all three bear an August 1833 date.[13] They appear in Revelation Book 1 in the order in which they appear in the letter. Manuscript pages 177–201 contain nine revelations that were all copied chronologically; however, the first four revelations in this group are dated before the August revelations found in the aforementioned letter. Manuscript pages 202–203 contain the final two items in Revelation Book 1: a heading for minutes of the February 1834 meeting to organize a standing "high counsel" in Ohio (likely indicating an intention to copy the minutes from this meeting) and the second copy of a revelation that was copied

---

8. See Revelation, ca. 8 Mar. 1831–B, pp. 131–133 herein [D&C 47].

9. Revelation, ca. early 1830, pp. 31–33 herein.

10. Revelation, 20 July 1831, p. 161 herein [D&C 57:11].

11. Revelation, 23 Feb. 1831 [D&C 42:78–93] does not appear in Revelation Book 1.

12. Revelation Book 2 does not contain the revelations dated 10 Jan. 1832 [D&C 73], 25 Jan. 1832 [D&C 75], and 26 Apr. 1832 [D&C 82].

13. Sidney Rigdon et al., Kirtland, OH, to Edward Partridge et al., Independence, MO, 6 Aug. 1833, JS Collection, CHL.

into the book twice.[14] Following this last revelation, there are three blank pages before a two-page index that Whitmer created for the first ninety-eight pages of the manuscript book.

Editorial redactions in Revelation Book 1 demonstrate that it was used as a source for publishing the Book of Commandments in 1833. Thirty-one revelations in Revelation Book 1 contain added verse numbers and punctuation that usually match verse numbers and punctuation in the Book of Commandments.[15] Items found in the later portion of the manuscript book were not printed in the Book of Commandments and contain few redactions.

After the 1833 destruction of the Saints' printing office in Missouri, efforts to publish the revelations shifted to Ohio, beginning in late 1834. Those preparing the revelations for publication in the 1835 Doctrine and Covenants did not initially have access to Revelation Book 1 because it was in Missouri. After John Whitmer returned to Kirtland in the middle of May 1835, evidently bringing the manuscript book with him, it became a supplemental source for the publication effort. Revelation Book 1 includes twenty-one items that contain redactions made for the 1835 Doctrine and Covenants.[16] These redactions show an effort to clarify wording in the revelations and other items on the part of those selecting, arranging, and preparing them for publication.

A comparison of Revelation Book 1 with the Book of Commandments and with the 1835 Doctrine and Covenants indicates that Revelation Book 1 is a relatively comprehensive collection of revelations. It contains 64 of the 65 items published in the 1833 Book of Commandments,[17] as well as 95 of the 103 sections published in the 1835 Doctrine and Covenants.[18] Of the many revelations and other items copied into the manuscript book, only 11 do not appear in either the Book of Commandments or the 1835 Doctrine and Covenants.[19]

In November 1831, JS and his associates were appointed by church conferences to prepare the revelations and other items in Revelation Book 1 for publication by correcting and modifying the text. JS was to "correct those errors or mistakes which he m[a]y discover by the holy Spirit."[20] Many redactions were made before selected items were published in Missouri, while others were made in Ohio before the 1835 publication of the Doctrine and Covenants. Changes made in Sidney Rigdon's hand are among the earliest, and evidence indicates that he made them in Ohio before the book went to Missouri in November 1831. Rigdon frequently altered the language in the revelations from the biblical "thee," "thy," and "thine" to the more modern "you," "your," and "yours." He also corrected grammar and changed some of the language to clarify and modify words and meaning.

John Whitmer and Oliver Cowdery could have made redactions in either Ohio or Missouri as early as 1831 or as late as 1835, though the majority of redactions they made first appear in print in 1833 or earlier. Whitmer's marks often reversed changes made by Sidney Rigdon, and his later editing also modified some of the wording in the revelations. Though not as frequent, changes in Cowdery's hand were often more substantive in nature, clarifying and expanding the meaning of

14. The revelation copied twice is Revelation, 25 Dec. 1832, pp. 291, 381–383 herein [D&C 87].

15. See Book of Commandments, chaps. 9, 16, 18–21, 27, 31–40, 42–44, 50, 54–59, 61, and 63–65.

16. See Doctrine and Covenants, 1835 ed., secs. 17–18, 20–29, 73–77, 84, 86–87, and 98.

17. The single revelation published in the Book of Commandments but not found in Revelation Book 1 is Revelation, May 1829–B, in Book of Commandments, chap. 11 [D&C 12].

18. The eight items published in the 1835 Doctrine and Covenants but not found in Revelation Book 1 are Revelation, May 1829–B, in Doctrine and Covenants 38, 1835 ed. [D&C 12]; Revelation, Oct. 1830–A, in Doctrine and Covenants 54, 1835 ed. [D&C 32]; Revelation, 9 Mar. 1833, in Doctrine and Covenants 92, 1835 ed. [D&C 91]; Revelation, 15 Mar. 1833, in Doctrine and Covenants 93, 1835 ed. [D&C 92]; Revelation, 12 Oct. 1833, in Doctrine and Covenants 94, 1835 ed. [D&C 100]; Revelation, 25 Nov. 1834, in Doctrine and Covenants 99, 1835 ed. [D&C 106]; "Marriage," ca. Aug. 1835, in Doctrine and Covenants 101, 1835 ed.; and "Of Governments and Laws in General," ca. Aug. 1835, in Doctrine and Covenants 102, 1835 ed. [D&C 134].

19. See the following herein: Revelation, ca. June 1829, pp. 21–23; Revelation, ca. early 1830, pp. 31–33; Revelation, 15 May 1831, p. 143; Testimony, ca. 1 Nov. 1831, p. 215; Answers to questions, ca. Mar. 1832, pp. 259–265 [D&C 77]; Sample of pure language, ca. Mar. 1832, p. 265; Revelation, 20 Mar. 1832, p. 273; Revelation, 25 Dec. 1832, p. 291 [D&C 87]; Revelation, 24 Feb. 1834, pp. 355–361 [D&C 103]; Revelation, 28 Apr. 1834, p. 373; and Revelation, 22 June 1834, pp. 375–379 [D&C 105].

20. Minute Book 2, 8 Nov. 1831.

several items in preparation for the publication of the Book of Commandments and the 1835 Doctrine and Covenants.

William W. Phelps had neither reason nor opportunity to edit the items in Revelation Book 1 until he and his associates began preparing the texts for publication in Missouri. As printer of *The Evening and the Morning Star* and the Book of Commandments, Phelps provided much of the punctuation and versification and many of the other copyediting changes. Only rarely did he alter the original language.

JS likely reviewed some of his associates' editorial changes and made slight alterations in his own hand before the book was taken to Missouri in late 1831 for publication of the Book of Commandments in 1833, although he may have reviewed the selection, editing, and publication process as late as April 1832 when he visited Missouri. He made additional changes, including adding the surnames of some individuals named in the revelations, just before the Doctrine and Covenants was published in 1835.[21] The extent to which JS influenced the redactions made by other individuals is unknown.

In addition to marking corrections, those preparing the items in Revelation Book 1 for publication used pins or adhesive wafers to attach slips of paper to pages of the manuscript book. The slips, one of which is extant in Revelation Book 1, contained additions to or clarifications of the original text. The extant slip is transcribed as a separate leaf where it appears in the manuscript book. Visible pinholes or wafer residue likely mark where additional slips were fastened to the page as texts were copied or prepared for publication.[22] This physical evidence, which suggests how the manuscript book was used by those preparing the texts for publication, is noted in the textual annotation.

A loose copy of a revelation in the handwriting of Sidney Rigdon was inserted into Revelation Book 1 at an unknown time, thereby becoming associated with the manuscript book though not physically part of it. This document is reproduced at the end of Revelation Book 1 as an appendix.

---

21. JS et al., Kirtland, OH, to Edward Partridge et al., Independence, MO, 25 June 1833, JS Collection, CHL.

22. See p. 107 herein for an example of a slip of paper that was pasted to the page. A series of pinholes is also visible on manuscript page 85 (p. 143 herein).

A Book of Commandments & Revelations
of the Lord given to Joseph the Seer & others by the
Inspiration of God & gift & power of the Holy Ghost which
beareth Record of the Father & Son ~~& Holy Ghost~~ which is
one God Infinite & eternal World without end Amen
— July one Thousand Eighthundred & Twenty Eight

Given to Joseph the Seer after he had lost certain writ=
ings which he had Translated by the gift & Power of God

Saying the works & the designs & the Purposes of God cannot
be frustrated neither can they come to naught for God
doth not walk in crooked Paths neither doth he turn to
the right hand nor to the left neither doth he vary from
that which he hath said therefore his paths are strait & his
course is one eternal round Remember Remember that it
is not the work of God that is frustrated but the work of
men for although a man may have many Revelations &
have power to do many Mighty works yet if he boast in
his own strength & sets at naught the councils of God &
follows after the dictates of his own will & carnal desires he
must fall ~~to the earth~~ & incur the vengence of a just God
upon him behold you have been intrusted with those
things but how strict were your commandments & Remember
also the Promises which were made to you if you did not
transgress them & behold how oft you have transgressed the
commandments and the Laws of God & have gone on in the Persuasions of men for
behold you should not have feared man more then God alth=
=ough men set at naught the councils of God & dispise his
words yet you should have been faithful & he would have
extended his arm & supported you against all the firey darts
of the adversary & he would have been with you in every time
of trouble behold thou art Joseph & thou wast chosen to do
the work of the Lord but because of transgression if thou art not
aware thou wilt fall but remember God is merciful therefore repent of
that which thou hast done & he will only cause thee
to be afflicted for a season & thou art still chosen &
will & will again be called to the work & except

/²A Book of Commandments & Revelations

of the Lord given to Joseph the Seer & others by the

Inspiration of God & gift & power of the Holy Ghost which

Beareth Re[c]ord of the Father & Son ~~& Holy Ghost~~ which is

one God Infinite & eternal World without end Amen

♦ ³July one Thousand Eighthundred & Twenty Eight

Given to Joseph the Seer after he had lost certan writ

=ings which he had Translated by the gift & Power of God

           the

Saying the wor{d\⟨k⟩}s {of\&} designs & the Purposes of God cannot

               naught

be frustrated neither can they come to {naught\ground} for God

  l

doth not wak in crooked Paths neither doth he turn to

              he

the right hand nor to the left neither doth vary from

that which he hath said therefore his paths are strait & his

course is one eternal round Remember Remember that it

is not the work of God that is frustrated but the works of

men for although a man ma{◊\y} have many Revelations &

have power to do many Mighty works yet if he boast in

his own strength & Sets at naught the councils of God &

             own

follows after the dictates of his will & carnal desires he

must fall ~~to the Earth~~ & incur the vengence of a Just God

upon him behold you have been intrusted with those

      how   were

things but strict ~~was~~ your commandments & Remember

                  did not

also the Promises which were made to you if you transgre

              commandments

ss~~ed~~ them & behold how oft you have transgressed the{m\se}

and the

Laws of God & have gone on in the Persuasions of men for

behold you should not have feared m{e\a}n more then God alth-

=ough men set at naught the councils of God & dispise his

words yet you should have been faithful & he would have

extended his arm & supported you against all the firey darts

of the advisary & he would have been with you in evry time

of trouble behold thou art Joseph & thou wast chosen to do

             if   art not

the work of the Lord but because of transgression thou ~~mayest~~

aware thou wilt ~~fall~~

fall but remember God is merciful therefore repent of

that which thou hast done & he will only cause thee

to be afflicted for a season & thou art still chosen &

will ~~& will~~ again be called to the work & e{s\xcept}

ORIGINAL INSCRIPTION
John Whitmer

REVISIONS
Oliver Cowdery
William W. Phelps
Sidney Rigdon
Joseph Smith
John Whitmer
Unidentified

1. John Whitmer some-times numbered pages as he copied items into the manuscript book and other times numbered a series of pages at once. Because it is often difficult to tell when Whitmer inscribed page numbers, the transcript identifies (by color) the handwriting of all page numbers, whether they were written at the time of original inscription or inserted later.

2. John Whitmer hand-writing begins.

3. The first publication reflecting most redactions in this revelation is the Book of Commandments (chapter 2).

Thou do this thou shalt be delivered up & become as other
men & have no more gift & when thou deliveredst up
which that which God had given thee sight and power to Translate
thou deliveredest up that which was Sacred into the hands
of a wicked man who has Set at naught the Councils of God
& has broken the most sacred promises which were made before
God & has depended upon his own judgement & boasted in
his own wisdam & this is the Reason that thou hast
lost they Privileges for a season for thou hast suffered
that the council of thy director to be trampeled upon from
the begining for as the knowledge of a Saveeaur nevertheless my work shall go forth & accomplish my purposes come
into the world even so shall the Knowledge of my People the Nephities
& the Jacobites & the Josephites & the Zoramites Jeremiites come to the
Zoramites knowledge of the Zoramites, & the Lamenites &
the Ishmaelites which dwindeled in unbelief because of
the iniquities of their Fathers who have been suffered to
destroy their Brethren because of their iniquities & their
Abominations & for this very Purpose are these Plates
preserved which contain these Records that the Promise
of the Lord might be fulfilled which he made to his
People & that the Lamanites might come to the knowledge
of their Fathers & that they might know the Promises of
the Lord that they may believe the Gospel & rely upon the
merits of Jesus Christ & that they might be glorified
through faith in his name & that through their
they might
be saved Amen Received in Harmony Susquehannah Penn

Feb AD 1829 A Revelation to Joseph the Father of the
Seer he desired to know what the Lord had for him to do
& this is what he Received as follows

Saying now Behold a Marvelous work is about
to come forth among the children of men therefore
O ye that embark in the service of God seethat ye
serve him with all your heart might mind & strength
that ye may stand blameless before God at the last day
therefore if ye have desires to serve God ye are called to the

Thou do this thou shalt be delivered up & become as other

men & have no more gift & when thou deliveredst up that

and power
Which ~~that which~~ God had given thee {r\s}ight to Translate

thou deliveredest up that which was Sacred into the hands

of a wicked man who has Set at naught the Councils of God

has   were
& ~~hath~~ broken the most Sacred promises which ~~was~~ made before

has
God & ~~hath~~ depended upon his own Judgement & boasted in

his own ~~arm~~[4] wisdom & this is the reason that thou hast

lost thy ~~Pr◊~~[5] Privileges for a Season for thou hast suffered

~~that~~ the council of thy directors to be trampeled upon from
nevertheless my work shall go forth & accomplish ~~its~~ ⟨my⟩ purposes /[6] has
the begining for as the knowledge of a Saveiour ~~hath~~ come

even
into the world so shall the knowledge of my People the Nephiti{s\es}

Zorumites ~~& the Lemuelites~~
& the Jacobites & the Josephites & the ~~Lamanites~~ come to the

uel
~~Lamanites~~ knowledge of the Lamanites, & the L{a\e}manites &

the Ishmaelites which dwindeled in unbelief because of

have
the iniquities of their Fathers who ~~hath~~ been suffered to

destroy their Brethren because of their iniquities & their

Abominations & for this very Purpose are these Plates
preserved
~~prepared~~ which contain these Records that the Promises

of the Lord might be fulfilled which he made to his

People & that the Lamanites might come to the knowledge

t   might
of their Fahers & that they ~~may~~ know the Promises of

&
the Lord that they may believe the Gospel & rely upon the

merits of Jesus Christ & ~~that they might~~ be glorified
through their
through faith {i\o}n his name & that ~~they might~~ repent
they might
& be Saved Amen Received in Harmony Susquehannah Penn

Feb[r.]
♦ AD 182{8\9} A Revelation to Joseph [Smith Sr.] the Father of the

Seer he desired to know what the Lord had for him to do

& this is what he Received as follows

Saying now Behold a Marvelous work is about

to come forth among the children of men therefore

O ye that embark in the service of God see that ye

Serve him with all your heart might mind & Strength

that ye may stand blameless before God at the last day

therefore if ye have desires to serve God ye are Called to the [*pages 3–10 missing*]

ORIGINAL INSCRIPTION
John Whitmer

REVISIONS
Oliver Cowdery
William W. Phelps
Sidney Rigdon
Joseph Smith
John Whitmer
Unidentified

4. Two layers of deletion: first layer by John Whitmer at the time of original inscription and second layer by Sidney Rigdon.

5. "Pr◊" wipe-erased and then stricken.

6. Sidney Rigdon inserted "/" to separate insertions in the manuscript.

shall publish it as the Record of Nephi; & thus I will confound those ~~who~~ have altered my words. I will not suffer that they shall destroy my work; yea, I will shew unto them that my wisdom is greater than the cuning of the Devil.[11] Behold they have only got a part, or an abridgement of the account of Nephi. Behold these are many things engraven on the Plates of Nephi, which do throw greater ~~light~~ views upon my Gospel; therefore, it is wisdom in me, that you ~~ye~~ should translate this first part of the engravings of Nephi, & send ~~forth~~ them in this ~~a~~ work. & behold ~~all~~ the remainder of this work does ~~it~~ contain all those parts of my Gospel which my ~~the~~ Holy Prophets; yea, & also my Disciples desired in their Prayers, should come forth unto this People. & I said unto them that it should be granted unto them ~~them~~ according to their faith in their Prayers; yea & this was ~~is~~ their faith, that my Gospel which I gave unto them, that they might Preach in their days, might come unto their Brethren, the Laman= =ites, & also, all that had become Lamanites, because of their dissentions. [12] now this is not all; their faith in their Prayers were ~~was~~ that this Gospel should be made known also, if it were posible ~~to that~~ that other nations who ~~should~~ possess this Land; & thus they did leave a blessing upon this Land in their prayers, that whosoever should believe in this Gospel, in this land, might have Eternal life; yea, that it might be free unto all of whatsoever Nation, Kindred, Tongue, or People, they may be.[13] & now, Behold, according to their faith in their Prayers, will I bring this part of my Gospel to the knowledge of my People. Behold I do not bring it to destroy that which they have received, but to build it up.[14] & for this cause have I said, if this generation harden not their hearts, I will establish my Church among them. now I do not say this to destroy my Church, but I say this to build up my Church: therefore, whosoever belongeth to my Church need not fear, for such shall inherit the Kingdom of Heaven: but it is they who ~~who~~ do not fear me, neither keep my commandments, but buildeth up Churches unto themselves, to get gain; yea, & all those that do wickedly, & buildeth up the Kingdom of the Devil; yea, Verily, Verily I say unto you, that it is they that I will disturb, distirub, & cause to tremble & shake to the Center.[15] Behold I am Jesus Christ, the Son of God: I came unto my own, & my own received

♦ ⁷Shall publish it as the Record of Nephi, & thus I will confound
　　　who　　　　　　　　　　　&
those ~~which~~ have altered my words. I will not suffer that they

shall destroy my work; yea, I will shew unto them that my wisdom
　　　　　　　　　　　　　　　　11
is greater than the cuning of the Devil. Behold th{y\ey} have only

got a part, or an abridgement of the account of Nephi. Behold there

are many things engraven on the Plates of Nephi, which do throw
　　　~~light~~ views
greater ~~views~~ upon my Gospel: therefore, it is wisdom in me, that
you
~~ye~~ should translate this first part of the engravings of Nephi,
　　them　　　　　　　all
& send forth in this ◊⁸ work. & behold ~~all~~ the remainder of this work
does　　^　　all　　　　　　　　　{my\my}
~~doth~~ contain ~~all~~ those parts of my Gospel which ~~the~~ Holy Prophets;
　　　　　　　　　　　　　　　　　^
yea, & also my Deciples desired in their Prayers, should come forth
　　　　　　　　　　　　　　　　　　　　　unto
unto this People. & I said unto them that it should be granted ~~unto~~
　them　　　　　　　　　　　　　　was
~~them~~ according to their faith in their Prayers; yea & this ~~is~~ their

faith, that my Gospel which I g{iv\av}e unto them, that they might

Preach in their days, might come unto their Brethren, the Laman

=ites, & also, all that had become Lamanites, because of their d{s\issentions}
12　　　　　　　but　　　　　　　were,
now this is not all, their faith in their Prayers ~~where~~ that this
　　　　　　　　^
　　　　　　　　　　　　　　　　　　to
Gospel should be made known also, if it were {so\posible} ~~that~~ that
　　who　　　　　　　　　　　　　　^
other Nations should p[o]ssess th{e\is} Land; & thus they did leave a
　　　　^
blessing upon this Land in their prayers, that whosoever should

believe in this Gospel, in this land, might have Eternal life;

yea, that it might be free unto all of whatsoever Nation, Kindred,
　　　　　　　　　　　　　　13
Tongue, or People, they may be{;\.} & now, Behold, according to their

faith in their Prayers, will I bring this part of my Gospel
　　　　　　　　　　^
to the knowledge of my People. Behold I do not bring it to
　　　　　　　　　　　　　　　14
destroy that which they have received, but to build it up. & for

this cause have I said, if this generation harden not their hearts, I

will establish my Church among them. now I do not say this

to destroy my Church, but I say this to build up my Church: therefore,

whosoever belongeth to my Church need not fe{◊r\ar}, for such shall inheri
　　　　　　　　　　　　　　who
=t the Kingdom of Heaven: but it is they ~~which~~ do not fear me, neither

keep my commandments, but buildeth up {◊\Churches} unto themselves, to get

gain; yea, & all those that do wickedly, & buildeth up the Kingdom of
　　　　　　　　　　　　　　　　that
the Devil; yea, Verily, Verily I say unto you, it is they that I will ~~disturb~~
　　　　　　　　　　　　　　　^　15
disturb, & cause to tremble & shake, to the center. Behold I am Jesus

Christ, the Son of God: I came unto my own, & my own received

ORIGINAL INSCRIPTION
John Whitmer

REVISIONS
Oliver Cowdery
William W. Phelps
Sidney Rigdon
Joseph Smith
John Whitmer
Unidentified

7. The first publication reflecting most redactions in this revelation is the Book of Commandments (chapter 9).

8. Possibly "R" or the initial strokes of a misshapen "w".

Me not. I am the light which shineth in darkness & the darkness comprehendeth it not. I am he who said other sheep have I which are not of this fold, unto my Disciples, & many there were that understood me not. 16 & I will shew unto this People, that People, that I had other sheep, & that they were a branch of the House of Jacob; & I will bring to light their marvelous works, which they did in my name; yea, & I will also bring to light my Gospel, which was ministered unto them, & behold they shall not contradict deny you that which I have received, but they shall bring it up, & shall bring to light the true points of my doctrine, yea, & the only doctrine which is in me; & this I do that I may establish my Gospel, that there may not be so much contention; yea, Satan doth stir up the hearts of the People to contention, concerning the points of my doctrine; & in these things they do err, for they do wrest the Scriptures, & do not understand them. therefore, I will unfold unto them, this great mystery, for behold, I will gather them to go as a hen gathereth her Chickens under her wings, if they will not harden their hearts; yea, if they will come, they may & partake of the waters of life freely. 17 Behold this is my doctrine: whosoever repenteth, & cometh unto me, the same is my Church; whosoever declareth more or less then this, the same is not of me, but is against me: therefore, he is not of my Church. 18 And now, Behold whosoever is of my Church, & endureth of my Church to the end, him will I establish upon my Rock, & the gates of Hell shall not prevail against them him 19 & now, remember the words of him who is the life & the light of the world, your Redeemer, your Lord & your God; Amen.

6th Commandment AD 1829

A Revelation to Oliver he being desirous to know whether the Lord would grant him the gift of Revelation & Translation given in Harmony Susquehannah Pennsylvania April 1829

Oliver Verily Verily I say unto you that assuredly as the Lord liveth which is your God & your Redeemer even so sure you shall receive a knowledge of whatsoever things you shall ask with an honest heart believing that you

12 [verso]

Me not. I am the light which shineth in darkness & the

         who
darkness comprehendeth it not. I am he ~~which~~ said ot{◊◊r\her} sheep

have I which are not of this fold, unto my Deciples, & many there
   that   16   ~~People~~
were ~~which~~ understood me not. & I will shew unto this ~~that~~ People,
             ^

that I had other sheep, & that they were a branch of the House

        their
of Jacob; & I will bring to light ~~these~~ marvelous works, which

they did in my name; yea, & I will also bring to light my

                  it
Gospel, which was m{inistered\anifested} unto them, & behold {~~they~~\they} shall not
~~contradict~~ deny you
            it
deny that which ~~ye~~ have received, but {~~they~~\th[e]y} shall build it up, & shall
^

bring to light the true points of my doctrine; yea, & the only

         m{y\ay}
doctrine which is in me; & this I do that I establish my Gospel,
         ^

that there may not be so much contention; yea, Satan doth

Stir up the hearts of the People to contention, concerning

the points of my doct{◊\rine}; & in these things they do err, for
    wrest
they do ~~arrest~~ the Scriptures, & do not understand them:
   ~~arrest~~
therefore, I will unfold unto them, this great mystery, for

Behold, I will gether them ~~to ge~~ as a hen gethereth her

Chickens under her wings, if they will not harden their
           ~~come~~
hearts; yea, if they will come, they may & partake of the waters
            ^
   17
of life freely. Behold this is my doctrine: whosoever repenteth, &
        of
cometh unto me, the same is my Church: whos[o]ever declareth
        ^
   the same
more or less then this, is not of me, but is against me: therefore,
    ^18 And
he is not of my Church. now, Behold whosoever is of my Church, &

& endureth {in\of} my church to the end, him will I establish upon

my {r\R}ock, & the gates of Hell shall not prevail against ~~him~~
 th{i\e}m.   him
~~them~~ 19 & now, remember the words of {◊\who} h{a\i}s the life & the light
              ^

of the world, your {r\R}edeemer, your Lord & your God: Amen.—

♦ ⁹6ᵗʰ⁻ Commandment AD 1829

A Revelation to Oliver [Cowdery] he being desirous to know whether

the Lord would grant him the gift of ~~Revelation~~ {& th◊\Translation}

given in Harmony Sus{◊\quehannah} Pennsylvania April 1829

  Oliver Verily Verily I say unto you that as a~~Sh~~uredly

as the Lord liveth which is your God & your Redeemer even
   you ~~you~~
so ~~sh~~ure shall ~~ye~~ receive a knowledge of whatsoever things
you ^   you
~~ye~~ shall ask with an honest heart believeing that ~~ye~~

Original Inscription
John Whitmer

Revisions
Oliver Cowdery
William W. Phelps
Sidney Rigdon
Joseph Smith
John Whitmer
Unidentified

9. The first publication reflecting most redactions in this revelation is the Book of Commandments (chapter 7).

shall receive, a knowledge concerning the engravings of old
Records which are ancient which contain those parts of my
Scriptures of which has been spoken by the manifestation
of my spirit yea Behold I will tell you in your mind & in your
heart by the Holy Ghost which shall come upon you & which
shall dwell in your heart now Behold this is the spirit of
Revelation Behold this is the spirit by which Moses brought the
Children of Israel through the Red Sea on dry ground there
=fore this is thy gift apply unto it & blessed art thou for
it shall deliver you out of the hands of your enemies when if it
were not so they would slay you & bring your soul to distruction
O Remember these words & keep my commandments remem=
=ber this is your gift now this is not all for you have another
gift which is the gift of working with the rod Behold
it has told you things Behold there is no other power save
God that can cause this rod of Nature to work in your
hands for it is the work of God & therefore whatsoever you shall
ask me to tell you by that means that will I grant unto you
that you shall know remember that without faith you can do
nothing triffle not with these things do not ask for that
which you had not ought ask that you may know the mysteries
of God & that you may Translate all those ancient Records which
have been hid up which are sacred & according to your faith
shall it be done unto you Behold it is I that have spoken it
& I am the same which spake unto you from the begining amen

7th COMMANDMENT AD 1829

A Revelation to Joseph & Oliver concerning John the
Beloved Deiple who leaned on his Saveiours breast
given in Harmony Susquehannah County Pennsylvania April 1829
And the Lord said unto me. John my Beloved what deriver=
=dst thou & I said Lord give unto me power that I may bring
souls unto thee & the Lord said unto me Verily Verily I say
unto thee because thou deseredst this thou shalt tarry until
I come in my glory & for this cause the Lord said unto
Peter if I will that he tarry till I come what is that to thee

Shall receive, a knowledge concerning the engraveings of old

Records which are ancient which contain those parts of my

Scriptures ~~of~~ which ~~hath~~ has been spoken by the manifestation

of my Spirit yea Behold I will tell you in your mind & in your

heart by the Holy Ghost which Shall come upon you & which

shall dwell in your heart now Behold this is the spirit of

Revelation Behold this is the spirit {w\by} which Moses brought the

children of Israel through the red Sea on dry ground there=

=fore this is thy gift apply unto it & blessed art thou for

it shall deliver you out of the hands of your enemies when if it

were not so they would sl{e\a}y ~~thee~~ you & bring ~~thy~~ your soul to distruction

O remember these words & keep my commandments remem-

=ber this is ~~thy~~ your gift now this is not all for ~~thou hast~~ you have another

gift which is the gift of working with the ~~sprout~~ rod Behold

it ~~hath~~ has told you things Behold there is no other power save

God that can cause this ~~thing of Nature~~ rod to work in your

hands for it is the work of God & therefore whatsoever ~~ye~~ you shall

ask to tell you by that means that will ~~he~~ I grant unto you me

that ~~ye~~ you shall know remember that without faith ~~ye~~ you can do

nothing trifle not with these things do not ask for that

which ~~ye had not~~ you ought not ask that ~~ye~~ you may know the mysteries

of God & that ~~ye~~ you may Translate all those ancient Records which

have been hid up which are Sacred & according to your faith

~~shall~~ shall it be done unto you Behold it is I that have spoken it

& I am the same which spake[10] unto you from the begining amen

ORIGINAL INSCRIPTION
John Whitmer

REVISIONS
Oliver Cowdery
William W. Phelps
Sidney Rigdon
Joseph Smith
John Whitmer
Unidentified

10. Or "spoke".

♦ 7ᵗʰ· Commandment AD 1829

A Revelation to Joseph & Oliver [Cowdery] concerning John the

Beloved Deciple who leaned on his Saveiours breast

given {o\in} Harmony Susquehannah County Pennsylvania April 1829

And the Lord said unto me. John my Beloved what desires=

=dst thou & I said Lord give unto me power that I may bring

souls unto thee & the Lord said unto me Veriley Verily I say

unto thee because thou desiredst this thou shalt tarry until

I come in my glory & for this cause the Lord said unto

Peter if I will that he tarry till I come what is that to thee

For he desiredst of me that he might bring souls unto
me but thou desiredst that thou mightest come unto me
in my Kingdom I say unto thee Peter this was a good
desire but my beloved ~~has~~ has undertaken a greater work
Verily I say unto you ye shall both have according to
your desires for ye hath ~~joy~~ rejoice in that which ye desired

8ᵗʰ Commandment AD 1829

A Revelation to Oliver he was desirous to
know the reason why he could not Translate & thus said the Lord
unto him

Rec'd in harmony Susquehanah County Pennsylvania April 1829
Behold I say unto you my Son that because ~~ye~~ you did not
Translate according to that which ~~ye~~ you desired of me & did
commence again to write for my servent Joseph even so
I would that ~~ye~~ now should continue until ye have finished
this Record which I have entrusted unto you & then Behold
other Records have I that I will give unto you power
that ~~ye~~ you may assist to Translate be patient my Son
for it is wisdom in me & it is not expedient that ~~ye~~ you
should translate at this time Behold ~~this~~ the work
which ~~ye~~ you are called to do is to write for my Servent Joseph &
Behold it is because that ~~ye~~ you did not continue as ~~ye~~ you commenced
when ~~ye~~ you began ~~commenced~~ to Translate that I have taken away this
privilege from you do not murmer my Son for it is
wisdom in me that I have dealt with you after this man-
ner Behold ~~ye~~ you have not understood ~~ye~~ you have supposed that I
would give it unto you when ~~ye~~ you took no thought
save it was to ask me but Behold I say unto you
that ~~ye~~ you must study it out in your mind then ~~ye~~ you must ask
me if it be right & if it is right I will cause that your bosom
shall burn within you therefore ~~ye~~ you shall feel that it is
right but if it be not right ~~ye~~ you shall have no such feelings but ~~ye~~ you shall have stupor of thought that shall cause
you to forget the thing which is wrong there ~~ye~~ fore you cannot write that which is sacred save it be given unto you

14 [verso]

For he desiredst of me that he might bring souls unto

me but thou desiredst that thou mightest come unto me

in my kingdom I say unto thee Peter this was a good

desire but my beloved ~~hath~~ ^has[11]^ undertaken a greater work

Verily I say unto you ye {s0h\shall} both have according to

your desires for ye both ~~Joy~~ ^rejoice[12]^ in that which ye desired

◆ ¹³8ᵗʰ· Com{a\mandment} AD 1829

A Revelation to Oliver [Cowdery] he was disrous [desirous] to

know the reason why he could not Translate ^&^ thus said the Lord

unto him

Recᵈ· in harmony Susquehannah County Pennsylvania *April 1829*

Behold I say unto you my Son that because ~~ye~~ ^you^ did not

Translate according to that which ~~ye~~ ^you^ desired of me & did

commence again to write for my servent Joseph even so

I would that ~~ye~~ ^ye^ ^now^ Should continue until ye have finished

this Record which I have entrusted unto you & then Behold

other Records have I that I will give unto you power

that ~~ye~~ ^you^ may assist to Translate be patient my Son

for it is wisdom in me & it is not expedient that ~~ye~~ ^you^

should translate at this time Behold ~~this is~~ the work

which ~~ye~~ ^you^ are called to do is to write for my Servent ^Joseph^ &

Behold it is because that ~~ye~~ ^you^ did not continue as ~~ye~~ ^you^ commenced

when ~~ye~~ ^you^ ~~commenced~~ ^began^ to Translate that I have taken away this

privilege from you do not murmer my Son for it is

wisdom in me that I have dealt with you after this man=

=ner Behold ~~ye~~ ^you^ have not understood ~~ye~~ ^you^ have Supposed that I

would give it unto you when ~~ye~~ ^you^ took no thought

save it was to ask me but Behold I say unto you

that ~~ye~~ ^you^ must study it out in your mind then ~~mu~~ ⟨you⟩ must ask

me if it be right & if it is right I will cause that your bosom

shall burn within you therefore ~~ye~~ ^you^ shall feel that it is

right but if it be not right ~~ye~~ ^you^ shall have no such feeli=

=ngs but ~~ye~~ ^you^ shall have stupor of thought that shall cause

you to forget the thing which is wrong there- ~~ye~~ ^-fore you^ can-

=not wriete that which is sacred save it be given unto you *[pages 15–22 missing]*

Oʀɪɢɪɴᴀʟ Iɴꜱᴄʀɪᴘᴛɪᴏɴ
John Whitmer

Rᴇᴠɪꜱɪᴏɴꜱ
Oliver Cowdery
William W. Phelps
Sidney Rigdon
Joseph Smith
John Whitmer
Unidentified

11. "has" first appears in print in the Book of Commandments (chapter 6).

12. "rejoice" does not appear in any JS-era publication.

13. The first publication reflecting most redactions in this revelation is the Book of Commandments (chapter 8).

Christ to bless & sanctify this bread to the Souls of all those
who partake of it that they may eat in Rememberance of the
Body of thy son & witness unto thee O God the Eternal Father
that they are willing to take upon them the name of thy Son
& always Remember him & keep his commandments which he
has given them that they may always have his spirit to be
with them amen then shall ye take the Cup & say O God
the eternal Father we ask thee in the name of thy son Jesus
Christ to bless & Sanctify this wine to the Souls of all
those who drink of it that they may do it in Remember-
-ance of the Blood of thy Son which was shed for them that they
may witness unto the O God the Eternal Father that they do always
remember him that they may have his spirit to be with them
amen & now Behold I give unto you a commandment that ye
shall not Suffer any one knowingly to partake of my flesh
& blood unworthily when ye shall minister it for Whoso eateth
& drinketh my flesh & blood unworthily eateth & drinketh damnat
=ion to his soul therefore if you know that a man is unworthy
to eat & drink of my flesh & blood ye shall forbid him never-
=theless ye shall not cast him out from among you but ye shall
minister unto him & ye shall pray for him unto the Father in
my name & if so be that he repenteth & is baptized in my name
then ye shall receive him & shall minister unto him of my flesh
& blood but if he repenteth not he shall not be numbered among
my People that he may not destroy my People for Behold I
know my sheep & they are numbered Nevertheless ye shall not
cast him out of your Synagogues or your Places of worship for
unto such ye shall continue to minister for ye know not but
what they will return & repent & come unto me with full purpose
of heart & I shall heal them & ye shall be the means of bringing
salvation unto them therefore keep these sayings which I have
commanded you that ye come not under condemnation for wo
unto him whom the father condemneth & the Church shall
meet together oft for Prayer & suplication casting out none
from your places of worship but rather invite them to
come & each member shall speak & tell the Church of their

♦ [14]Christ to bless & Sanctify this {b̶o̶\bread} to the Souls of all those

who partake of it that they may eat in Rememberance of the

Body of thy son & witness unto thee O God the Eternal Father

that they are willing to take upon them the name of thy Son

& always Remember him & keep his commandments which he

  has
h̶a̶t̶h̶ given them that they may always have his spirit to be

with them amen then shall ye take the Cup & say O God

the eternal Father we ask thee {t̶\in} the name of thy son Jesus

Christ to bless & Sanctify this wine to a̶l̶l̶ the Souls of all

those who drink[15] of it that they may do it in t̶h̶e̶ rem{b̶\ember=}

=ance of the Blood of thy Son which was shed for them that they

may witness unto the[e] O God the Eternal Father that they do always

rem{b̶\ember} him that they may have his spirit to be with them

                       ye
amen & now Behold I give unto you a commandment that y̶e̶

shall not Suffer any one knowingly to partake of my flesh

& blood unworthily when ye shall minister it for whoso eateth

& drinketh my flesh & blood unworthily eateth & drinketh damnat-

=ion to his soul therefore if you know that a man is unworthy

to eat & drink of my flesh & blood ye shall forbid him Never=

=theless ye shall not cast him out from among you but ye shall

minister unto him & ye shall pray for him unto the Father in

my name & if so be that he repenteth & is baptized in my name

then t̶h̶e̶n̶
ye shall receive him & shall minister unto him of my flesh

& blood but if he repenteth not he shall not be numbered among

my People that he may not destroy my People for Behold I

know my sheep & they are numbered Nevertheless ye shall not

cast him out of your Synegogues or your Places of worship for

unto such ye shall continue to minister for ye know not but

what they will return & repent & come unto me with full purpose

of heart & I shall hea{r\l} them & ye shall be the means of bringing

salvation unto them therefore keep these sayings which I have

commanded you that ye come not under condemnation for wo

unto him whom the father Condemneth & the Church shall

meet to gether oft for Prayer & suplication casting out none

from your places of worship but rather invite them to

come & each member shall speak & tell the Church of their

ORIGINAL INSCRIPTION
John Whitmer

REVISIONS
Oliver Cowdery
William W. Phelps
Sidney Rigdon
Joseph Smith
John Whitmer
Unidentified

14. Although most items in Revelation Books 1 and 2 are attributed to JS, an earlier, complete version of this revelation attributes it to Oliver Cowdery. (Oliver Cowdery, Revelation, ca. June 1829, CHL.)

15. An impression of "\" above "drink" may be from a similar mark etched into an earlier page that is now missing.

Progress in their way to eternal life & there shall be no
pride nor envying nor strifes nor malice nor Idolitry nor
whitchcraft nor whoredoms nor fornications nor lying nor
deceits nor no iniquity & if any one is guilty of any of the
least of these & doth not repent & shew fruits meet for
repentance they shall not be numbred among my People
that they may not destroy my People & now I speak unto
the Church again Behold this shall ye say Repent all ye ends of the Earth & come unto me
& be baptized in my name which is Jesus Christ & endure
to the end & ye shall be saved Behold Jesus Christ is the
name which is given of the father & there is none other
name given whereby man can be saved wherefore all
men must take upon them the name which is given
of the Father for in that name shall they be called at
the last day wherefore if they know not the name by
which they are called they cannot have place in the king=
=dom of my Father Behold ye must walk uprightly
before me & sin not & if ye do walk uprightly before
me & sin not my grace is sufficient for you that ye
shall be lifted up at the last day Behold I am Jesus Christ
the Son of the living God I am the same which came
unto my own & my own Received me not I am the light
which shineth in darkness & the darkness comprehendeth it not
these words are not of man nor of men but of me now
remember the words of him who is the first & the last the
light & the life of the world & I Jesus Christ your Lord &
your God & your Redeemer by the power of my spirit hath spoken
it amen & now if I have not authority to write these things
Judge ye Behold ye shall know that I have authority when
you & I shall be brought to stand before the Judgement seat
of Christ now may the grace of God the Father & our Lord
Jesus Christ be & abide with you all & finally save you
eternally in his kingdom through the infinite atonement
which is in Jesus Christ amen Behold I am Oliver
I am an Apostle of Jesus Christ by the will of God
the Father & the Lord Jesus Christ Behold I have written

24 [verso]

Progress in their way to eternal life & there shall be no

pride nor envying nor strifes nor mal{lice\ice} nor Idolitry nor

whitchcraft nor whoredoms nor fornications nor lying nor

deceits nor no iniquity & if any one is guilty of any or the

least of these & doth not repent & shew fruits meet for

repentance they shall not be numbered among my People

that they may not destroy my People & now I speak unto
Elders of again Behold thus shall ye say
the Church repent all ye ends of the Earth & come unto me
{^\^}
& be baptized in my name which is Jesus Christ & endure

to the end & ye shall be saved Behold Jesus Christ is the

name which is given of the father & there is none other

name given whereby man can be saved wherefore all

men must take upon them the name which is given

of the Father for in that name shall they be called at

the last day wherefore if they know not the name by

which they are called they cannot have place in the King=

=dom of my Father Behold ye must walk uprightly

before me & Sin not & if ye do walk uprightly before

me & Sin not my grace is Sufficient for you that ye

shall be lifted up at the last day Behold I am Jesus Christt

the Son of the living God I am the same which came

unto {hθ\my} own & my own Received me not I am the light

which shineth in darkness & the darkness comprehendeth it not

these words are not of man nor of men but of me now

remember the words of him who is the first & the last the

light & the life of the world & I Jesus Christ your Lord &

your God & your redeemer by the power of my spirit hath spoken

it amen & now {I\if} I have not authority to write these things

Judge ye Behold ye shall know that I have authority when

you & I shall be brought to stand before the Judgement seat

of Christ now may the grace of God the Father & our Lord
Amen
Jesus Christ be & abide with you all & finally save you
^
eternally in his Kingdom thorough the infinite atonement

which is in Jesus Christ amen Behold I am Oliver[16]

I am an Apostle of Jesus Christ by the will of God

the Father & the Lord Jesus Christ Behold I have written [*pages 25–26 missing*]

ORIGINAL INSCRIPTION
John Whitmer

REVISIONS
Oliver Cowdery
William W. Phelps
Sidney Rigdon
Joseph Smith
John Whitmer
Unidentified

16. Oliver Cowdery.

By my Almighty power that ye confess your sins lest you
suffer these punishments of which I have spoken of which in
the smalest yea even the least degree ye have tasted at the time
when I withdrew my spirit & I command you that you preach naught
but repentance & shew not these things neither speak these
things unto the World for they cannot bear meat but milk
they must Recieve Wherefore they must not know these things
lest they perish Wherefore learn of me & listen to my
words walk in the meekness of my spirit & you shall have peace
in me (Jesus Christ) by the will of the Father & again I
command you that thou shalt not covet thy Neibours wife
nor seek thy Neibours life & again I command you that thou
shalt not covet thine own Property but impart it freely to
the printing of the Book of Morman which contains the truth and the
word of God which is my word to the Gentiles that soon it may
go to the Jews of which the Lamanites are a Remnant that
they may Believe the Gospel & look not for a Masiah to come
for he which has already come & again I command you that thou
shalt pray vocally as well as to thyself yea before the World
as well as in secret in Publick as well as in private &
thou shalt declare glad tidings yea Publish it upon the
Mountains & upon every high place & among every People which
thou shalt be permited to see & thou shalt do it with all
humility trusting in me Reviling not against Revilers &
of tenets thou shalt not talk but thou shalt declare
Repentance & faith on the Saviour & Remissions of Sins by
Baptism & by fire yea even the Holy Ghost Behold this is a
great & the last commandment which I shall give unto you
for this shall suffice for thy daily walk even unto the end
of thy life & misery thou shalt Recieve if thou wilt
sleight these Councils yea even distruction of thyself &
Property Impart a portion of thy Property yea even a part
of thy lands & all save the support of thy family Pay the
Printers debt Release thyself from Bondage Leave thy House
& home except when thou shalt desire to see them & speak
freely to all yea Preach exhort declare the truth even

♦ ¹⁷By my Almighty power ~~that ye~~ confess your sins lest ~~ye~~
that ye to   you

suffer these punishments of which I have spoken of which in
                even   you ye have   the
the smalest yea ~~in~~ the least decree ~~ye have~~ tasted at ~~a~~ time
when   &   you¹⁸
I withdrew my spirit I command you that ~~ye~~ preach naught

but repentance & shew not these things neither speak these

things unto the World. for they cannot bear meat but milk

they must receive. Wherefore, they must not know these things

lest they perish Wherefore learn of me & listen to my
                                            you
words walk in the meekness of my spirit & ~~ye~~ shall have peace

in me (Jesus Christ) by the will of the Father & again I

command you that thou shalt not covet thy Neibours wife.

nor seek thy Neibours life. & again I command you that thou

shalt not covet thine own Property but impart it freely to
                                            the truth and the
the printing of the Books ~~of~~ Mormon {e\which} contains ~~of the~~
                                    the
word of God which is my word to Gentiles that soon it may

go to the Jews of which the Lamanites {~~of~~\are} a Remnant that

they may Believe the Gospel & look not for a Masiah to come
~~for he~~ which
~~which~~ has al{~~ra~~\ready} come & again I command you that thou

shalt pray vocally as well as to thyself yea before the World

as well as in seecret in Publick as well as in private &

thou shalt declare glad tidings yea Publish it upon the

Mountains & upon evry high place & among evry People which

thou shalt be permited to see & thou shalt do it with all

humility trusting in me Reviling not against Revilers &

of tenets thou shalt not ~~ta{k◊\lk}~~¹⁹ talk but thou shalt declare

Repentance & faith on the Saveiour & Remissions of Sins by

Baptism & by fire yea even the Holy Ghost Behold this is a
                        the
great & last commandment which I shall give unto you

for this shall suffice for thy daily walk even unto the end
                        thou
of thy life & misery shalt ~~thou~~ Receive if thou wilt

sleight these Councils yea even distruction of thyself &

Property. Impart a portion of thy Property yea even a part

of thy lands & all save the support of thy family Pay the

Printers debt Release thyself from Bondage Leave thy House

& home except when thou shalt desire to see them & speak

freely to all yea Preach exhort declare the truth even

ORIGINAL INSCRIPTION
John Whitmer

REVISIONS
Oliver Cowdery
William W. Phelps
Sidney Rigdon
Joseph Smith
John Whitmer
Unidentified

17. The first publication reflecting most redactions in this revelation is the Book of Commandments (chapter 16).

18. John Whitmer likely intended to insert "ye" after striking "you," as he did above the previous line.

19. "k◊" wipe-erased and written over; then whole word stricken.

With a loud voice with a sound of rejoiceing crying
Hozannah Hozannah blised be the name of the Lord God
pray always & I will pour out my spirit upon you, & great
shall be your Blessing: yea, even more than if you should
Obtain treasures of Earth, & corruptableness to the extent
thereof. Behold, canst thou read this without Rejoiceing, &
lifting up thy heart for gladness; or canst thou runabout
longer as a blind guide; or canst thou be humble & meek
& conduct thyself wisely before me; yea, come unto me
thy Saviour. amen.

17th Commandment AD April 6 1830

A Revelation to Joseph the Seer by way of comm=
=andment to the Church given at Fayette Seneca County
State of New York   A Revelation to me Joseph by way
of commandment to the Church Behold these shall be a Record kept among you
& in it thou shalt be called a Seer a Translater a Prophet
an Apostle of Jesus Christ an Elder of the Church through
the will of God the Father & the grace of our Lord Jesus Christ
being inspired of the Holy Ghost to lay the foundation
thereof & to build it up unto the most holy faith which
Church was Organized & established in the year of our Lord
one thousand Eight Hundred & Thirty in the forth Month
on the Sixth day of the month which is called April
Wherefore meaning the Church thou shalt give heed unto
all his words & commandments which he shall give unto
you as he receiveth them walking in all holyness before
me for his word ye shall receive as if from mine own
mouth in all Patience & faith for by doing these things
the gaits of Hell shall not prevail against you yea & the
Lord God will disperse the Powers of darkness from before
you & cause the Heavens to shake for your Good & his
names glory for thus saith the Lord God him have I inspired
to move the cause of Zion in Mighty power for good &
his dilligence I know & his prayers I have heard yea
his weeping for Zion I have seen & I will cause that

30 [verso]

Behold I speak a few words unto you, Samuel. {th\for} thou

also art under no condemnation,,[29] & thy calling is to Exhortation, and

to strengthen the Church. & thou art not yet called to prea[c]h

before the world. Amen.

♦ [30]21st Comandment AD 1830

A Commandment to given to {◊\Joseph} [Smith Sr.] at Manchester

Ontario County State of New York

~~unto you Joseph f~~[31]   Behold I speak a few words

unto you, Joseph: for thou art under no condemnation,

& thy calling also is to Exhortation, & to strengthen the

Church. & this is thy duty from henceforth & forever. amen.

♦ [32]22nd Commandment AD 1830

A Commandment to Joseph Knight given at

Manchester Ontario County State of New York
                    by   you
Behold I manifest unto you these words, that ~~thou~~ must
     your   you
take up ~~thy~~ Cross, in the which ~~thou~~ must pray vocally,
                              your
before the World, as well as in Seecret,, & in ~~thy~~ family &
     your   2 {&\and}   your
among ~~thy~~ friends, & in all Places. Behold it is ~~thy~~ duty
                 give ~~thy~~   ~~let your~~
to unite with the true Church, & ~~give thy~~ Language {to\be given}[33]
to   you
Exhortation continually, that ~~thou~~ may~~est~~ Receive the

reward of the Labou{◊◊\rer}.[34] amen.

♦ 23 Comandment AD 1830

A Revelation given to ~~Joseph~~ Oliver [Cowdery] Hyram [Hiram Page] Josiah [Stowell]

& Joseph Knight given at Manchester Ontario C[ounty] New York

Behold I the Lord am God I Created the Heavens & the Earth

& all things that in them is wherefore they are mine & I sway

my scepter over all the Earth & ye are in my hands to will &

to do that I can deliver you o{◊\ut} of evry difficulty & affliction

according to your faith & dilligence & uprightness Before me
                                   Joseph
& I have cov{◊\enanted} with my Servent that earth nor Hell

combined againsts him shall not take the Blessing out of

his hands which I have prepared for him if he walketh

uprightly before me neither the spiritual nor the temporal

ORIGINAL INSCRIPTION
John Whitmer

REVISIONS
Oliver Cowdery
William W. Phelps
Sidney Rigdon
Joseph Smith
John Whitmer
Unidentified

29. Or ",x".

30. The first publication reflecting most redactions in this revelation is the Book of Commandments (chapter 20).

31. "unto you Joseph f" partially wipe-erased and then stricken.

32. The first publication reflecting most redactions in this revelation is the Book of Commandments (chapter 21).

33. Two layers of deletion: one layer by John Whitmer and one layer by an unidentified scribe. The order of cancellation is unknown.

34. Possibly "Labou{rs\rer}" or "Labou{◊r\rer}".

Blessing & Behold I also covenanted with those who have assisted
him in my work that I will do unto them even the same
Because they have done that which is pleasing in my sight
(yea even all save ~~————————~~ it be one only) Wherefore be
dilligent in securing the Copy right of my ~~servent~~ work
upon all the face of the Earth of which is known by you
unto ~~unto~~ my servent Joseph & unto him whom he willeth
according as I shall command him that the faithful & the
righteous may retain the temporal Blessing as well as the
Spiritual & also that my work be not destroyed by the workers
of iniquity to their own distruction & damnation when they
are fully ripe & now Behold I say unto you that I have coven=
=anted & it Pleaseth me that Oliver Cowdery Joseph Knight Hyram
Page & Josiah Stowel shall do my work in this thing yea
                    Copy
even in securing the ^Right & they shall do it with an eye single
to my glory that it may be the means of bringing souls
~~unto me~~ Salvation through mine only Begotten Behold I am
God I have spoken it ~~it is expedient in me~~ Wherefore I say
unto you that ye shall go ~~————~~ seeking me Continually
through mine only Begotten & if ye do this ye shall have my
Spirit to go with you & ye shall have an addition of all things
which is expedient in me & I grant unto my servent a privelige
        a copyright
that he may sell ^through you speaking after the manner of
men for the four Provinces if the People harden not their hearts
against the enticeings of my spirit & my word for Behold it
lieth in themselves to their condemnation or to their Salvation
Behold my way is before you & the means I will prepare
& the ~~Blessing I hold in mine own~~ hand & if ye are faithful
I will pour out upon you even as much as ye are able to
Bear & thus it shall be Behold I am the father & it is through
mine only begotten which is Jesus Christ your Redeemer amen

Blessing & Behold I also covenanted with those who have assisted

him in my work that I will do unto them even the same

Because they have done that which is pleasing in my sight

³⁶(yea even all save M◊◊tin only³⁵ it be one o{l\nly}) Wherefore be

dilligent in Securing the Copy right of my ~~Servent~~ work

upon all the face of the Earth of which is known by you

unto ~~unto~~ my Servent Joseph & unto him whom he willeth

accordinng as I shall command him that the faithful & the

righteous may retain the temperal Blessing as well as the

Spirit[u]al & also that my work be not destroyed by the workers

of iniquity to the{r\ir} own distruction & damnation when they

are fully ripe & now Behold I say unto you that I have coven=

=anted & it Pleaseth me that Oliver Cowderey Joseph Knight Hyram

Pagee & Josiah Stowel shall do my work in this thing yea

Copy
even in securing the right & they shall do it with an eye single
     ^

to my Glory that it may be the means of bringing souls

unto ~~me~~ Salvation through mine only Be{t\gotten} Behold I am

God I have spoken it ~~& it is expedient in me~~ Wherefor I say

unto you that ye shall go ~~to Kingston~~ seeking me continually

through mine only Be{t\gotten} & if ye do this ye shall have my

spirit to go with you & ye shall have an addition of all things

      amen³⁷
which is expedient in me. & I grant unto my servent a privelige

   a copyright
that he may sell through you speaking after the manner of
     ^

men for the four Provinces if the People harden not their hearts

against the enticeings of my spirit & my word for Behold it

lieth in themselves to their condemnation &{◊\or} to th{er\eir} salvation

Behold my way is before you & the means I will prepare

& the Blessing I hold in mine own hand & if ye are faithful

I will pour out upon you even as much as ye are able to

Bear & thus it shall be Behold I am the father & it is through

mine o{◊\nly} begotten which is Jesus Christ your Redeemer amen

ORIGINAL INSCRIPTION
John Whitmer

REVISIONS
Oliver Cowdery
William W. Phelps
Sidney Rigdon
Joseph Smith
John Whitmer
Unidentified

35. Likely "Martin [Harris]". "M◊◊tin" and "only" have two layers of deletion: first layer by John Whitmer at the time of original inscription and second layer possibly by John Whitmer at a later time. "M◊◊tin" was also stricken a third time by an unidentified scribe. (See also pp. xli and xliii herein.)

36. Opening and closing parentheses possibly inserted at a later time.

37. An unidentified scribe crossed out the text from this point to the end of the revelation, presumably indicating that the revelation should end with "amen." The ink flow of the lines used to cross out the text possibly matches the ink flow of the inserted "amen".

24 Commandment AD 1830

A Revelation given to Joseph the Seer Same were
anxious to join the Church without Rebaptism & joseph
enquired of the Lord & he received as follows

[A commandment unto the Church of Christ which
was established in there ~~the day~~ last days one thousand eight
hundred & thirty on the forth month & in the sixth day of
the month which is called April] Behold I say unto you that
all old covenants have I ~~called~~ caused to be done away in
this thing & this is a New & an everlasting covenant even
~~the that~~ ~~the Same~~ which was from the begining wherefore although a
man^ shouldest be baptized an hundred times it availeth
him nothing for ye cannot enter into the strait gate
by the law of Moses neither by your dead works; for it
is because of your dead works, that I have caused this
last covenant, & this Church to be built up unto me; even
as in days of old. wherefore, enter ye in at the gate as
I have commanded, & seek not to Counsil your God. Amen.

25th Commandment. AD July 1830

A Revelation to Joseph & Oliver given at Harmony
Susquehannah County Pennsylvania telling them concerning two
Calls &c

Behold thou wast called & chosen to write the Book of Mormon
~~& to my~~ ministry & I have lifted thee up out of thine afflictions
& have counseled thee that thou hast been delivered from all
thine enemies & thou hast been delivered from the power
of satan & from darkness Neverthele∫s thou art not excusa-
-ble in thy Transgre∫sions Neverthele∫s go thy way & sin
no more magnify thine ~~thy~~ office & after ~~that~~ thou hast sowed
thy fields & secured them then go speedily unto the Church
which is in Colesvill Fayette & Manchester & they shall
support thee & I will ble∫s them both spiritually &
temporally but if they receive thee not I will send
upon them a Cursing instead of a ble∫sing & thou shalt
continue in calling upon me in my name & writing the

32 [verso]

◆ ³⁸24 Com{a\mandment} AD ₁₈₃₀

A Revelation {ᴓ\given} to Joseph the Seer Some were

anxious to Join the Church {~~they~~\without} Rebaptism & Joseph

enquired of the Lord & {~~rece~~\he} received as follows

³⁹[A commandment unto the Church of Christ which

these

was established in {~~these\the~~} ~~day~~⁴⁰ last days one thousand {s\eight}

hundred & thirty on the forth month & on the sixth day of

the month which is called April] Behold I say unto you that

all old covenants have I ~~called~~⁴¹ caused to be done away in

this thing & this is a New & an everlasting covenant even

that

{~~wherefore\the same~~} which was from the begining wherefore although a

man shouldest be baptized an hundred times it availeth

at

him nothing for ye cannot enter in~~to~~ the strait gate

by the law of Moses neither by your dead works; for it

is because of your dead works, that I have caused this

last covenant, & this church to be built up unto me; even

as in days of old. wherefore, enter ye in at the {~~at\gt~~\gate} as

I have commanded, & seek not to Coun{ci\se}l your God. Amen.

July

◆ ⁴²25ᵗʰ· Commandment AD 183{1\0}⁴³

A Revelation to Joseph & Oliver [Cowdery] given at Harmony

Susquehannah County Pennsylvania telling them concerning their

Calls &c

Behold thou wast called & Chosen to write the Book of Mormon

& to my ministery & I have lifted thee up out of thine afflictions

& have counseled thee that thou hast been delivered from all

thine enemies & thou hast been delivered from the power

of satan & from darkness Nevertheless thou art not excusa=

=ble in thy Transgressions Nevertheless go thy way & sin

thine

no more magnify ~~thy~~ office & after ~~that~~ thou hast sowed

thy fields & Secured them th{ᴓ\en} go speedily unto the Church

which is in Colesvill Fayette & Manchester & they shall

support thee & I will bless them both spiritually &

temporally but if they receive thee not I will send

upon them a cursing instead of a blessing & thou shalt

⟨God⟩ ~~me~~ in {m\my} name

continue in calling upon ~~in my name~~ & writing the

ᴏʀɪɢɪɴᴀʟ ɪɴsᴄʀɪᴘᴛɪᴏɴ
John Whitmer

ʀᴇᴠɪsɪᴏɴs
Oliver Cowdery
William W. Phelps
Sidney Rigdon
Joseph Smith
John Whitmer
Unidentified

38. The first publication reflecting most redactions in this revelation is the June 1832 issue of *The Evening and the Morning Star.*

39. The text enclosed in brackets did not appear in *The Evening and the Morning Star,* but a modified version appeared as a heading when this revelation was published in the Book of Commandments (chapter 23).

40. "day" stricken by John Whitmer at the time of original inscription, leaving "in these last days". "the" written over "these" and then "{these\the} day" stricken when "these" inserted.

41. "called" wipe-erased and then stricken.

42. The first publication reflecting most redactions in this revelation is the Book of Commandments (chapter 25). Other redactions do not appear in any JS-era publication.

43. This scribal error suggests that John Whitmer copied this revelation into the manuscript book in 1831.

things which shall be given thee by the Comforter & thou
shalt and expounding all scriptures unto the Church & it shall be
given thee in the very moment what thou shalt speak &
write & they shall hear it or I will send unto them a cursing
instead of a blessing for thou shalt devote all thy service in
Zion & in this thou shalt have strength be patient in afflictions
for thou shalt have many but endure them for Lo! I am
with thee our even unto the end of thy days & in temporal labors
thou shalt not have strength for this is not thy calling attend
to thy calling & thou shalt have wherewith to magnify thine
Office & to expound all scriptures & continue in the laying
on of the hands & confirming the Churches & thy brother Oliver
shall continue in bearing my name before the world & also to
the Church & he shall not suppose that he can say enough in
my cause & lo! I am with him to the end in me he shall have
glory & not of himself whether in weakness or in strength
whether in bands or free & at all times & in all places he
shall open his mouth & declare my Gospel as with the voice
of a Trump both day & night & I will give unto him
strength such as is not known among men require not
Miracles except I shall command you except casting out Devils
healing the sick & against Poisons Serpents & against deadly
Poison & these things ye shall not do except it be required of you
by them who desire it that the Scriptures might be fulfilled
for ye shall do according to that which is written
& in whatsoever place ye shall enter in & they receive you not in
my name ye shall leave a cursing instead of a blessing by
casting off the dust of your feet against them as a testim
-ony & cleansing your feet by the wayside & it shall come to
pass that whosoever shall lay their hands upon you by
violence ye shall command to be smitten in my name & behold I will
smite them according to your words in mine own due time
& whosoever shall go to law with you shall be cursed by the law
& thou shalt take no purse nor scrip neither staves neither
two coats for the Church shall give unto you in the very
hour what you need for food & for raiment. for shoes & for

Things which shall be given thee by the Comforter & ~~thou~~
              and
~~shalt~~ expounding all scriptures {to\unto} the Church & it shall be
       ^
given thee in the very moment what thou shalt speak &

write & they shall hear it or I will send unto them a cursing

instead of a blessing for thou shalt devote all thy ser{◊◊\vice} {to\in}

Zion & in this thou shalt have strength be patient in afflictions

for thou shalt have many but endure them for Lo! I am
            you
with ~~thee~~ even unto the end of thy days & in temporal labo{◊◊\◊◊}[44]
       ^
{=rs\thou} shalt not have strength for this is not thy calling attend

to thy calling & thou shalt have wherewith to magnify thine

Office & to expound all scriptures & continue in the laying

{of\on} of the hands & confirming the Churches & thy brother Oliver

Shall continue {to\in} bearing my name before the world & also to

the Church & he shall not suppose that he can say enough in
            I
my cause & lo! am with him to the end in me he shall have
       ^
glory & not of himself whether in weakness or in strength

whether in bonds o{n\r} free & at all times & in all places he

shall open his mouth & declare my Gospel as with the voice

of a Trump both day & night & I will give unto him

strength such as is not known among men require not
                                         out
Miracles except I shall command you except casting Devils
                                         ^
healing the sick & against Poisones [poisonous] Serpents & against deadly

Poison & these things ye shall not do except it be required of you

by them who desire it that the Scriptures might be ful{◊\filled}

for ye shall do according to that which is written ~~in the Scriptures~~

& in whatsoever place ye shall enter in & they receive you not in

my name ye shall leave a cursing instead of a blessing by

casting off the dust of your feet against them as a testim

=ony & cleansing your feet by the wayside & it shall come to

pass that whosoever shall lay their hands upon you by
                        in my name[45]
violence ye shall command to be smitten & behold I will
                        ^
             thy your
smite them according to ~~their~~ words in mine own due time
                   ^   ^   you thee
& whosoever shall go to law with ~~thee~~ shall be cursed by the Law
                              ^
& thou shalt tak[e] no purse nor scrip neither staves neither
                           you
two Coats for the Church shall give unto ~~thee~~ in the verry
       you
hour what ~~thou~~ needest for food & for raiment for shoes & for

Original Inscription
John Whitmer

Revisions
Oliver Cowdery
William W. Phelps
Sidney Rigdon
Joseph Smith
John Whitmer
Unidentified

44. Possibly "{r=\r}",
"{r=\rs}", or "{r\rs}".

45. Although the ink flow
of "in my name" appears to
match the original ink flow,
this phrase was possibly
inserted by John Whitmer at
a later time.

Money & for scrip for the art called to prune my vineyard
with a mighty pruning yea even for the last time yea &
also all those whom thou hast ordained & they shall do even
according to this pattern amen

26th Commandment AD 1830

A Revelation to Joseph Oliver & John given at Harmony
Susquehannah County State of Pennsylvania

Behold, I say unto you, that ye shall let your time
be devoted to the studying the Scriptures, & to preaching, &
to confirming the Church at Colesvill; & to performing
your labours on the Land, such as is required until after
ye shall go to the west, to hold the next conference;
then it shall be made known what they shall do, &
all things shall be done by common consent in the
Church, by much prayer & faith; for all things ye
shall receive by faith. amen

27th Commandment AD 1830

A Revelation to Emma given at Harmony Susquehannah
County State of Pennsylvania giving her a command to
select Hymns &c Emma my daughter in Zion

A Revelation I give unto you concerning my will
Behold thy sins are for given thee & thou art an Elect
Lady whom I have called murmer not because of the
things which thou hast not seen for they are withheld
from thee & the World which is wisdom in me in a time
to come & the office of thy calling shall be for a comfort
unto my Servent Joseph thy husband in his afflictions
with consoleing words in the spirit of meekness & thou
shalt go with him at the time of his going & be unto
him for a Scribe that I may send Oliver whithersoever I will
& thou shalt be ordained under his hand to expound Scriptures
& exhort the Church according as it shall be given thee
by my spirit for he shall lay his hands upon the & thou
shalt receive the Holy Ghost & thy time shall be

34 [verso]

Money & for scrip for ~~thou art~~ you are called to prune my vineyard

with a mighty pruneing yea even for the last time yea &

also all those wh{ich\om} thou hast ordained & they shall do even

according to this pattern amen

♦ 46 26th Commandment AD 1830

A Revelation to Joseph Oliver [Cowdery] & John [Whitmer] given at Harmony

Susquehannah County State of Pennsylvania

Behold, I say unto you, that ye shall let your time

be devoted to the studying the Scriptures, & to preaching, &

to confirming the Church at Colesvill; 2 & to performing

~~thy~~ your labours on the Land, such as is required until after

ye shall go to the west, to hold the next conference; 3

then it shall be made known what ~~thou~~ ye shal{t\l} do{.\,} 4 &

all things shall be done by common consent in the

Church, by much prayer & faith; 5 for all things ye

shall receive by faith. ~~& thus it is~~ {a◊◊n\amen}

♦ 47 27th Commandment AD 1830

A Revelation to Emma [Smith] given at Harmony Susquehan[na]

County state of Pennsylvania giving her a command to

select {h\Hymns} &c Emma my daughter in Zion—

— A Revelation I give unto you concerning my will

Behold thy sins are for given thee & thou art an Elect

Lady whom I have called murmer not because of the

things which thou hast not seen for they are withheld

from thee & the World from which is wisdom in me in a time

to come & the office of thy calling shall be for a comfort

unto my Servent Joseph thy husband in his afflictions

with consoleing words in the spirit of meekness & thou

shalt go with him at the time of his going & be unto

him a Scribe for that I may send Oliver [Cowdery] whithersoever I will

& thou shalt be ordained under his hand to expound Scriptures

& exhort the Church according as it shall be given thee

by my spirit for he shall lay his hands upon the[e] & thou

shalt receive the Holy Ghost & thy time shall be

ORIGINAL INSCRIPTION
John Whitmer

REVISIONS
Oliver Cowdery
William W. Phelps
Sidney Rigdon
Joseph Smith
John Whitmer
Unidentified

46. The first publication reflecting most redactions in this revelation is the Book of Commandments (chapter 27). Although William W. Phelps inserted verse numbers while preparing this revelation for publication in the Book of Commandments, the verse numbers printed therein are slightly different from those that appear here.

47. The first publication reflecting most redactions in this revelation is the Book of Commandments (chapter 26).

given to writing & to Learning must & then needest not for for
thy husband shall support thee from the Church for unto
them is his calling that all things might be revealed unto them
whatsoever I will according to their faith & verily I say unto
thee ~~that~~ thou shalt lay aside the things of this world &
seek for the things of a better & it shall be given thee also
to make a selection of sacred Hymns as it shall be given
the ~~as~~ pleasing unto me to be had in my Church
for my Soul delighteth in the song of the heart yea the
song of the righteous is a prayer unto me & it shall be
answered with a blessing upon their heads wherefore lift up
thy heart & rejoice & cleave unto the covenants which thou hast
made continue in the spirit of meekness & beware of Pride
let thy soul delight in thy husband & the glory which
shall come upon him keep my commandments continually
& a crown of righteousness thou shalt receive & except thou
do this where I am thou canst not come & verily I say unto
thee that this is my voice unto all even so amen

28th Commandment AD 1830

A Revelation to the Church given at Harmony Susquehana
County State of Pennsylvania given to Joseph the seer at a time
that he went to purchase wine for Sacrament & he was stoped by
an Angel & he spok to him as follows Saying

Listen to the voice of Jesus Christ your Lord
your God & your Redeemer whose word is quick & powerful
for Behold I say unto you it mattereth not what ye shall eat
or what ye shall drink when ye partake of the Sacrament
if it so be that ye do it with an eye single to my glory
Remembering unto the Father my Body which was laid down
for you & my blood which was shed for the Remission of
your sins Wherefore a Commandment I give unto you that
ye shall not Purchase Wine neither strong drink of your
enemies Wherefore ye shall partake of none except it is made
new among you yea in this my Fathers Kingdom which
shall be built up on the earth Behold this is wisdom in me

much
Given to writings & to Learning & thou needest not fear for

thy husband shall support thee from the Church for unto

them is {thy\his} calling that all things might be reve{l\aled} unto them

whatsoever I will according to their faith & verily I say unto

that
{you\thee} that thou shalt lay aside the things of this world &

seek for the things of a better & it shall be given thee also

be given
to make a selection of Sacred Hymns as it shall be given

thee as⁴⁸ {it shall\which} ⟨be⟩ is

thee which is pleasing unto me to be had in my Church

for my Soul delighteth in the song of the heart yea the

song of the heart righteous is a prayer unto me & it shall be

answered with a blessing upon their heads wherefore lift up

thy heart & rejoice & cleave unto the covenants which thou hast

made continue in the spirit of meekness & beware of Pride

let thy soul delight in thy husband & the glory which

shall come upon him keep my commandments continually

& a crown of righteousness thou shalt receive & except thou

thou   not   verily
do this where I am {thou\ye}⁴⁹ can{not\st} come & verily I say unto

thee
you that this is my voice unto all even so amen

♦ ⁵⁰28th· # Commandment AD 1830

h
A Revelation to the Church given at Harmony susquehann[a]

County State of Pennsylvania given to Joseph the Seer at a time

that he went to purch{◊s\ase} wine {it\for} Sacrament & he was stoped by

an {a\⟨A⟩}ngel & he he spok to him as follows Saying

Ł Listen to the voice of Jesus Christ your Lord

your God & your Redeemer whose word is quick & powerful

shall
for Behold I say unto you it mattereth not what ye {◊◊\eat}

or what ye shall drink when ye partake of the sacrament

if it so be that ye do it with an eye single to my glory

was
Remembering unto the father my Body which laid down

for you & my blood which was shed for you the Remission of

y{◊\our} sins Wherefore a commandment I give unto you that

ye shall not Purchase Wine neither strong drink of your

of
enemies Wherefore ye shall partake none except it is made

new among you yea in this my Fathers Kingdom which

shall be built up on the earth Behold this is wisdom in me

ORIGINAL INSCRIPTION
John Whitmer

REVISIONS
Oliver Cowdery
William W. Phelps
Sidney Rigdon
Joseph Smith
John Whitmer
Unidentified

48. "as" possibly wipe-erased.

49. "thou" wipe-erased and written over; then whole word stricken.

50. The first publication reflecting most redactions in this revelation is the March 1833 issue of *The Evening and the Morning Star*.

Wherefore marvel not for the hour cometh that I will
drink of the fruit of the Vine with you on the Earth &
with Jabez those whom my father hath given me out of
the world Wherefore lift up your hearts & rejoice & gird
up your loins & be ~~faithat~~ faithful untill I come
even so amen

29th Commandment AD September 1830

A Revelation to ~~Sixed~~ Elders of the Christ &
these members they understood from Holy Writ that the
time had come that the People of God should see eye to eye
& they seeing somewhat different upon the death of Adam
(that is his transgression) therefor they made it a subject
of Prayer & enquired of the Lord & thus came the word of
the Lord through Joseph the Seer saying given at Fayette Seneca
County State of New York

Listen to the voice of Jesus Christ your Redeemer the
great I am whose ~~arm~~ blood of mercy ~~has~~ atoned for your sins
who will gather his People even as a hen gathereth her
Chickens under her wings even as many as will hearken
to my voice & humble themselves before me & call upon
me in mighty prayer Behold Verily Verily I say unto you
at this time your sins are forgiven you Therefore ye receive
these things but remember to sin no more lest perils shall
come upon you Verily I say unto you that ye are chosen
out of the World to declare my Gospel with the sound of
Rejoicing as with the voice of a Trump lift up your hearts
& be glad for I am in your midst & am your advocate
with the Father & it is his good will to give you the
kingdom & as it is written Whatsoever ye shall ask in faith
being united in prayer according to my command ye shall
receive & ye are called to bring to pass the gathering of
mine Elect for mine Elect hear my voice & harden
not their hearts wherefore the decree hath gone forth
from the father that they shall be gathered in unto one
place upon the face of this land to prepare their

Wherefore marvel not for the hour cometh that I will

drink of the fruit of the Vine with you on the Earth &

with {you\all} those whom my father hath given me out of

the world Wherefore lift up your hearts & rejoice & Gird

up your loins & be ~~faitful~~ faithful untill I come

even so amen

♦ ⁵¹29ᵗʰ Commandment AD ^September^ 1830

A Revelation to Six {eders\el\Elders} of the Church &

three members they understood from Holy Writ that the

time had come ^that^ the People of God should see eye to eye

& they seeing somewhat different upon the death of Adam

(that is his transgression) therefor they made it a subject

of Prayer & enquired of the Lord & thus came the word of

the Lord through Joseph the seer ^saying given^ At Fayette Seneca

County State of New York

Listen to the voice of Jesus christ your Redeemer the

great I am whose ~~arm~~ ^alms^ of mercy ~~hath~~ ^has^ atoned for your sins

who will gether his People even as a hen gethereth her

Chickens under her wings even as many as will hearken

to my voice & humble themselves before me & call upon

me in mighty prayer Behold Verily Verily I say unto you

at this time your sins are forgiven you Therefore ye Receive

these things but remember to sin no more lest perils shall

come upon you Verily I say unto you that ye are chosen

out of the World to declare my Gospel with the sound of

Rejoiceing as with the voice of a Trump lift up your hearts

& be glad for I am in your midst & am your advocate

with the Father & it is his good will to give you the

kingdom & as it is written Watsoever ye shall ask in faith

being united in prayer according to my command ye shall

receive & ye are called to bring to pass the gethering of

mine Elect for mine Elect hear my voice & harden

not their hearts wherefore the decree hath gone forth

f{◊\rom} the father that they shall be gethered in unto one

place upon the ~~the~~ face of this land to prepare their

ORIGINAL INSCRIPTION
John Whitmer

REVISIONS
Oliver Cowdery
William W. Phelps
Sidney Rigdon
Joseph Smith
John Whitmer
Unidentified

51. The first publication reflecting most redactions in this revelation is the September 1832 issue of *The Evening and the Morning Star,* although some revisions—including those made by Oliver Cowdery and John Whitmer—first appear in print in the Book of Commandments (chapter 29).

Hearts & be prepared in all things against the day ~~of~~ ^when^ tribulation
& desolation ^are^ sent forth upon the wicked for the hour is nigh
& the day ^is^ soon at hand when the Earth ~~is~~ ^will be^ ripe & all the proud &
they that do wickedly shall be as stuble & I will burn them up
^saith the Lord of hosts^
that wickedness shall not be upon the Earth for the hour is nigh &
that ~~day soon at hand~~ which was spoken by mine Apostles
must be fulfilled for as they spake so shall it come to pass
for I will reveal myself from Heaven with Power & great
glory with all the hosts thereof & dwell in righteousness with
men on Earth a thousand Years & the wicked shall not stand
& again Verily Verily I say unto you & it ~~is~~ ^has^ gone forth in
a firm decree by the will of the father that mine Apostles
the twelve which were with me in my ministery at Jerusalem
shall stand at my right hand at the day of my comeing in
a piller of fire being clothed with Robes of righteousness with
crowns upon their heads in glory even as I am to judge the whole
House of Israel even as many as have loved me & kept my
commandments & none else for a trump shall sound both long
& loud even as upon mount Sinai & all the Earth shall quake
& they shall come forth yea even the dead which died in me
to receive a Crown of righteousness & to be Clothed upon even
as I am to be with me that we may be one, but, Behold I
say unto you that before this great day shall come the Sun
shall be darkened & the moon shall be turned into blood &
the ^the^ stars shall fall from Heaven & there shall be great
signs in the Heavens above & in the Earth beneath & there shall
be weeping & wailing among the ~~sons of men~~ ^inhabitants of the earth^ & there shall
be a great hailstorm sent forth to destroy the Crops of the
Earth & it shall come to pass because of the wickedness of the World
that I will take vengeance upon the Wicked for they will not
Repent for the cup of mine indignation is full for Behold my
blood shall not cleanse them if they ~~hear~~ ^hear me^ not therefore I will ^as the Lord God^
send forth flies upon the face of the Earth which shall take hold of
the inhabitants thereof & shall eat their flesh & shall cause
maggots to come in upon them & their tongues shall be
stayed that they shall not utter against me & their flesh shall

when
Hearts & be prepared in all things against the day ~~of~~ tribulation

are
& desolation ~~is~~ sent forth upon the wicked for the hour is nigh

is   will be
& the day soon at hand when the Earth ~~is~~ ripe & all the proud &

they that do wickedly shall be as stuble & I will burn them up
saith the Lord of hosts
that wickedness shall not be upon the Earth for the hour is nigh &

th{e\⟨at⟩} ~~day soon at hand~~ which was spoken by mine Apostles

must be fulfilled for as they spoke so shall it come to pass

for I will reveal myself from Heaven with Power & great

g{r\lory} with all the hosts thereof & dwell in righteousness with

men on Earth a thousand Years & the wicked shall not stand

has
& again Verily Verily I say unto you & it ~~hath~~ gone forth in

a firm decree by the will of the father that mine Apostles

the twelve which were with me in my ministry at Jerusalem

shall stand at my right hand at the day of my comeing in

a piller of fire being clothed with robes of righteousness with

crowns upon their heads in g{r\lory} even as I am to Judge the {hole\whole}

House of Israel even as many as have loved me & kept my

commandments & none else for a Trump Shall sound both long

& loud even as upon mount Sin{ia\ai} & all the Earth shall quake

& they shall come forth yea even the dead which died in me

to receive a Crown of righteousness & to be Clothed upon even

as I am to be with me that we may be one, but, Behold I

say unto you that before this great day shall come the Sun

shall be darkened & the moon shall be turned into b{o\⟨l⟩}ood &
the
~~some~~ stars shall fall from Heaven & there shall be greate~~r~~

signs in the Heavens above & in the Earth beneath & there shall
inhabitanets of the earth
be weeping & waileing among the ~~host of men~~ & there shall ~~be~~

be a great hailstorm sent forth to destroy the Crops of the

Earth & it shall come to pass because of the wickedness of the World

that I will take vengeance upon the Wicked for they will not

Repent for the cup of mine indignation is full for Behold my
hear me   the Lord God
blood shall not cleanse them if they ~~repent~~ not W{◊\herefore} I will
forth
send flies upon the face of the Earth which shall take hold of

the inhabitants thereof & shall eat their flesh & shall cause

magots to come in upon them & their tongues shall be

stayed that they shall not utter against me & their flesh shall

ORIGINAL INSCRIPTION
John Whitmer

REVISIONS
Oliver Cowdery
William W. Phelps
Sidney Rigdon
Joseph Smith
John Whitmer
Unidentified

fall from off their Bones & their eyes from their sockets
& it shall come to pass that then the Beasts of the forest
& the fowls of the air shall devour them up & that great
& abominable church which is the whore of all the Earth
shall be cast down by devouring fire according as it was
spoken by the mouth of Ezekiel the Prophet which spoke
of these things which have not come to pass as yet but
shurely must as I live for abominations shall not reign
& again verily verily I say unto you that when the thousand
years are ended & men again begin to deny their god then
will I spare the Earth but for a little season & the
end shall come & the Heaven & the Earth shall be consumed
& pass away & there shall be a New Heaven & a New Earth
for all old things shall pass away & all things shall
become New even the Heaven & the Earth & all the
fulness thereof both men & beasts the fowls of the air
& the fishes of the Sea & not one hair neither mote
shall be lost for it is the workmanship of mine hand
But Behold verily I say unto you before the Earth shall pass
away Michael mine Archangel shall sound his trump
& then shall all the dead awake for their graves shall
be opened & they shall come forth yea even all & the
righteous shall be gethered on my right hand unto eternal
life & the wicked on my left hand will I be ashamed to
own before the father Wherefore I will say unto them
depart from me ye cursed into everlasting fire prepared
for the devil & his Angels & now Behold I say unto you
never at any time have I declared from mine own mouth
that they should return for where I am they cannot come
for they have no power but remember that all my judgem-
-ents are not given unto men & as the words have gone
forth out of my mouth even so shall they be fulfilled
that the first shall be last & that the last shall be first
in all things Whatsoever I have created by the word of
my Power which is the Power of my spirit for by the
Power of my Spirit created I them yea all things both

Die as to the temporal death untill I the Lord God

should send forth Angels to declare unto them Repent~~ance~~

=ance & redemption through faith on the name of mine

only begotten Son & thus did I the Lord God appoint

unto man the days of his probation that by his natural

death he might be raised in immortality unto eternal

life even as many as would believe ~~on my name~~ & they

that believe not unto eternal damnation for they cannot

be redeemed from their spiritual fall Because they

repent not for they _{will} love da{ɵ\rkness} ~~more~~ _{rather} than light &

their deeds are evil & they receive their wages of whom

they list to obey But Behold I say unto you {ɵɵɵ\that} little

children are redeemed from the foundation of the wor{d\ld}

through mine only begotten Wherefore they cannot

sin for power is not given ~~unto~~ Satan to tempt little children

until they begin to be _{come} accountable before me for it is given

unto them even as I will according to mine own ~~will~~

pleasure that great things may be required at the

hand of their fathers & again I say unto you that

whoso having knowledge have not I commanded to

Repent & he that hath no understanding it remaineth

in me to do according as it is written & now behold

I declare no more unto you at this time amen

ORIGINAL INSCRIPTION
John Whitmer

REVISIONS
Oliver Cowdery
William W. Phelps
Sidney Rigdon
Joseph Smith
John Whitmer
Unidentified

53. The first publication reflecting several redactions in this revelation is the Book of Commandments (chapter 30). Many of Sidney Rigdon's redactions do not appear in any JS-era publication.

54. Evidence, including the date listed in the index of this manuscript book, indicates that this revelation should be dated September 1830. This scribal error suggests that John Whitmer copied this revelation in 1831.

♦ ⁵³30 **Commandment AD** 1831⁵⁴

A Revelation to Oliver [Cowdery] his Call to the Lamanitse &c

given at Fayette Seneca County State of New York

Behold I say unto you Oliver that it shall be given ~~thee~~

_{unto} thee that thou shalt be heard by the Church in all things

Whatsoever thou shalt teach _{them} by the Comforter concerning

the Revelations & commandments which I have given

But Behold Verily Verily I say unto you no one shall

be appointed to Receive commandments & Revelations

in this Church excepting my Servent Joseph for he

Receiveth them even as Moses & thou shalt be obed=

-ient unto the things which I shall give unto him

Even as Aaron to declare faithfully the commandments &
the Revelations with power & authority unto the Church & if
thou art led at any time by the comforter to speak or
teach or at all times by the way of Commandment unto
the Church thou mayest do it But thou shalt not write
by way of Commandment ~~unto the Church~~ but by
wisdom & thou shalt not command him ~~which~~ who is at the
head & at the head of the Church for I have given him
the keys of the mysteries of the Revelations which are
sealed until I shall appoint unto ~~them~~ another in his
stead & now Behold I say unto you ~~that~~ you shalt go unto
the Lamanites & Preach my Gospel unto them & cause my
Church to be established among them & you shall have
Revelations But write them not by the way of Commandment
& Now Behold I say unto you that it is not Revealed & no man
knoweth where the City shall be built But it shall be given
hereafter Behold I say unto you that it shall on the borders by
Lamanites you shalt not leave this place until after the
Conference & my servant Joseph shall be appointed to rule
the Conference by the voice of it & what he saith to you
that you shall tell And again you shall take your
Brother Hyram Between him & you alone & tell him
that those things which he hath written from that Stone
are not of me & that Satan deceiveth him for Behold
those things have not been appointed unto him Neither
shall any thing be appointed unto any of this Church
contrary to the Church ~~articles~~ Covenants for all things
must be done in order & by common consent in the Church
by the prayer of faith & you shall settle all these things
according to the Covenants of the Church before you shall
take your journey among the Lamanites & it shall be
given you from the time that you shalt go until the
time that you shalt return what you shalt do & you
must open your mouth at all times declaring my
Gospel with the sound of Rejoicing ~~amen~~ amen

Even as Aaaron to declare faithfully the commandments &

the Revelations with power & authority unto the Church & if

thou art led at any time by the comforter to speak or

teach or at all times by the way of Commandment unto

the Church thou mayest do it But thou shalt not write

by way of Commandment ~~unto the Church~~ but by
                                                   who
wisdom & thou shalt not command him ~~which~~ is at thy
                                            ^
head & at the head of the Church for I have given him

the keys of the myster{i\y}es of the Revelations which are
                                            them
sealed until I shall appoint unto ~~him~~ another in his
                                       that you
stead & now Behold I say unto you ~~that thou~~ shal{t\l} go unto

the Lamanites & Preach my Gospel unto them & cause my
                                            you
Church to be established among them & ~~thou~~ shal{t\l} have
                                                        t
Revelations but write them not by the way of Commandmen

& Now Behold I say unto you that it is not Revealed & no man

knoweth where the City shall be built Bu{tt\t} it shall be given
                                            on the borders by
hereafter Behold I say unto you that it shall be ~~among~~ the
                                                     ^
            you
Lamanites ~~thou~~ shal{t\l} not l[e]ave this place until after the

Conference & my servent Joseph shall be appointed to rule
                                                       you
the conference by the voice of it & what he saith to ~~thee~~
        you   you   your
that ~~thou~~ shal{t\l} tell And again ~~thou~~ shal{t\l} take ~~thy~~
                                                   you
Brother Hyram [Hiram Page] Between him & ~~thee~~ alone & tell him
                                          has
that those things which he ~~hath~~ written from that {s\⟨S⟩}ton{∅\e}

are not of me & that Satan deceiveth him for Behold

those things have not been appointed unto him Neither

shall any thing be appointed unto any of this Church

contrary to the Church ~~Articles &~~ Covenants for all things

must be done in order & by Common; consent in the Church
                        you sh
by the prayer of faith & ~~thou~~ shal{t\l} settle all these things
                                            you
according to the Covenants of the Church before ~~thou~~ shal{t\l}
        your
take ~~thy~~ Journey among the Lamanites & it shall be
        you   you
given ~~thee~~ from the time that ~~thou~~ shal{t\l} go until the
            you   you   you
time that ~~thou~~ shal{t\l} return what ~~thou~~ shal{t\l} do & ~~thou~~
            your
must open ~~thy~~ mouth at all times declaring my

Gospel with the sound of Rejoiceing ~~even so~~ amen

L [55]

ORIGINAL INSCRIPTION
John Whitmer

REVISIONS
Oliver Cowdery
William W. Phelps
Sidney Rigdon
Joseph Smith
John Whitmer
Unidentified

55. Possibly a stray ink mark rather than a deliberate printer's mark.

81 # Commandment AD 1830

A Commandment to David telling him that he
feared man more then god &c given at fayette Seneca
County NewYork

1 Behold I say unto you, David, that the Last peared man
& had not Relyed upon me for strength, as you ought
aught: But my mind has been on the things of Earth
more then on the things of me, your Maker & the ministers
wherunto you have been Called; & you had not given
heed unto my Spirit, & to those who were set over you,
But I have been perswaded by those whom I have
not Commanded: wherefore you are left to enquire for
your-self, at my hand & ponder upon the things which
you have Received. & your Lause shall be at your father's
Lause until I give unto you other commandments.
5 & you shall attend to the ministery in the Church,
& before the world, & in the regions round about. amen

32nd # COMMANDMENT AD 1830

A Revelation to Peter his calling to the Lamanites &c
given at Fayette Seneca County state of NewYork

1 Behold I say unto you Peter, that you shall take your
journey with your Brother oliver, for the time has come, that
it is expedient in me, that you shall open your mouth
to declare my Gospel: 2 therefore, fear not but give heed unto
the words & advice of your Brother, which he shall give you.
3 & be you afflicted in all his afflictions, ever lifting up your
heart up unto me in prayer, & faith, for his & your deliv-
-erance: 4 for I have given unto him to build up my Church
among your Brethren, the Lamanites. 5 & none have I appointed
to be ouer him in the Church, except it is his Brother
Joseph. 6 wherefore give heed unto these things & be
dilligent in keeping my commandments, & you shall
be blessed unto eternal life, & thus is amen

♦ ⁵⁶31 Commandment AD 1830

A Commandment to David [Whitmer] tellilg [telling] him that he

feared man more than god &c given at fayette Seneca

County New York

you   have
1   Behold I say unto you, David, that ~~thou hast~~ feared man
have   you
& ~~hast~~ not relyed upon me for strength, as ~~thou ha{st\dt}~~⁵⁷
2   your   the
ought: But ~~thy~~ mind has been on the things of Earth
your   ^
more than on the things of me, ~~thy~~ Maker, & the ministry
you   have   you have
whereunto ~~thou hast~~ been called; & ~~thou hast~~ not given

heed unto my Spirit, & to those who were set over ~~thee~~ you,
have
But ~~hast~~ been persuaded by those whom I have
3   you are
not commanded: wherefore ~~thou art~~ left to enquire for
your-
~~thy~~ -self, at my hand, & ponder upon the things which
^
4   your   your
you have Received. & ~~thy~~ home shall be at ~~thy~~ father's
you   other
house until I give unto ~~thee~~ ~~further~~ commandments.
5   you
& ~~thou~~ shal{t\l} attend to the ministry in the Church,

& before the world, & in ~~these~~ regions round about. amen

♦ ⁵⁸32ⁿᵈ Commandment AD 1830

A Revelation to Peter [Whitmer Jr.] his calling to the Lamanites &c

given at Fayette Seneca County state of New York

you
1   Behold I say unto you, Peter, that ~~thou~~ shal{t\l} take ~~thy~~ your
your
Journey with ~~thy~~ Brother oliver [Cowdery], for the time has come, that
you   your
it is expedient in me, that ~~thou~~ shal{t\l} open ~~thy~~ mouth

to declare my Gospel: Therefore, fear⁵⁹ not but give heed unto
your   you.
the words & advice of ~~thy~~ Brother, which he shall give ~~thee~~
3   you   up
& be ~~thou~~ afflicted in all his afflictions, ever lifting ~~thy~~ your
his^   your
h{◊◊◊\⟨ear⟩}t ~~up~~ unto me in prayer, & faith, for ~~thine~~ & ~~his~~ deliv=
4   up
-erance: for I have given unto him to build my Church
your   5   ^
among ~~thy~~ Brethren, the Lamanites. & none have I appointed

to be over him in the Church, except it is his Brother
6   these
Joseph. wherefore give heed unto ~~th{o\⟨e⟩}se~~⁶⁰ things & be
you
dilligent in keeping my commandments, & ~~thou~~ shal{t\l}

be blessed unto eternal life. & ~~thus it is~~ amen—

ORIGINAL INSCRIPTION
John Whitmer

REVISIONS
Oliver Cowdery
William W. Phelps
Sidney Rigdon
Joseph Smith
John Whitmer
Unidentified

56. The first publication reflecting most redactions in this revelation is the Book of Commandments (chapter 31).

57. "dt" appears to have been written after Sidney Rigdon canceled "hast".

58. The first publication reflecting most redactions in this revelation is the Book of Commandments (chapter 32).

59. Although "fear" appears to be stricken, the ink blot is actually offsetting from the opposite leaf (manuscript page 43).

60. "⟨e⟩" possibly inserted by Sidney Rigdon.

33 Commandment AD 1830.

A Revelation to John, his call to the Ministery &c
given at Fayette Seneca County State of New York

1 Behold I say unto John, that you shall commence
from this time forth to proclaim my Gospel, as with the
voice of a Trump; 2 & your Labour shall be at your Brother
Philips, & in that region round about; 3 yea, wheresoever you
canst be heard until I command you to go from hence;
4 & your whole Labour shall be in my Zion, with all your
Soul; from henceforth; yea, you shall ever open your mouth
in my cause not fearing what man can do, for I am
with you. amen

34th Commandment AD 1830

A Revelation to Thomas his call to the ministry &c
given at Fayette Seneca County State of New York

1 Thomas, my son, Blessed are you Because of your faith in
my work. 2 Behold you have had many afflictions because of your
family; Nevertheless I will bless you & your family; 3 yea your little
ones, & the day cometh that they will believe & know the
truth & be one with you in my Church. 4 lift up your heart &
rejoice for the hour of your mission is come; & your
tongue shall be loosed; & you shall declare glad tidings of
great joy unto this generation. 5 you shalt declare the things
which have been revealed to my Servent Joseph. 6 you shall
begin to preach from this time forth; yea, to Reap in the field
which is white already to be burned; 7 Therefore thrust in your
Sickle with all your Soul; & your Sins are forgiven you, & you
shall be laden with sheaves upon your Back, for the labourer is
worthy of his hire. 8 Therefore your family shall live. 9 Behold
Truely, I say unto you, go from them only for a little time, &
declare my word, & I will prepare a place for them, yea I will
open the hearts of the People & they will Receive you. 10 I will
establish a church by your hand; & you shall strengthen them
& prepare them against the time when they shall be gathering. 11
be patient in afflictions, & sufferings, revile not against

♦ ⁶¹33 Commandment AD 1830⁶²

A Revelation to John [Whitmer] his call to the Ministery {give\&c}

given at Fayette Seneca County State of New York

1 Behold I say unto John, that ~~thou~~⁶³ you my servent, shal{t\l} shall commence

from this time forth to proclaim my Gospel, as with the

2 your voice of a Trump{;\.} & ~~thy~~ Labour shall be at ~~thy~~ Brother

your 3 you Philip [Burroughs]'{s\ˢ}, & in that region roun{ʘʘ\d} about: yea, wheresoever ~~thou~~

you can~~st~~ be heard until I command ~~thee~~ to go from hence.

4 your & ~~thy~~ {h\whole} Labour shall be in my Zion, with all ~~thy~~ your

you your Soul, from henceforth; yea, ~~thou~~ shal{t\l} ever open ~~thy~~ mouth

in my cause not fearing what man can do, for I {aʘ\am}

you. with ~~thee~~ ~~even so~~ amen

♦ ⁶⁴34ᵗʰ Commandment AD 1830

A Revelation to {tʘ\Thomas} [B. Marsh] his call to the ministiry &c

gaven at Fayette Seneca County State of New York

are you your 1 Thomas, my Son, Blessed, ~~art~~ ~~thou~~ Be[c]ause of ~~thy~~ faith in

you have your my wor{ds\k}.⁶⁵ Behold ~~thou hast~~ had many afflictions because of ~~thy~~

you, your your family: Nevertheless I will bless ~~thee~~ & ~~thy~~ family: yea ~~thy~~ little

ones, & the day cometh that they will believe & know the

you 4 truth & be one with ~~thee~~ in my Church{;\.} lift up your heart &

your rejoice for the hour of your ~~Mishion~~ mission is come; &⁶⁶ ~~thy~~

you tongue shall be loosed; & ~~thou~~ shal{t\l} declare glad tidings of

5 you {J\great} joy into this generation. ~~thou~~ shal{t\l} declare the things

6 you which have been revealed ~~unto~~ my Servent Joseph. ~~thou~~ shal{t\l}

begin to preach from this time forth; yea, to Reap in the field

7 your which is white already to be burned: Therefore thrust in ~~thy~~

your your you; you Sickle with all ~~thy~~ Soul; & ~~thy~~ sins are forgiven ~~thee~~ & ~~thou~~

your shal{t\l} be laden with sheaves upon ~~thy~~ Back, for the labourer is

8 your 9 worthy of his hire. Wherefore ~~thy~~ family shall live. Behold,

Verily, I say {ʘ\unto} you, go from them only for a~~l~~ little time, &

declare my word, & I will prepare a place for them; yea, I will

you. 10 open the hear{tʘ\ts} of the People & they will Receive ~~thee~~ & I will

your you, establish a church by ~~thy~~ hand; & ~~thou~~ shal{t\l} strengthen them

shall be & prepare them against the time when th{e\ey} gether{ing\ed}. ~~shall~~

11 in 12 ~~be~~ be patient in afflictions, & sufferings, revile not ag{ʘʘ\⟨ai⟩}nst

ORIGINAL INSCRIPTION
John Whitmer

REVISIONS
Oliver Cowdery
William W. Phelps
Sidney Rigdon
Joseph Smith
John Whitmer
Unidentified

61. The first publication reflecting most redactions in this revelation is the Book of Commandments (chapter 33).

62. The later addition of "o" in graphite may indicate that John Whitmer was uncertain when the revelation should be dated, or perhaps his initial omission of this numeral was simply a scribal error.

63. Throughout this page, Sidney Rigdon changed "shalt" to "shall" by changing the last letter from a "t" to an "l". He also deleted "thou" and inserted "you". In this case, Rigdon likely intended to change "thou" to "you" but wrote "shall" instead. Another scribe (likely William W. Phelps) inscribed a dotted line beneath "thou", indicating that the word should be left as originally written. The repeated "shall" was left uncorrected in this manuscript.

64. The first publication reflecting most redactions in this revelation is the Book of Commandments (chapter 34).

65. Possibly "wor{{d\k}s\k}" or "wor{{d\k}s\d}".

66. Single underlining beneath "&" wipe-erased.

Those that we will govern your house in meekness, & be
steadfast. 13 Behold I say unto you that you shall be a Physician
unto the Church, but not unto the World, for they will not
receive you. 14 go your way whithersoever I will, & it shall be
given you by the Comforter what you shall do, &
whither you shall go. 15 pray always, lest you enter into
temptation, & loose your reward. 16 be faithful unto the end
& lo, I am with you. these words are not of man nar
of men, but of me, even Jesus Christ, your Redeemer, by
the will of the father. amen

35 & 36th Commandment AD Oct 1830

A Commandment to Ezra & Northrop their call to the
ministery &c, given at Fayett Seneca County State of New York
1 saying, behold I say unto you my servants Ezra, & Northrop, open ye your ears
& hearken to the voice of the Lord your God, whose word is
quick & powerfull, sharper than a twoedged sword, to the
dividing asunder of the joints & marrow, Soul & spirit; & is
a discerner of the thaughts & intents of the heart. 2 for verily, verily
I say unto you, that ye are called to lift up your voices as with the
sound of a Trump, to declare my Gospel unto a Crooked &
a perverse generation: 3 for Behold the field is white already
to harvest; & it is the Eleventh hour, & for the last time that I
shall call labourers into my vineyard. 4 & my vineyard has become
corrupted every whit; & there is none which that doeth good save it be a few;
& they err in many instances, because of Priest crafts,
all having Corrupt minds. 5 & verily, verily I say unto you, that
this Church have I established & called forth out of the Wilderness:
6 & even so will I gather mine elect from the four quarters
of the Earth, even as many as will believe in me, &
hearken unto my voice: 7 yea, verily, verily I say unto you, that
the field is white already to harvest; 8 wherefore thrust in your
sickles & reap with all your might, mind, & strength. 9 open your
mouth & it shall be filled, & you shall become even as
Nephi of old, who journed from Jerusalem in the wilderness:
10 yea, open your mouth & spare not, & you shall be loaden with
Sheaves upon your Backs, for lo I am with you; 11 yea,

Those that revile. govern[67] ~~thy~~ ^your^ house in meekness, & be

steadfast. Behold I say unto you that ~~thou~~ shal{t\l} ^you^ be a P[h]ysician

unto the Church, but not unto the World, for they will not

receive ~~thee~~ go[68] ~~thy~~ ^your^ you. 14 way whithersoever I will, & it shall be

given ~~thee~~ ^you^ by the Comf{◊◊\(or)}ter what ~~thou~~ shal{t\l} ^you^ do, &

whither ~~thou~~ ^you^ shal{t\l} go. pray always, 15 lest y{e\ou} enter into

temptation, & loose ~~thy~~ ^your^ reward. 16 be faithful unto the end

& {Lo\lo},![69] I am with you. 17 these words are not of man ~~neither~~ ^nor^

of men, but of me, even Jesus Christ, your Redeemer, by

the will of the father. ~~even so~~ amen

♦ [70]35 & 36th **Command{s\ment}** AD 1830 ^Oct.^

    A Commandment to Ezra [Thayer] & Northrop [Sweet] th[e]ir call to the

ministery &c {◊◊\given} at Fayette Seneca County State of New York

1   ^behold^ Saying I say unto you, Ezra, & Northrop, ^my servents^ open ye your ears

& hearken to the {◊\voice} of the Lord your God, whose word is

quick & powerfull, sharper than ~~any~~ a ^a^ twoedged sword, to the

dividing asunder of the Joints & marrow, Soul & spirit; &[72] ~~2~~[71] is

a decerner of the thoughts & intents of the heart. 2 for Verily, Verily

I say unto you, that ye are called to lift up ^your^ voices as with the

sound of a Trump, to declare my Gospel unto a Crooked &

a perverse generation: 3 for Behold the field is white already

to harvest; & it is the Elvenenth hour, & for the last time that I

shall call labouerers into my vineyard. 4 & my vineyard has become

corrupted evry whit: & there is none ~~that~~ ^which^ doeth good save it ~~is~~ a ^be^ few;
 & they ~~do~~ err, in many instances, because of Priest crafts,
~~only~~ all having corrupt minds. 5 & Verily, Verily I say unto you, that
^ {^\^}
this Church have I established & called forth out of the Wilderness:
6
& even so will I gether mine ~~ele(c)t~~ elect from the four quarters
of◊ the Earth, even as many as will believe {i\(o)}~~n my name~~ ^in me,^ &
hearken unto my voice: 7 yea, Verily, Verily I say unto you, that
the field is white already to harvest: 8 Wherefore thrust in ~~thy~~ ^your^
sickles & reap with all ~~thy~~ ^your^ might~~s~~, mind, & strength. 9 open ~~thy~~ ^your^
mouth & it shall be filled; & ~~thou~~ shal{t\l} ^you^ become even as
Nephi of old, who Journ[ey]ed from Jerusalem in the wilderness:
10 yea, open ~~thy~~ ^your^ mouth & spare not, & ~~thou~~ shal{t\l} ^you^ be laden with
Sheaves upon ~~thy~~ ^your^ Backs, 11 for lo I am with ~~thee~~ you: yea,

Original Inscription
John Whitmer

Revisions
Oliver Cowdery
William W. Phelps
Sidney Rigdon
Joseph Smith
John Whitmer
Unidentified

67. Triple underlining beneath "g" possibly stray ink marks.

68. Triple underlining beneath "g" possibly stray ink marks.

69. Or "~~Lo~~,!".

70. The first publication reflecting most redactions in this revelation is the Book of Commandments (chapter 35).

71. "2" wipe-erased and then stricken.

72. Triple underlining beneath "&" wipe-erased.

Open your mouths & they shall be filled, saying, Repent, repent &
prepare ye the way of the Lord, & make his path strait: for
the Kingdom of Heaven is at hand: [12] yea Repent & be Baptized
every one of you, for the remission of your sins; yea be baptized
even by water, & then cometh the Baptism of fire & of the Holy
Ghost. [13] Behold, Verily Verily I say unto you, this is my Gospel
& Remember that they shall have faith in me, or they can in no
wise be saved: [14] & upon this Rock I will build my Church; yea,
upon this Rock ye are built, & the gaits of Hell shall not prevail
against you & ye shall remember the Church Articles & Coven
ants to keep them: [15] & in so having faith you shall confirm
in my Church, by the laying on of the hands, & I will
bestow the gift of the Holy Ghost upon them: [16] & the Book
of Mormon, & the Holy Scriptures are given of me for your instruction;
& the power of my spirit quickeneth all things: [17] Wherefore be
faithful, praying always, having your lamps trimmed &
burning, & oil with you, that you may be Ready at the coming
of the Bride groom; for Behold, verily, Verily I say unto you
that I come quickly; even so: amen:

37th Commandment A D 1830

A Commandment to Orson his Call to the ministry &c
given at Fayette Seneca County State of New York
[1] My Son Orson, hearken & hear & Behold what I the Lord God
shall say unto you, even Jesus Christ your Redeemer, the light & the
life of the world; [2] a light which shineth in darkness & the
darkness Comprehendeth it not: [3] who so loved the world that
he gave his own life, that as many as would believe might
become the Sons of God: [4] Wherefore you are my Son, &
blessed are you because you have believed, & more blessed are
you because you are called of me to Preach my Gospel; to lift
up your voice as with the sound of a Trump, both long
& loud, & cry repentance unto a crooked & perverse generation; preparing
the way of the Lord for his second coming: [5] for Behold, Verily Verily
I say unto you, the time is soon at hand, that I shall come in a
cloud with power & great glory, & it shall be a great day at the

your   they
Open ~~thy~~ mouths & ~~it~~ shall be filled, saying, Repent, repent &

prepare ye the way of the Lord, & make his paths[73] strait: for

12
the Kingdom of Heaven is at hand: yea, Repent & be Baptized

a   your
evry one of you, for ~~the~~ remission of sins; yea, be baptized

of ~~of~~
even by water, & then cometh the Baptism of fire & the Holy

13
Ghost. Behold, Verily, Verily I say unto you, th{◊s\is} is my Gospel
~~that you must~~ that they Shall ~~h~~ th[e]y ~~you~~
& Remember ~~they shall~~ have, faith in me, or ~~they~~ can in no

14
wise be saved: & upon this Rock I will build my Church; yea,

you
upon this Rock ~~ye~~ are built, & the gaits of Hell shall not preva

=il against you; & ye shall remember the Church Articles & Coven

15   you
=ants to keep them: & whoso haveing faith ~~ye~~ shall confirm

in my Church, by the laying on of the hands, & I will

16
bestow the gift of the Holy Ghost upon them. & the Book
Holy Scriptures,   your
of Mormon, & the ~~Bible~~ {is\are} given of me for ~~thine~~ instructio[n];

17
& the power of my spirit quickeneth all things: Wherefore be

faithful, praying always, having your lamps trimmed &

you
burning, & oil with you, that ~~ye~~ may be Ready at the coming

of the Bride groom; for Behold, Verily, Verily I say unto you

that I come quickly; even so: amen.

♦ [74]37th Commandment AD 1830

A Commandment to Orson [Pratt] his {s\call} to the ministery &c

given at Fayette Seneca county {sta\State} of New York
hear, &
1 My Son Orson, hearken ~~ye~~ & Behold what I the Lord God
shall
say unto you, even Jesus Christ your Redeemer, the light & the

2
life of the world: {&\a}[75] light which shineth in darkness & the

3
darkness Comprehendeth it not: who so loved the world that

he gave his own life, that as many as would believe might

4   you
become the Sons ~~& daughter~~ of God: Wherefore ~~ye~~ are my Son, &

you
blessed are ~~ye~~ because y{e\ou} have believed, & more blessed {◊◊\are}

y{e\ou} because y{e\ou} are called of me to Preach my Gospel; to lift

up~~o~~ your voice as with {a\the} sound of a Trump, both long

& loud, & cry repentance unto a crooked & perverse generation; prepareing
~~the time of~~   5
the way of the Lord for his second Coming: for Behold, Verily, Verily
shall
I say unto you, the time is soon at hand, that I ~~will~~ come in a

cloud with power & great glory, & it shall be a great day at the

ORIGINAL INSCRIPTION
John Whitmer

REVISIONS
Oliver Cowdery
William W. Phelps
Sidney Rigdon
Joseph Smith
John Whitmer
Unidentified

73. "s" wipe-erased and then stricken.

74. The first publication reflecting most redactions in this revelation is the Book of Commandments (chapter 36). Although William W. Phelps inserted verse numbers while preparing this revelation for publication in the Book of Commandments, the verse numbers printed therein are slightly different from those that appear here.

75. "a" possibly inserted by an unidentified scribe.

6 time of my coming, for all nations shall tremble.
but before that great day shall come, the sun shall
be darkened, & the moon be turned into blood, & the
stars shall refuse their shineing, & some shall fall,
& great distructions await the wicked: 7 Wherefore lift up
your voice & spare not, for the Lord God hath spaken:
8 therefore Prophecy & it shall be given by the power of the
Holy Ghost; & if you are faithful behold I am with you
until I come: 9 & Verily Verily I say unto you I come
quickly, 10 of and your Lord & your Redeemer even so: amen.

38th Commandment AD 1830. Dec.y 7th

A Commandment to Joseph & Sidney. Sidneys Call
to writing for Joseph &c

Saying Listen to the voice of the Lord your God, even
Alpha & Omega, the begining & the end, whose course is
one eternal round, the same to day as yesterday & for ever.
2 I am Jesus Christ, the son of God, who was crucified for
the sins of the World, even as many as will believe on my name,
that they may become the sons of God, even one in me
as I am in the Father as the Father is one in me, that
we may be one. 3 Behold, Verily, Verily I say unto my servent
Sidney, I have looked upon thee & thy works. 4 I have heard
thy prayers & prepared thee for a greater work. 5 thou art
blessed for thou shalt do great things. 6 Behold thou wast
sent forth, even as John to prepare the way before me, & before
Elijah which should come, & thou knew it not. 7 thou didst
Baptize by water unto Repentance but they received not the
Holy Ghost; but now I give unto thee a Commandment,
that thou shalt Baptize they shall receive by water & the Holy Ghost
by the laying on of hands, even as the Apostles of old. 8 & it shall
come to pass, that there shall be a great work in the land
even among the gentiles for their folly & their abominations
shall be made manifest, in the eyes of all People: 9 for
I am God & mine arm is not shortened & I will shew
miricles, signs & wonders, unto all those who believe

46 [verso]

time of my coming, for all nations shall tremble.

6

but before that great day shall come, the sun shall

be darkened, & the moon be turned into blood, & the

stars shall refuse their shineing, & some shall fall,

7

& great distructions await the wicked: Wherefore lift up

your   has

~~thy~~ voice & spare not, for the Lord God ~~hath~~ spoken:

8

therefore Prophecy & it shall be given by the power of the

you

Holy Ghost; & if ~~ye~~ are faithful behold I am with you

9

until I come: & Verily Verily I say unto you I come

10 I am   even so:

quickly. ~~even so~~ your Lord & your redeemer, amen.

♦ 76 38th **Commandment** AD 1830.. Dec.ᵐ· 7th

A Commandment to Joseph & Sidney [Rigdon]. Sidneys call

to writing for Joseph &c

I

Saying {l\⟨L⟩}isten to the voice of the Lord your God, even

gi

Alpha & Omega, the bening & the end, whose course is

one eternal round, the same to day as yesterday & for ever.

2

I am Jesus Christ, the son of God, who was crusified for

many as

the sins of the World, even as will believe on my name,

that they may become the sons of God, even one in me

as I am in the Father as the Father is one in me, that

3

we may be one. Behold, Verily, Verily I say unto my Servent

4

Sidney, I have looked upon thee & thy works. I have heard

5

thy prayers & prepared thee for a greater work. thou art

6

blessed for thou shalt do great things. Behold thou wast

sent forth, even as John to prepare the way before me, & ~~before~~

before

Elijah which should come, & thou knew it not. thou didst

7

Baptize by water unto Repentance but they received not the

thee

Holy Ghost; but now I give unto ~~you~~ a commandment,

they shall receive & ~~they shall receive~~ give

that thou shalt Baptize by water & ~~give~~ the Holy Ghost

the   8

by laying on of hands, even as the Apostles of old. & it shall

come to pass, that there shall be a great work in the land

&   &

even among the gentiles for their folly their abominations

9

shall be made manifest, in the eyes of all People: for

not

I am God & mine arm is shortened & I will shew

miricles, signs & wonders, unto all those who believe

ORIGINAL INSCRIPTION:
John Whitmer

REVISIONS
Oliver Cowdery
William W. Phelps
Sidney Rigdon
Joseph Smith
John Whitmer
Unidentified

76. The first publication
reflecting most redactions in
this revelation is the Book of
Commandments (chapter 37).
Although William W. Phelps
inserted verse numbers while
preparing this revelation for
publication in the Book of
Commandments, the verse
numbers printed therein are
slightly different from those
that appear here.

who believe on my name. [10] & whoso shall ask it in my name in faith, they shall cast out Devils; they shall heal the sick; they shall cause the blind to receive their sight, & the deaf to hear, & the dumb to speak, & the lame to walk: [11] & the time speedily cometh, that great things are to be shewn forth unto the Children of men: [12] but without faith shall not any thing be shewn forth except desolations upon Babylon, the same which has made all Nations drink of the wine of the wrath of her fornication: [13] & there are none that doeth good except those who are ready to receive the fulness of my gospel, which I have sent forth to this generation: [14] wherefore I have called upon the weak things of the world those who are unlearned & despised, to thresh the Nations by the Power of my spirit: [15] & their arm shall be mine arm, & I will be their shield & their Buckler; & I will gird up their loins, & they shall fight manfully for me: [16] & their enemies shall be under their feet; & I will let fall the sword in their behalf; & by the fire of mine indignation will I preserve them. [17] & the poor & the meek shall have the gospel preached unto them, & they shall be looking forth for the time of my coming, for it is nigh at hand: [18] & they shall learn the Parable of the figg tree: for even now already summer is nigh, & I have sent forth the fulness of my gospel by the hand of my servant Joseph: [19] & in weakness have I blessed him, & I have given unto him the keys of the mystery of those things which have been sealed, even things which were from the foundation of the world, & the things which shall come from this time until the time of my coming, if he abide in me, & if not, another will I plant in his stead: [20] wherefore watch over him that his faith fail not, & it shall be given by the Comforter the Holy Ghost, that knoweth all things: [21] & a commandment I give unto thee that thou shall write for him: [22] & the scriptures shall be given even as they are in mine own bosom, to the salvation of mine own elect: [23] for they will hear my voice, & shall see me, & shall not be asleep, & shall abide the day of my coming; for they shall be purified, even as I am pure. [24] & now I

~~who believe~~ on my name. & whoso shall ask it in my name,

in faith, they shall cast out Devils; they shall heal the sick;

they shall cause the blind to receive their sight, & the deaf

{~~the~~\to} hear, & the dumb to speak, & the lame to walk: & the time

speedily cometh, that great things are to be shewn forth unto

                     shall
the Children of men: but without faith not any thing ~~shall~~

be shewn forth except desolations upon {b\⟨B⟩}ab{i\⟨y⟩}lon, the same

which has made all Nations drink of the wine of the wrath

                                      those
of her fornication. & there are none that doeth good except ~~they~~

who ~~that~~ are ready to receive the fulness of my Gospel, which I have

sent forth to this generation: Wherefore I have called upon

        of the world, those who
the weak things ~~of the world~~ ~~they~~ ~~that~~ are unlearned &

dispised, to thresh the Nations by the Power of my spirit:

& their arm shall be mine arm, & I will be their shield & their

Buckler; & I will gird up their loins, & they shall fight manf

=ully for me: & their enemies shall be under their feet; & I will

let fall the sword in their behalf; & by the fire of mine indig-

=nation will I preserve them. & the poor & the meek shall have

the Gospel preached unto them, & they shall be looking forth

for the time of my coming, for it is nigh at hand: & they shall

learn the Par{i\a}ble of the figg tree: for even now already sum-

                                  my
=mer is nigh, & I have sent forth the fullness of ~~the~~ Gospel

by the hand of my servent Joseph: & in weakness have I blessed

him, & I have given unto him the Keys of the mystery of

                                      were
those things which have been sealed, even things which ~~was~~

from the foundation of the world, & the things which shall

come from this time until the time of my coming, if he

abide in me, & if not, another will I plant in his stead.:

Wherefore watch over him that his faith fail not, & it shall

                                  that
be given by the comforter, ⟨the Holy Ghost,⟩ ~~Which~~ knoweth

                            thee, thou ⟨you⟩
all things: & a commandment I give unto ~~you~~ that ~~thou~~

shal{t\l} write for him: & the scriptures shall be given even as

they are in mine own bosom, to the salvation of mine

own elect:: for th[e]y will hear my voice, & shall see me, &

shall not be asleep, & shall abide the day of my coming,

for they shall be purified, even as I am pure. & now I

ORIGINAL INSCRIPTION
John Whitmer

REVISIONS
Oliver Cowdery
William W. Phelps
Sidney Rigdon
Joseph Smith
John Whitmer
Unidentified

48

Say unto you, tarry with him & he shall journey
with you. forsake him not & surely these things shall
be fulfilled. [25] in as much as ye do not write. behold it
shall be given him to prophecy. [26] & thou shalt Preach my
gospel, & call on the Holy Prophets to prove his words,
as they shall be given him. [27] Keep all the commandments
& covenants by which ye are bound, & I will cause the
Heavens to Shake for your good; [28] & satan shall tremble; &
Zion shall rejoice upon the Hills, & florish; & Israel shall
be saved in mine own due time. [29] & by the Keys which have
given, shall they be led & no more be confoun=
=ded at all. [30] lift up your hearts & be Glad. your redemption
draweth nigh. [31] fear not little flock the kingdom is yours
untill I come. [32] Behold I come quickly; even so: amen.

39th Commandment Decr 9th AD 1830

A Commandment to Edward his call to the Ministery &c
Saying [1] Thus saith the Lord God, the mighty one of
Israel, behold I say unto you my Servent Edward, that you are
blessed, & your Sins are forgiven you, you are called to
preach my Gospel as with the voice of a Trump; & I will
lay my hand upon you by the hand of my Servent Sidney,
& you shall Receive my spirit, the Holy Ghost, even the
Comforter, which shall teach you the peacible things of
the kingdom; & you shall declare it with a loud voice
Saying Hosannah, blessed be the name of the most high God. —
[3] And now this calling & commandment give I unto all
men, that as many as shall come before my Servent Sidney
& Joseph, embracing this calling & commandment, shall be
ordained & sent forth to preach the everlasting gospel
among the Nation, crying Repentance, saying save yourselves
from this untoward generation, & come forth out of the
fire, hating even the garment spotted with the flesh
[4] And this commandment shall be given unto the Elders
of my Church, that every man which will embrace it
with singleness of heart, may be ordained & sent

48 [verso]

Say unto you, tarry with him & he shall Journey

you;
with ~~thee~~ forsake him not & shurely these things shall

25
be fulfilled,. & in as much as ye do not write,⁷⁷ behold it

unto   26
shall be given him to prophecy. & thou shalt Preach my
        ^

gospel, & call on the Holy Prophets to prove his words,

27
as they shall be given him. keep all the commandments

& covenants by which ye are bound, & I will cause the

28
Heavens to shake for your Good: & satan shall tremble; &

Zion shall rejoice upon the Hills, & florish; & Israel shall

29   I
be saved in mine own due time. & by the Keys which have
                                                      ^

~~shall been~~ given, shall they be led & no more be confoun=

30
=ded at all. lift {θ\up} your hearts & be Glad{;\:} your redemption

31
draweth nigh. fear not little flock the Kingdom is yours

32
untill I come. Behold I come quickly; even so: amen.

♦ ⁷⁸39ᵗʰ **Commandment** Decᵐ⁻ 9ᵗʰ⁻ AD 1830
                            ⟨w⟩ w
A Commandmen{d\t} to Edard [Partridge] his call to the Ministery &c
                         ^
        I
Saying {t\T}hus saith the Lord God, the mighty one of
                                        that   you are
Israel, behold I say unto you, my Servent Edward, ~~thou art~~
        your   you, you are
blessed, & ~~thy~~ sins are forgiven ~~thee~~ & ~~thou art~~ called to
                                      ^
preach my Gospel as with the voice of a Trump; & I will

lay my hand upon you by the hand of my Servent sidney [Rigdon],
    you
& ~~thou~~ shal{t\l} Receive my spirit, ⟨the Holy Ghost,⟩⁷⁹ even the

comfort{t\er},⟩ which shall teach you the peacible things of
        2   you
the Kingdom: & ~~thou~~ shal{t\l} declare it with a loud voice
    Hosanna,
Saying Blessed be the name of the most high God.—
      ^
₃ And now this calling & commandment give I unto all

men, that as many as shall come before my Servent Sidney

& Joseph, embracing this calling & commandment, shall be

ordained & sent forth to preach the everlasting gospel

among the Nation, crying Repentance, saying save yourselves

from this untoward generation, & come forth out of the

fire, hating even the garment spotted with the flesh.=
₄
And this commandment shall be given unto the Eld{◊\ers}

of my Church, that every man which will embrace it

with singleness of heart, may be ordained & sent

ORIGINAL INSCRIPTION
John Whitmer

REVISIONS
Oliver Cowdery
William W. Phelps
Sidney Rigdon
Joseph Smith
John Whitmer
Unidentified

77. Offsetting from the opposite page makes this comma appear to be a semicolon.

78. The first publication reflecting the redactions in this revelation is the Book of Commandments (chapter 38).

79. Closing parenthesis wipe-erased, leaving "(the Holy Ghost even the | comfort{t\er})". Then all three parentheses stricken.

forth, even as I have spoken: I am Jesus Christ the Son of
God: Wherefore gird up your loins & I will suddenly come to
my temple; even so: amen:

40th Comandment AD 1830

A Revelation to Sidney & Joseph at a time that they
went from Fayette to Canandaigua to translate &c
given at Canandaigua Ontario County State of New York

A Commandment to Sidney & Joseph Saying Behold I say
unto you, that it is not expedient in me, that ye shall
translate any more until ye shall go to the Ohio; & this
because of the enemy & for your sakes: & again, I say unto
you, that ye shall not go until ye have Preached my
Gospel in those parts, & have strengthened up the Church
whithersoever it is found, & more especially in Coleshille:
for Behold they pray unto me in much faith: & again
a Commandment I give unto the Church, that it is
expedient in me that they should assemble together at
the Ohio, against the time that my Servent Oliver shall
return unto them: Behold here is wisdom, & let every
man Choose for himself until I come. amen, even so amen

41st Commandment Jan 2nd AD 1831

Received at fayette Seneca County State of New york
A Commandment to the Churches in New york, at a Conference
they being Commanded to flee to Ohio &c

Saying thus saith the Lord your God, even Jesus Christ.
the great I am, Alpha & Omega, the begining & the end,
the same which looked upon the wide expance of eternity; & all
the Seraphick hosts of Heaven, before the world was made, the
same which knoweth all things, for all things are present
before mine eyes: I am the same which spake & the world was
made, & all things came by me: I am the same which
hath taken the Zion of Enoch into mine own bosom:
& verily I say, even as many as have believed on my name,
for I am Christ, & in mine own name by the ve

forth, even as I have spoken. I am Jesus Christ, the Son of

God: Wherefore gird up your loins & I will suddenly come to

my temple; even so: amen.

♦ 80 40th Com^mandment AD 1830

A Revelation to Sidney [Rigdon] & Joseph at at time that they

went from Fayette to Canandaigua to translate &c

given at Canandaigua O{0\ntario} County State of New York

A Commandment to sidney & Joseph saying Behold I say

unto {ye\you}, that it is not Expedient in me, that ye should

Translate any more until ye shall go to the Ohio; & this

because of the enemy & for your sakes: & again, I say unto

you, that ye shall not go untill ye have Preached my

Gospel in those parts, & have strengthened up the Church

whithersoever it is found, & more especially in Colesville:

for Behold they pray unto me in much faith. & again

a commandment I ~~give~~ say give, unto the Church, that it is

expedient in me that they should assemble together at

the Ohio, ~~by~~ against the time that my Servent Oliver [Cowdery] shall

return unto them. Behold here is wisdom, & let evry

man Choose for himself until I come. amen, even so amen

♦ 81 41st Commandment Jan 2nd AD 1831

Rec{0\〈ei〉}ved at fa{r\y}ette Seneca County State of New york

A Comandment to the Churches in New Y{00\ork} at a conference

they being Commanded to flee to Ohio &c

Saying {t\T}hus saith the Lord your God, even Jesus Christ

the great I am, Alph & Omega, the begining & the end,

the same which looked upon the wide expance of eternity, & all

the Scerifick [seraphic] hosts of Heaven, before the world was made, the

same which k[n]oweth all things, for all things are present

before mine eyes: I am the same which spoke & the world was

made, & all things came by me: I am the same 〈which〉 ~~who~~

~~hath~~ has hath taken the Zion of Enoch into mine own bosom:

3 & verily I say, even as many as have believed on my name,

for I am Christ, & in mine own name by the ~~vi~~

ORIGINAL INSCRIPTION
John Whitmer

REVISIONS
Oliver Cowdery
William W. Phelps
Sidney Rigdon
Joseph Smith
John Whitmer
Unidentified

80. The first publication reflecting most redactions in this revelation is the Book of Commandments (chapter 39).

81. The first publication reflecting most redactions in this revelation is the January 1833 issue of *The Evening and the Morning Star.* Other redactions first appear in print in the Book of Commandments (chapter 40).

69

...ture of the blood which I have spilt, have I pled before
the Father for them; but Behold the residue of the wicked
have I kept in chains of darkness untill the judgement
of the great day, which shall come at the end of the
Earth, & even so will I cause the wicked to be kept that will not
hear my voice but harden their hearts; & wo. wo. wo.
is their doom. But Behold, Verily, Verily I say unto you,
that mine eyes are upon you; I am in your midst
& ye cannot see me, but the day soon cometh that
ye shall see me & know that I am, for the vails
vail of darkness shall soon be rent, & he that is not
purified shall not abide the day: wherefore, gird
up your loins & be prepared. Behold the kingdom
is yours & the enemy shall not overcome. Verily I
say unto you, that ye are clean but not all; &
there is none else with whom I am well pleased, for
all flesh is corruptable before me & the powers of dark
=ness prevail upon the Earth, among the children of
men, in the presence of all the hosts of Heaven, which
causeth silence to reign, & all eternity is pained, &
the Angels are waiting the great command, to Reap
down the Earth, to gether the tares that they may be
burned: & Behold the enemy is combined.. & now I shew
unto you a Mystery, a thing which is had in secret
chambers, to bring to pass even your distruction, in
process of time, & ye knew it not, but now I tell it unto you,
& ye are blessed not because of your iniquity, neither
your hearts of unbelief, for Verily some of you are guilty before me:
but I will be merciful unto your weakness.
Therefore, be ye strong from henceforth; fear not for
the Kingdom is yours; & for your Salvation I give unto
unto you a commandment, for I have heard your prayers
& the poor have complained before me, & the rich have I
made, & all flesh is mine, & I am no respecter to
persons: & I have made the earth rich, & Behold it is
my footstool: wherefore, again I will stand upon it
& I hold forth & deign to give unto you greater

Virtue of the b{o\lood} which I have spilt, have I pled before

the Father for them{◊\:} but Behold the residue of the wicked

have I kept in Chains of darkness untill the Judgement

of the great day, which shall come at the end of the

Earth, & even so will I cause the wicked that will not   ^to be kept^

hear my voice but harden their hearts; & wo, wo, wo,

is their doom. But Behold, Verily, Verily I say unto you,

that mine eyes are upon you; I am in your midst

& ye cannot see me, but the day soon cometh that

ye shall see me & know that I am, for the ~~chains of~~ ^vails^

vails of darkness shall soon be rent, & he that is not

purified shall not abide the day: wherefore, gird

up your loins & be prepared. Behold the Kingdom

is yours & the enemy shall not overcome. Verily I

say unto you, that ye are clean but not all; &

there is none else with whom I am well pleased, for

all flesh is corruptabl before me & the powers of dark-

=ness prevail upon the Earth, among the Children of

men, in the presence of all the hosts ⟨of⟩ Heaven, which

causeth silence to reign, & all eternity is pained, &

the Angels are waiting the great command, to Reap

down the Earth, to gether the tears [tares] that they may be

burned: & Behold the enemy is combined. & now I shew

unto you a Mystery, a thing which is had in seecret

Chambers, to bring to pass even your distruction, in

process of t{◊\ime}, & ye knew it not, but now I tell it ^unto^ you,

& ye are blessed not because of your iniquity, neither

your hearts of unbelief⟨,⟩ for Verily ^some of^ y{e\ou} are guilty before me:

but I will be merciful unto your weakness.

Therefore, be ye strong from henceforth; fear not for

the Kingdom is yours; & for your Salvation I g~~ave it~~ ^ive^

unto you a commandment, for I have heard your prayers

& the poor have complained before me, & the rich have I

made, & all flesh is mine, & I am no re{p\spector} to ~~& I~~[82]

persons: & I have made the earth rich, & Behold it is

my footstool: Wherefore, again I will stand upon it

& I hold forth & deign to give unto you greater

ORIGINAL INSCRIPTION
John Whitmer

REVISIONS
Oliver Cowdery
William W. Phelps
Sidney Rigdon
Joseph Smith
John Whitmer
Unidentified

82. "I" wipe-erased and then "& I" stricken.

Riches, even a land of promise, a land flowing with milk & Honey, upon which there shall be no curse [when the Lord come] & I will give it unto you for the land of your inheritance, if you seek it with all your hearts:

12 & this shall be my covenant with you ye shall have it for the land of your inheritance, & for the inheritance of your Children forever, while the Earth shall stand, & ye shall Possess it again in eternity, no more to pass away. But Verily I say unto you, that in time ye shall have no King nor Ruler, for I will be your King & watch over you:

13 Wherefore, hear my Voice & follow me, & ye shall be a free People, & ye shall have no laws but my laws, [when I come,] for I am your Law giver & what can stay my hand.

14 But Verily I say unto you, teach one another according to the Office wherewith I have appointed you, & let every man esteem his brother as himself & practice Virtue & Holyness before me.

15 & again I say unto you let every man esteem his Brother as himself, for what man among you, having twelve sons & is no respector to them, & they serve him obediently, & he saith unto the one be thou clothed in Robes & sit thou here; & to the other, be thou clothed in Raggs & sit thou there, & looketh upon his sons & saith I am just.

16 Behold this I have given unto you a Parable, & it is even as I am, I say unto you be one & if ye are not one ye are not mine.

17 & again I say unto you that the enemy in the Secret Chambers, seeketh your lives: ye hear of wars in far Countries, & you say in your hearts there will soon be great wars in far Countries, but ye know not the hearts of them in your own Land. I tell you these things because of your prayers:

18 Wherefore, treasure up Wisdom in your bosoms, lest the wickedness of men reveal these things unto you, by their wickeness in a manner, which shall speak in your ears, with a voice louder than that which shall shake the Earth: but if ye are prepared, ye shall not fear.

19 & that ye might escape the power of the enemy & be gathered unto me a Righteous people without spot & blameless:

20 Wherefore, for this cause I gave unto you

Riches, even a land of promise; a land flowing with
when the Lord come, eth
milk & Honey, upon which there shall be ~~no~~ ⟨no⟩ curse
^
& I will give it unto you for the land of your

enheritance, if you seek it with all your hearts:
12
& this shall be my covenant with you ye shall have

it for the land of your inheritence, & for the inheritance

of your Children forever, while the Earth shall stand, & ye shall

Possess it again in eternit{t\y}, no more to pass away. But Verily

I say unto you, that in time ye shall have no King nor Ruler,
13
for I will be your King & watch over you: Wherefore, hear my

voice & follow me, & ye shall be a free {p\⟨P⟩}eople, & ye shall
when I come,
have no laws but my laws, for I am your Law giver & wh{o\at}
^
14
can stay my hand. But Verily I say unto you, teach

one another according to the Office wherewith I have appoi

=nted you, & let evry man esteem his brother as himself
15
& practice Virtue & Holyness before me. & again I say unto

you let evry man esteem his Brother as himse{f\lf} for

what man among you, having twelve sons, & is no respector

to them, & they Serve him obediently, & he saith unto the

one, be thou clothed in Robes & sit thou here; & to the other,

be thou clothed in Raggs & sit th{oou\ou} there, & looketh upon
16   this
his sons & saith I am Just. Behold I have given unto you
^
a Parable, & it is even as I am, I say unto you be one & if
17
ye are not one ye are not mine. & again I say unto you
th
that the Enemy in the Seecret Chambers, seek your lives:
y{e\ou}   ^
ye hear of wars in far Countries, & ~~you~~ say in your hearts

there will soon be great wars in far Countries, but ye know
them
not the hearts of ~~they~~ in your own Land. I tell you these
^   18
things because of your prayers{;\:} Wherefore, treasure up
l
Wisdom in your bosoms, lest the wickedness of men ~~revea~~

reveal these things ~~in your~~ unto you, by their wicke[d]ness

in a manner, which shall speak in your ears, with a voice

louder than that which shall shake the Earth: but if ye are
shall   19
prepared, ye ~~need~~ not fear. & that ye might escape the power
^
of the enemy & be gethered unto me a Righteous people without
20
spot & blameless: Wherefore, for this cause I gave unto you

ORIGINAL INSCRIPTION
John Whitmer

REVISIONS
Oliver Cowdery
William W. Phelps
Sidney Rigdon
Joseph Smith
John Whitmer
Unidentified

the commandment, that you should go to the Ohio; & there
I will give unto you my law & there you shall be endowed
with power from on high, & from thence, whomsoever I will,
shall go forth among all nations, & it shall be told them what
they shall do, for I have a great work laid up in store; [21] for
Israel shall be saved, & I will lead them whithersoever I will,
& no power shall con stay my hand. [22] And now I give unto the
Church in these parts, a commandment, that certain men among
them shall be appointed, & they shall be appointed by the
voice of the Church; & they shall look to the poor & the
needy, & administer to their relief, that they shall not suffer;
& send them forth to the place which I have commanded
them; & this shall be their work, to govern the affairs
of the Church Property of this Church. [23] & they who have
farms, that cannot be sold, let them be left or rented
as seemeth them good. [24] See that all things are preserved,
& when men are endowed with power from on high,
& are sent forth, all these things shall be gethered unto
the Bosom of the Church. [25] & if ye seek the riches which
it is the will of the Father to give unto you, ye shall be
the richest of all People, for ye shall have the riches of
eternity. & it must needs be that the riches of the Earth is
mine to give; [26] but beware of Pride lest ye become as
the Nephites of old. [27] & again: I say unto you, I give unto
you a commandment, that every man both Elder, Priest,
or Teacher & also Member, go to with his might, with the
Labour of his hands, to prepare & accomplish these things,
which I have commanded. [28] & let your preaching be the
warning voice, every man to his Neighbour, in mildness,
& in meekness. [29] & go ye out from among the wicked, save
yourselves. [30] be ye clean that bear the vessels of the Lord. even so. amen.

Church Articles & Covenants.

Received in Fayette Seneca County New York April 10th 1830
Given to Joseph the seer, & given in spirit, by the gift & power of God &c

The commandment, that y{e\ou} should go to the Ohio; & there

I will give unto you my law & there you shall be endowed

with power from on high, & from thence, whomsoever I will,

shall go forth among all Nations, & it shall be told them what

they shall do, for I have a great work laid up in store: for ²¹

Israel shall be saved, & I will lead them whithersoever I will,

& no power ~~can~~ ^shall^ stay my hand. And now I give unto the ²²

church in these parts, a commandment, that certain men among

them shall be appointed, & they shall be appointed by the

voice of the Church; & they shall look to the poor & the

needy, & administer to their relief, that they shall not suffer;

& send them forth to the place which I have commanded

them; & this shall be their Work, to govern the affairs

of the ~~Church~~ Property of th{is\e\is} Church. & they ~~that~~ ^who^ have ²³

farms, that cannot be sold, let them be left or rented ~~as~~

as seemeth them good. see that all things are preserved, ²⁴

& when men are endowed with power from on high,

& are sent forth, all these things shall be gethered unto

the Bosom of the Church. & if ye seek the riches which ²⁵

^it^ is the will of the Father to give unto you, ye shall be

the richest of all People, for ye shall have the riches of

eternity. & it must needs be that the riches of the Earth is

mine. to give: but beware of Pride lest ye become as ²⁶

the Nephites of old. & again: I say unto you, I give unto ²⁷

you a commandment, that evry man both {e\Elder}, ~~Priest~~, ^Priest,^

& Teacher & also Member, go to with his might, with the

Labour of his hands, to prepare & accomplish these things,

which I have commanded. & let your preaching be the ²⁸

warning voice, evry man to his Neighbour, in mildness,

& in meekness. & go ye out from among the wicked. save ²⁹

yourselves. be ye clean that bear the vesels of the Lord, even so: = ³⁰ -amen

⁸³Church Articles & Covenants.

⁸⁴{ Received in Fayette Seneca County New York April 10ᵗʰ· 18{θ\30}
        & Oliver [Cowdery] an Apostle
  Given to Joseph {S\the} seer by the gift & power of God &c

  ~~soon aft{t\er} the Ch{h}r~~ }

ORIGINAL INSCRIPTION
John Whitmer

REVISIONS
Oliver Cowdery
William W. Phelps
Sidney Rigdon
Joseph Smith
John Whitmer
Unidentified

83. The first publication reflecting most redactions in this item is the June 1832 issue of *The Evening and the Morning Star.* Throughout this item, much of the ink used by Oliver Cowdery and John Whitmer to make changes appears to match, possibly indicating that they made changes at the same time.

84. The text enclosed in this series of braces does not appear in any JS-era publication.

The rise of the Church of Christ in these last days,
being one Thousand eight Hundred & thirty years since the com
=ing of our Lord & Saveiour Jesus Christ, in the flesh; it being
regularly organized & established agreeable to the Laws of our
Country, by the will & commandments of God in the fourth Month
& on the sixth day of the Month, which is called April: which
Commandments were given to Joseph the seer who was called of God
& ordained an Apostle of Jesus Christ, an Elder of this Church,
& also to Oliver who was also called of God ~ordained~ an
Apostle of Jesus Christ, an Elder of this Church & ordained under
his hand, & this according to the grace of our Lord & saveiour
Jesus Christ to whom be all glory both now & forever. AMEN

For after that truly was manifested unto this first Elder,
that he had Received a remission of his sins he was entangeled
again in the vanities of the world but after truly Repenting
God ministered unto him by an Holy Angel whose countinan
=ce was as Lightning & whose garments were pure & white above
all whiteness & gave unto him Commandments which insp-
=ired him from on high & gave unto him power by the means
which were before prepared that he should translate a
Book which Book contained a record of a fallen People &
also the fulness of the Gospel of Jesus Christ to the Gentiles
& also to the Jews proveing unto them that the Holy Scriptures
are true & also that God doth inspire men &
& call them to his Holy work in these last days as well as
in days of old that he might be the same God forever amen
Which Book was given by inspiration & is called the Book
of Marmon & is confirmed to others by the ministering of
Angels & declared unto the World by them Wherefore having
so great witnesses by them shall the world be judged even
as many as shall hereafter receive this work either to faith
& Righteousness or to the hardness of heart in unbelief to their
own condemnation for the Lord God hath spoken it for we
the Elders of the Church have heard & bear witness to
the words of the glorious majesty on high to whom be glory
for ever & ever amen

The rise of the Church of Christ in these last days,

being one Thousand eight Hundred & thirty years since the com

=ing of our Lord & Saveiour Jesus Christ in the flesh; it being

regularly organized & established agreeable to the Laws of our

Country, by the will & commandments of God in the fourth Month

& on the Sixth day of the Month, which is called April: which

Commandments were given to Joseph{,\,} ~~the seer,~~ who was called of God

& ordained an Apostle of Jesus Christ, an Elder of th{e\is} Church,

& also to Oliver who was also called of {go\God} ~~& ordained~~ an

Apostle of Jesus Christ, an Elders of th{e\is} Church & ordained under

his hand, & this according to the grace of our Lord & saveiour

Jesus Christ to whom be all glory both now & forever. {a\A}men.

                  it
For after that ‸truly was manifested unto this first Elder,

that he had Received a remission of his sins he was entangeled

again in the vanities of the world but after truly Repenting

God ministered unto him by an Holy Angel whose countenan

=ce was as Lightning & whose garments were pure & white above

all whiteness & gave unto him Commandments which insp=

=ered [inspired] him from on high & gave unto him power by the means

            were
~~of~~ which ~~was~~ before prepared that he should translate a

Book which {bo\⟨B⟩}ook contained a record of a fallen People &

also the fulness of the Gospel of Jesus Christ to the Gentiles

& also to the Jews proveing unto them that the Holy Scriptures

are tru{◊\e}l & also that God doth ~~Minister~~ inspire men ~~in~~

& call them to his Holy work in these last days as well as ~~in~~

in days of old that he might be the same God forever amen

                           &
Which Book was given by inspiration ‸is Called the Book

of Mormon & is confirmed to others by the ministering of

Angels & declared unto the World by them Wherefore having

so great witnesses by them shall the world be Judged even

as many as shall hereafter receive this work either to faith

& righteousness or to the hardness of heart in unbelief to the{◊\⟨i⟩}r

                ~~has~~ hath
own condemnation for the Lord God ~~hath~~ spoken it for we

the Elders of the Church have heard & bear witness to ~~his~~

the words of {his\the} glorious majesty on high to whom be glory

for ever & ever amen

ORIGINAL INSCRIPTION
John Whitmer

REVISIONS
Oliver Cowdery
William W. Phelps
Sidney Rigdon
Joseph Smith
John Whitmer
Unidentified

85. "◊" possibly "1" or "o".

Wherefore by these things we know that there is a God
in Heaven who is infinite & Eternal from everlasting to
everlasting the same unchangeable God the Maker of Heaven
& Earth & all things that in them is & that he created man
Male & female & after his own image & in his own likeness
created he them & that he gave unto the Children of men
Commandments that they should love & serve him the only
being whom they should worship but by the Transgression
of these Holy Laws man became sensual & devilish & became
fallen man Therefore the almighty God gave his only begotten
Son as it is Written in those Scriptures which have been
given of him that he suffered temptations but gave no
heed unto them that he was crucified died & rose again
the third day & that he ascended into Heaven to sit down
on the right hand of the Father to reign with almighty
Power according to the will of the Father therefore as
many as would believe & were Baptized in his Holy name
& endured in faith to the end should be saved yea even as
many as were before he came in the flesh from the
beginning which believed in the words of the Holy Prophets
which were inspired by the gift of the Holy Ghost which
truly testify of him in all things as well as those who
should come after who should believe in the gifts &
Callings of God by the Holy Ghost which beareth Record of
the Father & of the Son which Father & Son is & Holy
Ghost is one God infinite & eternal without end amen.

And we know that all men must Repent & believe
on the name of Jesus Christ & worship the father in
his name & endure in faith on his name to the end or
they cannot be saved in the Kingdom of God & we know
that Justification through the grace of our Lord & Saviour
Jesus Christ is just & true & we also know that Sanctification
through the grace of our Lord & Saviour Jesus Christ is
just & true to all those who love & serve God with all
their mights minds & strength but there is a posibility that
men may fall from grace & depart from the living

Wherefore by these things we know that there is a God

in Heaven who is infinite & Eternal from everlasting to

everlasting the same uncha{◊\ngeable} God the Maker of Heaven

& Earth & all things that in them is & that he {h◊◊\created} man

male & female & after his own Image & in his ^own^ likeness

created he them & that he gave unto the Children of men a

commandments that they should love & serve him the only

being whom they should wor{◊\ship} but by the Transgression

of these Holy Laws man became sensual & devlish & became

fallen man Wherefore the almighty God gave his only begotten

Son as it is Written in those Scriptures which have been

given of him that he suffered temptations but gave no

heed {h◊◊\unto}[86] ^unto^ them that he was crusified died & rose again

the third day & that he ascended into Heaven to sit down

on the right hand of the Father to reign with almighty

Power according to the will of the Father therefore as

many as would believe & were Baptized in his Holy name

& endured in faith to the end should be saved yea even as

many as were before he came in the flesh from the

begining which believed in the words of the Holy Prophets

which were inspired by the gift of the Holy Ghost which

truly testif{y\ie\y}s[87] of him in all things {&\as} well as ~~they which~~ ^those who^

should come after ~~which~~ ^who^ should believe in the gifts &

callings of God by the Holy Ghost which beareth Record of

the Father & of the Son which Father & Son ~~is~~ & ~~the~~ Holy

Ghost is one God {in\Infinite} & eternal without end amen.=

And we know that all men must Repent & believe

on the name of Jesus Christ & worship the father in

his name & endure in faith on his name to the end or

they cannot be saved in the Kingdom of God & we know

that Justification through the grace of our Lord & saveiour

Jesus Christ is Just & true & we ~~also~~ ^also^ know that Sanctification

through the grace of our Lord & Saveiour {is Just\Jesus} Christ is

Just & true to all those who love & serve God with all

their mights minds & strength but there is a posibility that

men may fall from grace & depart from the living

ORIGINAL INSCRIPTION
John Whitmer

REVISIONS
Oliver Cowdery
William W. Phelps
Sidney Rigdon
Joseph Smith
John Whitmer
Unidentified

86. "h◊◊" wipe-erased and written over; then whole word stricken.

87. Sidney Rigdon changed "testify" to "testifies" but then restored "testify" by retracing the "y". He may have also stricken "ies", but the deletion appears to be in a different ink flow.

God therefore let the Church take heed & pray always
lest they fall into temptation. yea & even he that is sanc
-tified also & we know that these things are true & agreable
to the Revelations of John neither ading to nor diminishing from
the Holy Scriptures Prophecy, of his Book neither to the Holy
scriptures neither to the Revelations of God which shall come
hereafter by the gift & power of the Holy Ghost neither by the
voice of God neither by the ministering of the Holy Ghost Ange
=els & the Lord God hath spoken it & honour Power & glory
be rendered to his holy name both now & ever Amen.

And again, by way of Commandment to the Church,
Concerning the manner of Baptism: Behold whosoever
humbleth himself before God, & desireth to be Baptized, &
comes forth with a broken heart & a contrite spirit, & witnesse
=eth unto the Church, that they have truly Repented of all
their sins & are willing to take upon them the name of
Christ, having a determination to serve him unto the end,
& truly manifest by their works that they have received the
spirit of Christ unto the remission of their sins, then shall they
be received unto Baptism into the Church of Christ.

The duty of the Elders, Priests, Teachers, Deacons & Members
of the Church of Christ. An Apostle is an Elder & it is his
calling to Baptize & to ordain other Elders, Priests, Teachers &
Deacons, & to administer the flesh & blood of Christ accord
=ing to the scriptures, & to teach, expound, exhort, & to Baptize,
& to watch over the Church, & to confirm the Church by
the laying on of the hands, & the giving of the Holy Ghost,
& to take the lead of all Meetings.

The Elders are to conduct the Meetings as
they are led by the Holy Ghost.

The Priests duty is to preach, teach, expound, exhort
& baptize, & administer the sacrement, & visit the House of each
member, & exhort them to pray vocally & in secret, & also to
attend to all family duties; & ordain other Priests, Teachers & Deacons
& take the lead of meetings but none of these offices is he
to do when there is an Elder present, but in all cases is

God therefore let the Church take heed & pray always

lest {th◊y\ye}[88] fall into temptation yea & even he that is sanc=

-tified also & we know that these things are true & agreeable

to the Revelations of John neither ad[d]ing nor diminishing to

the Holy Scriptures Prophecy of his Book neither to the Holy

Scriptures neither to the Revelations of God which shall come

hereafter by the gift & power of the Holy Ghost neither by the

voice of God neither by the ministering of the Holy {g\Ghost} Ang{es\=}

=els & the Lord God hath spoken it & honour Power & glory

be rend{◊\ered} to his holy name both now & ever amen.

    And again, by the way of Commandment to the Church,

    Con{◊\cerning} the manner of Baptism: Behold whosoever

humbleth himself before God, & desireth to be Baptized, &

comes forth with a broken heart & a contrite spirit, & witness=

=eth unto the Church, that they have truly Repented of all

their sins & are willing to take upon them the name of

Christ, having a determination to serve him unto the end,

& truly manifest by their works that they have received the

spirit of Christ unto the remision of their sins, th{◊◊\en} shall they

be received unto Baptism into the Church of Christ.

    The duty of the Elders, Priests, Teachers, Deacons & Members

of the Church of Christ. {a\A}n Apostle is an Elder & it is his

calling to Baptize & to ordain other Elders, Priests, Teachers &

Deacons, & to administering the flesh & blood of Christ accord=

=ing to the scriptures, & to teach, expound, exhort, & to Baptize,

& to watch {◊\over} the Church, & to confirm the Church by

the laying on of the hands, & the giving of the Holy Ghost,

& to take the lead of all Meetings. &c.[89]

    The Elders are to conduct the Meetings according as

they are led by the Holy Ghost.

    The Priests duty is to preach, teach, expound, {◊\exhort}

& baptize, & administer the Sacrament, & visit the House of each

member, & exhort them to pray vocally & in seecret, & also to

attend all familiy duties; & ordain other Priests, Teachers & Deacons,

& take the lead in meetings but none of these {◊◊ti◊◊\{o\o}ff{ices\ices}}[90] is they

to do when there is an Elder present, but in all cases are[92]

ORIGINAL INSCRIPTION
John Whitmer

REVISIONS
Oliver Cowdery
William W. Phelps
Sidney Rigdon
Joseph Smith
John Whitmer
Unidentified

88. "th◊y" wipe-erased and written over; then whole word stricken.

89. John Whitmer (or possibly Oliver Cowdery) drew two lines to join this paragraph and the next two paragraphs.

90. Initial layer possibly "duties".

91. Or "t".

92. "to" possibly written over "are". Alternative reading: "also".

to assist the Elders

The Teachers duty is to watch over the Church always
& be with them & strengthen them & see that there is no iniquity
in the Church neither hardness with each other neither
lying nor backbiting neither nor evil speaking & see that the
Church meets to gether often & also that all the members do
their duty & he is to take the lead of Meetings in the absence
of the Elder or Priest & is to be assisted always & in all
his duties in the Church by the Deacons but neither the
Teacher nor the Deacons have authority to Baptize nor admin=
=ister the sacrement but are to warn expound exhort &
teach & invite all to come unto Christ.

Every elder Priest Teacher & Deacon is to be ordained
according to the gifts & callings of God unto him by the
the Power of the Holy Ghost which is in tow are who
ordains him

The several elders composing this Church of Christ
are to meet in conference once in three Months or from time to time as they shall direct or appoint to do Church
business whatsoever is nessessary And each Priest or
Teacher who is ordained by a Priest is to take a cirtificate
from him at the time which when presented to an Elder he is
to give him a licence which shall authorize him to perform
the duty of his calling.
The Duty of the members after they are Received by
Baptism the Elders or priests are to have a sufficient
time to expound all things concerning this Church of
Christ to their understanding previous to their partakeing
of the Sacrament & being confirmed by the laying on of
the hands of the Elders so that all things may be done in
order & the members shall manifest before the Church &
also before the Elders by a Godly walk & conversation that
they are worthy of it that there may be works & faith agree=
=able to the Holy Scriptures walking in holyness before the
Lord.

Every member of this Church of Christ having children
is to bring them unto the Elders before the Church

5{◊\6} [verso]

to assist the Elders &c⁹³

The Teachers duty is to watch over the Church always

& be with them & strengthen them & see that there is no iniquty

neither   neither
in the Church nor no hardness with each other nor no

^   neither nor
lying nor backbiteing nor no evil speaking & see that the

^   ^   see   all the
Church meets to gether often & also that evry members does do

^   ^
th{is\eir} duty & he is to take the lead of Meetings in the absence

of the Elder or Priest & is to be assisted always & in all

the
his duties in the Church by the Deacons but neither the

Teachers nor the Deacons have authority to Baptize nor admin=

=ist{◊\er} the Sacrament {nor\But} {to\are} to warn expound exhort &

teach & invite all to come unt{o\o} Christ.

or
Every elder Priest Teacher {or\&} Deacon is to be ordained

him
according to the gifts & callings of God unto them by the

the Power of the Holy Ghost which is in the one who

ordains them{.\him}

The several elders composing this Church of {◊h\Christ}
or from time to time as they Shall direct or appoint—⁹⁴ do
are to meet in conference once in three Month to Church

^   ^
business whatsoever is n{◊e\essessary} &c {&\And} each Priest or

a
Teacher who is ordained by any Priests is to take a cirtificate

^   presented
from him at the time which when shewn to an Elder he is

^
to give him a licen{s\⟨c⟩}e which shall authorize him to perform

the duty of his calling.

The Duty of the members after they are Received by

Baptism the Elders or priests are to have a sufficient

time to expound all things conce{◊in\rning} this Church of

Christ to their understanding previous to their partakeing

of the sacrament & being confirmed by the laying on of

the hands of the Elders so that all things may be done in

order & the members shall manifest before the Church &

also before the Elders by a Godly walk & conversation that

they are worthy of it that there may be works & faith agree=

=able to the Holy scriptures walking in holyness before the

Lord.

Every member of this Church of Christ having children
is
are to bring them unto the Elders before the Church

Original Inscription
John Whitmer

Revisions
Oliver Cowdery
William W. Phelps
Sidney Rigdon
Joseph Smith
John Whitmer
Unidentified

93. John Whitmer (or possibly Oliver Cowdery) drew a line joining this paragraph with the following paragraph.

94. Because of the proximity of printing dates, it is unclear whether this insertion first appears in print in the Book of Commandments (chapter 24) or the June 1833 issue of *The Evening and the Morning Star*.

Who are to lay their hands upon them in the name of the Lord & bless them in the name of Christ.

There cannot any one be received into this Church of Christ who has not arrived to the years of accountability before God & is not capable of repentance.

And the way of Baptism is to be administered in the following manner unto all those who Repent; whosoever being called of God & having authority given them of Jesus Christ shall go down into the water with them, & shall say calling them by name: Having authority given me of Jesus Christ I baptize you in the name of Jesus Christ the Father & of the Son & of the Holy Ghost. Amen. Then shall he immerse them in the water & come forth again out of the water. And it is expedient that the Church meet together oft to partake of bread & wine, in Remembrance of the Lord Jesus & the Elder or Priest shall administer it, & after this manner shall he do; he shall kneel with the Church & call upon the Father in mighty prayer saying: O God the Eternal Father, we ask thee in the name of thy Son, Jesus Christ, to Bless & sanctify this bread to the souls of all those who partake of it, that they may eat in Remembrance of the body of thy Son, & witness unto thee, O God the Eternal Father, that they are willing to take upon them the name of thy Son, & always Remember him & keep his commandments, which he has given them, that they may always have his spirit to be with them. Amen.

The manner of administering the wine: Behold they shall take the cup & say, O God the Eternal Father, we ask thee in the name of thy Son, Jesus Christ, to bless & sanctify this wine to the souls of all those who drink of it, that they may do it in Remembrance of the blood of thy Son, which was shed for them, that they may witness unto thee, O God the Eternal Father, that they do always Remember him; that they may have his spirit to be with them. Amen.

Any member of this Church of Christ, transgressing or being over taken in a fault, shall be dealt with according as the scriptures direct.

upon⁹⁵
Who {a\a}re to lay their hands u̶p̶o̶n̶ them in the name of the
^

Lord & bless them in the name of Christ.

There cannot any one be received into this Church of Christ
has
who h̶a̶v̶e̶ not arive{n\d} to the years of accountability before God
is
& a̶r̶e̶ not capable of repentance.
ad-
And t̶h̶e̶ ̶w̶a̶y̶ ̶o̶f̶ Baptism is to be -ministered in the foll-
^

-owing manner unto all those who Repent; whosoever being

called of God & having authority given them of Jesus Christ

shall go down into the water with them, & shall say, calling

them by name: {h\H}aving authority given me of Jesus Christ I
you
baptize t̶h̶e̶e̶ in the name of J̶e̶s̶u̶s̶ ̶C̶h̶r̶i̶s̶t̶ the Father & of the
^

Son & of the Holy Ghost. amen. {t\T}hen Shall he immerse them

in the water & come forth again o{t̶\ut} of the water. And it is

expedient that the Church meet together oft to partake of bread

& wine, in Rememberance of the Lord Jesus & the Eld{er\er} or Priest

shall administer it, & after this manner shall he do; he shall

kneel with the Church & call upon the Father in mighty

prayer saying. O God the Eternal Father, we ask thee in the

name of thy son, Jesus Christ, to Bless & sanctify this bread

to the souls of all those⁹⁶ who partake of it, that they may eat

in Rememberance of the body of thy son, & witness unto

thee, O God the Eternal Father, that they are willing to take

upon them the name of thy son, & always Remember him
has⁹⁷
& keep his commandments, which he h̶a̶t̶h̶ given them, that

they may always have his spirit {w̶i̶\to} be with them. amen.

The manner of administering the wine: Behold they shall

take the cup & say, O God the Eternal Father, we ask thee

in the name of thy Son, Jesus Christ, to bless & sanctify this
those   m{a\a}y
wine to the souls of all who drink of it, that they do it in
^   ^

Rememberance of the blood of thy Son, which was shed for them,

that they may witness unto thee, O God the Eternal Father,

that they do always Remember him, that they may have his

spirit to be with them. amen..

Any member of this Church of Christ, transgressing or being

over taken in a fault, shall be dealt with according as the

scriptures directs. &̶c̶

ORIGINAL INSCRIPTION
John Whitmer

REVISIONS
Oliver Cowdery
William W. Phelps
Sidney Rigdon
Joseph Smith
John Whitmer
Unidentified

95. Because of the proximity of printing dates, it is unclear whether "upon" first appears in print in the Book of Commandments or *The Evening and the Morning Star.*

96. Or "these".

97. Although "has" first appears in print in the 1835 Doctrine and Covenants (section 2), the ink flow of this revision appears to match the ink flow of Sidney Rigdon's other redactions, indicating that this revision was likely intended for earlier publications but overlooked.

It shall be the duty of the several Churches, composing this Church of Christ, to send one or more of their Teachers to attend the several Conferences, held by the Elders of this Church, with a list of the names of the several members, uniting themselves to the Church since the last conference, or send by the hand of some Priest, so that there can be kept a regular list of all the names of the members of the whole Church, in a book kept by one of the Elders; whomsoever the other Elders shall appoint from time to time; & also, if any have been expelled from the Church, so that their names may be blotted out of the general Church Record of names.

Any member removing from the Church where he resides, if going to a Church where he is not known, may take a letter certifying that he is a regular member & in good standing; which certificate may be signed by any Elder or Priest, if the member recieving the letter is personally acquainted with the Elder or Priest, or it may be signed by the Teachers or Deacons of the Church.

42ⁿ Commandment A.d Jany 5th 1831

There was a man by the name of James who covenanted with the Lord that he would obey any commandment that the Lord would give through his servant Joseph & he enquired accordingly of the Lord & he received these words as following

given at Fayette Seneca County State New York

Saying hearken & listen to the voice of him who is from all eternity to all eternity the great I am even Jesus Christ the light & the life of the world a light which shineth in darkness & the darkness comprehendeth it not the same which come in the maridian of time unto my own & my own Recieved me not but to as many as recieved me gave I power to become my Sons & even so will I give unto as many as recieve me power to become my Sons. & verily verily I say unto you he that recieveth my Gospel recieveth me. & he that recieveth not my Gospel, recieveth not me. & this is my Gospel Repentance & Baptism by water & then

58 [verso]

It shall be the duty of the⁹⁸ several Churches, composing

this Church of Christ, to send one or more of their Teachers

to attend the several conferences, held by the Elders of this

Church, with a list of the names of the several members,

uniting themselves to the Church since the last conference,

or send by the hand of some Priest, so that th{ey\ere} can be

kept a regular li{◊\⟨s⟩}t of all the names of thei members of

the whole Church, in a bo{◊\ok} kept by one of the Elders;
                                                                    h
whomesoever the other Elders sall appoint from time
                                                   ^
to time{,\:} & also, if any have been expelled from the Church,

so that their names may be blotted out of the general

Church Record of names{◊\.}

Any member removeing from the Church where he
              resides,
belongs, if going to a Church where he is not known,
       ^
may take a letter certifying that he is a regular member

& in good standing; which cirtificate may be signed by

any Elder or Priest, if ~~the~~ the member receiving the

letter is personally acquainted with the Elder or Priest,
     it
& or may be signed by the Teachers or Deacons of the Church.
   ^

♦ ⁹⁹42ⁿᵈ Commandment Recᵈ Jan. 5ᵗʰ· 1831

there was a man by the name of James [Covill] who covenanted with

the Lord that he would obey any commandment that the
                                            accordingly
Lord would give through his servent Joseph & he enquird
                                              ^
of the Lord & he received these words as follows

given at Fayette Seneca County state New York

Saying hearken ~~ye~~ & listen to the voice of him who is from

all eternity to all eternity the great I am even Jesus Christ th[e]

light & the life of the world a light which shineth in

darkness & the darkness comprehendeth it not the same which

came in the maridian of time unto my own & my own

Received me not but to as many as received me gave I

power to become my Sons & even so will I give unto as

many as Receive me power to become my Sons. & Verily Verily

I say unto you he that receiveth my Gospel Receiveth me. & he
¹⁰⁰that receiveth not my Gospel, receiveth not me
& this is my Gospel Repentance & Baptism by water & then
^

ORIGINAL INSCRIPTION
John Whitmer

REVISIONS
Oliver Cowdery
William W. Phelps
Sidney Rigdon
Joseph Smith
John Whitmer
Unidentified

98. Uninked "/" etched into the paper. This mark corresponds to a line break in *The Evening and the Morning Star.*

99. The first publication reflecting most redactions in this revelation is the Book of Commandments (chapter 41).

100. John Whitmer drew a line indicating where this inserted phrase should be placed.

Cometh the Baptism of fire & the Holy ghost ~~even the~~
comforter which Showeth all things & teacheth the peaceble things
of the Kingdom & Now Behold I say unto you my servant
James I have looked upon ~~they~~ thy works & I know thee
& ~~~~ verily I say unto thee ~~this is~~ heart is right before me
at ^this time ~~~~ Behold I have bestowed great blessings upon thy
head nevertheless thou hast seen great sorrow for thou hast
rejected me many times because of pride & ~~the~~ cares of the
world but behold the days of thy deliverance ^are come
arise & be baptized & wash away your sins calling on my
name & you shall receive my ^Spirit a blessing so great
as you ~~~~ never ^have known & ^if thou do this I have prepared thee for a great
work thou shalt ^Preach the fulness of my Gospel which
I have sent forth in these last days ~~~~ the Covenant
which I ~~have~~ sent forth to recover my People which are
of the house of Israel & it shall come to pass that power
shall rest upon thee thou shalt have great faith & I will
be with thee & go before thy face ~~~~ thou art called to
labour in my Vineyard & to build up my Church & to bring
forth Zion that it may rejoice upon the hills & flourish Behold
^verily verily I say unto ~~thou you are at~~ ^thee ~~~~ ~~~~ not called to go unto
the Eastern Countries but ~~thou are~~ ^you are called to go to ^the Ohio & in
asmuch as my People shall assemble themselves ~~to~~ the Ohio
I have kept in store a blessing such as is not known among
the Children of men & it shall be poured forth upon ~~your~~
their heads & from thence ~~they~~ ^men shall go forth into all Nations
Behold verily verily I say unto you that the people in Ohio
call upon me in much faith ~~thinking~~ I ~~will~~ ^will stay my
hand in judgement upon the Nations but I cannot deny
my word wherefore lay to with your might & call forth
Labourers into my Vineyard that it may be pruned for the
last time & inasmuch as they do Repent & receive the fulness
of my Gospel & become sanctified I will stay mine hand
in judgement wherefore go forth crying with a loud voice
saying the Kingdom of Heaven is at hand crying Hosannah
blessed be the name of the most high God go forth

Cometh the Baptism of fire & the Holy ghost ~~yea~~[101] even the

comforter which {kn**Sh**}oweth all things & teacheth the peacibl things

of the Kingdom & Now Behold I say unto you my servent

James I have looked {◊p\upon} ~~thee &~~ thy works & I know thee

thy ~~is now~~ now
& {◊◊**now**}[102] verily I say unto thee ~~thine~~ heart is right before me

this time
{◊\at**at**} ~~present~~ Behold I have bestowed great blessings upon thy

head Nevertheless thou hast seen great Sorrow for thou hast

rejected me many times because of pride & {be**the**} cause of the

are
world but behold the days of thy deliverance ~~is~~ come

arise & be baptized & wash away your sins calling o{◊\n} my

name & y{e\ou} shall receive my spirit & a blessing so great

have   if thou do this
as y{e\ou} ~~have~~ never known & I have prepared thee for a greater

work thou shalt Preach the fulness of my Gospel which

I have sent forth in these last days. ~~yea even~~ the covenant

which {cove\I} have sent forth to recover my People which are

of the house of Israel & it shall come to pass that power

shall rest upon thee thou shalt have great faith & I will

be with th{◊◊\ee} & go before thy face ~~yea~~ thou art called to

Labour in my Vineyard & to build up my Church & to bring

forth Zion that it may Rejoice upon the hills & flourish Behold

thee thou ~~you are~~ **art**
Verily Verily I say unto ~~you~~ ~~thou art~~ not called to go {to\unto}

~~you are~~   the
the Eastern countries but ~~thou art~~ called to go to Ohio & in

[t]**hou**[103] **art**
asmuch as my People shall assemble themselves {at**to**} the Oohio

I have kept in store a blessing such as is not known among

the {◊\⟨c⟩}hildren of men & it shall be poured forth upon ~~your~~

~~they~~ **men**
their heads & from thence ~~ye~~ shall go forth into all Nations

Be{◊\hold} Verily Verily I say unto you that the people in Ohio

thinking   will
call upon me in much faith ~~believeing~~ I ~~would~~ stay my

hand in Judgement upon the Nations but I cannot deny

my word Wherefore lay to with your might & call forth

Labourers into my Vinyard that it may be pruned for the

last time & inasmuch as they do {wi\Repent} & receive the fulness

of my Gospel & become sanctified ~~&~~ I will stay m{y**ine**} hand

in Judgement wherefore go forth cr{i\ying} with a loud voice

saying the Kingdom of Heaven is at hand crying Hosannah

blessed {is**be**} the name of the most high God go forth

ORIGINAL INSCRIPTION
John Whitmer

REVISIONS
Oliver Cowdery
William W. Phelps
Sidney Rigdon
Joseph Smith
John Whitmer
Unidentified

101. Strikethrough bar partially wipe-erased. Alternative reading: "{◊◊\yea}", with "◊◊" wipe-erased and written over; then whole word stricken.

102. "◊◊" wipe-erased and written over; then whole word stricken.

103. JS wrote "thou" by using the "t" in the original "thou" for the first letter.

Baptizing with water preparing the way before my face for the time of my coming is at hand the day nor the hour no man knoweth but it shurely shall come & he that Receiveth these things Receiveth me & they shall be gethered into me in time & in eternity & again it shall come to pass that in as many as ye shall baptize with water ye shall lay your hands ~~in the name of Christ~~ they shall receive the gift of the Holy ghost & shall be a looking forth for the Signs of my coming & shall know me Behold I come quickly even so amen

43d COMANDMENT January 6th 1831

A Revelation to Joseph & Sidney Rd at Fayette Seneca County State of N.Y. telling them why James Received obeyed not the command which he Received &c

1 Behold, verily I say unto you, that his heart was right before me, for he covenanted with me, that he would obey my word & he Received the word with Gladness, but Straitway Satan ~~tempted him~~ tempted him; & the fear of persecution & the cares of the world, caused him to reject the word: Wherefore he broke my ~~the~~ Covenant, ~~and it he had made~~ & it Remaineth in me to do with him as seemeth me good. Amen.

Not to be printed AN EXPLANATION of the (or the covenants) Epistle to th first Corinthians 7 Chapter & 14th versi given to Joseph the Seer at Wayne County N.Y 1831

For the unbelieving husband is sanctified by the wife, & the unbelieving wife is sanctified by the husband, else were your children unclean, but now are they holy.

2 Now in the days of the Apostles the law of circumcision was had among ~~them~~ all the Jews, which believed not the Gospel of Jesus Christ; & it came to pass that there arose a great contention among the People concerning the law of circumcision, for the unbelieving husband was desirous that his children should be circumcised & become subject to the law of Moses, which law was

REVELATION BOOK 1
5 January 1831 [D&C 39]
6 January 1831 [D&C 40]
Circa December 1830 [D&C 74]

the way before my face
Baptizing with {ab◊◊\water} preparing for the time of my
{◊**for**} **the time**
coming is at hand the day nor the hour no man knoweth
^

but it shurely shall come & he that Receiveth these

things receiveth me & they shall be gethered unto me

{i\⟨u⟩}nto¹⁰⁴ in time & in eternity & again it shall come to

pass that on as many as ye shall baptize with water
              on   **&**
ye shall lay your hands in the name of Christ & they
              ^   **gift of the**   ^
shall receive the Holy ghost & shall be a looking forth
        Signs ^
for the time of my coming & shall know me Behold

I come quickly even so amen

♦ ¹⁰⁵43ʳᵈ· Com**m**andment January {◊\6}ᵗʰ· ¹⁰⁶ 1831
              ^
A Revelation to Joseph & Sidney [Rigdon] Recᵈ at {fay\Fayette}

Seneca County state of NY telling them why James [Covill] Receivd

{not the\obeyed} not the Command which he Received &c

₁ Behold, verily I say unto you, that his heart was

right before me, for he covenant{t\ed} with me, that he would
                                            2
obey my word{,\.} & he Received the word with Gladness, but

Straitway Satan came & tempted him; & the fear of persecutions

& the cares of the world, caused him to reject the word:
3   my
wherefore he br{o\o}ke¹⁰⁷ the covenant, which he had made
                                  ^
{th◊◊\& it} Remaineth in me to do with him as seemeth

me good.   Amen.
                               · (For the covenants)
♦ ¹⁰⁸Not to be printed An explanation of the

{first\Epistle} to the first Corinthians 7 Chapter & 14ᵗʰ verse:—

given to Joseph the Seer at Wayne County. N.Y 1830

For the unbelieveing {wife\husband} is sanctified by the

wife, & the unbelieveing wife is sanctified by the husband,

else were your Children unclean, but now ere [are] they holy.

₂ Now in the days of the Apostles the law of circum=

cision was had among them all the Jews, wh{i\o}ch believed

not the Gospel of Jesus Christ{,\.} & it came to pass that

there arose a great contention among the People concerning

the law of circumcision, for the unbelieveing husband

was desirous that his children should be circumcised

& become subject to the law of Moses, which law was

ORIGINAL INSCRIPTION
John Whitmer

REVISIONS
Oliver Cowdery
William W. Phelps
Sidney Rigdon
Joseph Smith
John Whitmer
Unidentified

104. "⟨u⟩" wipe-erased and then whole word stricken.

105. The first publication reflecting the redactions in this revelation is the Book of Commandments (chapter 42).

106. "◊" likely a misshapen "6".

107. Possibly "br{a\o}ke".

108. The first publication reflecting most redactions in this item is the 1835 Doctrine and Covenants (section 73).

fulfilled. & it come to pass that the Children being brought up in subjection to the law of moses, & gave heed to the traditions of their Fathers, & believed not the Gospel of Christ, wherein they became unholy: wherefore, for this cause the Apostle wrote unto the Church, giving unto them a commandment, not of the Lord, but of himself, that a believer should not be united to an unbeliever except the law of Moses should be done away among them, that their Children might remain without circumcision; & that the tradition might be done away, which saith, that little children are unholy: for it was had among the Jews: but little Children are holy being sanctified through the atonement of Jesus Christ: & this is what their Scriptures mean.

44 Commandment given Feb 4th 1831.

at Kirtland Geauga County Ohio given to the Church in these parts & pointing out the office at Edward &c & there was a man by the name of Copley in the Township of Thompson who had requested Brother & Sidney to live with him & he would furnish them houses & provisions on then Joseph enquired of the Lord & received as follows

1 Hearken & hear, O ye my People, saith your lord & your God, ye whom I delight to bless with the greatest of blessings, ye that hear me: & ye that hear me not, will I curse, that have professed my name, with the heaviest of all cursings. 3 Hearken O ye Elders of my Church whom I have called; 4 Behold I give unto you a commandment, that ye shall assemble yourselves to gether to agree upon my word, & by the prayer of your faith ye shall receive my law, that ye may know how to govern my Church, & have all things right before me. 5 & I will be your ruler when I come: and behold, I come quickly: & ye shall see that my law is kept. 6 he that receiveth my law & doeth it the same is my Disciple; 7 & he that saith he receiveth it & doeth it not, the same is not my Disciple, & shall be cast out from among you; 8 for it is not meet that the things which belong to the

{F\f}ulfilled. & it came to pass that the Children being brought

up in subjection to the law of moses, & gave heed to the tradit

=ions of their Fathers, & believed not the Gospel of Christ,

wherein they became unholy: wherefore, for this cause the Apo

=stle wrote unto the Church, giving unto them a comman

=dment, not of the Lord, but of himself, that a believer should

not be united to an unb{l\eliever} except the law of {m\⟨M⟩}oses

should be done away among them, that their Children

might remain without circumcision; & that the tradition

might be done away, which saith, that little children

are unholy: {f\F}or it was had among the Jews: but little

children are holy being sanctified through the atonement of

Jesus Christ: & this is w⟨h⟩at these scriptures mean.

♦ ¹¹⁰44 Commandment given Feb. 4th. 1831

at Kirtland Geauga County Ohio given to the Church

in these parts it pointing ⟨out⟩at the office of Edward [Partridge] &c & there

was a man by the name of [Leman] Copl[e]y in the Township of

Thompson who had requested ~~his~~ Brother ⟨Joseph⟩ & Sidney [Rigdon] {&\to} live with

him & he would furnish them houses & provisions &c then

{~~By~~\Joseph} enquired of the lord & Received as follows

1   Hearken & hear, oh! ⟨ye⟩my People, saith your lord & your

God, ye whom I delight to bless with the greatest of

blessings. ye that hear me. & ye that hear me not will I

curse, ~~with~~ ⟨ye⟩that have professed my name, with the heaviest

of all cursings. hearken ~~oh~~ ye Elders of my Church

whom I have called; Behold I give unto you a commandm

=ent, that ye shall assemble yourselves to gether to agree

upon my ~~my~~ word, & by the prayer of {fo\your} faith ye shall

receive my law, that ye may know h{⟨⟩\ow} to govern my ~~Chur⟨h⟩~~

Church, & have all things right before me. & I will be

~~when I come: and behold, I come quickly:~~ your ruler & ye shall see that my law is kept. he that

Receiveth my law & doeth it the same is my Deciple; &

he that saith he Receiveth it & Doeth it not, the same is

not my Deciple, & shall be cast out from among you;

for it is not meet that the things which belong to the

ORIGINAL INSCRIPTION
John Whitmer

REVISIONS
Oliver Cowdery
William W. Phelps
Sidney Rigdon
Joseph Smith
John Whitmer
Unidentified

109. "1" possibly inserted at a later time by an unidentified scribe.

110. The first publication reflecting most redactions in this revelation is the Book of Commandments (chapter 43).

62 given to them that are not worthy, or to dogs, or the pearl to be

children of the Kingdom, should be cast before swine. & again, it is meet that my servant Joseph should have a house built, in which to live & translate. & again it is meet that my servant Sidney should live as ~~comfortable room to live in~~ suiteth him good. & again, I have called my servant Edward, & give ~~him~~ a commandment, that he should be appointed by the voice of the Church, & ~~be~~ ordained a bishop unto the Church, to leave his merchandise & to spend all his time in the labours of the Church; to see to all things as it shall be appointed unto him in my Laws in the day that I shall give ~~them~~ & this because his heart is pure before me, for he is like unto Nathaniel of old, in whom there is no guile. These words are given unto you, & they are pure before me: wherefore ~~let~~ beware ~~ye~~ how you hold them, for they are to be answered upon your souls in the day of judgement; even so. Amen.

The Laws of the Church of Christ Received in or Kirtland Geauga County State of Ohio in the Presence of twelve elders February Ninth one thousand eight hundred & thirty one

1 Hearken, O ye Elders of my Church, who have assembled yourselves together, in my name, even Jesus Christ, the Son of the living God, the Saviour of the World; in as much as they believe on my name & keep my Commandments; again I say unto you, hearken & hear & obey the Law which I shall give unto you: for verily I say, as ye have assembled yourselves together according to the Commandment wherewith I commanded you, & are agreed as touching this one thing, & have asked the Father in my name, even so ye shall receive. Behold, verily I say unto you, I give unto you this first Commandment, that

6{3\2} [verso]
given to them that are not worthy, or to dogs, or the pearl to be
Children of the Kingdom, should be cast before
{6\9}
Swine. & again, it is meet that my servent Joseph

should have a house built, in which to live &

translate. & again, it is meet that my Servent Sidney
Seemeth him good.
should {ha\li}ve as ~~comfortable Room to live in~~ & again,

I have called my Servent Edward, & give ~~him~~ a

commandment, that he should be appointed by the

voice of the Church, & ~~be~~ ordained a bishop unto
to
the Church, {&\to} l{a\eave} his merchandise & spend all

his time in the labours of the Church; {&\to} see to
u[n]to him,   -s
all things as it shall be appointed in my Law-~~s~~
them ~~it.~~
in the day that I shall give ~~them~~ & this because

his heart is pure before me, for he is like unto

Nathaniel of old, in whome there is no guile. these

words are given unto you, & they are pure before
beware
me: wherefore ~~be ye aware~~ how you hold them,

for they are to be answered upon your souls

in the day of Judgement; even so. amen.

♦   ¹¹¹The Laws of the Church of

Christ Received in Kirtland Geauga County

State of Ohio in the Presence of twelve elders

February Ninth one thousand eight hundred & thirty one

~~First Shall the Church come to gether into one~~

~~place or continue in seperate establishments?~~

1 Hearken, ~~oh~~ ye Elders¹¹² of my Church who have

assembled yourselves together, in my name, even Jesus

Christ, the Son of the living God, the Saveiour of the
2
World; in as much as they believe on my name & keep
3
my Commandments; again I say unto you, hearken & hear
4
& obey the Law which I shall give unto you: for Verily

I say, as ye have assembled yourselves together according
the
to commandment wherewith I commanded you, & are agreed
the Father
as touching thi{θ\s} one thing, & have asked ~~me~~ in my
5
name, even so ye shall receive. Behold, verily I say unto

you, I give unto you this first commandment, that

ORIGINAL INSCRIPTION
John Whitmer

REVISIONS
Oliver Cowdery
William W. Phelps
Sidney Rigdon
Joseph Smith
John Whitmer
Unidentified

111. The first publication reflecting most redactions in this revelation is the July 1832 issue of *The Evening and the Morning Star*. Verse numbers as inserted here first appear in print in the Book of Commandments (chapter 44).

112. Uninked horizontal line etched into the paper above "~~oh~~ ye Elders".

ye shall go forth in my name, every one of you, excepting
my servents Joseph & Sidney & I give unto them a command
=ment that they shall go forth for a little season, & it shall
be given by the power of my spirit when they shall return
return, & ye shall go forth in the power of my spirit, preach
=ing my Gospel, two by two, in my name, lifting up your
voices as with the voice of a Trump, declaring my word
like unto Angels of God: & ye shall go forth baptizing
with water, saying, Repent ye, Repent ye, for the Kingdom
of Heaven is at hand & from this place ye shall go forth
into the region westward, & in as much as ye shall find
them that will receive you you shall build up my Church in every region,
untill the time shall come when it shall be revealed
unto you from on high, when the city of the New
Jerusalem shall be prepared that ye may be gethered in
one, that ye may be my people & I will be your God
& again, I say unto you, that my servent Edward shall
stand in the office wherewith I have appointed him & it
shall come to pass that if he transgress another shall be
appointed in his stead, verse. amen.

2nd The Law

Again I say unto you that it shall not be given to any
one to go forth to preach my Gospel or to build up my
Church except he be ordained by some one who has auth
=ority & it is known to the Church that he has authority &
has been regularly ordained by the heads of the Church &
again the Elders Priests & Teachers of this Church shall teach
the scriptures which are in the Bible & the Book of mormon
in the which is the fulness of the Gospel & they shall obse
=rve the Covenants & Church Articles to do them & this shall
be their teachings & they shall be directed by the Spirit which
shall be given them by the prayer of faith & if they receive
not the spirit they shall not teach & all this they shall
observe to do as I have commanded concerning their
teaching untill the fulness of my scriptures are given
& as they shall lift up their voices by the Comforter they shall

ye shall go forth in my name, every one of you, excepting

my servents Joseph & Sidney [Rigdon]{,\;} ^6^ & I give unto them a comman

=dment that they shall go {th\forth} for a little Season, & it shall

be given by the power of my spirit when they shall ~~retun~~

^7^ return; & ye shall go forth in the power of my spirit, preachi

=ng my Gospel, two by two, in my name, lifting up your

voices as with the voice of a Trump, declaring my word

like unto {a\⟨A⟩}ngels of God: ^8^ & ye shall go forth baptizing

with water, saying, repent ye, repent ye, for the Kingdom

of Heaven is at hand. ^8^ & from this place ye shall go forth

into the region westward, & in as much as ye shall find
them that will receive, ye
~~my Deciples~~ y{e\ou} shall build up my Church in evry region,
^
until the time shall come when it shall be revealed
when
unto you, from on high, & the city of the New

Jerusalem shall be prepared that ye may be gethered in

one{◊\,} ^9^ that[113] ye may be my people & I will be your God{,\.}

^9^ & again, I say unto you, that my servent Edward [Partridge] shall

stand in the office wherewith I have appointed him{,\,} ^10^ & it

shall come to pass that if he transgress another shall be

appointed in his stead; even so. amen. ⌇

2nd ~~Thee~~[114] ~~Law~~

Again I say unto you that it shall not be given to any

one to go forth to preach my Gospel or to build up my
he   who   has
Church except ~~they~~ be ordained by some one ~~that hath~~ auth
has
=orit{t\y} & it is known to the Church that he ~~hath~~ authority &

{◊◊◊\has} been regularly ordained by the heads of the Church &

again the Elders {p\⟨P⟩}riests & Teachers of th{◊\is} Church shall teach

the scriptures which are in the Bible & the Book of mormon

in the which is the fulness of the Gospel & th{ou\ey} sh{alt\all} obse-

=rve the Covenants & Church Articles to do them & this shall
which
be th{y\eir} teachings & th{ou\ey} sh{a\a}l{t\l} be directed by the Spirit ~~it~~

shall be given the{e\m} by the prayer of faith & if {ye\they} receive

not the spirit {ye\they} shall not teach & all this {ye\they} shall

observe to do as I have commanded concerning {y◊◊\th◊◊r\their}

teaching untill the fulness of my scriptures are given
their   they
& as {ye\they} shall lift up ~~your~~ voices by the comforter ~~ye~~ shall

ORIGINAL INSCRIPTION
John Whitmer

REVISIONS
Oliver Cowdery
William W. Phelps
Sidney Rigdon
Joseph Smith
John Whitmer
Unidentified

113. Triple underlining beneath the first "t" wipe-erased and then stricken. The underlining was inscribed over a wipe-erased "◊◊".

114. Second "e" wipe-erased and then stricken with the entire phrase.

Speak & prophecy as seemeth me good, for behold the
Comforter knoweth all things & beareth record of the
Father & the Son. & now behold I speak unto the Church
Thou shalt not kill. & he that killeth shall not
have forgiveness neither in this world nor in the world to come
& again thou shalt not kill, he that killeth shall die —
thou shalt not steal. & he that stealeth & will not
repent shall be cast out — thou shalt not lie he that lieth
& will not repent shall be cast out thou shalt love
thy wife with all thy heart & shall cleave unto her & none
else & he that looketh upon a woman to lust after her shall
deny the faith & shall not have the spirit & if he repent
not he shall be cast out. — —
Thou shalt not commit adultery & he that committeth adultery
& Repenteth not shall be cast out & he that committeth adultery
& Repenteth with all his heart & forsaketh & doeth it no more
thou shalt forgive him but if he doeth it again he shall
not be forgiven but shall be cast out. Thou shalt not
speak evil of thy neighbour or do him any harm. thou knowest
my Laws. they are given in my Scriptures he that sinneth &
Repenteth not shall be cast out — If thou lovest me thou
shalt serve me & keep all my commandments & Behold thou
shalt consecrate all thy properties that which thou hast unto
me with a covenant & a deed which cannot be broken. & they
shall be laid before the Bishop of my Church & two of the
Elders such as he shall appoint & set apart for that purpose
& it shall come to pass that the Bishop of my Church after
that he has received the properties of my Church that it cannot
be broken taken from the Church he shall appoint every man
a steward over his own property or that which he has
received in as much as it shall be sufficient for himself
& family & the Residue shall be kept to administer to
him who has not that every man may receive according
as he stands in need. & the Residue shall be kept in my
Store house to administer to the poor & needy as shall be
appointed by the Elders of the Church & the Bishop

Speak & prophecy as seemeth me good, for behold the

Comforter knoweth all things & beareth record of thee
       of
Father & the son. & now behold I speak unto the Church
     ^

    Thou shalt not kill. & he that k[i]lleth shall not
               in world
have forgiveness neither in this world nor the to come
                         ^   ^

& again thou shalt not kill. he that k[i]lleth shall die—

thou shalt not steal. & he that stealeth & will not

Repent shall be cast out— thou shalt not lie he that lieth

& will not repent shall be cast out thou shalt love
                    shall
thy wife with all thy heart & Cleave unto her & none
               ^
                             her
else & he that looketh upon a woman to lust after shall
                                  ^

deny the faith & shall not have the spirit. & if he repent

⟨not⟩ he shall be cast out. — — —

    Thou shalt not commit adu{r\ltery} & he that commiteth adultery

& Repenteth not shall be cast out & he that commiteth adultery

& Repenteth with all his heart & forsaketh & doeth it no more

thou shalt forgive him but if he doeth it again he shall

not be forgiven but shall be cast out. Thou shalt not

speak evil of thy neighbour or do him any harm. thou knowest

my Laws they are given in my Scriptures he that sinneth &

Repenteth not shall be cast out— If thou lovest me thou
    thou
shalt serve me & keep all my commandment{s\s} & Behold thou

shalt consecrate all thy properties that which thou hast unto

me with a covenant & a deed which cannot be Broken. & they

shall be laid before the Bishop of my Church & two of the

Elders shuch as he shall appoint & Set apart for that purpose

& it shall come to pass that the Bishop of my Church after

that he has Received the properties of my Church that it cannot
                the chirch
be ~~broken~~ taken from ~~you~~ he shall appoint evry man
                    ^
                               has
a stewart over his own proper{y\ty} or that which he ~~hath~~

Received in as much as it shall be sufficient for himself

& family & the Residue shall be kept to administer to
    who   has
him ~~that hath~~ not that evry man may Receive according

as he stands in need. & the Residue shall be kept in my
                       as
Store house to administer to the poor & needy & shall be
                                    ^

appointed by the Elders of the Church & the Bishop

ORIGINAL INSCRIPTION
John Whitmer

REVISIONS
Oliver Cowdery
William W. Phelps
Sidney Rigdon
Joseph Smith
John Whitmer
Unidentified

But for the purpose of purchaseing lands & the building
up of the New Jerusalem which is hereafter to be revealed that
my Covenant people may be gethered in one in the day that I
shall come to my temple & this I do for the salvation of my
people. & it shall come to pass that he that sineth & repentith
not shall be cast out & shall not receive again that which he
hath consecrated unto me for it shall come to pass that which
I spake by the mouths of my Prophets shall be fulfilled for I
will consecrate the riches of the Gentiles unto my People
which are of the House of Israel & again thou shalt not be
proud in thy heart. let all thy garments be plain & their
beauty the beauty of the work of thine own hands & let all things
be done in cleanlyness before me —

Thou shalt not be idle; for he that is idle shall not eat the
bread, nor wear the garments of the labourer; & whosoever among
you that are sick, & have not faith to be healed, but believeth,
shall be nourished in all tenderness with herbs & mild food, &
that not of the World; & the Elders of the Church, two or more,
shall be called & shall pray for, & lay their hands upon them in
my name; & if they die, they shall die unto me; & if they
live, they shall live unto me. Thou shalt live together in
love, insomuch that thou shalt weep for the loss of them that
die, & more especially for those that have not hope of a glorious
resurrection. & it shall come to pass, that they that die in me
shall not taste of death, for it shall be sweet unto them,
& they that die not in me, woe unto them, for their death is bitter.
& again, it shall come to pass, that he that hath faith in me
to be healed, & is not appointed unto death, shall be healed.
he who hath faith to see, shall see; he who hath faith to
hear, shall hear; the lame who have faith to leap, shall
leap, & they who have not faith to do these things, but believ
-eth in me, have power to become my sons; & in as much as
they break not my Laws, thou shalt bear their infirmities. thou
shalt stand in the place of thy stewardship; thou shalt not
take thy Brother's garment; thou shalt pay for that which
thou shalt receive of thy Brother; & if thou obtainest more

And for the purpose of purchaseing lands & the building

up of the New Jerusamlm which is hereafter to be revealed that

my Covenant people may be gethered in one in the day that I

shall come to my temple & this I do for the salvation of my

p{o\eople}. & it shall come to pass that he that sin[n]eth & repenteth

not shall be cast out & shall not receive again that which he

has ~~hath~~ consecrated unto me for it shall come to pass that which

I spake[115] by the mouths of my Prophets shall be fulfilled for I

will consecrate the riches of the Gentiles unto my People

which are of the House of Isra{le\el} & again thou shalt not be

proud in thy heart. let all thy Garments be plain & their

beauty the beauty of the work of thine own hands & let all things

be done in cleanlyness before me—

Thou shalt not be id{el\le}; for he that is idle, shall not {at\eat} the

bread, nor wear the garments of the labourer{,\:}[116] & whos{e\oever} among

h{as\ave}
you that {is\are} sick, & ~~hath~~ not faith to be healed, but believeth,

shall be nourished in all tenderness with Herbs & mild food, &

that not of the World; & the Elders of the Church, two or more,

shall be called & shall pray for, & lay their hands upon them in

my name, & if they die, they shall die unto me; & if they ~~shall~~

live, they shall live unto me. ◊Thou shalt live together in

love, insomuch that thou shalt weep for the loss of them that

die, & more especially for those that have not h{ope\ope} of a glorious

resurrection. & it shall come to pass, that they that die in me

Shall not taste of death, for it shall be sweet unto them,

unto
& they that die not in me, w{oe\o} ~~is~~ them, for their death is bitter.

has
& again, it shall come to pass, that he that ~~hath~~ faith in me

to be healed, & is not appointed unto death, shall be healed.

who   has
he ~~that hath~~ faith to See, shall see; he ~~that hath~~ faith to

who
hear, shall hear; the lame ~~that~~ have faith to leap, shall

who
leap, & they ~~that~~ have not faith to do these things, but belie

have[117]
=ve in me, ~~hath~~ power to become my sons; & in as much as

they break not my Law{◊\s}, tho{◊\u} Shalt bear their infirmities. thou

sh{◊l\(al)}t stand in the place of thy st{◊\ewardship}{,\:}[118] thou shalt not

take thy Brother's garment, thou shalt pay for that which

-est
thou shalt receive of thy Brother, & if thou {◊\obtain}- more
^

ORIGINAL INSCRIPTION
John Whitmer

REVISIONS
Oliver Cowdery
William W. Phelps
Sidney Rigdon
Joseph Smith
John Whitmer
Unidentified

115. Or "spoke".

116. Or "{:\:}".

117. Uninked "/" etched into the paper. This mark corresponds to a line break in *The Evening and the Morning Star.*

118. Or "{:\:}".

then that which would be for thy support, then thou shalt give it into my Store House, that all things may be done according to that which I have spoken. Thou shalt ask & my scriptures shall be given as I have appointed; & for thy safety it is expedient that thou shalt held thy peace concerning them, untill ye have received them; then I give unto you a commandment that ye shall teach them unto all men; & they also shall be taught unto all Nations, Kindreds, tongues & People. Thou shalt take the things which thou hast received, which thou knowest to have been my law, to be my law to govern my Church; & he that doeth according to these things shall be saved, & he that doeth them not shall be damned, if he continue. If thou shalt ask, thou shalt receive Revelation upon Revelation, Knowledge upon Knowledge, that thou mayest know the mysteries & the peaceable things of the Kingdom; that which bringeth Joy, that which bringeth life Eternal. thou shalt ask, & it shall be revealed unto you in mine own due time, where the New Jerusalem shall be built. & behold, it shall come to pass, that my Servants shall be sent both to the East, & to the West, to the North, & to the South; & even now let him that goeth to the East, teach them that shall be converted to flee to the West. & this in consequence of that which is to come on the earth, & of secret combinations. Behold, thou shalt observe all these things, & great shall be thy reward; thou shalt observe to keep the mysteries of the Kingdom unto thyself, for it is not given to the World to know the mysteries. The laws which ye have received & shall hereafter receive shall be sufficient for you, both here & in the New Jerusalem. he that lacketh knowledge, let him ask of me & I will give him liberally, & upbraid him not; lift up your hearts & rejoice, for unto you the Kingdom has been given; even so. Amen

3d how the Elders are to dispose of their families while they .... otherwise engaged in the service of the Church

Then that which would be for thy support, thou shalt

give it into my {s\⟨S⟩}tore House, that ~~it~~ all things may be done according

to that which I have spoken. Thou shalt ask & my scriptures

shall be given as I have appointed; & for thy ~~salvation~~ safety it is

thou shalt hold thy peace concerning them, untill ye have expedient that

received them; & then I give unto you a[119] commandment that

ye ~~should~~ shall teach them unto all men{;\.} & they also shall be

taught unto all Nations, Kindreds, tongues & People.— Thou

shalt take the things which thou hast Received, which thou

knowest to have been my law, to b{y\e} my law to govern

my Church{;\,} & he that d{e\oeth} according to these things shall

be saved, & he that doeth them not shall be damned, if

he continue— If thou shalt ask, thou shalt receive Revelation

u{◊\pon} Revelation, Knowledge upon Knoweledge, that thou

mayest know the mysteries & the peacible things of the

Kingdom; that which bringeth Joy, that which bringeth

life Eternal{—\.} thou shalt ask, & it shall be reve{◊\aled}

unto you in mine own due time, whe{n\re} the New Jerusalem

shall be built. ~~thou shalt ask & it shall be revealed in~~

~~mine own due time~~. & behold, it shall come to pass,

that my Servents shall be sent both to the East, & to

the west, to the North, & to the South; & even now let

him that ~~goes~~ goeth to the East, teach them that {g◊\are}[120] shall be converted

to flee to the West. & this ~~because~~ in consequence of that which is to

come. & of Secret combinations. Behold, thou sha{l\lt} observe on the earth,

all these things, & great shall be thy[121] reward; thou shalt

observe to keep the mysteries of the Kingdom unto thyself,

for it is not given to the {w◊rld\World} to know the mysteries.

& {t\T}hese laws which ye have received, ~~are~~ & shall hereafter receive,| shall be sufficient for

you, both here & in the New Jerusalem. ~~But~~ therefore ^~~Therefore~~ he that lacketh

knowledge, let him ask of me & I will give him liberally,

& upbraid him not{;\:} lift up your hearts & rejoice, for unto

you the Kingdom has been given{,\;} ~~unto you~~ even so. amen[122]

3rd ~~How the Elders are to dispose of their families while~~

~~they are proclaiming repentance or are otherwi{◊\se} engaged~~

~~in the service of the Church.—~~[123]

ORIGINAL INSCRIPTION
John Whitmer

REVISIONS
Oliver Cowdery
William W. Phelps
Sidney Rigdon
Joseph Smith
John Whitmer
Unidentified

119. Uninked "|" etched into the paper. This mark corresponds to a line break in *The Evening and the Morning Star.*

120. "g◊" wipe-erased and written over; then whole word stricken.

121. Uninked "|" etched into the paper. This mark corresponds to a line break in *The Evening and the Morning Star.*

122. Uninked horizontal line etched into the paper beneath "even so. amen".

123. Dash included in cancellation.

The Priests, & Teachers, shall have their stewardship given them even as the members; & the Elders are to assist the Bishop in all things, & he is to see that their Families are supported out of the property which is consecrated to the Lord, either a stewardship, or otherwise, as may be thought best by the Elders & Bishop. —

4th ~~Now it is the ~~~ ~~of the Lord that we should~~ ~~meetings with the ~~~ ~~we should conduct our~~ ~~dealings with them—~~

except thou art commanded.

Thou shalt contract no debts with ~~them~~ the world, & again, the Elders & Bishop, shall counsel together, & they shall do by the directions of the spirit as it must needs be nessessary. —

5th ~~~ ~~~ ~~~

There shall be as many appointed as must needs be nessessary to assist the Bishop in obtaining places for the heathering ~~from New York, that~~ they may be to gether as much as can be, & as they are directed by the Holy Spirit; & evry family shall have ~~after~~ a place that they may live by themselves. & evry Church shall be organiz= ed in as close bodies as they can be: and this for a wise purpose: even so. Amen.

45th Commandment AD 1831

given to the Elders of this Church at Kirtland Geauga Ohio

Oh hearken ye Elders of my Church & give ear to the words which I shall speak unto you for Behold verily verily I say unto you that ye have received a commandment for a law unto my Church through him whom I have appointed unto you to receive commandments & Revelations from my hand & this ye shall know assuredly that there is none other appointed unto you to receive commandments & Revelations untill he be taken if he abide in me. but verily verily I say unto you that none else shall be appointed unto this gift except it be through him for if it be taken from him he shall not have power except to appoint another in his stead & this shall be a law unto you that ye receive not the teachings of any that shall

Come before you {◊\with}[129] as {◊\Revelations} or commandments

& this I give unto you that you may not be deceived, that

you may know they are not of me for Verily I say unto

you that he that is ordained of me shall come in at the

gate & be ordained as I have told you before to teach those

Revelations which you have received & shall receive

through him whom I have appointed— & now Behold

I give unto you a commandment that when ye are

assembled yourse{◊\lves}[130] together ye shall note with a

Pen how to act, & for my Church to act upon

the points of my law. & commandments which I have

given & thus it shall become a law unto you being

Sanctified by that which ye have received that ye

shall bind yourselves to act in all holiness before

me that in as much as ye do this glory shall be

ad[d]ed to the Kingdom which ye have received, inasmuch

as ye do it not it shall be taken even that which

ye have received, purge ye out the iniquity which

is among you Sanctify yourselves before me & if ye

desire the glories of the Kingdom appoint ye my

Joseph
Servent & uphold him before me by the prayer of faith

& again I say unto you that if y{o\e}u desire the mysteries

of the Kingdom provide for him food & raiment &

whatsoever isthing he needeth to accomplish the work

wherewith
wh{i\e}ch I have commanded him & if ye do it not he shall

who
remain unto them that have received him, that I may

reserve unto myself a pure People before me ✍ —

//[131]{a\⟨A⟩}gain, I say hearken, ye Elders of my Church whom I

have appointed{,\:} ye are not sent forth to be taught, but to

teach the Children of men the things which I have put

{in\into} your hands, by the power of my Spirit; & ye are

to be taught from on high: Sanctify yourselves & ye

shall be endowed with power, from on high that ye

may give even as I have spoken{,\:} hearken ye, for

Behold, the great day of the Lord is nigh at hand; for the

day cometh that the Lord shall utter his voice {◊\out} of

ORIGINAL INSCRIPTION
John Whitmer

REVISIONS
Oliver Cowdery
William W. Phelps
Sidney Rigdon
Joseph Smith
John Whitmer
Unidentified

129. "◊" wipe-erased and written over; then whole word stricken.

130. "◊" wipe-erased and written over; then whole word stricken.

131. Possibly a double quotation mark. This mark corresponds to a similar mark at the end of the revelation (manuscript page 70), and the text enclosed within these marks was published in *The Evening and the Morning Star,* where most redactions in this section first appear in print.

heaven, the Heavens shall shake & the Earth shall tremble, &
the Trump of God shall sound, both long & loud, & shall
say to the sleeping Nations, Ye saints arise & live; ye
sinners stay & sleep untill I shall call again. Wherefore,
gird up your loins, lest ye are found among the wicked.
Lift up your voices & spare not, call upon the Nations
to repent, both old & young, both bond & free; saying,
Prepare yourselves for the great day of the Lord, for if
I who am a man, do lift up my voice & call upon you
to repent, & ye hate me, what will you say when the
day cometh, when the Thunders shall utter ~~their~~ her voice
from the ends of the Earth, speaking in the ears of all
that live, saying, Repent, & prepare for the great day of the
Lord; yea, & again, when the lightnings shall streak
forth from the East unto the west, & shall utter forth their
voices unto all that live, & make the ears of all tingle
that hear, saying these words, Repent ye, for the great day
of the Lord is come. And again, the Lord shall utter his voice
out of Heaven, saying, Hearken, O ye Nations of the
Earth, & hear the words of that God who made you. O ye
Nations of the Earth, how often would I have gathered you
as a hen gathereth her chickens under her wings, but
ye would not; how oft have I called upon you by the
mouth of my Servants, & by the ministering of Angels,
& by mine own voice & by the voice of thunderings
& by the voice of lightnings, & by the voice of tempests,
& by the voice of Earthquakes, & great hailstorms, & by the
voice of famines, & pestilences of every kind, & by the great
sound of a trump, & by the voice of judgements, & by the
voice of mercy all the day long, & by the voice of Glory, & to
honour, & the riches of eternal life, & would have saved you
with an everlasting salvation, but ye would not; Behold,
the day has come when the cup of the wrath of mine
indignation is full. Behold verily, I say unto you, that
these are the words of the Lord your God. Wherefore Labour
ye, Labour ye, in my vineyard, for the last time, for the last
time call ye upon the inhabitants of the Earth; for in mine

Heaven, the Hevens shall shake & the Earth shall tremble, &

the Trump of God shall sound, both long & loud, & shall

say to the sleeping Nations, {y\Y}e saints arise & live;. ye

sinners stay & sleep unt{◊◊\ill} I shall call again. Wherefore,

gird up your loins, lest ye are found among the wicked;

lift up your voices & spare not, call upon the Nations

to repent, both old & young, both bond & free; saying,

{p\P}repare yourselves for the great day of the Lord, for if

I, who am a man, do lift up my voice & call upon you

to repent, & ye hate me{n\,} what will you say when the

day cometh, when the Thunders shall utter ~~their~~ her voices

from the ends of the Earth, speaking in the ears of all

that live, saying, {r\R}epent, & prepare for the great day of the

Lord; yea, & again, when the lightnings shall streak

forth from the East unto the west, & shall utter forth their

voices unto all that live, & make the {◊\ears} of all tingle

that hear,— saying, these words, {r\R}epent ye, for the great day

of the Lord is come. {&\And} again, the {l\L}ord shall utter his voice

out of Heaven, saying, {h\H}earken, O ye Nations of the

Earth, & hear the words of that God who made you, O ye

Nations of the Earth, how often would I have gethered you,

as a hen gethereth her chickens under her wings, but

ye would not; how oft have I {◊\called} upon you by the

mouth of my Servents & by the ministering of Angels,
& by mine own voice & by the voicce of thunderings
& by the voice of lightnings, |[132] & by the voice of tempests,

& by the voice of Earthquakes, & great hailstorms, & by the

{v◊\voice} of famines, & pestilences, of evry kind, & by the great

sound of a trump, & by the voice of Judgements, & by the

voice of mercy all the day long, & by the voice of Glory, & ~~hon~~[133]

honour, & the riches of eternal life; & would have saved you

with an everlasting salvation, but ye would not; Behold,

the day has come when the cup of the wrath of mine

indignation is full. Behold verily, I say unto you, that

these are the words of the Lord your God. Wherefore Labour

ye, Labour ye, in {◊\⟨m⟩}y vineyard, for the last time, for the last

time call ye upon the inhabitants of the Earth{,\:} for in mine

ORIGINAL INSCRIPTION
John Whitmer

REVISIONS
Oliver Cowdery
William W. Phelps
Sidney Rigdon
Joseph Smith
John Whitmer
Unidentified

132. This mark corresponds to a line break in *The Evening and the Morning Star.*

133. "hon" stricken and then wipe-erased.

Own due time will I come upon the Earth in judgement,
& my People shall be redeemed, & shall reign with me
on Earth, for the great Millenial which I have spoken
by the mouth of my Servants, shall come; for satan
shall be bound, & when he is loosed again, he shall only
reign for a little season, & then cometh the end of the
~~Earth~~ & he that liveth in righteousness, shall be changed
in the twinkling of an eye, & the Earth shall pass
away so as by fire, & the wicked shall go away into
unquenchable fire, & their end no man knoweth on
Earth, nor ever shall know untill they come before
me in judgement. Hearken ye to these words, Behold
I am Jesus Christ, the saviour of the World; treasure
these things up in your hearts, & let the Solemnities
of Eternity rest upon your minds, be sober, keep
all my Commandments, even So: AMEN!

46th COMMANDMENT Feby 1831

A Revelation to Joseph & Sidney Received at
Kirtland Geauga Ohio a call to the Elders of the ~~Church~~
Church &c

Behold thus saith the Lord unto you my Servents
it is expedient in me that the Elders of my Church
should be called together from the East & from the
West & from the North & from the South by letter or
some other way in as much as they are faithful and exercise faith in me & it shall come to pass that I will pour
out my Spirit upon them in the day that they assemble
themselves together & it shall come to pass that they
shall go forth into the regions round about & preach
repentance unto the People & many shall be converted
insomuch that ye shall obtain power to organize
yourselves according to the laws of man that
your enemies may not have power over that you may be preserved
in all things that you may ~~be enabled~~ to keep my laws
that every band may be broken wherewith the
enemy seeketh to destroy my People Behold I say unto

70 [verso]

Own due time will I come upon the Earth in Judgement,

& my People shall be redeemed, & shall reign with me

on Earth, for the great Millenial which I have spoken

by the mouths of my Servents, shall come; for satan

shall be bound, & when he is loosed again, he shall only

r{i\eign} for a little Season, & then cometh the end of the
Earth;
world & he that liveth in righteousness, shall be changed

in the twinkling of an eye, & the Earth shall pass

away so as by fire, & the wicked shall go {◊\away} into

unquinchable fire, & their end no man knoweth, on

Earth, nor ever shall know untill they come before

me in Judgement. {h\H}ear{◊◊\ken} ye to these words, Behold

I am Jesus Christ, the saveiour of the World; treasure

these things up in your hearts, & let the Solemn[i]ties

of Eternity rest upon your minds, be sober, keep
my
all the commandments, even So: amen.\\¹³⁴

♦ ¹³⁵46ᵗʰ **Commandment** Febu. 1831

    A Revelation to Joseph & Sidney [Rigdon] Receivd at

Kirtland Geauga Ohio a call to the Eldrs of this ~~Church &c~~

Church &c

    Blehold thus saith the Lord unto you my Servents

it is expedient in me that the Elders of my Church

should be called to gether from the East & from the

West & from the North & from the South by letter or
in as much as they are faithful and exercise faith in me
some other way & it shall come to pass that I will pour

out my Spirit upon them in the day that they assemble

thems{◊◊l\elves} ~~to~~together & it shall come to pass that they

shall go forth unto the regions round about & preach

repentance unto th{i\e}s People & many shall be converted

insomuch that ye shall obtain power to organize

yourselves according {◊\to} the laws of man that
    not have power over that you may be preserved
your enemies may ~~be under~~ your ~~feet in all~~
in all   ~~not have power over you~~
things that y{e\ou} may be enabled to keep my laws

that evry band¹³⁶ may be broken wherewith the

enemy s{◊◊\eeketh} to destroy my People Behold I say unto

ORIGINAL INSCRIPTION
John Whitmer

REVISIONS
Oliver Cowdery
William W. Phelps
Sidney Rigdon
Joseph Smith
John Whitmer
Unidentified

134. Possibly a double quotation mark. This mark corresponds to a similar mark halfway through the revelation (manuscript page 68), and the text enclosed within these marks was published in *The Evening and the Morning Star,* where most redactions in this section first appear in print.

135. The first publication reflecting the redactions in this revelation is the Book of Commandments (chapter 46).

136. Or "bond".

you that ye must visit the poor & the needy &
administer to their releaf that they may be kept untill
all things may be done according to my law which
ye have received amen

47 A prophecy March 7th 1831
given to Joseph the seer at Kirtland geauga
County Ohio

Saying hearken O ye people of my Church to whom
the kingdom has been given hearken ye & give ear to him
who laid the foundation of the Earth who made the Heavens
& all the hosts thereof & by whom all things were made
which live & move & have a being & again I say hearken
unto my voice lest death shall overtake you in an hour
when you think not the summer shall be past & the harvest
ended & your souls not saved listen to him who is your
advocate with the Father who is pleading your case before
him saying Father behold the sufferings & death of him
who did no sin in whom thou wast well pleased Behold
the blood of thy son which was shed the blood of him whom
thou gavest that thyself might be glorified wherefore Father
spare these my Brethren that believe on my name that they
may come unto me And have everlasting life Hearken
O ye people of my Church & ye Elders listen together & hear
my voice whilst it is called to day & harden not your hearts
For verily I say unto you that I am Alpha & Omega the
Begining & the end the light & the life of the world a light
that shineth in darkness & the darkness comprehendeth it not
I came unto my own & my own received me not but unto
as many as received me gave I power to do many Miracles
& to become the Sons of God & even unto them that
believed on my name gave I power to obtain eternal
life & even so I have sent mine everlasting covenant into the
World to be a light to the world & to be a standard for
my people & for the gentiles to seek to it And to be a
messenger before my face to prepare the way before me

you that ye must visit the poor & the needy &

administer to their releaf that they may be kept unt{ɵ\ill}

all things may be done according to my law which

ye have receivd amen

◆ ¹³⁷47 A prophecy March 7ᵗʰ· 1831

//¹³⁸given to Joseph the seer at Kirtland geauga

County Ohio

Saying hearken {o\O} ye people of my Church to whom

the Kingdom {~~was~~\has} been given hearken ye & give ere [ear] to him

who laid the foundation of the Earth who made the Heavens

& all the hosts thereof & by whom all things were made

which live & move & have a being & again I say hearken

unto my voice lest death shall overtake you in an hour

when y{e\ou} think not the Summer shall be past & the harvest

ended & your souls ᴬʳᵉ not saved listen to him who is ~~the~~ ʸᵒᵘʳ

advocate with the Father who is pleading your case before

him saying Father behold the sufferings & death of him

who did no sin in whom thou wast well ple{s\ased} Behold

the Blood of thy son which was shed the blood of him whom

thou gavest that thyself might be glorified wherefore Father

spare these my Brethren that Believe on my name that they

may come unto me And have everlasting life Hearken

O ye people of my Church & ye Elders listen together & hear

my voice whilest it is called to day & harden not your hearts

For verily I say unto you that I am Alpha & Omega the

Begining & the end the light & the life of the world a light

that shineth in darkness & the darkness comprehendeth it not

I came unto my own & my own Received me not but unto

as many as received me gave I power to do many M{i\a}ricles

& to become the {s\Sons} of God & even unto them that

believed on my name gave I power to obtain eternal

life & even so I have sent mine everlasting covenant unto the

World to be a light to the world & to be a standerd for

my people & for the gentiles to seek to it And to be a

mesinger before my face to prepare the way before me

ORIGINAL INSCRIPTION
John Whitmer

REVISIONS
Oliver Cowdery
William W. Phelps
Sidney Rigdon
Joseph Smith
John Whitmer
Unidentified

137. The first publication reflecting most redactions in this revelation is the June 1832 issue of *The Evening and the Morning Star.*

138. This mark corresponds to a similar mark at the end of the revelation (manuscript page 76) and possibly indicates intent or instruction to publish this revelation in *The Evening and the Morning Star.*

Wherefore came ye unto it, and with him that cometh, I will reason as with men in days of old, And I will shew unto you my strong reasoning; Wherefore hearken ye together & let me shew it unto you, even my wisdom, the wisdom of him whom ye say is the God of Enoch, & his Brethren, who were seperated from the Earth, & were reserved unto myself, a City reserved untill a day of righteousness shall come, a day which was sought for by all holy men, & they found it not Because of wickedness & abominations, & confessed that they were strangers & pilgrims on the Earth; but obtained a promise that they should find it, & see it in their flesh. Wherefore hearken & I will reason with you, & I will speak unto you & prophecy as unto men in days of old, & I will shew it plainly as I shewed it unto my Disciples, as I stood before them in the flesh & spoke unto them saying, As ye have asked of me concerning the signs of my coming, in the day when I shall come in my glory, in the clouds of Heaven to fulfill the promises that I have made unto your fathers; for as you have looked upon the long absence of your spirits, from your bodies to be a bondage, I will shew unto you how the day of redemption shall come, & also the restoration of the scattered Israel. And now ye behold this temple which is in Jerusalem, which ye call the house of God, & your enemies say that this House shall never fall. But verily I say unto you, that desolation shall come upon this generation as a thief in the night, And this people shall be destroyed & scattered among all Nations, & this Temple which ye now see shall be thrown down that there shall not be left one stone upon another. And it shall come to pass, that this generation of jews shall not pass away untill every desolation which I have told you concerning them shall come to pass. Ye say that ye know, that the end of the World cometh; ye say also that ye know, that the Heavens & the Earth shall pass away.

Wherefore come ye unto it; and With him that cometh,

{wi\I} will reason as with men ~~of old~~ in days of old, And

I will shew unto you my strong reasoning; Wherefore hearken

ye tog{g\ether} & let me shew it unto you, even my wisdom,

the wisdom of him whom ye say is the God of Enoch, &

his Brethren, who were seperated from the Earth, & were

reserved unto mysel{f\f}, a City reserved untill a day of

righteousness shall come, a day which was sought for by

all Holy men, & they found it not Because of wickedness

& abominations, & confessed that they were strangers &

pilgrims on the Earth; but obtained a promise that

they should find {◊◊\it}, & see it in their flesh. {w\W}herefore

hearken & I will reason with you, & I will speak

unto you & prophecy as unto men in days of old, & I

will shew it plainly as I shewed it unto my Deciples,

as I stood before th{i\em} in the flesh & spake[139] unto them

saying: {⟨as⟩\As} ye have asked of me concerning the~~se~~ signs of my

coming, in the day when I shall come in my glory,

in the clouds of Heaven to fulfill the promises that

I have made unto your fathers; for {y\as} you have

looked upon the long absence of your spirits from

your bodies, to be a bondage, I will shew unto

you how the day of redemption shall come, & also

the restoration of the scattered Israel. {&\And} now ye behold

this temple which is in Jerusalem, which ye call the

House of God, & your enemies say that this House shall

never fall. {b\B}{◊t\ut} verily I say unto you, that desolation

shall come upon this generation as a thief in the night,

And this people shall be destroyed & scattered among all

Nations, & this Temple which ye now see shall be thrown

down that there shall not be le{◊◊\ft} an stone upon another.

{&\And} it shall come to pass, that this generation of Jews

untill ~~the~~ eve{◊◊\ry}

shall not pass away, desolation which I have told you

concerning them shall come to pass. ¶ye say that ye

know, that the end of the World cometh; ye say also

that ye know, that the Heavens & the Earth shall pass away.

Original Inscription
John Whitmer

Revisions
Oliver Cowdery
William W. Phelps
Sidney Rigdon
Joseph Smith
John Whitmer
Unidentified

139. Or "spoke".

And in this ye say truely, forso it is; But these things which I have told you, shall not pass away untill all shall be fulfilled; & this I have told you concerning Jerusalem & when that day shall come, shall a remnant be scattered among all Nations, but they shall be gathered again; but they shall remain untill the times of the gentiles be fulfilled. & in that day shall be heard of wars & rumours of wars, & the whole Earth shall be in commotion, & mens hearts shall fail them, & shall say that Christ delayeth his coming untill the end of the Earth & the love of men shall wax cold, & iniquity shall abound; & when the times of the gentiles is come in, a light shall break forth among them that sit in darkness, & it shall be the fulness of my gospel; but they receive it not, for they percieve not the light, & they turn their hearts from me because of the precepts of men, & in that generation shall the times of the gentiles be fulfilled: & there shall be men standing in that generation, that shall not pass untill they shall see an overflowing scourge; for a desolating sickness shall cover the land. but my Disciples shall stand in Holy places & shall not be moved, but among the wicked, men shall lift up their voices & curse God & die; & there shall be earthquakes, also, in diverse places, & many desolations, yet men will harden their hearts against me; & they will take up the sword one against another & they will kill one another: And now, when I the Lord had spaken these words unto my Disciples, they were troubled, & I said unto them, be not troubled, for when all these things shall come to pass, ye may know that the promises which have been made unto you, shall be fulfilled; & when the light shall begin to break forth, I shall be unto them like unto a Parable which I will shew you: ye look & behold the figtrees, & ye see them with your eyes, & ye say when they begin to shoot forth & their leaves are yet tender, ye say that summer

And in this ye say truly, for so it is; But these things

which I have told you, shall not pass away ~~but~~ all shall
                                         untill

be fulfilled; & this I have told you concerning Jerusalem;

& when that day shall come, shall a remnant ~~shall a~~ be

scattered among all Nations{;\,} but they shall be gethered

again; but they shall remain untill the times of the

gentiles be fulfelled. & in that day shall be heard of

wars & rumours of wars, & the whole Earth shall be in

commotion, & mens hearts shall fail them; & {&\shall} say

that Christ delayeth |140 his coming until the end of the Earth
                                                            world
~~world~~ & the love of men shall wa{ɵ\x} cold, & in{i\⟨e⟩}quity shall
                                              Shall be   are is
abound; & when the times of the gentiles ~~shall be~~141 ~~is~~ come;

in ~~in~~ ~~And~~ a light shall break forth among them that sit in

darkness, & it shall be the fulness of my Gospel; but they

receive it not, for they perceive not the light, & they turn their

hearts from me because of the precepts of men; & in that

generation shall the times of the gentiles be fulfilled: &

there shall be men standing in that generation, that shall

not pass, untill they shall see an overflowing scourge{;\,}142

for a desolating sicknes shall cover the land; ~~& shall not be~~

~~moved~~ but my D{e\is}ciples shall stand in Holy places & shall

not be moved, but among the wicked, men shall lift

up their voices & curse God & die; & there shall be earthq

=akes, also, in diverse places, & many desolations, yet men

will harden th{◊◊\eir} hearts against me; & they will take

up the sword one against another & they will kill one

another: And now, when I the Lord had spoken these words

unto my Deciples, they were troubled, ~~for when all these~~

~~things shall come~~ & I said unto them, be not troubled, for

when all these things shall come to pass, ye may know

that the promises which have been made unto you, shall

be fulfilled, & when the light shall begin to break

forth, it shall be with them like unto a Parable which

I will shew you: ye look & behold the figgtrees, & ye see

them with your eyes, & ye say when they begin to shoot

forth & th{◊◊◊\eir} leaves are yet tender, ye say that summer

ORIGINAL INSCRIPTION
John Whitmer

REVISIONS
Oliver Cowdery
William W. Phelps
Sidney Rigdon
Joseph Smith
John Whitmer
Unidentified

140. This mark corresponds to a line break in *The Evening and the Morning Star.*

141. "shall be" canceled at the time of original inscription, leaving "when the times of the gentiles is come in a light shall break forth". An unidentified scribe later changed "is" to "are" and canceled "in". John Whitmer later reversed the redaction, canceling "are" and rewriting "Shall be" and "is". He also inserted a dotted line under the original "shall be" to indicate that the phrase should be left as originally inscribed. Whitmer then canceled the original "shall be" again and canceled the "Shall be" he had inserted, likely upon realizing "shall be" had been canceled at the time of original inscription.

142. Possibly ";". However, it appears that the dot in the semicolon was stricken, forming a comma.

is now nigh at hand; even so it shall be in that day
when they shall see all these things, then shall they
know that the hour is nigh. & it shall come to pass that
he that feareth me shall be looking for the great
day of the Lord to come, even for the signs of the coming
of the son of man; & they shall see signs & wonders,
for they shall be shewn forth in the heavens above,
& in the Earth beneath; & they shall behold blood &
fire, & vapours of smoke; & before the day of the
Lord shall come, the sun shall be darkened, & the moon
be turned into blood, & stars shall fall from
Heaven; & the remnant shall be gethered unto this
place; & then they shall look for me, & Behold I
will shall come; & they shall see me in the clouds of heaven,
clothed with power & great glory, with all the holy
Angels; & he that watches not for me shall be cut off.
¶ But before the arm of the Lord shall fall, an angel
shall sound his Trump, & the saints that have slept shall
come forth to meet me in the cloud wherefore if ye
have slept in peace blessed are you for as you now
Behold me & know that I am even so shall ye come unto
me & your souls shall live. And your redemption shall
be perfected And the saints shall come forth from the
four quarters of the Earth then shall the arm of the Lord
fall upon the nations & then shall the Lord set his foot
upon this mount & it shall cleave in twain & the Earth
shall tremble & reel to & fro & the Heavens also shall
shake & the Lord shall utter his voice & all the ends of the
Earth shall hear it & the nations of the Earth shall mourn
& they that have laughed shall see their folly & calamity
shall cover the mocker & the scorner shall be consumed &
they that have watched for iniquity shall be cut off hewn
down & cast into the fire & then shall the Jews look upon
me & say what are these wounds in thine hands & in
thy feet then shall they know that I am the Lord
for I will say unto them; these wounds are the wounds

is now nigh at hand; even so it shall be in that day,

when they shall see all these things, then shall they k̶[143]

know that the hour is nigh. & it shall come to pass that

he that feareth me shall be looking for the great

day of the {l\L}ord to come, even for the signs of the coming

of the son of man; & they shall see signs & wonders,

for they shall be shewn forth in the heavens above,

& in the Earth beneath; & they shall behold blood &

fire{s\s}, & vapor{s\s} of smoke; & before the day of the

       shall[144]
lord come, the sun shall be darkened, & the m{◊\oon}

b̶e̶ turned i̶n̶t̶o̶ blood, & s̶o̶m̶e̶ stars shall fall from

Heaven; & the remnant shall be gethered unto this

place; & then they shall look for me, & Behold I

      shall[145]
will come; & they shall see me in the clouds of heaven,

clothed with power & great glory, with all the holy

Angels; & he that watches not for me shall be cut off.

                   an
¶But before the arm of the Lord shall fall, & t̶h̶e̶[146] Angel

shall sound his Trump, & the saints that have slept shall

come forth to meet me in the cloud wherefore if ye

have slept in peace blessed are you for as you now

Behold me & know that I am even so shall ye come unto

me & your souls shall live And your redemption shall

be perfected And the saints shall come forth from the

four quarters of the Earth then shall the arm of the Lord

fall upon the Nations & then shall the lord set his foot

upon this mount & it shall cl{◊\eave} in twain & the Earth

shall tremble & reel to & fro & the Heavens also shall

shake & the Lord shall utt{◊\⟨e⟩}r his voice & all the ends of the

Earth {h\shall} hear it & the Nations of the Earth shall mourn

& they that have laughed shall see their folly & calamity

        Seize cover
shall c̶e̶a̶s̶e̶ the mocker & the scorner shall be consumed &

they that have watched for iniquity shall be c̶u̶t̶ ̶o̶f̶f̶ hewn

down & cast into the fire & then shall the Jews look upon

me & say what are these wou{◊\nds} in thine hands & in

thy feet then shall they know that I am the Lord

for I will say unto them these wounds are the wounds

ORIGINAL INSCRIPTION
John Whitmer

REVISIONS
Oliver Cowdery
William W. Phelps
Sidney Rigdon
Joseph Smith
John Whitmer
Unidentified

143. "k" wipe-erased and then stricken.

144. "**shall**" first appears in print in the Book of Commandments (chapter 48).

145. "**shall**" stricken and then wipe-erased.

146. "& the" deleted; the ink used in the cancellation spread and appears to be an ink blot.

With which I was wounded in the house of my friends
I am he that was lifted up I am Jesus which was crucified
I am the Son of God & then shall they weep because of their
iniquities then shall they lament because they persecuted
their King & then shall the heathen Nations be redeemed
& they which knew no law shall have part in the first
Resurrection & it shall be tolerable for them & Satan shall
be bound that he shall have no place in the hearts of the
Children of men & at that day when I shall come in my
Glory. Shall the parable be fulfilled which I spoke
Concerning the ten virgins for they that are wise & have received
the truth & have taken the Holy Spirit for their guide &
have not been deceived Verily I say unto you they shall
not be hewn down & cast into the fire but shall abide
the day & the Earth shall be given unto them for an inher
itance & they shall multiply & wax strong & their children
shall grow up without sin unto salvation for the Lord
shall be in their midst & his glory shall be upon them &
he will be their King & their law giver & now behold I
say unto you it shall not be given unto you to know
any farther than this until the New Testament be transla
ted & in it all these things shall be made known. Wherefore
I give unto you that ye may now Translate it that ye
may be prepared for the things to come. for Verily I say unto
you that great things await you ye hear of wars in foreign
lands but behold I say unto you they are nigh even unto
your doors & not many years hence ye shall hear of wars
in your own lands wherefore I the Lord have said gather
ye out from the Eastern lands assemble ye yourselves toge
ther ye Elders of my Church go ye forth into the western
countries call upon the inhabitants to Repent & in as much as
they do repent build up Churches unto me & with one
heart & with one mind gather up your riches that you
may purchase an inheritance which shall hereafter be appo
inted you & it shall be called the New Jerusalem a land
of peace a city of refuge a place of safety for the saints of

With which I was wounded in the house of my friends

I am he that was lifted up I am Jesus which was crusified

I am the Son of God & then shall they weep {◊\because} of their

iniquities then shall they lament because they persecuted

their King & then shall the heathen Nations be redeemed

& they which knew no law shall have p{◊\art} in the first

resurrection & it shall be tolerable for them & Satan shall

be b{◊\◊o)}und that he shall have no place in the hearts of the

children of men & at that day when I shall come in my

glory, Shall the palable [parable] be fulfilled of ¹⁴⁷ which I spoke

concerning the ten virgins for they that {is\are} wise & ha{th\ve} received

the truth & ha{s\ve} taken the Holy Spirit for their guide &

have not been deceived Verily I say unto you they shall

not be hewn down & cast into the firee but shall abide

the day & the Earth shall be given unto them for an inher

=itance & they shall multiply & wax strong & their children

shall g[row]¹⁴⁸ up without Sin unto salvation for the Lord

shall be in their midst & his glory shall be upon them &

he s̶h̶a̶l̶l̶ ^{will} be their King & their law giver. & now behold I

say unto you, it shall not be given unto you to know

any farther then this, until the New Testament be transla

=ted, & {it\in} it ^{these} all things shall be made known: Wherefore

I give unto you that ye may now Translate it, that ye

may be prepared for◊ the things to come. for Verily I say unto

you that great things await you ye hear of wars in foreign

lands but behold I say unto you they are nigh even unto

your doors & not many years hence ye Shall hear of wars

in your own lands wherefore I the Lord have said gether

ye out from the Eastern lands assemble ye yourselves toge

=ther ye Elders of my Church ge [go] ye forth into the western

countries call upon the inhabitants to repent & in as much as

they do repent build up Churches unto me & with one

heart & with one mind gether up your riches that you

may purchase an inheritance which shall hereafter be appo

=inted you & it shall be called the New Jerusalem a land

of peace a City of refuge a place of s{a◊\af)}ety for the saints of

ORIGINAL INSCRIPTION
John Whitmer

REVISIONS
Oliver Cowdery
William W. Phelps
Sidney Rigdon
Joseph Smith
John Whitmer
Unidentified

147. Two layers of deletion: first layer by an unidentified scribe and second layer in the same ink flow as the corrections made by an unidentified scribe on the next line.

148. Deletion of "& the" on manuscript page 74 created an ink blot over this word, leaving it partially illegible. All early manuscripts and JS-era published versions read "grow".

the most high God & the glory of the Lord shall be
there & the terror of the Lord also shall be there, insomuch
that the wicked will not come unto it; & it shall be called
Zion: & it shall come to pass, among the wicked, that
every man that will not take his sword against his
neighbour, must needs flee unto Zion for safety. &
there shall be gethered unto it out of every nation under
Heaven: & it shall be the only people that shall not be
at war one with another. & it shall be said among the
wicked, let us not go up to battle against Zion, for
the inhabitants of Zion are terible: wherefore we cannot
stand. & it shall come to pass that the righteous shall
be gethered out from among all nations, & shall come
to Zion singing, with songs of everlasting Joy. & now
I say unto you, keep these things from going abroad
unto the world, ^(while it is coexpedient in me) that ye may accomplish this work in
the eyes of the people, & in the eyes of your enemies,
that they may not know your works untill ye have
accomplished the thing which I have commanded you,
that ^when the Lord shall appear he shall ^they shall know it. ^(that they may consider these things; for) ^may be terrible unto
them, that fear may siese upon them, & they shall
stand afar off & tremble: & all nations shall be afraid
because of the terror of the Lord, & the power of his might
even so amen

(Compared this far by J & O)

48th Commandment March 8th 1831

A given at Kirtland geauga County Ohio to the
church concerning Confirmation & sacrament meetings &
        Hearken Oh ye my people of my Church for
Verily I say unto you that these things were spoken unto
you for your profit & learning but notwithstanding these
things which are written it always has been given to the
Elders of my Church from the begining & ever shall be
to conduct all meetings as they are directed & guided
by the Holy spirit nevertheless ye are commanded never
to cast any one out from your publick meetings

The most high God & the glory of the Lord shall be

there & the terer of the Lord also shall be there, insomuch

that the wicked will not come unto it: & it shall be called

Zion: & it shall come to pass, among the wicked, that

evry man that will not take his sword against his

Neighbour, must needs flee unto Zion for safety. &

there shall be getherd unto it out of evry Nation under

Heaven: & it shall be the only people that shall not be

at war one with another. & it shall be said among the

wicked, let us not go up to battle against Zion, for

the inhabitants of Zion are terible: wherefore we cannot

stand. & it shall come to pass that the righteous shall

be gethered o{◊\ut} from among all Nations, & shall come

to Zi{◊\on} singing, with songs of everlasting Joy.[149] & now

I say unto you, keep these things from going a{b◊\broad}
{◊◊**until**} **it is expe**{◊**dient**} **in me**,
unto the world, that ye may accomplish this work in

the eyes of the people, & in the eyes of your enemies,

that they may not know your works untill ye have

accomplished the thing which I have commanded you:
that they ~~may~~ consider these things for
that when they shall know it, ~~it~~ may be terible unto
when the Lord shall appear he shall ^
them, that fear may sieze upon them, & they shall

stand afar off & tremble: & all nations shall be afraid

because of the teror of the lord, & the power of his might;

even so: amen//[150]

(Compared thus far by J & O)[152]
[151]48th Commandment March {◊\7\8}th. [153] 1831

♦

//[154]given at Kirtland geauga County Ohio to the

Church concerning conformation & sacrament meetings &c
of
Hearken {O\oh} ye ~~my~~ people of my Church for
were
Verily I say unto you that th{e\o}se things ~~are~~ spoken unto

you for your profit & l{ae\〈ea〉}rning but notwithstanding those

things which are written it always has been given to the

Elders of my Church from the begining & ever shall be
di[r]ected
to conduct all meetings as they are ~~conducted~~ & guided

by the Holy spirit nevertheless ye are commanded never

to cast any one out from your publick meetings

ORIGINAL INSCRIPTION
John Whitmer

REVISIONS
Oliver Cowdery
William W. Phelps
Sidney Rigdon
Joseph Smith
John Whitmer
Unidentified

149. *The Evening and the Morning Star* publication ends here; redactions after this point in the revelation first appear in print in the Book of Commandments (chapter 48).

150. This mark corresponds to a similar mark at the beginning of the revelation (manuscript page 71) and possibly indicates intent or instruction to publish this revelation in *The Evening and the Morning Star,* where a portion of the revelation was published. (See preceding note.)

151. Most of John Whitmer's redactions in this revelation that were made in darker ink first appear in print in the Book of Commandments (chapter 49).

152. Because this notation was written by John Whitmer, "J" likely refers to Whitmer and "O" likely refers to Oliver Cowdery. The ink flow of this notation appears to match the ink flow of a similar notation on manuscript page 146, but its meaning is unknown. (See 269n388 herein.)

153. The original layer of this date is almost completely obscured by subsequent layers; remnants of the original layer indicate that it was likely "8". The second layer is "7" with a thick stem. The "7" was later altered with an S-like shape to restore the "8".

154. This mark corresponds to a similar mark at the end of the revelation (manuscript page 78) and possibly indicates intent or instruction to publish this revelation in *The Evening and the Morning Star,* where it was published in August 1832.

which are held before the world ye are also commanded
not to cast any one — who belongeth to the Church out
of your sacrament meetings nevertheless if any have trespas
-sed let him not partake untill he makes reconciliation
And again I say unto you ye shall not cast any out of
your sacrament meetings who is earnestly seeking the
Kingdom I speak this concerning those who are not of the
Church And again I say unto you concerning your conf
-irmation meetings that if there be any that is not of the
Church that is earnestly seeking after the Kingdom ye shall
not cast them out but ye are commanded in all things
to ask of God who giveth liberally & that which the spirit
testifies unto you even so I want that ye should do in all
holyness of heart walking uprightly before me considder
-ing the end of your salvation doing all things with prayer
& thanksgiving that ye may not be seduced by evil spirits
or doctrines of Devils or the commandments of men for some
are of men & others of Devils Wherefore beware lest ye are
deceived & that ye may not be deceived seek ye earnestly
the best gifts always remembering for what they are
are given for verily I say unto you they are given for the
benefit of those who love me & keep all my commandments
& he who seeketh so to do that all may be benefitted that
seeketh or that asketh of me that asketh & not for a sign
that he may consume it upon his lusts And again
Verily I say unto you I would that ye should always remember
& always retain in your minds what those gifts are that are
given unto the Church for all have not every gift given
unto them for there are many gifts & to every man is given
a gift by the spirit of God to some is given one & to some
is given another that all may be profited thereby to some
is given by the Holy Ghost to know that Jesus Christ is
the son of God & that he was crucified for the sins of the
World to others it is given to believe on their words that they
also might have eternal life if they continue faithful And
again to some it is given by the Holy Ghost to know the

which are held before the world ye are also commanded

not

~~never~~ to cast any one ~~out~~ who belongeth to the Church out
^

of your sacrament meetings nevertheless if any have trespas

=sed let him not partake untill he makes reconciliation

And again I say unto you ye shall not cast any out of

your sacrement meetings who is earnestly seeking the

Kingdom I speak this concerning th{is\ose} who are not of the

Church And again I say unto you concerning your conf=

-irmation meetings that if there be any that is not of the

Church that is earnestly seeking after the Kingdom ye {s\⟨S⟩}hall

not cast them out but ye are commanded in all things

to ask of God who giveth liberally & that which the spirit

testifies unto you even so I would that ye should do in all

Holyness of heart walking uprightly before me consider=

=ing the end of your salvation doing all things with prayer

& thanksgiving that ye may not be seduced by evil spirits

or doctrines of Devils or the commandments of men for some

are of men & others of Devils Wherefore beware lest ye are

deceived & that ye may not be deceived seek ye earnestly

the best gifts always remembering for what they ~~were~~

are given for verily I say unto you they are given for the

benefit of those who love me & keep all my commandments

he who[155]

& ~~him that~~ seeketh so to do that all may be benefitted that

seeketh or that asketh of me that asketh & not for a sign

that he may consume it upon his lusts And again

Verily I say unto you I would that ye should always remember

& always retain in your minds what th{e\o}se gifts are that are

given unto the Church for all have not every gift given

unto them for there are many gifts & to evry m{0n\an} is given

it

a gift by the spirit of God to some is given one & to some
^

is given another that all may be profited thereby to some

is given by the Holy Ghost to know that Jesus Christ is

the son of God & that he was crusified for the sins of the

World to others it is given to believe on their words that they

also m{ay\ight} have eternal life if they continue faithful And

again to some it is given by the Holy Ghost to know the

ORIGINAL INSCRIPTION
John Whitmer

REVISIONS
Oliver Cowdery
William W. Phelps
Sidney Rigdon
Joseph Smith
John Whitmer
Unidentified

155. This revision does not appear in any JS-era publication.

Differences of administration as it will be pleasing
unto the same Lord according as the Lord will suiting
his mercies according to the conditions of the children
of men And again it is given by the Holy Ghost to
some to know the diversities of operations whether
it be of God that the manifestations of the
spirit may be given to every man to profit withall
And again Verily I say unto you to some it is given by
the spirit of God the word of wisdom to another it
is given the word of knowledge that all may be taught
to be wise & to have knowledge & again to some it is
given to have faith to be healed & to others it is given
to have faith to heal And again to some it is given
the working of miracles & to others it is given to
prophecy & to others the decerning of spirits & again
it is given to some to speak with tongues & to another
it is given the interpretation of tongues & all these
gifts cometh from God for the benefit of the children of God
& unto the Bishop of the Church & unto such as God
shall appoint & ordain to watch over the Church &
to be Elders unto the Church are to have it given
unto them to decern all these gifts lest there shall be any
among you professing & yet be not of God & it shall
come to pass that he that asketh in spirit shall receive
in spirit that unto some it may be given to have
all these gifts that there may be a head in order that
every member may be profited profited thereby he that
asketh in the spirit asketh according to the will of God
wherefore it is done even as he asketh & again I say unto
you all things must be done in the name of Christ
whatsoever you do in the spirit & ye must give thanks
unto God in the spirit for whatsoever blessing ye
are blessed with & ye must practice virtue & holyness
before me continually even so Amen

Defferences of administeration as it will be pleasing

unto the same Lord according as the Lord will suiting

his mercies according to the conditions of the children

of men And again it is given by the Holy Ghost to

some to know the diversities of opperations whether

it be of God ~~or not so~~ that the manifestations of the

spirit may be given to evry man to ~~prophet~~ profit withall

And again Verily I say unto you to some it is given by

the spirit of God the word of wisdom to another it

is given the word of Knowledge that all may be taught

to be wise & to have knowledge & again to some it is

given to have faith to be healed & to others it is given

to have faith t{t\o} heal And again to some it is given

the working of mira{l\cles} & to others it is given to

prophecy & to others the decerning of spirits & again

it is given to some to speak with tongues & to a{◊\⟨n⟩}other

it is given the interpretation of ton{◊gs\gues} & all these[156]

gifts cometh from ~~the Lord~~ God for the benefit of the children of God

& unto the Bishop of the Church {^\^} & unto such as God

sahall appoint & ordain to watch over the Church &

to ~~the~~ be Elders unto the Church are to have it given

unto to decern them all those gifts lest there shall be any if

among you ~~prophecying~~ profesing & yet ~~not~~ not be of God ~~behold~~ & it shall

come to pass that he that asketh in spirit shall receive

in spirit that unto some it may be given to have

all those gifts that there may be a head in order that

evry member may be ~~propheted~~ profited thereby he that

asketh in the spirit asketh according to the will of God

wherefore it is done even as he a{◊\sketh} & again I say unto

you all things must be done in the name of Christ

whatsoever you do in the spirit {y\&} ye must give thanks

unto God in the spirit for whatsoever blessing ye

are blessed with & ye must practice virtue & holyness

before me continually even so amen\\[157]

ORIGINAL INSCRIPTION
John Whitmer

REVISIONS
Oliver Cowdery
William W. Phelps
Sidney Rigdon
Joseph Smith
John Whitmer
Unidentified

156. Or "there".

157. This mark corresponds to a similar mark at the beginning of the revelation (manuscript page 76) and possibly indicates intent or instruction to publish this revelation in *The Evening and the Morning Star.*

49 Commandment March 10th 1831

A Revelation And received at Kirtland Geauga County Ohio concerning the Brethren in New York how to Manage with their property &c

It is nessessary that ye should remain for the present time in your places of abode as it shall be suitable to your circumstances & inasmuch as ye buy lands ye shall import to the Eastern Brethren & in as much as ye have not lands let them buy for the present time in those regi =ons round about as seemeth them good for it must needs be nessessary that they have places to live for the present time it must needs be nessessary that ye save all the money that ye can (& that ye obtain all that ye can in righteousness) that in time ye may be enabled to purch =ase lands for an inheritance (even the City) the place is not yet to be revealed but after your Brethren come from the East there are to be certain men to be app =ointed & to them it shall be given to know the place or to them it shall be revealed & they shall be appoin =ted to purchase the lands & to lay the foundation make a commencement to lay the foundation of the City & then ye shall begin to be gathered with your families every man according to his family according to his circumstances & as is appointed to him lay the Bishop & Elders of the Church according to the laws & commandments which ye have received & which ye shall hereafter receive even so Amen.

50th COMMANDMENT March 8th 1831

given at Kirtland Geauga Ohio — given to John being desireth to write at the request of joseph with

Behold it is expedient is me that my servent John should write & keep a regular history & assist you my servent joseph in transcribing all things which shall be given you And again verily I say unto you that god he can also lift

82 [verso]

Unto the place which I have appointed behold I say

unto you go forth as I have commanded you repent of all

your sins ask & ye shall receive knock & it shall be

opened unto you behold I will go before you & be your

rearward & I will be in your midst & you shall not be

confounded behold I am Jesus Christ & I come quickly

even so Amen———

♦ ¹⁶³52ⁿᵈ Commandment May 9ᵗʰ· 1831

//¹⁶⁴A Revelation to the Elders of this Church given

at Kirtland geauga Ohio in consequence of their

not being perfectly acquainted with the different

opperations of the Spirits which are abroad in the {◊\E}arth

& th{◊s\us} saith the Lord unto them as follows

Hearken o ye Elders of my Church & give ear to the voice of

the living God & attend to the words of wisdom which shall be

given unto you according as ye have asked & are agreed as touch-

=ing the Church & the spirits which have gone abroad in the

Earth Behold verily I say unto you that there are many spirits

which are false spirits which have gone forth in the Earth

deceiving the world & also Satan ~~hath~~ ^has^ sought to deceive you that

he might {◊\overthrow} you Behold I the Lord have looked upon you

& have seen abominations in the Church which profess my name

but blessed are they who are faithfull & endure whe{◊\ther} in life

or in death for they shall inherit eternal life but wo ~~be~~

unto them that are deceivers & hypocrit{s\es} for thus saith the

Lord I will bring them to Judgement behold verily I say unto

you there are hypo{r\crites} among you & have deceived some which

~~have~~ ^has^ given the adversary power but behold such shall be recla-

=imed but the hypo{◊\crites} shall be detected & shall be cut off

either in life or in death even as I will & wo ^is^ unto ~~is~~ them ~~that is~~ ^who^ are

cut off from my Church for the same is overcome of the

world wherefore let every man be aware lest he do that

which is not in truth & righteousness before me & now

come saith the Lord by the spirit ~~by~~ ^unto^ the Elders of his

Church & let us reason together that ye may understand

Original Inscription
John Whitmer

Revisions
Oliver Cowdery
William W. Phelps
Sidney Rigdon
Joseph Smith
John Whitmer
Unidentified

163. Most of John Whitmer's redactions in this revelation first appear in print in the August 1832 issue of *The Evening and the Morning Star;* most of Sidney Rigdon's redactions first appear in either that issue of the *Star* or the Book of Commandments (chapter 53); all of Oliver Cowdery's redactions first appear in the Book of Commandments; and most of JS's redactions first appear in the 1835 Doctrine and Covenants (section 17).

164. This mark corresponds to a similar mark at the end of the revelation (manuscript page 85) and possibly indicates intent or instruction to publish this revelation in *The Evening and the Morning Star.* The introduction was not published, despite its inclusion within the printer's marks.

let us reason even as a man reasoneth one with another
face to face now when a man reasoneth he is understood of man
because he reasoneth as a man even so will I the Lord
reason with you that you may understand wherefore I the Lord
asketh you this question unto what were ye ordained to
Preach my Gospel by the spirit even the comforter which
was sent forth to teach the truth & then received ye spirits
which ye could not understand & received them to be of God
& in this are ye justified? Behold ye shall answer this
question yourselves nevertheless I will be mercyfull unto you he that
is weak among you hereafter shall be made strong verily I
say unto you he that is ordained of me & sent forth to preach
the word of truth by the comforter in the Spirit of truth doth
he preach it by the spirit of truth or some other way & if by
some other way it be not of God & again he that receiveth the
word of truth doth he receive it by the spirit of truth or
some other way if it be some other way it be not of God therefore
why is it that ye cannot understand & know that he that receiveth the
word by the spirit of truth receiveth it as it is preached by
the spirit of truth wherefore he that preacheth & he that receiveth understandeth
one another & both are edified & rejoice together & that which
doth not edify is not of God & is darkness that which is of God
is light & he that receiveth light & continueth in god receiveth
more light & that light groweth brighter & brighter untill
the perfect day & again verily I say unto you & I say it that
you may know the truth that you may chase darkness
from among you for he that is ordained of God & sent forth
the same is appointed to be the greatest notwithstanding he
is least & the servant of all wherefore he is possessor of all
things for all things are subject unto him both in Heaven & on the Earth
the life & the light the spirit & the power sent forth by the
will of the father through Jesus Christ his son but no man
is possessor of all things except he be purified & cleansed
from all sin & if ye are purified & cleansed from all sin
ye shall ask whatsoever you will in the name of Jesus
& it shall be done but know this it shall be given

which is more then is needful for the want of this People

be kept in the hands of the Bishop & let him also reserve

unto himself for his own wants & for the wants of his family

as he shall be employed in doing this Business & thus I

grant unto this People a privelige of organizeing themselves

according to my laws & I consecrate unto them this land for

a little season untill I the Lord shall provide for them othe

=rwise & command them to go hence & the hour & the day is

not given unto them wherefore let them act upon this land as

for years & this shall turn unto them for their good Behold this

shall be an exa~~m~~ple unto my Servent Edward in other places

in all Churches & whoso is found a faithful & Just & a wise

stewart shall enter into the Joy of his lord & shall inherit

eternal life verily I say unto you I am Jesus Christ who

cometh quickly in an hour you think not even so Amen

♦ 180 55th **Comandment** given at Kirtland June 6th 1831

Directions to the Elders of the Church of Christ &c

Behold, thus saith the Lord unto the Elders whom he hath called & chosen,

in these last days, by the voice of his Spirit, saying, I the Lord will make

known unto you what I will ~~make known~~ that ye sh◊◊ld do from this

time untill the next conference, which shall be held in Missorie, upon

the land which I will consecrate unto my People, which are a remnant of

Jacob, & th{◊\ose}^182 who are heirs according to the covenant. wherefore, verily I say

unto you, let my Servents Joseph & Sidney [Rigdon] take their Journey as Soon as

preperations can be made to leave their homes, & Journey to the land of

Missorie. & in as much as they are faithfull unto me, it shall be made

known unto them what they shall do: & it shall also, in as much as they

are faithfull, be made known unto them the land of your inheritance.

& in as much as they are not faithfull, they shall be cut off, even as I will,

as Seemeth me good. & again verily I say unto you, let my Servent

Lyman (Wight.) & my Servent John ({c\⟨C⟩}orrill) take their Journey speedily.

& also my Servent John (Murdock) & my Servent^183 Hyram [Hyrum] (Smith) take

their Journey unto the Same place by the way of Detroit. & let them

Journey from thence preaching the word by the way, saying none

other things than the Prophets & Apostles have written, & that which is

ORIGINAL INSCRIPTION
John Whitmer

REVISIONS
Oliver Cowdery
William W. Phelps
Sidney Rigdon
Joseph Smith
John Whitmer
Unidentified

180. The first publication reflecting most redactions in this revelation is the Book of Commandments (chapter 54). Although William W. Phelps inserted verse numbers while preparing this revelation for publication in the Book of Commandments, the verse numbers printed therein are slightly different from those that appear here.

181. "2" wipe-erased and then stricken.

182. "◊" wipe-erased and written over; then whole word stricken.

183. There is a pinhead impression above "Servent", indicating that the pin in the previous leaf remained in the same general location for some time. (See 145n178 herein.)

Taught them by the comforter, through the prayer of faith. [9] let them go two by two, & thus let them Preach by the way in every congregation, Baptizing by water & the laying on of the hands by the water side: [10] for thus sayeth the lord, I will cut my work short in righteousness: [11] for the days cometh that I will send forth Judgement unto victory. [12] & let my Servent Lyman be aware, for Satan desireth to sift him as Chaff. [13] & behold, he that is faithfull shall be made ruler over many things. [14] & again, I will give unto you a Pattern in all things, that ye may not be deceived, for Satan is abroad in the land & he goeth forth deceiving the Nations: [15] wherefore he that prayeth, whose spirit is contrite, the same is accepted of me if he obey mine ordinances; [16] he that speaketh, whose spirit is contrite, whose language is meek, & edifieth, the same is of God, if he obey mine ordinances: [17] & again, he that trembleth under my power, shall be made strong, & shall bring forth fruits of Praise & wisdom, according to the Revelations, & truths which I have given you. [18] & again, he that is overcame & bringeth not forth fruits, even according to this Pattern, is not of me: [19] wherefore by this Pattern ye shall know the spirits in all cases, under the whole Heavens. [20] & the days have came, according to men's faith it shall be done unto them. [21] behold this command- ment is given unto all the Elders whom I have chosen. [22] & again, verily I say unto you, let my Servent Thomas (Marsh) & my Servent Ezra (Thayer) take their journey, also preaching the word by the way, unto this same land. [23] & again, let my servent Isaac (Morly) & my Servent Ezra (Booth) take their journey, also preaching the word by the way unto the same land. [24] and again Let my Servent Edward (Patridge) & Martin (Harris) take their journey with my Servents Sidny & Joseph. [25] let my Servent David (Whitmer) & Harvy Whitlock, also take their journey & preach unto this same Land by the way [26] let my Servent Parly (Pratt) & Orson (Pratt) take their journey & Preach by the way even unto this same land. [27] & let my Servent Solomon (Hancock) & simeon (Carter) also take their journey to the same land & preach by the way. [28] let my Servent Edson (Fuller) & Jacob (Scott) also take their journey. [29] let my servent Levi Hancock & Zebedee (Coltrin) also take their journey. [30] let my Servent Reynolds (Cahoon)

Taught them by the Comforter, through the prayer of faith. let them

go two by two, & thus let them Preach by the way in every congregation,

Baptizing by water & the laying on of the hands by the water side: for

thus sayeth the lord, I will cut my work short in righteousness:

for the days cometh that I will send forth Judgement unto victory.

& let my Servent Lyman be aware, for Satan desireth to sift him

as Chaff. & behold, he that is faithfull shall be made ruler over many

things. & again, I will give unto you a Pattern in all things,

that ye may not be deceived, for Satan is abroad in the land &

he goeth forth deceiveing the Nations: wherefore he that prayeth,

whose spirit is contrite, the same is accepted of me if he obey

〈16〉 and
mine ordinances: he that speaketh, whose spirit is contrite, whose

langue i{n\s} meek, & edifieth, the Same is of God, if he obey

mine ordinances. & again, he that trembeleth under my power,

shall be made strong, & shall bring forth fruits of Praise, &

wisdom; according to the Revelations, & truths which I have

given you. & again, he that is overcometh & bringeth not forth

fruits, even according to this Pattern, is not of me: wherefore

by this Pattern ye shall know all the spirits in all cases,

{10◊\20}[184]
under the whole Heavens. & the days have come, according to

men's faith it shall be done unto them. behold this command-

=ment is given unto all the Elders whom I have chosen. &

again, verily I say unto you, let my Servents Thomas [B.] (Marsh)

& my Servent Ezra (Thayer) take their Journey, also, preaching the

word by the way, unto this same land. & again, let my servent

Isaac (Morl[e]y) & my Servent Ezra (Booth) take their Journey, also

〈24〉 and again
preaching the word by the way unt{o\o} the same land. let my Servent

Edward (Pa[r]tridge) & Martin (Harris) take their Journey with my

servents Sidney & Joseph. let my Servent David (Whitmer) & Harvey

unto this same Land.
Whitlock, also take their Journey & preach by the way 26 let my

Servent Parl[e]y [P.] (Pratt) & Or[s]on (Pratt) also take their Journey &

even   27 let
Preach by the way, unto this {la\same} land. & my Servent Solomon

(Hancock) & simeon (Carter) also take their Journey to the same

land & preach by the way. let my Servent Edson (Fuller) & Jacob

(Schott [Scott]) also take their Journey. let my servent Levi Hancock & Zebedee

(Coltrin) also take their Journey. let my Servent Reynolds (Cahoon)

ORIGINAL INSCRIPTION
John Whitmer

REVISIONS
Oliver Cowdery
William W. Phelps
Sidney Rigdon
Joseph Smith
John Whitmer
Unidentified

184. Likely "{19\20}".

& Samuel (Smith) also take their journey. [31] let my servant
Wheeler (Baldwin) & william (Carter) also take this journey. [32] and let
my servant Newel Knight & (Sealy [Griffin]) both be ordained &
also take their journey. [33] yea, verily I say unto you let all these take
their journey unto one Place, in their several courses & one man
shall not build upon another's foundation. [34] niether journey in an
other's tracks. [35] he that is faithfull, the same shall be kept &
blest with much fruit. [36] & again, I say unto you let my servant
Joseph (Wakefield) & Soloman (Humphrey) take their journey into
the eastern lands, [37] & let them labour with their families, declaring
none other things than the Prophets & Apostles, that which they have
seen & heard, & most assuredly believe. that the Prophecies may be fulfilled.
[38] in consequence of transgression, let that which was bestowed upon
Heman (Bassett) be taken from him. & placed upon the head of Simonds
Simonds (Rider). [39] & again verily I say unto you, let Jared (Carter) be
ordained a Priest & also George (James) be ordained a Priest. [40] let the
residue of the Elders watch over the Churches, & declare the word in
the regions among them. [41] & let them labour with their own hands
that there be no Idolitry nor wickedness, practiced. [42] & remember in
all things, the poor & the Needy, the Sick & the afflicted, for he that
doeth not these things the same
is not my Disciple. [43] & again let my servant Joseph & Sidney & Edward
take with them a recommend from the Church. [44] & let there be one
obtained for my servant Oliver also. [45] & thus, even as I have said, if
ye are faithfull, ye shall assemble yourselves together to rejoice upon
the land Missouri which is the Land of your inheritance, which is now the land of your enemies
[46] but behold I the lord will hasten the city in its time; [47] & will
crown the faithfull with joy & rejoicing. [48] Behold I am Jesus Christ
the Son of God & I will lift them up at the last day; even so amen

56th COMMANDMENT June 8th 1831

A Revelation to Sidney Gilbert his call &c
Behold I say unto you, my servant Sidney, that I have heard your
prayers, & you have called upon me, that it should be made known
unto you, of the lord your God, concerning your calling & election
in this Church, which I the lord have raised up in these last days

& Samuel (Smith) also take their Journey. ³¹let my Servent

Wheeler (Baldwin) & william (Carter) also take their Journey. ³²and let

my Servent Newel Knight & {Sealy [Selah]}\(}Griffin) both be ordained &

also take their Journey: ³³yea, verily I say ~~unto you~~ let all these take

their Journey unto one Place, in their Several courses & one man

shall not build upon another's foundation. ³⁴neither Journey in an

other's tracks.¹⁸⁵ ³⁵he that is faithfull, the same shall be kept &

blest with much fruit. ³⁶& again, I say unto you let my servent

Joseph (Wakefield) & Solomon (H[u]mphrey) [Jr.] take their Journey into

the east{ern\eren} lands. ³⁷& let them labour with their families, declaring

none other things than the Prophets & Apostles, that which they have

seen, & heard, & most as--shuredly believe, that the Prophecies may be fulfilled.

◊³⁸in consequence of transgression, let that which was bestowed upon

Heman (Bassett) be taken from him & placed upon the head of ~~Simon~~ ds¹⁸⁶

Simonds (Rider.) ³⁹& again verily I say unto you, let Jared (Carter) be

ordained a Priest & also George (James) be ordained a Priest{₃\.} {₃\⁴⁰}let the

residue of the Elders watch over the Churches, & declare the word in

th{e\ose} regiones among them. ⁴¹& let them labour with their own hands,

that there be no Idolitry nor wickedness, practiced. ⁴²& remember in

all things, the poor & the Needy, the {si\Sick} & the afflicted, for he that

doeth not these things ~~is not my deciple these things~~ the same

is not my Deciple. ⁴³& again let my Servent Joseph & Sidney & Edward

take with them a recomend from the Church. ⁴⁴& let there be one

obtained for my Servent Oliver [Cowdery] also{₃\.} ⁴⁵& thus, even as I have said, if

ye are faithfull, ye shall assemble yourselves together to rejoice upon

Missorie, which is the Land of¹⁸⁷ in
the land of your inheritance, which is now the land of your enemies

⁴⁶but behold I the lord will haste{◊\n} the City in its time; {₅\⁴⁷}& will

crown the faithfull with Joy & rejoicing. with ⁴⁸Behold I am Jesus Christ,

the Son of God & I will lift them up at the last day; even so. amen

---

♦ ¹⁸⁸5{5\6}ᵗʰ **Commandment** June 8ᵗʰ· 1831

A Revelation to Sidney Gilbert his Call &c

Behold I say unto you, my servent Sidney, that I have heard your

prayers, & ~~ye~~ you have called upon me, that it should be made known

unto you, of the lord your God, concerning your calling, & {◊◊◊◊◊◊\election}

in this Church, w{◊◊\hich} I the Lord have raised up in these last days

ORIGINAL INSCRIPTION
John Whitmer

REVISIONS
Oliver Cowdery
William W. Phelps
Sidney Rigdon
Joseph Smith
John Whitmer
Unidentified

185. "s" wipe-erased and then stricken.

186. "Simon⟨ds⟩" partially wipe-erased and then "Simon" stricken.

187. The ink flow of this insertion and of "in" one line above indicates that they were possibly written at the time of original inscription.

188. The first publication reflecting most redactions in this revelation is the Book of Commandments (chapter 55).

90

Behold I the Lord, who was crucified for the sins of the world,
giveth unto you a commandment, that you shall forsake the
world. [3] take upon you mine ordinances even that of an Elder
to Preach faith & repentance & remission of sins, according
to my word, & the reception of the Holy Spirit by the laying on
of hands, [4] & also to be an agent unto this Church, in the Place
which shall be appointed by the Bishop according to command-
=ments which shall be given hereafter. [5] & again, verily I say unto
you, you shall take your journey with my servent Joseph
& Sidney. [6] Behold these are the first ordinances which you shall
receive: [7] & the residue shall be made known unto you in a
time to come, according to your labours in my vineyard.
[8] & again, I would that ye should learn that it is the only
who is saved that endureth unto the end; even so: amen

57th COMMANDMENT June 10th 1831

A Revelation to the Church at Thompson giving them
Directions what to do &c &

Behold, thus saith the Lord, even Alpha & Omega, the begining & the
end, even he who was crucified for the sins of the World. [2] Behold, verily,
verily I say unto you, my servent Newel, you shall stand fast in the
office wherewith I have appointed you; [3] & if your Brethren desire to escape
their enemies let them repent of all their sins, & become truly humble
before me & contrite: [4] & as the covenant which they made unto me has
been broken, even so it has become void & of none effect; [5] & wo to him
by whom this offence cometh, for it had been better for him that he had
been drownded in the depth of the sea; [6] but blessed are they who have
kept the covenant, & observed this commandment, for they shall obtain
mercy: [7] wherefore, go to now & flee the land, lest your enemies
come upon you: [8] And take your journey & appoint whom you
will to be your leader, & to pay moneys for you. [9] & thus you shall
take your journey into the regions westward unto the land of Missouri, unto the
borders of the Lamanites. [10] & after you have done journeying, Behold I
say unto you seek ye a living like unto men, untill I prepare
a place for you: [11] & again be patient in tribulation untill I
come: [12] & Behold I come quickly, & my reward is with me,

90 [verso]

2
Behold I {my\the} Lord, who was crusified for the sins of the world,

giveth unto you a commandment, that you shall forsake the

3
world. take upon you mine ordinances even that of an Elder

to Preach faith & repentance & remission of sins, according

to my word, & the reception of the Holy spirit by the laying on

4
of hands. & also to be an agent unto this Church, in the P{◊◊\lace}

which shall be appointed by the Bishop according to command

5
=ments which shall be given hereafter. & again, verily I say unto

you, you shall take your Journey with my servent Joseph

6   first
& sidney [Rigdon]. Behold these are the ordinances which you shall
                                   ^
7
receive: & the residue shall be made known unto you in a

time to come, according to your labour in my vinyard.
8   he
& again, I would that ye should learn that it is hi◊ only

who is saved that endureth unto the end; even so: amen

Ꮯ

ORIGINAL INSCRIPTION
John Whitmer

REVISIONS
Oliver Cowdery
William W. Phelps
Sidney Rigdon
Joseph Smith
John Whitmer
Unidentified

189. The first publication reflecting most redactions in this revelation is the Book of Commandments (chapter 56).

190. The editing mark around "contrite" is a take mark; it indicates the final words of the fourth gathering ("D" signature) of the Book of Commandments (page 128).

191. "s" wipe-erased and then stricken.

♦ [189]57th. **Commandment** June 10th. 1831

 A Revelation {◊\to} the Church at Thompson giving them

 Directions what to do &c �

Behold, thus saith the Lord, even Alpha & Omega, the begining & the
                 he who   2
end, even him that was crusified for the sins of the World. Behold, verily,

verily I say unto you, my servent Newel [Knight], you shall stand fast in the

3
office wherewith I have appointed you{,\:} & if your Brethren desire to escape

their enemies, let them repent of all their sins, & become truly humble

4   4   made
before me, & contrite: [190] & as the covenant which they make unto me, has
             has   ^   5
been broken, even so it hath become void & of none affect; & wo to him

by whom this offence cometh, for it had been better for him that he had

6
been drownded in the depth of the sea; but blessed are they who have

kept the covenant, & observed the commandment, for they shall obtain

7
mercy: wherefore, go to now & flee the land, lest your enemies

8
come upon you: And take your Journey & appoint whom you

9
will to be your leader, & to pay moneyes for you. & thus you shall
                                   the Land of
take your Journeys[191] into the regions westward unto Missorie, unto the
10   ^
borders of the Lamanites. & after {◊\⟨y⟩}ou have done Journeying, Behold I

say unto you seek ye a living like unto men, untill I prepare
                     11
a place for you. & again be patient in tribulation untill I
12
come: & Behold I come quickly, & my reward is with me,

o thy who have sought me early, shall find rest to their souls; EVEN SO: AMEN

58 COMANDMENT June 14th 1831 A Revelation to William Phelps & Joseph Coe their Calling &c

Behold thus saith the lord unto you, my servent William; yea, even the lord of the whole earth, thou art called & chosen & after thou hast been baptized by water, which if you do with an eye single to my glory, you shall have a remission of your sins, & a reception of the Holy spirit, by the laying on of hands & then thou shalt be ordained by the hand of my servent Joseph, to be an Elder unto the Church, to preach repentance & remission of sins by way of baptism in the name of Jesus Christ, the son of the living God; & on whomsoever you shall lay your hands, if they are contrite before me you shall have power to give the holy spirit. & again you shall be ordained to assist my servent Oliver to do the work of Printing, & of selecting, & writing Books for Schools, in this Church, that little Children also may receive instruction before me as is pleasing unto me. & again verily I say unto you for this cause you shall take your journey with my servents Joseph & Sidney, that you mayest be planted in the land of your inheritance to do this work. & again let my servent Joseph (Coe) also take his journey with them. the residue shall be made known hereafter; even as I will. Amen

59th COMMANDMENT June 15th 1831

Thomas Marsh was desirous to know what he should do as the Lord had commanded him & Ezra Thayer to take their journey to the land of Missorie but Thayer could not get ready as soon as Thomas wanted that he should & then are the words of the Lord as fallaws Hearken O ye people which Profess my name, saith the lord your God, for Behold mine anger is kindeled against the rebelious, & they shall know mine arm & mine indignation in the day of visitation & of wrath upon the Nations. & he that will not take up his cross & fallow me, & keep my commandments, the same shall not be saved: behold I the lord commandeth, & he that will not obey shall be cut off in mine own due time;

91 [recto]

who ha{s\ve}
& {ɵ\t}h{e\ey} ~~that hath~~ sought me early, shall find rest to their

Souls: even So: amen ◈◈◈ — — — — — — —

◆ [192]58 Comandment June 14th 1831 A Revelation

to William [W.] Phelps & Joseph Coe their Calling &c——

Behold thus saith the lord unto you, my servent {w\⟨W⟩}illiam;

yea, even the lord of the whole {◊◊\Earth}, ²thou art called & chosen & ~~hast~~

after thou hast been baptized by water, which if you do with an eye

single to my glory, you shall have a remission of your sins, & a recep

=tion of the Holy spirit, by the laying on of hands & then thou shalt

be ordained by the hand of my servent Joseph, to be an Elder unto this

Church, to Preach repentance & remission of sins by way of baptism

in the name of Jesus Christ, the son of the living God; ³& on whom

soever you shall lay your hands, {&\if} they are contrite before me,

you shall have power t{◊\o} give the holy spirit. & ⁴{ag\ag}ain ~~thou~~ shal{t\l} ⟨you⟩

be ordained to assist my servent Oliver [Cowdery] to do the work of Print

=ing, & of Selecting, & writing Books for Schools, in this Church,

that little Children also may receive instruction before me as

is pleasing unto me. ⁵& again verily I say unto you for this cause

~~thou~~ ⟨you⟩ shal{t\l} take ~~thy~~ ⟨your⟩ Journey with my servents Joseph & Sidney [Rigdon], that

~~thou~~ ⟨you⟩ may~~est~~ be planted in the land of ~~thine~~ ⟨your⟩ inheritance to do

this work. ⁶& again let my servent Joseph (Coe) also take his

Journey with them. ⁷{t\T}he residue shall be made known hereaft{◊\er};

even as I will. Amen

◆ [193]59th Commandment June 15th 1831

Thomas [B.] Marsh was desirous to know what he should do as the

Lord had commanded him & Ezra Thayer to take their Journey to the

land of Missorie but {◊◊\Thayer} could not get ready as ~~he said~~ soon as

Thomas wanted that he should & these are the words of the Lord a{◊\s} follows

Hearken O ye people which Profess my name, saith the lord your God,

for Behold mine anger is kindeled against the rebelious, & they shall know

mine arm & mine indignation in the day of visitation & of wrath upon

the Nations. ²& he that will not take up his cross & follow me, & keep

my commandments, the same shall not be saved. ³behold I the Lord comman

=deth, & he that will not obey shall be cut off in mine own due time;

And after that I have commanded & the commandment is broken, Wherefore I the Lord command & revoke, as it seemeth me good; & all this to be answered upon the heads of the rebellious saith the Lord: Wherefore I revoke the commandment which was given unto my servant Thomas & Ezra, & give a new commandment unto my servant Thomas, that he shall take up his journey speedily to the land of Missorie; & my servant Sealy Griffin shall also go with him! for behold I revoke the commandment which was given unto my servants Sealy & Newel, in consequence of the stiffneckedness of my people which are in Thompson; & their rebellions: Wherefore let my servant Newel remain with them, & as many as will go may go, that are contrite before me, & be led by him to the land which I have appointed; & again, verily I say unto you, that my servant Ezra Thayer must repent of his pride, & his selfishness, & obey the former commandment which I have given him concerning the place upon which he lives; & if he will do this, as there shall be no divisions made upon the land, he shall be appointed still to go to the land of Missorie; otherwise he shall receive the money which he has paid, & shall leave the place, & shall be cut off out of my Church, saith the Lord god of hosts; & though the Heavens & the Earth pass away, these words shall not pass away, but shall be fulfilled. & if my servant Joseph must needs pay the money, behold I the Lord will pay it unto him again in the land of Missorie, that those of whom he shall receive may be rewarded again for the thing according to that which they do, & they shall receive mine in lands for their inheritance. Behold thus saith the Lord unto my people you have many things to do, & to repent of; for behold your sins have come up unto me & are not pardoned, because you seek to council in your own ways. & your hearts are not satisfied & obey not the truth, but have pleasure in unrighteousness. Wo unto you rich men, that will not give your substance to the poor, for your riches will canker your souls!. And this shall be your lamentation in the day of visitation, & of judgement, & of indignation; the Harvest is past, the summer is ended, & my soul is not saved! Wo unto you poor men, whose hearts are not broken, whose spirits are not contrite, & whose bellys are not satisfied, & whose hands are not stayed from laying hold upon other men's goods, whose eyes are full of greediness, who will not labour with their own hands!

92 [verso]

4
And after that I have commanded & the commandment is broken,

Wherefore I the lord command & revoke, as it seemeth me good; &

all this to be answered upon the heads of the rebelious saith the Lord:

5
Wherefore I revoke the commandment which was given unto my servant

Thomas & Ezra, & give a new commandment unto my Servent Thomas,

6
that he shall take up his Journey speedily to the land of Missorie; & my

7
servent Sealy [Selah] Griffin shall also go with him: for behold I revoke the

commandment which was given unto my servents Sealy & Newel [Knight], in con=

=sequence of the stiffneckedness of my people which are in Thompson; &

8
their rebelions: Wherefore let my servent Newel remain with them, & as

many as will go may go, that are contrite before me, & be led by him

9
to the land which I have appointed. & again, verily I say unto you, that

of
my servent Ezra Thayer must repent of his pride, & his selfishness, &

obey the former commandment which I have given him concerning

10   be
the place upon which he lives; & if he will do this, as there shall no

be
divisions be[194] made upon the land, he shall be appointed still to go

11
to the land of Missorie; otherwise he shall receive the money which

he has paid, & shall leave the place, & shall be cut off out of my Church,

12
saith the Lord god of hosts: & though the Heavens & the Earth pass away,

13
these words shall not pass away, but shall be fulfilled. & if my servent

it
Joseph must needs pay the money, {B\b}ehold I the Lord will pay unto

him again in the land of Missorie, that those of whom he shall receive

⟨14⟩ for they according to that which they do,
may be rewarded. again, according to that which they do, they shall receive

15
even in lands for their in heritance. Behold thus saith the lord unto

16
my people you have many things to do, & to repent of: for behold

your sins have come up unto me & are not pardoned, because you

17
seek to council, in your own ways. & your hearts are not satisfied

18 ye   19
& y{◊\ou} obey not the truth, but have pleasure in unrighteouness. wo!

unto you rich men, that will not give your substance to the poor,

for your riches will kanke{◊\r} your souls!. And this shall be your

lamentation in the day of visitation, & of Judgement, & of indignation:

20   21
the Harvest is past, the sum{er\mer} is ended, & my soul is not saved! wo!

unto you poor men, whose hearts are not broken, whose spirits are

not contrite, & whose bellys are not satisfied, & whose hands are not

stayed from laying hold upon other men's goods, whose eyes are

full of greediness, whos will not labour with their own hands!

ORIGINAL INSCRIPTION
John Whitmer

REVISIONS
Oliver Cowdery
William W. Phelps
Sidney Rigdon
Joseph Smith
John Whitmer
Unidentified

194. Two layers of deletion: first layer by John Whitmer at the time of original inscription and second layer by Oliver Cowdery.

22 who are pure in heart, whose hearts are broken, &

But blessed are the poor, whose spirits are contrite, for they
shall see the Kingdom of God coming in power & great glory
unto their deliverance! for the fatness of the Earth shall be theirs:
for Behold the Lord shall come, & his recompence shall be with
him, & he shall reward every man, & the poor shall rejoice! & their
generations shall inherit the Earth from generation to generation
for ever & ever, & now, I make an end of speaking unto you;
EVEN SO, AMEN.

60 COMMANDMENT (No 6)

Given in Missorie Independence Jackson Co. July 20th 1831
to the Bishop & Agents.
giving directions, how to proceed concerning purchasing Lands &c.

[Not to be printed at present]

Hearken Oh ye Elders of my Church, saith the Lord your God,
Who have assembelled yourselves together, according to my commandment
in this land which is the land of Missorie which is the Land which I,
have appointed & consecrated for the gathering of the Saints. Wherefore,
this is the land of promise & the place for the City of Zion.
thus saith the Lord your God, If you will receive wisdom here is wisdom
Behold the place which is now called Independence is the centre
place, & the spot for the Temple is lying westward upon a lot which
is not far from the court-house. Wherefore it is wisdom that the
land should be purchased by the saints & also every tract lying westward even unto the line running directly between Jew & gentile
And also every tract bordering by the Prairies in as much as my
Deciples are enabled to buy lands. Behold this is wisdom that they
may obtain it for an everlasting inheritance & let my servent Sidny
Gilbert stand in the office which I have appointed him to receive moneys
to be an agent unto the church to buy lands in all the regions round
about in as much as can be in righteousness, & as wisdom shall direct,
And let my servent Edward Partridge stand in the office which I have appointed him
divide unto the saints their inheritence even as I have commanded & also
them whom he has appointed to assist him And again verily I say unto
you let my servent Sidny Gilbert plant himself in this place, & establi
-lish a store that he may sell goods without fraud that he may
obtain money to buy lands for the good of the saints & that he may

22 who are pure in heart, whose hearts are broken, &

But blessed are the poor whose spirits are contrite, for they

shall see the {◊\Kingdom} of God coming ~~with~~ ^in^ power & great glory

unto their deliverance: 23 for the fatness of the Earth shall be theirs:

24 for Behold the lord shall come, & his recompence shall be with

him, & he shall reward every man, & the poor shall rejoice: & their

generations shall inherit the Earth from generation to generation,

for ever & ever{,\.} 25 & now I make an end of speaking unto you;

even So: amen.

◆ 195 60 Commandment (N° 6) 196

Given in Missorie Independence Jackson Co July 20th. 1831
to the Bishop & Agent
giving directions how to preceed concerning purchuseing Lands &c. &c.

[Not to be printed at present] 197

Hearken Oh ye Elders of my Church, saith the Lord your God,

Who have assembelled yourselves together, according to my commandment

in this land which is the land of Missorie which is the Land which I,

have appointed & consecrated for the gethering of the Saints. Wherefore,

this is the land of promise & the place for the City of Zion. ~~yea~~ ^&^

thus saith the Lord your God, If y{e\ou} will receive wisdom here is wisd

=om. Behold the place which is now called Independence is the centre

place, & the spot for the Temple is lying westward upon a lot which

is not far from the court-house. Wherefore it is wisdom that the

land should be purchased by the saints & also every tract lying west-

-ward even unto the line run{◊\ing} directly betwen Jew & gentile

And also every tra{t\ct} bordering by the Prairies in as much as my

Deciples are enabled to buy lands. Behold this is wisdom that they

may obtain it for an everlasting inheritance & let my Servent Sidney

Gilbert stand in the office which I have appointed ^him^ to receive moneys

to be an agent unto the church to buy lands in all the regions round

about in as much as can be in righteousness, & as wisdom shall direct.

And let my servent Edward ^Partridge^ stand in the office which I have appointed him

^divide^ to unto the saints their inheritance even as I have commanded & also

them whom he has appointed to assist him And again verily I say unto

you let my servent Sidney Gilbert p{◊\lant} himself in this place, & estab

-lish a store that ~~his~~ he may sell goods without frauds that he may

obtain money to buy lands for the goods of the Saints & that he may

195. The first publication reflecting most redactions in this revelation is the 1835 Doctrine and Covenants (section 27).

196. Seven of the eight revelations published as sections 22–29 in the 1835 Doctrine and Covenants bear a similar notation in Revelation Book 1. John Whitmer numbered these revelations from "N° 1" to "No 8", omitting "N° 2". "N° 1" appears on manuscript page 113, "N° 3" on 112, "N° 4" on 114, "N° 5" on 124, "N° 6" on 93, "N° 7" on 122, and "No 8" on 146.

197. This revelation was first published in the 1835 Doctrine and Covenants.

ORIGINAL INSCRIPTION
John Whitmer

REVISIONS
Oliver Cowdery
William W. Phelps
Sidney Rigdon
Joseph Smith
John Whitmer
Unidentified

94

Obtain provisions & whatsoever things the Desiples may need to plant them in their inheritance & also let my servent Sidney Gilbert obtain a license (behold here is wisdom & whoso readeth let him under stand) that he may send goods also unto the people even by whom he will as clerks. employed in his service & thus let them as and preach provide for my saints, that my gospel maybe preached unto the gospel unto those who sit in darkness and in the region of the shadow of death And again verily I say unto you let my servent William W. Phelps also be planted in this place & be established as a Printer unto the Church & lo! if the world recieveth his writings (behold this is wisdom) let him obtain whatsoever he can obtain in righteousness for the good of the saints. And let my servent Oliver assist him even as I have commanded in whatsoever place I shall appoint unto him to copy & to correct & select so that all things may be right before me as it shall be proved by the spirit through him & thus let those of whom I have spoken be planted in the Land of Zion as speedely as can be with their families to do these things even as I have spoken And now concerning the gathering let the bishop & the agent make preperations for those families which have been commanded to come to this land as soon as possible & plant them in their inheritance & unto the residue of both Elders & members further directions shall be given hereafter even so Amen ————————

61 COMMANdMENT August 1st 1831

A Revelation given to the Elders who were assembled on the land of Zion Directions what to do &c &c &c &c

Hearken O ye Elders of my Church, & give ear to my word, & learn of me what I will concerning you, & also concerning this land unto which I have sent you; for verily I say unto you, blessed is he that keepeth my commandments, whether in life or in death; & he that is faithfull in tribulation the reward of the same is greater in the kingdom of heaven. Ye cannot behold with your natural eyes, for the present time, the design of your God concerning those things which shall come hereafter, & the glory which shall follow— after much tribulation, for after much tribulation cometh the blessings. Wherefore, the day cometh that ye shall be crowned with much glory, the hour is not yet but is nigh at hand. Remember this which I tell you before, that you

94 [verso]

Obtain provisions & whatsoever things the Deciples may need to

plant them in their inheritance & also let my servents Sidney gilbert

obtain a license (behold here is wisdom & whoso readeth let him under

=stand) that he may send goods also unto the ~~lamanites~~ people

even by whom he will as clerks employed in his service & thus
~~let them go and peach~~ provide for my saints, that my gospel may be preached unto ~~the people~~
~~the gospel~~ ~~may be preached unto them~~ And again verily I say unto
^ those who sit ⟨in⟩ darkness and in the region of the shadow of death
you let~~t~~ my servent ⟨^⟩William ⟨W Phelps⟩ also be planted in this place & be

established as a Printer unto the Church & lo{.\!} if the world receiveth

{to\his} writings (behold this is wisdom) l{t\et} him obtain whatsoever
obtain
he can in righteousness for the good of the saints. And let my
^
servent~~s~~ Oliver [Cowdery] assist him even as I have commanded in Whatsoever

place I shall appoint unto him to copy & to correct & select &c that

all things may be right before me as it shall be proved by the

Spirit through him & thus let those of whom I have spoken be

planted in the Land of Zion as speedily as can be with their
now
families to do these things even as I have spoken And concer
^
=ning the gethering let the bishop & the agent make preperations

for th{◊\o}se families which have been commanded to come to this

land as soon as posible & plant them in their inheritance & unto

the residue of both Elders & members further directions shall be

given hereafter even So Amen———

♦ ¹⁹⁸61 Commandment August 1ˢᵗ· 1831

A Revelation given to the Elders who were assembeled {in\on}

the land of Zion Directions what to do &c &c &c ↵

Hearken {oh\O} ye Elders of my Church, & give ear to my word, & learn of

me what I will concerning you, & also concerning this land unto which I
2
have sent you: for verily I say unto you, blessed is he that keepeth my
3
commandments, whether in life or in death; & he that is faithfull in

tribulation the reward of the same is greater in the kingdom of
4
heaven. ye cannot behold with your natural eyes, for the present

time, the design of your God concerning those things which shall come
5   5
hereafter, & the glory which shall follow,— after¹⁹⁹ much tribulation. for
6
after much tribulation cometh the blessings. Wherefore, the day cometh

that ye shall be crowned with much glory, the hour is not yet but
7
is nigh at hand. remember this which I tell you before, that you

ORIGINAL INSCRIPTION
John Whitmer

REVISIONS
Oliver Cowdery
William W. Phelps
Sidney Rigdon
Joseph Smith
John Whitmer
Unidentified

198. The first publication reflecting most redactions in this revelation is the Book of Commandments (chapter 59).

199. Triple underlining beneath "a" wipe-erased.

may lay it to heart, & receive that which shall follow. behold,
verily I say unto you, for this cause I have sent you that you might
be obedient, & that your hearts might be prepared to bear testimony
of the things which are to come; & also, that you might be honoured
of laying the foundation, & of bearing record of the land upon which
the Zion of God shall stand; & also, that a feast of fat things might
be prepared for the poor; yea, a feast of fat things, of wine on the
lees well refined, that the earth may know that the mouths of the
Prophets shall not fail; yea, a supper of the house of the Lord, well
prepared, unto which all nations shall be invited. firstly the rich,
& the learned, the wise & the Noble; & after that cometh the day of my
Power; then shall the poor, the lame and the blind, & the deaf, come
in unto the marriage of the lamb, & partake of the supper of the
Lord prepared for the great day to come. Behold I the Lord have spoken
it. & that the testimony might go forth from Zion; yea, from the
mouth of the city of the heritage of God; yea, for this cause I have
sent you hither; & I have selected my servant Edward & appointed
unto him his mission in this land: but if he repent not of his sins, which
are unbelief & blindness of heart, let him take heed lest he fall..
behold his mission is given unto him & it shall not be given
again. & whoso standeth in this mission, is appointed to be a judge
in Israel, like as it was in ancient days, to divide the lands of
the heritage of God unto his children; & to judge his people by the
testimony of the just, & by the assistance of his councillors, according
to the laws of the kingdom which are given by the Prophets of
God: for verily I say unto you, my laws shall be kept on this land.
Let no man think that he is ruler, but let god rule him
that judgeth according to the council of his own will; or in other
words, him that councileth, or sitteth upon the judgement seat:
let no man break the laws of the land, for he that keepeth
the laws of God, hath no need to break the laws of the land:
Wherefore be subject to the powers that be, untill he reigns
whose right it is to reign, & subdues all enemies under his feet
behold the laws which ye have received from my hand, are the
laws of the Church, & in this light ye shall hold them forth.
behold here is wisdom. & now, as I spoke concerning my

may lay it to heart, & receive that which shall follow. behold,

verily I say unto you, for this cause I have sent you that you might

be obedient, & that your hearts might be prepared to bear testimony

of the things which are to come; & also, that you might be honoured

of laying the foundation, & of bearing record of the land upon which

the Zion of God shall stand; & also, that a feast of fat things might

be prepared for the poor; yea, a feast of fat things, of wine on the

lees well refined, that the earth may know that the mouths of the

Prophets shall not fai{s\l}; yea, a supper of the house of the Lord, well

prepared, unto which all nations shall be invited. firstly the rich,

& the learned, the wise & the Noble; & after that cometh the day of my

Power: then shall the poor, the lame and the blind, & the deaf, come

in unto the marriage of the lamb, & partake of the supper of the

Lord, prepared for the great day to come. Behold I the Lord have spoken

it. & that the testimony might go forth from Zion; yea, from the

mouth of the City of the heritage of God: yea, for this cause I have

Sent you hither; & have Select{t\ed} my Servent Edward [Partridge] & appointed

unto him his mission in this land: but if he repent not of his sins, which

~~is~~ are unbelief & blindness of heart, let him take heed lest he fall.

behold his mission is given unto him & it shall not be given

again. & whoso standeth in ~~that~~ this mission, is appointed to be a Judge

in Israel, like as it was in ancient days, to divide the lands of

the heritage of God unto his ch{d\ildren}; & to Judge his people by the

testimony of the Just, & by the assistance of his councillors, according

to the laws of the kingdom which are given by the Prophets of

God: for verily I say unto you, my laws shall be kept on this land.

{le\Le}t n{o⊕\o} man think that he is ruler, but let god rule him

that Judgeth according to the council of his own will: (or in other

words} him that councileth, or set{t\eth}[200] upon the Judgement Seat{;\:}

let no man break the laws of the land, for he that keepeth

the laws of God, hath no need to break the laws of the land:

Wherefore be subject to the powers that be, untill he reigns

whose right it is to reign, & subdues all enemies under his feet.

behold the laws which ye have received from my hand, are the

laws of the Church; & in this light ye shall hold them forth.

behold here is wisdom. & now, as I spoke concerning my

ORIGINAL INSCRIPTION
John Whitmer

REVISIONS
Oliver Cowdery
William W. Phelps
Sidney Rigdon
Joseph Smith
John Whitmer
Unidentified

200. Or "sit{t\eth}".

96

(Partrage)

Servant Edward: this land is the land of his residency, & those whom he has appointed for his councillors [32] & also the land of the residence of him whom I have appointed to keep my storehouse: [33] Wherefore let them bring their families to this land, as they shall council between themselves & me; [34] for behold it is not meet that I should command in all things, for he that is compelled in all things, the same is a sloth-full & not a wise servant: [35] Wherefore he receiveth no reward. [36] Verily I say, men should be anxiously engaged in a good cause, and do many things of their own free will, & bring to pass much righteousness; [37] for the power is in them, wherein they are agents unto themselves. [38] & in-as-much as men do good, they shall in no wise loose their reward. [39] but he that doeth not any thing until he is commanded, & receiveth a commandment with a doubtfull heart, & keepeth it with slothfullness, the same is damned. [40] Who am I that made man, saith the Lord, that will hold him guiltless, that obey not my commandments? [41] who am I saith the Lord, that have promised & have not fulfilled? [42] I command & a man obeys not, I revoke & they receive not the blessing: [43] then they say in their hearts, this is not the work of the Lord, for his promises are not fulfilled. [44] but wo unto such, for their reward lurketh beneath, & not from above. [45] & now I give unto you further directions concerning this land. [46] It is wisdom in me, that my servant Martin should be an example unto the church, in laying his moneys before the bishop of the church; [47] & also this is a law unto every man that cometh unto this land, to receive an inheritance; [48] and he shall do with his moneys according as the law directs. [49] & it is wisdom also, that there should be lands purchased in Independence, for the place of the storehouse, & also for the house of the Printing. [50] & other directions concerning my servant Martin shall be given him of the spirit, that he may receive his inheritance as seemeth him good. & let him repent of his sins, for he seeketh the praise of the world. [52] & also let my servant William W Phelps stand in the office which I have appointed him, & receive his inheritance in the land. [53] & also, he hath need to repent, for I the Lord am not pleased with him, for he seeketh to excell & he is not sufficiently meek before me: [54] behold he that tho hes repented of his sins the

96 [verso]

(Partrage)²⁰¹

Servent Edward: this land is the land of his residence, &

those whom he has appointed for his councillors. ³² & also the

land of the residence of him whom I have appointed to keep

my storehouse: ³³ Wherefore let them bring their families to

this land, as they shall council between them- -selves ³⁴ & me: for

behold it is not meet that I should command in all things,

for he that is compelled in all things, the same is a sloth

=full & not a wise Servent: ³⁵ Wherefore he receiveth no reward.

³⁶ verily I say, men should be anxiou{l\sly} engaged in a good

cause, and do many things of their own free will, &

bring to pass much righteousness{;\:} ³⁷ for the power is in them,

wherein they are agents unto themselves. 3{7\8} & in-as-much as men

do
~~are~~ good, they shall in no wise loose their reward. ³⁹ but he that doeth

not any thing untill he is commanded, & receiveth a commandment with

a doubtfull heart, & keepeth it with slothfullness, the same is damned.
{3\40}
Who am I that made man, saith the Lord, that will hold him guil{ty\l\tless},

that obey not my commandments? ⁴¹ who am I saith, the Lord, that have

promised & have not fulf{if\illed}? ⁴² I command & a man obeys not, I

revoke & they receive not the blessing: ⁴³ then they say in their hearts,

this is not the work of the Lord, for his promises are not fulfilled.

⁴⁴ but wo unto such, for their reward lurketh beneath, & not from

above. ⁴⁵ & now I give unto you further directions concerning this Land.

⁴⁶ it is wisdom in me, that my servent Martin [Harris] should be an example

unto the church, in laying his moneys²⁰² before the bishop of the

Church{;\.} ⁴⁷ & also, this is a law unto every man that cometh unto th{e\is} Land,

to receive an inheritance; ⁴⁸ and he shall do with his moneys according

as the law directs. ⁴⁹ & it is wisdom also, that {it\there} should be lands purch

=ased, in Independence, for the place of the storehouse{;\.} ⁵⁰ & also for the house
Harris
of the Printing. ⁵¹ & other directions, concerning my servent {m\⟨M⟩}artin{,\,} shall

be given him of the spirit, that he may receive his inheritance as

seemeth him good. & let him repent of his sins, for he seeketh the
W Phelps
praise of the world. ⁵² & also let my servent {w\⟨W⟩}illiam stand in the

office which I have appointed him, & receive his inheritance in

has
the Land. ⁵³ & also, he ~~hath~~ need to repent, for I the lord am not pleased

with him, for he seeketh to excell & he is not sufficiently ~~humble~~²⁰³
who has
before me. ⁵⁴ meek ~~in his heart~~ behold he ~~that hath~~ repented of his sins the

Original Inscription
John Whitmer

Revisions
Oliver Cowdery
William W. Phelps
Sidney Rigdon
Joseph Smith
John Whitmer
Unidentified

201. The first publication reflecting the surnames inserted in this revelation by JS is the 1835 Doctrine and Covenants (section 18).

202. Tail of "y" stricken, making the intent of the revision read "mon{ey\ie}s"; then strikethrough bar wipe-erased, changing word back to "moneys."

203. "humble" wipe-erased and then stricken.

same is forgiven, & I the Lord remembereth them no more. [55] by this ye may know if a man repenteth of his sins. [56] behold he will confess them & forsake them, [57] & now verily I say, concerning the residue of the Elders of my Church, the time has not yet come for many years for them to receive their inheritance in this land; except they desire it through the prayer of faith only, as it shall be appointed unto them of the Lord. [58] for Behold they shall push the people together from the ends of the Earth, [59] wherefore assemble yourselves together, & they who are not appointed to stay in this land, let them preach the gospel in the regions round about; [60] & after that, let them return to their homes. [61] let them preach by the way, & bear testimony of the truth in all places, & call upon the rich, the high, & the low, & the poor, to repent; [62] & let them build up churches inasmuch as the inhabitants of the Earth will repent. [63] & let there be an agent appointed unto the church in Ohio, by the voice of the Church, to receive moneys to purchase lands & give unto my servent Sidney Rigdon a commandment, that he shall write a discription of the Land of Zion, & a statement of the will of God, as it shall be made known by the spirit, unto him; and an Epistle & subscription, to be presented unto all the Churches to obtain moneys, to be put into the hands of the Bishop, to purchase lands for an inheritance for the children of God, of himself or the agent, as seemeth him good, or as he shall direct. [65] for behold, verily I say unto you the lord willeth that the disciples, & the children of men, should open their hearts, even to purchase this whole region of country, as soon as time will permit. [66] behold here is wisdom let them do this lest they reserve none inheritance, save it be by the sheding of blood. [67] & again, in as much as there is lands obtained, let there be workmen sent forth, of all kinds, unto this land, to labour for the saints of God. [68] but let all these things be done in order; [69] & let the priveliges of the lands be made known from time to time, by the Bishop, or the agent of the Church. [70] & let the work of the gathering be not in haste, nor by flight, but let it be done as it shall be counseled by the Elders of the Church at the conferences, according to the knowledge which they receive from time to time. [71] & let my servent Sidney Rigdon consecrate & dedicate this land, & the spot of the temple, unto the lord. [72] & let a conference meeting be called, & after that let my servent Sidney Rigdon & Joseph Smith Jr. return, & also Oliver Cowdery with them, to ———

same is forgiven, & I the Lord remembereth them no more. ⁵⁵ by this

ye may know if a man repenteth of his sins. ⁵⁶ behold he will

confess them & forsake them. ⁵⁷ & now verily I say, concerning the residue

of the Elders of my Church, the time has not yet come for many years,

for them to receive their inheritance in this land; except they desire

the ⎯⎯ **of faith** ⎯⎯⎯⎯⎯⎯⎯⎯⎯ of the Lord.
it through prayer only, as ~~they~~ it shall be appointed unto them ₅₈ for
    ^   ^   ^

Behold they shall push the people together from the ends of the Earth:
₅₉   who are
wherefore assemble yourselves together, & they ~~that is~~ not appointed to

stay in this land, let them preach the gospel in the regions round

⎯⎯⎯⎯⎯ ⁶⁰   ⁶¹
about; & after that, let them return to their homes. let them preach

by the way, & bear testimony of the truth in all places, & call upon

                                              ⁶²
the rich, the high, & the low, & the poor, to repent; & let them build

up churches in-as-much as the inhabitants of the Earth will repent.
₆₃   unto the church in Ohio, to receve moneys to purchase lands ⟨in Zion.⟩
& let there be an agent appointed by the voice of the Church, ₆₄ & I
                            Rigden [Rigdon]
give unto my servent Sidney a commandment, that he shall write
                            ^

a discription of the Land of Zion, & a statement of the will of God,

as it shall be made known by the {~~ooi~~\spirit}, unto him; and an Epi

=stle & subscription, to be presented unto all the Churches to obtain

moneys, to be put into the hands of the Bishop, to purchase lands

for an inheritance for the children of God, of him{~~se~~\self} or the agent,
                                                  ⁶⁵
as seemeth him good, or as he shall direct. for behold, verily I say

unto you the Lord willeth that the deciples, & the children of men,

should open their hearts, even to purchase this whole region of

                                          ⁶⁶
country, as soon as time will permit. behold here is wisdom let

them do this lest they reserve none inheritance, save it be by

                      ⁶⁷
the sheding of blood. & again, in as much as there is lands obtained,

let there be workmen sent forth, of all kinds, unto this land, to

                              ⁶⁸
labour for the saints of God{₅\.} let all these things be done in order.
₆₉
& let the priveliges of the lands be made known from time to time,

                                      ⁷⁰
by the Bishop, or the agent of the Church{₅\.} & let the work of the gether

ing be not in haste, nor by flight, but let it be done as it shall be

councelied by the Elders of the Church at the conferences, according to

                                          ⁷¹
the knowledge which they receive from time to time. & let my serv
                            Rigden
=ent Sidney consecrate & dedicate this land, & the spot of the temple,
              ^   ⁷²
unto the Lord. & let a conference meeting be called, & after that let my
                Rigden   **Smith Jr**   **Cowdrey** [Cowdery]
servent Sidney & Joseph return, & also Oliver with them, to ~~accom~~²⁰⁴
            ^   ^   ^

ORIGINAL INSCRIPTION
John Whitmer

REVISIONS
Oliver Cowdery
William W. Phelps
Sidney Rigdon
Joseph Smith
John Whitmer
Unidentified

204. "accom" wipe-erased
and then stricken.

amongst the residue of the work, which I have appointed unto them in their own land. [73] & the residue as shall be ruled by the conference. [74] & let no man return from this land, except he bear record by the way, of that which he knows & most assuredly believes. [75] Let that which has been bestowed upon Ziba Peterson be taken from him: [76] & let him stand as a member in the Church, & labour with his own hands, with the brethren, untill he is sufficiently chastened for all his sins, for he confesseth them not, & he thinketh to hide them. [77] but the residue of the Elders of this church, which are coming to this land, some of whom are exceedingly blessed upon this land. [78] & let my servant direct the conference, from above measure, also, hold a conference, which shall be held by them. [79] & let them also return, preaching the gospel by the way, bearing record of the things which are revealed unto them: [80] for verily the sound must go forth from this place into all the world, & unto the uttermost parts of the Earth. [81] the gospel must be preached unto every creature, with signs following them that believe. [82] & behold the son of man cometh. Amen.———

62 COMMANDMENT

Given in Missori Jindipendence Jackson Co Aug 7th 1831 instructing the saints how to keep the sabath & how to fast and pray & what it was &c &c———

Behold, blessed, saith the Lord, are they who have come up unto this land with an eye single to my glory, according to my commandments, for them that live shall inherit the earth, & they that die shall rest from all their labours, & their works shall follow them, & they shall receive a crown in the mansions of my father, which I have prepared for them; yea, blessed are they whose feet stand upon the land of Zion, who have obeyed my gospel, for they shall receive for their reward the good things of the Earth, & it shall bring forth in its strength; & they also shall be crowned with blessings from above; yea & with commandments not a few; and with revelations in their time, they that are faithfull & dilligent before me. Therefore I give unto them a commandment, saying thus, thou shalt love the Lord thy god with all thy heart, with all thy might, mind, & strength; & in the name

98 [verso]

accomplish the residue of the work, which I have appointed unto

them in their own land: ⁷³& the residue as shall be ruled by

the conferenc{e\es}. ⁷⁴& let no man return from this land, except he

bear record by the way, of that which he knows & most {◊h◊◊\assuredly}

Peterson

believes. ⁷⁵let that which has been bestowed upon Ziba, be taken
^

from him: ⁷⁶& let him stand as a member in the Church, & labour

with his own hands, with the brethren, untill he is sufficiently

chastened for all his sins, for he confeseth them not, & he think

=eth to hide them. ⁷⁷let the residue of the Elders of this church, which

are coming to this land, some of whom are exceedingly blessed

upon this land{,\:} 78 and let my Servent ~~direct~~ Edw[ard Partridge] direct the conference,

even above measure, also, hold a conference which shall be
^

held by them. ⁷⁹& let them also return, preaching the gospel by

the way, bearing record of the things which are revealed unto

them: ⁸⁰for verily the sound must go forth from this place

into all the world, & unto the uttermost parts of the Earth. ⁸¹the

gospel must be preached unto every creature, with signs

following them that believe: ⁸²& behold the son of man cometh.

Amen. {——\——}²⁰⁵

♦ ²⁰⁶62 Commandment

Given in Missorie Independence Jackson Co Aug 7ᵗʰ· 1831

instructing the sa[i]nts how to {◊\keep} the sabath & how to fast

and pray & what it was &c &c — — — — — — —

Behold, blessed, saith the Lord, are they who have come up unto this

Land with an eye single to my glory, according to my commandments,

~~those who~~ them that   ~~tho◊◊ who~~ them that
for ~~them that~~ live shall {live i\inherit} the earth, & ~~them that~~ die shall rest
^   ^

from all their labours, & their works shall follow them, & they shall

receive a crown in the mans{s\ions} of my father, which I have prepared

for them; yea, blessed are they whose feet stand upon the Land of Zion,

who have obeyed my Gospel, for they shall receive for their reward the

its
good things of the Earth, & it shall bring forth in ~~his~~ strength; & they

also shall be crowned with blessings from above; yea & with comm

=andments not a few; And with revelations in their time, they that

are faithfull & dilligent before me{,\.} Wherefore I give unto them a

commandment, saying,²⁰⁷ thus{◊\:} thou shalt love the Lord thy good with

all thy heart, with all thy might, mind, & strength; & in the name

ORIGINAL INSCRIPTION
John Whitmer

REVISIONS
Oliver Cowdery
William W. Phelps
Sidney Rigdon
Joseph Smith
John Whitmer
Unidentified

205. First dash wipe-erased or written in lighter ink before second dash written.

206. The first publication reflecting most redactions in this revelation is the July 1832 issue of *The Evening and the Morning Star.*

207. "," wipe-erased and then stricken.

of Jesus Christ thou shalt serve him. Thou shalt love thy neighbour as thyself. Thou shalt not steal, neither commit adultery, nor kill, nor do any thing like unto it. Thou shalt thank the Lord thy God in all things. Thou shalt offer a sacrifice unto the Lord thy God in righteousness, even that of a broken heart & a contrite spirit; & that thou mayest more fully keep thyself unspotted from the world, thou shalt go to the house of prayer & offer up thy sacraments upon my holy day, for verily this is a day appointed unto you to rest from your labours, & to pay thy devotions unto the most high: nevertheless thy vows shall be offered up in righteousness on all days, & at all times, but remember that on this, the Lord's day, thou shalt offer thine oblations, & thy sacraments, unto the most high, confessing thy sins unto thy brethren, & before the Lord; &, on this day thou shalt do none other thing, only let thy food be prepared with singleness of heart, that thy fasting may be perfect; or in other words, that thy joy may be full. Verily this is fasting & prayer; or, in other words, rejoicing & prayer. & in as much as ye do these things with thanksgiving, with cheerful hearts, & countenances, (not with much laughter for this is sin) but with a glad heart, & a cheerful countenance, verily I say, that in as much as ye do this, the fullness of the earth is yours; the beasts of the fields, & the fowls of the air, & that which climbeth upon the trees, & walketh upon the earth; yea, & the herb, & the good things which cometh of the earth, whether for food or for raiment, or for houses, or for barns, or for orchards, or for gardens, or for vineyards; yea, all things which cometh of the earth, in the season thereof, is made for the benefit & the use of man, both to please the eye, & to gladden the heart; yea, for food & for raiment, for taste, & for smell, to strengthen the body, & to enliven the soul; & it pleaseth God that he hath given all these things unto man; for unto this end were they made, to be used with judgement, not to excess, neither by extortion; & in nothing doth man offend God, or against none is his wrath kindled save those who confess not his hand in all things, & obey not his commandments. Behold this is according to the law & the Prophets. Wherefore trouble me no more concerning this matter, but learn that he who doeth the works of righteousness, shall receive his reward, even peace in this

of Jesus Christ thou shalt serve him. {t\T}hou shalt love thy neighbour

as thyself. {t\T}hou shalt not steal, neither commit adultery, nor kill,

nor do any thing like unto it. {t\T}hou shalt thank the Lord thy God

in all things. {t\T}hou shalt offer a Sacrifice unto the Lord thy God in

righteousness, even that of a broken heart & a contrite spirit; & that

thou mayest more fully keep thyself unspoted from the world,

thou shalt go to the house of prayer & offer up thy Sa{◊\craments} upon

my holy day, for verily this is a day appointed unto you to rest from

your labours, & to pay thy devotions unto the most high: nevertheless

thy vows shall be offered up in righteousness {in\on} all days, & at all

times, but remember that on this, the Lord's day, thou shalt offer thine

oblations, & thy sacraments, unto the most high, confessing thy sins

unto thy brethren, & before the Lord; &, on this day thou shalt do

none other thing, only let thy food be prepared with singleness of

heart, that thy fasting m[a]y be perfect; or in other words, that thy

Joy may be full. {v\V}erily this is fasting & prayer; or, in other word,

rejoicing & prayer. & in as much as ye do these things with than

=ksgiving, with cheerful hearts, & countenances, (not {with much laugh

=ter for this is sin,) but with a glad heart, & a cheerfull countenance:

verily I say, that in as much as ye do this the fullness of the Earth

is yours; the beasts of the fields, & the fowls of the air, & that which

     the

climbeth upon trees, & walketh upon the Earth; yea, & the herb, &

the good things which cometh of the Earth, whether for food or for

raiment, or for houses, or for barns, or for orchards, or for gardens,

or for vineyards; yea, all things which cometh of the Earth, in the

season thereof, is made for the benefit & the use of man, both to

please the eye, & to gladden the heart; yea, for food & for {◊◊\raiment},

for taste, & for smell, to strengthen the body, & to enliven the soul;

& it pleaseth God that he hath given all these things unto m{◊\a}n;

for unto this end were they made, to be used with Judgement,

not to excess, neither by extortion; & in nothing doth man offend

God, or against none is his wrath kinde{◊\⟨l⟩}ed save those who confess

not his hand in all things, & obey not his commandments. {b\B}ehold

this is according to the law & the Prophets: Wherefore trouble me

no more concerning this matter, but learn that he who doeth the

works of righteousness, shall receive his reward, even peace in this

ORIGINAL INSCRIPTION
John Whitmer

REVISIONS
Oliver Cowdery
William W. Phelps
Sidney Rigdon
Joseph Smith
John Whitmer
Unidentified

Word, & eternal life in the world to come, I the lord
~~have~~ spoken it & the spirit beareth record, Amen,

63 COMMANDMENT given in

Missouri Jackson County Independence August 8th 1831
directions to some of the Elders to return to this ~~town~~
own land &c &c !! — [~~Not to be printed now~~]
& &

Behold, thus saith the lord unto the Elders of the Church, who are to
return speedily to the land from whence they came.[2] behold it
pleaseth me, that you have come up hither;[3] but with some
I am not well pleased, for they will not open their mouths,
but hide the talent which I have given unto them, because of
the fear of man.[4] we unto such, for mine anger is kindled
against them.[5] & it shall come to pass, if they are not more
faithfull unto me, it shall be taken away, even that which
they have for I the lord ruleth in the heavens above, & among
the armies of the earth:[6] And in the day when I shall make
up my jewels, all men shall know what it is that bespeak
eth the power of God.[7] but verily I will speak unto you
concerning your journey unto the land from whence you
came.[8] let there be a craft made or bought, as seemeth
you good, it mattereth not unto me, & take your journey
speedily for the place which is called St. Lewis.[9] & from thence
let my servant Sidney, & Joseph, & Oliver take their journey for
Cincinnati:[10] & in this place let them lift up their voice, &
declare my word with loud voices, without wrath or doubting,
lifting up holy hands upon them:[11] for I am able to make
you holy, & your sins are forgiven you.[12] & let the residue
take their journey from St. Lewis, two by two, & preach the
word, not in haste, among the congregations of the wicked, untill
they return to the churches from whence they came.[13] & all this
for the good of the churches; for this intent have I sent them.[14] & let
my servant Edward impart of the money which I have given him,
a portion unto mine Elders, which are commanded to return:[15] &
he that is able, let him return it, by the way of the agent, & he
that is not of him it is not required.[16] And now I speak of the

World, & eternal life in the world to come. I the lord
have
~~hath~~ spoken it & the spirit beareth record. Amen.

♦ [208]63 Commandment given in

Missorie Jackson County Independence August 8th 1831

directions to some of the Elders to return to their ~~homes~~

{& &\own} land &c &c ✧✧✧ ~~[Not to be printed now]~~[209]

his
Behold, thus saith the Lord unto the Elders of ~~this~~ Church, who are to

return speedily to the land from whence they came. behold it

pleaseth me, that you have come up~~o~~ hither; but with some

I am not well pleased, for they will not open their mouths,
unto
but hide the tallent which I have given them, because of

the fear of man. wo unto such, for mine anger is kindelled

against them. & it shall come to pass, if they are not more

faithfull unto me, it shall be taken away, even that which

they have for I the Lord ruleth in the heavens above, & among

the armies of the Earth: And in the day when I shall make

up my Jewels, all men shall know what it is that bespeak

=eth the power of God. but verily I will speak unto you

concerning your Journey unto the Land from whence you

came. let there be a craft made or bought, as seemeth

you good, it mattereth not unto me, & take your Journey

speedily for the place which is called St. Lewis. & from thence

let my Servent Sidney [Rigdon], & Joseph, & Oliver [Cowdery] take their Journey for

Cincinnati: & in this place let them lift up their voice, &

declare my word with loud voices, without wrath or doubting,

lifting up holy hands upon them: for I am able to make

you holy, & your sins are forgiven you. & let the residu{ǫ\e}

take their Journey from St. Lowis, two by two, & preach the

word, not in haste, among the congregations of the wicked, untill

they return to the churches from whence they came. & all this

for the good of the churches{,\;} ~~14~~[210] for[211] this intent have I sent them. & let

my servent Edward [Partridge] impart of the money which I have given him,

a portion unto mine Elders, which are commanded to return: &

he that is ab{ǫ\le}, let him return it, by the way of the agent, & he

that is not of him it is not required. And now I speak of the

ORIGINAL INSCRIPTION
John Whitmer

REVISIONS
Oliver Cowdery
William W. Phelps
Sidney Rigdon
Joseph Smith
John Whitmer
Unidentified

208. The first publication reflecting most redactions in this revelation is the Book of Commandments (chapter 61). Although William W. Phelps inserted verse numbers while preparing this revelation for publication in the Book of Commandments, the verse numbers printed therein are slightly different from those that appear here.

209. This revelation was first published in the Book of Commandments.

210. "14" wipe-erased and then stricken.

211. Triple underlining beneath "f" wipe-erased.

residue which ~~is~~ are to come ~~unto~~ into this ~~Land~~ [17] Behold they have been sent to preach my gospel among the congregations of the wicked: [18] wherefore I give unto them a commandment .. thus: [19] thou shalt not Idle away thy time: [20] neither shalt thou bury thy tollent that it may not be known [21] & after thou hast come up unto the land of Zion & [22] hast proclaimed my word, thou shalt speedily return proclaim~~ing~~ the word among the congregations of the wicked, not in haste, neither in wrath, nor with strife; [23] & shake off the dust of thy feet against those who receive thee not, not in their presence lest thou provoke them, but in secret & wash thy feet as a testimony against them [24] in the day of judgement this is sufficient for you, & the will of him who hath sent you. [25] & by the mouth of my servent Joseph, it shall be made known concerning, Sidney & Oliver. [26] the residue hereafter; even so: amen ———————

64 Commandment given Aug 12th 1831
in the Bank of the River Distruction (or Missorie) unfolding
some mysteries &c &c ((——————— ?

Behold & horken unto the voice of him who ~~hath~~ has all power who is from everlasting to everlasting even alpha & omega the begining & the end Behold verily thus saith the lord unto you O ye Elders of my Church who are assembled upon this spot whose sins are now forgiven you for I the Lord forgiveth sins & am mercyfull unto those who confess their sins with humble hearts but verily I say unto you that it is not needpull for this whole company of mine Elders to be moveing swiftly upon the waters whilst the Inhabitants on either sides are perishing in unbelief neverthelefs I suffered it that ye might bear record Behold ~~there~~ are many dangers upon the waters & more especially hereafter & for I the Lord have decreed in mine anger many distructions upon the waters yea & especially upon these waters neverthelefs all flesh is in mine hand & he that is faithfull among you shall not perish by the waters wherefore it is expedient that my servent Sidney Gilbert & my servent William Phelps be in haste upon their errand & mission neverthelefs I would not suffer that ye should part untill ye are chastened for all your sins that you might be one that you might not perish in wickednefs but now verily I say it residue which ~~is~~ ^are^ to come unto this {s̶l̶o̶o̶\Land}. Behold they have been

sent to preach my gospel among the congregations of the wicked; ^17^

^18^ wherefore I give unto them a commandment. {T\t}hus; ^19^ thou shalt not

Idle away thy time; ^20^ neither shalt thou bury thy tallent that it

may not be known. ^21^ & after thou hast come up unto the land

of Zion, & ha{ve\st} proclaimed my word, thou shalt speedily return

pr{eaching\oclaim}^-ing^ the word among the congregations ⟨22⟩ ^of the wicked,^ not in haste, neither

in wrath, nor with strife; ^23^ & shake off the dust of thy feet against

those who receive thee not, not in their presence, lest thou provoke

them, but in secret & wash thy feet as a testimony against them,

^24^ {i\I}n the day of Judgement, ~~25~~ ^Behold^ this is sufficient for you, & the will of

him who hath sent you. ^25^ & by the mouth of my servent Joseph,

it shall be made known concerning, sidney & Oliver. {t\T}he residue ^26^

hereafter; even so; amen——

♦ [212]64 **Commandment** given Aug 12th. 1831

on the Bank of the River Distruction (or Missorie) unfolding

some mysteries &c &c ∽ —— ∽

Behold & hearken unto {h̶i̶m̶\the} voice of him who ~~hath~~ ^has^ all power who is

from everlasting to everlasting even alpha & omega the begining & the

end Behold verily thuss saith the lord unto you O ye Elders of my

Church who are assembled upon this spot whose sins are now forgiven

you for I the Lord forgiveth sins & am mercyfull unto those who confess

their sins with humble hearts but verily I say unto you that it is not

needfull for this whole company of mine Elders to be moveing swiftly

upon the waters whilst the Inhabitants on either sides are perishing

in unbelief nevertheless I suffered it that ye might bear record Behold

there are many dangers upon the waters & more especially hereafte

-r for I the Lord have decreed in mine anger many distructions

upon the waters yea & especially upon these waters nevertheless

all flesh is in mine ^&^ hand he that is faithfull among you shall

not perish by the waters wherefore it is expedient that my servent

Sidney Gilbert[213] & William [W.] {o̶o̶\Phelps}[214] ^my servent^ be in haste upon their errand

& mission nevertheless I would not suffer that ye should part

untill y{e\ou} are chastened for all your sins that you might be one

that you might not perish in wickedness but now verily I say it

ORIGINAL INSCRIPTION
John Whitmer

REVISIONS
Oliver Cowdery
William W. Phelps
Sidney Rigdon
Joseph Smith
John Whitmer
Unidentified

212. The first publication reflecting most redactions in this revelation is the December 1832 issue of *The Evening and the Morning Star.*

213. The circle around "ilbert" appears to be in the same ink flow as William W. Phelps's redactions in the previous revelation. The name was printed as "Sidney (G.)" in *The Evening and the Morning Star* and the Book of Commandments (chapter 62); the full name was first printed in the 1835 Doctrine and Covenants (section 71).

214. The circle around "Phelps" appears to be in the same ink flow as William W. Phelps's redactions in the previous revelation. The name was printed as "William, (P.)" in *The Evening and the Morning Star* and as "William" in the Book of Commandments; the full name was first printed in the 1835 Doctrine and Covenants.

behooveth me that ye should part wherefore let them my servants
Sidney & William take their former company & let them
take their journey in haste that they may fill their mission
& through faith they shall overcome & in as much as they are
faithful they shall be preserved & I the Lord will be with
them & let the residue take that which is needful for
clothing let my servant Sidney take that which is not needful
with him as you shall agree & now behold for your good
I give unto you a commandment concerning these things & I
the Lord will reason with you as with men in days of old
Behold I the Lord in the begining blessed the waters but in
the last days by the mouth of my servant John I cursed
the waters wherefore the days will come that no flesh shall
be safe upon the waters & it shall be said in days to come
that none is able to go up to the land of Zion upon the
waters but he that is upright in heart & as I the Lord in
the begining cursed the land even so in the last days have
I blessed it in its time for the use of my saints that they
may partake the fatness thereof & now I give unto you a
commandment & what I say unto one I say unto all that
you shall forewarn your brethren concerning these waters
that they come not in journeying upon them lest their faith
fail & they are caught in her snares I the Lord have decreed
& the destroyer rideth upon the face thereof & I revoke not
the decree I the Lord was angry with you yesterday but to day
mine anger is turned away wherefore let those whom I have
spoken that should take their journey in haste again I say
unto you let them take their journey in haste & it mattereth
not unto me after a little if it so be that they fill their
mission whether they go by water or by land let this be as it is
made known unto them according to their judgements & now hereafter
concerning my servants Sidney Joseph & Oliver let them come
not again upon the waters save it be upon the canal while
journeying unto their homes or in other words they shall not
come upon the waters to journey save upon the canal Behold I
the Lord have appointed a way for the journeying of my saints

102 [verso]

Behooveth me that ye should part wherefore let them my servents

Sidney [Gilbert] & William take their former company & let them

take their Journey in haste that they may fill their mission

& through faith they shall overcome & in as much as they are

faithfull they shall be preserved & I the Lord will be with

them & let the residue take that which is needfull for

clothing let my servent sidney [Gilbert] take that which is not needfull

with {them\him} as you shall agree & now behold for your good

I give unto you a commandment concerning these things & I

the Lord will reason with you as with men in days of old

Behold I the Lord in the begining belessed the waters but in

the last days by the mouth of my servent John I cur{s◊\⟨s⟩}ed

the waters wherefore the days will come that no flesh shall

be safe upon the waters & it shall be said in days to come

that none is able to go up to the land of Zion upon the

waters but he that is upright in heart & as I the Lord in

the begi{ng\ning} cursed the land even so in the last days have

I blessed it in its time for the use of my saints that they

may partake the fatness thereof & now I give unto you a

commandment & what I say unto one I say unto all that

you shall forewarn your brethren concerning these waters

that they come not in Journeying {on\upon} them lest their faith

fail & they are caught in her snares I the Lord ~~hath~~ ^have^ decreed

& the destroyer rideth upon the face thereof & I revoke not

the decree I the Lord was angery with you yesterday but to day

mine anger is turned away wherefore let those whom I have

spoken that should take their Journey in haste ~~of~~ ^concerning^ {^\^} again I say

unto you let them take their Journey in haste & it mattereth

not unto me after a little if it so be that they fill their

mission whether they go by water or by land let this be as it is

made known unto them according to their Judgements & ^hereafter^ now

concerning my servents Sidney [Rigdon] ^&^ Joseph & Oliver [Cowdery] let them come

not again {◊◊◊\upon} the waters save it be upon the canal while

Journeying unto their homes or in other words they shall not

come upon ~~upon~~ ^to Journey^ the waters save upon the canal Behold I

the Lord have appointed a way for the Journeying of my saints

ORIGINAL INSCRIPTION
John Whitmer

REVISIONS
Oliver Cowdery
William W. Phelps
Sidney Rigdon
Joseph Smith
John Whitmer
Unidentified

& behold this is the way that after they leave the canal they shall
journey by land in as much as they are commanded to journey
& go up unto the land of Zion & they shall do like unto the
children of Israel pitching their tents by the way & behold this
commandment you shall give unto all your brethren nevethe
=less unto whom it is given power to command the waters unto
him it is given by the spirit to know all his ways wherefore
let him do as the spirit of the living God commandeth him
whether upon the land or upon the waters as it remaineth with
me to do hereafter & unto you it is given the course for the saints or
the way for the saints of the camp of the Lord to journey & again
verily I say unto you my servants being Joseph & Oliver shall not
open their mouths in the congregations of the wicked until they
arrive at cincinnati & in that place they shall lift up their voices
unto god against that People yea unto him whose anger is kindled
against their wickedness a people which is well nigh ripened for distruc
=tion & from thence let them journey for the congregations of their
brethren for their labours even now are wanted more abundantly
among them then among the congregations of the wicked & now
concerning the residue let them journey & declare the word among
the congregations of the wicked inasmuch as it is given & inasmuch
as they do this they shall rid their garments & they shall be spot
=less before me & let them journey together or two by two as
seemeth them good only let my servant Reynolds & my servant
Samuel with whom I am well pleased be not seperated until
they return to their homes & this for a wise purpose in me
& now verily I say unto you & what I say unto one I say unto
all be of good cheer little children for I am in your midst
& I have not forsaken you & in as much as you have humb
=led yourselves before me the blessings of the kingdom are yours
gird up your loins & be watchfull & be sober looking forth
for the coming of the son of man for he cometh in an hour you think not
pray always that you enter not into temptation that you
may abide the day of his coming whether in life or in death
even so Amen

& behold this is the way that after they l{◊◊\ea}ve the canal they shall

Journey by land in as much as they are commanded to Journey ~~by~~

& go up unto the land of Zion & they shall do like unto the

children of Israel pitching their tents by the way & behold this

commandment you shall give unto all your brethren neverthe

=less unto whom it is given power to command the waters unto

him it is given by the spirit to know all his ways wherefore

let him do as the spirit of the living God commandeth him

whether upon the land or upon the waters as it remaineth with

me to do hereafter & unto you it is given the course ~~ofor~~²¹⁵ ^{for} the saints or

the way for the saints of the camp of the Lord to Journey & again

verily I say unto you my Servents Sidney [Rigdon] [&] Joseph & Oliver shall not

open ~~open~~ their mouths in the congregations of the wicked untill they

arrive at cincinnati & in that place they shall lift up their voices

unto god against that People yea unto him whose anger is kindelled

against their wick{n\edness} a people which is well ^{nigh²¹⁶} ripened for distruc

=tion & from thence let them Journy for the congregations of their

brethren for their labours even now are wanted more abundantly

among them then among the congregations of the wicked & now

concerning the residue let them Journey & declare the word among

the congregations of the wicked inasmuch as it is given & in as much

as they do this they shall rid their garments & they shall be spot

=less before me & let them Journey together or two by two as

seemeth them good only let my servent reynolds [Cahoon] & my Servent

Samuel [Smith] with whom I am well pleased be not seperated untill

they return to their homes & this for a wise purpose in me

& now verily I say unto you & what I say unto one I say unto

all be of good cheer little children for I am in your midst

& I have not forsaken you & in as much as y{e\ou} have humbe

=lled yourselves before me the blessings of the kingdom ^{are} ~~is~~ yours

gird up your loins & be watchfull & be sober looking forth

for the coming of the Son of man ^{for he cometh} in an hour you think not

pray always that you enter not into temptation that you

may abide the day of his coming whether in life or in death

even So Amen

ORIGINAL INSCRIPTION
John Whitmer

REVISIONS
Oliver Cowdery
William W. Phelps
Sidney Rigdon
Joseph Smith
John Whitmer
Unidentified

215. "o" in "of" stricken and "or" inserted after "f" by same unidentified scribe, leaving "for"; then entire word stricken by John Whitmer and "for" inserted above.

216. "nigh" first appears in print in the Book of Commandments.

65 Commandment given Aug 13th 1831

on the Bank of the river Missorie at a meeting of some of the Elders which had not yet arived at their journeys end

Behold & hearken, oh ye Elders of my Church, saith the Lord your God, even Jesus Christ, your advocate who knoweth the weakness of man & how to succour them who are tempted; & verily mine eyes are upon those who have not as yet gone up unto the land of Zion; wherefore your mission is not yet full; nevertheless ye are blessed for the testimony which ye have borne, is recorded in heaven for the Angels to look upon; & they rejoice over you; & your sins are forgiven you; & now continue your journey, assemble yourselves upon the land of Zion, & hold a meeting, & rejoice together, & offer a sacrament unto the most high; & then you may return to bear record, yea, even altogether, or two by two, as seemeth you good; it mattereth not unto me only be faithfull, & declare glad tidings unto the inhabitants of the earth, or among the congregations of the wicked. Behold I the Lord have brought you together, that the promise might be fulfilled that the faithfull among you should be preserved & rejoice together in the land of Missorie. I the Lord promised the faithfull, & cannot lie. I the Lord am willing, if any among you desireth to ride upon horses, or upon mules, or in chariots, shall receive this blessing, if he receive it from the hand of the Lord, with a thankfull heart in all things. These things remain with you to do according to judgement & the directions of the spirit. Behold the kingdom is yours. And Behold & lo I am with the faithfull always, even so. Amen

66 Commandment recived at Kirtland Geauga Ohio August 30th 1831 to the Church &c

Hearken, oh ye People & open your hearts & give ear from afar, & listen, you that call yourselves the people of God the Lord, & hear the word of the Lord, & his will concerning you; yea verily I say, hear the word of him whose anger is kindled against the wicked & rebelious, who willeth to take even them whom he will take; & preserveth in life them whom he will preserve; who buildeth up at his own will & pleasure & destroyeth when he please, & is able to cast the soul down to hell

♦ [217]65 Commandment given Aug 13th. 1831

on the Bank of the river Mis{o\⟨s⟩}orie at a meeting of

some of the Elders which had not yet arived at their Journeys end &c[218]

Behold & hearken, ~~oh~~ ye Elders of my Church, saith the Lord your

God; even Jesus Christ, your advocate who knoweth the weakness

of man & how to sucour ~~they that~~ ^them^ ^who^ are tempted: & verily mine eyes

are upon {~~you~~\those} who have not as yet gone up unto the Land of

Zion: wherefore your mission is not yet full: nevertheless ye are blessed

for the testimony which ye have borne, is recorded in heaven for the

Angels to look upon, & they rejoice over you; & your sins are forgiven

you: & now continue your Journey. assemble yourselves upon the

land of Zion, & hold a meeting, & rejoice together, & offer a sacrament

unto the most high; & then you may return to bear record; yea, even

all together, or two by two, as seemeth you good: it mattereth not unto

me only be faithfull, & declare glad tidings unto the inhabitants

of the Earth, or among the Congregations of the wicked. Behold I

the Lord have brought you together, that the promise might be

fulfilled that the faithfull among you should be preserved &

rejoice together in the Land of Missorie. I the Lord promised the

faithfull, & cannot lie{.\,} {I\I} the Lord am willing, if any among

you desireth to ride upon horses, or upon mules, or in chariots,

shall receive this blessing, if he receive it from the hand of the

Lord, with ^a^ thankfull~~ness~~[219] hearts in all things. {t\T}hese things remain

with you to do according to Judgement & the directions of the spirit.

Behold the kingdom is yours. And Behold & lo I am with the

faithfull always; even so: Amen——

♦ [220]66 Commandment received at Kirtland

Geauga Ohio August 30th 1831 to the Church &c

Hearken, {o\O}~~h~~ ye People & open your hearts & give ear from a-far,

& listen, you that call yourselves the people of ~~God~~ the Lord, & hear the

word of the Lord, & his will concerning you: yea verily I say, hear the word

of him whose anger is kindled against the wicked & rebelious, who

willeth to take even whom he will take; & preserveth in life ~~those~~ ^them^ ~~them~~ ^those^

whom he will preserve; who buildeth up at his own will & pleasure,

& destroy{s\eth} when he please, & is able to cast the soul down to ~~hell~~

ORIGINAL INSCRIPTION
John Whitmer

REVISIONS
Oliver Cowdery
William W. Phelps
Sidney Rigdon
Joseph Smith
John Whitmer
Unidentified

217. The first publication reflecting most redactions in this revelation is the Book of Commandments (chapter 63).

218. "&c" possibly inserted at a later time.

219. "ness" wipe-erased and then stricken.

220. The first publication reflecting most redactions in this revelation is the February 1833 issue of *The Evening and the Morning Star*. Some of Sidney Rigdon's revisions first appear in print in the Book of Commandments (chapter 64), and most of JS's revisions first appear in print in the 1835 Doctrine and Covenants (section 20). Although William W. Phelps inserted verse numbers while preparing this revelation for publication in the Book of Commandments, the verse numbers printed therein are slightly different from those that appear here.

hell. 5 Behold I the Lord uttereth my voice, & it shall be obeyed: 6 wherefore verily I say let the wicked take heed; & let the rebelious fear & tremble; 8 & let the unbelieving hold their lips, for the day of wrath shall come upon them as a whirlwind, & all flesh shall know that I am god: 9 & he that seeketh signs shall see signs, but not unto salvation. 10 verily I say unto you, there are those among you who seeketh signs & there have been such even from the beginning; 11 but behold faith cometh not by signs, but signs follow those that believe; 12 yea signs cometh by faith not by the will of men, nor as they please, but by the will of God: 13 yea signs cometh by faith unto mighty works: 14 for without faith no man pleaseth god; 15 & with whom god is angry: he is not well pleased; 16 wherefore, unto such he sheweth no signs, only in wrath unto their condemnation: 17 wherefore I the Lord am not pleased with those among you who have sought after signs & wonders for faith & not for the good of men, unto my glory; 18 nevertheless I gave commandments, & many have turned away from my commandments, & have not kept them. 19 there were among you adulterers & adulteresses; 20 some of whom have turned away from you, & others remain with you, that hereafter shall be revealed. 21 let such beware, & repent speedily, lest judgement shall come upon them as a snare, & their folly shall be made manifest, & their works shall follow them, in the eyes of the People. 22 & verily I say unto you as I have said before, he that looketh on a woman to lust after her, or if any shall commit adultery in their hearts, they shall not have the spirit, but shall deny the faith, & shall fear: 23 wherefore I the Lord have said that the fearful, & the unbelieving, & all liars, & whosoever loveth & maketh a lie, & the whoremanger, & the sorcerer, shall have their part in that lake which burneth with fire & brimstone, which is the second death. 24 verily I say, that they shall not have part in the first resurrection: 25 & now behold I the Lord saith unto you that ye are not justified because these things are among you: 26 nevertheless he that endureth in faith, & doeth my will, the same shall overcome, & shall receive an inheritance upon the earth, when the day of transfiguration shall come, when the earth shall be transfigured even according to the pattern

⁵ hell. Behold I the Lord uttereth my voice, & it shall be obeyed:

⁶ wherefore verily I say let the wicked take heed; ⁷ & let the rebelious

fear & tremble; ⁸ & let the unbelieving hold their lips, for the day of wrath

shall come upon them as a whirlwind, & all flesh shall know that I

am god: ⁹ & he that seeketh signs shall see signs, but not unto

salvation. ¹⁰ verily I say unto you, there are those among you

who {who\seeketh} signs & there ha{s\ve} been such even from the begining;

¹¹ but behold faith cometh not by signs, but signs follow those that

believe; ¹² yea signs cometh by faith not by the will of men, nor

as they please, but by the will of God: ¹³ yea signs cometh by faith

unto mighty works; ¹⁴ for without faith no man pleaseth God;

¹⁵ & with whom god is angery he is not well pleased: ¹⁶ wherefore,

unto such he sheweth no signs, only in wrath in ^unto their^ condemnation:

¹⁷ wherefore I the Lord am not pleased with those among you who

have sought after signs & wonders, ~~& not~~ for faith & not for

the good of men, unto my glory; ¹⁸ nevertheless I gave commandm

=ents, & many have turned away from my commandments, & have

not kept them. ¹⁹ there were among you {◊\adulter{es\s}} & ²⁰ adultereses; some

of whom have~~e~~ turned away from you, & others remain with you,

that hereafter shall be revealed. ²¹ let such be- ~~aware~~ ^-ware,^ & repent speedily,

lest Judgement shall come upon {you\them} as a snare, & their folly shall

be made manifest, & their works shall follow them, in the eyes

of the People. ²² & verily I say unto you as I have said before, he that

looketh on a wom{man\an} to lust after her, or if any shall commit

adultery in ~~his~~ ^their^ hearts, they shall not have the spirit, but shall

deny the faith, & shall fear: ²³ wherefore I the Lord have said that

the fearfull, & the unbelieving, & all liars, & whosoever loveth

& maketh a lie, & the whoremonger{s\,} & the sorcerers, should have

their part in that lake which burneth with fire & brimstone,

which is the second death. ²⁴ verily I say, that they shall not have

part in the first resurrection. ²⁵ & now behold I the lord ~~sa{i◊\y}th~~ ^**saith**^[221]

unto you that ye are not Justified because these things are among

you: ²⁶ nevertheless he that endureth in faith, & doeth my will,

the same shall overcome, & shall receive an inheritance upon

the earth, when the day of transfiguration shall come, when the

earth shall be transfigured, even {◊◊◊\according} to the pattern ~~shewn~~

ORIGINAL INSCRIPTION
John Whitmer

REVISIONS
Oliver Cowdery
William W. Phelps
Sidney Rigdon
Joseph Smith
John Whitmer
Unidentified

221. Likely "sa{ie\y}th" until "sa{ie\y}" stricken and "saith" inserted.

Which was shewn unto mine Apostles upon the mount
27 of which account, the fullness ye have not yet received 28 & now,
verily I say unto you that as I said that I would make it
my will, Behold I will make it known unto you
known unto you not by the way of commandment, for there are
many who observe not to keep my commandments, but unto
him that keepeth my commandments I will give the mysteries
of my kingdom & the same shall be in him a well of living
water, springing up unto everlasting life. 30 & now behold this is the will
of the Lord your god, concerning his saints, that they should assemble
themselves together unto the land of Zion not in haste lest there should
be confusion, which bringeth pestilence. 31 behold the land of Zion I the
Lord holdeth it in mine own hands: 32 nevertheless I the Lord rendereth
unto Cæsar the things which are Cæsars: 33 wherefore I the Lord willeth
that you should purchase the lands, that you may have advantage
of the world that you may have claim on the world that they may
not be stirred up unto anger for satan putteth it into their hearts
against you
to anger & to the sheding of blood wherefore the land of Zion shall
not be obtained but by purchase or by blood otherwise there is none
inheritance for you & if by purchase behold you are blessed & if by
blood as ye are forbidden to shed blood Lo your enemies are upon
you & ye shall be scourged from city to city & from synegogue to
synegogue & but few shall stand to receive an inheritance I the
Lord am angry with the wicked I am holding my spirit from the
inhabitants of the Earth I have sworn in my wrath & decreed wars
upon the face of the Earth & the wicked shall slay the wicked & fear
shall come upon every man & the saints also shall hardly escape
nevertheless I the Lord am with them & will come down in
heaven from the presence of my Father & consume the wicked with
unquenchable fire & behold this is not yet but by & by wherefore
seeing that I the Lord have decreed all these things upon the face
of the Earth I willeth that my saints should be assembled upon
the Land of Zion & that every man should take righteousness in his
hands & faithfulness upon his loins & lift a warning voice unto
the inhabitants of the Earth & declare both by word & by flight
that desolation shall come upon the wicked wherefore let my
Disciples in Kirtland arrange their temporal concerns which

106 [verso]

Which was shewn unto mine Apostles upon the mount,
27 of whi{00\ch} account, the fullness ye have not yet received. 28 & now,

verily I say unto you, that as I said that I would make it
my will, ⟨29⟩ **Behold I will make it known unto you**,
known unto you not by the way of commandment, for there are
{^\^}222
many who obser{00\ve} not to keep my commandments, but unto

him that keepeth my commandments, I will give the mysteries

of my kingdom, & the same shall be in him a well of living
everlasting 30
water, springing up unto ~~eternal~~ life. & now behold this is the will

of the lord your god, concerning his saints, that they should assemble

themselves together unto the land of Zion, not in haste lest there should
31
be confusion, which bringeth pestilence. behold the land of Zion I the
32
Lord holdeth it in mine own hands: nevertheless I the Lord rendereth
33
unto {Sez**Caes**}ar the things which are Seazer's: wherefore I the Lord willeth

that you should purchase the Lands, that you may have advantage

of the world that you may have claim on the world that they may

not be stirred up unto anger for satan puteth it into their hearts
against you
to anger & to the sheding of blood wherefore the land of Zion shall

not be obtained but by purchase or by blood otherwise there is none

inheritance for you & if by purchase behold you are blessed & if by

blood as ye are forbidden to shed blood Lo your enemies are upon

you & ye shall be scourged from city to city & from Synego{ug\gue} to

Synego{ug\gue} & but few shall stand to receive an inheritance I the

Lord am angery with the wicked I am holding my spirit from the

inhabitants of the Earth I have sworn in my wrath & decreed wars

upon the face of the Earth & the wicked shall slay the wicked & fear

shall come upon every man & the saints also shall hardly escape

nevertheless I the Lord am with them & will come down in ~~heaven~~223
my Father
heaven from the presence of ~~god~~ & consume the wicked with

unquenchable fire & behold this is not yet but by & by wherefore

seeing that I the Lord have decreed all these things upon the face

of the Earth I willeth that my saints should be assembelled upon

the Land of Zion & that every man should take righteousness in his

hands & faithfullness upon his loins & lift a warning voice unto

the inhabitants of the Earth & declare both by word & by flight

that desolation shall come upon the wicked wherefore let my

Deciples in Kirtland arrange their temporal concerns which

ORIGINAL INSCRIPTION
John Whitmer

REVISIONS
Oliver Cowdery
William W. Phelps
Sidney Rigdon
Joseph Smith
John Whitmer
Unidentified

222. Or "✦". The revised text could read either "I would make known my will unto you" or "I would make known unto you my will".

223. "heaven" wipe-erased and then stricken.

Dwell upon this farm, let my servent Titus, who has the case thereof dispose of the land that he may be prepared in the coming spring to take his journey up unto the land of Zion with those that dwell upon the face thereof excepting those whom I shall reserve unto myself that shall not go untill I shall command them & let all the moneys which can be spared (it mattereth not unto me whether it be little or much) sent up unto the Land of Zion unto them whom I have appointed to receive behold I the Lord will give unto my servent Joseph Smith jr power that he shall be enabled to decern by the spirit those who shall go up unto the Land of Zion & those of my Disciples who shall tarry let my servent Newel K Whitney retain his store or in other words the store yet for a little season nevertheless let him impart all the money which he can impart to be sent up unto the Land of Zion behold these things are in his own hands let him de according to wisdom verily I say let him be ordained as an agent unto the deciples that shall tarry & let him be ordained unto this power & now speedily visit the churches expanding these things unto them with my servent Oliver Cowdery Behold this is my will obtaining moneys even as I have directed: he that is faithfull & enduseth shall overcome the world he that sendeth up treasures unto the Land of Zion, shall receive an inherit =ance in this world, & his works shall follow him, & also, a reward in the world to come; yea, & blessed are the dead that die in the Lord from hence forth, when the Lord shall come & old things shall pass away, & all things become new, they shall rise from the dead & shall not die after, I shall receive an inherit -ance before the Lord, in the holy City, & he that liveth when the Lord shall come, & have kept the faith, blessed is he, nevertheless it is appointed to him to die at the age of man: wherefore child =ren shall grow up untill they became old, old men shall die but they shall not sleep in the dust, but they shall be changed in the twinkling of an eye: wherefore, for this cause preached the apostles unto the world, the resurrection of the dead: these things are the things that ye must look for, & speaking after the manner of the Lord, they are now nigh at hand; & in a time

&
Bil[l]ings
Dwell upon this farm let my servent {ΛΛ\Tit{a\u}s} who has the care
coming
thereof dispose of the Land that he may be prepared in the ~~following~~

spring to take his Journey up unto the land of Zion with those

that dwell upon the face thereof excepting those whom I shall
shall
reserve unto myself that shall not go untill I command them

& let all the moneys which can be spared (it mattereth not
~~they {little\be\have}~~[224] it be
unto me whether ~~it be~~ little or much) sent up unto the Land
it
of Zion unto them whom I have appointed to receive behold
Smith Jr
I the Lord will give unto my Servent Joseph power that he

shall be enabled to decern by the spirit those who shall go up
who
unto the Land of Zion & those of my Deciples ~~which~~ shall tarry
K
let my Servent Newel {w\Whitney} retain his store or in other

words th{i\e}s store yet for {al\a} little season nevertheless let him

impart all the money which he can impart to be sent up unto

the Land of Zion behold these things are in his own hands let
do   as
him according to wisdom verily I say let him be ordained ~~as~~[225]

an agent unto the deciples that shall tarry & let him be ordaned

unto this power & now speedily visit the churches expounding
Coudery [Cowdery]
these things unto them with my servent Oliver Behold this

is my will obtaining moneys even as I have directed: [226]⌐ he that is

faithfull & endureth, shall overcome the world{;\.} he that sendeth

up treasures unto the Land of Zion, shall receive an inherit

=ance in this world, & his works shall follow him; & also, a

reward in the world to[227] come; yea, & blessed are the dead that

die in the Lord from hence forth, when the Lord shall come

& old things shall pass away, & all things become new, they shall
after
rise from the dead & shall not die, & shall receive an inherit

-ance before the Lord, in the holy City, & he that liveth when the

Lord shall come, & have kept the faith, blessed is he, nevertheless

it is appointed to him to die at the age of man: wherefore child

=ren shall grow up untill they become old. old; men shall die but

they shall not sleep in the dust, but they shall be changed in the

twinkling of an eye: wherefore, for this cause preached the

apostles unto the world, the resurrection of the dead: these things

are the things that ye must look for, & speaking after the

manner of the Lord, they are now nigh at hand; & in a time

ORIGINAL INSCRIPTION
John Whitmer

REVISIONS
Oliver Cowdery
William W. Phelps
Sidney Rigdon
Joseph Smith
John Whitmer
Unidentified

224. Possibly "~~they {little\be\~~
have} it be". Sidney Rigdon
possibly did not write "be"
over "little" but instead wipe-
erased "little" on this line and
the strikethrough bar in "be"
on the line below.

225. Possibly two layers of
deletion, both layers by an
unidentified scribe.

226. An unidentified scribe
inserted punctuation between
this mark and a similar mark
on the following page. The
redacted punctuation is found
only within the marks; no
punctuation was added to the
revelation immediately before
or after these marks.

227. Uninked "/" etched into
the paper. This mark corresponds to a line break in *The
Evening and the Morning Star*.

to come, even in the day of the coming of the Son of man, & untill that hour there will be foolish virgins among the wise; & at that hour cometh an entire seperation of the righteous & the wicked; & in that day will I send mine angels to pluck out the wicked, & cast them into unquenchable fire. & now behold verily I say unto you I the Lord am not well pleased with my servent Sidney Rigdon he exhalted himself in his heart & received not counsel but grieved the spirit wherefore his writing is not exceptable unto the Lord & he shall make an other & if the Lord receive it not Behold he standeth no longer in the office which I have appointed him, & again verily I say unto you. let those who desire in their hearts in meekness to warn sinners to repentance let them be ordained unto this power for this is a day of warning & not a day of many words for I the Lord am not to be mocked in the last days behold I am from above & my power lieth beneath I am over all & in all & through all & searcheth all things & the days cometh that all things shall be subject unto me Behold I am alpha & Omega even Jesus christ wherefore let all men beware have they take my name in their lips for behold verily I say that many there be who are under this condemnation who useth the name of the Lord & useth it in vain having not authority wherefore let the Church repent of their sins & I the Lord will own them otherwise they shall be cut off Remember that. That which cometh from above is sacred & must be spoken with care & by constraint of the spirit & in this there is no condemnation & ye receive the spirit through prayer wherefore without this there remaineth condemnation. let my servent Joseph Smith jr & Sidney Rigdon seek them a home as they are taught through prayer, by the spirit. ¶ these things remain to over come through patience, that such may receive a more exceeding & eternal weight of glory; otherwise, a greater condemnation. Amen

67 REVELATION Kirtland Sept 11th 1831

Directions to the Elders &c &c———————

Behold, thus saith the Lord your God unto you, O ye Elders

to come, even in the day of the coming of the {s\S}on of man,

hour[228]
& untill that ~~time~~, there will be foolish virgins among

the wise, & at that hour cometh an entire seperation of the

righteous & the wicked; & in that day will I send mine angels

to pluck out the wicked, & cast them into unquenchable fire.⌉[229]

~~well~~
& now behold verily I say unto you I the Lord am not pleased

Rigdon   -d
with my servent Sidney he exhalteth himself in his heart &

received not {in atr◊◊tion\Coun{ci\se}l}[230] but grieved the spirit wherefore his

writing is not exceptable unto the Lord & he shall make an

Behold
=other & if the Lord receive it not he standeth no longer in the

I have
office which ~~he hath~~ appointed him. & again verily I say unto

you let those who desire in their hearts in meekness to

warn sinners to repentance let them be ordained unto this

power for this is a day of warning & not a day of many

words for I the Lord am not to be mocked in the last days

behold I am from above & my power lieth beneath I am over

& through all
all & in all & searcheth all things & the days cometh that

all things shall be subject unto me Behold I am alpha &

-ware
Omega even Jesus christ wherefore let all men be- ~~aware~~

how they take my name in their lips for behold verily I

say that meny there be who are under this condemnation

who useth the name of the Lord & useth it in vain having

of their Sins ~~of~~
not authority wherefore let the Church repent & I the Lord

will own them otherwise they shall be cut off remember

which
that. That cometh from above is sacred & must be spoken

with care & by constra⟨i⟩nt of the spirit & in this there is no

condemnation & ye receive the spirit through prayer wherefore

70
without this there remaineth condemnation. let my servent

Smith Jr   Rigden
Joseph & Sidney, {sek\seek} them a home as they are taught through

71
prayer, by the spirit. these things rema[i]n to over come, through

patience, that such may receive a more exceeding & eternal

72
weight of glory; otherwise, a greater condemnation. Amen

♦ [231]67 Revelation Kirtland Sept 11th. 1831

Directions to the Elders &c &c ⧟⧟⧟⧟⧟⧟

Behold, thus saith the Lord your God unto you, O ye Elders

ORIGINAL INSCRIPTION
John Whitmer

REVISIONS
Oliver Cowdery
William W. Phelps
Sidney Rigdon
Joseph Smith
John Whitmer
Unidentified

228. "hour" possibly retraced at a later time.

229. An unidentified scribe inserted punctuation between this mark and a related mark on the previous page. The redacted punctuation is found only within the marks; no punctuation was added to the revelation immediately before or after these marks.

230. John Whitmer possibly inserted "Council" at a later time.

231. The first publication reflecting most redactions in this revelation is the Book of Commandments (chapter 65), but the first publication reflecting JS's revisions is the 1835 Doctrine and Covenants (section 21). Although William W. Phelps inserted verse numbers while preparing this revelation for publication in the Book of Commandments, the verse numbers printed therein are slightly different from those that appear here. This revelation had been only partially printed for the Book of Commandments when the printing office was destroyed in 1833.

of my Church, hearken ye, & hear, & receive my will concerning you; [2] for verily I say unto you I will that ye should overcome the world; [3] wherefore I will have compassion upon you; [4] there are those among you who have sinned; but verily I say for this once, for mine own glory, & for the salvation of souls, I have forgiven you your sins. [6] I will be mercyfull unto you for I have given unto you the Kingdom; [7] & the keys of the mysteries of the kingdom, shall not be taken from my Servant Joseph, while he liveth, inasmuch as he obeyeth mine ordinances. [8] there are those who have sought occasion against him without a cause; [9] nevertheless he has sinned; but verily I say unto you I the Lord forgiveth sins unto those who confess their sins before me, & ask forgiveness, who have not sinned unto death. [10] my Disciples, in days of old, sought occasion against one an other, & forgave not one an other in their hearts; & for this evil they were afflicted, & sorely chastened; [11] wherefore I say unto you, that ye ought to forgive one another; for he that forgiveth not his brother his trespasses, standeth condemned before the Lord, for there remaineth in him the greater Sin. [12] I the Lord will forgive whom I will forgive, but of you it is required to forgive all men; [13] & ye ought to say in your hearts let god judge between me & thee, & reward thee according to thy deeds. [14] & he that repenteth not of his sins, & confesseth them not, then ye shall bring him before the church, & do with him as the scriptures saith unto you, either by commandment, or by revelation. [15] & this ye shall do that God might be glorified not because ye forgive not, having not compassion, but that ye may be justified in the eyes of the law, that ye may not offend him who is your lawgiver. [16] verily I say, for this cause ye shall do these things. [17] Behold, I the Lord was angry with him who was my Servant Ezra; [18] & also my servant Isaac, for they kept not the law, neither the commandment; they sought evil in their hearts, & I the Lord withheld my spirit. [19] they condemned for evil, that thing in which there was no evil; [20] nevertheless I have forgiven my servant Isaac; [21] & also my servant Edward; [22] Behold he hath sinned, & satan seeketh to destroy his soul; but when these things are made known unto them, they repent

of my Church, hearken ye, & hear, & receive my will conce

=rning you: for verily I say unto you, I will that ye should over

=come the world: wherefore I will have compassion upon you. there

are those among you who have sinned; but verily I say for this

once, for mine own glory, & for the salvation of Souls, I have

forgiven you your sins. I will be mercyfull unto you for I

have given unto you the Kingdom{,\:} & the keys of the mysteries

                                                             Smith Jr

of the kingdom, shall not be taken from my Servent Joseph, while

he liveth, in-as-much as he obeyeth mine ordinances. there are those

who have sought occation against him without a cause; nevertheless

has

he ~~hath~~ sinned, but verily I say unto you I the Lord forgiveth

sins unto those who confess their sins before me, & ask forgiveness,

who have not sinned unto death. my Deciples, in days of old,

sought occasion against one an other, & forgave not one an

other in their hearts, & for this evil they were afflicted, & sorely

chastened: wherefore I say unto you, that ye ~~had~~ ought to forgive one

another, for he that forgiveth not his brother his tresspasses, stand=

=eth condemned before the Lord, for there remaineth in him the

greater sin. I the Lord will forgive whom I will forgive, but

of you it is required to forgive all men; & ye ~~had~~ ought to say

in your hearts let God Judge between me & thee, & reward thee

according to thy deeds. & he that repenteth not of his sins, & confesseth

them not, then ye ~~ye~~ shall bring him before the church, & do

with him as the Scriptures ~~direct~~ Saith unto you, either by comm

        by

=andment, or revelation. & this {s\ye} shall do that God might be glorif

=ied not because ye forgive not, having not compassion, but that

ye may be Justified in the eyes of the law, that ye may not

offend him who is your lawgiver. verily I say, for this cause

ye shall do these things. Behold I the Lord was angery with

       18 **Booth**   **Morl**[e]**y**

him who was my Servent Ezra; & also, my Servent Isaac for

they kept not the Law, neither the commandment; they sought

evil in their hearts, & I the Lord withheld my spirit. they condem

=ned for evil, that thing in which there was no evil: nevertheless

       2{0\1} **Morley**   **Partrage** [Partridge]

I have forgiven my Servent Isaac{,\.} & also my Servent Edward,

{B\b}ehold he hath sinned, & Satan Seeketh to destroy his soul{,\;} but

when these things are made known unto them, they repent~~eth~~

ORIGINAL INSCRIPTION
John Whitmer

REVISIONS
Oliver Cowdery
William W. Phelps
Sidney Rigdon
Joseph Smith
John Whitmer
Unidentified

of the evil; & they shall be forgiven. [23] & now verily I say, that it is expedient in me that my servant Sidney (Gilbert) after a few weeks, should return upon his business, & to his agency in the Land of Zion; [24] & that which he hath seen & heard may be made known unto my Disciples, that they perish not. [25] & for this cause have I spoken these things. [26] & again, I say unto you, that my servant Isaac Morley may not be tempted above that which he is able to bear, & council wrongfully to your hurt, I gave commandment that this farm should be sold. [27] I willett not that my servant Frederick G Williams should sell his farm, for I the Lord willett to retain a strong hold in the Land of Kirtland, for the space of five years; in the which I will not overthrow the wicked, that thereby I may save some; [28] & after that day I the Lord will not hold any guilty, that shall go, with an open hearts, up to the Land of Zion: for I the Lord requireth the hearts of the children of men. [29] Behold now it is called to day, (until the coming of the son of man) & verily it is a day of sacrifice, & a day for the tithing of my People; [30] for he that is tithed shall not be burned, (at his coming) for after to day cometh the burning; this is speaking after the manner of the Lord; [31] for verily I say, tomorrow all the proud & they that do wickedly shall be as stubble; & I will burn them up, for I am the Lord of hosts; [33] & I will not spare any that remaineth in Babylon. [34] wherefore, if ye believe me ye will labour while it is called to day. [35] & it is not meet that my servants, Newel K Whitney & Sidney Gilbert should sell their Store, & their Passessions here, for this is not wisdom untill the residue of the Church, which remaineth in this place, shall go up unto the Land of Zion. [36] behold it is said in my Laws, or forbidden to get in debt to thine enemies; [37] but Behold it is not said at any time, that the Lord should not take when he please & pay as seemeth him good: [38] wherefore as ye are agents, & ye are on the Lord's errand; & whatever ye do according to the will of the Lord is the Lord's business; & his is the Lord's business to provide for his saints in these last days, that they may obtain an inheritance in the Land of Zion; [39] & Behold I the Lord declare unto you, & my words are sure & shall not fail that they shall obtain it; [40] but all things must come

Of the evil, & they shall be forgiven. & now verily I say, that

²³ it is expedient in me that my servent Sidney (G)ilbert)²³² after a

few weeks, should return upon his business, & to his agency

in the Land of Zion; & that which he hath seen & heard may be

made known unto my Deciples, that they perish not. & for this

cause have I spoken these things. & again, I say unto you, that

Morley
my servent Isaac may not be tempted above that which he is

able to bear, & council wrongfully to your hurt, I gave

commandment that this farm should be sold. I willeth not
G Williams
that my servent {f\Frederick}, should sell his farm, for I the Lord

willeth to retain a strong hold in the Land of Kirtland, for

the space of five years, in the which I will not overthrow

the wicked, that thereby I may save some; & after that day I
an
the Lord will not hold any guilty, that shall go, with open

hearts, up to the Land of Zion: for I the Lord requireth the hearts
(until the Coming of the son of man)
of the Children of men. Behold now it is called to day, & verily

it is a day of Sacrifice, & a day for the tithing of my People;
{ᴓ\(at} **his Coming)**
for he that is tithed shall not be burned; for after to day cometh

the burning: this is speaking after the manner of the Lord: for
ly
verily I say, tomorrow all the proud & they that do wickedly shall

be as {ᴓ\stuble}; & I will burn them up, ~~saith the Lord~~ for I am

the Lord of hosts; & I will not spare any that remaineth in Babylon.

wherefore, if ye believe me ye will labour while it is called
K Whitney |²³³ Gilbert
to day. & it is not meet that my servents, Newel & sidney, should

sell their Store, & their Possessions here, for this is not wisdom

untill the residue of the Church, which remaineth in this place,

shall go up unto the Land of Zion. behold it is said in my Laws,

or forbidden to get in debt to thine enemies; but Behold it is

not said at any time, that the Lord should not take when he

please & pay as seemeth him good: wherefore as ye are agents,

& ye are on the Lord's errand; & whatever ye do according to
this
the will of the Lord, is the Lord's business, & ~~it~~ is the Lord's busi
and he hath set you
=ness to provide for {ᴓ\his} saints in these last days, that they

may obtain an in heritance in the Land of Zion: & Behold

I the Lord declare unto you, & my words are shure & shall not

fail that they shall obtain it; but all things must come

ORIGINAL INSCRIPTION
John Whitmer

REVISIONS
Oliver Cowdery
William W. Phelps
Sidney Rigdon
Joseph Smith
John Whitmer
Unidentified

232. The circle around "ilbert" appears to be in the same ink flow as William W. Phelps's other redactions on this page. The name was printed as "Sidney (G.)" in the Book of Commandments; the full name was first printed in the 1835 Doctrine and Covenants.

233. JS inserted this line to separate insertions in the manuscript.

to pass in its time; wherefore be not weary in well doing, for ye are laying the foundation of a great work, & out of small things proceedeth that which is great; behold the Lord requireth the heart, & a willing mind, & the willing & obedient shall eat the good of the Land of Zion in these last days; & the rebelious shall be cut off out of the Land of Zion, & shall be sent away & shall not inherit the Land: for verely I say that the rebelious are not of the blood of Ephraim wherefore they shall be plucked out. Behold I the Lord have made my Church in these last days, like unto a judge setting on an hill, or in an high place, to judge the Nations: for it shall come to pass, that the inhabitants of Zion shall judge all things; & all liars & hypocrites shall be proved by them, & they which are not Apostles & prophets shall be known; & even the judge & his councellors, if they are not faithfull in their stewardships, shall be condemned, & others shall be planted in their steads; for behold I say unto you that Zion shall flourish, & the glory of the Lord shall be upon her, & she shall be an ensign unto the People, & there shall come unto her out of every Nation under heaven. & the days shall come, when the Nations of the Earth shall tremble because of her, & shall fear because of her terrible ones: the Lord hath spoken it. amen.

Given at Kirtland September the 11th 1831

A Revelation to Wm E. McLelin Reced Oct 29th 1831

Behold thus saith the Lord unto you my Servent William (E.) McLelin, blessed are you, in as much as you have turned away from your iniquities & have received my truths, saith the Lord your Redeemer, the Saviour of the World of as many as believe on my name: verily I say unto you, blessed are you for receiving mine everlasting covenant, even the fulness of my gospel, sent forth unto the children of men, that they might have life & be made partakers of the glories which are to be revealed in the last days, as it was written by the Prophets & Apostles in days of old; verily I say unto you my Servent Wm (E.) that you are clean but not all; repent therefore of those things which are not pleasing in my sight, saith the Lord, for the Lord will shew them unto you. & now verily I the Lord will shew unto you what I will concerning you, or what is my will concerning you. Behold, verily I say unto you, that it is my will that you should proclaim my gospel from land to land, & from city to city; yea in those regions

⁴¹
²³⁴to pass in its time; wherefore be not weary in well doing,

{◊\4}2

for ye are laying the foundation of a great work. & out of ~~sm~~²³⁵

⁴³
small things proceedeth that which is great. behold the Lord

⁴⁴
requireth the hear{ts\t} & a willing mind; & the willing & obedient

shall eat the good of the Land of Zion in these Last days{◊\.}

⁴⁵
& the rebelious shall be cut off out of the Land of Zion, & shall be

⁴⁶
sent away & shall not inherit the Land: for verily I say that the

⁴⁷
rebelious are not of the blood of Ephraim :²³⁶ wherefore, they shall

⁴⁸
be plucked out. Behold I the Lord have made my Church in

these last days like unto a Judge, setting on an hill, or in an

⁴⁹
high place, to Judge the Nations: for it shall come to pass, that
pertaining ₅₀ **to Zion**
the inhabitants of Zion, shall Judge all things; & all liars &

⁵¹
hypocrites shall be proved by them; & they which are not Apostles
& prophets ₅₂
— shall be known. & even the Judge & his councellors, if they are

not faithfull in their stewardships, shall be condemned, & ~~an~~ oth

⁵³
=ers shall be planted in their stead: for behold I say unto you,

that Zion shall flourish, & the glory of the Lord shall be upon

⁵⁴
her, & she shall be an ensighn unto the People. & these ~~shall~~

⁵⁵
shall come unto her out of every Nation under heaven. & the

days shall come, when the Nations of the Earth shall

tremble because of her, & shall fear, because of her terable

ones: the Lord hath spoken it. amen

Given at Kirtland September the 11th. 1831

◆ ²³⁷A Revelation to W^{m.} E Mc lel[l]in Rec^{d.} Oc^{t.} 29th. 1831

Behold thus saith the Lord unto you my Servant William (E.) Mclel{~~lin~~\in}) blessed

are you, in as much as you have turned away from your iniquities, & have receiv

even
=ed my truths, saith the Lord, your redeemer, the saveiour of the World, of as many

²
as believe on my name. verily I say unto you, blessed are you for receiving mine ever[la]

=sting ~~truths~~²³⁸ Covenant, even the fullness of my gospel, sent forth unto the Children of
are
men, that they might have life & be made partakers of the glories which ~~was~~ to be revealed
^3
in the last days, as it was written by the Prophets & Apostles in days of old. verily I say unto

⁴
you, my Servant W^{m.} (E.) that you are Clean but not all; repent therefore of those things
them
which are not pleasing in my sight, saith the Lord, for the Lord will shew unto you.
^
⁵
~~what~~ {◊~~hat~~\I &}²³⁹ now verily I the Lord will shew unto you what I will concerning you, or

⁶
what is my will concerning you. Behold, verily I say unto you, that it is my will that you

⁷
should proclaim my Gospel from land to land, & from City to City: yea, in those regions

---

ORIGINAL INSCRIPTION
John Whitmer

REVISIONS
Oliver Cowdery
William W. Phelps
Sidney Rigdon
Joseph Smith
John Whitmer
Unidentified

234. This leaf, containing manuscript pages III–II2, was removed from the manuscript book at some point and is located at the Community of Christ Library-Archives.

235. "sm" wipe-erased and then stricken.

236. The editing mark around "of Ephraim" is a take mark; it indicates the final word of the fifth gathering ("E" signature) of the Book of Commandments (page 160).

237. Although most redactions in this revelation were made in preparation for publication of the Book of Commandments, this revelation was not printed therein because the printing office was destroyed in 1833. A few additional redactions, such as JS's insertions, were likely made for publication in the 1835 Doctrine and Covenants, where most redactions in this revelation first appear (section 74).

238. "truths" wipe-erased and then stricken.

239. "I" has two layers of deletion: first layer by John Whitmer at the time of original inscription and second layer by William W. Phelps.

this place. go not up unto the land of Zion as yet in as much as you can send, send; otherwise think not of thy property. go unto the Eastern lands, bear testimony unto every people & in every place & in their synagogues, reasoning with the people. let my Servant Samuel go with you, & forsake him not, & give him thine instructions, & he that is faithfull shall be made strong in every place, & I the Lord will go with you. lay your hands upon the sick, & they shall recover. return not untill I the Lord shall send you. be patient in afflictions. ask & ye shall receive; knock & it shall be opened unto you. seek not to be cumbered. forsake all unrighteousness. commit not adultery, a temptation with which thou hast been troubled. keep their sayings true & faithfull, & thou shalt magnify thine office, & push many people to Zion with songs of everlasting joy upon their heads. continue in those things even unto the end & you shall have a crown of eternal life on the right hand of my father, who is full of grace & truth. verily, thus saith the Lord your God your Redeemer, even Jesus Christ. AMEN.

a Revelation (No 3) Oct 30th 1831

Hearken & lo a voice as one sent down from on high who is mighty & powerfull whose going forth is unto the ends of the Earth yea whose voice is unto men prepare ye the way of the Lord make his paths straight The keys of the kingdom of God are committed unto man on the Earth & from thence shall the gospel roll forth unto the ends of the Earth as the stone which is Cut out of the Mountain without hands shall roll forth untill it has filled the whole Earth yea a voice crying prepare ye the way of the Lord prepare ye the supper of the Lamb make ready for the Bridegroom pray unto the Lord call upon his holy name make known his wonderfull works among the people call upon the Lord that his kingdom may go forth upon the Earth that the inhabitents thereof may receive it & be prepared for the days to come in the which the son of man shall come down in heaven clothed in the brightness of his glory to meet the kingdom of God which is set up on the Earth Wherefore may the kingdom of God go forth that the kingdom of heaven may come that thou O God may be glorified in heaven so on Earth that thine enemies may be subdued for thine is the kingdom honour power & glory forever & ever. Amen.

[112] [verso]   [h]as hath   8
240[round a]bout, whe[r]e it ~~hath~~ not been proc[l]aimed. tarry not many days in
                                          ^   as yet,
                   9
this place. go not up unto the land of Zion but in as much as you can send,
               10   11   12
send; otherwise think not of thy property. go unto the Eastern lands. bear testimony
                                   unto every people,
~~unto every people~~ & in every Place, & in their synnagogues, reasoning with the people.
    13   **H Smith**
let my Servant Samuel go with {thee\you}, & forsake him not, & give him thine instructions.
    1{0\4}   ^
& he that is faithfull shall be made strong in every place, & I the Lord will go with you.
    15   16
lay your hands upon the sick, & they shall r[e]cover. return not untill I the Lord shall
                17   18
send you{.\.} be patiant in afflictions. ask & ye shall receive; knock & it shall be
                      19   20   21
opened unto you. seek not to be Cumbered. forsake all unrighteousness. commit
                                  you have thou hast 22
not Adultery, a temptation with which ~~thou hast~~ been troubled. keep these
    for they are   you shall thou shalt^ your thine
Sayings, true & faithfull, & ~~thou shalt~~ magnify ~~thine~~ office, & push many people
             ^   ^   ^   23   even
to Zion with songs of everlasting Joy upon their heads. continue in those things unto
        even   ^
the end & you shall have a crown of eternal life on the right hand of my father,
       ^
                              24
who is full of grace & truth. verily, thus saith the Lord your God, your redeemer,

even Jesus Christ. Amen.

                                (Nᵒ 3)²⁴² 65²⁴³
♦ ²⁴¹69 Revelation Octᵗ· 30ᵗʰ· 1831

//²⁴⁴Hearken & Lo a voice as one sent down from on high who is mighty

& powerfull whose going forth is unto the ends of the Earth yea whose voice

is unto men prepare ye the way of the Lord make his paths strait

The keys of the kingdom of God {is\are} committed unto man on the Earth & from

thence shall the Gospel roll forth unto the ends of the Earth as the stone
        cut out of²⁴⁵
which is ~~hew{n\e} from~~ the Mountain without hands shall roll forth
            has   ^²⁴⁶
untill it ~~hath~~ filled the whole Earth yea a voice crying prepare ye the

way of the Lord prepare ye the supper of the Lamb make ready for the

Bridegroom pray unto the Lord call upon his holy name make

known his wonderfull workˢ· among the people call upon the Lord

that his kingdom may go forth upon the Earth that the inhabitants

thereof may received it & be prepared for the days to come in the

which the Son of man Shall come down in heaven Clothed in the

brightness of his glory to meet the kingdom of God which is set up on

the Earth Wherefore may the kingdom of {g\⟨G⟩}od go forth that the kingdom

of heaven may come that thou O God may be glorified in heaven

so on Earth that thine enemies may be subdued for thine is the

~~kingdom~~ honour power & glory forever & ever. Amen\\.²⁴⁷

ORIGINAL INSCRIPTION
John Whitmer

REVISIONS
Oliver Cowdery
William W. Phelps
Sidney Rigdon
Joseph Smith
John Whitmer
Unidentified

240. This leaf, containing manuscript pages 111–112, was removed from the manuscript book at some point and is located at the Community of Christ Library-Archives.

241. The first publication reflecting most redactions in this revelation is the September 1832 issue of *The Evening and the Morning Star*.

242. For an explanation of this numbering, see 159n196 herein.

243. "65" written and circled in graphite and then erased. This revelation has appeared as section 65 in all editions of the Doctrine and Covenants published by the RLDS church (now Community of Christ).

244. This graphite mark corresponds to a similar mark at the end of the revelation and possibly indicates intent or instruction to publish this revelation in *The Evening and the Morning Star*, where it was published in September 1832.

245. "**cut out of**" first appears in print in the 1835 Doctrine and Covenants (section 24); "**cut**" possibly written in a different ink flow than "**out of**", indicating that these words were possibly written at different times.

246. "**^**" possibly a stray ink mark.

247. This graphite mark corresponds to a similar mark at the beginning of the revelation and possibly indicates intent or instruction to publish this revelation in *The Evening and the Morning Star*, where it was published in September 1832.

70 A Revelation to Orson Luke & Lyman. & William
The mind & will of the Lord, as made known by the voice of the
Spirit ~~~ known to a conference, held November first. 1831, concerning
certain Elders, who requested of the Lord to know his will concerning
them, & also certain items, as made known in addition to the Laws
& commandments, ~~which have been~~ given to the church, firstly,
my servant Orson was called by his ordinance to proclaim the
everlasting Gospel by the spirit of the living God from people
to people & from land to land ~~from~~ in the congregations of the wicked
in their Synagogues reasoning with & expounding all scriptures unto
them & behold & lo this is an ensample unto all those who are
ordained unto this priesthood whose mission is appointed unto
them to go forth & this is the ensample unto them that they shall
speak as they are moved upon by the Holy Ghost & whatsoever they
shall speak when moved upon by the Holy Ghost shall be scrip
ture shall be the will of the Lord shall be the mind of the Lord
shall be the word of the Lord
shall be the voice of the Lord & ~~shall be~~ the power of God unto
Salvation behold this is the promise of the Lord unto you O ye my
servants wherefore be of good cheer & do not fear for I the Lord
am with you & will stand by you & ~~you~~ ye shall bear record
of me even Jesus Christ that I am the Son of the living God that
I was that I am & that I am to come this is the mind
of the Lord unto you my Servant Orson & also unto ~~to~~ my Ser
vant Luke & unto my servant Lyman & unto my servant
William & unto all the faithful Elders of my church
go ye into all the world preach the gospel to every creature
acting in the authority which I have given you baptizing
in the name of the Father & of the Son & of the Holy Ghost & he that
believeth & is baptized shall be saved & he that believeth not shall
be damned & he that believeth shall be blessed with signs
following even as it is written & unto you it shall be given to
know the signs of the times & the signs of the coming of the Son of man
& of as many as the Father shall bear record to you it shall be
given power to seal them up unto Eternal life Amen. ———
And now concerning the items in addition to the Laws & com
mandments they are these that there remaineth hereafter in the due

248given in Hiram Nov. 1. 1831   (N° 1.)249   113 [recto]
70 A Revelation to /250Orson [Hyde] Luke [Johnson] & Lyman [Johnson] & William ⏎
[E. McLellin]

The mind & will of the Lord, as made known by the voice of the

~~known~~ to
spirit ~~made~~ a confrence, held November first, 1831, concerning
           ^

certain Elders, who requested of the Lord to kno{◊\w} his will concerning

them, & also certain items, as made known in addition to the Laws

& commandments, ~~which have been~~ given to the church, firstly:

my servant Orson was called by his ordinance to proclaim the

everlasting Gospel by the spirit of the living God from people
                                        in the
to people & from land to land ~~from~~ congregtions of the wicked
                                ^   un
in their Synagogues reas[o]ning with & expounding all scriptures to
                                                                 ^
them & behold & lo this is an ensample unto all those who {were\are}

ordained unto this priesthood whose mission is appointed unto

them to go forth & this is the ensample unto them that they shall

speak as they are moved upon by the Holy Ghost & whatsoever they

shall speak when moved upon by the Holy Ghost shall be Scrip-

=ture shall be the will of the Lord shall be the mind of the Lord
shall be the word of the Lord
shall be the voice of the Lord & ~~shall be~~ the power of God unto
^   O
Salvation behold this is the promise of the Lord unto you ~~o~~ ye my
                                                          ^
servants wherefore be of good cheer & do not fear for I the Lord
                                          ye
am with you & will stand by you & ~~you~~ shall bear record
                                       ^
                        the living
of me even Jesus christ that I am the Son of God that
                                            ^
I was that I am & that I am to come this is the word
                                       unto
of the Lord unto you my Servant Orson & also ~~to~~ my ser-

=vant Luke & unto my servant Lyman & unto my servant

William & unto all the faithful Elders of my church

go ye {u\i}nto all the world preach the gospel to every creature

acting in the authority which I have given you baptising
                      of   of the
in the name of the Father & ~~of~~ the Son & ~~of~~ Holy Ghost & he that
                            ^   ^
believeth & is baptised shall be saved & he that believeth not shall

be damned & he that believeth shall be blessed with signs

following even as it is written & unto you it shall251 be given to

know the signs of the times & the signs of the coming of the Son of man

& of as many as the Father shall bear record to you it shall be
     power
given to seal them up unto Eternal life Amen—
     ^
And now conc[e]rning the items in addition to the Laws & com

=mandments they are these there rema[i]neth hereafter in the due

Original Inscription
John Whitmer
Oliver Cowdery

Revisions
Oliver Cowdery
William W. Phelps
Sidney Rigdon
Joseph Smith
John Whitmer
Unidentified

248. The first publication reflecting most redactions in this revelation is the October 1832 issue of *The Evening and the Morning Star,* although some of Oliver Cowdery's redactions first appear in print in the 1835 Doctrine and Covenants (section 22).

249. For an explanation of this numbering, see 159n196 herein.

250. John Whitmer handwriting ends; Oliver Cowdery begins.

251. Or "sha⟨l⟩lt".

time of the Lord other Bishops to be set apart unto the Church
to minister even according to the first wherefore it shall be an
high priest who is worthy & he shall be appointed by ~~a conference of~~ the presidency of
high priests And again, no Bishop, or ~~priest~~ high priest which shall be set apart
for this ministry shall be tried or condemned for any crime save
it be before ~~a conference of high priests~~ the first presidency of the church & inasmuch as he is found guilty
before ~~a conference of high priests~~ this presidency & by testimony that cannot be impeached
he shall be condemned or forgiven according to the ~~laws~~ Covenants of the church
✗ or in any of her stakes which are duly organized
And again inasmuch as parents have children in Zion, that teach them
not to understand the doctrine of repentance faith in Christ the Son of the
living God & of baptism & the gift of the Holy Spirit by the laying on of the
hands when eight years old, the sin be upon the head of the parents for
this shall be a law unto the inhabitants of Zion or her stakes which are regularly organized & their children shall
be baptized for the remission of their sins when eight years old &
receive the laying on of the hands & they also shall teach their children to pray
& to walk uprightly before the Lord & the inhabitants of Zion shall also
observe the Sabbath day to keep it holy & the inhabitants of Zion also
shall remember their labors inasmuch as they are appointed to labor
in all faithfulness for the idler shall be had in remembrance before
the Lord now I the Lord am not well pleased with the inhabitants
of Zion for there are idlers among them & their children are also growing
up in wickedness they also seek not earnestly the riches of
eternity but their eyes are full of greediness these things ought not
to be & must be done away from among them wherefore let my
servant Oliver Cowdery carry these sayings unto the land of Zion & a commandment I give unto them that ~~he which~~ he who observeth not his prayers
before the Lord in the season thereof let them be had in remembrance before the judge of my people these sayings are true & faithful wherefore transgress them not neither take therefrom behold
I am Alpha & Omega & I come quickly Amen
given in in Hiram November first 1831 by Joseph the Seer

11th Revelation (No 4) given Nov 2nd 1831

Behold & hearken, oh ye Elders of my Church, who have
assembled yourselves together, whose prayers I have heard
& whose hearts I know & whose desires have come up before me, behold &

♦ ²⁵⁹72 A Revelation Recd. Nov 3, 1831²⁶⁰

Hearken, oh ye People of my Church,—— saith the
God,
Lord {—\your}²⁶¹ & hear the word of the Lord, concerning you the Lord

who shall suddenly come to his temple; the Lord who
upon the world
shall come down with a curse to Judgement; yea, upon

all the Nations that forget god & upon all the ungodly amongst
2
you: for he shall make bear his holy arm in the eyes of

all the Nations, & all the ends of the earth shall see the
3
salvation of their god: wherefore prepare ye, prepare ye, {oh\O}

ye my People: Sanctify yourselves: gether ye together, oh ye

People of my Church, upon the Land of Zion, all you that
4
have not been commanded to tarry{,\.} go ye out from

Babylon. be ye clean that bear the vessels of the Lord. call
5
your solom assemblies, & speak often one to another. &

let every man call upon the name of the Lord; yea, verily

I say unto you, again, the time has come when the voice

of the Lord is unto you, go ye out of Babylon: gether ye

out from among the nations, from the four winds, from one
6
end of Heaven to the other. send forth the Elders of my Church

unto the nations which are afar off; unto the ilands of the {s\S}ea;

send forth unto foreign lands: call upon all nations: firstly, upon
7
the gentiles, & then upon the Jews. & Behold & Lo this shall be their

Cry, & the voice of the Lord unto all People: {g\G}o ye forth unto

the Land of Zion, that the borders of my People may be enlarged,

& & that her stakes may be strengthened, & that Zion may go forth—
8
unto the regions round about:— yea let the cry go forth

among all people: awake & arise & go forth to meet the
9
Bride-groom: Behold & Lo the Bride-groom Cometh— go ye

out to meet him. {p\P}repare yourselves for the great day of the

Lord. {w\W}atch, therefore, for ye know neither the day nor the
10
hour{,\.} let them, therefore, wh{i\o}ch are among the gentiles—
them who
flee unto Zion. & let they which be of Judah f{◊ee\lee} unto
11
Jerusalem, unto the Mountains of the Lord's house. go ye

out from among the Nations, even from Babylon

ORIGINAL INSCRIPTION
John Whitmer

REVISIONS
Oliver Cowdery
William W. Phelps
Sidney Rigdon
Joseph Smith
John Whitmer
Unidentified

259. The first publication reflecting most redactions in this revelation is the May 1833 issue of *The Evening and the Morning Star*. Although many redactions in this revelation were made in preparation for publication of the Book of Commandments, this revelation was not printed therein because the printing office was destroyed in 1833.

260. After manuscript pages 116–129 were inscribed, John Whitmer gave each item a number and supplied some items with generic titles. The ink flow suggests that he numbered and titled these items in one sitting.

261. Dash wipe-erased and then written over.

From the midst of wickedness, which is spiritual Babylon.
12 But verily thus saith the Lord, let not your flight be in haste, but let all things be prepared before you: & he that goeth, let him not look back — lest sudden distruction shall come upon him.
13 Hearken & hear oh ye inhabitants of the Earth: listen ye Elders of my Church together, & hear the voice of the Lord, for he calleth upon all men & he commandeth all men every where to repent: 14 for behold the Lord God hath sent forth the angel crying through the midst of Heaven, saying: prepare ye the way of the Lord, & make his paths strait, for the hour of his coming is nigh, when the Lamb shall stand upon Mount Zion, & with him an hundred & forty-four thousand, having his father's name written in their foreheads:—
15 wherefore, prepare ye for the coming of the Bridegroom; go ye go ye out to meet him, for Behold he shall stand upon the Mount of Olivet, & upon the mighty Ocean, even the great deep, & upon the Islands of the Sea, & upon the Land of Zion:— & he shall utter his voice out of Zion, & he shall speak from Jerusalem, & his voice shall be heard among all people, & it shall be as the voice of many waters, & as the voice of a great thunder, which shall break down the Mountains, & the vallies shall not be found: 16 he shall command the great deep & it shall be driven back into the North countries; & the Islands shall become one land, & the land of Jerusalem & the Land of Zion, shall be turned back into their own place, & the earth shall be like as it was in the days before it was divided. 17 & the Lord even the Saviour shall stand in the midst of his people, & shall reign over all flesh; & they who are in the North countries shall come in remembrance before the Lord, & their Prophets shall hear his voice, & shall no longer stay themselves & they shall smite the rocks, & the ice shall flow down at their presence. 18 & an high way shall be cast up in the midst of the great deep. Their enemies shall become a prey unto them, & in the barren deserts there shall come forth pools of living water; & the parched ground shall no longer be a thirsty land; & they shall bring forth their rich treasures

117 [recto]

~~DC~~ 1²⁶²
~~108~~²⁶³ From the midst of wickedness, which is spiritual {b\B}abylon.

12

But verily thus saith the Lord, let not your {f◊◊\flight} ~~not~~ be in

h{◊\a}ste, but let all things be prepared before you: & he that goeth, let

look

him not back{—\—}²⁶⁴ lest sudden distruction shall come upon him.

13

{h\H}earken & hear oh ye inhabitants of the Earth. & listen ye

Elders of my Church together, & hear the voice of the Lord,

for he calleth upon all men & he comandeth all men every

where to repent: for behold the Lord God hath sent forth the

Angel ~~with the everlasting gospel~~ crying through the midst of

Heaven, saying: prepare ye the way of the Lord, & make his

paths strait, for the hour of his coming is nigh, when the Lamb

an

Shall stand upon Mount Zion, & with him {a\a }hundred & forty-four

thousand, having his father's name written in their foreheads:—

15

wherefore, prepare ye for the coming of the Bride-gr{◊◊\oom}: {g\G}o ye, g[o]

y{◊◊\e} out to meet him, for Behold he shall stand upon the

Mount of Olivet{◊\,} & upon the mighty Ocean, even the great deep,

& upon the Islands of the Sea, & upon the Land of Zion;— & he shall

utter his voice out of Zion, & he shall speak from Jerusalem, &

a voice ~~a voice~~

his voice shall be heard among all people, & it shall be as

the voice of many waters, & as the voice of a great thunder,

which shall break down the Mountains, & the valies shall not

16

be found: he shall command the great deep & it shall be driven

back into the North countries{;\,} & the Islands shall become one

land, & the land of Jerusalem & the Land of Zion, shall be turned

back into their own place, & the earth Shall be like as it was in

17

the days before it was ~~before it was~~ divided. & the Lord even

& shall reign

the Saviour shall stand in the midst of his people, over all ~~the~~

~~Earth~~ flesh{;\.} & they ~~which~~ who are in the North countries shall come

in rememberanc before the Lord, & their Prophets shall hear his

voice, & shall {l\no} longer stay themselves & they shall smite

18

the rocks, & the ice shall folow down at their presenc[e]. & an high

way shall be cast up in the midst of the great deep. {t\T}heir

enemies shall become a prey unto them, & ⟨in⟩ the barren deserts

there shall come forth pools of living water; & the parched

no

ground shall longe[r] be a thirsty land; & they shall bring forth

th[e]ir rich treasures

ORIGINAL INSCRIPTION
John Whitmer

REVISIONS
Oliver Cowdery
William W. Phelps
Sidney Rigdon
Joseph Smith
John Whitmer
Unidentified

262. This leaf, containing manuscript pages 117–118, was removed from the manuscript book at some point and is located at the Community of Christ Library-Archives. "1" is written and circled in graphite, possibly a twentieth-century method of numbering the leaves located at the CCLA.

263. "DC | 108" written and circled in graphite and then erased. This revelation has appeared as section 108 in all editions of the Doctrine and Covenants published by the RLDS church (now Community of Christ). Multispectral imaging made recovery of the notation possible. (See pp. xli and xliii herein.)

264. "{—\—}" possibly "◊".

unto the Children of Ephraim my servants. & the boundaries
of the everlasting hills shall tremble at their presence. & the
shall they fall down & be crowned with glory, even in
Zion, by the hands of the servants of the Lord, even the Child
=ren of Ephraim; & they shall be filled with songs of everla
=sting joy. 20 Behold this is the blessing of the everlasting God
upon the tribes of Israel, & the richer blessing
upon the head of Ephraim & his fellows. 21 & they also of the
tribe of Judah, after their pain, shall be sanctified in
holiness before the Lord to dwell in his presence day & night
forever & ever. 22 & now verily saith the Lord, that these things
might be known among you, oh inhabitants of the
Earth, I have sent forth mine Angel, flying through the
midst of heaven having the everlasting Gospel, who hath
appeared unto some, & hath committed it unto man, who shall
appear unto many that dwell on the Earth, & this gospel
shall be preached unto every Nation, & kindred, & tongue, &
People & the servants of God shall go forth, saying, with a loud
voice: Fear God & give glory to him: for the hour of his judgement
is come: & worship him that made heaven, & earth, & the sea,
& the fountains of waters, calling upon the Lord day & night,
saying: 24 Oh that thou wouldst rend the heavens, that thou
wouldst come down, that the mountains might flow
down at thy presence. & it shall be answered upon
their heads for the presence of the Lord shall be as the
melting fire that burneth & as the fire which causeth the
waters to boil. 25 Oh Lord, thou shalt come down to make
known thy name known to thine adversaries & all nations shall
tremble at thy presence. When thou doest terrible things,
things they look not for; yea, when thou camest down
& the Mountains flowed down at thy presence, thou shalt
meet him who rejoiceth & worketh righteousness, who remembereth
thee in thy ways: 25 for since the beginning of the world have not
man heard nor perceived by the ear, neither hath the eye seen,
O God, besides thee how great things thou hast prepared for him that
waiteth for thee; 26 & it shall be said who is this that cometh

118 [verso]

²⁶⁵unto the Children of Ephraim my servents. ¹⁹& the boundaries

of the everlasting hills shall trembl at their presence. & these

shall ~~thy~~ ^{they} fall down & be crowned with glory, even in

Zion, by the hands of the Servents of the Lord, even the child

=ren of Ephraim; & they shall be filled with songs of everla

=sting Joy. ²⁰{b\B}ehold this is the blessing of the everlasting God

upon the ~~heads of the~~ tribes of Israel, & the richer blessing

upon the head of Ephraim & his fellows. ²¹& they also o{n\f} the

tribe of Judah, aft{ter\er} their pain, shall be Sanctified in

holiness before the Lord t{o\o} dwell in his presenc[e] day & night

forever & ever. ²²& now verily saith the Lord, that these things

might be known among you, oh inhabitants of the

Earth, I have sent forth mine Angel, flying throug[h] the

midst of heaven having the everlasting Gospel, who hath

appeard unto some, & hath commit{e\t}^ed it unto man, who shall

appear unto many that dwell on the Earth, & this gospel

shall be preached unto every Nation, & kindred, & tongue, &

People, & the Servents of God shall go forth, saying, with a loud

voice: ²³{f\F}ear God & give glory to him: for the hour of his Judgement

is come: & worship him that made Heaven, & earth, & ~~the~~ Sea,

& the fountain{s\s}, of waters, calling upon the Lord day & night,

saying: ^{2{0\4}}{o\O}h that thou wouldst rend the heavens, that thou

wouldest come down, that the mountains ~~would~~ ^{might} flow

down at thy presence. & it shall be answered upon

their heads for the presence of the Lord shall be as the

melting fire that burneth & as the fire ~~that~~ ^{which} causeth the

waters to boil. ²⁵{o\O}h Lord, thou shalt come down to make

~~known~~ ^{known} thy name to thine advisar{y\ies} & all nations shall

trembl at thy presence. {w\W}hen thou doeth ter{a\i}bl things,—

things ~~that~~ they look not for; yea, when thou comest down

& the Mountains flow down at thy presenc[e], thou shalt

meet him ~~that~~ ^{who} rejoiceth & worketh righteousness, who remember ¬²⁶⁶

thee in thy ways: ²⁵for sinc[e] the begining of the world have not

man heard nor perceived by the {e\⟨E⟩}ar, neither hath ~~the~~ ^{any} eye seen,

O God, {G\besid{s\es}} thee, {0000\how} great things thou ^{hast} prepared for him that

waiteth: ²⁶for thee{;\.} ^{it} & shall be said who is this that cometh

Original Inscription
John Whitmer

Revisions
Oliver Cowdery
William W. Phelps
Sidney Rigdon
Joseph Smith
John Whitmer
Unidentified

265. This leaf, containing manuscript pages 117–118, was removed from the manuscript book at some point and is located at the Community of Christ Library-Archives.

266. "¬" possibly an ink blot.

down from god in heaven with ~~their~~ ^{died} garments; yea,
from the regions ~~that are~~ ^{which are} not known, clothed in his glorious
apparel, traveling in the greatness of his strength. ²⁷ & he
shall ~~put~~ ^{say} I am he ^{who spake} in righteousness, mighty to save.
= & the Lord shall be red ~~~~ in his apparel, & his gar-
ments like him that treadeth in the wine ^{vat} ~~fat~~ & so
great shall be th glory of his presence, that the Sun
shall hide his face in shame; & the moon shall ~~~~ ^{with hold its}
^{light}; ~~~~ & the stars shall be hurelled from their place;
~~~~ ²⁸ & his voice shall be heard, I have trodden the ~~~~
wine ~~~~ ^{press} alone, & have brought judgement upon all
people; & none ~~was~~ ^{were} with me; & I have trampelled
them in my fury, & I did tread upon them in mine
anger, & their blood have I sprinkled upon my garments, & ~~have~~ stained all my raiment; for this was the day
of vengeance which was in my heart. ²⁹ & now the year
of my redeemed is come, & they shall mention the loving
kindness of their Lord, & all that he ~~has~~ ^{has} bestowed upon
them, according to his goodness, & according to his loving
kindness, forever & ever, in all their affliction he was afflicted,
³⁰ & the angel of his presence saved them; & in his love, & in
his pity, he redeemed them, & ~~carried~~ ^{he} bear them & ~~~~ carryed
them all the days of old; yea, & Enoch also, & they ^{who}
were with him; the Prophets ~~which~~ ^{that} were before him
& Noah also, & they ~~which~~ ^{who} were before him, & ^{Moses)} ~~~~ also,
& they ~~which~~ ^{who} were before him, & from ~~Moses~~ to ~~Elijah~~
& from ~~Moses~~ ^{Elijah} to John, who were with Christ in his
resurrection, & the Holy Apostles, with Abraham, Isaac
& Jacob, shall be in the presence of the Lamb. ³¹ & the graves
of the saints shall be opened, & they shall come forth & stand
on the right hand of the Lamb, when he shall stand upon
mount Zion, & upon the Holy City, the New Jerusalem, ~~where~~
& they shall sing the Song of the lamb day & night for ever
& ever.— ³² & for this cause, that men might be ^{made} partakers
of the glories which were ^{to be} revealed, the Lord sent forth the
fullness of ~~the~~ ^{his} gospel, ~~the~~ ^{his} everlasting covenant,

died
²⁶⁸down from god in heavn with ~~thy~~ garments; yea,
                which are
from the regions ~~that is~~ not known, clothed in his gloriou[s]
                                                      27
appearl, travling in the greatness of his strength? & he
       say,   who spake²⁶⁹
shall ~~speak~~ I am he in righteousness, mighty to save.

& the Lord shall {re\be} read ~~read~~ in his appearl, & his garm
                                                      vat,
=ents like him that treadeth in the wine ~~path~~ {&\&} so

great shall be the glory {in\of} his presence, that the Sun
                                        with hold its
shall hide his face in shame; & the moon shall ~~be~~
     light;
~~blown out~~ & the Stars shall be hurrelled from their place
     28   :
~~sockets~~ & his voice shall be heard, I have trodden the ~~place²⁷⁰~~
     vat press
wine ~~press²⁷¹~~ alone, & have brought Judgement upon all
                    were
people; & none ~~was~~ with me; & I have trampelled

them in my fury, & I did tread upon them in mine

anger{;\,} & {◊\their} blood have I sprinkeled upon my garme

-nts, & ~~have~~ stained all my r{◊\⟨a⟩}iment: for this was the day
                                        29
of vengeance which was in my heart. & now the year

of my redeemed is come, & they shall mention the loveing
                                      has
kindness of their Lord; & all that he ~~hath~~ bestowed upon

them, according to his goodness, & according to his loving

kindness, forever & ever; in all their affliction he was afflicted.
30
& the angel of his presenc[e] saved them; & in his love, & in
                              he
his pity, he redeemed them, & ~~did~~ bear them & ~~did~~ carr{y\ied}
                                                    who
them all the days of old; yea, & Enoch also, & they ~~which~~
                              that
were with him; the Prophe{ts\ts} ~~which~~ were before him,
              who   ^   Moses
& Noah also, & they ~~which~~ were before him,◊²⁷² {◊\&}; ~~Elijah~~ also
        who   Mosses   Elijah,
& they ~~which~~ were before him, & from ~~Elijah~~ to ~~Moses~~
     Elijah
& from ~~Moses~~ to John, who were with Christ in his

resurrection, & the Holy Apostles, with Abraham, Isaac
                                                31
& Jacob, shall be in the presenc[e] of the lamb.²⁷³ & the graves

of the saints shall be opened, & they shall come forth & stand

on the right hand of the Lamb,²⁷⁴ when he shall stand upon
                              l
mount Zion, & upon the Hoy City, the New Jerusalem, ~~wherefo~~

& they shall sing the Song of the lamb day & night for ever
                                    made
& ever.— & for this cause, that men might be partakers
                    to be
of the glories which were revealed the Lord sent forth the
          his   ^ his
fullness of ~~the~~ gospel, & ~~the~~ everlasting covenant,

ORIGINAL INSCRIPTION
John Whitmer

REVISIONS
Oliver Cowdery
William W. Phelps
Sidney Rigdon
Joseph Smith
John Whitmer
Unidentified

267. The stem of the "9" is visible, but the rest of the numeral is missing because the corner of the leaf is torn.

268. This leaf, containing manuscript pages 119–120, was removed from the manuscript book at some point and is located at the Community of Christ Library-Archives.

269. Or "spoke".

270. "place" was inserted on the wrong line and then stricken. Because the edge of the leaf worn, the line endings are obscured, and both this insertion and the inserted "place" one line above may be "places".

271. Two layers of deletion: first layer by Sidney Rigdon and second layer by John Whitmer.

272. "◊" likely a punctuation mark.

273. Triple underlining beneath "l" wipe-erased.

274. "b" possibly retraced by a later scribe.

Reasoning in plainness, & simplicity, to prepare the weak for those things which are coming upon the earth; & for the Lords errand in the day when the weak should confound the wise & little one become a strong nation, & two shall put their tens of thousands to flight; & by the weak things of the Earth, the Lord shall thresh the Nations of the by the power of his Spirit. [& for this cause these commandments were given; they were commanded to be kept from the world in the day that they were given, but now are to go forth unto all flesh.] 33 & this according to the mind & will of the Lord, who reigneth over all flesh & unto him that repenteth & sanctifieth himself before the Lord shall be given eternal life, & they upon them that hasken not to the voice of the Lord, shall be fulfilled that which was written by the Prophet Moses, that they should be cut off from among the people. 34 & also that which was written by the Prophet, Malichi for Behold the day cometh that shall burn as an oven, & all the proud; & they that do yea, & all that do wickedly, shall be stubble; & the day that cometh shall burn them up with the Lord of hosts, that it shall leave them neither root nor branch. 35 wherefore this shall be the answer of the Lord unto them in that day when I came unto my own. no man among you received me, & you were driven out; when I called again there was none of you to answer, yet my arm was not shortened at all, that I could not redeem, neither my power to deliver; 36 Behold at my rebuke I dry up the Sea. I make the rivers a wilderness: their fish stinketh, & dieth for thirst. I Clothe the Heavens with blackness, & make sackcloth their covering; 37 & this shall ye have of my hand, ye shall lay down in sorrow. 38 Behold & lo there are none to deliver you, for ye obeyed not my voice, when I called unto you out of the Heavens, ye believed not my servants; & when they were sent unto you ye received them not; wherefore they sealed up the testimony & bound up the law, & ye were delivered over unto darkness: there shall go away into outer

²⁷⁵{r\R}eas[o]ning in plainness, & simplisity, to prepare the weak

for those things which are coming ~~upon~~ the earth: & for

weak should confound the wise;
the Lords E{rre\rrand} in the days when the & {◊◊\the} little one become

a strong nation, & two should put their tens of thousands

to flight; & by the weak things of the Earth, the Lord should

thresh the Nations²⁷⁶ ~~of the Earth~~ by the power of his spirit.

⌈²⁷⁷ & for this cause these commandments were given; they

were commanded to be kept from the world in the

that
day they were given, but now are to go forth unto all

33
flesh.⌉ & this according to the mind & ~~the~~ will of the Lord,

ruleth
who ~~reigneth of~~ over all flesh & unto him that repenteth

& sanctifieth himself before the Lord shall be given eternal

upon them
life. & ~~they~~ that harken not to the voice of the Lord, shall

be fulfilled that which was written by the Prophet

Moses, ~~& also~~²⁷⁸ that they should be cut off from among the

34
people. & also that which was written by the Prophet, M{◊\a}lichi{◊\e}²⁷⁹

shall burn
for Behold the day cometh that ~~burneth~~ as an Oven, & all

the proud; ~~& they that do~~ yea, & all that do wickedly, shall be

stuble; & the day that cometh shall burn them up saith the

Lord of hosts, that it shall l[e]ave them neither root nor

35
branch. wherefore this shall be the answer of the

unto them
Lord in that day when I come unto my own. no man

were
among you received me, & y{e\ou} ~~are~~ driven out. when I

called again there was none of you to answer, yet

my arm was not shortened at all, that I could not

36
redeem, neither my power to deliver. Behold at my

rebuke I dry up the Sea. {is\I}²⁸⁰ make the rivers a wild-

=erness: their fish stinketh, & dieth for thirst. I

Clothe the Heavens with blackness, & make sackloth

37   ye
their covering: & this shall have ~~at~~ of my hand, ye shall

in   ^38
l{ay\ie} down ~~with~~ sorrow. Behold & Lo there {is\are} none to deliver

voice,
you, for ye obeyed not my ~~voice~~ when I called ~~unto~~ you {all\out}

of the Heavens, ye believed not my Servants; & when they

were sent unto you ye received them not: wherefore they

sealed up the testimony & bound up the Law, & ye were

as over
delivered ~~up~~ unto darkness: these shall go away into outer

ORIGINAL INSCRIPTION
John Whitmer

REVISIONS
Oliver Cowdery
William W. Phelps
Sidney Rigdon
Joseph Smith
John Whitmer
Unidentified

275. This leaf, containing manuscript pages 119–120, was removed from the manuscript book at some point and is located at the Community of Christ Library-Archives. The leaf contains residue from an adhesive wafer on the top right corner, indicating that it was at one time attached to the following leaf.

276. "s" possibly inserted.

277. Similar brackets elsewhere in the manuscript book identify portions of the text that were to be changed or omitted before publication, especially in *The Evening and the Morning Star* and the 1835 Doctrine and Covenants. Although many redactions in this revelation, including these brackets, were made in preparation for publication of the Book of Commandments, this revelation was not printed therein because the printing office was destroyed in 1833. The phrase enclosed in these brackets is found in each version of this revelation printed in JS-era publications, but it may not have appeared in the Book of Commandments if this revelation had been printed in that volume.

278. "& also" wipe-erased and then stricken.

279. Final "◊" possibly ",", or "s".

280. Possibly "in".

darkness, where there is weeping, & wailing, & gnash
-ing of teeth. Behold the Lord your God hath spoken
it. AMEN

       Given In Hyrum Portage Co Ohio
       November 3rd 1831

73   Revelation

The Testimony of the witnesses to the Book of the Lords comm
-andments which he gave to his church through Joseph Smith jr
who was appointed by the voice of the Church for this purpose.
We the undersigners feel willing to bear testimony to all
the world of mankind to every creature upon the face of
all the Earth & upon the Islands of the Sea that god hath
born Record to our souls through the Holy Ghost shed forth
upon us that these commandments are given by inspiration
of God & are profitable for all men & are verily true we
give this testimony unto the world the Lord being our
helper & it is through the grace of God the father & his Son
Jesus Christ that we are permitted to have this privilege of
bearing this testimony unto the world in the which we rejoice
exceedingly praying the Lord always that the children of
men may be profited thereby   AMEN

                            Sidney Rigdon

Joshua Fairchild   Orson Hyde
Peter Dustin   Wm. E. McLellin
Newel Knight   Luke Johnson
Levi Hancock cause to be noted Lyman Johnson
Thomas B Marsh   Reynolds Cahoon
                         John Corrill
                         Parley P Pratt
                         Harvey Whitlock
                         Lyman Wight
                         John Murdock
                         Calvin Beebe
                         Zebedee Coltrin

281darkness, where there is weeping, & wailing, & gnash

-ing of theeth. Behold the Lord your God hath spoken

it. Amen.

Given In H{yr\iram}Portage Co Ohio

Novembr 3rd. 1831

♦ 73 Revelation282

The Testimony of the witnesses to the Book of the Lords comm

-andments which he gave to his church through Joseph Smith Jr

who was appointed by the v̶o̶s̶ ^voice^ of the Church for this purpose

We the undersigners feel willing to bear testimony to all

the world of mankind to every creature upon a̶ll̶ the face of

all the Earth ^&^ upon the Islands of the Sea that god hath b̶o̶r̶

born record to our souls through the Holy Ghost shed forth

upon us that these commandments are given by inspiratio{◊\n}

of God & are profitable for all men & are verily true we

give this testimony unto the world the Lord being m̶y̶ ^our^

helper & it is through the grace of God the father & his Son

Jesus Christ that we are permitted to have this privelege of

bearing this testimony unto the world in the which we rejoice

exceedingly b̶y̶ praying the Lord always that the children of

men may be p{◊◊\rofited} thereby Amen

Joshua Fairchild

Peter Dustin

Newel Knight

Levi Hancock; never to be eraised284

Thomas B Marsh

Sidney Rigdon283

Orson Hyde

Wm. E. Mc.l{l\el[l]in}

Luke Johnson

Lyman Johnson

Reynolds Cahoon

John Corrill

   Parley [P.] Pratt

Harv[e]y Whitlock

Lyman Wight

John Murdock

Calvin Beebe

Zebedee Coltrin

ORIGINAL INSCRIPTION
John Whitmer

REVISIONS
Oliver Cowdery
William W. Phelps
Sidney Rigdon
Joseph Smith
John Whitmer
Unidentified

281. Red adhesive wafers on the top and bottom left corners of this leaf attached it to the previous leaf. The leaves are now separated.

282. After manuscript pages 116–129 were inscribed, John Whitmer gave each item a number and supplied some items with generic titles. The ink flow suggests that he numbered and titled these items in one sitting. Because Whitmer inserted this title at a later time, it is unknown whether "Revelation" accurately reflects JS's or other early Saints' view of this item.

283. John Whitmer copied the signatures of Sidney Rigdon, Orson Hyde, William E. McLellin, Luke Johnson, and Lyman Johnson. The others appear to have signed the manuscript book themselves.

284. Or "era{◊\sed}" or "excised".

74

Hearken unto me saith the Lord for verily I say unto you, for my servant Oliver's sake, it is not wisdom in me, that he should be intrusted with the commandments & the moneys which he shall carry unto the Land of Zion, except one go with him, who will be true & faithfull; wherefore I the Lord willeth that my servant John (Whitmer) should go with my servant Oliver & also that he observe to continue in writing & makeing a history of all the important things which he shall observe & know, concerning my Church; & also that he receive counsil & assistance from my servant Oliver, & others, & also that my servants which are abroad in the Earth should send forth their accounts of their stewardships to the Land of Zion; for the Land of Zion shall be a seat & a place to receive & do all these things: nevertheless let my servant John travel many times, from place to place, & from Church to Church, that he may the more easily obtain knowledge; & Preaching & expounding, writing, copying, & selecting, & obtaing all things, which shall be for the good of the Church, & for the rising generations which shall grow up on the Land of Zion, to possess it from generation to generation, forever & ever, Amen.

75 A REVALATION given at Hiram Portage Co Nov 11th 1831

To the Church of Christ in the Land of Zion in addition to the Church Laws respecting Church business, verily I say unto you, saith the Lord of hosts there must needs be presiding Elders to preside over those who are of the office of an Elder; & also Priests over those who are of the office of a Priest; & also Teachers over those who are of the office of a Teacher, in like manner; & also the deacons; wherefore from deacon to Teacher, & from Teacher to Priest, & from Priest to Elder, severally as they are appointed according to the Church Articles & Covenants; then cometh the high Priesthood, which is the greatest of all; wherefore it must needs be that one be appointed of the high Priesthood to preside over the Priesthood, & he shall be called President of the high Priesthood of the Church; or in other words the Presiding high Priest over the high Priesthood of the Church; from the same cometh the administering of ordinances & blessings upon the Church by the laying on of the hands; wherefore the office of a Bishop is not equal unto it, for the office of a Bishop is in administering all temporal things; nevertheless a Bishop must be chosen from the high Priesthood, that he may be set apart unto the ministering of temporal things, having a knowledge of them by the Spirit of truth; & also to be a judge in Israel to do the business of the Church, to sit in judgement

Nov
◆ ²⁸⁵74²⁸⁶   Received on ^the· 11 of O̶c̶t̶ 1831 (N° 7)²⁸⁷

Hearken unto me saith the Lord, for verily I say unto

you, for my Servent Oliver [Cowdery]'s sake, it is not wisdom

in me, that he should be intrusted with the commandments

the
& moneys which he shall carry unto the Land of Zion,
^

except one go with him, who will be true & faithfull;

2
wherefore I the Lord willeth that my Servent John (Whitmer)
= Should
s̶h̶a̶l̶l̶ go with my servent Oliver· & also that he observe to
^   3

continue in writing & makeing a history of all the

important things which he shall observe & know, concerning

4
my Church; & also that he receive council & assistance

5   Servants
from my Servent Oliver, & others{;\.} & also that my S{◊◊◊\⟨ain⟩}ts
who   ^
w̶h̶i̶c̶h̶ are abroad in the Earth, should send forth their accounts
of ^their Stewardship, 6
to the Land of Zion; for the Land of Zion shall be a seat
^   =
7
& a place to receive & do all these things: nevertheless
                                         =

let my Servnt John travel many times, from place

to place, & from Church to Church, that he may the more

8
easily obtain knowledge; Preaching & expounding, writing

cop[y]ing, & selecting, & obtain[in]g all things, which shall be

for the good of the Church, & for the rising generations

which shall grow up on the Land of Zion, to possess

it from generation̶s̶ to generation{s\,} forever & ever. Amen.

◆ ²⁸⁸75²⁸⁹ # A Revelation given at Hiram Portage Co Nov 11ᵗʰ· 1831

²⁹⁰·To the Church of Christ in the Land of Zion in addition to the Church Laws
respecting Church business verily I say unto you, saith the Lord of hosts there
must needs be p̶{◊\r̶e̶s̶i̶d̶i̶n̶g̶}²⁹¹ presiding Elders to preside over th{em\ose} who are of the
office of an Elder: ⟨2⟩ & also Priests over th{em\ose} who are of the office of a Priest;
⟨3⟩ & also Teachers o{◊\ver} th{em\ose} who are of the office of a Teacher, in like manner.
⟨4⟩ And also the deacons; ⟨5⟩ wherefore from Deacon to Teacher, & from Teacher to Priest,
& from Priest to Elder; severally as they are appointed, according to the Church
Articles & Covenants: ⟨6⟩ {t\T}hen cometh the high Priest hood, which is the greatest
of all: ⟨7⟩ wherefore it must needs be that one be appointed of the high Priest
    hood to preside over the Priest hood: ⟨8⟩ & he shall be called President of the
-̶h̶o̶o̶d̶²⁹² high Priest hood of the Church; ⟨9⟩ or in o̶ other h̶i̶g̶h̶ words the Presiding
high Priest h̶o̶o̶d̶ over the high Priesthood of the Church; ⟨10⟩ from the same
cometh the administring of ordinances & blessings upon the Church,
by the Laying on of the hands: ⟨11⟩ wherefore the office of a Bishop is not equal
unto it; ⟨12⟩ for the office of a Bishop is in administering all t̶h̶i̶n̶g̶s̶ temporal
things: ⟨13⟩ nevertheless a Bishop must be c{h◊◊◊\hosen} from the high Priesthood, that
he may be set apart unto the ministering of temporal things, having a
knowledge of them by the Spirit of truth; ⟨14⟩ & also to be a Judge in
Israel to do the business of the Church, to sit d̶o̶w̶n̶²⁹³ in Judgement

ORIGINAL INSCRIPTION
John Whitmer

REVISIONS
Oliver Cowdery
William W. Phelps
Sidney Rigdon
Joseph Smith
John Whitmer
Unidentified

285. Although most redac-
tions in this revelation were
made in preparation for
publication of the Book of
Commandments, this revelation was not printed therein
because the printing office was
destroyed in 1833. The first
publication reflecting several
redactions in this revelation is
the 1835 Doctrine and
Covenants (section 28).

286. After manuscript pages
116–129 were inscribed, John
Whitmer gave each item a
number and supplied some
items with generic titles. The
ink flow suggests that he
numbered and titled these
items in one sitting.

287. For an explanation of
this numbering, see 159n196
herein.

288. Although most redac-
tions in this revelation were
made in preparation for
publication of the Book of
Commandments, this revelation was not printed therein
because the printing office was
destroyed in 1833.

289. After manuscript pages
116–129 were inscribed, John
Whitmer gave each item a
number and supplied some
items with generic titles. The
ink flow suggests that he
numbered and titled these
items in one sitting.

290. Interlinear insertions in
this section of the revelation
are transcribed in angle
brackets because the lines are
so close together.

291. "◊" wipe-erased and
written over; then whole word
stricken.

292. "-hood" was likely
meant as a continuation of
"Priest" two lines above.

293. "down" partially wipe-
erased and then stricken.

upon transgressors upon testimony as it shall be laid before them according to the Laws, by the assistance of his councillors whom he hath chosen or will choose among the Elders of the church, thus shall he be a judge even a common judge among the inhabitants of Zion, until the borders are enlarged, & it becomes necessary to have other bishops or judges, & inasmuch as there are other bishops appointed they shall act in the same office, again verily I say unto you, the most important business of the church, & the most difficult cases of the church, inasmuch as there is not sufficient satisfaction upon the decision of the judge, it shall be handed over & carried up unto the court of the church before the president of the high priesthood, & the president of the court of the high priesthood shall have power to call other high priests even twelve to assist as councillors, & thus the president of the high priesthood & his councillors shall have power to decide upon testimony according to the laws of the church, & after this decision it shall be had in remembrance no more before the Lord; for this is the highest court of the church of God & a final decision upon controversies that is not any person belonging to the church who is not exempt from this court of the church, & inasmuch as the president of the high priesthood shall transgress, he shall be had in remembrance before the Common court of the church, who shall be assisted by twelve councillors of the high priesthood, & their decision upon his head shall be an end of controversy concerning him; thus none shall be exempt from the justice & the Laws of God, that all things may be done in order, & in solemnity before me, according to truth & righteousness, Amen. A few more words in addition to the Laws of the church. And again, verily I say unto you, the duty of a president over the office of a Deacon is to preside over twelve Deacons, to set in council with them, & to teach them their duty, edifying one another as it is given according to the covenants. And also the duty of the president over the office of the Teachers, is to preside over twenty four of the Teachers, & to set in council with them, teaching them the duties of their office as given in the Covenants. Also the duty of the president over the priesthood, is to preside over forty eight priests, & to set in council with them, & to teach them the duties of their office, as given in the covenants. And again the duty of the president over the office of the Elders, is to preside over ninety six Elders, & to set in council with them, & to teach them according to the Covenants. And again the duty of the president of the office of the High Priesthood, is to preside over the whole Church, & to be like unto Moses, behold here is wisdom; yea, to be a Seer, a revelator, a translator, & a prophet, having all the gifts of God, which he bestoweth upon the head of the church; Wherefore now let every man learn his duty, & to act in the office in which he is appointed, in all diligence; he that is slothful shall not be counted worthy to stand, & he that learneth not his duty & sheweth himself not approved, shall not be counted worthy to stand, even so, Amen.

upon transgressors upon testimony ⟨as⟩ it shall be laid before ⟨him,⟩ ~~them~~ according
to the Laws, by the assistance of his ⟨^⟩ councillors whom he hath⟨^⟩ chosen or
will choose /²⁹⁴among the Elders of the church. ⟨15⟩ thus shall he be a judge even a ↵
    common judge among
the inhabitants of Zion until the borders are enlarged, & it becomes necessary to have ↵
    other Bishops
or judges. ⟨16⟩ & inasmuch as there are other Bishops appointed, they shall act in the same ↵
    office. ⟨17⟩ & again,
verily I say unto you, the most important business of the church, & the most difficult cases
of the church, inasmuch as there is not ~~sufficient~~ satisfaction upon the dec{s\ision} of the ↵
    judge, it
shall be handed over, & carried up unto the court of the church before the president of the high
Priesthood; ⟨18⟩ & the president of the Court of the high priesthood shall have power to call ↵
    other high
priests, even twelve to assist as counsellors, ⟨19⟩ & thus the president of the high priesthood, ↵
    & his coun
=cellors, shall have power to decide upon testimony, according to the laws of the church; ↵
    ⟨20⟩ & after this

²¹
desision it shall be had in remembrance no more before the Lord; for this is the highest court of
    there is not any
the church of God & a final desision upon controvers[i]es, ⟨~~there no~~⟩ all persons belonging ↵
    who is
      to the church ~~are not~~ exempt
    ^ ²²
from this court of the church: & inasmuch as the president of the high priesthood shall transgress,

he shall be had in remembrance before the common court of the church, who shall be assisted by

twelve counsellors of the high Priesthood, & their desicision upon his head shall be an end of
    ²³   &
controversy concerning him. thus none shall be exempt from the justice of the Laws of God,
      ^
that all things may be done in order, & in solemnity before me, {in\according} to truth & righteousness.
   ²⁴   ²⁵
Amen. A few more words in addition to the Laws of the church. And again, verily I say

unto you, the duty of a president over the office of a Deacon, is to preside over twelve Deacons,

to set in council with them, & to teach them their duty, edifying one another as it is
    ²⁶
given according to the covenants. And also the duty of the president over the office of the

Teachers, is to preside over twenty four of the Teachers, & to set in council with them, teaching them
    ²⁷
the duties of their office as given in the covenants. Also the duty of the president over the priest

=hood, is to preside over forty eight priests, & to set in council with them, & to teach them
    ²⁸
the duties of their office, as given in the covenants. And again the duty of the president over the
                        teach
office of the Elders, is to preside over ninety six Elders, & to set in council with them, & to ^
    2{8\9}
them according to the covenants. And again the duty of the president of the office of the
                        ³⁰
High Priesthood, is to preside over the whole church, & to be like unto Moses. behold
    ³¹
here is wisdom: yea, to be a Seer, a revelator, a translator, & a prophet, having
                      ³²
all the gifts of God, which he bestoweth upon the head of the chuch: Wherefore now

let every man learn his ~~duly~~ duty, & to act in the office in which he is appointed, in
          ³³
    all diligence. he that is slothful shall not be counted worthy to stand.
   ³⁴
    & he that learneth not his duty, & sheweth himself not approved, shall

    not be counted worthy to stand; even so: Amen. ✌

ORIGINAL INSCRIPTION
John Whitmer
Oliver Cowdery

REVISIONS
Oliver Cowdery
William W. Phelps
Sidney Rigdon
Joseph Smith
John Whitmer
Unidentified

294. John Whitmer hand-
writing ends; Oliver Cowdery
begins.

Revelation

76 Hiram Nov. 12. 1831

Behold & hearken, o ye inhabitants of Zion, & all ye people of my church, which are far off & hear the word of the Lord, which I give unto my servant Joseph, & also unto my servant Martin; & also unto my servant Oliver; & also unto my servant William; & also unto my servant John; & also unto my servant Sidney; by the way of commandment unto them, for I give unto them, a commandment: wherefore hearken & hear, for thus saith the Lord unto them, I the Lord have appointed them, & ordained them to be stewards over the revelations & commandments which I have given unto them, & which I shall hereafter give unto them, & an account of this stewardship will I require of them in the day of judgement: wherefore I have appointed unto them, & this is their business in the church of God, to manage them & the concerns thereof, yea the benefits thereof: wherefore a commandment I give unto them, that they shall not give these things unto the church, neither unto the world: nevertheless, inasmuch as they receive more than is needful for their necessities, & their wants, it shall be given into my storehouse, & the benefits thereof shall be consecrated unto the inhabitants of Zion, & unto their generations, inasmuch as they become heirs according to the laws of the kingdom: behold this is what the Lord requires of every man in his stewardship; even as I the Lord have appointed, or shall hereafter appoint unto any man, & behold none is exempt from this law, who belong to the church of the living God; yea, neither the bishop, neither the agent, who keepeth the Lords storehouse; neither he who is appointed in a stewardship over temporal things; he who is appointed to administer spiritual things, the same is worthy of his hire; even as those who are appointed to a stewardship to administer in temporal things; yea, even more abundantly which abundance is multiplied unto them through the manifestations of the spirit; nevertheless in your temporal things, you shall be equal, & this not grudgeingly, otherwise the abundance of the manifestations of the spirit shall be withheld. now this commandment I give unto my servants for their benefit while they remain, for a manifestations of my blessings upon their heads, & for a reward of their diligence, & for their security for food & for raiment; for an inheritance; for houses & for lands, in whatsoever circumstances I the Lord shall place them, & whithersoever I the Lord shall send them:

◆ 124 [verso] ²⁹⁶Revelation (Nº 5)²⁹⁵

²⁹⁷76²⁹⁸ Hiram Nov. 12. 1831

Behold & hearken, o ye inhabitants of Zion, & all ye people of my
off,²⁹⁹
Church, which are far ~~off~~ & hear the word of the Lord, which I give unto my

     2
servant Jos[e]ph; & also unto my servant Martin [Harris]; & also unto my servant ↵
     Oliver [Cowdery];

4   unto   5   ⟨6⟩ & also unto my servant William [W. Phelps]
& also my servant John [Whitmer]; & also unto my servant Sidney [Rigdon]; by the ↵
     way of com
                                                            h
=mandmen{ts\t} unto them, for I give unto them a commandment: Werefore

hearken & hear, for thus saith the Lord unto them, I the Lord have appointed

them, & ordained them to be stewards over the revelations & com-

=mandments which I have given unto them, & which I shall hereafter
          7
give unto them; & an account of this stewardship will I require of them
                    8
in the day of judgement: wherefore I have appointed unto them, & this is

their business in the church of God, to manage them & the concerns
     9   benefits   9
thereof, yea³⁰⁰ the ~~profits~~ thereof: wherefore a commandment I give unto

them, that they shall not give these things unto the church, neither unto
     10   needful
the world: nevertheless, inasmuch as they receive more than is for their

necessities, & their wants, it shall be given into my storehouse, & the

benefits thereof shall be consecrated unto the inhabtants of Zion, &

unto their generations, inasmuch as they become heirs according to the
                    11
laws of the kingdom. behold this is what the Lord requires of every

man in his stewardship; even as I the Lord have appointed, or shall
          p   any   12
hereafter apoint unto ~~any~~ man. & behold none is exempt from this
                         13   the
law, who belong to the church of the Living God; yea, neither Bishop, neither
                                        who
the agent, who keepeth the Lord's storehouse; neither he ~~that~~ is appointed
                         who
in a stewardship over temporal things; he ~~that~~ is appointed to ad=
                              those
minister spiritual things, the same is worthy of his hire; even as ~~they~~
          to
who are appointed ~~in~~ a stewardship to administer in temporal things;
14
yea even more abundantly which abundance is multiplied unto them
                         15
through the manifestations of the spirit.: nevertheless in your temporal
               16
things, you shall be equal; ~~in all things~~; & this not grudgeingly, otherwise

the abundance of the manifestations of the spirit, shall be withheld.
17   for their benefit
now this commandment I give unto my servants, while they remain, for

a manifestations of my blessings upon their heads, & for a reward of
               18
their diligence; & for their security for food & for raiment, for an

inheritance; for houses & for lands,³⁰¹ & in whatsoever circumstances

I the Lord shall place them, & {h\whithersoever} I the Lord shall send them:

ORIGINAL INSCRIPTION
Oliver Cowdery

REVISIONS
Oliver Cowdery
William W. Phelps
Sidney Rigdon
Joseph Smith
John Whitmer
Unidentified

295. For an explanation of this numbering, see 159n196 herein.

296. This leaf contains residue from adhesive wafers on the top and bottom right corners, indicating that it was at one time attached to the following leaf.

297. Although most redactions in this revelation were made in preparation for publication of the Book of Commandments, the first publication reflecting several of them is the 1835 Doctrine and Covenants (section 26). This revelation was not printed in the Book of Commandments because the printing office was destroyed in 1833.

298. After manuscript pages 116–129 were inscribed, John Whitmer gave each item a number and supplied some items with generic titles. The ink flow suggests that he numbered and titled these items in one sitting.

299. Oliver Cowdery's revisions throughout this revelation are possibly in the same ink flow as the original text, which would indicate that he made them at the time of original inscription.

300. Triple underlining beneath "y" wipe-erased.

301. "s" possibly inserted.

for they have been faithful over many things, & have done well ever much as they have not sinned. Behold I the Lord am merciful & will bless them & they shall enter into the joy of these things; even so Amen.

~~even so Amen~~ ~~now again verily I say unto you that~~ ~~William shall be included in this~~ ~~you in this~~

77 Revelation

Given in Hiram Novr 1st 1831

A Preface or instructions upon the Book of commandments which were given of the Lord unto this Church through him whom he appointed to this work by the voice of his Saints through the prayer of faith this church being organized according to the will of him who rules all things on the sixth day of April in the year of our Lord 1830.

Hearken O ye People of my Church saith the voice of him who dwells on high & whose eyes are upon all men, yea verily I say hearken ye People from afar & ye that are upon the Islands of the sea listen together for verily the voice of the Lord is unto all men & there is none to escape & there is no eye that shall not see neither ear that shall not hear neither heart that shall not be penetrated & the rebellious shall be pierced with much sorrow for their iniquities shall be spoken upon the house tops & their secret acts shall be revealed & the voice of warning shall be unto all people by the mouth of my Disciples whom I have chosen in these last days they shall go forth & none shall stay them for I the Lord have commanded them Behold this is mine authority & the authority of my servants & my preface unto the Book of my Commandments which I have given them to publish unto you O Inhabitants of the Earth wherefore fear & tremble O ye People for what I the Lord have decreed in them shall be fulfilled & verily I say unto you that they who go forth bearing these tidings unto the Inhabitants of the Earth to them is power given to seal both on earth & in heaven the unbelieving & rebellious yea verily to seal them up unto the day when the wrath of God shall be poured out upon the wicked without measure unto the day when the Lord shall come to recompense unto every man according to his works & measure to every man according to the measure which he has measured to his fellow man wherefore the voice of the Lord ~~unto~~ ~~his fellow~~ unto the end of the Earth that all that will

19
[302]for they have been faithful over many things, & have done well

20
inas much as they have not sin[n]ed. behold I the Lord am merciful

& will bless them & they shall enter into the joy of these things;
even so: Amen.
~~even so Amen and again verily I say unto you that my~~

~~servant William shall be included in this commandment with~~

~~you in this same stewardship even so Amen~~[303]

♦ 77   Revelation[304]

/[305]Given in Hiram Nov.^m 1.st 1831

A Preface or instructions upon the Book of Commandments which

were given of the Lord unto his Church through him whom he appoin

=ted to this work by the voice of his Saints through the prayer of faith

this church being organized according to the will of him who rules all

things on the Sixth day of April in the year of our Lord 1830 ↩

Hearken O ye {~~Chure~~\People} of my Church saith the voice of him who

dwells on high & whose eyes are upon all men yea verily I say hearken

ye People from afar & ye[306] that are upon the Islands of the sea listen

to gether for verily the voice of the Lord is unto all men & there is

none to escape & there is no eye that shall not see neither ear that

shall not hear neither heart that shall not be penetrated & the rebelious

shall be pier{~~d~~\ced} with much sorrow for their iniquities shall be spoken

upon the house tops & their seceret acts shall be revealed & the voice

of warning shall be unto all people by the mouth of my Deciples

whom I have chosen in these last days they shall go forth & none

shall stay them for I the Lord have commanded them Behold this is

mine authorit{~~t~~\y} & the authority of my servents & my preface unto the

Book of my Commandments which I have given them to Publish unto you

O Inhabitants of the Earth wherefore fear & tremble O ye People for what

I the Lord have decreed in them shall be fulfilled & verily I say unto

you that they who go forth bearing these tidings unto the Inhabitants of

the Earth to them is power given to seal both on Earth & in Heaven the

unbelieveing & rebelious yea verily to seal them up unto the day when

the wrath of God shall be poured out upon the wicked without measure

unto the day when the Lord shall come to recompence unto every man

according to his works & measure to every man according to the measure

which he has measured to his fellow man wherefore the voice of the Lord

is unto ~~his fellow man~~ unto the end of the Earth that all that will

Original Inscription
Oliver Cowdery
John Whitmer

Revisions
Oliver Cowdery
William W. Phelps
Sidney Rigdon
Joseph Smith
John Whitmer
Unidentified

302. This leaf is connected to the sixth gathering. Red adhesive wafers on the top and bottom left corners of this leaf formerly attached it to the previous leaf, which was cut or torn from the manuscript book and is no longer connected to the original binding.

303. Portions of this line and the preceding one were deleted a second time by an unidentified scribe.

304. After manuscript pages 116–129 were inscribed, John Whitmer gave each item a number and supplied some items with generic titles. The ink flow suggests that he numbered and titled these items in one sitting.

305. Oliver Cowdery handwriting ends; John Whitmer begins.

306. Or "yet".

ears may hear prepare ye prepare ye for that which is to come for the Lord is nigh & the anger of the Lord is kindled & his sword is bathed in heaven & it shall fall upon the inhabitants of the Earth & the arm of the Lord shall be revealed & the day cometh that they who will not hear the voice of the Lord neither his servants neither give heed to the words of the Prophets & Apostles shall be cut off from among the People for they have strayed from mine ordinances & have broken mine everlasting Coven= ant they seek not the Lord to establish his righteousness but every man walketh in his own way & after the ~~~~~ Image of his own God whose Image is in the likeness of the world & whose substance is that of an Idol which waxeth old & shall perish in Babylon even Babylon the great. which shall fall wherefore I the Lord knowing the calamity which should come upon the inhabitants of the Earth called upon my Servant Joseph & spake unto him from heaven & gave him commandment & also gave commandment to others that they should proclaim these things unto the world & all this that it might be fulfilled which was written by the Prophets the weak things of the world should come forth & break down the mighty & strong ones that man should not counsel his fellow man neither trust in the arm of flesh but that every man might speak in the name of God the Lord even the Saviour of the world that faith also might increase in the Earth that mine everlasting Covenant might be established that the fullness of my gospel might be proclaimed by the weak & the simple unto the ends of the world & before kings & Rulers Behold I am God & have spoken it these ~~ commandments are of me & were given unto my Servants in their weakness after the manner of their language that they might come to understanding & in as much as they erred it might be made known & in as much as they sought wisdom it might be ~~ ~~~~~ instructed & in as much as they sinned they might be chastened that they might repent & in as much as they were humble they might be made strong & blessed from on high & receive knowledge from time to time. After they having received the record of the Nephites yea even my Servant Joseph might have power to translate through the mercy of God by the power of the Book of Mormon & also those to whom these commandments were given might have power to lay the foundation of this Church & to bring it forth out of obscurity & out of darkness the only true & living Church upon the face of the whole Earth with which I

126 [verso]

hear may hear prepare ye prepare ye for that which is to come for

the Lord is nigh & the anger of the Lord is kindled & his sword is bathed in

heaven & it shall fall upon the inhabitants of the {ᴇ\Earth} & the arm of the

Lord shall be revealled & the day cometh that they who will not hear the

voice of the Lord neither his servants neith[er] give heed to the words of the

Prophets & Apostles shall be cut off from among the People for they

have strayed from mine ordinances & have broken mine everlasting Coven

=ant they seek not the Lord to establish his righteousness but every man

walketh in his own way & after the ~~imge~~ Image of his own God

whose Image is in the likeness of the world & whose substance is that

of an Idol which waxeth old & shall perish in Babylon even Babylon

the great, which shall fall wherefore I the Lord knowing the calamity

which should come upon the inhabitants of the Earth called upon my

Servents Joseph & spake[307] unto him from heaven & gave him commandment

& also {&\gave} commandments to others that they should proclaim these things

unto the world & all this that it might be fulfilled which was written by

the Prophets the w{a\eak} things of the world should come forth & break

down the mighty & strong ones that m{e\⟨a⟩}n should not council his fellow

man neither trust in the arm of flesh but that every man might

Speak in the name of God the Lord even the Saveiour of the world

that faith also might in{~~crease~~\crease} in the Earth that mine everlasting

Covenant might be established that the fullness of my Gospel might

be proclaimed by the weak & the Simple unto the ends of the world

& before kings & Rulers Behold I am God & have spoken it these ~~are~~

commandments are of me & were given unto my Servents in their weakness

after the manner of their Language that they might come to understanding

& in as much as they erred it might be made known & in as much as they

sought wisdom it might be ~~made known~~ instructed & in as much

as they sinned they might be chastened that they might repent & in as

much as they were humble they might be made strong & ble{~~st~~\ssed} from

on high & receive knowledge from time to time After they having

received the record of the Nephites yea even my Serv{e\⟨a⟩}nt Joseph might have

power to translate through the mercy of God by the power of the

Book of {m\⟨M⟩}ormon & also those to whom these commandments

were given might have power to lay the foundation of this Church

& to bring it forth out of obscurity & out of darkness the only true

& living Church upon the face of the whole Earth with which I

ORIGINAL INSCRIPTION
John Whitmer

REVISIONS
Oliver Cowdery
William W. Phelps
Sidney Rigdon
Joseph Smith
John Whitmer
Unidentified

307. Or "spoke".

the Lord am well pleased speaking unto the Church collectively & not individually for I the Lord cannot look upon sin with the least degree of allowance nevertheless he that repenteth & doeth the commandments of the Lord shall be forgiven & he that repenteth not from him shall be taken even the light which he has received for my spirit shall not always strive with man saith the Lord of hosts & again verily I say unto you O inhabitants of the earth for I the Lord am willing to make these things known unto all flesh for I am no respecter to persons & willeth that all men shall know that the day speedily cometh the hour is not yet but is nigh at hand when peace shall be taken from the earth & the Devil shall have power over his own dominion & also the Lord shall have power over his saints & shall reign in their midst & shall come down in judgement upon Idumea (or the World) search these commandments for they are true & faithfull & the Prophecies & promises which are in them shall all be fulfilled what I the Lord have spoken I have spoken & I excuse not myself & though the heaven & the earth pass away my word shall not pass away but shall all be fulfilled whether by mine own voice or by the voice of my servants it is the same for Behold & lo the Lord is God & the Spirit beareth Record & the is true & the truth abideth for ever & ever AMEN

127 [recto]

the Lord am well pleased speaking unto the Church collectively & not

individually for I the Lord cannot look upon sin with the least degree

of allowance nevertheless he that repenteth & doeth the commandments of

the Lord shall be forgiven & he that repenteth not from him shall be

taken even the light which h{◊s\e} has received for my spirit shall not

always strive with man saith the Lord of hosts & again verily I say unto

you O inhabitants of the Earth for I the Lord am willing to make

these things known unto all {◊◊\flesh} for I am no respector to persons

& willeth that all men shall know that the day speedily cometh the hour

is not yet but is nigh at hand when peace shall be taken from the

Earth & the Devil shall have power {◊\over} his own dominion & also the

Lord shall have power over his saints & shall reign in their midst & shall

come down in Judgement upon Idumea (or the World) search these com

=mandments for they are true & faithfull & the Prophecies & promises

which are in them shall all be fulf{l\illed} what I the Lord have spoken

I have spoken & I excuse not myself & though the Heaven & ^the^ Earth

pass away my word shall not pass away but shall all be fulfilled

whether by mine own voice or by the voice of my Serv{◊\⟨a⟩}nts it is the

same for Behold & Lo the Lord is God & the Spirit beareth record & the

is true & the truth abideth for ever & ever Amen[308]

ORIGINAL INSCRIPTION
John Whitmer

REVISIONS
Oliver Cowdery
William W. Phelps
Sidney Rigdon
Joseph Smith
John Whitmer
Unidentified

308. There are two small holes near the bottom of this page. (See 229n313 herein.)

Revelation [Not to be published now]

Independence Jackson County Missouri April 26, 1832

Verily Verily I say unto you my servants that inasmuch as
ye have forgiven one another your trespasses even so I the
Lord forgive you nevertheless there are those among you who
have sinned exceedingly yea even all of you have sinned but
verily I say unto you beware from henceforth & refrain from
sin lest sore judgements fall upon your heads for unto
whom much is given much is required & he who sinneth
against the greater light shall receive the greater condemna-
-tion ye call upon my name for revelations & I give them
unto you & inasmuch as ye keep not my sayings which I give
unto you ye become transgressors & justice & Judgement is
the penalty which is affixed unto my law therefore what I
say unto one I say unto all watch for the adversary spreadeth
his dominions & darkness reigneth & the anger of God kindleth
against the inhabitants of the Earth & none doeth good for all
have gone out of the way & now verily I say unto you I the
Lord will not lay any sin to your charge go your ways & sin
no more but unto that soul who sinneth shall the former
sins return saith the Lord your God. And again I say unto
you I give unto you a new commandment that you may
understand my will concerning you or in other words I give
unto you directions how you may act before me that
it may turn to you for your salvation, I the Lord am bound
when ye do what I say but when ye do not what I say
ye have no promise therefore verily I say unto you it is exp-
-edient for you my servants Edward & Newel Sidney Gilbert &
Sidney Rigdon & my servant Joseph & John & Oliver &
William & Martin be bound together by a bond & Covenant
-ment that cannot be broken in your several Stewardships to
manage the literary & Mercantile concerns & the Bishoprick
both in the Land of Zion & in the Land of Kirtland for I
have consecrated the land of Kirtland in mine own due
time for the benefit of the saints of the most high God
& for a stake to Zion for Zion must increase in beauty
& in holiness her borders must be enlarged

◆ 78   Revelation[309] [Not to be published now][310]

128 [verso]

Independence Jackson County Missori {a\April} 2{6\6}. 1832

Verily Verily I say unto you my Servents that inasmuch as

ye have forgiven one another your tresspasses even so I the

Lord forgive you nevertheless there are those among you who

have sinned exceedingly yea even all of you have sinned but

Verily I say unto you beware from henceforth & refrain from

sin lest sore Judgements fall upon your heads for unto

whom much is given much is required & he who sinneth

against the greater light shall receive the greater condemna=

=tion ye call upon my name for revelations & I {J\give} them

unto you & inasmuch as ye keep not my sayings which I give

unto you ye become[311] transgressors & Justice & Judgement is

the panalty which is affixed unto my law therefore what I

say unto one I say unto all watch for the advisary spreadeth

his dominions & darkness reigneth & the anger of God kindleth

against the inhabitants of the Earth & none doeth good for all

have gone out of the way & now verily I say unto you I the

Lord will not lay any sin to your charge go your ways & Sin

no more but unto that soul who sin[n]eth shall the former

sins return saith the Lord your God. And again I say unto

you I give unto you a new commandment that you may

understand my will concerning you or in other words I give

unto you directions how you may act before me that

it may turn to you for your salvation, I the Lord am bound

when ye do what I say but when ye do not what I say

ye have no promise*[312] therefore verily I say unto you it is exp=

=edient for you my Serv{◊\⟨a⟩}nts Edward [Partridge] & Newel [K. Whitney] Sidney ↵
Gilbert &

Sidney Rigdon & my Servant Joseph & John [Whitmer] & Oliver [Cowdery] &

William [W. Phelps] & Martin [Harris] be bound together by a bond & Coven~~ant~~

=nant that cannot be broken in your several Stewartships to

manage the literary & Mercantile[313] concerns & the Bishoprick~~s~~

both in the Land of Zion & in the Land of Kirtland for I

have consecrated the land of Kirtland in mine own due

time for the benefi{ts\t} of the Saints of the most high ~~God~~

& for a stake to Zion for Zion must increase in beauty

& in holy-ness her {◊\borders} must ~~increase~~ be enlarged

ORIGINAL INSCRIPTION
John Whitmer

REVISIONS
Oliver Cowdery
William W. Phelps
Sidney Rigdon
Joseph Smith
John Whitmer
Unidentified

309. After manuscript pages 116–129 were inscribed, John Whitmer gave each item a number and supplied some items with generic titles. The ink flow suggests that he numbered and titled these items in one sitting.

310. This revelation was first published in the 1835 Doctrine and Covenants (section 86).

311. Or "became".

312. The 1835 Doctrine and Covenants uses code words for ten proper nouns found between this asterisk and an asterisk on the following page. The asterisks are likely part of a key used by copyists or typesetters to include these code words in publication.

313. There are two small holes near "Mercantile", suggesting that a slip of paper was pinned to the page. The slip may have contained editorial corrections keyed to the asterisks inserted on this page and the following page.

her stakes must be strengthened yea verily I say unto you
Zion must arise & put on her beautyful garments
Therefore I give unto you this commandment that ye bind
yourselves by this covenant & it shall be done according
to the Laws of the Land behold here is wisdom also in
in me for your good & you are to be equal as in
other words you are to have equal claims on the proparties
for the benefit of managing the concerns of your stew
-ardship every man according to his wants & his needs ina
much as his wants are just & all this for the benefit
of the Church of the living god that every man my improve
upon his tallents that he may gain other tallents yea even
an hundred fold to be cast into the Lords Storehouse &
become the common property of the whole Church
every man seeking the interest of his neighbour & doing all
things with an eye single to the glory of god this order I have
appointed to be an everlasting order unto you & unto your successor
inasmuch as you sin not & the soul that sins against this
covenant & hardeneth his heart against it shall be
dealt with according to the laws of my Church &
shall be delivered over to the buffetings of Satan until the
day of Redemption And now verily I say unto you &
this is wisdom make unto yourselves friends with the
mammon of unrighteness & they will not destroy you leave
judgement alone with me for it is mine & I will repay
Peace be with you my blessings continue with you for
even yet the kingdom is yours & shall be forever if ye
fall not from your steadfastness even so Amen

Section LXXXVII

79 ☩ REVELATION

given at Amherst in conference assembled to
the Elders January 1832.

1 Verily, verily I say unto you, who speak even by the
voice of my spirit; even alpha & omega, your Lord &
your God; Hearken, O ye who have given your names
to go forth to proclaim my Gospel, & to prune my

³¹⁵her stakes must {in\be} strengthened yea {I\verily} I say unto you

Zion must arise & put on her beautyful garments

Therefore I give unto you this commandment that ye bind

yourselves by this covenant & it shall be done according

to the Laws of the Land,*³¹⁶ behold here is wisdom also ~~in~~

in me for your {G\good} & you~~r~~ are to be {ꝕ\equal} or in

other words you are to have equal claims on the properties

for the benefi~~ts~~ of managing the concerns of your stew-

=ar{t\d}ship every man according to his wants & his needs inas

=much as his wants are Just & all this for the benefit

of the Church of the living God that every man may improve

upon his tallent~~s~~ that h{y\e} may gain other tallents yea even

an hundred fold to be cast into the Lords Storehouse to

become the common property of the whole ~~conduct~~ Churc[h]

every man seeking the interest of his neighbour & doing al[l]

                             order³¹⁷

things with an eye single to the glory of God this ~~firm~~ I have
  appointed   order

to be an everlasting ~~firm~~ unto you & unto your Successor◊³¹⁸

inasmuch as you sin not & the soul that sins against th[e]

covenant & ~~holdeth~~ hardeneth his heart against it shall be

dealt with according ~~according~~ to the laws of my Church &

shall be delivered over to the buffitings of Satan untill the

day of Redemtion And now verily I say unto you &

this is wisdom make unto yourselves friends with the ~~mam~~

mamon of unrightness & they will not destroy you leave

Judgement alone with me for it is mine & I will repay

Peace be with you my blessings continue with you for

even yet the kingdom is yours & shall be forever if ye

fall not from your Steadfastness even so Amen

♦ 79 A Revelation³²⁰   ³¹⁹Section LXXXVII

      given at ~~Amherst in a conference held there to~~

      ~~ten Elders.~~ January 25. 1832.——

1 Verily, Verily I say~~u~~ unto you, I who speak even by the ~~Spirit~~

voice of my Spirit; even alpha & omega, your Lord &

       ²

your God: Hearken, {o\O} ye who have given your names³²¹

to go forth to proclaim my Gospel, & to prune my [v]in[e]y[ard]³²²

ORIGINAL INSCRIPTION
John Whitmer

REVISIONS
Oliver Cowdery
William W. Phelps
Sidney Rigdon
Joseph Smith
John Whitmer
Unidentified

314. The stem of the "9" is visible, but the rest of the numeral is missing because the corner of the leaf is torn.

315. The remainder of this revelation is crossed out with a large X in graphite and red grease pencil.

316. Between this asterisk and an asterisk on the previous page, there are ten code words in the 1835 Doctrine and Covenants. The asterisks are likely part of a key used by copyists or typesetters to include these code words in publication.

317. The first publication reflecting this revision and the two revisions on the next line is the 1835 Doctrine and Covenants.

318. Final character possibly "s", "&", or an overextended ink mark; line ending obscured by a badly worn edge.

319. This revelation was not printed in the Book of Commandments because the printing office was destroyed in 1833. A few redactions, including the insertion of paragraph markers and surnames, were likely made for publication in the 1835 Doctrine and Covenants, where most redactions in this revelation first appear (section 87).

320. See 205n260 herein.

321. Possibly a comma following "names"; line ending obscured by a badly worn edge.

322. William W. Phelps likely added punctuation following this word because Phelps inserted triple underlining and a verse number on the top of the following page. The corner of the leaf is worn, making it impossible to definitively identify the punctuation.

3 Behold I say unto you, that it is my will that you should
go forth & not tarry, neither be idle, but labour with your might
—in lifting up your voices as with the sound of a trump proclai=
=ming the truth according to the revelations & commandments which
I have given you, 4 & thus if ye are faithful ye shall be laden
with many sheaves, & crowned with honor, & glory, & immortality,
& eternal life: 5 Therefore verily I say unto my servant William
E. McLellin I revoke the commission which I gave unto him, to go into
the eastern countries, & I give unto him a new commission
& a new commandment, in the which I the Lord chasteneth
him for the murmurings of his heart; & he sinned, nevertheless
I forgive him & say unto him again, go ye into the south
countries; 6 & let my servant Luke Johnson go with him & proclaim
the things which I have commanded them, calling on the name
of the Lord for the comforter, which shall teach them all
things that is expedient for them, 7 praying always that they
faint not; & in as much as they do this, I will be with them
even unto the end. 8 Behold this is the will of the Lord your
God concerning you; even so: amen.

9 And again, verily thus saith the Lord, let my servant Orson
Hyde & my servant Samuel H. Smith take their journey into the eastern
countries, & proclaim the things which I have commanded
them; 10 & in as much as they are faithful, I will be with them
even unto the end. 11 And again verily I say unto my servant
Lyman Johnson & unto my servant Orson Pratt, they shall also
take their journey into the eastern countries; 12 & behold & lo!
I am with them also, even unto the end.
13 And again I say unto my servant Asa Dodds & unto my servant
Calvin Wilson; that they also shall take their journey into the
western countries, & proclaim my Gospel even as I have
commanded them. 14 & he who is faithful shall overcome
all things, & shall be lifted up at the last day.
15 And again, I say unto my servant Major N. Ashley & my
servant Burr Riggs let them take their journey also into the south
countries: 16 yea, let all these take their journeys as I have
commanded them, going from house to house, & from
village to village, & from city to city; 17 & in whatsoever

130 [verso]
³²³3 Behold I say unto you, that it is my will that your should

go forth & not tarry, neither be Idle, but labour with your migh

=ts lifting up your voices as with the sound of a trump proclai=

=ming the truth according to the revelations & commandments which

I have given you. ⁴& thus if ye are faithful ye shall be laden

with many sheaves, & crowned with honor, & glory, & immortallity,

{5\#¶}
& eternal life: Therefore verily I say unto my Servant William, (E)
E McLellin
I revoke the commission which I {◊◊\gave} unto him, to go unto
^
the eastern Countries, & I give unto him a new commission

& a new commandment, in the which I the Lord chaste{◊\⟨n⟩}eth

him for the murm{e\u}rmings of his heart; & he sinned, nevertheless

I forgive him & say unto him, again, go ye {u\⟨i⟩}nto the south
⁶   Johnson
countrie{s\s}; & let my servent Luke go with him & proclaim
^
the things which I have commanded them, calling on the name

of the Lord for the comforter, which shall teach them all

things that is expedient for them, praying always that they
⁷
faint not; & in asmuch as they do this, I will be with them
⁸
even unto the end. Behold this is the will of the Lord your

God concerning ~~them~~ you; even so: amen.
{9\#¶}
And again, verily thus saith the Lord, let my servent Orson
a   H Smith   Journey
(H)yde & my Servnt Samuel, {th\take} their into the Eastern
^   ^   ^
countries, & proclaim the things which I have command{◊de\ed}
1{◊\◊}³²⁴   1o
them; & in as much as they are faithful, I will be with them
^
even unto the end. And again verily I say unto my servant
Johnson
Lyman (J) & unto my Servant Orson, Pratt——³²⁵ they shall also
^
take their Journey into the eastern countries: & behold & Lo:
¹²
I am with them also, even unto the end.
13   Dodds
And again I say unto my servant Asa & unto my Servant
Wil{lso\son}   ^
Ca{rl\lves}, that they also shall take their Journey unto the

western countries, & proclaim my Gospel even as I have
¹⁴
commanded them. & he who is faithful shall overcome

all things, & shall be lifted up at the last day.
15   N. Ashley
And again, I say unto my Servant Major, & ~~unto~~ my
Riggs   let them   ^
servant Burr{\⟨⟩} take their Journey also unto the south
^
countr{y\ies}: yea, let all these take their Journeys as I have
¹⁶
commanded them, going from house to house, & from
¹⁷
Vil[la]ge to Village, & from Citty to Cit{t\y}{;\;} & in whatsoever

ORIGINAL INSCRIPTION
John Whitmer

REVISIONS
Oliver Cowdery
William W. Phelps
Sidney Rigdon
Joseph Smith
John Whitmer
Unidentified

323. The right side of the page contains residue from three adhesive wafers on the upper, middle, and lower portions, indicating where it was attached to the following leaf. The two leaves are still attached at the lower right corner of this page. The reason for attaching the leaves is unknown.

324. "◊" possibly "9" or "1".

325. "Pratt" is circled. This mark was likely made for publication in the Book of Commandments as an instruction to shorten or eliminate the last name. (See 175nn213–214 herein.)

House ye enter, & they receive you, leave your blessing
upon that house; & in whatsoever house ye enter, & they
receive you not ye shall depart speedily from that house,
& shake off the dust of your feet as a testimony against
them; & you shall be filled with joy & gladness & know
this, that in the day of judgement you shall be judges of
that house, & condemn them; & it shall be more tolerable for the heathen in the day of judgment, than for that
house; therefore gird up your loins & be faithful & ye shall
overcome all things & be lifted up at the last day;
even so: Amen.

Another Revelation Received at the same time & place

Connect #1

And again verily I say unto you thus saith the Lord unto you, O ye elders of my church, who have given your names
that you might know his will concerning
you: Behold I say unto you that it is the duty of the Church to
assist in supporting the families of those, & also to support
the families of those who are called & must needs assunt
unto the world to proclaim the Gospel unto the world; &
I the Lord give unto you this commandment, that ye obtain
places for your families in as much as your brethren are
willing to open their hearts; & let all such as can obtain
places for their families, & support of the Church for them,
not fail to go into the world; whether to the East, or to the
West, or to the North, or to the South, let them ask & they
shall receive; knock & it shall be opened unto them, & made
known from on high, even by the Comforter, whither they
shall go. & again verily I say unto you that every man
who is obliged to provide for his own family, let him provide & he shall in no wise loose his crown; & let him
labour in the Church. let every man be dilligent in all
things. & the Idler shall not have place in the Church
except he repents & mends his ways. Wherefore let my
servant Simeon Carter & my servant Emer Harris be united in the
ministry. & also my servant Ezra Thayre

[326]House ye enter, & they receive you, leave your blessings

[18] upon that house; & in whatsoever house ye enter, & they

receive you not ye shall depart speedily from that house,

& shake off the dust of your feet as a testimony against

[19] them: & you shall be filled with Joy & gladness & know

this, that in the day of Judgement you shall be Judges of

that house, & condemn them; & it shall be more tolerab

=le for the heathen in the day of Judgment, than for that

[20] house: therefore gird up your loins & be faithful & ye shall

overcome all things & be lifted up at the last day;

even So: Amen.——

Connected

Another Revelation Received at the same time[327]

#¶ & place

[21] And again verily I say unto you thus saith the Lord unto

you, O ye elders of my Church, who have given your names

that ye m{ay\ight} know you might know his will concerning

[22] you: Behold I say unto you that it is the duty of the Church to

assist in supporting the families of those, & also to supp[or]t[328]

the families of those who are called & must needs [be sent]

[23]
unto the world to proclaim the Gospel unto the wor[ld. wherefore]

I the Lord give unto you this commandment, that ye obtain

places for your families in as much as your brethren are

[24] willing to open their hearts; & let all such as can obtain

places for their famili{s\es}, & support of the Church for them,

[25] not fail to go into the world; whether to the East, or to the

west, or to the North, or to the South, let them ask & they

shall receive; knock & it shall be opened unto them, & made

known from on high, even by the comforter, whither they

[26] #¶
shall go. & again verily I say unto you that every man

who is obliged to provide for his own family, let him pro

crown; [27]
=vide & he shall in no wise loose his reward & let him

[28] labour in the Church. let every man be dilligent in all

[29] things. & the Idler shall not have place in the Church,

except he repents & mends his ways. Wherefore let my

Carter   Harris
servnts Simeon, & my Servant Emer, be united in the

[29]   Thayre [Thayer] B. Mar[sh]
ministery. & also my Servant Ezra, & my Servant Thomas

ORIGINAL INSCRIPTION
John Whitmer

REVISIONS
Oliver Cowdery
William W. Phelps
Sidney Rigdon
Joseph Smith
John Whitmer
Unidentified

326. The left side of the page contains three adhesive wafers on the upper, middle, and lower portions, indicating where it was attached to the previous leaf. The two leaves are still attached at the lower left corner of this page. The reason for attaching the leaves is unknown.

327. Two layers of deletion: first layer in ink by William W. Phelps and second layer in red grease pencil by an unidentified scribe. The first layer appears to have been done in preparation for the Book of Commandments and the second layer for the 1835 Doctrine and Covenants. Both layers seem to be an attempt to join the two revelations.

328. Reconstruction of this line and the following two lines is based on other versions of this revelation. Reconstruction of the verse number and punctuation after "world" is based on William W. Phelps's surrounding versification and punctuation. Portions of the redacted punctuation mark are visible, indicating that it was likely a period rather than a semicolon or a comma.

also my servant Hiram [Smith] & my servant Reynolds [Cahoon] & also my servant Daniel [Stanton] & my servant Seymaur [Brunson] & also my servant Silvester [Smith] & my servant Gideon [Carter] & also my servant Ruggles [Eames] & my servant Stephen [Burnett] & also my servant Micah, [B. Welton] & also my servant Eden [Smith] him so amen

80 A REVELATION received in Zion Apr 30, 1832

Verily thus saith the Lord in addition to the laws of the Church concerning women & children [those] who belong to the Church who have lost their husbands or fathers women have claim on their husbands untill they are taken & if they are not found transgressors they remain upon their inheritances all children have claim upon their parents untill they are of age & after that they have claim upon the Church or in other words the Lords storehouse for inheritances.

81 A REVELATION Rec'd in Kirtland December 4, 1831 the Appointment of Bishop his duty &c

Hearken & listen to the voice of the Lord, O ye who have assembled yourselves together who are the High Priests of [my] Church & the Kingdom & Power have been given for verily thus saith the Lord it is expedient in me for a Bishop to be appointed unto you of you unto the Church in this part of the Lords vineyard & verily in this thing ye have done wisely for it is required of the Lord at the hand of every Steward to render an account of his stewardship both in time & in eternity for he who is faithfull & wise in time is accounted worthy to inherit the mantions prepared for them of my father verily I say unto you the Elders of the Church in this part of my vineyard shall render an account of their stewardship unto the Bishop which shall be appointed unto of me, in this part of my vineyard these things shall be had on record to be handed over unto the Bishop in Zion & the duty of the Bishop shall be made known by the commandments which have been given & by the voice of the conference & now I say unto you my servant Newel (Whitney) is the man who shall be appointed & ordained unto this power this is the will of [verily] & amen

132 [verso]

                              Smith   Cahoon 31
³²⁹30   also my Servant Hiram [Hyrum], & my Servant Reynolds; &
                    Stanton   Brunson
also my servant Dani{l\el}, & my Servant Seymour; ⟨32⟩ & also
                    Smith   Carter
my servant Silvester [Sylvester], & my servant Gideon; ⟨33⟩ & also my
                Eames   ^   Burnett
Servant Rug{l\gles}, & my Servant Stephen; ⟨34⟩ & also my
              B. Welton   Smith
Servant Micah, & also my Servant Eden; even so: amen—
                              ^

♦ ³³⁰80   **A Revelation** Received in Zion Apr 30, 1832

X   Verily thus saith the Lord in adition to the laws of the
                                            those
Church concerning women & children, who bel{l\ong} {if\to} the
                                    ^
Church who have lost their husbands or fathers women have

claim on their husbands untill they are taken & if they are not

found transgressors they remain upon their inheritances all

children have claim upon the{r\ir} parents untill they are of age &

after that they have claim upon the Church or in other words

the Lords storehouse for inheritances.

        X
♦ ³³¹81 **A Revelation** Rec^d. in Kirtland Decem=

        ber 4, 1831 the Aappointment³³² of Bishop his duty &c

        Hearken & listen to the voice of the Lord, O ye who have
                                                      my
[ca]lled yourselves together who are the High Priests of the Church
                                                      ^
[to who]m the Kingdom & Power have been given for verily thus saith

the Lord it is expedient in me for a Bisho{◊\p} to be appointed unto you

or of you unto the Church in this part of the Lords vinyard & verily

in this thing ye have done wisely for it is required of the Lord at the

hand of every Stewart to render an account of his Stewartship both

in time & in eternity for he who is faithfull & wise in time is

accounted worthy to inherit the mansions prepared for th{i\em} of my

father verily I say unto you the Elders of the Church in this part

of my Vineyard shall render an account of their stewartship unto

the Bishop which shall be appointed unto m{◊\e}³³³ of me in this part

of my vineyard these things shall be had on record to be

handed over unto the Bishop in Zion & the duty of the Bishop

shall be be made known by the commandments which have
                                                verily
been given & by the voice of the conferences & now I say unto
                                              ^
[y]ou my Servant Newel is the man ([K.] Whitney) is the man who

[s]hall be appointed & ordained unto this power this is the will of

[t]he Lord your God your redeemer even so Amen—

Original Inscription
John Whitmer

Revisions
Oliver Cowdery
William W. Phelps
Sidney Rigdon
Joseph Smith
John Whitmer
Unidentified

329. Remnants of two adhesive wafers are present on the top and bottom right corners of this leaf, indicating that it was attached to the following leaf. The leaves are now separated.

330. A large X is written over this revelation with red grease pencil. This revelation was first published in the January 1833 issue of *The Evening and the Morning Star*.

331. Two large Xs are written over parts of this revelation with red grease pencil. The first publication reflecting most redactions in this revelation is the December 1832 issue of *The Evening and the Morning Star*.

332. "Aapp" appears to have been triple underlined in light ink or ink that was later wipe-erased; an illegible stroke—possibly the beginning of a bracket—is written between "A" and "a" in the same light ink or ink that was later wipe-erased.

333. "◊" wipe-erased and written over; then stricken with entire phrase.

[The duty of the Bishop as made known at the same time

The word of the Lord in addition to the law which has been given making known the duty of the Bishop which has been ordained unto the Church in this Part of the vineyard which is verily this to keep the Lords store house to receive the funds of the Church in this part of the vineyard to take an account of the Elders as before has been commanded & to administer to their wants who shall pay for that which they receive in as much as they have wherewith to pay that this also may be consecrated to the good of the Church to the poor & needy & he who has not wherewith to pay an account shall be taken & handed over to the Bishop in Zion who shall pay the debt out of that which the Lord shall put into his hands & the labours of the faithful who labour in spiritual things in administering the Gospel & the things of the Kingdom unto the Church & unto the World shall answer the debt unto the Bishop in Zion thus it cometh out of the Church for according to the Law every man ^that^ cometh up to Zion must lay all things before the Bishop in Zion & now verily I say unto you that as every Elder in this part of the vineyard must give an account of his stewardship unto the Bishop in this part of the vineyard a certificate from the Judge or Bishop in this part of the vineyard unto the Bishop in Zion rendereth every man acceptable & answereth all ^things^ for an inheritance & to be received as a wise steward & as a faithful labourer otherwise ^he^ shall not be acceptable of the Bishop in Zion And now verily I say unto you let every Elder who shall give an account unto the Bishop of the Church in this part of the vineyard be recommended by the Church or Churches in which he labours that he may render himself & his accounts approved in all things And again let my servants who are ~~bound~~ appointed as stewards over the literary concerns of my Church have claim for assistance upon the Bishop or Bishops in all things that the Revelations may be published & go forth unto the ends of the Earth that they also may obtain funds which shall benefit the Church in all things that they also may render themselves approved in all things & be ^accounted^ as wise stewards And ^now^ Behold this shall be an ensample for

³³⁴[The duty of the Bishop as made known at the same time]³³⁵

The word of the Lord in a{⊘\dition} to the law which has been

given making known the duty of the Bishops which ha{v\⟨s⟩}~~e~~ been

ordained unto the Church in this Part of the vinyard which is

verily this to keep the Lords store house to receive the funds of

the Church in this part of the vineyard to take an account of

the Elders as before has been commanded & to administer to

their wants who shall pay for that which they receive in{~~as~~\ as}

much as they have wherewith to pay that this also may be con=

=secrated to the good of the Church to the poor & needy & he who has not

wherewith to pay an {co\account} shall be taken & handed over to the

Bishop in Zion who shall pay the de{⊘\bt} out of that which the Lord

shall put into his hands & the labours of the faithful who labor

in spiritual things in administering the Gospel & the things of the

Kingdom unto the Church & unto the World shall answer the debt

unto the Bishop in Zion thus it cometh out of the Church for

according to the Law every man ~~who~~ ᴬthat cometh up to Zion must lay

all things before the Bishop in Zion & now verily I say unto you

that as every Elder in this part of the vineyard must give an account

of his stewartship unto the Bishop in this part of the vineyard a

certificate from the Judge or Bishop in this part of the vineyard

unto the Bishop in Zion rendereth every man acceptable & answer

=eth all ᴬthings for an inheritance & to be received as a wise stewart &

as a faithful laborer otherwise ᴬhe shall not be acceptable of the

Bishop in Zion And now verily I say unto you let every Elder

who shall give an acc{◊\⟨o⟩}unt unto the Bishop of the Church in this

part of the vineyard be recomended by the Church or Churches

in which he lab{◊\⟨o⟩}urs that he may rende{⊘\r} himself & his accounts

approved in all things And again let my servants who are

~~abroad~~ appointed as stewarts over the lit{~~te~~\erary} concerns of my

Church have claims for assistance upon the Bishop or Bishops

in all things that the Revelations may be published & go forth

unto the ends of the Earth that they also may obtain funds

which shall benefit the Church in all things that they also

may render themselves approved in all things & be ~~accepted~~ ᴬaccounted as

wise stewarts And Behold this shall be an ᴬnow ensample for

Original Inscription
John Whitmer

Revisions
Oliver Cowdery
William W. Phelps
Sidney Rigdon
Joseph Smith
John Whitmer
Unidentified

334. Remnants of two adhesive wafers are present on the top and bottom left corners of this leaf, indicating that it was attached to the following leaf. The leaves are now separated.

335. The text enclosed within these brackets does not appear in any JS-era publication. The brackets appear to be written in the same ink flow as the redactions throughout this revelation that first appear in print in *The Evening and the Morning Star.*

all the extensive branches of my Church in whatsoever land they shall be established & now I make an end of my sayings amen.

A few words in addition to the laws of the Kingdom respecting the members of the Church they that are appointed by the Holy spirit to go up unto Zion & they who are priviliged to go up unto Zion let them carry up unto the Bishop a certificate from three Elders of the Church or a certificate from the Bishop otherwise he who shall go up unto the land of Zion shall not be accounted as a wise steward this also an ensample amen

82 A Revelation to Joseph & Sidney
given Hiram Portage County Ohio Decmr 1, 1831

Behold, thus saith the Lord unto you my servants, that the time has verily come, that it is nessesary & expedient in me, that you should open your mouths in proclaiming my Gospel, the things of the Kingdom, expounding the Misteries thereof out of the scriptures, according to that portion of spirit & power, which shall be given unto you, even as I will. 2 verily I say unto you, proclaim unto the world in the regions round about, & in the Church also, for the space of a season, even untill it shall be made known unto you. 3 verily this is a mission for a season, which I give unto you. 4 wherefore labor ye in my vineyard. 5 call upon the inhabitants of the Earth & bear record & prepare the way for the Commandments & the Revelations which are to come. 6 Now, behold this is wisdom; whoso readeth let him understand & receive also: for unto him who receiveth it shall be given more abundantly, even power; 8 Wherefore confound your enemies call upon them to meet you, both in publick & in private, & in as much as ye are faithful their shame shall be made manifest. 10 Wherefore let them bring forth their strong reasons against the Lord. 11 Verily thus saith the Lord unto you, there is no weapon that is formed against you shall prosper; 12 & if any man lift his voice against you he shall be confounded in mine own due time; 13 Wherefore keep these commandments. 14 they are true & faithful; even so: amen

134[a] [verso]
all the extensive branches of my Church in whatsoever

land they shall be established & now I make an end of my

sayings amen.

A fi{w\ew} words in adition to the laws of the Kingdom resp[e]cting

that
the members of the Church they ~~who~~ are appointed by the Holy spirit

to go up unto Zion & they who are privil{i\⟨e⟩}ged to go up unto Zion let them

carry up unt[o] the Bish{ig\op} a certificate from three Elders of

the Church or a certificate from the Bishop otherwise he who

shall go up unto the land of Zion shall not be accounted as

a
wise stewart this also an ensample amen—

♦ ³³⁶82 A Revelation to Joseph & Sidney [Rigdon]

given Hiram Portage County Ohio Dec^m. 1, 1831

Behold, thus saith the Lord unto you my servants, that the

time has verily come, that it is nessessary & expedient in me,

that ~~that~~ you should open your mouths in proclaming my Gospel,

the things of the Kingdom, expounding the Misteries thereof o{t\ut} of the Scriptu

=res, according {th\to\to} that portion of spirit & power, which shall be given

2
unto you, even as I will. verily I say unto you, proclaim unto the world

in the regions round about, & in the Church also, for the space of

3
a season, even untill it shall be made known unto you. verily

4
this is a mission for a season, which I give unto you: wherefore labor ye

5
in my ~~Church~~³³⁷ vineyard. call upon the inhabitants of the Earth

the
& bear record & prepare the way for the Commandments & {re\Revelations}

6   7
which are to come. Now, behold this is wisdom; whoso readeth let him

7
understand & receive also: for unto him who receiveth it shall be

8
gi{◊◊\ve}n more abundantly, even Power{,\:} Wherefore confo[u]nd your enemies;

9
call upon them to meet you, both in publick & in private, & in as

much as ye are faithful their shame shall be made manifest.

10
Wherefore let them bring forth th[e]ir strong reasons against the

11
Lord. Verily thus saith the Lord unto you, there is no weapon

12
that is formed against you ~~that~~ shall prosper; & if any man lift his

voice against you, he shall be confounded in mine own due time;

13   14
Wherefore keep these commandments. ~~for~~³³⁸ they are true & faith=

=ful; even so: amen

ORIGINAL INSCRIPTION
John Whitmer

REVISIONS
Oliver Cowdery
William W. Phelps
Sidney Rigdon
Joseph Smith
John Whitmer
Unidentified

336. Although redactions throughout this revelation were made in preparation for publication of the Book of Commandments, this revelation was not printed therein because the printing office was destroyed in 1833.

337. "Church" partially wipe-erased and then stricken.

338. Double underlining beneath "f" written and then wipe-erased by William W. Phelps.

A Vision of Joseph and Sidney.

February the 16. 1832 given in Portage County Hiram Township State of Ohio in North America which they saw concerning the Church of the first born & concerning the ^economy^ ~~the economy the~~ of God & his vast creation throughout all eternity.

Hear, O ye heavens, & give ear, O earth, & rejoice ye inhabitants thereof, for the Lord he is God, & beside him there is none else; & great is his wisdom; marvelous are his ways; & the extent of his doings, none can findout; his purposes fail not, neither are there any who can stay his hand: from eternity to eternity, he is the same, & his years never fail.

I the Lord am merciful & gracious unto them who fear me, and delight to honor them who serve me in righteousness, & in truth; great shall be their reward, & eternal shall be their glory, & unto them will I reveal all mysteries; yea, all the hidden mysteries of my Kingdom from days of old; & for ages to come will I make known unto them the good pleasure of my will concerning all things; yea, even the wonders of eternity shall they know, & things to come will I shew them, even the things of many generations; their wisdom shall be great, & their understanding reach to heaven; before them the wisdom of the wise shall perish, & the understanding of the prudent shall come to naught; for by my spirit will I enlighten them, & by my power will I make known unto them the secrets of my will; yea, even those things which eye has not seen, nor ear heard, nor yet entered into the heart of man.—

We, Joseph & Sidney, being in the spirit on the ~~sixteenth~~ of Feb. in the year of our Lord, ~~1832~~ one thousand, eight hundred & thirty two, and through the power of the spirit our eyes were opened, & our understandings were enlightened, so as to see & understand the things of God; even things which were from the beginning before the World was, which was ordained of the Father, through his only begotten Son, who was in the bosom of the father even from the beginning; of whom we bear record, & the record which we bear is the fulness of the Gospel of Jesus Christ, who is in the Son whom we saw & with whom we conversed in the heavenly vision, for as we sat doing the work of translation, which the Lord had appointed unto us, we came to the twenty ninth verse of the fifth Chapter

³³⁹A Vision of Joseph and Sidney [Rigdon]

Febuary the 16. 1832 given in Portage County Hiram

Township State of Ohio in North America which they saw

concerning the Church of the first born & concerning the ~~coming~~ Economy

~~the coming the~~³⁴⁰ {g\of} God & his vast creation throughout all eternity.

Hear, O ye heavens, & give ear, O earth, & rejoice ye inhabitants

thereof, for the Lord he is God, & beside him there is none else; & great

is his wisdom; marvelous are his ways; & the extent of his doings, none

can find out; his purposes fail not, neither are there any who can stay

his hand: from eternity to eternity, he is the same, & his y{◊\ears} never

fail.

I the Lord am mercyful & gracious unto them who fear me,

and delight to honor them who serve me in righteousness, & in ~~truth~~³⁴¹

truth; great shall be their reward, & eternal shall be their glory, &

unto them will I reveal all m{i\⟨y⟩}steries; yea, all the hidden m{i\⟨y⟩}ster

=ies of my Kingdom from days of old; & for ages to come will I make

known unto them the good pleasure of my will concerning all

things; yea, even the wonders of eternity shall they know, & things

to come will I shew them, even the things of many generations; their

wisdom shall be great, & their understanding reach to heaven; before

them the wisdom of the wise shall perish, & the understanding of the

prudent shall come to naught; for by my spirit will I enlighten

them, & by my power will I make known unto them the secrets of my

will; yea, even those things which ey{es\e} has not seen, nor ear heard, nor

yet entered into the heart of man.—

We, Joseph, & Sidney, being in the spirit on th{e\is} {16 day of\Sixteenth} of Febʳ,

in the year of our Lord, 1832 one thousand, eight hundred, &, thirty two, and through the power of the spirit,

our eyes were opened, & our understandings were enlightened, so as to

see & understand the things of God; even things which were from the

begining before the World was, which was ordained of the Father, through

his only begotten Son, who was in the bosom of the father{s\,} even from

the begining, of whom we bear record, & the record which we bear is

the fulness of the Gospel of {G\Jesus} Christ, wh{o\ich} is in the Son whom we

saw & with whom we conversed in the heaven{s\ly} vision, for as we

sat doing the work of translati{n\on}, which the Lord had appointed

unto us, we came to the twenty ninth verse of the fifth Chapter

ORIGINAL INSCRIPTION
John Whitmer

REVISIONS
Oliver Cowdery
William W. Phelps
Sidney Rigdon
Joseph Smith
John Whitmer
Unidentified

339. The first publication reflecting most redactions in this item is the July 1832 issue of *The Evening and the Morning Star.*

340. "the coming the" has two layers of deletion: first layer by John Whitmer at the time of original inscription and second layer by the same unidentified scribe who wrote "Economy".

341. "truth" wipe-erased and then stricken.

of John, which was given unto us thus: Speaking of the resurrection
of the dead who should hear the voice of the Son of man, & shall
come forth; they who have done good in the resurrection of the
just, & they who have done evil in the resurrection of the
unjust. Now this caused us to marvel, ~~greatly~~ for it was given
us of the spirit; & while we meditated upon these things, the Lord
touched the eyes of our understanding, & they were opened, & the glory
of the Lord shone round about; & we beheld the glory of the
Son, on the right hand of the Father, & received of his fulness; &
saw the holy angels, & they who are sanctified before his throne,
worshiping God & the Lamb forever & ever. And now after the many
testimonies which have been given of him, this is the testimony,
last of all, which we give of him, that he lives, for we saw
him even on the right hand of God; & we heard the voice bearing
record that he is the only begotten of the Father; that by him, &
through him, & of him, the worlds are made, & were created;
& the inhabitants thereof are begotten sons and daughters
unto God. This we saw also & bear record that an Angel of God,
who was in authority in the presence of God, who rebelled against
the only begotten ~~Son~~ whom the father loved, & who was on the
bosom ~~of~~ the Father, was thrust down from the presence of
God & the Son, & was called perdition; for the heavens wept over
him; for he was Lucifer, even the son of the morning; & we beheld
& lo, he is fallen! is fallen! even the son of the morning. and while
we were yet in the spirit, the Lord commanded us that we should
write the vision; for behold Satan, that old Serpent, even the Devil,
who rebelled against God, & sought to take the Kingdoms of our God,
& of his Christ; wherefore he maketh war with the saints of God,
& encompasses them about; and we saw a vision of the eternal
sufferings of those with whom he maketh war & overcometh, for
thus came the voice of the Lord unto us.

Thus saith the Lord, concerning all those who know my power,
& have been made partakers thereof, & suffered themselves, through the power
of the Devil, to be overcome unto the denying of the truth, and the
defying of my power: they are they who are the sons of perdition, of
whom I say it had been better for them never to have been born;
for they are vessels of wrath doomed to suffer the wrath of God,

134[b]³⁴² [verso]

of John, which was given unto us thus: Speaking of the resurrection

of the dead who should hear the voice of the Son of man, & shall

come forth; they who have done³⁴³ good in the resurrection of the

Just, & they who have done evil in the resurrection of the

unjust. Now this caused us to mar{◊\vel}, ~~greatly~~ for it was given

us of the spirit; & while we meditated upon these things, the Lord

touched the eyes of our understandings, & they were opened, & the glory

of the Lord shone round about; & we beheld the glory of the

Son, on the right hand of the father, & received of his fulness; &

saw the holy angels, & they who are sanctified before his throne,

worshiping God & the Lamb forever & ever. And now after the many

testimonies which have been given of him, this is the testimony,

last of all, which we give of him, that he lives, for we saw

him even on the right hand of God; & we heard the voice bearing

record that he is the only begotten of the father; that by him, &

through him, & of him, the worlds are made, & were created;

& the inhabitant thereof are begotten Sons {of\and} daughters ~~of~~

unto God. This we saw also & bear record that an Angel of God,

who was in authority in the presence³⁴⁴ of God, who rebelled against

                   in³⁴⁵

the only begotten S{on\on}, whom the father loved, & who was ~~in~~ the

    of

Bosom ~~with~~ the father◊ was thrust down from the presence of

God & the Son, & was called perdition; for the heavens wept over

him; for he was {l\L}ucipher, even the son of the morning; & we beheld

& lo{!\,} he is fallen! is fallen! even the Son of the morning. and while

we were yet in the spirit, the Lord commanded us that we should

write the vision; for behold Satan, that old Serpent, even the Devil,

who rebelled against God, & sought to take Kingdoms of our God,

& of his Christ; wherefore he maketh war with the saints of God,

& incompasses them about; and we saw a vision of the eternal

sufferings of those with whom he maketh war & overcometh, for

            of the Lord

thus came the voice unto us.

    Thus saith the Lord, concerning all those who know my power,

& have been made partakers thereof, & suffered themselves, through the power

of the Devil, to be overcome unto the denying of the truth, and the~~y~~

     of

def{i\ying} my power: they are they who are the Sons of perdition, of

whom I say it had been better for them never to have been born;

for they are vessils of wrath doomed to suffer the wrath of God,

---

ORIGINAL INSCRIPTION
John Whitmer

REVISIONS
Oliver Cowdery
William W. Phelps
Sidney Rigdon
Joseph Smith
John Whitmer
Unidentified

342. John Whitmer misnumbered this page; it should be manuscript page 136. Page numbers remain two off throughout the rest of the manuscript book.

343. Uninked "/x" etched into the paper. This mark corresponds to a line break in *The Evening and the Morning Star.*

344. Uninked "x" etched into the paper. This mark corresponds to a line break in *The Evening and the Morning Star.*

345. Although many of John Whitmer's changes throughout this item appear to match the original ink flow, Whitmer may have made the changes at a later time.

with the Devil & his angels, throughout eternity; concerning whom I have said there is no forgiveness for them in this world nor in the world to come; having denied the holy Ghost after having received it, & having denied the only begotten Son of the father, crucifying him unto themselves, & putting him to an open shame: these are they who shall go away into the lake of fire & brimstone, with the Devil & his angels, & the only ones on whom the second death shall have any power; yea, verily the only ones who shall not be redeemed in the due time of the Lord, after the sufferings of his wrath, who shall be brought forth by the resurrection of the dead, through the triumph & glory of the Lamb; who was slain, who was in the bosom of the father before the worlds were made. and this is the Gospel the glad tidings which the voice out of the heavens bore record unto us, that he came into the world, even Jesus to be crucified for the world, & to bear the sins of the world, & to sanctify the world, & to cleanse it from all unrighteousness; that through him all might be saved, whom the father had put into his power; & made by him who glorifieth the father; & saveth all the work of his hands, except those sons of perdition, who denyeth the son after the father hath revealed him: wherefore he saveth all save them, & there shall go away into everlasting punishment, which is endless punishment, which is eternal punishment, to reign with the Devil & his angels throughout eternity, where their worm dieth not & the fire is not quenched, which is their torment, but the end thereof, neither the place thereof, & their torment, no man knoweth, neither was revealed, neither is, neither will be revealed unto man, save to them who are made partakers thereof: nevertheless I the Lord sheweth it by vision unto many, but straitway shutteth it up again: wherefore the end, the width, the height, depth, & the misery thereof, he understandeth not, neither any man save them who are ordained unto this condemnation. & we heard the voice saying write the vision for lo, this is the end of the vision of the eternal sufferings of the ungodly!

And again, we bear record for we saw & heard, & this is the testimony of the Gospel of Christ, concerning them who come forth in the resurrection of the just; they are they who received the

with the Devil & his angels, throughout eternity: concerning whom

I have said there is no forgiveness for them in this world nor in

the world to come; having denied the holy ghost after having

received it, & having denied the only begotten Son of the father,

crusifying him unto themselves, & puting him to an open shame:

these are they who shall go away into the lake of fire & brimston[e],

with the Devil & his angels, & the only ones ^on^ whom the second death

shall have any power; yea, verily the only ones who shall not be

redeemed in the due³⁴⁷ time of the Lord, after the sufferings of his

wrath, who shall be brought forth by the resurrection of the dead,

through the ~~the~~ triumph & glory of the lamb; who was slain,

who was in the bosom of the father before the worlds were made.

and this is the Gospel the glad tidings which the voice out of

the heavens bore record unto us, that he came into the world,

even Jesus to be crusified for the world, & to bear the sins of the ^world,^

& to sanctify the world, & to cleans it from all unrighteousness;

that through him all might be saved, whom the father had put

{u\i}nto his³⁴⁸ power; & made by him who glorifieth the father; & saveth

all the work of his hands, except those sons of perdition, who

den{i\⟨y⟩}eth the son after the father hath revealed him: wherefore he

~~saith~~ ^saveth^ all save them, & these shall go away into everlasting punishm

=ent, which is endless punishment, which is eternal punishment, to

reign with the {de\Devil} & his angels throughout eternity, where

their worm dieth not & the fire is not quenched, which is

their torment, but the end thereof, neither the place thereof,

& their torment, no man knoweth, neither was revealed, neither

is, neither will be revealed unto man, save to them who are

made partakers thereof: nevertheless I the Lord showeth it by

vision unto many, but straitway shuteth it up again: wherefore

the end, the width, the hi{t\gth}, ^the^ depth, & the misery thereof, he

understandeth not, neither any man save them who are orda

-ined unto this condemnation. & we heard the voice saying write

the vision for lo, this is the end of the vision of the eternal

sufferings of the ungodly!

And again, we bear record for we saw & heard, & this is the tes=

=timony of the Gospel of Christ, concerning them who come forth

in the resurrection of the Just: they are they who received the

ORIGINAL INSCRIPTION
John Whitmer

REVISIONS
Oliver Cowdery
William W. Phelps
Sidney Rigdon
Joseph Smith
John Whitmer
Unidentified

346. John Whitmer mis-
numbered this page; it should
be manuscript page 137. Page
numbers remain two off
throughout the rest of the
manuscript book.

347. Uninked "/" etched into
the paper. This mark corresponds to a line break in *The
Evening and the Morning Star.*

348. Uninked "x" etched into
the paper. This mark corresponds to a line break in *The
Evening and the Morning Star.*

testimony of Jesus, & believed on his name, & were baptized after the manner of his burial, being buried in the water in his name, & this according to the commandment which he hath given, that, by keeping the commandment, they might be washed & cleansed from all their ~~their~~ sins, & receive the holy Ghost by the laying on of the hands of ~~him~~ him who is ordained & sealed unto this power; & who overcame by faith, & are sealed by that holy Spirit of promise, which the father sheddeth forth upon all those who are just & true: they are they who are the church of the first born; they are they into whose hands the father hath given all things; they are they who are Priests & Kings, who having received of his fulness, & of his glory, are Priests of the most high after the order of Melchisidec, which was after the order of Enoch, which was after the order of the only begotten Son: wherefore, as it is written, they are gods, even the Sons of God: wherefore all things are theirs, whether life or death, or things present, or things to come, all are theirs, & they are Christ's, & Christ is God's; & they shall overcome all things: wherefore let ~~all things~~ no man glory in man, but rather let him glory in God, who shall subdue all ~~enemies~~ under his feet; these shall dwell in the presence of God & his Christ forever & ever: these are they whom he shall bring with him, when he shall come in the clouds of Heaven, to reign on the earth over his People: these are they who shall have part in the first resurrection: these are they who shall come forth in the resurrection of the just: these are they who ~~have~~ [are] come unto Mount Zion, & unto the city of the living God, the heavenly place the holiest of all: these are they who have come to an innumerable company of Angels; to the general assembly & Church of Enoch, & of the first born: these are they whose names are written in heaven, where God & Christ is the ~~their~~ judge of all: these are they who are just men made perfect through Jesus the mediator of the new Covenant, who wrought out this perfect atonement through the shedding of his own blood: these are they whose bodies are celestial, whose glory is that of the Sun, even of God the highest of all; which glory the sun of the

136 [verso]
testimony of Jesus, & believed on his name, & were baptized

aft{r\er} the manner of his buri{e\a}l, being buried in the water

in his name, & this according to the commandment which

he hath given, that, by keeping the commandment, they

might be washed & cleansed from all their ~~their~~ sins, &

receive the holy Ghost by the laying on of the hands of ~~him~~³⁴⁹

him who is ordained & sealed unto this power; & who overcome³⁵⁰

by faith, & are sealed by that holy spirit of promise, which the

father sheddeth forth upon all those who are Just & true:

they are they who are the church of the first born; they are

they into whose hands the father hath given all things; they

are they who are Priests & Kings, who having rec{◊◊◊d\eived} of his

fullness, & of his Glory, are Priests of the most high after

the order of Mel{k\chisidec{k\,}} which was after the order of Enoch,

which was after the order of the only begotten Son: wherefore,

as it is written, they are Gods,³⁵¹ even the Sons of God: wherefore

all things are theirs, whether life or death, or things present,

or things to come, all are theirs, & they are Christ's, & Christ~~s~~

is God's; & they shall overcome all things: wherefore let ~~all things~~

no man glory in man, but rather let him glory in God,

who shall {◊\subdue} all {~~things~~\enemies} under his feet; these shall

dwell in the presence of God & his Christ forever & ever: these

are they whom he shall bring with him, when he shall come

in the clouds of Heaven, to reign on the Earth over his People: these

are they who shall have part in the first resurrection: these

are they who shall come forth in the resurrection of the Just:

these are they who ~~have~~ ᵃʳᵉ come unto Mount Zion, & unto the

City of the living God, the heavenly place the holiest of all:

these are they who have come to an innumerable company

of Angels; to the general assembly {~~of~~\&} Church of Enoch, & of the

first born: these are they whose names are written³⁵² in heaven,

where god & Christ {is\{are\is}} the ~~Chur~~ {ch\Judge} of all: these are they who

are Just men made p{r\erfect} through Jesus the mediator of

the new Covenant, who wrought out this perfect atonement

through the sheding of his own blood: these are th[e]y whose

bodies are celestial, whose glory is that of the Son, even of

God the highest of all; which glory the Sun of the

ORIGINAL INSCRIPTION
John Whitmer

REVISIONS
Oliver Cowdery
William W. Phelps
Sidney Rigdon
Joseph Smith
John Whitmer
Unidentified

349. "him" wipe-erased and then stricken.

350. Or "overcame".

351. Uninked "x" etched into the paper. This mark corresponds to a line break in *The Evening and the Morning Star.*

352. Uninked "x" etched into the paper. Unlike most uninked marks in this section of the manuscript, this mark does not correspond to a line break in *The Evening and the Morning Star.*

firmament is written of as being typical.—

And again, we saw the Terrestrial world, & behold & lo! these are they who are of the Terrestrial, whose glory differeth from that of the Church of the first born, who have received of the fulness of the father, even as that of the Moon differeth from the Sun of the firmament. Behold, these are they who died without law; & also they who are the spirits of men kept in prison, whom the Son visited & preached the gospel unto them, that they might be judged according to men in the flesh, who received not the testimony of Jesus in the flesh, but afterwards received it: these are they who are honorable men of the Earth, who were blinded by the craftiness of men: these are they who receive of his glory, but not of his fulness: these are they who receive of the presence of the Son, but not of the fulness of the father: wherefore, they are bodies Terrestrial & not bodies Celestial, & differeth in glory as the Moon differeth from the Sun: these are they who are not valiant in the testimony of Jesus: wherefore they obtained not the Crown over the Kingdoms of our God. & now this is the end of the vision which we saw of the Terrestrial, that the Lord commanded us to write while we were yet in the spirit.

And again, we saw the glory of the Telestial, which glory is that of the lesser, even as the glory of the Stars differeth from that of the Moon glory of the Moon in the firmament: these are they who receive not the gospel of Christ, neither the testimony of Jesus: these are they who deny not the Holy Ghost: these are they who are thrust down to Hell: there are they who shall not be redeemed from the Devil, untill the last resurrection, untill the Lord, even Christ the Lamb, shall have finished his work: there are they who receive not of his fulness in the eternal world, but of the Holy Ghost through the administration of the Terrestrial; & the Terrestrial through the administration of the Celestial; & also the Telestial receive it of the administering of angels, who are appointed to minister for them, or who are appointed to be ministering spirits for them, for they shall be heirs of salvation. & thus we saw, in the Heavenly vision, the glory of the Telestial which surposeth all understanding; & no man knoweth it except

firmament is written of as being typical.—

And again, we saw the Terrestrial world, & behold & lo! these

are they who are of the Terrestrial, whose glory differeth from

that of the Church of the first born, who have received of the

fulness of the father, even a{s\s} that of the Moon differeth from

the Sun of the firmament. Behold, these are they who died with

=out law; & also they who are the spirits of men kept in

prison, whom the Son visited & preached the gospel unto them,

that they might be Judged according to men in the flesh,

who received not the testimony of Jesus, in the flesh, but

afterwards received it: these are they who are honorable men

of the Earth, who were blinded by the craftiness of men: these

are they who receive of his glory, but not of his fulness: these

are they who receive of the presence of the Son, but not of

the fulness of the father: wherefore◊ they are bodies Ter{◊◊\restrial}

& not bodies Ceelestial, & differeth in glory as the Moon {◊\diff}

=ereth from the Sun: these are they who are not[353] valient in the

testimony of Jesus: wherefore they obtained not the Crown over

the Kingdoms of our God. & now this is the end of the vision

which we saw of the Terrestrial, that the Lord commanded

us to write while we were yet in the Spirit.

And again, we saw the glory of the Telestial, wh{ose\ich} glory is ~~of~~

that of the lesser, even ~~of~~ ^{as} the glory of the Stars differeth from that

of the ~~Moon~~ glory of the Moon in the firmament: these are they

who receive not the gospel of Christ, neither the testimony of Jesus:

these are they who deny not the {h\⟨H⟩}oly Ghost: these are they who

are thrust down to {h\⟨H⟩}ell: these are they who shall not be redee

=med from the Devil, untill the last resurrection, untill the Lord,

even Christ the Lamb, shall have finished his work: these are

they who receive not of his fulness in the eternal world, but of

the Holy Ghost through the administration of the Terrestrial;

& the Terrestrial through the administration of the Celestial; &

also the {t\⟨T⟩}elestial receive it of[354] the administering of angels, who

are appointed to minister for them, or who are a{◊\ppointed} to be min=

=istering Spirits for them, for they Shall be heirs of salvation{◊\.}

& thus we saw, in the Heavenly vision, the glory of the Telestial

which surpaseth all understanding; & no man knoweth it except

ORIGINAL INSCRIPTION
John Whitmer

REVISIONS
Oliver Cowdery
William W. Phelps
Sidney Rigdon
Joseph Smith
John Whitmer
Unidentified

353. Uninked "/" etched into the paper. This mark corresponds to a line break in *The Evening and the Morning Star.*

354. Uninked "x" etched into the paper. This mark corresponds to a line break in *The Evening and the Morning Star.*

him to whom God hath revealed it, and thus we saw the glory
of the ~~Celestial~~ Terrestrial which excelleth in all things. the glory of the
Telestial, even in glory, & in power, & in might, & in dominion. &
thus we saw the glory of the Celestial, which excelleth in all things
where God, even the father, reigneth upon his throne for ever &
ever; before whose throne all things bow in humble reverence
& giveth him glory for ever & ever. they who dwell in his presence
are the Church of the first born; & they see as they are seen
& know as they are known, having received of his fulness & of
his grace; & he maketh them equal in power, & in might, & in
dominion. & the glory of the Celestial is one, even as the glory of the Sun is
one. & the glory of the Terrestrial is one, even as the glory of the
Moon is one. & the glory of the Telestial is one, even as the
glory of the stars is one; for as one star differeth from another
star in glory, even so differeth one from another in glory in
the Telestial world; for these are they who are of Paul, & of
Apollos, & Cephas: they are they who say, there are some of one &
some of another; some of Christ; & some of John; & some of
Moses; & some of Elias; & some of Esaias; & some of Isaiah; & some
of Enoch; but received not the gospel; neither the testimony of
Jesus; neither the Prophets; neither the everlasting Covenant:
last of all: these are they who will not be gathered with the
saints, to be caught up into the Church of the first born;
& received into the Cloud: these are they who are liars, & sorcerers
& adulterers, & whoremongers, & whosoever loveth & maketh a lie:
these are they who suffer the wrath of God on the earth: these
are they who suffer the vengeance of eternal fire: these are they who
are cast down to Hell, & suffer the wrath of almighty God until
the fulness of times, when Christ shall have subdued all enemies
under his feet, & shall have perfected his work, when he shall
~~have~~ deliver up the Kingdom & present it unto his father
spotless, saying; I have over come & have trodden the winepress
alone, even the winepress of the fierceness of the wrath of
almighty God: then shall he be crowned with the crown of his
glory, to sit on the throne of his power, to reign for ever &
ever: but behold & lo, we saw the glory of the Telestial world,
that they were in number as innumerable as the stars in the

138 [verso]

  him to whom God hath revealed it. and th{is\us} we saw the glory

  Terrestrial

of the ~~Telestial~~ which excelleth in all things the glory of the

  ^

             in   in

Telestial, even in glory, & in power, & might, & dominion. &

             ^   ^

thus we saw the glory of the Celestial, which excelleth in all things

where God, even the father, reigneth upon his throne for ever &

ever: before whose throne all things bow in humble reverance

& giveth him glory forever & ever. they who dwell in his presence

are the Church of the first born; & they see as they are seen

& know as they are known, having received of his fulness & of

his grace; & he maketh them equal in power, & in might, & in

                glory of the

dominion. & the glory of the Celestial is one, even as the Son is

                     ^

one. & the glory[355] of the Terrestrial is one, even as the glory of th[e]

Moon is one. & the glory of the Telestial is one, even as the

{g◊\glory} of the Stars is one: for as one Star differeth from another

                  in

star in glory, even so differeth one from another ~~from~~ glory in

                    ^

the Telestial world: for these are they who are of Paul, & of

Apollis, & Ceph{a\es}: they are they who say, there are some of one &

some of another; some of Christ; & some of John; {◊\&} some of

Moses; & some of Elias; & some of Esaias; & some of Isaiah; & some

of Enoch, but received not the gospel; neither the testimony of

Jesus; neither the Prophets; neither the everlasting Covenant;

last of {◊◊\all}: these are they who will not be gethered with the

saints, to be caught up {u\i}nto the Church of the first born,

& received into the Cloud: these are they who are liars, & {◊\Sorcerers}

& adultere{s\rs},[356] & whoremongers, & whosoever loveth & maketh a lie:

these {◊◊\are} they who suffer the wrath of God on the Earth: these

are they who suffer the vengence of eternal fire: these are they who

are cast down to[357] Hell, & suffer the wrath of almighty God untill

the fulness of times, when Christ shall have subdued all enemies

under his feet, & shall have perfected his work, when he shall

~~have~~ delivered up the Kingdom & present it unto his father

spotless, saying: I have over come & have trodden the winepress

alone, even the winepress of the fierceness of the wrath of

almighty God: then shall he be crowned with the crown of his

{G\glory}, to sit on the throne of his power, to reign for ever &

ever. but behold & lo, we Saw the glory of the Telestial world,

that they were in number as innumerable as the stars in the

Original Inscription
John Whitmer

Revisions
Oliver Cowdery
William W. Phelps
Sidney Rigdon
Joseph Smith
John Whitmer
Unidentified

355. Uninked "x" etched into the paper. This mark corresponds to a line break in *The Evening and the Morning Star.*

356. At this point the page bears traces of offsetting from redactions to manuscript page 139, indicating that page 139 was likely still part of the manuscript book when the redactions were made.

357. Uninked "x" etched into the paper. This mark corresponds to a line break in *The Evening and the Morning Star.*

firmament of Heaven, or as the sand upon the sea shore, &
heard the voice of the Lord saying: these all shall bow the knee,
& every tongue shall confess to him who sitteth upon the throne
forever & ever; for they shall be judged according to their works;
& every man shall receive according to his own works, & his own
dominion, in the mansions which are prepared; & they shall be
servants of the most high, but where God & Christ dwells they
cannot come, worlds without end. this is the end of the vision
which we were commanded to write while we were yet in
the Spirit.

But great & marvelous are the works of the Lord & the mysteries
of his kingdom which he shewed unto us, which surpasseth all
understanding in glory, & in might, & in dominion, which he
commanded us we should not write, while we were yet
in the Spirit, & are not lawful for man to utter; neither
is man capable to make them known, for they are only to
be seen & understood by the power of the holy Ghost; which God
bestows on them who love him & purify themselves before
him; to whom he grants this privilege of seeing & knowing for
themselves; that through the power & manifestation of the spirit,
while in the flesh, they may be able to bear his presence in
the world of glory. & to God & the Lamb be glory, & honor, &
dominion, forever & ever. amen.

83 REVELATION given to F. G. Williams

Portage, March 15. 1832 &c Ohio   Frederick G Williams

Verily I say unto you my servant listen to the voice of
him who speaketh, to the word of the Lord your God, & hearken to
the calling wherewith you are called, even to be a high Priest in
my Church & counsellar unto my servant Joseph, unto whom
I have given the keys of the Kingdom which belong always to
the presidency of the high Priest Hood, therefore verily I acknowl
edge him & will bless him, & also thee, inasmuch as thou
art faithful in Counsel, in the office which I have appointed
unto you, & in prayer always vocally & in thy heart in publ
ick & in private also in thy ministry, in proclaiming the
gospel in the land of the living & among thy brethren;

139³⁵⁸ [recto]

³⁵⁹firmament of Heaven, or as the sand upon the sea shore, &

heard the voice of the Lord saying: these all shall bow the knee,

& every to{ung\ngue} shall confess to him who³⁶⁰ sitteth upon the throne

forever & ever: for they shall be Judged according to their works;

& every man shall receive according to his own works, & his own

dominion, in the mansions which are prepared; & they shall be

servants of the most high, but where God &³⁶¹ Christ dwells they

cannot come, worlds without end. this is the end of the vision
                    saw, which we
which we were commanded to write while we were yet in
          ^

the Spirit.

　　But great & marvelous are the works of the Lord & the m{i\y}steries

of his Kingdom which he shewed unto us, which surpaseth all

understanding in glory, & in might, & in dominion, which he

commanded us ~~that~~ we should not write, while we were yet

in the Spirit, & are not Lawful for men³⁶² to utter; neither

is man capa{◊◊\ble} to make them known, for they are o{◊\nly} to

be seen & understood by the power of the holy Gohost; which God

bestows on those who love him & purify themselves before

him; to whom he grants this privelege of seeing & knowing for

themselves; that through the power & manifestation of the spirit,

while in the flesh, they may be able to bear his presence in

the world of Glory. & to God & the Lamb be glory, & honor, &

dominion, forever & ever. amen{.\.}

　　　　　　　　　　F[rederick] G Williams
◆　83　**Revelation** {◊◊\given} to ~~Jesse Gause~~ Hiram

Portage ^{# 363} March 15. 1832 [#]C^{o.} Ohio
          verily　　　　　　　Frederick G Wllams
　　Verily I say unto you my serv{◊◊\ant} ~~Jesse~~ listen to the voice of
         ^

him who speaketh, to the word of the Lord your God, & hearken to

the calling wherewith you are called, even to be a high Priest in

my Church & coun{c\⟨s⟩}ellor unto my Servant Joseph, unto whom

I have given the keys of the Kingdom which belongs always to

the presidency of the high Priest Hood, therefore verily I acknowl

=edge him & will bless him, & also thee, in as much as thou

art faithful in Counsel, in the office which I have appointed

unto you, & in prayer always vocally & in thy heart in publ-

-ick & in private also in thy minist{er\ry}, in proclaiming the

gospel in the Land of the Living & among thy brethren;

ORIGINAL INSCRIPTION
John Whitmer

REVISIONS
Oliver Cowdery
William W. Phelps
Sidney Rigdon
Joseph Smith
John Whitmer
Unidentified

　358. The stem of the "9" is visible, but the rest of the numeral is missing because the corner of the leaf is worn.

　359. This leaf, containing manuscript pages 139–140, was removed from the manuscript book at some point and is located at the Community of Christ Library-Archives. It was likely still part of the book when the redactions on this page were made. (See 253n356 herein.)

　360. There are three small holes, apparently made by a pin, below "to him who". No pinhead impressions are visible on the surrounding pages, indicating that the holes were likely made after this page was separated from the manuscript book. A pin may have secured this leaf to another leaf not found in this manuscript book.

　361. Uninked "/" or "^" etched into the paper. This mark corresponds to a line break in *The Evening and the Morning Star*.

　362. Possibly "m{a\e}n", but more likely "e" retraced over a misshapen "e".

　363. "#" likely inserted to indicate where the county and state information inserted at the end of the line should be placed.

and in doing these things, thou wilt do the greatest good unto thy fellow beings, & will promote the glory of him who is your Lord. wherefore, be faithful, stand in the office I have appointed you succor the weak; lift up the hands which hang down, & strengthen the feeble knees; & if thou art faithful unto the end thou shalt have a crown of immortality & eternal life in the mansions which I have prepared in the house of my father behold & lo these are the words of Alpha & Omega even Jesus Christ AMEN

140 [verso]
³⁶⁴and in doing these things thou {◊\wilt} do the greatest good

unto thy fellow beings, & will promote the g{r◊\lory} of him
lo

who is your Lord. wherefore be faithful,³⁶⁵ stand in the office

I have appointed you succor the weak, lift up the hands

which hang down, & strengthen the feeble knees; & if thou

art faithful unto the end thou shalt have a crown

of immortal{◊◊\ity} & eternal life in the mans{ti◊ns\ion} which

I have prepared in the house of my father b{i\ehold} & lo

these are the words of Alpha & Omega even Jesus

Christ amen

ORIGINAL INSCRIPTION
John Whitmer

REVISIONS
Oliver Cowdery
William W. Phelps
Sidney Rigdon
Joseph Smith
John Whitmer
Unidentified

364. This leaf, containing manuscript pages 139–140, was removed from the manuscript book at some point and is located at the Community of Christ Library-Archives.

365. There are three small holes below "wherefore be faithful". (See 255n360 herein.)

Revelation Explained

What is the sea of glass spoken of by John 4 Chap. and sixth verse of revelations?

It is the Earth in its sanctified immortal and eternal state

What are we to understand by the four beasts spoken of by John in the 4 Chapt. & 6 verse of Revelations?

They are figurative expressions used by the revelator John in describing heaven the paradise of God the happiness of men and of beasts and of creeping things and of the fowls of the air that which is spiritual being in the likeness of that which is temporal and that which is temporal in the likeness of that which is spiritual the spirit of man in the likeness of his person as also the spirit of the beast and every other creature which God has created

Are the four beasts limited to individual Beasts or do they represent classes or orders?

They are limited to four individual beasts which were shewn to John to represent the glory of the classes of beings in their destined order or sphere of creation in the enjoyment of their eternal felicity.

What are we to understand the eyes and wings which the beasts had?

Their eyes are a representation of light and knowledge that is they are full of knowledge and their wings are a representation of power to move to act &c.

What are we to understand by the four and twenty elders spoken of by John?

We are to understand that these Elders whom John saw were Elders who had been faithful in the work of the ministry and were dead who belonged to the seven Churches and were then in the paradise of God.

What are we to understand by the Book which John saw which was sealed on the back with seven seals?

Revelation Explained

What is the Sea of Glass spoken of by John 4 Chap. and

sixth verse of revelations?

Ans   {ⱷ\It} is the Earth in its sanctified immortal and eternal

state

Q   What are we to understand by the four beasts spoken of

by John in the 4 Chap^t. & 6 verse of Revelations?

A^366   They are figurative Expressions used by the revelator

John in disscribing heaven the paradise of God the

hapiness of men and of beasts and of creeping things

and of the fowls of the air that which is spiritual being

{ⱷⱷⱷ\in} the likeness of that which is temporal and that

which is temporal in the likeness of that which is spirit-

=ual the Spirit of man in the likeness of his person

as also the spirit of the beast and every other creature

which God has created

Q   {W\Are} the four beasts limited to individual Beasts or do

they represent classes or orders?

Ans   They are limited to four individual beasts which were

shewn to John to represent the g{r\lory} of the classes of

beings in their destined order or sphere of creation in the

enjoyment of their eternal felicity.

Q   What are we to understand the Eyes and wings which the

beasts had?

A   The{y\ir} eyes are a representation of light and knowledge

that is they are full of knowledge and their wings are a

representation of power to move to act &c.

Q   What are we to understand by the four and twenty Elders

spoken of by John?

A   We {ⱷ\are} to understand that these Elders whom John saw

were Elders who had been faithful in the work of the mini

=stry and were dead who belonged to the Seven Churches

and were then in the paradise of God.

Q   What are we to understand by the Book which John saw
                    on the {ⱷ\back}
          which was sealed with seven Seals ~~which John?~~
                              ^

ORIGINAL INSCRIPTION
John Whitmer

REVISIONS
Oliver Cowdery
William W. Phelps
Sidney Rigdon
Joseph Smith
John Whitmer
Unidentified

366. A large X appears in the left margin below "A". The X presumably marked this item for exclusion from publication. The item was published in the August 1844 issue of the *Times and Seasons,* shortly after JS's death. ("History of Joseph Smith," *Times and Seasons,* 1 Aug. 1844, 5:595–596.)

Ans. We are to understand that it contains the revealed
will. mysteries and works of God. the hidden things
of his œconomy concerning this earth during the
seven thousand years of its continuance or its
temporal existence.

What are we to understand by the seven seals with
which it was sealed?

We are to understand that the first seal contains
the things of the first thousand years and the second
also of the second thousand years and so on until
the seventh.

What are we to understand by the four Angels
spoken of by John 9 Chap & first verse of Revelations?

We are to understand that they are four angels sent
forth from God to whom is given power over
the four parts of the earth to save life and to
destroy these are they who have the everlasting
gospel to commit to every nation kindred tongue
and people having power to shut up the heavens
to seal up unto life, or to cast down to the
regions of darkness.

What are we to understand by the angel ascending
from the east Rev 9 Chap. & 2 verse?

We are to understand that the angel ascended from
the east is he to whom is given the seal of the
living God over the twelve tribes of Israel
wherefore he crieth unto the four angels having
the everlasting gospel ~~temporal~~ saying hurt not
the earth neither the sea nor the trees till we have
sealed the servants of our God in their foreheads
and if you will receive it this is Elias which
was to come to gather together the tribes of Israel
and restore all things.

What time are things spoken of in this chapter
to be accomplished?

Q   What is to be understood by the two witnesess {◊\in}

the {◊\eleventh} Chapt. of Rev.?

A   They are two prophets that are to be raised up to

the Jewish nation in the last days at the time

of the restoration and to prophesy to the Jews after

they are gathered and have built the city of Jerusalem

in the Land of their Fathers ◊

sample of pure language

[370]A Sample of pure Language

given by Joseph the Seer ~~as copied by Br Johnson~~[371]

~~Question~~ What is the name of God in pure Language

~~Answer~~   Awm{e\a}n.[372]

Q   The meaning of the pure word Am{e\a}n

A   It is the being which made all things in all its parts.

Q   What is the name of the Son of God.

A   {◊◊\The} Son[373] Awm{e\a}n.

Q   What is the Son Awm{e\a}n.

A   It is the greatest of all the parts of {◊\Awm{e\a}n} which

is the Godhead the first born.

Q   What ~~is~~ is man.

A   This signifies Sons Awm{e\a}n. the human family the

children of men the greatest parts of Awm{e\a}n Sons

the Son Awm{e\a}n

Q   What are Angels called in pure language.

A   Awm{e\a}n Angls-men

Q   {w\⟨W⟩}hat are the meaning of these words.

A   Awm{e\a}n's {Ser◊◊◊ts\Ministerring} serv{◊\⟨a⟩}nts Sanctified who are

sent forth from heaven to minister for or to Sons

Awm{e\a}n the greatest part of Awm{e\a}n Son. Sons

Awmen Son Awmen Awm{e\a}n

ORIGINAL INSCRIPTION
John Whitmer

REVISIONS
Oliver Cowdery
William W. Phelps
Sidney Rigdon
Joseph Smith
John Whitmer
Unidentified

370. A large X appears in the left margin. (See 259n366 herein.)

371. Likely John Johnson Sr.

372. Throughout this item, "Awm{e\a}n" could possibly be "Awm{e\⟨a⟩}n" or "Awm{e\a}n". John Whitmer's *a* and *o* are almost always indistinguishable; thus if Whitmer made the correction, the *a* could be an *o*.

373. Or "San". After this point in the item, this reading is possible each time "Son" appears. Similarly, "Sans" is possible when "Sons" appears.

Revelation given Kirtland March 4, 1832

1 Hearken unto me saith the Lord your God O ye who are ordained unto the high priesthood of my church who have assembled [yourselves together and listen to the counsel of him who has ordained you from on high who shall speak in your ears the words of wisdom that salvation may be unto you in that thing which you have presented before me saith the Lord God for verily I say unto you the time has come and is now at hand and behold and lo it must needs be that there be [an organization of the litterary and 2^d Mercantile establishments of my Church both in this place and in 2 the land of Zion for a permanent and everlasting establishment and firm unto my Church] to advance the cause which ye have espaused to the salvation of man and to the glory of your Father who is in heaven that you may be equal in the bands of heavenly things yea and earthly things also for the attaining of heavenly things for if ye are not equal in earthly things ye cannot be equal in obtaining heavenly things for if ye will that I give unto you a place in the Celestial kingdom world ye must prepare yourselves by doing the things which I have commanded and required of you and now verily thus saith the Lord it is expedient that all things be done unto my glory that ye should who are joined together in this order or in other words that my servant Ahashdah and my servant Gazelam or Enoch and my servant Pelagoram set in counsel with the Saints who are in Zion otherwise Satan seeketh to turn their hearts away from the truth that they become blinded and understand not the things which are prepared for them wherefore a commandment I give unto you to prepare and organize yourselves by a bond or an everlasting covenant that cannot be broken and he who breaketh it shall loose his office and standing in the church and shall be delivered over unto the buffetings of satan until the day of redemption behold this is the preparation wherewith

[374]Revelation[375] given Kirtland March 1, 1832

1[376] Hearken unto me saith the Lord your God O ye

who are ordained unto the high priests hood of my church

who have assembled [377][yourselves together and listen to

the counsel of him who has ordained you from on high

who shall speak in your ears the words of wisdom that

salvation may be unto you in that thing which you
have
presented before me saith the Lord God for verily
^
I say unto you the time has come and is now at hand

and behold and lo it must needs be that there be
                                        the
[378][an organization of the litterary and Mercantile establi=
                               ^
=shments of my Church both in this place and in

2 the Land of Zion for a permanent and everlasting

establishment and firm unto my church] to advance

the cause which ye have espoused to the Salvation

of man and to the glory of your Father who is in

heaven that you may be equal in ~~all~~ the bonds of

heavenly things yea and earthly things also for the obtain=

-ing of heavenly things for if ye are not equal in earthly things

ye cannot be equal in obtaining heavenly things for if ye

will that I give unto you a place in the Celestial ~~Kingdom~~

world ye must prepare yourselves by doing the things

which I have commanded and required of you and now

verily thus saith the Lord it is expedient that all things be

done unto my glory that ye should who are Joined together
        order   Ahashdah
in this ~~firm~~ or in other words that my Servant ~~Whitney~~[379] and
     Gazelam or Enoch   Pelagoram
my Servant ~~Joseph~~ and my Servant ~~Sidney~~[380] sit in counsel

with the Saints who are in Zion otherwise Satan Seeketh

to turn their hearts away from the truth that they become

blinded and understand not the things[381] which are prepared

for them wherefore a commandment I give unto you to

prepare and organize yourselves by a bond or an everlasting

covenant that cannot be broken and he who bre⟨a⟩keth it

shall loose his office and standing in the church and shall

be delivered over unto the buffittings of Satan until the

day of redemption behold this is the preperation wherewith

ORIGINAL INSCRIPTION
John Whitmer

REVISIONS
Oliver Cowdery
William W. Phelps
Sidney Rigdon
Joseph Smith
John Whitmer
Unidentified

374. The first publication reflecting most redactions in this revelation is the 1835 Doctrine and Covenants (section 75).

375. There are two small holes above "Revelation", suggesting that a slip of paper was pinned to the page. The paper may have contained editorial corrections keyed to the three numbers inserted in this revelation.

376. The three numbers inserted in this revelation likely directed a copyist or typesetter to insert text not found in the manuscript book. Such text appears in the 1835 Doctrine and Covenants, the first published version of this revelation. A new heading was also added in the 1835 Doctrine and Covenants.

377. The text from the beginning of this revelation up to this bracket was modified in the 1835 Doctrine and Covenants.

378. The text enclosed within these brackets was modified in the 1835 Doctrine and Covenants.

379. Newel K. Whitney.

380. Sidney Rigdon.

381. "s" possibly inserted.

I prepare you and the foundation and the insample
which I give unto you whereby you may accomplish
the commandments which are given you that through my
providence of your father notwithstanding the tribulations
which shall decend upon you that the church may stand independent
above all other creatures beneath the Celestial world
that you may come up unto the crown prepared for
you and be made rulers over many kingdoms saith
the Lord God the holy one [of Zion] verily verily I say
unto you ye are little children and ye have not as
yet understood how great blessings the father hath put
into his own hands and prepared for you and ye can not
bear all things now nevertheless be of good cheer for I
will lead you along the kingdom is yours and the blessings
thereof are yours and the riches of eternity are yours and he
who receiveth all things with thankfulness shall be made
glorious and the things of this earth shall be added unto him
an hundred fold
yea more: wherefore do the things which I have command
=ed you saith your Redeemer even the Son Ahman
=eth all things before he taketh you who prepar
the church of the first born and he will take
you up
in the cloud and appoint every man his portion and
he that is a faithful and wise steward shall inherit
all things Amen.

[Read] A Revelation (108) Compared
given Hiram
Portage County Ohio January 10. 1832
A Revelation to Joseph and Sidney the word of the Lord
unto them concerning the Elders of the Church of the living
God established in the last days making known the will
of the Lord unto the Elders what they shall do untill conferenced
for verily thus saith the Lord it is expedient in me that they
should continue preaching the gospel and in exhortation
to the churches in the regions round about untill conferenced
and behold then it shall be made known unto them
by the voice of the conference their several missions
Now verily I say unto my servants Joseph and Sidney

146 [verso]

I prepare you and the foundation³⁸² and the ensample

which I give unto you whereby you may accomplish

the commandments which are given you that through ~~the~~ ^my^

providences ~~of your fa{◊◊\ther}~~³⁸³ notwithstanding the tribulations

which shall decend upon you, ~~you~~ may sta{d\nd} independent ^that the church^

above all other creatures beneath the Celestial world

that you may come up unto the crown prepared for

you and be made rulers over many kingdoms saith

the Lord God the holy one [of ~~Israel~~]³⁸⁴ verily verily I say ^3 Zion^

unto you ye are little children and ye have not as

yet understood how great blessings the father has ~~put~~

~~into~~ his own hands and prepared for you and ye can not

bear all things now nevertheless be of good cheer for I

will lead you along the kingdom is yours and the blessings

thereof are yours and the riches of eternity are yours and he

who receiveth all things with thankfulness shall be made

glorious {in\and} the things of this ~~world~~ ~~even an~~³⁸⁵ hundred fold ^earth shall be added unto him^

yea more: wherefore do the things which I have command ^even an^

=ed you saith your Redeemer even ~~Jesus Christ~~ who prepar= ^the Son Ahman^

=eth all things before he ~~cometh and then he will come~~ ^taketh you for ye are ◊◊^

~~even with~~ the church of the first born and ~~receive you~~ ^he will take^

^you up³⁸⁶^ in the cloud and appoint every man his portion and

he that is a faithful and wise stewart shall inherit

all things Amen.

♦ [Read]³⁸⁷ A Revelation ·(No 8)³⁸⁸ {Read\Compared} given Hiram

Portage County Ohio January 10. 1832

A Revelation to Joseph and Sidney [Rigdon] the word of the Lord

unto them concerning the Elders of the Church of the living

God established in the last days making known the will

of the Lord unto the Elders what they shall do untill conference

for verily thus saith the Lord it is expedient in me that they

should continue preaching the gospel and in exhortation

to the churches in the regions round about untill conference

and behold then it shall be made known unto them

by the voice of the conference their several missions

Now verily I say unto my servants Joseph and Sidney

ORIGINAL INSCRIPTION
John Whitmer

REVISIONS
Oliver Cowdery
William W. Phelps
Sidney Rigdon
Joseph Smith
John Whitmer
Unidentified

382. There are two small holes below "the foundation". (See 267n375 herein.)

383. "◊◊" wipe-erased and written over; then stricken with entire phrase.

384. The text at this point is significantly expanded in the 1835 Doctrine and Covenants.

385. The dotted underline indicates that the text should be left as it was originally written.

386. Or "into".

387. This notation appears to match the ink flow of a similar notation on manuscript page 76, but its meaning is unknown. (See 125n151 herein.)

388. For an explanation of this numbering, see 159n196 herein.

saith the Lord it is expedient to translate again and
inasmuch as it is practicable to preach in the regions
round about untill conference and after that it is expe
=dient to continue the work of translation untill it be
finished and let this be a pattern unto the Elders
until further knowledge even as it is written and
now I give no more unto you at this time gird
up your loins and be sober even so Amen.

A Revelation given Hiram

Portage County Ohio March 17, 1832

Verily thus saith the Lord unto you my servant Steppen
Burnett
Go ye go ye into the world and preach the Gospel to every
creature that cometh under the sound of your voice and in
asmuch as you desire a companion I will give unto
you my servant Eden smith wherefore go ye and preach
my gospel whether to the North or to the South to the East
or to the West it mattereth not for you cannot go amiss
therefore declare those things which you have heard and
verily believe and know to be true behold this is
the will of him who hath called you your Redeemer
even Jesus Christ Amen

Revelation given March 12

1832 Hiram Portage Ohio

Verily I say unto you that it is my will that mine
servant Jarad Carter should go again into the eastern countries
as from place to place and from city to city in
the power of the ordination wherewith he has been
ordained proclaiming glad tidings of great joy
even the everlasting Gospel and I will send upon
him the comforter which shall teach him the
truth and the way whether he shall go and inas=
=much as he is faithful I will crown him again with
sheaves wherefore let your heart be glad my servant
Jared Carter and fear not saith your Lord even Jesus
Christ Amen

Saith the Lord it is expedient to translate again and

inasmuch as it is practicable to preach in the regions

r{◊\ound} about untill conference and after that it is expe

=dient to continue the work of translation untill it be

finished and let this be a pattern unto the Elders

until further knowledge even as it is written and ~~now~~

now I give no more unto you at this time gird

up your loins and be sober even so Amen.

♦ # A Revelation given Hiram

Portage County Ohio March 17.³⁸⁹ 1832

Verily thus saith the Lord unto you my Servant~~s~~ Stephen
Burnett³⁹⁰
go ye go ye into the world and preach the Gospel to every

creature that cometh under the sound of your voice and in

asmuch as you desire a companion I will give unto

you my Servant Eden Smith wherefore go ye and preach

my gospel whether to the North or to the South to the East

or to the West it mattereth not for you cannot go amiss

therefore declare the~~se~~³⁹¹ things which you have heard and

verily belieeve and know to be true behold this is

the will of him who hath called you your Redeemer

even Jesus Christ Amen

♦ ³⁹²# Revelation given March 12

1832 Hiram Portage Ohio

Verily I say unto you that it is my wil{◊\l} that my

Servant³⁹³ Jarad [Jared] Carter should go again into the eastern countri

=es from place to place and from City to City in

the power of the ordination wherewith he has been

ordained proclaiming glad tidings of great Joy

even the everlasting Gospel and I will Send upon

him the comforter which shall teach him the

truth and the way whither he shall go and inas=

=much as he is faithful I will crown him again with

sheaves³⁹⁴ wherefore let your heart be glad my servant
Carter
Jared and fear not saith your Lord even Jesus

Christ Amen — — — —

ORIGINAL INSCRIPTION
John Whitmer

REVISIONS
Oliver Cowdery
William W. Phelps
Sidney Rigdon
Joseph Smith
John Whitmer
Unidentified

389. The ink flow of "1" is heavier than the surrounding text, perhaps indicating that this numeral was inserted later. This revelation should be dated 7 March 1832. For more information on this dating, see the discussion of this revelation in the Documents series.

390. "Burnett" first appears in print in the 1835 Doctrine and Covenants (section 77).

391. "se" wipe-erased and then stricken.

392. The first publication reflecting the redactions in this revelation is the 1835 Doctrine and Covenants (section 76).

393. This insertion is possibly in the same ink flow as the original text, which would indicate that John Whitmer made the change at the time of original inscription.

394. Final "s" possibly inserted.

Revelation given March 20.th
1832 Portage Co Ohio.

It is expedient with the Lord unto you that the paper shall be purchased for the printing of the Book of the Lords commandments and it must needs be that you take it with you for it is not expedient that my servant Marten should as yet go up unto the Land of Zion let the purchase be made by the Bishop if needs must be by him whatsoever is done let it be done in the name of the Lord.

Revelation given Hiram
Portage County August 29. 1832

Behold thus saith the Lord unto you my servant John (Murdock) thou art called to go into the eastern countries from house to house and from Village to Village and from City to City to proclaim mine everlasting gospel unto the inhabitants thereof in the midst of persecution and wickedness and whoso receiveth you receiveth me and you shall have power to declare my word in the demonstration of my Holy Spirit and whoso receiveth you as a little child receiveth my kingdom and blessed are they for they shall obtain mercy and whoso rejecteth you shall be rejected of my father and his house and you shall cleanse your feet in the secret places by the way for a testimony against them. And behold, and lo I come quickly to judgement to convince all of their ungodly deeds which they have committed against me as it is written of me in the volume of the Book. And now verily I say unto you that it is not expedient that you should go untill your children are provided for and kindly sent up unto the bishop in Zion and after a few years if thou desirest of me thou mayest go up also unto the goodly land to possess thine inheritance otherwise thou shalt continue proclaiming my gospel until thou be taken Amen.

148 [verso]

♦ ³⁹⁵**Revelation** given {m\⟨M⟩}arch 20.ᵗʰ

1832 Portage Co Ohio.

It is expedient Saith the Lord unto you that the

paper shall be purchased for the printing of the

Book of the Lord's commandments and it must needs

be that you take it with you for it is not

expedient that my Servent Martin [Harris] should as yet go

up unto the Land of Zion let the purchase be

made by the Bishop if needs must be by ~~him~~ hire

whatsoever is done let it be done in the name

of the Lord.

♦ **Revelation** given Hiram

Portage County {◊◊\August} 29. 1832

Behold thus saith the Lord unto you my servant John (Murdock)

thou art called to go unto the eastern countries from house to house

and from Village to Village and from City to City to proclaim

mine everlasting gospel unto the inhabitants thereof in the midst of

persecution and wickedness and whoso~~ever~~ receiveth you receiveth

me and you shall have power to declare my word in the demm=

=onstration of my Holy Spirit and whoso receiveth you as a little

child receiveth my kingdom and blessed are they for they shall

obtain mercy and whoso rejecteth you shall be rejected of my

fa{r\ther} and his house and you shall cleanse your feet in the secret

                                                          and
places {◊◊\by} the way for a testimony against them. And behold, Lo
                                                           ^
I come quickly to Judgement to convin[c]e all of their ungodly deeds

which they have committed against me as it is written of me

in the volume of the Book. And now verily I say unto you

that it is not expedient that you should go untill your children
                    for
are provided ᶺ and kindly sent up unto the bishop in Zion and

after a few years if thou desirest of me thou mayest go

up also unto the goodly land to possess thine inheritanc[e]

otherwise thou shalt continue proclaiming my Gospel

until thou be taken Amen.

Oʀɪɢɪɴᴀʟ Iɴꜱᴄʀɪᴘᴛɪᴏɴ
John Whitmer

Rᴇᴠɪꜱɪᴏɴꜱ
Oliver Cowdery
William W. Phelps
Sidney Rigdon
Joseph Smith
John Whitmer
Unidentified

395. This entire revelation is crossed out with an X in what appears to match the ink flow of William W. Phelps's redactions on the previous page. The X presumably marked the revelation for exclusion from publication. This revelation did not appear in any JS-era publication.

A Revelation given at Kirtland
September 22 & 23, 1832.

A Revelation of Jesus Christ unto his servant Joseph and six elders as they united their hearts in lifting their voice on high yea the word of the Lord concerning his church established in the last days for the restoration of his people as he has spoken by the mouths of his prophets and for the gathering of his saints to stand upon mount Zion which shall be called the city New Jerusalem which city shall be built beginning at the Temple lot which is appointed by the finger of the Lord in the western boundaries of the state of Missouri and dedicated by the hand of Joseph and others with whom the Lord was well pleased verily this is the word of the Lord that the city New Jerusalem shall be built by the gathering of the saints beginning at this place even the place of the temple which temple shall be reared in this generation for verily this generation shall not all pass away untill an house shall be built unto the Lord and a cloud shall rest upon it which cloud shall be even the glory of the Lord which shall fill the house and the Sons of Moses according to the holy priesthood which he received under the hand of his father in law Jethro and Jethro received it under the hand of Caleb and Caleb received it under the hand of Elihu and Elihu under the hand of Jeremy and Jeremy under the hand of Gad and Gad under the hand of Esaias and Esaias received it under the hand of God Esaias also lived in the days of Abraham and was blessed of him which Abraham received the priesthood from Melchizedek who received it through the lineage of his father even till Noah and from Noah till Enoch through the lineage of their fathers and from Enoch to Abel who was slain by the conspiracy of his brother who received the priesthood by the commandment of God by the hand of his father Adam who was the first man which priesthood continueth in the church of God in all generations and is without beginning of days or end of years and the Lord

♦ # A Revelation given at Kirtland

September 22 & 23, 1832.

A Revelation of Jesus Christ unto his Servant Joseph and Six elders

as they united their hearts in lifting their voices on high y[e]a the

word of the Lord concerning his church established in the last

days for the restoration of his people as he has spok{ɵ\en} by

the mouths³⁹⁶ of his p{ɵ\rophets} and for the gathering of his

sa{nts\ints} to stand upon mount Z[i]on which Shall be called

the city New Jerusalem which city shall be built begin=

=ning at the Temple lot which is appointed by the finger

of the Lord in the westeren boundaries of the state of

Missouri and dedicated by the hand of Joseph and

others with the³⁹⁷ whom the Lord was well pleased verily this

is the word of the Lord that the city New Je{uɵ\rusalem} shall

be built by the gathering of the Saints beginning at this

place even the place of the temple which temple shall be

reared in this generation for verily this generation shall

not all pass away untill an house shall be built unto the

Lord and a cloud shall rest upon it which cloud shall be

even the glory of the Lord which shall fill the house and

the Sons of Mosses according to the holy priesthood which he

received under the hand of his father{in\ in} law Jethro and Jethro

received it under the hand of Caleb and Caleb received it under

the hand of Elihu and Elihu under the hand of Jeremy and

Jeremy under the hand of Gad and Gad under the han{ɵ\d} of

Esaias and Esaias received it under the hand of God Esaias

also lived in the days of Abraham and was blessed of him

which Abraham received the priesthood from Melch{ɵs\iz}ede{c\k}

who received it through the lineage of h{ɵs\is} father even till

Noah and from Noah till Enoch through the lineage of

their fathers and from Enoch to Abel who was Slain

by the conspiracy of his brother who received the priesthood

by the commandment of God by the hand of his father

Adam who was the first man which priesthood con=

=tinueth in the church of God in all generations and is

without begining of days or end of years and the Lord

ORIGINAL INSCRIPTION
John Whitmer

REVISIONS
Oliver Cowdery
William W. Phelps
Sidney Rigdon
Joseph Smith
John Whitmer
Unidentified

396. "s" wipe-erased and then stricken.

397. "the" partially wipe-erased and then stricken.

confirmed a priesthood also upon Aaron and his seed throughout all the generations of the Jews which priesthood continueth and abideth forever with the priesthood which is after the holiest order of God and this greater priesthood administereth the gospel and holdeth the keys of the mysteries of the kingdom even the key of the knowledge of God therefore in the ordinances thereof the power of godliness is manifest and without the ordinances thereof and the authority of the Priesthood the power of godliness is not manifest unto man in the flesh for without this no man can see the face of God even the father and live now this Moses plainly taught to the children of Israel in the wilderness and sought dilligently to sanctify his people that they might behold the face of God but they hardened their hearts and could not endure his presence therefore the Lord in his wrath for his anger was kindled against them swore that they should not enter into his rest which rest is the fulness of his glory while in the wilderness therefore he took Moses out of their midst and the holy priesthood also, and the lesser priesthood continued which priesthood holdeth the keys of the ministring of Angels and the preparatory gospel which gospel is the gospel of repentance and baptisam and the remission of sins and the law of carnal commandments which the Lord in his wrath caused to continue with the house of Aaron among the children of Israel untill John whom God raised up being filled with the Holy Ghost from his mothers womb for he was baptized while he was yet in the womb and was ordained by the Angel of God at the time he was eight days old unto this power to overthrow the kingdom of the Jews and to make strait the way of the Lord before the face of his people to prepare them for the coming of the Lord in whose hand is given all power. And again the offices of elder and bishop are necessary appendages belonging unto the high priesthood. And again the offices of teachers and deacons are necessary appendages belonging to the lesser priesthood which priesthood was confirmed

150 [verso]

confirmed a priesthood also upon Aaron and his seed

throughout all the generations of {his\the} Jews which priest=

-hood continueth and abideth forever with the priesthood

which is after the holiest order of God and this greater

priesthood administereth the gospel and holdeth the keys of

the mysteries of the kingdom even the key of the knowledge

of {g\God} therefore in the ordinances thereof the power of Godliness

is manifest and without the ordinances thereof and the authority

of the Priesthood the power of Godliness is not manifest unto

m{e\an} in the flesh for without this no man can see the face

of God even the father and live now this Moses plainly

taught to the children of Israel in the wilderness and ~~soug~~

sought dilligently to sanctify his people that they might

behold the face of God but th[e]y hardened the{r\ir} hearts and

could not endure his presence therefore the Lord in his for ^wrath^

his anger was kindled against them Swore that they should

not enter into his {~~glory~~\rest} which rest is the fulness of his

glory while in the wilderness therefore he took Mos{~~ses~~\es} out

of their midst and the holy priesthood also, and the lesser

priesthood continued which priesthood holdeth the keys of

the ministring of Angels and the preparatory gospel

which gospel is the gospel of repentance and baptisam and

the remission of sins and the law of carnal commandments

which the Lord in his wrath caused to continue with

the house of Aaron among the children of Israe{el\l} untill

John whom God raised up being filled with the Holy

Ghost from his mothers womb for he was baptized while

he was yet in the womb and was ordained by the

Angel of God at the time he was eight days old unto

this power to overthrow the kingdom of the Jews and to

make strait the way of the Lord before the face of his

people to prepare them for the coming of the Lord in

whose hand is given all power. And again the offices of

Elder and bishop are ~~nessessarery~~[398] necessary appendages belon=

-ging unto the high priesthood And again ^the^ offices of

teachers and deacons are necessary appendages belonging

to the lesser priesthood which priesthood was confirmed

ORIGINAL INSCRIPTION
John Whitmer

REVISIONS
Oliver Cowdery
William W. Phelps
Sidney Rigdon
Joseph Smith
John Whitmer
Unidentified

398. "nessessarery" wipe-erased and then stricken.

upon Aaron and his sons therefore as I said concerning the sons of Moses for the sons of Moses and also the sons of Aaron shall offer an acceptable offering and sacrifice in the house of the Lord which house shall be built unto the Lord in this generation upon the consecrated spot as I have appointed and the sons of Moses and of Aaron shall be filled with the glory of the Lord upon Mount Zion in the Lords house whose sons are ye and also many whom I have called and sent forth to build up my church for whoso is faithful unto the obtaining of these two priesthoods of which I have spoken and the magnifying their calling are sanctified by the spirit unto the renewing of their body that they become the sons of Moses and Aaron and the seed of Abraham and the church and kingdom and the elect of God and also all they who receive this priesthood receiveth me saith the Lord for he that receiveth my servants receiveth me and he that receiveth me receiveth my father and he that receiveth my father receiveth my fathers kingdom therefore all that my father hath shall be given unto him and this is according to the oath and the covenant which belongeth to the priesthood therefore all those who receive the priesthood receiveth this oath and covenant of my father which he cannot brake neither can it be moved but whoso braketh this covenant after he hath received it and altogether turneth therefrom shall not have forgiveness in this world nor in the world to come and all those who come not unto this priesthood which ye have received which I now confirm upon you who are present this day viz. the twenty third day of September one thousand eight hundred and thirty two eleven high priests save one by mine own voice out of the heavens and even I have given the heavenly hosts and mine Angels charge concerning you and I now give unto you a commandment to be wise concerning yourselves to give heed dilligently to the words of eternal life for you shall live by every word that proceedeth forth from the mouth of God for the word of the Lord is truth and whatsoever is truth is light and whatsoever is light is spirit even the spirit of Jesus Christ and the spirit giveth light to every man that cometh into the world and the spirit lighteneth every man through the world that hearkeneth to the voice of the spirit and every one that hearkeneth to the voice of

151 [recto]

upon Aaron and his Sons therefore as I said concer=
-ning the sons of {m\⟨M⟩}oses for the sons of Mos{~~s~~\es} and also
the sons of Aaron shall offer an acceptable offering and
sacrifice in the house of the Lord which house shall
~~shall~~ be built unto the Lord in this generation upon the con
=secrated spot as I have appointed and the sons of Moses and
of Aaron shall be filled with the glory of the Lord upon Mount
Zion in the Lords house whose sons are ye and also many
whom I have {~~◊◊◊~~\called} and sent forth to build up my church for
whoso is faithful unto the obtaining of these two priesthoods of
{~~◊~~\which} I have spoken and the magnifying their calling are sancti-
-fied by the spirit unto the renewing of their bod{~~ies~~\y} that they become[399]
the Sons of Moses and Aaron and the seed of Abraham and the chur=
=ch and kingdom and the elect of God and also all they who receive this
priesthood receiveth me saith the Lord for he that receiveth my ~~servant~~
servants receiveth me and he that receiveth me receiveth my father and
he that receiveth my father receiveth my father's {~~ki◊n~~\kingdom} Therefore
all that my father hath shall be given unto {~~◊◊~~\him} and this is according
to the oath and ^the covenant which belongeth to the priesthood therefore
all those who receive the priesthood {~~◊◊~~\receiveth} this oath and covenant
of my father which he cannot brake neither can it be moved but
{~~◊◊i◊◊◊~~\whoso} braketh this covenant after he hath received it and altogether
turneth therefrom shall not have forgiveness in this world nor
in the world to come and all those who come[400] not unto this
priesthood which ye have received which I now confirm upon you
who are present this day viz. the twenty third day of September
one thousand eight hundred and thirty two eleven high priests save
one by ~~my~~ mine own voice out of the heavens and even I have given
the heavenly hosts and mine Angels charge concerning you and I
now give unto you a commandment to be ware concerning your=
=selves to give heed dilligently to the words of eternal life for you
shall live by every word that proceedeth forth from the mouth
of God. for the word of the Lord is truth and {~~what◊◊◊~~\whatsoever} is truth is
light and whatsoever is light is spirit even the Spirit of Jesus Christ
and the spirit giveth light to every man that cometh into the world
and the Spirit lighteneth every man through the world that hearkeneth
to the voice of the Spirit {an\And} every one that hearkeneth to the voice of

Original Inscription
John Whitmer

Revisions
Oliver Cowdery
William W. Phelps
Sidney Rigdon
Joseph Smith
John Whitmer
Unidentified

399. Or "became".
400. Or "came".

152 the spirit cometh unto God even the father and the father teacheth him of the covenants which he hath renewed and confirmed upon you which is confirmed upon you for your sakes and not for your sakes only but for the sake of the whole world and the whole world lieth in sin and groaneth under darkness and under the bondage of sin and by this you may know they are under the bondage of sin because they come not unto me for whoso cometh not unto me is under the bondage of sin and whoso receiveth not my voice is not acquainted with my voice and is not of me And by this you may know the righteous from the wicked and that the whole world groaneth under sin and darkness even now and your minds in time past have been darkened because of unbelief and because you have treated lightly the things you have received which vanity and unbelief hath brought the whole church under condemnation and this condemnation resteth upon the children of Zion even all and they shall remain under this condemnation untill they repent and remember the new covenant even the Book of Mormon and the former commandments which I have given them not only to say but to do according to that which I have written that they may bring forth fruit meet for their fathers kingdom otherwise there remaineth a scourge and a judgement to be poured out upon the children of Zion for shall the children of the kingdom pollute my holy land verily verily I say unto you nay. Verily verily I say unto you who now hear my words which is my voice blessed are you inasmuchas you receive these things for I will forgive you of your sins with this commandment that you remain steadfast in your minds in solemnity and the spirit of prayer in bearing testimony to all the world of those things which are communicated unto you Therefore go ye into all the world and whatsoever place ye cannot go into ye shall send that the testimony may go forth from you into all the world unto every creature and as I said unto mine Apostles even so I say unto you for ye are mine Apostles even God's high Priests ye are they whom my father hath given me ye are my friends Therefore as I said unto mine Apostles I say unto you again that every soul who

152 [verso]
the Spirit cometh unto God even the father and the father

teacheth him the covenants which he hath renewed and confirmed
of
^

upon you which is confirmed upon you for your Sa{◊\kes} and

not for your Sakes only but for the Sake of the whole world

and the whole world lieth in sin and groaneth under darkness and under

the bondage of sin and by this you may know they are under the

bondage of sin because they come not unto me for whoso

cometh not unto me is under the bondage of sin and

whoso receiveth not my voice is not accquainted with my

voice and is not of me{◊.} And by this you may know the right=

=eous from the wicked and that the whole world groaneth under

sin and darkness even now and your minds in time past have

been darkened because of unbelief and because you have treated

lightly the things you have received which vanity and unbelief

hath brought the whole church under condemnation and this

condemnation resteth upon the children of Zion even all

and {shall\they} shall remain under this condemnation untill they

repent and remember the new covenant even the Book of

Mormon and the former commandments which I have

given them not only to say but to do {◊◊◊◊\according} to that

which I have written that they may bring forth fruit meet

for their fathers kingdom otherwise there remaineth a scourge

and a Judgement to be poured out upon the children of Zion

for shall the children of the kingdom pollute my holy land

verily verily I say unto you nay. Verily verily I say unto you who

now hear my words which is my voice blessed are you inasmuch as

you receive these things for I will forgive you of of your sins

with this commandment that you remain steadfast in your minds

in solemnity and the spirit of prayer in bearing testimony to

all the world of th{e\o}se things which are communicated unto

you Therefore go ye into all the world and whatsoever place

ye cannot go into ye shall send {t◊◊\that} the testimony may go

forth from you into all the world unto every creature and as

I said unto mine Apostles even so I say unto you for ye are

mine Apostles even God's high Priests ye are th{y\ey} whom my[401]

my father hath given me ye are my friends Therefore as I said

unto mine Apostles I say unto you again that every soul who

ORIGINAL INSCRIPTION
John Whitmer

REVISIONS
Oliver Cowdery
William W. Phelps
Sidney Rigdon
Joseph Smith
John Whitmer
Unidentified

401. "my" wipe-erased and
then stricken.

believeth on your words and are baptized by water for the
remission of their sins shall receive the holy Ghost and these signs
shall follow them in my name they shall do many wonderful
works in my name they shall cast out devils in my name they
shall heal the sick in my name they shall open the eyes of
the blind and unstop the ears of the deaf and the tongue of
the dumb shall speak and if any man shall administer poison
unto them it shall not hurt them & the poison of the serpent
shall not have power to harm them. But a commandment I
give unto them that they shall not boast themselves of
these things neither speak them before the world for these
things are given unto you for your profit and for salvation
Verily verily I say unto you he who believeth not on your words
and are not baptized by water in my name for the remission
of their sins that they may receive the holy Ghost shall be
damned and shall not come into my fathers kingdom where
I and my father & I am and this revelation unto you and command
-ment is in force from this very hour upon all the world
and this gospel is unto all who have not received it but verily
I say unto all those to whom the kingdom has been given
from you it must be preached unto them that they shall
repent of their former evil works for they are to be upbraided
for their evil hearts of unbelief and your brethren in Zion
for their rebellion against you at the time I sent you
And again I say unto you my friends for from henceforth I shall call
you friends it is expedient that I give unto you this command
-ment that you become even as my friends in days when
I was with them in travelling to preach this gospel in my
power for I suffered them not to have purse or scrip neither
two coats Behold I send you; out to prove the world and the laborer
is worthy of his hire and any man that shall go and preach
this gospel of the kingdom and fail not to continue faithful in
all things shall not be weary in mind neither darkened neither
body limb or joint and an hair of your heads shall not fall
to the ground unnoticed and they shall not go hungry neither
athirst Therefore take no thought for the morrow for what ye
shall eat or what ye shall drink or wherewithall ye shall be

~~belongeth~~[402]   153 [recto]

believeth on your words and are baptized by water for the ~~rem~~

remission of their sins shall receive the holy Ghost and these signs

shall follow them in my name they shall do many wonderful

works in my name they shall cast out devils in my name they

shall heal the sick in my name they shall open the eyes of

the blind and unstop the ears of the deaf and the tongue of

the dumb shall speak and if any man shall administer poison

unto {~~you~~\them} It shall not hurt them the poison of the Serpent

shall not have power to harm them. But a commandment I

give unto them that they shall not boast themselves of

these things neither speak them before the world for these

things are given unto you for your prophet [profit] and {◊◊◊\for} Salvation

Verily verily I say unto you he who believeth not on your words

and are not baptized by water in my name for the remission

of their sins that they may receive the holy Gost shall be ~~damnd~~[403]

damned and shall not come into my fathers kingdom where

~~I and~~ my father am and this revelation unto you and comm

-andment is in force from this {◊◊◊\very} hour upon all the world

and this gospel is unto all who have not received it but verily

I say unto all those to whom the kingdom has been given

from you it must be preached unto them that they Shall

repent of their former evil work for they are to be upbraided

for their evil hearts of unbelief and your brethren in Zion

for their rebellion against you at the time I sent you

And again I say unto you my friends for from henceforth I shall call

you ~~my~~ friends {i◊\it} is expedient that I give unto you this command-

=ment that you become even as my friends in days ~~of old~~ when

I was with them in travelling to preach this gospel in my

power for I suffered them not to have purse or scrip neither

two coats Behold I send you; out to prove the world and the laborer

is worthy of his hire and any man that shall go and preach

this gospel of the kingdom and fail not to continue faithful in

all things shall not be weary in mind neither darkened neither

body limb or Joint and an hair of your heads shall not fall

to the ground unnoticed and they shall not go hungary neither

athurst Therefore take no thought for the morrow for what ye

shall eat or what ye shall drink or wherewithall ye shall be

ORIGINAL INSCRIPTION
John Whitmer

REVISIONS
Oliver Cowdery
William W. Phelps
Sidney Rigdon
Joseph Smith
John Whitmer
Unidentified

402. It appears that John Whitmer deleted his false start "belongeth" and then continued writing below the deletion, gradually bringing the words up to the first line.

403. "damnd" wipe-erased and then stricken.

clothed for consider the lillies of the field how they grow
they toil not neither do they spin and the kingdoms of this
world and all their glory are not arrayed like one of these
for your father who is not in heaven knoweth that you have
need of all these things Therefore let the morrow take thought for
the things of itself. Neither take ye thought beforehand what
ye shall say but treasure up in your minds continually the
words of life and it shall be given you in the very hour
that portion that shall be meeted unto every man Therefore
let no man among you (for this commandment is unto all
the faithful who are called of God in the church unto the
ministry) therefore let no man from this hour take purse
or scrip that goeth forth to proclaim this gospel of the kingdom
behold I send you out to reprove the world of all their unright
-teous deeds and to teach them of a judgment which is to
come and whoso receiveth you there I will be also for I
will go before your face I will be on your right hand and on
your left and my spirit shall be in your hearts and mine
angels round about you to bear you up whoso receiveth you
receiveth me and the same will feed you and clothe you and
give you money and he who feedeth you and clotheth you or
giveth you money shall in no wise loose his reward And
he that doeth not these things is not my disciple by this you
may know my disciples He that receiveth you not go away
from him alone by yourselves and cleanse your feet even
with water pure water whether in heat or in cold and bear
testimony of it unto your father which is in heaven and return
not again unto that man. And in whatsoever Village or city ye
enter do likewise Nevertheless search dilligently and spare not
wo unto that house or that village or city that rejecteth you or
your words or testimony concerning me wo I say unto you
again unto that house or that village or city that rejecteth
you or your words or your testimony of me for I the Almighty
have laid my hand upon the Nations to scourge them for
their wickedness and plagues shall go forth and it shall
not be taken from the earth untill I have completed my
work which shall be cut short in righteousness untill all

154 [verso]

clothed for consider the lillies of the field how they grow

they toil not neither do they spin and the kingdoms of this

world and all their glory are not arrayed like one of these

for your father ~~which~~ ^who^ art in heaven knoweth that you have

^need^ of all these things Therefore let the morrow take thought for

the things of itself. Neither take ye thought beforehand what

ye shall say but treasure up in your minds continually the

words of life and it shall be given you in the very hour

that portion that shall be meeted unto every m{◊◊\an} Therefore

let no man among you (for this commandment is unto all

the faithful who are called of God in the church unto the

ministry) theref{◊◊\ore} let no man from this hour take purse

or scrip that goeth forth to proclaim this gospel of the kingdom

behold I {◊◊◊◊◊◊◊\⟨send you⟩} out to reprove the world of all their unrigh

=teous deeds and to teach them of a Judgment {t◊◊◊◊e\which is} to

come and whoso receiveth you th{em\ere} I will be also for I

will go before your face I will be on your right hand and on

your left and my Spirit shall be in your hearts and mine

angels round about you to bear you up whoso receiveth you

receiveth me and the same will feed you and clothe you and

give you money and he who feedeth you and clothes you or

giveth you money shall in no wise loose his~e~ reward And

he that doeth not these things is not my disciple by this you

may know my disciples He that receiveth you not go away

from him alone by yourselves and cleanse your feet even

with water pure water whether in heat or in cold and bear

testimony of it unto your father which is in heaven and return

not again unto that man. And in whatsoever Village or City ye

enter do likewise Nevertheless search dilligently and spare not

wo unto that house or that village or city that rejecteth you or

your words or testimony concerning me wo I say ~~unto you~~

again unto {◊◊◊◊\that}[404] house or that village or city that rejecte{d\th}

you or your words or your testimony of me for I the Almighty

have laid my hand upon the Nations to Scourge them for

their wick{ned\edness} and plagues shall go forth and it shall

not be taken from the earth untill I have completed my

work which shall be cut short in righteousness untill all

ORIGINAL INSCRIPTION
John Whitmer

REVISIONS
Oliver Cowdery
William W. Phelps
Sidney Rigdon
Joseph Smith
John Whitmer
Unidentified

404. "◊◊◊◊" wipe-erased and then partially knife-erased.

155

shall know me who remain even from the least unto the
greatest and shall be filled with the knowledge of the Lord and
shall see eye to eye and shall lift up the voice and with the
voice together sing this new song saying the Lord hath brought
again Zion the Lord hath redeemed his people Israel according to
the election of grace which was brought to pass by the faith
and covenant of their fathers the Lord hath redeemed his people
and Satan is bound and time is no longer the Lord hath gathered
all things in one the Lord hath brought down Zion from above
the Lord hath brought up Zion from beneath the earth hath
travelled and brought forth her strength and truth is establish=
=ed in her bowels and the heavens hath smiled upon her and she
is clothed with the glory of her God for he standeth in the midst of
his people. Glory and honor and power and might be ascribed to
our God for he is full of mercy justice grace and truth and
peace for ever and ever Amen

Received on the 23 day of September 1832
And Again Verily verily I say unto you it is expedient that every
man who goes forth to proclaim mine everlasting Gospel that
inasmuch as they have families and receive moneys by gift
they should send it unto them or make use of it for their
benefit as the Lord shall direct them. for thus it seemeth me
good and let all those who have not families who receive
moneys send it up unto the bishop in Zion or unto the
bishop in Ohio that it may be consecrated for the bringing
forth of the revelations and the printing thereof and for establi=
=shing of Zion and if any man shall give unto any of you a
coat or a suit take the old and cast it unto the poor and go
your way rejoicing And if any man among you be strong
in the spirit let him take with him he that is weak that he
may be edified in all meekness that he may become strong also.
Therefore take with you those who are ordained unto the lesser
priesthood and send them before you to make appointments and to
prepare the way and to fill appointments that yourselves are not able
to fill Behold this is the way that mine Apostles in ancient days
built up my church unto me therefore let every man stand
in his own office labor in his own calling and let not the head

shall know me who remain even from the least unto the

greatest and shall be filled with the knowledge of the Lord and

shall see eye to eye and shall lift up the voice and with the

voice together sing this new song Saying the Lord hath brought

again Zion the Lord hath redeemed his people Israel according to

the election of grace which was brought to pass by the faith

and covenant of their fathers the Lord hath redeemed his people

and Satan is bound and time is no longer the Lord hath gathered

all things in one the Lord hath brought down Zion from above

the Lord hath brought up Zion from beneath the earth hath

travelled and brought forth her strength and truth is establish=

=ed in her bowels and the heavens hath smiled upon her and she

is clothed with the glory of the {Lord\her} God for he standeth in the midst of

h{er\is} people. Glory and honor and power and might be asscribed to

our God for he is full of mercy Justice grace and truth and pe

peace for ever and ever Amen

Received on the 23 day of September 1832

And Again Verily verily I say unto you it is expedient that every

man who goes forth to proclaim mine everlasting Gospel that

inasmuch as they have families and receive moneys by gift

they should send it unto them or make use of it for the{◊◊\ir}

benefit as the Lord shall direct them. for thus it seemeth me

good and let all those who have not families who receive

money {who receive\send it} up unto the bishop ᵢₙ Zion or unto the

bishop ᵢₙ Ohio that it may be consecrated for the bringing

forth of the revelations and the printing thereof and for establi=

=shing of Zion and if any man shall give unto any of you a

coat or a suit take {it\the} old and cast it unto the poor and go

your way rejoicing And if any man among you be strong

in the spirit let him take with him he that is weak that he

may be edified in all meekness that he may become strong also.

Therefore take with you those who are ordained unto the lesser

priesthood and send them before you to make appointments and to {◊◊◊\pre=}

=pare the way and to fill appointments that yourselves are not able

to fill Behold this is the way that mine Apostles in ancient days

built up my church unto m{◊\e} therefore let every man stand

in his own office & labor in his own calling and let not the head

ORIGINAL INSCRIPTION
John Whitmer

REVISIONS
Oliver Cowdery
William W. Phelps
Sidney Rigdon
Joseph Smith
John Whitmer
Unidentified

say into the feet it hath no need of the feet for without the feet how shall the body be able to stand: Also the body hath need of every member that all may be edified together that the system may be kept perfect And behold the high-priesthood should travel and also the elders and also the lesser priests. But the Deacons and Teachers should be appointed to watch over the church to be ^a standing minister unto the church and the bishops also should travel ^and ^round about and among all the churches searching after the poor to ~~administer~~ minister to their wants by humbling the rich and the proud he should also employ ~~an~~ agents for to take charge and to do his secular business as he shall direct nevertheless let the bishop go unto the city of New York and also to the city of Albany and also to the city of Boston and warn the people of those cities with the sound of the gospel with a loud voice of the desolation and utter abolishment which awaits them if they do reject these things for if they do reject these things the hour of their judgment is nigh and their houses shall be left unto them desolate. Let him trust in me and he shall not be confounded and an hair of his head shall not fall to the ground unnoticed And verily I say unto you the rest of my servants go ye forth as your circumstances shall permit in your several callings unto the great and notable cities and villages reproving the world in righteous-ness of all their unrighteousness and ungodly deeds setting forth clearly and understandingly the desolation of abomination in the last days. For with you saith the Lord Almighty I will rend their kingdoms I will not only shake the earth but the starry ^heavens shall ~~tremble~~ also for I the Lord have put forth mine hand to exhert the powers of heaven ye cannot see it now yet a little while and ye shall see it and know that I am and that I will come and reign with my people I am Alpha and Omega the begining and the end AMEN

142
24
56 8
288
440,80   4,40

156 [verso]

      say {t͟o͟ ͟o͟o͟o͟\unto the} feet it hath no need of the feet for without

the feet how shall the body be able to stand: Alas the body

hath need of every member that all may be edified together

that the system may be kept perfect And behold the high-

priesthood should travel and also the elder's and also the lesser

priests But the Deacons and Teachers should be appointed to watch

over the church to be ^a^ standing minister unto the church and

the bishop also should travel ^round^ about and among all the churches

searching after the poor to ⟨ad⟩minister to their wants by humbling

the rich and the proud {◊\⟨H⟩}e should also employ {a͟n͟\an} agents for

to take charge and to do his secular business as he shall direct

nevertheless let the bishop go unto the c{t͟\ity} of New York and

also to the city of Albany and also to the city of Boston and

warn the peopl of those cities with the sound of the gospel

with a loud voi{◊\ce} of the desolation and utter abollishment

which awaits them if they do reject these things for if

they do reject these things the hour of their Judgment is nigh

and their houses shall be left unto them desolate Let him

trust in me and he shall not be confounded and an hair of

his head shall not fall to the ground unnoticed And verily I say

unto you the rest of my servants go ye forth as your circumstances

shall permit in your several callings unto the great and

notable cities and villages reproving the world in righteous=

=ness of all their unrighteousness and ungodly deeds setting forth

clearly and understandingly the desolation of abomination◊[405] in the

last days. For with you saith the Lord Almighty I will rend

their kingdoms I will not only shake the earth but the Starry

{◊◊◊◊◊◊◊◊\Shall tremble} ^heavens^ also for I the Lord have put forth mine hand

to exhert the powers of heaven ye cannot see it now yet a

little while and ye shall see it and know that I am and

that I will come and reign with my people I am Alpha

and Omega the begining and the end Amen.

Original Inscription
John Whitmer

Revisions
Oliver Cowdery
William W. Phelps
Sidney Rigdon
Joseph Smith
John Whitmer
Unidentified

405. "◊" possibly wipe-erased
and then knife-erased.

$$
\begin{array}{r}
142 \\
24 \\
\hline
568 \\
28\{◊\4\} \\
\hline
440,8͟o͟ \\
\end{array}
$$

    4,4;o

157

Prophey or Commandments given Decem. 25. 1832

Verily thus saith the Lord concerning the wars that will shortly
come to pass begining at the rebellion of south Carolina which will
eventually terminate in the death & misery of many Souls &
the days will come that war will be poured out upon all nations
begining at this place for behold the southern States shall be
divided against the northern States and the Southern States will
call on other nations ~~begining at this place for behold the south~~
~~ern States~~ even the nation of great Briton as it is called & they
shall also call upon other nations in order to defend themselves
against other nations & then war shall be poured out upon all
nations & it shall come to pass after many days Slaves shall rise up
against their masters who shall be marshaled & disciplined for war
& it shall come to pass ~~after many days~~ also that the remnant who
are left of the land will marshal themselves & shall become exceeding angry & shall vex the gentiles with a sore vexation & then
with the sword & by bloodshed the inhabitants of the Earth shall
mourn. and with famine & ~~pestilence~~ plague & earthquakes &
the thunder of heaven & the fierce & vivid lightning also shall
the inhabitants of the earth be made to feel the wrath & in=
=dignation & chastning hand of an Almighty God. untill the
consumption decreed hath made a full end of all nations that
the cry of the Saints & of the bloodshed of the saints shall cease to
come into the ears of the Lord of Sabaoth from the earth to be
avenged of their enemies; wherefore stand ye in holy places &
be not moved untill the day of the Lord come for Behold
it cometh quickly saith the Lord. Amen.

♦ ⟨Prophecy or⟩ **Commandments** given Decem. 25. 1832 ₁₅₇⁴⁰⁶ [recto]

Verily thus saith the Lord concerning the wars that will shortly

come to pass begining at the rebellion of South Carolina which will

eventually terminate in the death & misery of many Souls &

     come
the days will that war will be poured out upon all nations
    ^

begining at this place for behold the southeren States shall be

divided against the northeren States and the Southeren States will

call on⁴⁰⁷ other nations ~~begining at this place for behold the South=~~

~~=eren States~~ even the nation of great Bri{ttan\tan}⁴⁰⁸ as it is called & they

shall also call upon other nations in order to defend themselves

against other nations & then war shall be poured out upon all

nations & it shall come to pass after many days slaves shall rise up

against their masters who shall be mar{ti\sh}aled & disciplined for war

& it shall come to pass ~~after many day{◊s\s}⁴⁰⁹~~ also that the remnant who

are left of the Land will mar{ti\sh}al themselves & shall become exceed=

-ing angry & shall vex the gentiles with a sore vexation & thus

with the sword & by bloodshed the inhabitants of the Earth shall

mourn. and with famine & ~~pestilence~~ plague & earthquakes &
            &
the thunder of heaven & the fierce vivid lightning also shall
         ^

the inhabitants of the earth be made to feel the wrath & in=

-dignation & chastning hand of an Almighty God untill the

consumption decreed hath made a full end of all nations that
  the cry
~~the day~~ of the Saints of the bloodshed of the Saints shall cease to
  ^

come into the ears of the Lord of Sabaoth from the earth to be

avenged of their enemies: wherefore stand ye in holy places &

be not moved untill the day of the Lord come for Behold

it cometh quickly saith the Lord. Amen.

ORIGINAL INSCRIPTION
John Whitmer

REVISIONS
Oliver Cowdery
William W. Phelps
Sidney Rigdon
Joseph Smith
John Whitmer
Unidentified

406. Consistency of numbering style and ink flow suggests that William W. Phelps numbered the pages throughout the rest of the manuscript book in one sitting.

407. Or "an".

408. Or "Bri{tton\ton}".

409. "◊s" wipe-erased and written over; then stricken with the entire phrase.

158

A Revelation

given to the first Elders of the church of Christ, organized in these last days.

Given, December 27, 1832.

Verily thus saith the Lord to you who have assembled your-selves together to receive his will concerning you; behold this is pleasing unto your Lord and the Angels rejoice over you; the alms of your prayers have come up into the ears of the Lord of Sabaoth, & are recorded in the book of the names of the Sanctified, even they of the celestial world. wherefore I now send upon you another Comforter, even upon you my friends, that it may abide in your hearts, even the Holy Spirit of promise; which other Com-forter is the same that I promised unto my Disciples, as is recorded in the testimony of John: this comforter is the promise which I give unto you of eternal life, even the glory of the Celestial Kingdom; which glory is that of the Church of the first born, even of God the holiest of all, through Jesus Christ his Son; he that ascended up on high, as also he decended below all things, in that he comprehendeth all things, that he might be in all & through all things, the light of truth. therefore, which truth shineth; this is the light of Christ. as also he is in the Sun & the light of the Sun & the power thereof by which it was made as also he is in the Moon & is the light of the Moon & the power thereof by which it was made as also the light of the Stars & the power thereof by which they were made & the earth also & the power thereof even the earth upon which you stand & the light which now shineth which giveth you light is through him which enlighteneth your eyes which is the same light that quickeneth your understandings which light proceedeth forth from the presence of God to fill the immensity of space the light which is in all things which giveth life to all things which is the law by which all things are governed even the power of God who sitteth upon his throne who is in the bosom of eternity who is in the midst of all things. Now verily I say unto you that through the redemption which is made for you is brought to pass the resurrection from the dead and the spirit & the body is the soul of man & the resurrection from the dead is the redemption of the soul & the redemption of the soul is through him who quickeneth

....158 [verso]

♦ A Revelation given to the first

Elders of this church of Christ, organized in these last days:

Given, {d\⟨D⟩}ecember 27, 1832.

Verily thus saith the Lord to you who have assembled your

selves together to receive his will concerning you; behold this is

pleasing unto your Lord and the Angels rejoice over you; the alms

of your prayers have come up into the ears of the Lord of Sabaoth, & are

recorded in the book of the names of the Sanctified, {◊◊◊◊\even}⁴¹⁰ they of
                                                              even

the Celestial world. wherefore I now send upon you another

Comforter, even ~~p~~upon you my friends, that it may abide in

your hearts, ev{◊\en} the Holy Spirit of promise; which other com-

-forter is the same that I promised unto my Disciples, as is

recorded in the testimony of John: this comforter is the promise

which I gave unto you of eternal life, even the glory of the

Celestial Kingdom; Which glory is that of the Church of the first ~~born~~

born, even of God the holiest of all, through Jesus Christ his Son:

he that ascended up on high, as also he decended below all

things, in that he comprehendeth all things, that he might be in all

& through all things, the light of truth. therefore, whi{th\ch} truth

shineth; this is the light of Christ. as {A\also} he is in the Sun &

the light of the Sun & the power thereof by which it was made as

also he is ~~in~~ in the Moon & is the light of the Moon & the power

thereof by which it was made. as also the light of the Stars & the
also & the power thereof even the ~~upon which~~⁴¹¹ earth
power thereof by which they were made & the earth {◊◊\upon} which

you stand & the light which now shineth which giveth you light

is through him which enlighteneth your eyes which is the same

light that quickeneth your understandings which light proceedeth

forth from the presence of God to fill the immencity of space the

light which is in all things which giveth life to all things

which is the law by which all things are goverened even the power

of God who sitteth upon his throne who is in the bosom of eternity

who is in the midst of all things Now verily I say unto you

that through the redemption which is made for you is brought to

pass the resurrection from the dead and the Spirit & the body is the
                                                          from
soul of man & the resurrection ~~of~~ the dead is the redemption of the

soul & the redemption of the Soul is through him who quickeneth

ORIGINAL INSCRIPTION
John Whitmer

REVISIONS
Oliver Cowdery
William W. Phelps
Sidney Rigdon
Joseph Smith
John Whitmer
Unidentified

410. "◊◊◊◊" wipe-erased and
written over; then whole word
stricken.

411. "upon which" wipe-
erased and then stricken.

293

all things in whose bosom it is decreed that the poor & the meek
of the earth shall inherit it, therefore it must needs be sanctified
from all unrighteousness that it may be prepared for the Celestial glory for
after it hath filled the measure of its creation it shall be crowned with
a glory even with the presence of God the father that bodies who are
of the Celestial kingdom may possess it for ever & ever for for this
intent was it made & created & for this intent are they sanctified & they
who are not sanctified through the Law which I have given unto you
even the law of Christ must inherit an other kingdom even that
of a Terrestrial kingdom or that of a Telestial kingdom for he that is
not able to abide the law of a Celestial kingdom cannot abide a
Celestial glory & he who cannot abide the law of a Terrestrial kingdom
cannot abide a Terrestrial glory he who cannot abide the law of a Telesti
-al kingdom cannot abide a Telestial glory therefore he is not
(or must) prepared for a kingdom of glory therefore he must abide a kingdom
which is not a kingdom of glory. And again verily I say unto you
the earth abideth the law of a Celestial kingdom for it filleth the
measure of its creation & transgresseth not the law. wherefore it shall
be sanctified yea notwithstanding it shall die it shall be quickened again
& shall abide the power by which it is quickened & the righteous shall inherit
it for notwithstanding they die they also shall rise again a spiritual
body they who are of a celestial spirit shall receive the same body
which was a natural body even ye shall receive your bodies & your
glory shall be that glory by which your bodies are quickened ye who
are quickened by a portion of the Celestial glory shall then receive
of the same even a fulness & they who are quickened by a portion of the
Terrestrial glory shall then receive of the same even a fulness &
also they who are quickened by a portion of the Telestial glory shall
then receive of the same even a fulness & they who remain shall also
be quickened nevertheless they shall return again to their own
place to enjoy that which they are willing to receive because they
were not willing to enjoy that which they might have received for
what doth it profit a man if a gift is bestowed upon him & he
receive not the gift behold he rejoiceth not in that which is given
unto him neither rejoice in him who is the giver of the gift
And again verily I say unto you, that which is governed by law is
also preserved by law & perfected &

all things in whose bosom it is decreed that the poor & the meek

of the earth shall inherit it therefore it must needs be sanctified

from all unrighteousness that it may be prepared for the Celestial glory for

after it hath filled the measure of its creation it shall be crowned with

glory even with the presence of God the father that bodies who are

of the Celestial kingdom {kin\may} possess it for ever & ever for for this

intent was it made & created & for this intent are they Sanctified & they

who are not sanctified through the Law which I have given unto you

even the law of Christ must inherit an other kingdom even that

of a Terrestrial kingdom or that of a Telestial Kingdom for he that is

not able to abide the law of a Celestial Kingdom cannot abide a

Celestial glory & he who cannot abide the law of a Terrestrial Kingdom

cannot abide a Terrestrial glory he who cannot abide the law of a Telesti

=al Kingdom cannot abide {◊\the}⁴¹² Telestial glory {t\⟨T⟩}herefore he is not
(or meet.)
fruit for a Kingdom of glory Therefore he must abide a Kingdom

which is not a Kingdom of glory And again verily I say unto you

the earth abideth the Law of a Celestial Kingdom for it filleth the

measure of its creation & transgresseth not the law. wherefore it shall

be sanctified yea notwithstanding it shall die it shall be quickened again

& shall abide the power by which it is quickened & the righteous shall inherit

it for not withstanding they die they also shall rise again a Spiritual

body they who are of a celestial Spirit Shall receive a̶ c̶e̶l̶e̶s̶t̶i̶a̶l the same body

which was a natural body even y{o\⟨e⟩}u̶ shall receive your bodies & your

glory shall be that glory by which your bodies are quickened ye who

are quickened by a portion of the Celestial glory shall then receive

of the Same even a ful{l\ness} & they who are quickened by a portion of the

Terrestrial glory shall then receive {the\of} the Same even o̶f̶ t̶h̶e̶ a fulness &

also they who are quickened by a portion of the Telestial glory shall

then receive of the Same even a fulness & they who remain shall also

be quickened nevertheless they Shall return again to their own

place to enjoy that which they are willing to receive because t{◊◊\hey}

were not willing to enjoy that which they might have received for

what doth it profit a man if a gift is bestowed upon {a̶ m̶a̶n̶\him} & he

receive not the gift behold he rejoiceth not in that which is given

unto him neither rejoice in him who is the giver of the gift

And again verily I say unto you, that which is goverened by law is

also p̶e̶r̶f̶e̶c̶t̶e̶d̶ b̶y̶ l̶a̶w̶ &̶ s̶a̶n̶c̶t̶i̶f̶i̶e̶d̶ preserved by law & perfected &

ORIGINAL INSCRIPTION
John Whitmer

REVISIONS
Oliver Cowdery
William W. Phelps
Sidney Rigdon
Joseph Smith
John Whitmer
Unidentified

412. "◊" wipe-erased and written over; then whole word stricken.

sanctified by the same that which breaketh a law & abideth
not by law but seeketh to become a law unto itself & willeth to abide
in sin & altogether abideth in sin cannot be sanctified by law neither
by mercy justice or judgment Therefore they must remain filthy still
all kingdoms have a law given and there are many kingdoms for
there is no space in the which there is no kingdom & there is no kingdom
in which there is no space either a greater or lesser kingdom. & unto
every kingdom is given a law, & unto every law there are certain bounds
also, & conditions. all beings who abide not in those conditions are
not justified, for inteligence cleaveth unto inteligence wisdom receiveth
wisdom truth embraceth truth virtue loveth virtue light cleaveth unto
light mercy hath compassion on mercy & claimeth her own justice
continueth its course & claimeth its own judgment goeth before the face
of him who sitteth upon the throne & governeth & executeth all things
he comprehendeth all things & all things are before him & all things
& all things are round about him & he is above all things & in all
things & is through all things & is round about all things & all things are
by him & of him even God for ever & ever. And again verily I say unto
you he hath given a law unto all things by which they move in
their times & their seasons & their causes are fixed even the
causes of the heavens. & the earth which comprehend the earth &
all the planets & they give light to each other in their times & in
their seasons in their minutes & in their hours in their days
in their weeks in their months in their years. All these are
one year with God but not with man the earth rolls
upon her wings & the Sun giveth his light by day & the moon
giveth her light by night & the Stars also giveth their light as they
roll upon their wings in their glory in the midst of the power of
God. Unto what shall I liken these kingdoms that ye may
understand behold all these are kingdoms and any man who hath
seen any or the least of these hath seen God moving in his majesty
& power I say unto you he hath seen him nevertheless he who came
unto his own was not comprehended the light shineth in darkness
& the darkness comprehendeth it not nevertheless the day shall come
when you shall comprehend even God being quickened in him
& by him then shall ye know that ye have seen me that I
am & that I am the true light that is in you & that you are

160 [verso]

Sanctified by the same that which breaketh a law & abideth

not by law but seeketh to become a~~l~~ law unto itself & willeth to abide

in sin & altogether abideth in sin cannot be sanctified by law neither

of
by^ mercy Justice or Judgment Therefore they must remain filthy still

all Kingdoms have a law given and there are many Kingdoms for

there is no space in the which there is no Kingdom & there is no Kingdom

in which there is no space either a greater or lesser Kingdom. & unto

every Kingdom is given a law, & unto every law there are certain bounds

also, & conditions. all beings who abide not in th{e\o}se⁴¹³ conditions are

not Justified:⁴¹⁴ for inteligence {~~abideth~~\cleaveth} unto inteligence wisdom receiveth

wisdom truth embraceth truth virtue loveth virtue light cleaveth unto

light mercy hath compassion on mercy & claimeth her own Justice

continueth its course & claimeth i{s\ts} own Judgment goeth before the face

of him who sit{t\eth} upon the throne & governeth & executeth all things

he comprehendeth all things & all things are before him & all things

~~& all things~~ are r{u\ound} about him & he is above all things & in all

things & is through all things & is round about all things & all things are

by him & of him even God for ever & ever. And again verily I say unto

you he hath given a law unto all things by which they move in

th{er◊\eir} times & th{◊◊◊\eir} seasons & their courses are fixed even the

courses of the heavens & ~~of~~ the earth which comprehend the earth &

all the planets{—\.}⁴¹⁵ & they give light to each other in their times & in

their Seasons in their minutes & in their hours in their days

in their weeks in their months in their years. All these are

one year with God but not with man the earth rolls

upon her wings & the Sun giveth h{er\is} light by day & the moon

their
giveth her light by night & the Stars also giveth ~~her~~ light as they
^

roll upon their wings in their glory in the midst of the power of

God.   Unto {◊\what} shall I liken th{eir\ese} kingdoms that ye may

understand behold all these are kingdoms and any man who hath

have
seen any or the least of these ~~has~~ Seen God moveing in his majesty
^

& power I say unto you he hath seen him nevertheless he who came

unto his own was not comprehended the light shineth in darkness

& the darkness comprehendeth it not nevertheless the day shall come

when you shall comprehend even God being quickened in him

& by him then shall ye know that ye have seen me that I

am & that I am the true light that is in you & that you are

ORIGINAL INSCRIPTION
John Whitmer

REVISIONS
Oliver Cowdery
William W. Phelps
Sidney Rigdon
Joseph Smith
John Whitmer
Unidentified

413. Or "th{er\os}e".

414. ":" possibly a stray ink mark.

415. Original dash is stricken.

in me, otherwise ye could not abound. Behold I will liken
these kingdoms unto a man having a field & he sent forth
his servants into the field to dig in the field & he said unto the
first go ye & labor in the field & in the first hour I will come unto
you & ye shall behold the joy of my countenance & he said unto the
second go ye also into the field & in the second hour I will visit
you with the joy of my countenance & also unto the third saying
I will visit you & unto the fourth & so on unto the twelfth &
the Lord of the field went unto the first in the first hour & tarried
with him all that hour & he was made glad with the light
of the countenance of his Lord & then he withdrew from the
first that he might visit the second also the third & the fourth
& so on unto the twelfth & thus they all received the light of the
countenance of their Lord every man in his hour & in his time
& in his season begining at the first & so on unto the last & from
the last unto the first & from the first unto the
last every man in his own order untill his hour was finished
even according as his Lord had commanded him that his Lord
might be glorified in him & he in him that they all might
be glorified. therefore unto this parable will I liken all those King
-doms & the inhabitants thereof every kingdom in its hour & in its time
& in its season even according to the decree which God hath made.
And again verily I say unto you my friends I leave these sayings
with you to ponder in your hearts with this commandment which
I give unto you that ye shall call upon me while I am near
draw near unto me & I will draw near unto you seek me dilligently &
ye shall find me ask & ye shall receive knock & it shall be opened
unto you   Whatsoever ye ask the father in my name it shall be given
unto you that is expedient for you & if ye ask any thing that is not
expedient for you it shall turn unto your condemnation.
Behold that which you hear is as the voice of one crying in the wild
-erness in the wilderness because you cannot see him my voice because
my voice is Spirit my Spirit is truth truth abideth & hath no
end & if it be in you it shall abound & if your eye be single to
my glory your whole body shall be filled with light & there shall
be no darkness in you & that body which is filled with light
comprehendeth all things.

in me otherwise ye could not abound. Behold I will liken

these Kingdoms unto a man having a field & he sent forth

his servants into the field to dig in the field & he said unto the

first go ye & labor in the field & in the first hour I will come unto

you & ye shall behold the Joy of my countenanc[e] & he said unto the

{& ye sh\second} go ye also into the field & in the second hou{◊\r} I will visit

you with the Joy of my countenance & also unto the third saying

I will visit you & unto the fourth & so on unto the twelfth &

the Lord of the field went unto the first in the first hour & tarried

with him all that hour & he was made glad with the light

of the countenance of his Lord & then he withdrew from the

first that he might visit the second also the third & the fourth
&
^

& so on unto the twelfth & th{is\us} they all received the light of the

countenance of their Lord every man in his hour & in his time

& in his season begining at the first & so on unto the last & from

the last & from the last unto the first & from the first unto the

last every man in his own order untill his hour was finished

even according as his Lord had commanded him that his Lord

might be glorified in him & he in him that they all might

be glorified. therefore unto this parable will I liken all those King-

-doms & the inhabitants thereof every kingdom in its hour & in its time

& in its Season even according to the decree which God ha{s\⟨th⟩} made.

And again verily I say unto you my friend{◊s\s} I leave these sayings

with you to ponder in your hearts with this commandment which

I give unto you that ye shall call upon me while I am near

draw near unto me & I will draw near unto you seek me dilligently &

ye shall find me ask & ye shall receive knock & it shall be opened

unto you Whatsoever ye ask the father in my name it shall be given

unto you that is expedient for you & if ye ask any thing that is not

expedient for you it shall turn unto your condemnation.

Behold that which you hear is as the voice of one crying in the wild-

-erness in the wilderness because y{e\ou} cannot see him my voice because

my voice is {s\⟨S⟩}pirit my Spirit is truth truth abideth & hath no

end & if it be in you it shall abound & if your eye be single to

my glory your whole body shall be filled with {gl◊◊y\light} & there shall

be no darkness in you & that body which is filled with light

comprehendeth all things.

ORIGINAL INSCRIPTION
John Whitmer

REVISIONS
Oliver Cowdery
William W. Phelps
Sidney Rigdon
Joseph Smith
John Whitmer
Unidentified

Therefore sanctify yourselves that your minds became single to
God & the days will come that you shall see him for he will unveil
his face unto you & it shall be in his own time & in his own way
& according to his own will remember ~~remember~~ the great & last
promise which I have made unto you. Cast away your idle
thoughts & your excess of laughter far from you tarry ye tarry
you in this place & call a solemn assembly even of those who
are the first laborers in this last kingdom & let those whom
they have warned in their travelling call on the Lord & ponder the
warnings in their hearts which they have received for a little season
behold & lo I will take care of your flock & will raise up Elders
& send unto them   Behold I will hasten my work in its time &
I give unto you who are the first laborers in this last kingdom
A commandment ~~I give unto you~~ that you assemble yourselves
together & organize yourselves & prepare yourselves & sanctify yourselves
yea purify your hearts & clean your hands & your feet before me
that I may make you clean that I may testify unto your father &
your God & my God that you are clean from the blood of ~~this~~ this
wicked generation that I may fulfil this promise this great &
last promise which I have made unto you when I will.
Also I give unto you a commandment that ye shall continue
in prayer & fasting from this time forth & I give unto you
a commandment that you shall teach one another the doctrines
of the kingdom teach ye dilligently & my grace shall attend
you that ye may be instructed more perfectly in theory in princi=
=ple in doctrine in the law of the gospel in all things that pertain
unto the kingdom of God that is expedient for you to understand
of things both in heaven & in the earth & under the earth things
which have been things which are things which must shortly
come to pass things which are at home things which are abroad
the wars & the perplexities of the nations & the judgments which
are on the land. And a knowledge also: of countries & of kingdoms
that ye may be prepared in all things when I shall send you
again to magnify the calling whereunto I have called you & the
mission ~~with which~~ which I have commissioned you
Behold I sent you out to testify & warn the people & it becometh
every man. who hath been warned to warn his neighbors

Therefore sanctify yourselves that your minds become single to

God & the days will come that you shall see him for he will unveil

his face unto you & it shall be in his own time & in his own way

& {◊\according} to his own will remember ~~remember~~ the great & last

promise which I have made unto you. Cast away your idle

thoughts & your excess of laughter far from you tarry ye tarry

ye in this place & call a Sol{l\emn} assembly even of those who

are the first laborers in this last kingdom & let those whom

they have warned in their travelling call on the Lord & ponder the

warnings in their hearts which they have received for a little season

behold & lo I will take care of your flock & will raise up Elders

& send unto them Behold I will hasten my work in its time &

I give unto you who are the first laborers in this last Kingdom

A commandment ~~I give unto you~~ that you assemble yourselves

together & organize yourselves & prepare yourselves & sanctify yourselves

yea purify your hearts & clean your hands & your feet before me

that I may make you clean that I may testify unto your father &

your God & my God that you are clean from the blood of {b◊\this}

wicked generation that I may fulfil this promise this great &

last promise which I have made unto you when I will.

Also I give unto you a commandment that ye shall continue

in prayer & fasting from this time forth & I give unto you

a commandment that you shall teah one another the doctrines

of the kingdom teach ye dilligently & my grace shall attend

you that ye may be instructed more perfectly in theory in princi=

=ple in doctrine in the law of the gospel in all things that pertain

unto the kingdom of God that is expedient for you to understand

of things both in heaven & in the earth & under the earth things

which have been things which are things which must shortly

come to pass things which are at home things which are abroad

the wars & the perplexities of the nations & the Judgments which

are on the land. And a knowledge also: of countries & of kingdoms

that ye may be prepared in all things when I shall send you

again to magnify the calling whereunto I have called you & the

mission w{h◊re w◊th\ith which} I have commissioned you

Behold I sent you out to testify & warn the people & it becometh

every man who hath been warned to warn his neighbors

ORIGINAL INSCRIPTION
John Whitmer

REVISIONS
Oliver Cowdery
William W. Phelps
Sidney Rigdon
Joseph Smith
John Whitmer
Unidentified

therefore they are left without excuse & their sins are upon
their own heads.. He that seeketh me early shall find me: & shall
not be forsaken Therefore tarry ye & labor dilligently that you may
be perfected in your ministry to go forth among the gentiles for
the last time as many as the mouth of the Lord shall name to
bind up the law & seal up the testimony & to prepare the
saints for the hour of judgment which is to come that their
souls may escape the wrath of God the desolation of abominati
=on. which awaiteth the wicked hath in this world & in the
world to come. Verily I say unto you let those who are not the first
Elders continue in the vineyard untill the mouth of the Lord
shall call them for their time is not yet come their garments
are not clean from the blood of this generation. Abide ye
in the Liberty wherewith ye are made free entangle not your
-selves in sin but let your hands be clean untill the Lord come
for not many days hence & the earth shall tremble & reel to
& fro as a drunken man & the sun shall hide his face &
shall refuse to give light & the moon shall be bathed in
blood & the stars shall become exceeding angry & shall
cast themselves down as a fig that falleth from off a fig tree
& after your testimony cometh wrath & indignation upon the people
for after your testimony cometh the testimony of earthquakes
that shall cause groanings in the midst of her & men shall fall
upon the ground & shall not be able to stand. & also cometh
the testimony of the voice of thunderings & the voice of lightnings
& the voice of tempests & the voice of the waves of the Sea. heaving
themselves beyond their bounds & all things shall be in com-
-motion & surely mens hearts shall fail them for fear shall
come upon all people & angels shall fly through the
midst of heaven crying with a loud voice sounding the trump
of God saying prepare ye prepare ye O inhabitants of the earth
for the judgment of our God is come. Behold & lo the bridegroom
cometh go ye out to meet him. And immediately there shall
appear a great sign in heaven & all people shall see it together
And another angel shall sound his trump saying that great church
the mother of abominations that made all nations drink of the
wine of the wrath of its fornication that persecuteth the saints of

therefore they are left without excuse & their sins are upon

their own heads. He that seeketh me early shall find me: & shall

not be forsaken Therefore tarry ye & labor dilligently that you may

be perfected in your minist{ery\ry} to go forth among the gentiles for

the last time as many as the mouth of the Lord shall name to

bind up the law & seal up the testimony & to prepare the

saints for the hour of Judgment which is to come that their

souls may escape the wrath of God the desolation of abominati

=on which a waiteth the wicked both in this world & in the

world to come. Verily I say unto you let those who are the first

Elders continue in the vineyard untill the mouth of the Lord

shall call them for their time is not yet come their garments

are not clean from the blood of this generation. Abide ye

in the Liberty wherewith ye are made free entangle not your

-selves in sin but let your hands be clean untill the Lord come

for not many days hence & the earth shall tremble & reel to

& fro as a drunken man & the Sun shall hide his face &

shall refues to give light & the moon shall be bathed in

blood & the stars shall become exceeding angry & shall

cast themselves down as a fig that falleth from off a fig tree

& after your testimony cometh wrath & indignation upon the people

for after your testimony cometh the testimony of earthquakes

that shall cause groanings in the midst of her & men shall fall

upon the ground & shall not be able to stand: & also, cometh

the testimony of the voice of thunderings & the voice of lightnings

& the voice of tempests & the voice of wa{v\ves} of the Sea. heaving

themselves beyond their bounds & all things shall be in com-

-motion & surely mens hearts shall fail them for fear shall

come upon ~~them~~ all people & angels shall fly through the

midst of heaven crying with a loud voice sounding the trump

of God saying prepare ye prepare ye O inhabitants of the earth

for the Judgments of our God is come. Behold & lo the bridegroom

cometh go ye out to meet him. And immediateely there shall

appear a great sign in heaven & all people shall see it together

And another angel shall sound his trump saying that great church

the mother of abominations that made all nations drink of the ~~wine~~

wine of the wrath of its fornication that pursecuteth the Saints of ~~God~~

ORIGINAL INSCRIPTION
John Whitmer

REVISIONS
Oliver Cowdery
William W. Phelps
Sidney Rigdon
Joseph Smith
John Whitmer
Unidentified

164 God ~~the saints of god~~ that shed their blood her who
sitteth upon many waters & upon the islands of the sea behold.
she is the ~~tares~~ of the earth she is bound in bundles her bands
are made strong no man can loose them therefore she is ready
to be burned: & he shall sound his trump both long & loud
& all nations shall hear it & there shall be silence in heaven
for the space of half an hour And immediately after shall the
curtain of heaven be unfolded as a scroll is unfolded after it
is rolled up And the face of the Lord shall be unveiled: & the saints
that are upon the ~~earth~~ who are alive shall be quickened & be
caught up to meet him & they who have slept in their graves
shall come forth for their graves shall be opened & they also shall be
caught up to meet him in the midst of the pillar of heaven
they are Christs the first fruits they who shall descend with him
first. ~~And~~ they who are on the earth & in their graves who are first
caught up to meet him & all this by the voice of the sounding of
the trump of the Angel of God & after this another trump shall
sound which is the second trump & then cometh the redemption of those
who are Christs at his coming who have received their part in that
prison which is prepared for them that they might receive the
gospel and be judged according to men in the flesh. And again another
trump shall sound which is the third trump & then cometh the
spirits of men who are to be judged & are found under condem-
-nation & these are the rest of the dead & they lived not again untill
the thousand years are ended Niether again until the end of the earth
And another trump shall sound which is the fourth trump
saying there are found among those who are to remain untill
that great & last day: even the end: who shall remain filthy
still And another trump shall sound which is the fifth trump
which is the fifth angel who committeth the everlasting gospel
flying through the midst of heaven unto all nations kindreds
tongues & people & this shall be the sound of ~~his~~ his trump
saying to all people both in heaven & in earth & that are under
the earth for every ear shall hear it & every knee shall bow &
every tongue shall confess while they hear the sound of the
trump: saying fear God & give glory to him who ~~that~~ sitteth upon
the throne for ever & ever for the hour of his judgment is

God ~~the saints of God~~ that shed their blood her who

set{t\eth} upon many waters & upon the {il\islands} of the sea behold

she is the {ΦΦs\tares} of the earth she is bound in bundles her bands

are made Strong no man can loose them therefore she is ready

to be burned: & he shall sound his trump both long & loud

& all nations shall hear it & th{er\er}e shall be silence in heaven

for the space of half an hour And immediately after shall the

curtain of heaven be unfolded as a scroll is unfolded after it

is rolled up And the face of the Lord shall be unveiled: & the Saints

that are upon the earth who are alive shall be quickened & be

caught up to meet him & they who have slept in their graves

shall come forth for their graves shall be opened & they also shall be

caught up to meet him in the midst of the pillars of heaven

they are C^h^rist's the first fruits they who shall decend with him

first. {&\And} they who are on the earth & in their graves who are first

caught up to meet him & all this by the voice of the sounding of

the trump of the Angel of God & after this another trump shall

sound which is the second trump & then cometh the redemption of those

who are Christs at his coming who have received their part in that

prison which is prepared for them that they might receive the

gospel and be Judged according to men in the flesh. & ^And^ again another

trump shall sound which is the third trump & then cometh the

spirits of men who are to be Judged & are found under condem-

-nation & these are the rest of the dead & they lived not again untill

the thousand years are ended Neither again until the end of the earth

And another trump shall sound which is the fourth trump

saying these are found among those who are to remain until

that great & last day: even the end: who shall remain filthy

still And another trump shall sound which is the fifth trump

which is the fifth angel who commiteth the everlasting gospel

flying through the midst of heaven unto all nations kindreds

tongues & people & this shall be the sound of ~~this~~ ^his^ trump

saying to all people both in heaven & in earth & that are under

the earth for every ear shall hear it & every knee shall bow &

every tongue shall confe{ΦΦ\ss} while they hear the sound of the

trump: saying fear God & give glory to him ~~that~~ ^who^ siteth upon

the throne for ever & ever for the hour of his Judgment ~~a~~ is

ORIGINAL INSCRIPTION
John Whitmer

REVISIONS
Oliver Cowdery
William W. Phelps
Sidney Rigdon
Joseph Smith
John Whitmer
Unidentified

come. And again another angel shall sound his trump which is the sixth angel saying she is fallen who made all nations drink of the wine of the wrath of her fornication she is fallen is fallen. And again another angel shall sound his trump which is the seventh angel saying it is finished it is finished the Lamb of God hath over come & troden the wine press alone even the wine press of the fierceness of the wrath of Almighty God And then shall the angel be crowned with the glory of his might & the saints shall be filled with his glory & receive their inheritance & be made equal with him And then shall the first angel again sound his trump in the ears of all living & reveal the secret acts of men & the mighty works of God in the first thousandth year. And then shall the second angel sound his trump & reveal the secret acts of men & the thoughts & intents of their hearts & the mighty works of God in the second thousandth year And so on untill the seventh angel shall sound his trump & he shall stand forth upon the land & upon the sea & swear in the name of him who sitteth upon the throne that there shall be time no longer & Satan shall be bound that old Serpent who is called the devil & shall not be loosed for the space of a thousand years And then he shall be loosed for a little season that he may gether together his armies & Michael the seventh angel even the archangel shall gether together his armies even the hosts of heaven & the devil shall gether his armies even the hosts of hell & shall come up to battle against Michael & his armies & then cometh the battle of the great God and the devil & his armies shall be cast away into their own place that they shall not have power over the saints any more at all: for Michael shall fight their battles & shall overcome him who seeketh the throne of him who sitteth upon the throne even the Lamb this is the glory of God & the sanctified & they shall not any more see death.

Therefore verily I say unto you my friends call your solemn assembly as I have commanded you & as all have not faith seek ye dilligently & teach one another words of wisdom yea seek ye out of the best Books words of wisdom seek learning even by study & also by faith organize yourselves prepare every needful thing & establish an house even an house of prayer an house of fasting an house of faith an house of learning an house of glory an house of order an house of God that your incomings may be in the name of the Lord that your outgoings may be in the name of the Lord that all your salutations may be in the name of the Lord with uplifted hands unto the

come. And again another angel his trump which is the sixth
^

angel saying she is fallen who made all nations drink of the wine of

the wrath of her fornication she is fallen is fallen. And again anoth

=er angel shall sound his trump which is the seventh {t̶o̶o̶o̶p̶\angel} saying it

⟨is⟩ finished it is fini{h̶\shed} the Lamb of God hath over come & {d̶o̶\troden} the

wine press alone even the wine press of the fierceness of the wrath of

Almighty God And then shall the angel be crowned with the glory

of his might & the saints shall be filled with his glory & receive

                                                    And
their inheritanc[e] & be made equal with him & then shall the first angel
                                                  ^
                                        living
again sound his trump in the ears of all b̶e̶i̶n̶g̶s̶ & reveal the secret
                                        ^

acts of men & the mighty works of God in the first thousand{o̶o̶o̶\th} year. And

then shall the second angel sound his trump & reveal the Secret acts of
                              & the
men i̶n̶ ̶t̶h̶e̶ ̶s̶e̶c̶o̶n̶d̶ {t̶h̶o̶u̶s̶o̶n̶d̶t̶h̶\and the thoughts} & intents of their hearts & the migh-
                              ^
=ty works of God in the second thousandth year. & {s̶\And} so on untill the seventh angel

shall sound his trump & he shall stand forth upon the land & upon the sea

& swear in the name of him who siteth upon the throne that there shall

be time no longer & satan shall be bound that old serpent who is

called the devil & shall not be loosed for the space of a thousand years

    And then he shall be loosed for a little season that he may gether togeth

-er his armies & {m̶o̶h̶\Michael} the seventh angel even the archangel shall

gether together his armies even the hosts of heaven & the devil shall gat{o̶o̶\her}

his armies even the hosts of hell & shall come up to battle against Michael

& his armies & then cometh the battle of the great God and the devil &

his armies shall be cast away into their own place that they shall not

have power over the Saints any more at all: for Michael shall

fight their battles & shall overcome him who seeketh the throne of

him who siteth upon the throne even the Lamb this is the glory of

God & the sanctified & they shall not any more see death.

    Therefore verily I say unto you my friends call your solemn assemb{o̶o̶\ly}

as I have commanded you & as all have not faith seek ye dilligently &

teach one another words of wisdom yea seek ye out of the best Books

words of wisdom seek learning even by Study & also by faith organize
                                                        even an house
yourselves prepare every needful thing & establish an house of prayer an
                                                        ^
house of fasting an house of faith an house of learning an house of glory

an house of order an house of God that your incomings may be in the name

of the Lord that your outgoings may be in the name of the Lord that all your

salutations may be in the name of the Lord with uplifted hands unto the

ORIGINAL INSCRIPTION
John Whitmer

REVISIONS
Oliver Cowdery
William W. Phelps
Sidney Rigdon
Joseph Smith
John Whitmer
Unidentified

166

Most High. Therefore cease from all your light speeches from all your laughter from all your lustful desires from all your pride & light mindedness & from all your wicked doings appoint among yourselves a teacher & let not all be spokesman at once but let one speak at a time & let all listen unto his sayings that when all have spoken that all may be edified of all & that every man may have an equal privilege. See that ye love one another cease to be covetous learn to impart one to an other as the gospel requires cease to be idle cease to be unclean cease to find fault one with another cease to sleep longer than is needful retire to thy bed early that ye may not be weary arise early that your bodies & your minds may be invigorated & above all things clothe yourselves with the bonds of charity as with a Mantle which is the bonds of perfectness & peace pray always that you may not faint untill I come Behold & lo I will come quickly & receive you unto myself Amen

A Revelation given Jany 3. 1833 Kirtland

The order of the house prepared for the presidency & instructions in all things that is expedient for the officers or in other words them who are called to the ministry in the church begining at the high priests even down to the deacons & this shall be the order of the house he that is appointed to be a teacher shall be found standing in his place which shall be prepared for him in the house of God in a place that the congregation in the house may hear his words correctly & distinctly not with loud speach. And when he cometh into the house of God for he should be first in the house behold this is beautiful that he may be an example let him offer himself in prayer upon his knees before God in token of the everlasting covenant & when any shall come in after him let the teacher arise & with uplifted hands to heaven yea even directly & salute his brother or brethren with these words saying art thou a brother or brethren I salute you in the name of the Lord Jesus Christ in token of the everlasting covenant in which covenant I receive you to fellowship in a determination that is fixed immoveable and unchangable to be your friend & brother through the grace of God in the bonds of love to walk in all the commandments of God blameless in thanksgiving forever & ever. And he that cometh in & is a brother or brethren shall salute the Teacher with uplifted hands to heaven with this same prayer & covenant or by saying amen

166 [verso]

Most High. Therefore cease from all your light speeches from

all ~~your~~ laughter from all your lustful desires from all your light-

^{pride &}

ed

=mindness & from all your wicked doings appoint among yourselves

a teacher & let not all be spokesman at once but let one speak

at a time & let all listen unto his sayings that when all have

spoken that all may be edified of all & that every man may have an

equal privilege. {~~see that~~\See that} y{o\⟨e⟩}~~u~~ love one another cease to be cove{◊◊t◊\tous}

learn to impart one to an other as the gospel requires cease to be

{d\idle} cease to be unclean cease to find fault one with another cease

to sleep longer than is needful retire to thy bed early that ye may not

be weary arise early that your bodies & your minds may be invigorated

& abo{◊\ve} all things clothe yourselves with the bonds of charity as

with a Mantle which is the bonds of perfectness & peace pray always

^{will}

that you may not faint untill I come Behold & lo I come quickly

& receive you unto myself Amen

ORIGINAL INSCRIPTION
John Whitmer

REVISIONS
Oliver Cowdery
William W. Phelps
Sidney Rigdon
Joseph Smith
John Whitmer
Unidentified

♦ A Revelation given Jany 3. 1833 Kirtland

The order of the house prepared for the presidency & instructions in all

things that is expedient for the officers or in other words them who are called

to the ministry in the church begining at the high priests {~~hood~~\even} down

to the deacons & this shall be the order of the house he that is appointed

to be a teacher shall be found standing in his place which shall be prepa-

=red for him in the house of God in a place that the congregation in the house

may hear his words correctly & distinctly not with loud speach. And when

he cometh into the house of God for he should be first in the house behold

this is beautiful that he may be {~~an ensample~~\an example} let him offer himself in

prayer upon his knees before God in token of the everlasting covenant &

when any shall come in after him let the {~~T~~\teacher} arise & with uplifted

hands to heaven yea even directly & salute his brother or brethren

with these words saying art thou a brother or brethren I salute you in the name

of {◊◊◊\the} Lord Jesus Christ in token of the everlasting covenant in which covenant I receive

you to fellowship in a determination that is fixed immoveable ~~and~~

~~thanksgiving~~ & unchangable to your friend & brother through the grace

of God in the bonds of love to walk in all the commandments of

God blameless in thanksgiving for ever & ever. And he that cometh

in & is a brother or brethren shall salute the {◊\Teacher} with uplifted

hands to heaven with this same prayer & covenant or by saying amen

In token of the same. Behold verily I say unto you, this is a sample unto you for a salutation to one another in the house of God & to you the called to the ministry of the ordinances of the house of God & ye are called to do this by prayer & thanksgiving as the spirit shall give utterance in all your doings in the house of the Lord that it may become a sanctuary a tabernacle of the Holy Spirit to your edification Amen.

A Revelation for the benefit of the saints, given in Kirtland, February 27, 1833.

A word of wisdom, for the benefit of the council of high priests, assembled in Kirtland, and church; and also the saints in Zion, to be sent greeting: not by commandment or constraint, but by revelation and the word of wisdom; showing forth the order and will of God in the temporal salvation of all saints in the last days: given for a principle with promise, adapted to the capacity of the weak, and the weakest of all saints, who are, or can be called saints.

Behold verily, thus saith the Lord unto you, in consequence of evils & designs, which do and will exist in the hearts of conspiring men in the last days, I have warned you, and forewarn you, by giving unto you this word of wisdom, by revelation: That inasmuch as any man drinketh wine or strong drink among you, behold it is not good, neither meet in the sight of your Father, only in assembling yourselves together, to offer up your sacraments before him: and behold, this should be wine, yea, pure wine, of the grape of the vine of your own make.

And again, strong drinks are not for the body, but for the washing of your bodies. And again, Tobacco is not for the body, neither for the belly, and is not good for man, but is an herb for bruises and all sick cattle; to be used with judgment and skill. And again, hot drinks are not for the body, or belly.

And again, verily I say unto you, all wholesome herbs, God hath ordained for the constitution, nature and use of man: every herb in and every ~~and all~~ fruit in the season thereof:
the season thereof; all these to be used with ~~judgment~~ prudence and thanksgiving: Yea, flesh also of beasts and of the fowls of the air, I the Lord hath ordained for the use of man, with thanksgiving: nevertheless, they are to be used sparingly; and it is pleasing unto me, that they should not be used only in times of winter, or of cold, or famine.

All grain is ordained for the use of man and of beasts, to be the staff of life, not only for man, but for the beasts of the field, and

In token of the Same Behold verily I say unto you this is a sample

unto you for a salutations to one another in the house of God {t\&} to you

the called to the ministry of the ordinances of the house of God & ye are

called to do this by prayer & thanksgiving as the spirit shall give ~~utteran~~[416]

uterance in all your doings in the house of the Lord that it may become

a sanctuary a tabernacle of the Holy Spirit to your edification Amen

---

♦ /[417]A Revelation for the benefit of the saints, given in Kirtland,

February 27, 1833.

A word of wisdom, for the benefit of the council of high priests assem=

=bled in Kirtland, and church; and also the saints in Zion, to be sent greeting: not

by commandment or constraint, but by revelation and the word of wisdom;

showing forth the order and will of God in the temporal salvation of all saints

in the last days: given for a principle with promise, adapted to the capacity of the

weak, and the weakest of all saints, who are, or can be called saints.

Behold, verily, thus saith the Lord unto you, in consequence of evils &

designs, which do and will exist in the hearts of conspiring men in the

last days, I have warned you, and forewarn you, by giving unto you

this word of wisdom, by revelation: That inasmuch as any man drinketh

wine or strong drink among you, behold it is not good, neither meet

in the sight of your Father, only in assembling yourselves together, to of=

=fer up your sacraments before him{;\:} and behold, this should be wine, yea

pure wine, of the grape of the vine of your own make.

And again, strong drinks are not for the body, but for the washing of

your bodies. And again, Tobacco is not for the body, neither for the belly,

and is not good for man, but is an herb for bruises and all sick cattle;

to be used with judgment and skill. And again, hot drinks are not for

the body, or belly.

And again, verily I say unto you, all wholesome herbs, God hath

ordained for the constitution, nature and use of man: every herb in
and every ~~and all~~ fruit in the season thereof:[418] prudence
the season thereof; all these to be used with ~~judgment~~ and thanksgiving:

Yea, flesh also of beasts and of the fowls of the air, I the Lord hath or=

=dained, for the use of man, with thanksgiving: Nevertheless, they are

to be used sparingly; and it is pleasing unto me, that they should not

be used only in times of winter, or of cold, or ~~of~~ famine.

All grain is ordained for the use of man and of beasts, to be the

staff of life, not only for man, but for the beasts of the field, and

ORIGINAL INSCRIPTION
John Whitmer
Oliver Cowdery

REVISIONS
Oliver Cowdery
William W. Phelps
Sidney Rigdon
Joseph Smith
John Whitmer
Unidentified

416. "utteran" wipe-erased and then stricken.

417. John Whitmer handwriting ends; Oliver Cowdery begins.

418. Although the ink flow of Oliver Cowdery's changes throughout this revelation all appears to match the original ink flow, he may have made the changes at a later time.

the fowls of heaven, and all wild animals, that run or creep on the earth; and these hath God made for the use of man, only in times of famine and excess of hunger.

All grain is good for the food of man, as also the fruit of the vine, that which yieldeth fruit, whether in the ground, or above the ground. Nevertheless, wheat for the man, and corn for the Ox, and oats for the horse, and rye for the fowls, and for swine, and for all beasts of the field; and barley for all useful animals, and for mild drink, as also other grain.

And all saints who remember to keep and do these sayings, walk= =ing in obedience to the commandments, shall receive health in their naval, and marrow to their bones, and shall find wisdom and great treasures of knowledge; even hidden treasures; and shall run and not be weary, and shall walk and not faint: and I the Lord give unto them a promise, that the destroying angel shall pass by them, as the children of Israel, and not slay them. Amen.

Kirtland, March 8, 1833.

A Commandment given unto Joseph, saying, Thus saith the Lord, verily, verily I say unto you, my son, thy sins are forgiven thee, according to thy petition, for thy prayers and the prayers of thy brethren, have come up unto my ears; therefore thou art blessed from henceforth that bear the keys of the kingdom given unto you; which kingdom is coming forth for the last time.

Verily, I say unto you, the keys of this kingdom shall never be taken from you, whilst thou art in the world, neither in the world to come: Nev= =ertheless, through you shall the oracles be given unto another, yea, even unto the church. And all they who receive the oracles of God, let them be aware how they hold them, lest they are accounted as a light thing, and are brought under condemnation thereby, and stumble and fall, when the storms descend, and the winds blow, and the rains descend, and beat upon their house.

And again, verily I say unto thy brethren, Sidney Rigdon and Frederick G. Williams, their sins are forgiven them also, and they are accounted as equal with thee in holding the keys of this last kingdom: as also through your administration the keys of the school of the prophets, which I have commanded to be organ= =ized, that thereby they may be perfected in their ministry for the salva= =tion of Zion, and the nations of Israel, and of the Gentiles, as many as will

168 [verso]

the fowls of heaven, and all wild animels, that run or creep on the

earth; and these hath God made for the use of man, only in times of

famine and excess of hunger.

All grain is good for the food of man, as also the fruit of the vine,

that which yieldeth fruit, whether in the ground, or above the ground:

Nevertheless, wheat for ~~the~~ man, and corn for the ox, and oats for the

horse, and rye for the fowls, and for swine, and for all beasts

of the field; and barley for all useful animals, and for mild drink,

as also other grain.

And all saints who remember to keep and do these sayings, walk,

=ing in obedience to the commandments, shall receive health in

their naval, and marrow to their bones, and shall find wisdom

and great treasures of knowledge; even hidden treasures; and shall

run and not be weary, and shall walk and not faint: and I the

Lord give unto them a promise, that the destroying angel shall

pass by them, as the children of Israel, and not slay them. Amen.

♦ ⁴¹⁹Kirtland, March 8, 1833.

A Commandment given unto Joseph, saying, {t\T}hus saith the Lord,

verily, verily I say unto you, my son, thy sins are forgiven thee, according to thy

petition, for thy prayers and the prayers of thy brethren, have come up unto

my ears{;\:} therefore thou art blessed from henceforth that bear the keys of the

kingdom given unto you; which kingdom is coming forth for the last time.

Verily, I say unto you, the keys of this kingdom shall never be taken from

you, whil{ls\st} thou art in the world, neither in the world to come: Nev=

=ertheless, through you shall the oracles be given unto another; yea, even

unto the church. And all they who receive the oracles of God, let them

be {w\aware} how they hold them, lest they are accounted as a light

thing, and are brought under condemnation thereby, and stumble

and fall, when the storms descend, and the winds blow, and the rains

descend, and beat upon their house.

¶⁴²⁰   Rigdon   G. Williams
And again, verily I say unto thy brethren, Sidney and Frederick{,\ˆ} their

sins are forgiven them also, and they are accounted as equal with thee in

holding the Keys of this last kingdom: as also through your administration

the keys of the school of the prophets, which I have commanded to be organ=

=ized, that thereby they may be perfected in their ministry for the salva=
                              of ⁴²¹
=tion of Zion, and the nations of Israel, and of the Gentiles, as many as will

---

ORIGINAL INSCRIPTION
Oliver Cowdery

REVISIONS
Oliver Cowdery
William W. Phelps
Sidney Rigdon
Joseph Smith
John Whitmer
Unidentified

419. The first publication reflecting most redactions in this revelation is the 1835 Doctrine and Covenants (section 84).

420. The paragraph markers in this revelation mark the beginning of some verses as published in the 1835 Doctrine and Covenants.

421. Although the ink flow of Oliver Cowdery's changes throughout this revelation all appears to match the original ink flow, he may have made the changes at a later time.

believe, that through your administration, they may receive the word, and through their administration, the word may go forth unto the ends of the earth, unto the Gentiles first, and then behold, and lo, they shall turn unto the Jews: and then cometh the day when the arm of the Lord shall be revealed in power, in convincing the nations, the heathen nations, the house of ~~Joseph~~ of the gospel of their salvation.

For it shall come to pass in that day, that every man shall hear the fulness of the gospel in his own tongue, and in his own language, through those who are ordained unto this power, by the administration of the Comforter shed forth upon them, for the revelation of Jesus Christ.

And now verily I say unto you, I give unto you a commandment, that you continue in this ministry and presidency, and when you have finished the translation of the prophets, you shall from thenceforth preside over the affairs of the church and the school; and from time to time as shall be manifest by the Comforter, receive revelations to unfold the mysteries of the kingdom, and set in order the churches, and study, and learn, and become acquainted with all good books, and with languages, tongues, and people. And this shall be your business and mission in all your lives to preside in council and set in order all the affairs of this church and kingdom. Be not ashamed, neither confounded; but be admonished in all your high mindedness and pride, for it bringeth a snare upon your souls. Set in order your houses; keep slothfulness and uncleanness far from you.

Now verily, I say unto you, let there be a place provided as soon as it is possible, for the family of thy counsellor and scribe, even Frederick: and let mine aged servant Joseph continue with his family upon the place where he now lives, and let it not be sold until the mouth of the Lord shall name. And let thy counsellor, even Sidney, remain where he now resides, until the mouth of the Lord shall name.

And let the bishop search diligently to obtain an agent; and let it be a man who has got riches in store; a man of God and of strong faith: that thereby he may be enabled to discharge every debt, that the store house of the Lord may not be brought into disrepute before the eyes of the people. Search diligently, pray always, and be believing, and all things shall work together for your good, if ye walk uprightly, and remember the covenant wherewith ye have covenanted one with another. Let your families be small, especially mine aged servant Joseph, as

believe, that through your administration, they may receive the word, and

through their administration, the ~~work~~ word may go forth unto the ends of the

earth, unto the Gentiles first, and then behold, and lo, they shall turn unto

the Jews: and then cometh the day when the arm of the Lord shall be revealed

in power, in convincing the nations, the heathen nations, the house of ~~Israel~~ Joseph of

the gospel of their salvation.

¶For it shall come to pass in that day, that every man shall hear the ful=

=ness of the gospel in his own tongue, and in his own language, through those who

are ordained unto this power, by the administration of the Comforter shed forth

upon them, for the revelation of Jesus Christ.

And now verily I say unto you, I give unto you a commandment, that you con=

=tinue in this ministry and presidency, and when you have finished the trans=

=lation of the prophets, you shall from thence forth preside over the affairs

of the church and the school; and from time to time as shall be manifest

by the Comforter, receive revelations to unfold the mysteries of the

kingdom, and set in order the churches, and study, and learn, and become

acquainted with all good books, and with languages, ~~and~~ tongues, and people{s\s}. ~~&c. &c.~~ And this shall be your business

and mission in all your lives to preside in council and set in order all the affairs of this

church and kingdom. Be not ashamed, neither confounded; but be admon=

=ished in all your high-mindedness and pride, for it bringeth a snare

upon your souls. Set in order your houses; ~~kep~~ keep slothfulness and un=

=cleanness far from you.

¶   Now verily, I say unto you, let there be a place provided as soon as it

is possible, for the family of thy counsellor and scribe, even Frederick: and

let mine aged servant Joseph [Smith Sr.] continue with his family up on the place

where he now lives, and let it not be sold until the mouth of the Lord

shall name. And let thy counsellor, even Sidney, remain where he now

resides, until the mouth of the Lord shall name.[422]

And let the bishop ~~search~~ search[423] diligently to obtain an agent; and let it be a

man who has got riches in store; a man of God and of strong faith: that thereby

he may be enabled to discharge every debt; that the store house of the Lord

may not be brought into disrepute before the eyes of the people. Search

diligently, pray always, and be believing, and all things shall work

together for your good, if ye walk uprightly, and remember the

covenant wherewith ye have covenanted one with another. Let

your families be small, especially mine aged servant Joseph [Smith Sr.], as

ORIGINAL INSCRIPTION
Oliver Cowdery

REVISIONS
Oliver Cowdery
William W. Phelps
Sidney Rigdon
Joseph Smith
John Whitmer
Unidentified

422. A line joining this paragraph with the following
paragraph was drawn in the
same ink flow as that of Oliver
Cowdery's redactions.

423. Or "sear~~(c)~~h".

pertaining to those who do not belong to your families: that those
things that are provided for you, to bring to pass my work, are
not taken from you and given to those that are not worthy, and
thereby you are hindred in accomplishing those things which I have
commanded you.

And again, verily I say unto you, it is my will that my handmaid,
Viana Jaques should receive money, to bear her expences, and go up unto the
land of Zion; and the residue of the money may be consecrated unto me,
and she be rewarded in mine own due time. Verily, I say unto you, that it is
meet in mine eyes that she should go up unto the land of Zion, and
receive an inheritance from the hand of the bishop, that she may
settle down in peace inasmuch as she is faithful, and not be idle
in her days from thenceforth.

And behold, verily I say unto you, that ye shall write this com=
=mandment, and say unto your brethren in Zion; In love greeting:
that I have called you also to preside over Zion in mine own
due time. Therefore, let them cease wearying me concerning this
matter. Behold I say unto you, that your brethren in Zion, be=
=gin to repent, and the angels rejoice over them; nevertheless, I
am not well pleased with many things: and I am not well
pleased with my servant, Wm E. McLelin, neither with my
servant, Sidney Gilbert, and the bishop also: and many others
have many things to repent of: but verily I say unto you, that I
the Lord will contend with Zion, and plead with her strong
ones, and chasten her, until she overcomes and is clean before
me: for she shall not be moved out of her place: I the Lord have
spoken it. Amen.

pertaining to those who do not belong to your families: that those

things that are provided for you, to bring to pass my work, are

not taken from you and given to those that are not worthy, and

thereby you are hindred in accomplishing those things which I have

commanded you.

¶ And again, verily I say unto you, it is my will that my handmaid,

Jaques
Viana [Vienna Jacques] should receive money, to bear her expences and go up unto the

the   may be   me
land of Zion; and the residue of ~~her~~ money ~~I will~~ consecrated unto ~~myself,~~

She be   that
and rewarded ~~her~~ in mine own due time. Verily, I ~~say~~ say unto you, it is

meet in mine eyes that she should go up unto the land of Zion, and

receive an inheritance from the hand of the bishop, that she may

settle down in peace inasmuch as she is faithful, and not be idle

in her days from thenceforth.

And behold, verily I say unto you, that ye shall write this com=

=mandment, and say {to\unto} your brethren in Zion: In love greeting:

that I have called you also to preside over Zion in mine own

due time: Therefore, let them cease wearying me concerning this

matter. Behold I say unto you, that your brethren in Zion, be=

=gin to repent, and the angels rejoice over them; nevertheless, I

am not well pleased with many things: and I am not well

pleased with my servant, Wm E. McLel[l]in, neither with my

servant, Sidney Gilbert, and the bishop also: and ~~many~~ others

have many things to repent of: but verily I say unto you, that I

the Lord will contend with Zion, and plead with her strong

is
ones, and chasten her, until she overcomes and ~~are~~ clean before

me: for she shall not be moved out of her place: I the Lord have

spoken it. Amen.

ORIGINAL INSCRIPTION
Oliver Cowdery

REVISIONS
Oliver Cowdery
William W. Phelps
Sidney Rigdon
Joseph Smith
John Whitmer
Unidentified

Kirtland August 2nd 1833.

The word of the Lord unto Joseph Sidney & Frederick verily I
say unto you my friends, I speak unto you with my voice even the
voice of my spirit that I may shew unto you my will concerning
your brethren in the land of Zion, many of whom are truly
humble & are seeking dilligently to learn wisdom & to find
truth verily verily I say unto you blessed are all such for they
shall obtain for I the Lord sheweth mercy unto all the meek
& upon all whomsoever I will that I may be justified when I shall
bring them unto judgement

Behold I say unto you concerning the School in Zion I the Lord
am well pleased that there should be a School in Zion & also with my
servant Parley (P. Pratt) for he abideth in me & in asmuch as he
continueth to abide in me he shall continue to preside over
the School in the land of Zion & I will bless him with a multiplicity of blessings
in expounding all Scriptures & mysteries to the edification of the
School & of the Church of Zion & to the residue of the School I the Lord am willing
to shew mercy nevertheless there are those that must needs be
chastened & their works shall be made known the axe is laid at
the roots of the trees & every tree that bringeth not forth good fruit
shall be hewn down & cast into the fire I the Lord have spoken it
verily I say unto you, all among them who know their hearts are honest
& are broken, & their Spirits contrite, & are willing to observe their
covenant by Sacrifice yea every sacrifice which I the Lord shall command them are all accepted of me for I the Lord will cause them to
bring forth as a very fruitful tree which is planted in a goodly
land by a pure Stream that yieldeth much precious fruit

Verily I say unto you that it is my will that an house should be built
unto me in the land of Zion, like unto the pattern which I have
given you yea let it be built speedily by the tithing of my people behold this is the tithing & the Sacrifice which I the Lord require at
their hand that there may be a house built unto me for the salvation of Zion & for a place of thanksgiving for all Saints & for a
place of instruction for all those who are called to the work
of the ministry in all their several callings & offices that they may
be perfected in the understanding of their ministery in theory

◆ /⁴²⁴Kirtland August ◊.⁴²⁵ 1833. 2ⁿᵈ

The word of the Lord unto Joseph Sidney [Rigdon] & Frederick [G. Williams] verily I

say unto you my friends, I speak unto you with my voice even the

voice of my spirit that I may show unto you my will concerning

your brethren in the land of Zion, many of whom are truly

humble & are seeking dilligently to learn wisdom & to find

truth verily verily I say unto you blessed are all such for they

shall obtain for I the Lord showeth mercy unto all the meek

& upon all whomsoever I will that I may be Justified when I shall

bring them unto Judgement

Behold I say unto you concerning the School in Zion I the Lord

am well pleased that there should be a School in Zion & also with my

Servant {p\⟨P⟩}arl[e]y (P. Pratt) for he abideth in me & in asmuch as he

continueth to abide in me he shall continue to preside over
the land of⁴²⁶
the School in Zion & I will bless him with a multiplicity of blessings
             ^

in expounding all scriptures & mysteries to the edification of the
                                in   of the School
School & of the Church of Zion & to the residue I the Lord am willing
                        ^   ^

to show mercy nevertheless there are those that must needs be

chastened & their works shall be made known the axe is laid at

the roots of the trees & every tree that bringeth not forth good fruit

shall be hewn down & cast into the fire I the Lord have spoken it

verily I say unto you, all among them, who know their hearts are honest;⁴²⁷

& are broken, & their Spirits contrite, & are willing to observe thei{◊\r}

covenant by sacrifice yea every sacrifice which I the Lord shall com-

-mand them are all accepted of me for I the Lord will cause them to

bring forth as a very fruitful tree which is planted in a goodly

land by a pure stream that yieldeth much precious fruit
                             that
    Verily I say unto you it is my will that an house should be built
                           ^

unto me in the land of Zion, like unto the pattern which I have

given you yea let it be built speedily by the tithing of my peo-
                                       the
-ple behold this is the tithing & Sacrifice {&\which} I the Lord require at
                                 ^

their hand that there may be a house built unto me for the Salva

-tion of Zion & for a place of thanksgiving for all Saints & for a

place of instruction for all t{h◊s◊\hose} who are called to the m{y\ini}⁴²⁸ work

of the ministry in all their several callings & offices that they may

be perfected in the understanding of their ministery in theory &

ORIGINAL INSCRIPTION
John Whitmer

REVISIONS
Oliver Cowdery
William W. Phelps
Sidney Rigdon
Joseph Smith
John Whitmer
Unidentified

424. Oliver Cowdery hand-writing ends; John Whitmer begins.

425. Or "{◊\◊}" or "{◊\◊}".

426. Although the ink flow of John Whitmer's changes throughout this revelation appears to match the original ink flow, he may have made the changes at a later time.

427. Or ",".

428. "y" partially wipe-erased and written over; then whole word stricken.

in principle & in doctrine in all things pertaining to the
kingdom of God on the Earth the keys of which kingdom have been
confered upon you & inasmuch as my people build an house
unto me in the name of the Lord & do not suffer any unclean
thing to come into it that it be not defiled my glory shall rest
upon it & my presence shall be there for I will come into it
& all the pure in heart that shall come into it shall see God
but if it be defiled I will not come into it & my glory shall
not be there for I will not come into an unholy Temple And
now behold if Zion do these things she shall prosper & spread
herself & become very glorious very great & very terable & for the
Nations of the Earth shall honor her & shall say surely Zion is
the City of our God & surely Zion cannot fall neither be removed
out of her place, for God is there & the hand of the Lord is there
& he hath sworn by the power of his might to be her salvation
& her high tower therefore verily thus saith the Lord let Zion
rejoice (for this is Zion the pure in heart) therefore let Zion
rejoice while all the wicked shall mourn for behold & lo. vengeance
cometh speedily or the wicked upon the ungodly as the sickle as
the whirlwind & who shall escape it the Lords scourge shall
pass over by night & by day & the report thereof shall vex all people
yet it shall not be stayed untill the Lord came. for the indignation
of the Lord is kindled against their abominations & all their
wicked works nevertheless Zion shall escape if she observe to do
all things whatsoever I have commanded her but if she observe
not whatsoever I have commanded her I will visit her according
to all her works with sore affliction with pestilence with plague
with sword with vengeance with devouring fire Nevertheless
let it be read this once in their ears that I the Lord have accepted of
their offering & if she sin no more none of these things shall
come upon her but I will bless her with blessings & multi
-ply a multiplicity of blessings upon her & upon her generations
for ever & ever saith the Lord your God Amen

And again verily I say unto you my friends a commandment I give
unto you that ye shall commence a work of laying out & preparing
a begining & foundation of the City of the stake of Zion here in the
land of Kirtland begining at my house & behold it must be done

in principle & in doctrine in all things partaining to the

kingdom of God on the Earth the keyes of which kingdom have been

confered upon you & inasmuch as my people build an house

unto me in the name of the Lord & do not suffer any unclean

thing to come into it that it be not defiled my glory shall rest

upon it yea & my presence shall be there for I will come into it

& all the pure {♦\in} heart that shall come into it shall see God

but if it be defiled I will not come into it & my glory shall

not be there for I will not come in⟨to⟩ an unholy Temple And

now behold if Zion do these things she shall prosper & spread

herself & become very glorious very great & very terable & for the

Nations of the Earth shall honor her & shall say sur[e]ly Zion is

the City of our God & Sur[e]ly Zion cannot fall neither be removed

out of her place, for God is there & the hand of the Lord is there

& he hath sworn by the power of his might to be her salvation

& her high tower therefore verily thus saith the Lord let Zion

rejoice (for this is Zion the pure in heart) therefore let Zion

rejoice while all the wicked shall mourn for behold & lo. vengea

-nce cometh speedily ~~as the whir~~ upon the ungodly {as th\& ~~who sha~~}⁴²⁹ as

the whirlwind & who shall escape it the Lords scourge shall

pass over by night & by day & the report thereof shall ~~be to~~ vex all people

yet it shall not be stayed untill the Lord come. for the indignation

of the Lord is kindled againnst their abominations & all their

wicked works nevertheless Zion shall escape if she observe to do

all things whatsoever I have commanded her but if she observe

not whatsoever I have commanded her I will visit her according

to all her works with sore affliction with pestilence with plague

with sword with vengeance with devouring fire Nevertheless

let it be read this once in their ears that I the Lord have accepted of

their offering & if she sin no more none of these things shall

come upon her but I will bless her with blessings & multi

-ply a multiplicity of blessings upon her & upon her generations⁴³⁰

for ever & ever saith the Lord your God Amen

♦   And again verily I say unto you my friends a commandment I give

unto y{e\ou} that y{♦♦\e} shall commence a work of laying out & preparing

a begining & foundation {i\o}f the {&\City} of the Stake of Zion here in the

land of Kirtland begining at my house & behold it must be done

ORIGINAL INSCRIPTION
John Whitmer

REVISIONS
Oliver Cowdery
William W. Phelps
Sidney Rigdon
Joseph Smith
John Whitmer
Unidentified

429. "as th" wipe-erased and written over; then stricken with entire phrase.

430. "s" possibly inserted.

according to the pattern which I have given unto you & let the first lot on the south be consecrated unto me for the building of an house for the Presidency in obtaining revelations & for the work of the ministery of the Presidency in all things pertaining to the Church & king- dom verily I say unto you that it shall be built fifty five by sixtyfive in the width thereof & in the length thereof in the inner court & there shall be a lower court & a higher court according to the pattern which shall be given unto you hereafter & it shall be dedicated unto the Lord from the foundation thereof according to the order of the priesthood according to the pattern which shall be given unto you hereafter & it shall be wholly dedicated unto the Lord for the work of the Presidency & ye shall not suffer any unclean thing to come into it & my glory shall be there & my presence shall be there but if there shall come into it any unclean thing my glory shall not be there & my presence shall not come in to it.

And again verily I say unto you the second lot on the south shall be dedicated unto me for the work of the printing of the transla- tion of my Scriptures & all things whatsoever I shall command you & it shall be fifty five by sixtyfive in the width thereof & in the length thereof in the inner court there shall be a lower & a higher court & this house shall be wholly dedicated unto the Lord from the foun- dation thereof for the work of the Printing in all things whatsoever I shall command you to be holy & undefiled according to the pat- tern in all things as it shall be given unto you & on the third lot shall my servant Hyrum (Smith) receive his inheritance & on the first & second lots on the north shall my servant Reynolds Cahoon & Jared Carter receive their inheritance that they may do the work which I have appointed unto them, to be a committee to build my house according to the commandment which I the Lord God have given unto you & now I give unto you no more at this time.

Kirtland August 6, 1833.

verily I say unto you my friends fear not let your hearts be comforted yea rejoice evermore & in every thing give thanks waiting patiently on the Lord for your prayers have entered into the ears of the Lord of Sabaoth & are recorded with this seal & testament according to the pattern which I have given unto you & let the

first lot on the south be consecrated unto me for the building of

an house for the Presidency in obtaining revelations & for the work
in all things
of the ministery of the Presedency partaining to the Church & King-
you
-dom verily I say unto that it shall be built fifty five by sixty five
^

in the wi{ΘΘ\dth} thereof & in the length thereof in the inner court & there

shall be a lower Court & a higher court according to the pattern which

shall be given unto you hereafter & it shall be dedicated unto the Lord

from the foundation thereof according to the order of the priesthood

according to the pattern which shall be given unto you hereafter &

it shall be wholly dedicated unto the Lord for the wor{d\k} of the Presidency

& ye shall not suffer any unclean thing to come {in\⟨into⟩} it & my glory

shall be there & my presence shall be there but if there shall come

into it any unclean thing my glory shall not be there & my presence

shall not come in to it.

And again verily I say unto you the second lot on the South

shall be dedicated unto me for the work of the printing of {my\the} transla-

-tion of my Scriptures & all things whatsoever I shall command you

& it shall be fifty five by Sixty five in the width thereof & in the length
&
thereof in the inner court there ⟨&⟩ shall be a lower & a higher court
^

& this house shall be wholly dedicated unto the Lord from the found

-ation thereof for the work of the Printing in all things whatsoever

I shall command you to be holy & undefiled {in\according} to the pat

-tern in all things as it shall be given unto you & on the third
Servant
lot shall my Hyrum (Smith) receive his inheritance & on the
^

first & second lots on the north shall my Servant Reynolds

Cahoon & Jar{d\ad} [Jared] Carter receive their inheritance that they may do the

work which I have appointed unto them, to be a committee to

build my house according to the commandment which I the Lord

God have given unto you & now I give unto you no more at

this time.

Kirtland August {2\6}, 1833.

Verily I say unto you my friends fear not let your hearts be

comforted yea rejoice evermore & in every thing give thanks waiting

patiently on the Lord for your prayers have entered into the ears

of the Lord of Sabaoth & are recorrded with this seal & testament

ORIGINAL INSCRIPTION
John Whitmer

REVISIONS
Oliver Cowdery
William W. Phelps
Sidney Rigdon
Joseph Smith
John Whitmer
Unidentified

the Lord hath sworn & decreed that they shall be granted therefore he giveth this promise unto you with an immutable covenant that they shall be fulfilled & all things wherewith you have been afflicted shall work together for your good & to my names glory saith the Lord God.

And now verily I say unto you concerning the laws of the land it is my will that my people should observe to do all things whatsoever I command them & that law of the land which is constitutional supporting the principals of freedom in maintaining rights & priveleges to all mankind & is justifiable before me therefore I the Lord justifieth you & your brethren of my Church in befriending that law which is the constitutional law of the land & as pertaining to law of man whatsoever is more or less than this cometh of evil I the Lord your God maketh you free therefore you are free indeed & the Law also maketh you free nevertheless when the wicked rule the people mourn wherefore honest men & wise men should be sought for dilligently & good men & wise men ye should observe to uphold otherwise whatsoever is less than this cometh of evil & I give unto you a commandment that ye shall forsake all evil & cleave unto all good that ye shall live by every word that proceedeth forth out of the mouth of God for he will give unto the faithful line upon line precept upon precept & I will try you & prove you herewith & whoso layeth down his life in my cause for my names sake shall find it again even life eternal therefore be not afraid of your enemies for I have decreed in my heart saith the Lord that I will prove you in all things whether you will abide in my covenant even unto death that you may be found worthy for if you will not abide in my covenant you are not worthy of me therefore renounce war & proclaim peace & seek dilligently to turn the hearts of the children to the fathers & the hearts of the fathers to the children & again the hearts of the Jews to the Prophets & the Prophets to the Jews lest I came & smite the whole earth with a curse & all flesh be consumed before me let not your hearts be troubled for in my

182 [verso]

my will that you should build an house. If ye keep

my commandments ye shall have power to build it: If ye

keep not my commandments, the love of the Father shall not

continue with you{,\.} Therefore, ye shall walk in darkness{,\.} Now

here is wisdom, and the mind of the Lord: Let the house be

built, not after the manner of this world; for I give not unto you

that ye shall live after the manner of the world. Therefore, let

it be built after the manner ~~of those of you~~ which I shall show

unto those of whom ye shall appoint and ordain unto this

power; and the size thereof shall be fifty &^ five feet in width,

& let it be sixty & five feet in length in the inner court thereof,

and let the lower part of the inner court be dedicated unto m{◊,\e}
    and for your preaching & your fasting & your praying
for your Sacrament offering{s\,}, & the offering up your most holy

desires unto me saith your Lord. And let the higher part of the

inner court be dedicated unto me for the school of mine apos-

-tles, saith Son[439] awman,[440] or in other words, Alpha, or in other words

Omegas, even Jesus Christ your Lord: Amen.

♦ # Revelation given Kirtland, June{,\ 4}, 1833.

Behold I say unto you, here is wisdom, whereby ye may know

how to act concerning this matter. For it is expedient in me, that

this stake that I have set for the strength~~ning~~ of Zion, should be

made strong. Therefore, let my servant Newel [K. Whitney] take charge of the

place which is named among you, upon which I design to

build mine holy house. And again, let it be divided into lots

according to wisdom, for the benefit of those who seek inheritan-

-ces, as it shall be determined in counsel among you{,\.} Therefore,

take heed that y{ou\e} see to this matter; and that portion that is necessa-

-ry to benefit the Firm for the purpose of bringing forth my word

to the children of men. For behold verily I say unto you, this is the

most expedient in me, that my word should go forth unto the

children of men, for the purpose of subdueing the he{◊◊\ar}ts of the

children of men, for your good even so: {am\Amen}.

And again, verily I say unto you, it is wisdom, and expedient

in me, that my servant John Johnson, whose offering I have

accepted, {◊\and} whose prayers I have heard, unto whom I give

a promise of eternal life, in as much as he keepeth my

ORIGINAL INSCRIPTION
John Whitmer

REVISIONS
Oliver Cowdery
William W. Phelps
Sidney Rigdon
Joseph Smith
John Whitmer
Unidentified

439. Or "San".
440. Or "awmon".

341

commandments from henceforth, for he is a descendant of
Joseph, and a partaker of the blessings of the promise made
unto his fathers. Verily I say unto you, it is expedient in me that
he should become a member of the Firm; that he may assi-
-st in bringing forth my word unto the children of men. Therefore,
ye shall ordain him unto this blessing, and he shall seek
dilligently to take away incumbrances that are upon the house
named among you, that he may dwell therein; even so, Amen.

Revelation Given Kirtland December 16 & 17, 1833.

Verily I say unto you, concerning your brethren, who have been afflic-
-ted, and persecuted, and cast out from the land of their inheritances,
I the Lord have suffered the affliction to come upon them wherewith
they have been afflicted in consequence of their transgressions; yet,
I will own them, and they shall be mine in the day when I shall come to make
up my jewels.

Therefore, they must needs be chastened, and tried, even as Abraham,
who was commanded to offer up his only Son. For all those who
will not endure chastisening but deny me, cannot be sanctified.

Behold, I say unto you, there were jarrings, and contentions, and
stripes, and lustful and covetous desires among them. Therefore,
by these things they polluted their inheritances: They were slow to
hearken unto the voice of the Lord their God; therefore, the Lord their
God is slow to hearken unto their prayers, to answer them in the
day of their trouble. In the day of their peace they esteemed lightly
my counsel; but in the day of their trouble, of necessity, they feel of
after me.

Verily, I say unto you, notwithstanding their sins my bowels are filled with
compassion towards them; I will not utterly cast them off; and in the day
of wrath I will remember mercy.

I have sworn and the decree hath gone forth by a former command-
-ment which I have given unto you, that I would let fall the sword of
mine indignation in the behalf of my people; and even as I have said
it shall come to pass. Mine indignation is soon to be poured out without
measure upon all nations and this will I do, when the cup of their iniquity
is full. And in that day all who are found upon the watchtower,

commandments from henceforth, for he is a decendant of

Joseph, and a partaker of the blessings of the promise made

unto his fathers. Verily I say unto you, it is expedient in me that

he should become a member of the Firm, that he may assi-

-st in bringing forth my word unto the children of men. Therefore,

ye shall ordain him unto this blessing, and he shall seek

dilligently to take away incumberences that are upon the house

named among you, that he may dwell theiri{◊\n}; even so, Amen

ORIGINAL INSCRIPTION
John Whitmer

REVISIONS
Oliver Cowdery
William W. Phelps
Sidney Rigdon
Joseph Smith
John Whitmer
Unidentified

441. "so" wipe-erased and then stricken.

◆ ## Revelation Given Kirtland December 16 & 17, 1833.

Verily I, say unto you, concerning your brethren, who have been affli

-cted, and pursecuted, and cast out from the land of their inheritances,

I the Lord have suffered the affliction to come upon them wherewith

they have been afflicted in consequence of their {s\transgressions}: yet,

I will own them, and they shall be mine in the day when I shall make [come to]

up my Jewels.

Therefore, they must needs be chastened, and tried, even as Abraham,

who was commanded to offer up his only Son. For all those who

will not endure chastingning [chastening] but deny me, cannot be sanctified.

Behold, I say unto you, there were Jarrings, and contentions, and

strifes, and lustful and covetous desires among them. Therefore,

by these things they polluted their inheritances: They were slow to

hearken unto the voice of the Lord their God; therefore, the Lord their

God is slow to hearken unto their prayers, to answer them in the

day of their trouble. In the day of their peace they esteemed light

-ly my {c◊\counsel}; but in the day of their trouble, of necesity, they feel af

after me.

Verily, I say unto you, notwithstanding their sins my bowels are filled with

compassion towards them; I will not utterl{l\y} cast them off; and in the day

of wrath I will remember mercy.

I have sworn and the decree hath gone forth by a former command-

-ment which I have given unto you, that I would let fall the sword of

mine in{g\dignation} in the behalf of my people, and even as I have said s̶o̶[441]

it shall come to pass. Mine indignation is soon to be poured out without

measure upon all nations and this will I do, when the cup of their iniqity

is full. And in that day all who are found upon the watchtower, or in other words, all mine Israel shall be saved; and they that have been scattered shall be gathered; and all they who have mourned shall be comforted; and all they who have given their lives for my name shall be crowned. Therefore let your hearts be comforted concerning Zion, for all flesh is in mine hands: be still, and know that I am God. Zion shall not be moved out of her place; notwithstanding her children are scattered, they that remain and are pure in heart, shall shall return and come to their inheritances, they and their children with songs of everlasting joy, to build up the waste places of Zion. And all these things that the prophets might be fulfilled.

And behold, there is none other place appointed, than that which I have appointed; neither shall there be any other place appointed, than that which I have appointed for the work of the gathering of my saints, untill the day cometh, when there is found no more room for them; and then I have other places which I will appoint unto them, and they shall be called stakes, for the curtains or strength of Zion.

Behold it is my will, that all who call on my name, and worship me according to mine everlasting gospel, should gather together, and stand in holy places, and prepare for the revelation which is to come, when the veil of the covering of my temple in my tabernacle, which hideth the earth shall be taken off, and all flesh shall see me together; and every corruptable thing, both of man and of the beasts of the field, or of the fowls of heaven, or of the fish of the sea, that dwell upon all the face of the earth, shall be consumed; and also, that of element, shall melt with fervent heat; and all things shall become new; that my knowledge and glory, may dwell upon all the earth. And in that day the enmity of man, and the enmity of beasts, yea, the enmity of all flesh shall cease from before my face.

And in that day whatever any man shall ask it shall be given unto him. And in that day Satan shall not have power to tempt any man; and there shall be no sorrow; because there is no death. in that day an infant shall not die untill he is old, and his life shall be as the age of a tree; and when he dies he shall not sleep, (that is to say in the earth,) but shall be changed in the twinkling of an eye, and shall be caught up and his rest shall be glorious.

Yea, verily I say unto you, in that day when the Lord shall come

184 [verso]

or in other words, all mine Israel shall be saved; and they that

have been scattered shall be gathered; and all they who have {◊\mourned}

shall be comforted; and all they who have given their lives for my

name shall be crowned. Therefore let your hearts be comforted concer=

-ning Zion, for all flesh is in mine hands: be still, and know that

I am God. Zion shall not be moved out {her\of} her place; notwithstanding

her children are scattered, they that remain and are pure in heart, ~~shall~~

shall return and come to their inheritances, they and their children with

songs of everlasting Joy, to build up the waste places of Zion. And

all these things that the prophets might be fulfilled.

And behold, there is none other place appointed, than that

which I have appointe{◊\d}; neither shall there be any other place ap-

-pointed, than that which I have appointed for the work of the geth-

-ering of my Saints, untill the day cometh, when there is found no

more room for them; and then I have other places which I will

appoint unto them, and they shall be called stakes, for the curtains

or strength of Zion.

Behold it is my will, that all who call on my name, and worship-[442]

me according to mine everlasting gospel, should g{e\a}ther together, and stand

in holy places, and prepare for the revelation which is to come, when the

veil of the covering of my temple in my tabernacle, which hideth the

earth shall be taken off, and all flesh shall see me together; and every

corruptabe [corruptible] thing, both of man and of the beasts of the field, or of the

fowls of heaven, or of the fish of the sea, that dwell upon all the face

of the earth, shall be consumed; and also, that of element, shall melt

with fervent heat; and all things shall become new; that my knowledge

and glory, may dwell upon all the earth. And in that day the enmity of

man, and the enmity of beasts, yea, the enmity of all flesh shall cease

from before my face.

And in that day whatever any man shall ask it shall be given

unto him. And in that day sat{◊◊\an} shall not have power to tempt any

man; and there shall be no sorrow; because there is no death. in that

day an infant shall not die until he is old, and his life shall be as the

age of a tree; and when he dies he shall not sleep, (that is to say in the

earth,) but shall be changed in the twi{i\nkling} of an eye, and shall

be caught up and his rest shall be glorious.

Yea, verily I say unto you, in that day when the Lord shall come

Original Inscription
John Whitmer

Revisions
Oliver Cowdery
William W. Phelps
Sidney Rigdon
Joseph Smith
John Whitmer
Unidentified

442. Hyphen wipe-erased, likely indicating that John Whitmer began to write "worshiping" or "worshiped" before realizing the word should be "worship".

he shall reveal all things; things which have passed, and hidden things which no man knew; things of the earth, by which it was made, and the purpose and the end thereof; things things most precious; things that are above and things that are beneath; things that are in the earth, and upon the earth, and in heaven. And all they who suffer persecution for my name, and endure in faith, though they are called to lay down their lives for my sake, yet shall they partake of all this glory.

Wherefore, fear not, even unto death, for in this world your joy is not full, but in me your joy is full. Therefore, care not for the body, neither for the life of the body; but care for the soul, and for the life of the soul; and seek the peace of the Lord always, that in patience you may possess your souls, and ye shall have eternal life.

When men are called unto mine everlasting gospel, and covenant with an everlasting covenant, they are accounted as the salt of the earth and the saviour of men; they are called to be the saviour of men. Therefore, if that salt of the earth, loose its saviour, behold it is thenceforth good for nothing, only to be cast out and trodden under the feet of men.

Behold, here is wisdom concerning the children of Zion, even many, but not all; they were found transgressors, therefore they must needs be chastened. He that exalteth himself shall be abased, and he that abaseth himself shall be exalted.

And now I will show unto you a parable, that you may know my will concerning the redemption of Zion:

A certain nobleman had a spot of land very choice, and he said unto his servants, Go ye into my vineyard, even upon this very choice piece of land, and plant twelve olive-trees, and set watchmen about them, and build a tower, that one may overlook the land round about, to be a watchman upon the tower, that mine olive-trees may not be broken down, when the enemy shall come to spoil and take unto themselves the fruit of my vineyard.

Now, the servants of this nobleman went and did as their lord commanded them, and planted the olive-trees and built a hedge round about, and set watchmen, and began to build the tower. And while they were yet laying the foundation thereof, they began to say among themselves, And what need hath my lord of this Tower? and consulted for a long time, saying among themselves, What need hath my Lord of this Tower?

he shall reveal all things; things which have {p◊◊\passed}, and hid-

-den things which no man knew; things of the earth, by which ~~it~~

it was made, and the purpose and the end thereof; things ~~things~~ most

precious; things that are above and things that are beneath; things that

are in the earth, and upon the earth, and in heaven. And all they

who suffer persecut{◊◊\io}n for my name, and endure in faith though

they are called to lay down their lives for my sake, yet shall they

partake of all this glory.

Wherefore, fear not, even unto death, for in this world your Joy is not full,

but in me your Joy is full. Therefore, care not for the body, neither for the life of the

body; but ^care^ for the soul, and for the life of the soul; and seek the peace of the

Lord always, that in patience you may possess your souls, and ye shall have

eternal life.

When men are called unto mine everlasting gospel, and covenant with

an everlasting covenant, they are accounted as the salt of the earth and the

savio{r\ur} of men, they are called to be the saviour of men. Therefore, if that

salt of the earth, loose its saviour, behold it is thenceforth, good for noth-

-ing, only to be cast out and trodden under the feet of men.

Behold, here is wisdom concerning the children of Zion, ~~even many,~~

even many but not all; they were found transgressors, therefore they

must needs be chastened. He that exalteth himself shall be abased, and he that

abaseth himself shall be exalted.

And now I will show unto you a parable, that you may know

my will concerning the redemption of Zion:

A certain nobleman, had a spot of land very choice, and he said

unto his servants, Go ye into my vineyard, even upon this very choice piece

of land, and plant twelve olive-trees, and set watchmen about them, and

build a tower, that one may overlook the land roundabout, to be a

watchman upon the tower, that mine olivetrees may not be broken

down, when the enemy shall come to spoil and take unto themselves

the fruit of my vineyard

Now, the servants of this nobleman went and did as their lord com=

-manded them, and planted the olivetrees and built a hedge round a{◊◊◊\bout}

and set watchmen, and began to build the tower. and while they were

yet laying the foundation thereof, they began to say among themselves,

{a\⟨A⟩}nd what need hath my lord of {a ◊◊\this} Tower? and consulted for a long

time, saying among themselves, What need hath my Lord of this Tower?

ORIGINAL INSCRIPTION
John Whitmer

REVISIONS
Oliver Cowdery
William W. Phelps
Sidney Rigdon
Joseph Smith
John Whitmer
Unidentified

Seeing this is a time of peace? might not this money be given
to the exchangers? for there is no need of these things.

And while they were yet at variance one with another, they became very slothful, and they hearkened not unto the commandment of
their Lord; and the enemy came by night and brake down the hedge,
and the servants of the noble-man arose and were affrighted and fled,
and the enemy destroyed their works, and brake down the olive
trees.

Now behold the noble-man, the lord of the vineyard, called upon
his servants, and said unto them, Why! what is the cause of this great
evil! Ought ye not to have done even as I commanded you?
And after you had planted the vineyard, and built the hedge
round about, and set watchmen upon the walls thereof, built the
tower also, and set a watchman up on the tower? and watched
for my vineyard, and not have fallen asleep, lest the enemy should
come upon you? And behold the watchman upon the Tower,
would have seen the enemy while he was yet afar off; and then ye
could have made ready and kept the enemy from breaking down
the hedge thereof, and saved my vineyard from the hands of the destroyer.

And the Lord of the vineyard said unto one of his servants, Go & gather
together the residue of my servants, and take all the strength of
mine house, which are my warriors, my young men, and they
that are of middle age also, among all my servants, who are the
strength of my house, save those only whom I have appointed to
tarry; and go ye straightway unto the land of my vineyard, and
redeem my vineyard, for it is mine, I have bought it with
money.

Wherefore, get ye straightway to my land, break down the
wall of mine enemies, throw down their tower and scatter
their watchman; and inasmuch as they gather together against
you, avenge me of mine enemies, that by and by I may come
with the residue of mine house and possess the Land.

And the servant said unto his Lord, when shall all these
things be? and he said unto his servant, When I will; go ye
straightway and do all things whatsoever I have commanded you;
and this shall be my seal and blessing upon you. A
faithful and wise steward in the midst of mine house a ruler

188 [verso]

Zion. {t\⟨T⟩}here is even now already in st{r\ore} a sufficient; yea,

even abundance to redeem Zion, and establish her waste

places no more to be thrown down, were the churches who call

themselves after my name, willing to hearken to my voice.

And again, I say unto you, those who have been scattered

by their enemies, it is my will that they should continue to impor-

-tune for redreess and redemption by the hands of those who are

placed as rulers, and are in authority over you, according to the law

and constitution of the people which I have suffered to be

established; and should be maintained for the rights and pro-

-tection of all flesh, according to Just and holy principals, that

every man may act in doctrine and principal partaining to

futurity, according to the moral agency of {◊◊◊◊◊\which} I have given

unto them, that every man may be accountable for his own

sins in the day of Judgment.

Therefore, it is not right that any man should be in bondage one

to another. And for this purpose have I established the constitution

of this land by the hands of wise men, whom I raised up unto

this very purpose, and redeemed the land by the shedding of blood.

Now unto what shall I liken the children of Zion? I will

liken them unto the parable of the woman and the unjust Judge,

(for men ought always to pray and not faint) which saith, there, was in

a city a Judge which feared not God neither regarded m{e\⟨a⟩}n; and

there was a widow in that city, and she came unto him {◊◊\Saying},

Avenge me of mine advisary: and he would not for a while, but

afterwards he said within himself, though I fear not God nor regard

man; yet because this widow troubleth me I will avenge her, lest

by her continual coming she weary me.

Thus, will I liken the children of Zion, Let them importune

at the feet of the Judge; and if he heed them not, let them

importune at the feet of the Governor, and if the Governor heed them

not, let them importune at the feet of the President and if the

president heed them not, then will the Lord arise and come

forth out of his hiding place, and in his fury vex the nation;

and in his hot displeasure and in his fierce anger in his time

will he cut off these wicked unfaithful and unjust stewards,

and appoint them their portion among hypocrites and

ORIGINAL INSCRIPTION
John Whitmer

REVISIONS
Oliver Cowdery
William W. Phelps
Sidney Rigdon
Joseph Smith
John Whitmer
Unidentified

unbelievers, even in outer darkness, where there is weeping, and wailing, and gnashing of teeth.

Pray ye therefore, that their ears may be opened unto your cries, that I may be merciful unto them, that these things may not come upon them. What I have said unto you must needs be, that all men may be left without excuse, that wise men and rulers may hear and know that which they have never considered; that I may proceed to bring to pass my act, my strange act, and perform my work, my strange work, that men may discern between the righteous and the wicked, saith your God.

And again, I say unto you, it is contrary to my commandments and my will, that my servant Algernon Sidney Gilbert, should sell my storehouse which I have appointed unto my people, into the hands of mine enemies. Let not that which I have appointed be polluted by mine enemies, by the consent of those who call themselves after my name; for this is a very sore and grievous sin against me and against my people, in consequence of those things which I have decreed, and are soon to befall the nations.

Therefore, it is my will that my people should claim and hold claim upon that which I have appointed unto them, though they should not be permitted to dwell thereon. Nevertheless, I do not say that they shall not dwell thereon, for inasmuch as they bring forth fruit and works meet for my kingdom, they shall dwell thereon: They shall build and another shall not inherit it; they shall plant vineyards and they shall eat the fruit thereof: even so; Amen.

A REVELATION given at Kirtland, Ohio

Verily in the Spring of 1834, before Joseph Smith jr started to Zion. I say unto you, my friends, behold I will give unto you a Revelation and commandment, that you may know how to act in the discharge of your duties concerning the salvation and redemption of your brethren who have been scattered from the land of Zion: being driven and smitten by the hands of mine enemies on whom I will pour out of my wrath without measure in mine own time; for I have suffered these things for them thus far, that they might fill up the measure of their iniquities that their cup might be full, and that those who call themselves after my name might be chastened for a little season, with a sore and grievous

49 of these sacred things, for the purpose of printing these sacred

things, according as I have said; and the avails of these sacred

things shall be had in the treasury, and a seal shall be upon it,

and it shall not be used or taken out of the treasury by any one

neither shall the seal be loosed which shall be placed upon it,

50 only by the voice of the firm, or by commandment{, an\—} And thus

shall ye preserve all the avails of these sacred things in the treas-

-ury, for sacred and holy purposes, and this shall be called the

Sacred treasury of the Lord and a seal shall be kept upon it,

that it may be ~~kept~~ holy and consecrated unto the Lord.

And again, there shall be another treasury prepared

and a treasurer appointed to keep the treasury and a seal shall be

placed upon it, and all moneys that you receive in your stewardsh-

-ips by improving upon the properties which I have appointed unto

you, in houses {are\or} in lands, or in cattle {or\and} in all things, save it

be the Holy and sacred writings, which I have reserved unto myself

for holy and sacred purposes, shall be cast into the treasury as fast

as you receive ~~moneys~~ monies, by hundreds, or by fifties, or by

tw[e]nties, or by tens, or by fives, or in other words, if any man among

51 you, obtain five dollars, let him cast it into the treasury, or if he obtain

ten, or twenty, or fifty or a hundred, let him do like wise; and let

not any man among you, say that it is his {◊wn\,\own}; for it shall not

be called his, nor any part of it, and there shall not any part of it

&
used, or taken out of the treasury only by the voice ~~of~~ common con-
^

52
-sent of the firm. And this shall be the voice and common con-

5{2\3}
-sent of the Firm:— that any man among you, say unto the ~~treasury~~

treasurer, I have need of this to help me in my stewardship if it

54   55
be five dollars, or if it be ten dollars, or twenty, or fifty, or a hundred.

The treasurer shall give unto him the sum which he requires, to

help him, in his stewardship, until he be found a transgressor, and

56
it is manifest before the counsel of the Fi{◊\⟨r⟩}m, plainly that he is an

unfaithful and an unwise steward; but so long as he is in full

fellowship and is faithful and wise in his stewardship, this shall

be his token unto the treasurer, that the treasurer shall not withhold

but in case of transgression the treasurer shall be subject unto

57
the counsel and voice of the Firm, and in case the treasurer is

an
found an unfaithful and unwise steward, he shall be subject to
^

Original Inscription
John Whitmer

Revisions
Oliver Cowdery
William W. Phelps
Sidney Rigdon
Joseph Smith
John Whitmer
Unidentified

the counsel and voice of the Firm, and shall be removed out of his place and another shall be appointed in his stead.

And again, verily I say unto you, concerning your debts, behold it is my will that you should pay all your debts; and it is my will that you should humble yourselves before me, and obtain this blessing by your diligence, and humility, and the prayer of faith, and in as much as you are diligent and humble and exercise the prayer of faith; behold I will soften the hearts of those to whom you are in debt, until I shall send means unto you for your deliverance. Therefore write speedily unto New York, and write according to that which shall be dictated by my Spirit, and I will soften the hearts of those to whom you are in debt, that it shall be taken away out of their minds, to bring affliction upon you. And in as much as ye are humble and faithful and call on my name, behold I will give you the victory:— I give unto you a promise, that you shall be delivered this once out of your bondage—In as much as you obtain a chance to loan money by hundreds or by thousands, even until you shall *learn* obtain enough to deliver yourselves from bondage, it is your privilege, and pledge the properties which I have put into your hands this once by giving your names by common consent, or otherwise as it shall seem good unto you, I give unto you the privilege this once, and behold if you proceed to do the things which I have laid before you, according to my commandment, all these things are mine, and ye are my stewards, and the master will not suffer his house to be broken up; even so Amen.

Revelation given at Kirtland April 28, 1834.

Verily thus saith the Lord concerning the division and settlement of the United Firm. Let there be reserved three thousand dollars for the right and claim of the Firm in Kirtland for inheritances in due time, even when the Lord will; and with this claim to be had in remembrance when the Lord shall reveal it for a right of inheritance. Ye are *made* free from the Firm of Zion and the Firm in Zion is made free from the Firm in Kirtland thus saith the Lord Amen ——

the counsel and voice of the {f\⟨F⟩}irm, and shall be removed

out of his place and another shall be appointed in this stead.

And again, verily I say unto you, concerning your debts,

behold it is my will that you should pay all your debts; and it

is my will that you should humble yourselves before me,

and obtain this blessing by your diligence, and humility, and

the prayer of faith, and in as much as you are diligent and humble

and exercise the prayer of faith; behold I will soften the hearts of those

to whom you are in debt, until I shall send means unto you for

your deliverance. Therefore write speedily unto New **59** York, and

write according to that which shall be dictated by my Spirit, and

I will soften the hearts of those to whom you are in debt, that it

shall be taken away out of their minds to bring affliction upon

you. And in as much as ye are humble and faithful and call

on my name, behold I will give you the victory:— I give unto

you a promi{e\se}, that you shall be delivered this onc⟨e⟩ out of your

bondage— Inas much as you obtain a chanc[e] to loan money by

                                                                    loan
hundreds or by thousands, even until you shall ~~obtain~~ enough
                                                                    ^

to deliver yourselves from bonda{◊◊\ge}, it is your privilege, and pledge

the properties which I have put into your hands this once by giving

your names by common consent, or otherwise as it shall seem good

unto you, I give unto you the privilege this once, and behold if

you proceed to do the things which I have laid before you, according

to my commandment, all these things are mine, and ye are my

stewards, and the master will not suffer his house to be broken

up; even so Amen.

♦ Revelation given at Kirtland April 28, 1834.

Verily thus saith the Lord concerning the division and settlement

of the United Firm. Let there be reserved three thousand dollars for

the right and claim of the Firm, in Kirtland for inheritances in due

time, even when the Lord will; and with this claim to be had in

remembrance when the Lord shall reveal it for a right of inheri-
                                                        made[454]
-tance. Ye are free from the Firm of Zion and the Firm in Zion
                  ^

is made free {in\from} the Firm in Kirtland thus saith the Lord

Amen——

Original Inscription
John Whitmer

Revisions
Oliver Cowdery
William W. Phelps
Sidney Rigdon
Joseph Smith
John Whitmer
Unidentified

454. John Whitmer possibly made this change at a later time.

Revelation given June 22, 1834. Clay Co. Mo.

Verily I say unto you, who have assembled together that you may learn my will, concerning the redemption of mine afflicted people; behold I say unto you, were it not for the transgression of my peo- -ple speaking concerning the church and not individuals, they might have been redeemed even now; but behold, they have not learned to be obedient to the things which I require at their hands, but are full of all manner of evil and do not impart of their substance as becometh saints; to the poor and afflicted among them and are not united, according to the union required by the law of the celestial kingdom and Zion cannot be built up unless it is by the princi- -ples of the law of the celestial kingdom, otherwise, I cannot receive her unto myself and my people must needs be chastened, until they learn obedience if it must needs be by the things which they suffer. I speak not concerning those who are appointed to lead my people who are the first elders of my church for they are not all under this condem- -nation, but I speak concerning the church abroad, there are many who will say where is their god, Behold, he will deliver in time of trouble, otherwise we will not go up unto Zion, and will keep our monies.

Therefore in consequence of the transgression of my people, it is expedient in me that mine elders should wait for a little season for the redemption of Zion, that they themselves may be prepared and that my people may be taught more perfectly, and have experience and know more perfectly concerning their duty, and the things which I require at their hands, and this cannot be brought to pass until mine elders are endowed with power from on high, for behold I have prepared a great endowment and blessing to be poured out upon them — inasmuch as they are faithful and continue in humility before me. Therefore it is expedient in me, that mine elders should wait for a little season for the redemption of Zion, For behold I do not require at their hands, to fight the battles of Zion. for as I have said in a former commandment even so I will fulfil. I will fight your battles, behold the destroyer I have already sent forth to destroy and lay waste mine enemies, and not many years hence they shall not be left to pollute mine heritage, to blaspheme my name

Revelation given {~~22~~\June} 22, 1834. Clay Co. Mo.

Verily I say unto you, who have assembled together that you may learn my will, concerning the redemption of mine afflicted people; behold I say unto you, were it not for the transgression of my peo- -ple speaking concerning the church and not individuals, they might have been redeemed even now; but behold, they have not learned to be obedient to the things which I require at their hands, but are full of all manner of evil and do not impart of their substanc[e] as becometh saints; to the poor and afflicted among them and are not united, according to the union {~~of~~\required} by the law of the celestial kingdom and Zion cannot be built up unless it is by the princi- -poles of the law of the Celestial kingdom otherwise, I cannot receive her unto my-self and my people must needs be chastened, until they learn obedience if it must needs be by the things which they suffer. I speak not concerning those who are appointed to lead my people who are the first elders of my church for they are not all under this condem- -nation, but I speak concerning the church abroad, there are many who will say where is their god, Behold, he will deliver in time of trouble, otherwise we will not go up unto Zion, and will keep our monies.

Therefore in consequence of the transgression of my people, it is expedient in me that mine elders should wait for a little season for the redempti{◊n\on} of Zion, that they themselves may be prepared and that my people may be taught more perfectly, and have experience and know more perfectly concerning their duty, and the things which I require at their hands, and this cannot be brought to pass until mine elders are endowed with power from on high, for behold I have prepared a great endowment and blessing to be poured out upon them— in as much as they are faithful and continue in humility before me. Therefore it is expedient in me, that mine elders should wait for a little season for the redemption of Zion, For behold I do not require at their hands, to fight the battles of Zion. for as I have said in a former commandment even so I will fulfil. I will fight your battles, behold the destroyer I have {~~arl~~\already} sent forth to destroy and lay waste mine enemies, and not many years hence they shall not be left to pollute mine heritage, to & blaspheme my name.

ORIGINAL INSCRIPTION
John Whitmer

REVISIONS
Oliver Cowdery
William W. Phelps
Sidney Rigdon
Joseph Smith
John Whitmer
Unidentified

prepare the land which I have consecrated consecrated for the gathering together of my Saints,

Behold I have commanded my servant Joseph, to say to the strength of my house, even my warriors my young men and middle aged to gather together for the redemption of my people and throw down the tower of mine enemies, and scatter their watchmen — but the strength of my house has not hearkened unto unto my words, but in as much as there are those that have hearkened unto my words, I have prepared a blessing and an endowment for them, I have heard their prayers and will accept their offering, and it is expedient in me that they should be brought thus far, for a trial of their faith.

And now verily I say unto you, a commandment I give unto you, that as many as have come up hither that can stay in the region round about, Let them stay, and those who cannot stay, who have families in the east, let them tarry for a little season, in as much as my servant Joseph shall appoint unto them for I will counsel him concerning this matter, And all things whatsoever he shall appoint unto them shall be fulfilled. and let all my people who dwell in the region round about, be very faithful and prayerful and humble before me, and reveal not the things which I have revealed unto them, Talk not of judgment boast not of faith nor of mighty works, but carefully gather together in as much one region as can be consistently with the feeling of the people. And Behold I will give unto you favor and grace in their eyes, that you may rest in peace and safety, whilst you are saying unto the people execute judgment & Justice for us according to law, and redress us of our wrongs.

Now behold, I say unto you my friends, in this way you may find favor in the eyes of the people, until the armies of Israel become very great, and I will soften the hearts of the people as I did the heart of Pharaoh from time to time, until my servant Joseph and mine elders whom he shall appoint shall have time to gather up the strength of my house; and to have sent wise men to fulfil that which I have commanded concerning the purchasing of all the lands in Jackson County

100 [200] [verso]   F

upon the land which I have ~~consecanted~~ consecrated for the

gathering together of my Saints{,\.}

Behold I have commanded my servant Joseph, to say to the

strength of my house; even my wariers my young men and

middle aged to gather~~to~~ together for the redemption of my people

and throw down the tower of mine enemies, and scatter

their watchmen— but the strength of my house has not heark-

-ened unto ~~unto~~ my words, but in as much as there are those

that have hearkened unto my words, I have prepared a blessing

and an endowment for them, I have heard their prayers and

will accept their offering, and it is expedient in me that

they should be brought thus far, for a trial of their faith{,\.}

And now verily I say unto you, a commandment I give

unto you, that as many as have come up hither that can stay

in the region round about, Let them stay, and those who

cannot stay, who have families in the east, let them tarry for a

little season, in as much as my servant Joseph shall appoint unto

them for I will counsel him{,\concerning} this matter, And

all things whatsoever {is\he} shall appoint unto them shall be fulfilled

and let all my p{ep\eople} who dwell in the region round about,

be very faithful and prayerful and humb[l]e before me, and

reveal not the things which I have revealed unto them, Talk not

of Judgment b{◊\oast} not of faith nor of mighty works, but

carefully gather together in one region as can be consistently~~,~~ as much

with the feeling of the people. And Behold I will give unto

you favor and grace in their eyes, that you may rest in peace

and safety, whilst you are saying unto the people execute jud-

-gment Justice for us according to law, and redre{◊\⟨s⟩}s us of our &

wrongs.

Now behold, I say unto you my friends, in this way you

may find favor in the eyes of the people, until the armies of

Israel become very great, and I will soften the hearts of the

people as I did {I\the} heart of Pharioh[455] from time to time, until

my servant Joseph and mine elders whom he shall appoint shall

have time to gather up the strength of my house; and to have

sent wise men to fulfil {whi\that} which I have commanded

concerning the purchasing of all the lands in Jackson County

ORIGINAL INSCRIPTION
John Whitmer

REVISIONS
Oliver Cowdery
William W. Phelps
Sidney Rigdon
Joseph Smith
John Whitmer
Unidentified

455. Or "Phariah".

that can be purchased and in the adjoining counties round about, for it is my will, that these lands should be purchased and after they are purchased that my saints should possess them according to the laws of consecration, which I have given. And after these lands are purchased I will hold the armies of Israel guiltless in taking possession of their own lands and of throwing down the tower of mine enemies that may be upon them, and scattering their watchmen, and avenging me of mine enemies, unto the third and fourth generation of them that hate me. But firstly let my army become very great, and let it be sanctified before me, that it may become fair as the Sun and clear as the moon, and that her banners may be terrible unto all nations, that the kingdom of this world may be constrained to acknowledge that the kingdom of Zion, is in very deed the kingdom of our God, and his Christ;

Therefore let us become subject unto her laws. Verily I say unto you it is expedient in me, that the first elders of my church should receive their endowment from on high in mine house which I have commanded to be built unto my name in the land of Kirtland, and let those commandments which I have given concerning Zion: and her law be executed and fulfilled after her redemption. There has been a day of calling; but the time has come for a day of choosing, and let those be chosen that are worthy and it shall be manifest unto my servant Joseph by the voice of the spirit, those who are chosen, and they shall be sanctified, and in as much as they follow the counsels which they receive they shall have power after many days to accomplish all things pertaining to Zion.

And again I say unto you, sue for peace not only the people that have smitten you, but also to all people. and lift up an ensign of peace, and make a proclamation for peace unto the ends of the earth and make proposals for peace unto those who have smitten you, according to the voice of the spirit which is in you, and all things shall work together for your good, and be faithful and behold and lo I am with you even unto the end. even so Amen ————

that can be purchased and in the adjoining Counties round

about, for it is my will, that these⁴⁵⁷ lands should be purchased
and after they are purchased,
that my saints should possess them according to the law of conse-
^
-cration, which I have given. And after these⁴⁵⁸ lands are purchased

I will hold the armies of Israel guiltless in taking possessions of

their own lands and of throw[i]ng down the tower of mine enemies

that may be upon them, and scattering their watchmen, and

avengeing me of mine enemies, unto the third and fourth gener-

-ation of them that hate me{,\.} But firstly let my army become very

great, and let it be sanctified f before me, that it may become

fair as the Sun and clear as the moon, and that her banners

may be terrable unto all nations, that the kingdom of this

world may be constrainned to acknowledge that the kingdom

of Zion, is in very deed the kingdom of our God, and his Christ,

Therefore let us become subject unto her laws, Verily I say unto

you it is expedi{n\ent} in me, that the first elders of my church should

receive their endowment from on high in mine house which

I have commanded to be built unto my name in the land

of Kirtland, and let those commandments which I have given

concerning Zion, and her law be executed and fulfilled after

her redemption. There has been a day of calling. but the time

has come for a day of choosing, and let those be chosen that are

worthy and it shall be manifest unto my servant Joseph by

the voice of the Spirit, those who are chosen, and they shall be

sanctified, and in as much as they, follow the counsels which they

receive they shall have power after many days to accomplish

all things partaining to Zion{,\.}

⟨And⟩ {A\again} I say unto you, sue for peace not only the people that

have smitten you, but also to all people. and lift up an ensign

of peace, and make a proclamation {of\for} peace unto the ends of
                                    for
the earth and make proposals of peace unto those who have
                              ^
smitten you, according to the voice of the spirit which is in

you, and all thing shall work together for your good, and

be faithful and behold and low I am with you even unto

the end. even so Amen

ORIGINAL INSCRIPTION
John Whitmer

REVISIONS
Oliver Cowdery
William W. Phelps
Sidney Rigdon
Joseph Smith
John Whitmer
Unidentified

456. "◊" possibly misshapen "1".

457. Possibly "there".

458. Possibly "there".

Organization of high counsel
Kirtland February 17. 1834.

Kirtland, July 3, 1835.

Verily thus saith the Lord, concerning
the wars that will shortly come to pass, begining with uprising out of rebellions like unto the
One of South Carolina; and it will eventually come to pass, that wars shall break out
and terminate in the death and misery of
many souls; and the days will come
that war will be poured out upon
all nations, and it shall go forth, beginning
upon this Continent; for there will be
division among the people; for behold the southern states shall be divided
against the northern states, and other nations will be stirred up unto war also, and
even the nation of Great Britain, as it is called;
and they shall also call upon other nations,
in order to defend themselves against other
nations; and this war shall be poured out
upon all nations. And it shall come to pass
after many days, those who are held in bondage shall rise up against those who
hold them in bondage, and shall be martialed and disciplined for war.
And it shall come to pass also, that the remnants who are left of the land, will martial themselves, and shall become exceeding angry, and shall vex the Gentiles with a sore
vexation. And thus with the sword, and by bloodshed, the inhabitants of the earth shall mourn; and
with famine and plague, and earthquakes, and the
thunder of heaven, and the fierce and vivid
lightning also, shall the inhabitants of the earth

[202] [verso]

♦ # Organization of high counsel

Kirtland Fe{◊\bruary} 17, 1834.

♦ /⁴⁵⁹Kirtlnd, July 3, 1835.⁴⁶⁰

{◊\Verily} thus saith the Lord, concerning

the wars that will shortly come to pass, begin=

ning and arising out of rebellions like unto the

one of South Carolina{;\:} and it will eventu=

=ally come to pass, that war shall brake out

and te[r]minate in the death and miseary of

many souls; and the days will come

that war will be poured out upon

all nations, and it shall go forth, beginning

upon this continent; for there will be

a division among the people; for be=

=hold the southern states shall be divided

against the northern states, and other na

=tions will be stirred up unto war also, and

even the nation of Great Britain, as it is called;

and they shall a{s\lso} call upon other nations,

in order to defend themselves aga[i]nst other

nations{,\;} and thus war shall be pourd out

upon all nations. And it shall come to pass

those
after m[a]ny days, ~~slaves~~ who are held in bon=

=dage shall rise up against those who

hold them in bondage, and shall be mar=

=tialed and disiplined for war.

And it shall come to pass also, that the rem=

=nants who are left of the land, will mar=
and shall
=tial themselves ~~also~~ become exceeding an=
^   ^
=gery, and shall vex the Gentiles with a sore

vex{ing\ation}. And then with the sword, and by blood=

=shed, the inhabitants of the earth shall mourn; and

with famine and plague, and earthquakes, and the

thunder of heaven, and the fierce and vivid

lightning also, shall the inhabinants of the earth

ORIGINAL INSCRIPTION
John Whitmer
Oliver Cowdery

REVISIONS
Oliver Cowdery
William W. Phelps
Sidney Rigdon
Joseph Smith
John Whitmer
Unidentified

459. John Whitmer hand-
writing ends; Oliver Cowdery
begins.

460. This date likely indicates
when this revelation was copied into the manuscript book.
This revelation should be
dated 25 December 1832. (See
p. 291 herein.)

be made to feell the wrath and indignation of the chastning hand of an Almighty God, until the consumption decreed hath made a full end of all nations, that the cry of the saints, and of the blood of the saints, shall cease to come up into the ears of the Lord of Sabaoth, from the earth, to be avenged of their enemies.

Wherefore, stand ye in holy places, and be not moved, until the day of the Lord come, for behold, it cometh quickly, saith the Lord. Amen.

be made to feell the wrath and indignation
and
~~of~~ the chastning hand of an Almighty God, until
^

the consumption decreed hath made a full end

of all nations, that the cry of the saints, and

of the blood of the saints, shall cease to come

up into the ears of the Lord of Sabaoth,

from the earth, to be avenged of their enemies.

Wherefore, stand ye in holy places and be

not moved until the day of the Lord come;

for behold, it cometh quickly, saith the Lord.

Amen./[461] [*pages [204–206] blank*]

ORIGINAL INSCRIPTION
Oliver Cowdery

REVISIONS
Oliver Cowdery
William W. Phelps
Sidney Rigdon
Joseph Smith
John Whitmer
Unidentified

461. Oliver Cowdery hand-
writing ends.

"The Index of the contents of this Book

[207] [recto]

/⁴⁶²The Index of the contents of this Book

No. Pages

1828	first Commandment given to Joseph the Seer	1
1829	first Commandment given to Joseph [Smith Sr.] the father of the Seer	2
1829	Commandment to Joseph & Martin [Harris]	3
1829	first Commandment to Oliver [Cowdery]	5
1829	Second Commandment to Joseph the Seer	8
1829	Second Commandment to Oliver—	12
1829	A Revelation to {φ\Joseph} & Oliver	13
1829	third commandment to Oliver	14
1829	first Commandment to Hyram [Hyrum Smith]	15
1829	first Commandment to David [Whitmer]	17
1829	A Revelation to Oliver David & the twelve	18
1829	A Revelation to John [Whitmer]	20
1829	first Revelation to Peter [Whitmer Jr.]	21
1829	{th\{f}}ird 4ᵗʰ· Revelation to Oliver	21
1829	A Commandment to Oliver David & Martin	25
1829	A Revelation to Martin	25
1829	A Revelation to Joseph the Seer	28
18{29\30}	fifth Revelation to Oliver	29
1830	Second Commandment to Hyram	29
1830	A Commandment to Samuel [Smith]	29
1830	A Commandment to Joseph	30
1830	A Commandment to Joseph Knight	30
1830	A Revelation given to the Church concerning Baptism	32
1830	{φ\A} Revelation to Joseph & Oliver concerning their call	32
1830	A Revelation to Joseph Oliver & John	34
1830	A Commandment to Emma [Smith]	34
1830	A Revelation to the Church concerning Bread & Wine	35
1830	Sixth Commandment to Oliver	40
1830	Second Command to David	42
1830	Second Commandment to Peter	42
1830	Second Commandment to John	43
1830	A Commandment to Thomas [B. Marsh]	43
1830	A Commandment to Ezra [Thayer] & Northrop [Sweet]	44
1830	A Commandment to Orson [Pratt]	45

ORIGINAL INSCRIPTION
John Whitmer

REVISIONS
Oliver Cowdery
William W. Phelps
Sidney Rigdon
Joseph Smith
John Whitmer
Unidentified

462. John Whitmer handwriting begins.

[208] [verso]

[page [209] blank]

ORIGINAL INSCRIPTION
John Whitmer

REVISIONS
Oliver Cowdery
William W. Phelps
Sidney Rigdon
Joseph Smith
John Whitmer
Unidentified

463. "◊" possibly "6" or beginning of "o".

$$
\begin{array}{r}
5\,2 \\
\underline{2} \\
6\,)\,1\,0\,4\,(17\,1/3 \\
\underline{6} \\
4\,4 \\
\underline{4\,2} \\
2
\end{array}
\qquad 3
\qquad
\begin{array}{r}
5\,2 \\
\underline{3} \\
4\,.1\,6
\end{array}
\qquad
\begin{array}{r}
5\,2 \\
4\,0 \\
2\,0,8\,0 \\
4\,1\,6 \\
\overline{16,6\,4}
\end{array}
$$

77

$$52$$
$$\underline{2}$$
$$6)\overline{104}(17\frac{1}{3}$$
$$\underline{6}$$
$$44$$
$$\underline{42}$$
$$2$$

$$3$$

$$52$$
$$\underline{8}$$
$$4.16$$

$$52$$
$$\underline{40}$$
$$20.80$$
$$\underline{4[.]16}$$
$$16,64$$

$${}^{/464}70$$
$$\underline{7\lozenge}$$
$$49\lozenge$$

ORIGINAL INSCRIPTION
John Whitmer
Unidentified

REVISIONS
Oliver Cowdery
William W. Phelps
Sidney Rigdon
Joseph Smith
John Whitmer
Unidentified

464. John Whitmer hand-
writing ends; unidentified
begins.

ORIGINAL INSCRIPTION
Sidney Rigdon

REVISIONS
Sidney Rigdon
Unidentified

11. There is no evidence that "6" was written on the manuscript, but the corner of the leaf is missing.

12. Unidentified handwriting ends; Sidney Rigdon begins.

/¹²An appendix to Revelation

Revelation Book 2. From early 1832 to late 1834, Frederick G. Williams, Joseph Smith, and other scribes copied many of Smith's early revelations into this manuscript book. The book was used to prepare some of those revelations for publication in the first edition of the Doctrine and Covenants (1835) and was later used in the history-writing effort in Nauvoo, Illinois. Revelation Book 2, Revelations Collection, Church History Library, Salt Lake City.

REVELATION BOOK 2

Source Note

"Book of Revelations," Revelation Book 2, [ca. Feb. 1832–ca. Nov. 1834]; handwriting of Frederick G. Williams, Orson Hyde, Oliver Cowdery, and JS in both original inscription and later redactions; handwriting of William W. Phelps, Sidney Rigdon, and an unknown number of unidentified scribes in later redactions only; 121 pages and two inserted leaves; Revelations Collection, CHL. Includes redactions and archival marking. Volume also contains Willard Richards and William W. Phelps, "Facts left out Re[g]istered herei[n]," Notes for JS History, [Nauvoo, IL], [ca. 1843]; handwriting of Willard Richards and William W. Phelps; 4 pages and one inserted leaf.

This volume consists of 152 leaves—including three flyleaves in the front, three flyleaves in the back, and two pastedowns—measuring 11¹⁵⁄₁₆ x 7⅝ inches (30 x 19 cm). There are twelve gatherings of twelve leaves (twenty-four pages) each. All but the pastedowns and flyleaves are ruled paper with thirty-four horizontal lines in faded blue-green ink. The text block is sewn all along over recessed cords, and the front and back covers of the volume are pasteboard. The book has a tight-back case binding with a brown calfskin quarter-leather binding. The outside covers are adorned in shell marbled paper, with red and black body and veins of green. The bound volume measures 12¼ x 7⅞ inches (31 x 19 cm) and is ¹⁵⁄₁₆ inches (2 cm) thick. The front cover of the book is labeled "Book of Revelatio[ns] | ⟨{A\A}⟩ | ⟨B⟩" in black ink. It is unknown why an "A" was written over the inserted "A". The inserted "B" is written in a formal style that matches the covers of other manuscript volumes in the CHL's holdings.[1] The inside front cover has "c c/i | pep" or "c c/i | pe/=" written in graphite pencil. Although this notation was written at an unknown time, similar markings appear in at least three other extant volumes.[2] A slip of white paper pasted on the spine reads "KIRTLAND REVELATIONS".

Affixed to the inside front cover is a half-page sheet containing an index of the volume's contents through manuscript page 47. The partial index, written on cut ruled paper measuring 7¾ x 7⅝ inches (20 x 19 cm), was attached to the inside front cover with an adhesive wafer on each corner. The two upper wafers are now detached. On the verso of the index, "FGW" is written in the upper left-hand corner and a "J", "I", or "T" is centered along the top. What appears to be an "L" is written close to the bottom of the page. The index, which was inscribed by Frederick G. Williams, was likely begun before the revelation that begins at the bottom of manuscript page 13 was inscribed. All seven index entries up to that point appear to have been written in one sitting in the same ink flow, while the remaining entries indicate a continually updated index rather than a retrospective index. Williams interlineated the final three index entries (two for manuscript page 33 and one for manuscript page 37) where there was space in the existing text of the index, likely because no space remained at the bottom of the page. Three blank flyleaves follow the index.

The first fifteen pages contain six revelations, one vision, and one journal entry that were copied in February and March 1832. These eight items are dated circa March 1831–March 1832 and do not appear in chronological order. Manuscript pages 15–83 contain twenty-two revelations and one song, dated March 1832–December 1833, that are largely in chronological order. Manuscript pages 83–97 contain ten items, dated October 1830–April 1832, that were copied into the volume out of chronological order sometime before summer 1834. Manuscript pages 97–116 contain six items, dated February 1834–November 1834, that are out of chronological order. Manuscript pages 117–120 contain three items dated circa December 1830, 23 February 1831, and June 1829. The first two items were copied into the manuscript book at the same time. The final copied revelation is followed by eighty-one blank leaves, three leaves of historical notes, three blank flyleaves, and one final pastedown.

---

1. See, for example, JS, Journal, 1835–1836, in *JSP*, J1:52.
2. See JS Letterbook 1; Minute Book 1; and Quorum of the Twelve Apostles, Record.

Revelation Book 2 was used for the preparation of the 1835 Doctrine and Covenants circa 1834–1835 in Kirtland, Ohio. Because there is no known reference to this book in church records from 1836 to 1843—when the church's headquarters moved from Kirtland to Far West, Missouri, and then to Nauvoo, Illinois, and the book was not being used to record revelations—it is unknown who had possession of the manuscript book during this time. When compiling JS's history in 1843, Willard Richards and William W. Phelps turned the manuscript book upside down and used three blank leaves at the back of the volume for notations about their history-writing effort. The title on the back cover, partially worn off and written in black ink that later turned brown, reflects this usage: "Facts left out | Re[g]istered | herei[n]". Revelation Book 2 is listed on the Church Historian's Office 1846 inventory as "Book of 'Revelations B'". Subsequent inventories have listed similar titles, indicating continuous custody.[3]

Historical Introduction

Revelation Book 2, also known as "Book of Revelations" or "Kirtland Revelation Book," is a manuscript book of revelations and other items. Some of these items, such as a revelation to Lincoln Haskins, are not found anywhere else.[4] Items were copied into the manuscript book over a period of almost three years, from late February or early March 1832 to late 1834. Internal evidence, historical context, and comparison with other manuscript revelations suggest approximate dates that many items were copied. Specific dates are known for several other items, such as a single journal entry dated 8 March 1832.[5] Notations by Orson Hyde date the copying of three revelations, two on 18 August 1834 and one on 27 August 1834.[6] Only three revelations dated before 1831 were copied into the manuscript book.

Some items within Revelation Book 2 contain ink, graphite, or grease pencil editing marks made to prepare them for printing in publications such as the 1835–1836 reprint of *The Evening and the Morning Star* and the 1835 Doctrine and Covenants.[7] Similar marks appear in Revelation Book 1, which is even more heavily marked. Revelation Book 2 was used for the preparation of the 1835 Doctrine and Covenants circa 1834–1835 in Kirtland, Ohio. All but eight items in the manuscript book were published therein,[8] while just three revelations appear in both the manuscript book and the Book of Commandments.[9] Two revelations in the manuscript book were first published in the 1844 Doctrine and Covenants, although no evidence indicates that Revelation Book 2 was used as the source for publication.[10]

The first item in the manuscript book, titled "The Vision" and dated 16 February 1832, commands JS and Sidney Rigdon four times to commit the vision to paper. The version in Revelation Book 2 does not appear to be the original copy, although it was copied into the manuscript book shortly after the date it bears.[11] In fact, all of the revelatory items copied into the manuscript book appear to be copies from earlier manuscripts, not the original dictated versions, and more than half are in chronological order. Frederick G. Williams acted as principal scribe for Revelation Book 2 and inscribed full or partial copies of forty items. Orson Hyde, Oliver Cowdery, and JS inscribed

---

3. Historian's Office, "Schedule of Church Records," [1]; "Inventory," [1], Catalogs and Inventories, 1846–1904, CHL.

4. Revelation, 27 Feb. 1832, p. 433 herein.

5. Journal Entry, 8 Mar. 1832, pp. 433–435 herein.

6. See pp. 631 and 639 herein.

7. For an example of editing marks that were likely made in preparation for the 1835–1836 reprint of *The Evening and the Morning Star,* see Vision, 16 Feb. 1832, pp. 415–433 herein [D&C 76]. For an example of editing marks made in preparation for the 1835 Doctrine and Covenants, see Revelation, 2 Aug. 1833–A, pp. 537–543 herein [D&C 97].

8. The following items herein from Revelation Book 2 were not published in the 1835 Doctrine and Covenants: Revelation, 27 Feb. 1832, p. 433; Revelation, 20 Mar. 1832, p. 451; Revelation, 25 Dec. 1832, pp. 477–479 [D&C 87]; Song, 27 Feb. 1833, pp. 509–511; Revelation, 15 May 1831, pp. 599–601; Revelation, 22 June 1834, pp. 611–617 [D&C 105]; Revelation, 24 Feb. 1834, pp. 633–639 [D&C 103]; and Revelation, 28 Apr. 1834, p. 639.

9. The following revelations herein from Revelation Book 2 were published in the Book of Commandments: Revelation, ca. 8 Mar. 1831–B, pp. 437–439 [D&C 47]; Revelation, 4 Feb. 1831, pp. 603–605 [D&C 41]; and Revelation, 23 Feb. 1831, pp. 651–653 [D&C 42:74–77].

10. The following revelations herein from Revelation Book 2 were first published in the 1844 Doctrine and Covenants: Revelation, 22 June 1834, pp. 611–617 [D&C 105]; and Revelation, 24 Feb. 1834, pp. 633–639 [D&C 103].

11. See Vision, 16 Feb. 1832, pp. 415–433 herein [D&C 76].

full or partial copies of seventeen items (eight items in the manuscript book were inscribed by more than one person). These four men, as well as William W. Phelps and Sidney Rigdon, also made later corrections.

The first three items in Revelation Book 2 (manuscript pages 1–11) were likely copied between 16 February 1832, the date the first item bears, and 8 March 1832, the date the third item bears. This third item, a journal entry describing JS's recent activities, was probably a contemporary record. After these three items, the manuscript book appears to have been updated throughout March 1832 as new items were dictated by JS. The revelations on manuscript pages 11–19 were likely copied before JS left Hiram, Ohio, on 1 April 1832 to journey to Missouri, as commanded in a revelation in this portion of the manuscript book. JS dictated two known revelations while in Missouri, but his scribes did not copy them into the manuscript book when he returned to Ohio in early summer 1832. One of these revelations, dated 30 April 1832, was eventually copied into the manuscript book circa 1834. A second revelation, dated 26 April 1832, was never copied into Revelation Book 2, although it was copied into Revelation Book 1 shortly after the date it bears.

The next two revelations in the manuscript book (manuscript pages 19–31) are dated August and September 1832, and both are signed by Frederick G. Williams, who served as a scribe for JS during this period. He likely copied these revelations into Revelation Book 2 shortly after they were initially recorded. The next four revelations (manuscript pages 31–48), the first of which was signed by Williams as both scribe and counselor to JS, were likely copied after Williams was appointed as counselor, which occurred by 22 January 1833.[12] The next five items (manuscript pages 48–55) were likely copied soon after the dates they bear—late winter 1833.

Orson Hyde copied the next three revelations (manuscript pages 56–61), perhaps while acting as clerk for the presidency of the church, a service he performed starting 6 June 1833.[13] Hyde likely copied these revelations before he left on a proselytizing mission to Pennsylvania the last week of July 1833.[14] The three revelations on manuscript pages 61–71 were quoted in a letter dated 6 August 1833 and were likely copied into Revelation Book 2 about the same time.[15] The next revelation (manuscript pages 71–72) was copied by Oliver Cowdery, something Cowdery could have done only after his return to Kirtland in late October 1833.[16] The revelation following this (manuscript pages 73–83) was likely copied into the manuscript book before being published as a broadsheet circa January 1834.[17]

The next ten items (manuscript pages 83–97) are dated between October 1830 and the end of April 1832 and are not in chronological order. While three of the ten had been published previously (one in the 1833 Book of Commandments[18] and two in *The Evening and the Morning Star*[19]), the presence of the other seven items appears to be the result of an effort to collect revelations that were not in print by 1834. All are dated several years before they were copied into Revelation Book 2, and four of them were not included in the Book of Commandments although they were available for publication. Of these ten items, nine were later published in the 1835 Doctrine and Covenants.[20]

While Williams, the scribe for all ten items, might have copied this portion of the manuscript book in late 1833 or early 1834, internal and external evidence suggests that he copied the items following his return from the "Camp of Israel" expedition to Missouri in 1834 (later known as "Zion's

---

12. Minute Book 1, 22 Jan. 1833.

13. Minute Book 1, 6 June 1833.

14. Coltrin, Diary, 30 July 1833, [6].

15. Sidney Rigdon et al., Kirtland, OH, to Edward Partridge et al., Independence, MO, 6 Aug. 1833, JS Collection, CHL.

16. See Oliver Cowdery, Kirtland, OH, to Warren Cowdery, Freedom, NY, 30 Oct. 1833, in Cowdery, Letterbook, 1–3.

17. *Verily, I say unto you, concerning your brethren who have been afflicted,* [Kirtland, OH: ca. Jan. 1834], copy at CHL [D&C 101].

18. Revelation, 4 Feb. 1831, pp. 603–605 herein [D&C 41], was published as chapter 43 in the Book of Commandments.

19. Revelation, 30 Oct. 1831, p. 591 herein [D&C 65], was published in the September 1832 issue of *The Evening and the Morning Star*. Revelation, 30 Apr. 1832, p. 603 herein [D&C 83], was published in the January 1833 issue of *The Evening and the Morning Star*.

20. Revelation, 15 May 1831, pp. 599–601 herein, was not published in the 1835 Doctrine and Covenants.

Camp"). August 1834 is the most probable copying date for two reasons. First, Williams erroneously dated one revelation "August 20" rather than "May 20," suggesting that he copied it into the manuscript book in August.[21] Second, a committee to publish the revelations was appointed by late September 1834, indicating that church leaders had begun to plan for another publication of the revelations by that time, possibly as early as August.[22] Despite this evidence, however, late 1833 and early spring 1834 cannot be ruled out as the period Williams did this copying work.

Cowdery, Hyde, and Williams penned the next nine items (manuscript pages 97–120), perhaps as part of the continued attempt to collect revelations for publication. Hyde provided late August 1834 as the date he finished copying three of these items.[23] The fourth revelation penned by Hyde bears no date of copying. The next five items were copied sometime after 25 November 1834, the date of the first of these five items (manuscript page 116).

Though space remained, scribes copied no additional revelations into Revelation Book 2. It is unknown why later revelations were not copied or who possessed the book from 1834 to 1843. Revelations of that period were recorded in other places, such as JS's journals. When working on JS's history in Nauvoo, Illinois, in 1843, William W. Phelps and Willard Richards used three blank leaves in the back of Revelation Book 2 to record information not incorporated into the history, often citing sources for the new material. Information about such sources will accompany publication of these historical notes in the History series.

In addition to marking corrections, those preparing the items in Revelation Book 2 for publication pinned into the manuscript book slips of paper that contained additions or clarifications to the original text. Two such slips are extant in Revelation Book 2, and they are transcribed as separate leaves where they appear in the manuscript book. Elsewhere in Revelation Book 2, visible pinholes likely mark where additional slips were fastened to the page as texts were copied or prepared for publication.[24] This physical evidence, which suggests how the manuscript book was used by those preparing the texts for publication, is identified in the textual annotation.

The leaf containing pages 54–55 of JS's March–September 1838 journal, titled "Scriptory Book," was torn from that journal and inserted into Revelation Book 2, probably in the late nineteenth or early twentieth century when revelations from different locations in the Church Historian's Office were assembled into one collection. That leaf is no longer in Revelation Book 2; it remains separated from the journal and is in the Revelations Collection. The leaf includes two revelations dated 8 July 1838 and is transcribed in its original location in the first volume of the Journals series. A document related to the history-writing effort in Nauvoo was also inserted into Revelation Book 2 at some point, thereby becoming associated with the book though not physically part of it. That document, written by Thomas Bullock, is reproduced at the end of Revelation Book 2 as an appendix.

21. See Revelation, 20 May 1831, p. 591 herein [D&C 51].

22. Minute Book 1, 24 Sept. 1834; see also Frederick G. Williams, Kirtland, OH, to "Dear Brethren," Independence, MO, 10 Oct. 1833, in JS Letterbook 1, p. 58; and F. G. Williams and Company, Account Book, 1.

23. See the following herein: Revelation, 23 Apr. 1834, pp. 617–631 [D&C 104]; Revelation, 24 Feb. 1834, pp. 633–639 [D&C 103]; and Revelation, 28 Apr. 1834, p. 639.

24. See p. 535 herein for an example of a slip of paper that was pinned to the page. A series of pinholes is also visible on manuscript page 69 (p. 553 herein).

♦ /¹Page 1 first The Vision of Joseph & Sidney [Rigdon] Feb 16ᵗʰ· 1832

P 10 A Revelation to Lincoln Hasskin [Haskins] Feby 27— 1832

P 10 Ordination of Jesse Gause & his call to be councillor March {◊\8}—² 1832

P 11 A commandment to Joseph & Sidney to go into the world,³ ˄and warn the peopl

and call upon the people to repent Dec 1— 1832

12 A Revelation to Jerad [Jared] Carte[r] March 12— 1832—

12 A Revelation to John Whitmer calling him to be a hystorian

to the church March 7th 183{2\1}⁴

13 A Revelation given to choose a Bishop N[ewel]. K. Whitney

was chosen & was sanctioned by the lord

and also another in addition to the Law making known

the duty of the Bishop Kirtland Dec 4— 183{2\1}

15 A Revelation given for Sidney Joseph & Newel to go an[d]

sit in council with the elders in Zion March 1— 1832

17 Revelation to Jesse Gauze March 15— 1832

18 Revelation to Stephen Burnett March 7ᵗʰ 1832
47 A Revelation giving instructions how to regulate the Elders school Jan 3, 1833⁵
19 A commandment to Joseph Sidney & Newel {◊\to} purchase paper
and omit translating for the present time
March 20— 1832{—\↻} c◊◊sd

19 Revelation to John Mordock [Murdock] August 29th 1832—
33 A Rev given to the first Elders &c Dec 27— 1832
20 Revelation given to six Elder sept 22 & 23ᵈ of 1832

explaining the two priest hoods and commissioning

the Apostles {◊\to} preach the gospel
(1832
31 A Revelation explaining the parable of the wheat & tears [tares] Dec <u>6</u>
33 [32] Prophecy given Dec 25— 1832 concerning concerning the wars [*end of recto*]

FGW ◊⁶ [*end of verso; 6 pages blank*]⁷

ORIGINAL INSCRIPTION
Frederick G. Williams

REVISIONS
Oliver Cowdery
William W. Phelps
Joseph Smith
Frederick G. Williams
Unidentified

1. Frederick G. Williams handwriting begins. This partial index was attached to the inside front cover with an adhesive wafer on each corner. The two upper wafers are now detached. (See also pp. xli–xlii herein.)

2. "◊" likely "7" but possibly "1".

3. "," possibly a stray ink mark.

4. The change from "1832" to "1831" and a similar scribal error four lines below suggest that Frederick G. Williams created the index in 1832.

5. Frederick G. Williams interlineated the final three index entries where there was space in the existing text, likely because no space remained at the bottom of the page.

6. "J", "I", or "T". What appears to be an "L" is found near the bottom of the page but cannot be photographed because the bottom portion of the page is attached to the inside front cover of the manuscript book with adhesive wafers.

7. The first blank page has two adhesive wafers that contain paper residue, indicating that the wafers were used to attach a leaf to this page, perhaps in an effort to complete the index. The final blank leaf before the first item copied into the manuscript book has a tear—possibly caused by a pin—at the center. The verso of the same leaf bears offsetting from the opposite inscribed side (manuscript page 1).

— — — The Vision — — — — —

A vision of Joseph & Sidney February 16th 1832
given in Portage County Hiram Township State of Ohio
in North America which they saw concerning the
church of the first born and concerning the economy
of God and his vast creation throughout all eternity
Hear O ye heavens & give ear O earth and rejoice
ye inhabitants thereof for the lord he is God
and beside him there is no Savior for great is
his wisdom, marvilous are his ways and the
extent of his doings none can find out his
purposes fail not neither are there any who can
stay his hand from eternity to eternity, he is
the same and his years never fail for thus saith the lord The Lord
am merciful and gracious unto those who fear
me and delight to honor those who serve me
in righteousness and in truth unto the end great shall be
their reward and Eternal shall be their glory and unto
them will I reveal all misteries yea all the hiden
misteries of my Kingdom from days of old and for
ages to come will I make known unto them the good
pleasure of my will concerning all things pertaining to my Kingdom yea
even the wonders of eternity shall they know and things
to come will I shew them even the things of many
generations there wisdom shall be great and there
understanding reach to heaven and before them
the wisdom of the wise shall perish and the
understanding of the prudent shall come to naught
for by my spirit will I inlighten them and by
my power will I make known unto them the
secrets of my will yea even those things which
eye has not seen nor ear heard nor yet
entered into the heart of man
We Joseph Smith Jr & Sidney Rigdon being in the spirit on the

♦ [10]— — — The Vision — — — — —

A vision of Joseph & Sidney [Rigdon] February 16[th.] 1832

given in Portage County Hiram Township state of Ohio

in North Ame[r]ica which they saw concerning the

church of the first born and concerning the economy

of God and his vast creation througout all eternity

Here O ye heavens & give ere [ear] O earth and rejoice

ye inhabitants thereof for the lord he is God

                          Savior
and beside him there is none ~~else~~ for great is
                             ^

his wisdom, marvilous are his ways and the

extent of his doings none can find out his

purposes fail not neither are there any who can

stay his hand,[11] from eternity to eternity, he is

                    For thus saith the Lord,
the same and his years never fail{.\.} I the Lord
                                              ^
                                those
am merciful and gracious unto ~~them~~ who fear
                                    ^
                      those
me and delight to honor ~~them~~ who serve me
                            ^
                        unto the end
in righteousness and in truth great shall be
                                 ^

their reward and Eternal Shall be their glory and unto

them will I reveal all misteries yea all the hiden

misteries of my Kingdom from days of ol{l\d} and for

ages to come will I make Known unto them the good
                          pertaining to my Kingdom
pleasure of my will concerning all things ~~to come~~ yea
                                           ^

even the wonders of eternity shall they know and things

to co{◊\me} will I shew them even the things of many

generations there wisdom shall be great and there

understanding reach to heaven and before them

the wisdom of the wise shall perish and the

understanding of the prudent shall come to naught

for by my spirit will I enlighten them and by

{◊\my} my power will I make known unto them the

secrets of my will yea even those things which

eye has not seen nor ear heard nor yet

entered into the heart of man
           Smith Jr   Rigdon
We Joseph & Sidney being in the spirit on the
     ^   ^

ORIGINAL INSCRIPTION
Frederick G. Williams
Joseph Smith

REVISIONS
Oliver Cowdery
William W. Phelps
Joseph Smith
Frederick G. Williams
Unidentified

8. This identification matches others in Revelation Book 2 and is a mid-twentieth-century redaction; it also matches notations found on other manuscripts in the Revelations Collection, CHL.

9. The style and ink flow of the page numbers change frequently throughout the manuscript book, suggesting that Frederick G. Williams numbered most pages as he copied items into the book. The transcript identifies (by color) the handwriting of all page numbers, whether they were written at the time of original inscription or inserted later.

10. The first publication reflecting most redactions in this item is the February 1835 issue of *Evening and Morning Star,* which was an edited reprint of the July 1832 issue of *The Evening and the Morning Star.*

11. Possibly "hands" (without a comma).

sixteenth of February in the year of our Lord
one thousand eight hundred and thirty two
~~and they~~ by the power of the spirit our eyes
were opened and our understanding were enlarged
so as to see and understand the things of God even
those things which were from the begining before
the world was which were ordained of the Father
through his only begoten son who was in the
bosom of the father even from the begining
of whom we been record and the record which
we been is the fulness of the gospel of Jesus Christ
who is the son whom we saw and with whom
we conversed in the heavenly vision for while we
were doing the work of translation which the
Lord had appointed unto us we came to the
twenty ninth verse of ~~in~~ the fifth chapter
of John which was given unto us as follows
concerning those who shall
of the resurrection of the dead who shall hear
the voice of the son of man and shall come forth
they who have done good in the resurrection of the
Just and they who have done evil in the
resurrection of the unjust now this caused us
to marvel for it was given unto us of the spirit
and while we meditated upon these things
the Lord touched the eyes of our understanding
and they were opened and the glory of the
Lord shone round about and we beheld the
glory of the son on the right of the Father and
received of his fulness and saw the holy Angels
and they who are sanctified before his throne
who worship him
worshiping God and the lamb for ever and ever
and now after the many testimonies which
have been givin of him this is the testimony
last of all which we give of him that he lives

2 [verso]

sixteenth of February in the year of our Lord

one thousand eight hundred and— thirty two

by
~~and~~ ~~through~~ the power of the spirit our eyes

were opened and our understandings were enlarged

so as to see and understand the things of God even
those
~~the~~ things which were from the begining before

were
the world was which ~~was~~ ordained of the Father
^

through his only begoten son who was in the

bosom of the father even from the begining
we
of whom ~~be~~ bear reccord and the reccord which
^

we bear is the fulness of the gospel of Jesus Christ

who is the son whom we saw and with whom
while
we conversed in the heavenly vision for ~~as~~ we
were
~~sat~~ doing the work of translation which the

lord had appointed unto us we came to the

twenty ninth verse of ~~in~~ the fifth chapter
as follows
of John which was given unto us ~~thus~~ speak[i]ng
concerning^**those** |¹² **Shall**
of the reserection of the dead who ~~should~~ hear-
^   ^

the voice of the son of man and shall come forth

they who have done good in the resurection of the

just and they who have done evil in the

resurection of the unjust now this caused us
unto
to marvel for it was given us of the spirit
^

and while we meditated upon these thing{◊\s}

the Lord touched the eyes of our understandings

and they were opened and the glory of the

lord shone round about and we beheld the

glory of the son on the right of the Father and

received of his fulness and saw the holy Angels

and they who are sanctified before his throne
who worship him
worshiping God and the lamb for ever and ever
^

and now after the many testamonies which

have been given of him this is the testamony

last of all which we give of him that he lives

ORIGINAL INSCRIPTION
Frederick G. Williams

REVISIONS
Oliver Cowdery
William W. Phelps
Joseph Smith
Frederick G. Williams
Unidentified

12. JS inserted "|" to separate insertions in the manuscript.

for we saw him, even on the right hand of God & we
heard the voice bearing record that he is the only begotten of
the Father that by him and through him and of him the
worlds are and were created and the inhabitants
thereof are begotten sons and daughters unto God and
this we saw also and bear record that an angel of
God who was in authority in the presence of God who
rebelled against the only begotten son (whom the father
loved who was in the bosom of the father) and
was thrust down from the presence of the father
God and the son and was called perdition for the
heavens wept over him he was Lucifer
a son of the morning and we beheld
and lo he is fallen is fallen even a son
of the morning and while we were yet in the
Spirit the Lord commanded us that we should
write the vision for we beheld Satan that old
serpent even the devil who rebelled against
God and sought to take the kingdom of our God
and his Christ wherefore he maketh war with
the saints of God and encompasseth them round
about, and we saw a vision of the
sufferings of those with whom he made war
and overcame for thus came the voice of the
Lord unto us thus saith the lord concerning all
those who know my power and have been
made partakers thereof and suffered them
selves through the power of the devel to be over
come and to deny the truth and
defy my power they are they who are
the sons of perdition of whom I say it had
been better for them never to have been born
for they are vessels of wrath doomed to suffer
the wrath of God with the Devel and his angels

for we saw him, even on the right hand of God & we

heard the voice bearing reccord that he is the only begotten of

the Father that by him and through him and of him the

worlds are ~~made~~ and were created and the inhabitants

thereof are begotten sons and daughters unto God and

this we saw also and bear reccord that an angel of

God who was in authority in the presence of God who

rebelled against the only begotten son (whom the father

       of

loved who was in the bosom ~~with~~ the father) and

was thrust down from the presence of ~~the father~~

God and the son and was called perdition for the

heavens wept over him ~~for~~ he was Lucifer

 A

~~even the~~ son of the morning and we beheld

       A

and lo he is fallen is fallen even ~~the~~ son

of the morning, and while we were yet in the

      us

spirit the Lord commanded that we should

write the vision for we beheld satan that old

serpent even the devel ~~who~~ who rebelled against

God and saught to take the kingdom of our God

and his christ wherefore he maketh war with

the saints of God and encompasse~~sth~~ them round

about, and we saw a vision of the ~~eternal~~

sufferings of those with whom he made war

and overcame for thus came the voice of the

Lord unto us thus saith the lord concerning all

those ~~who~~ who know my power and have been

made partakers thereof and ~~have~~ suffered them

-selves through the power of the devel to be over-

  and to deny

come ~~unto the denying of~~ the truth and ~~the~~

defy~~ing of~~ my power they are they who are

the sons of perdition of whom I say it had

       to have

been better for them ~~to have~~ never been born

for they are vessels of wrath doomed to suffer

the wrath of God with the Devel and his angels

ORIGINAL INSCRIPTION
Frederick G. Williams

REVISIONS
Oliver Cowdery
William W. Phelps
Joseph Smith
Frederick G. Williams
Unidentified

through-out ~~will~~ eternity concerning whom
have said there is no forgiveness ~~for them~~ in this
world nor in the world to come having denied
the holy ^{Spirit} ~~ghost~~ after having received it and
having denied the only begotten son of the father
having crucified
~~crucifying~~ him unto themselves and put~~ting~~
him to an open shame these are they who
shall go away into the lake of fire and
brimstone with the devil and his angels
and the only ones on whom the second
death shall have any power yea verily the
only ones who shall not be redeemed in the
due time of the Lord after the sufferings of
his wrath who shall be brought forth by the
resurrection of the dead through the triumph
and glory of the lamb who was slain who
was in the bosom of the father before the
worlds were made and this is the gospel
the glad tidings which the voice out of the
heavens bore record unto us that he came
in to the world even Jesus to be crucified
for the world and to bear the sins of the
world and to sanctify the world and to
cleanse it from all unrighteousness that
through him all might be saved whom
the father had put into his power and
made by him who glorifyeth the father
and saveth all the works of his hands except
those sons of perdition who denyeth the son
after the father hath revealed him wherefore
he saveth all ^{except} ~~save~~ them, ~~and~~ they shall go
away into everlasting punishment which is
~~to reign~~ ~~Endless~~ punishment ^{which is} Eternal punishment
and his angels ~~through-out~~ ~~throughout~~ eternity ^{to reign with the devil}

through~~out~~ ~~all~~ eternity concerning whom I

have said there is no forgivness ~~for~~ ~~them~~ in this

world nor in the world to come having denied

      Spirit
the holy ~~ghost~~ after having received it and

having denied the only begoten son of the fathe[r]
haveing crucifyed
~~crucifying~~ him unto themselves and put~~ting~~

him to an open shame these are they who

shall go away into the lake of fire and

brimstone with the devel and his andels [angels]

and the only ones on whom the seccond

death shall have any power yea verely the

only ones who shall not be redeemed in the

due time of the Lord after the sufferings of

his wrath who shall be brought forth by the

resurection of the dead through the triumph

and glory of the lamb who was slain who

was in the bosom of the father before the

worlds were made and this is the gospel

the glad tidings which the voice out of the

heavens bore reccord unto us that he came

in to the world even Jesus to be crucified

for the world and to bear the sins of the

world and to sanctify the world and to

cleanse it from all unrighteousness that

through him all might be saved whom

the father had put into his power and

       es
made by him who glorify~~eth~~ the fathe[r]
     s
and save~~th~~ all the works of his hands except

those sons of perdition who den{ie**y**}~~th~~ thee [the] son
      s
after the father ha~~th~~ revealed him wherefore
   s   **except**
he save~~th~~ all ~~save~~ them, ~~and~~ the{se**y**} shall go

away into everlasting punishment which is
   En[d]less   **which is Eternal punishment**
~~eternal~~ punishment to reign with the devel

and his angels ~~throughout~~ ~~all~~ **in** eternity

ORIGINAL INSCRIPTION
Frederick G. Williams

REVISIONS
Oliver Cowdery
William W. Phelps
Joseph Smith
Frederick G. Williams
Unidentified

where their worm dies not and the fire is not quenched
which is their torment and the end thereof neither the place
thereof nor their torment no man knoweth neither was it revealed
neither is neither will be revealed unto none except to them
who are made pertakers thereof neverless the Lord sheweth
it by vision unto many but straight way shutteth it
up again wherefore the end the width the hight the depth
and the misery thereof he understandeth not neither any
man except them who are ordained unto this condemnation and we heard the voice saying write
the vision for lo this is the end of the vision of the
sufferings of the ungodly and again we
bear record for we saw and heard and this is
the testimony of the gospel of Jesus Christ concerning them who come forth in the resurrection
of the just they are they who received the testimony
of Jesus and believed on his name and were baptized
after the manner of his burial being buried in the
water in his name and this according to the commandment which he hath given that by keeping the commandments they might be washed and cleansed from
all their sins and receive the holy ghost by the
laying on of the hands of him who is ordained
and sealed unto this power and who overcome
by faith and are sealed by that holy spirit
of promise which the father shedeth forth upon
all those who are just and true they are they
who are the church of the first born they are
they into whose hands the father hath given
all things they are they who are priest and
kings who having received of his fulness and of his
glory and are priest of the most highest after
the order of Melchisedeck which was after the
order of Enoch which was after the order of the

their   **dies**
where ~~the~~ worm ~~dieth~~ not and the fire is not quenched

which is there torment and the end thereof neither the place

    nor   **s**   **it**
thereof ~~and~~ there torment no man knoweth neither was reve[a]led
                  except
neither is neither will be reveiled unto none ~~save~~ to them ~~to~~

who are made partakers thereof never[the]less I the Lord sh{e**o**}weth

it by vision unto many but straight way shut~~teth~~ it

up again wherefore the end the width the hight the depth

and the misery thereof he understandeth not neithe[r] any
    except
man ~~save~~ them who are ordained unto this con-

demnation and we heard the voice saying write

the vision for lo this is the end of the vision of the

~~eternal~~ sufferings of the undodly [ungodly] and again we

bear reccord for we saw and heard and this is

the ~~gospel~~ testamony of the gospel of Jesus Christ con-

cerning them who come forth in the resurection
    are
of the just they ~~were~~ they who received the testamony
           and
of Jesus and believed on his {◊\name} were baptized

after th{◊\e} manner of his buriel being buried in the

water in his name and this according to the command-

-ment which he hath given that by keeping the com-

mandments they might be washed and cleansed from

all there sins and receive the holy ghost by the

laying on of the hands of him who is ordained

and sealed unto this power and who overcome

by faith and are sealed by that holy spirit

of promise which the father shedeth forth upon

all those who ~~who~~ are just and true they are they

who are the church of the first born they are

they into whose hands the father hath given

all things they are they who are priests and
    recieved
kings who having of his fulniss and of his

glory and are priests of the most high after

the order of Melchesadeck which was after the

order of Enoch which was after the order of of the

ORIGINAL INSCRIPTION
Frederick G. Williams

REVISIONS
Oliver Cowdery
William W. Phelps
Joseph Smith
Frederick G. Williams
Unidentified

only begotten son wherefore as it is written they
are Gods even the sons of God wherefore all things are
theirs whether life or death or things present or
things to come, all are theirs and they are Christ's
and Christ is Gods and they shall overcome
all things wherefore let no man glory in man
but rather let them glory in god who shall
subdue all enemies under his feet then
shall dwell in the presence of God and his
Christ for ever and ever these are they whom
he shall bring with him when he shall come
in the clouds of heaven to reign on the
earth over his people these are they who
shall have part in the first resurrection
these are they who shall come forth in the
resurrection of the just these are they who
are come unto mount Zion and unto the
city of the Living God the heavenly place
the holiest of all these are they who have
come to an innumerable company of Angels
to the general assembly and Church of
Enoch and of the first born these are
they whose names are written in heaven
where God and Christ are the Judge of all these are
they who are just men made perfect through
Jesus the mediator of the new covenant who
wrought out this perfect atonement
through the shedding of his own blood
these are they whose bodies are celestial
whose glory is that of the sun even the glory of God the
highest of all whose glory the sun of the
firmament is written of as being typical
and again we saw the terrestrial world and behold
lo these are they who are of the Terrestial

6 [verso]

only begotten son wherefore as it is writen they

are Gods even the sons of God wherefore all things are

theres whethe[r] life or death or things present or

things to come, all are thers and they ar christs

and christ is Gods and they shall overcome

all things wherefore let no man glory in man

but rather let them glory in god who shall

subdue all enimies under his feet these

shall dwell in the presence of God and his

christ for ever and ever these are they whom

he shall bring with him when he shall come

in the clouds of heaven to reign on the

earth over his people these are they who

shall have part in the first resurection

these are they who shall come forth in the

resurection of the just these are they who

are come unto mount Zion and unto the

city of the Living God the heavenly place

the holiest of all these are they who ~~are~~ **have**

come to an innumerable company of Angels

to the general assembly and church of

Enoch and of the first born these are

they whose names are writen in heaven

where God and Christ ~~is~~ **are the** judge of all these are

they who are just men made perfect through

Jesus the {◊\mediator} of the new covenent who

wrought out this perfect attonement

through the shedding of his own blood

these are they whose bodies are celestial

whose glory is that of the s{◊\⟨u⟩}n even **the glory of** God the

highest of all whose glory the s{o\⟨u⟩}n of the

firmament is writen of as being typical

and again we saw the terest{t\rial} world and **behold**

and lo these are they who are of the Terestrial

ORIGINAL INSCRIPTION
Frederick G. Williams

REVISIONS
Oliver Cowdery
William W. Phelps
Joseph Smith
Frederick G. Williams
Unidentified

whose glory differeth from that of the church of the
first born who have received the fulness of the father
even as that of the moon differeth from the sun of
the firmament behold these are they who died with
out law and also they who are the spirits of men
kept in prison whom the son visited and preached
the gospel unto them that they might be judged
according to men in the flesh who received
not the testimony of Jesus in the flesh but
afterwards received it these are they who
are honorable men of the earth who were
blinded by the craftiness of men these are
they who receive of his glory but not of his
fulness these are they who receive of the presence
of the son but not of the fulness of the father
wherefore they are bodies terestrial and not
bodies celestial and differ in glory as the
moon differeth from the sun these are they who
were not valient in the testamony of Jesus
wherefore they obtained not the crown over
the kingdom of our God, and now this is
the end of the vision which we saw of the
terestrial that the lord commanded us to write
while we were yet in the spirit, and again we
saw the glory of the Telestial which glory is
that of the leser even as the glory of the stars
differeth from that of the glory of the moon in the firmament these are they who receive not the gospel
of Christ neither the testamony of Jesus these are they
who deny not the holy-ghost, these are they who are thrust
down to hell these are they who shall not be recumed from
the devil untill the last reserection untill the lord even
christ the lamb shall have finished his work these
are they who receive not of his fulness in the eternal

whose glory differeth from that of the church of the

first born who have received the fulnes of the father

even as that of the moon differe~~th~~ ^{rs} from the sun of

the firmament behold these are they who died with

out Law and also they who are the spirits of men

kept in prison whom the son visited and preached

the gospel unto them that they might be judged

according to men in the flesh who received

not the testamony of Jesus in the flesh but

afterwards received it these are they who

are honorable men of the earth who were

blinded by the craftiness of men these are

they who receive of ^{his} ~~th{is\is}~~[13] glory but not of ~~t~~h{e**is**}[14]

fulness these are they who receive of the presence

of the son but not ⟨of⟩ the fulness of the father

wherefore they are bodies Terestrial and not

bodies Celestial and differ~~eth~~ in glory as the

moon differ{e**s**}~~th~~ from the sun these are they who

^{were} ~~are~~ not valient in the testamony of Jesus

wherefore they obtained not the crown over

the kingdoms of our God, and now this is

the end of the vision which we saw of the

Terestrial that the lord commanded us to write

while we were yet in the spirit, and again we

saw the glory of the Telestial which glory is

that of the lesser even as the glory of the stars

differ~~eth~~ from {◊\that} of the ^{glory of the} moon in the firma-

-ment these are they who receive not the gospel

of christ neithe[r] the testamony of Jesus these are they

who deny not the holy ghost, these are they who are thrust

down to hell these are they who shall not be redeemed from

the devel untill the last reserection untill the lord even

christ the Lamb shall have finished his work these

are they who receive not of his f{i\ullness} in the eternal

ORIGINAL INSCRIPTION
Frederick G. Williams

REVISIONS
Oliver Cowdery
William W. Phelps
Joseph Smith
Frederick G. Williams
Unidentified

13. "t" knife-erased and "**is**" written over "is" to make "his"; then whole word stricken.

14. Possibly "~~t~~h{is**is**}".

world, but of the holy ghost through the ministration of the Terrestrial and the Terrestrial through the ministration of the Celestial and also the Telestial receive it of the administering of angels who are appointed to minister for them or who are appointed to be ministering spirits for them for they shall be heirs of salvation and thus we saw in the heavenly vision the glory of the Telestial which surpasseth all understanding and no man knoweth it except him to whom God hath revealed it and thus we saw the glory of the Terrestrial which excelleth in all things the glory of the Telestial even in glory and in power and in might and in dominion and thus we saw the glory of the Celestial which excelleth in all things where God even the father reigneth upon his throne forever and ever before whose throne all things bow in humble reverence and giveth him glory forever and ever, they who dwell in his presence are the church of the first born and they see as they are seen and know as they are known having received of his fulness and of his grace and he maketh them equal in power and in might and in dominion, and the glory of the celestial is one even as the glory of the son is one, and the glory of the Terrestrial is one even as the glory of the moon is one, and the glory of the Telestial is one even as the glory of the stars are one for as one star differeth from another star in glory even so differeth one from another in glory in the Telestial world for these are they who are of Paul, and of Apollos and of Cephas these are they who say they are some of one and some of another some of Christ & some of John and some of Moses and some of Elias and some of Esaias

world, but of the holy ghost through the ministration

of the Terestrial and the Terestrial through the ~~ad~~ministration

of the Celestial and also the Telestial receive it of the

administring of angels who are appointed to minister

for them or who are appointed to be ministering

spirits for them for they shall be heirs of salvation

and th{is**us**} we saw in the heavenly vision the glory

of the Telestial which surpasseth all understanding

and no man knoweth it except him to whom God

hath reveiled it and th{is**us**} we saw the glory of the

Terestrial which excell{e**s**}~~th~~ in all things the glory of

the Telestial even in glory and in power and might

and in dominion and thus we saw the glory of the

Celestial which excell{e**s**}~~th~~ in all things where God even

the father reigneth upon his throne forever and ever

    whose
before ~~his~~ throne all things bow in humble reverence

    him
and give~~th~~ glory forever and ever, they who dwell

in his presence are the church of the first born

and they see as they are seen and know as they are

known having received of his fulness and of his

grace and he make~~sth~~ them equal in power

and in might and in dominion, and the

glory of the celestial is one even as the

glory of the son is one, and the glory of the

Terestrial is one even as the glory of the

~~of the~~ moon is one, and the glory of the

Telestial is one even as the glory of the stars

are ~~is~~ one for as one star differ{e**s**}~~th~~ from another

star in glory even so differe~~sth~~ one from an

other in glory in the Telestial world for these are

they who are of Paul, and of Apolus and of cephus

these are they who say they are some of one and

some of another some of Christ & some of John and

some of Moses and some of Elius and some of Esaises [Esaias]

ORIGINAL INSCRIPTION
Frederick G. Williams

REVISIONS
Oliver Cowdery
William W. Phelps
Joseph Smith
Frederick G. Williams
Unidentified

and some of Isaiah and some of Enoch but received not the
gospel neither the testimony of Jesus neither the prophets
neither the everlasting covenant last of all these all
they who will not be gathered with the saints to be caught
up unto the church of the first born and received into
into the cloud these are they who are liars and sorcerers
and adulterers and whoremongers and whosoever loves
and makes a lie these are they who suffer the wrath of
God on the earth these are they who suffer the vengeance
of eternal fire these are they who are cast down to
hell and suffer the wrath of Almighty God until
the fulness of times when christ shall have subdued
all enemies under his feet and shall have perfected
his work when he shall deliver up the kingdom
and present it unto the father spotless saying I have
overcome and have trodden the winepress alone even
the winepress of the fierceness of the wrath of Alm-
-ighty God then shall he be crowned with the crown
of his glory to sit on the throne of his power to reign
for ever and ever, but behold and lo we saw the
                 and the inhabitants
glory of the Telestial world that they were in number
as innumerable as the stars in the firmament of
heaven, or as the sand upon the sea shore and heard
the voice of the Lord saying these all shall bow the
knee and every tongue shall confess to him who
sitteth upon the throne for ever and ever for
they shall be judged according to their works and
every man shall receive according to his own works
and his own dominion in the mansions which are
         and
prepared, they shall be servants of the most high
but where God and christ dwell they cannot come
worlds without end this is the end of the vision
which we saw which we were commanded to
write while we were yet in the spirit,

and some of Isaiah and some of Enoch but received not the

gospel neither the testamony of Jesus neither the prophets

neither the everlasting covenants last of all these are all

they who will not be gathered with the saints to be caught

up unto the church of the first born and received into

into the cloud these are they who are liars and sorseres [sorcerers]

and aduterers and whoremongers and whosoever love~~th~~ l

and make~~sth~~ a lie these are they who suffer the wrath of s

God on the earth these are they who suffer the vengence

of eternal fire these are they who are cast down to

hill [hell] and suffer the wrath of Almighty God untill

the fulness of times when christ shall have subdued

all enemies under his feet and shall have perfected

his work when he shall deliver up the Kingdom

and present it unto the father sp{t\otless} saying I have

overcome and have troden the winepress alone even

the winepress of the fierceness of the wrath of Alm-

-ighty God then shall he be crowned with the crown

of his glory to sit on the throne of his power to reign

for ever and ever, but behold and lo we saw the
and the inha[b]**itants**
glory of the Telestial world that they were in number

as innumerable as the stars in the firmament of

heaven, or as the sand upon the sea shore and herd

the voice of the Lord saying these all shall bow the

knee and evry tongue shall confess to him who

sitteth upon the throne for ever and ever for

they shall be judged according {~~accordin~~\to there} works and

every man shall receive according to his own works

and his own dominion in the mansions which are
and
prepared, they shall be servants of the most high

but where God and christ dwels they cannot come

worlds without end this is the end of the vision

which we saw which we were commanded to

write while we were yet in the spirit,

ORIGINAL INSCRIPTION
Frederick G. Williams

REVISIONS
Oliver Cowdery
William W. Phelps
Joseph Smith
Frederick G. Williams
Unidentified

But great and marvelous are the works of the Lord and the mistries of his kingdom which he shewed unto us which surpasses all understanding in glory and in might and in dominion which he commanded us we should not write while we were yet in the spirit and are not lawful for men to utter neither is man capable to make them known for they are only to be seen and understood by the power of the holy Spirit which God bestows on them who love him and purifies themselves before him to whom he grants the priviledge of seeing and knowing for themselves that through the power and manifestation of the spirit while in the flesh they may be able to bear his presence in the world of glory and to God and the Lamb be glory and honor and dominion for ever and ever Amen

Sidney Rigdon
Joseph Smith Jr

Hyram Portage County Ohio Feby 27th 1832
Behold thus saith the Lord unto you my servants that I have chosen Lincoln to be a servant unto me wherefore verily I say unto you let him be ordained and receive the articles and covenants which I have given unto you and some of the comm-andments that he may go forth and proclaim my gospel whithersover I will send him in the congregation of the wicked and in as much as he is faithful I will prosper him even so Amen

March 8th 1832
Chose this day and ordained brother Jesse Gause

But great and marvelous are the works of the Lord

and the mistries of his kingdom which he shewed

unto us which surpasse~~th~~ ^s^ all understanding in glory

and might ^in^ and in dominion which he commanded

us we should not write while we were yet in the

spirit and are not lawful for men to utter neither

is man capable to make them known for they

are only to be seen and understood by the power

of the holy ~~ghost~~ **Spirit** which God bestows on those who

love him and purifies themselves before him to

whom he grants the privalege of seeing and knowing

for themselves that through the power and manifestation

of the spirit while in the fles{s**h**} they may be able

to bear his presence in the world of glory and to

God and the Lamb be glory and honor and dominion

for ever and ever Amen

Sidney Rigdon

Joseph Smith Jr

Original Inscription
Frederick G. Williams

Revisions
Oliver Cowdery
William W. Phelps
Joseph Smith
Frederick G. Williams
Unidentified

15. This entire revelation is crossed out with an X in ink that appears to match the ink used to inscribe the X on manuscript page 19. The X presumably marked the revelation for exclusion from publication. This revelation did not appear in any JS-era publication.

◆ 15Hyram [Hiram] Portage County Ohio Febry. 27th. 1832

Behold thus saith the Lord unto you my servants

that I have chosen Lincoln [Haskins] to be a servant unto me

wherefore verily I say unto you lit [let] him be ordained

and receive the articles and covenants which I

have givin unto you and some of the comm-

-andments that he may go forth and proclaim

my gospel whithersover I will send him in the

congregrations of the wicked and in asmuch as he

is faithful I will prosper him even so Amen

◆ March 8th 1832

Chose this day and ordained brother Jesse Ga{s\use}

and Broth Sidney to be my councellers of the ministry
of the presidency of high Priesthood and from the 16th
of February up to this date have been at home
except a journey to Kirtland on the 29 Feby and
returned home on the 4th of March we received a
revelation in Kirtland and one since I returned
home blessed be the name of the Lord ———

~~~~~~

Sec. 71

Hiram Portage County Ohio Dec 1st, 1832
A commandment given to us Joseph and Sidney in these
words saying behold thus saith the Lord unto you my
servants that the time has verily come that it is
necessary and expedient in me that you should
open your mouth in proclaiming my gospel and the
things of the kingdom expounding the mysteries thereof
out of the scripture according to that portion of spirit
and power which shall be given unto you even as well
verily I say unto you proclaim unto the world in the
region round about and in the church also for
the space of a season even until it shall be made
known unto you, verily this is a mission for a season
which I give unto you wherefore labour ye in my
vineyard call upon the inhabitants of the earth and
bear record and prepare the way for the command-
-ments and the revelation which are to come
now behold this is wisdom whoso readeth let
him understand and receive also for unto him
who receiveth it shall be given more abundantly
even power wherefore confound your enemies call
upon them to meet you both in public and in
private and inasmuch as ye are faithful their shame
shall be made manifest wherefore let them bring
forth their strong reasoning against the Lord

and Broth[er] Sidney [Rigdon] to be my councillers of the ministry

of the presidency of high Pristhood and from the 16th.

of February up to this date have been at home

except a journey to Kirtland on the 29 Feby and

returned home one [on] the 4th of March we received a

revelation in Kirtland and one since I returned

home blessed be the name of the Lord — — — — — — — —

Sec. 71¹⁶

♦   Hiram Portage County Ohio Dec. 1th., 1832—¹⁷

A commandment given to us Joseph {S\and} Sidney [Rigdon] in these

words saying behold thus saith the Lord unto you my

servants that the time his [has] ~~come~~ verily come that it is

necessary and expeden{θy\t} in me that you should

open your mouth in proclaiming my gospel and the

things of the kingdom expounding the mysteries thereof

{of\out} of the scripture according to that po[r]tion of spirit

and power which shall be given unto you even as I will

verily I say unto you proclaim unto {you\the} w{ill\orld} in the

regions round about and in the church also for

the space of a season even until it shall be made

known unto you, verely this is a mission for a season

which I give unto you wherefore labour ye in my

vineyard call upon the inhabitants of the earth and

bear reccord and prepare the way for the command-

-ments and the revelations which are to come

now behold this is wisdom whoso readeth let

him understand and receive also for unto him

who receiveth it shall be given more abundantly

even power wherefore confound your enimies call

upon them to meet you both in public and in

private and inasmuch as ye are faithful there shame

shall be made manifest wherefore let them bring

forth there strong reason{ings\s} against the Lord

ORIGINAL INSCRIPTION
Frederick G. Williams

REVISIONS
Oliver Cowdery
William W. Phelps
Joseph Smith
Frederick G. Williams
Unidentified

16. This identification matches others in Revelation Book 2 and is a mid-twentieth-century redaction; it also matches notations found on other manuscripts in the Revelations Collection, CHL.

17. Evidence suggests that this revelation should be dated 1 December 1831. This scribal error suggests that Frederick G. Williams copied this revelation in 1832.

verily thus saith the Lord unto you there is no weapon
that is formed against you shall prosper and if any
man lift his voice against you he shall be confounded in mine own due time wherefore keep these
commandment they are true and faithful even so
— — — — — — — — — — — — — Amen —

Sec. 79

A Revelation given to Jared Carter March 12th 1832
in Hiram Portage County Ohio —
Verily verily I say unto you that it is my
will that my servant Jared should go again
into the eastern countries from place to place,
and from city, city, in the power of the ordinance
where with he has been ordained proclaiming
glad tidings of great joy even the everlasting
gospel and I will send upon him the comforter
which shall teach him the truth and his
way whither he shall go and in as much as he
is faithful I will crown him again with sheaves
wherefore let your heart be glad my servant
Jared and fear not saith your Lord even
Jesus Christ Amen

Sec. 47

Hiram Portage Co Ohio March 7th 1831
Behold it is expedient in me that my servant
John Whitmer should write and keep a regular
history and assist my servant Joseph in translating all things which shall be given
him, and again verily I say unto you
that ye can also lift up your voice in
meetings when ever it shall be expedient
and again I say unto you that it shall be

12 [verso]

verily thus saith the Lord unto you there is no weapon

that is formed against you shall prosper and if any

man lift his voice against you he shall be con-

-founde{r◊\d} in mine own due time wherefore keep these

commandments they are true and faithful even so

— — — — — — — — Amen—

ORIGINAL INSCRIPTION
Frederick G. Williams

REVISIONS
Oliver Cowdery
William W. Phelps
Joseph Smith
Frederick G. Williams
Unidentified

Sec 79[18]

♦   A Revelation given to Jerad [Jared] Carter March 12th 1832

in Hiram Pordage [Portage] County Oh{o\io}, — — —

Verily verily I say unto you that it is my

will that my Servant Jerad should go again

into the eastern countries from place, to place,

and from City, City, in the power of the ordinence

wherewith he has been ordained proclaiming

glad tidings of ɉ great joy even the everlasting

gospel and I will send upon him the comforter

which shall teach him the truth and his

way whither he shall go and in as much as he

is faithful I will crown him again with sheaves

wherefore let your heart be glad my servant

Jerad and fear not saith your Lord even

Jesus Christ Amen——

18. This identification and
that of "Sec 47" below match
others in Revelation Book 2
and are mid-twentieth-
century redactions; they also
match notations found on
other manuscripts in the
Revelations Collection, CHL.

19. Another version of this
revelation found in Revelation
Book 1 is dated 8 March 1831
(see pp. 131–133 herein). For
more information about this
dating, see the discussion of
this revelation in the
Documents series.

Sec 47

♦   Hiram Portage Co Ohio March 7[th.] 183{2\1}[19]

Behold it is expedient in me that my servent

John Whitmor [Whitmer] should write and keep a regular

history and assist my servant Joseph in trans-

-lating all things which shall be given

him, and again verily I say unto you

that ye can also lift up your voice in

meetings when ever it shall be expedient

and again I say unto you that it shall be

appointed unto you to keep the church record and history
continualy for Oliver I have appointed to an other office where
=fore it shall be given thee by the Comforter to write these
things even so Amen

~~~~~~

Kirtland December 4th 1831 Harken and listen
to the voice of the Lord Oh ye who have asembled yourselves
together who are the high Priest of my Church to whom the King
=dom and power have been given for verily Saith the Lord it is
expedient in me for a bishop to be appointed unto you or of you
unto the Church in this part of the Lords viniard and verily
in this thing ye have done wisely for it is required of the
Lord at the hand of every Steward to render an acount of
his Stewardship both in time and in eternity for he
who is faithful and wise in time is acounted worthy
to inherit the mantions prepared for him of my Father
verily I Say unto you the Elders of the Church in this
part of my vinyard I shall render an acount of their
Stewardship unto the Bishop which Shall be appointed
of me in this part of my vinyard these things shall
be had on record to be handed over to the Bishop
in Zion and the duty of the Bishop Shall be made
known by the commandments which have been
given and by the voice of the Conference and
verily I Say unto you my Servant Newel Whit
=ney is the man which Shall be appointed and or-
=dained unto this power this is the will of the Lord
your God your redeemer even So Amen

~~~~~~

Kirtland December 4th 1831 — — — — —
The word of the Lord in addition to the law
which has been given making known the duty

appointed unto you to keep the church record and history

continaly for Oliver [Cowdery] I have appointed to an other office wher-

=efore it shall be given thee by the comforter to write these

things even so Amen

♦   Kirtland December 4th 1831 Harken and listen

to the voice of the Lord Oh ye who have asembled yourselves

together who are the high Priest of my church to whom the King

       and   have been
=dom {◊◊◊\and} power ~~is~~ given for verily Saith the Lord it is

expedient in me for a bishop to be appointed u[n]to you or of you

unto the church in this part of the Lords viniard and verily

in this thing yea have done wisely for it is required of the

Lord at the hand of every Steward to render an acount of

his Stewardship both in time and in eternity for he

who is faithful and wise in time is acounted worthy

to inherit the mantions prepareed {of\for} him of my Father

Verily I Say unto you the Elders of the Church in this

                       their
part of my vineyard Shall render an acount of ~~his~~

                 who
Stewardship u[n]to the Bishop ~~which~~ Shall be appointed

of me in this part of my Vinyard these things Shall

be had on record to be handed over to the Bishop

in Zion and the duty of the Bishop Shall be made

known by the commandments which have been

given and by the voice of the conference and

verily I Say unto you my Servent Knewel [Newel K.] Whit-

=ney is the man which Shall be appointed and or-

=dained unto this power this is the will of the Lord

your god your redeemer even So Amen——

♦   Kirtland December 4th. 1831 — — — — —

The word of the Lord in addition to the Law

which has been given making known the duty

ORIGINAL INSCRIPTION
Frederick G. Williams
Joseph Smith

REVISIONS
Oliver Cowdery
William W. Phelps
Joseph Smith
Frederick G. Williams
Unidentified

of the Bishop who has been ordained unto
the church in this part of the vinyard which is verily this
to keep the Lords Store house to receive the funds of the ch-
-urch in this part of the vinyard to take an account of
the Elders as before has been commanded and to adm
-inister to their wants who shall pay for what they
receive inasmuch as they have wherewith to pay
that this also may be consecrated to the good of the
good of the church to the poor and needy and he
who not wherewith to pay an account shall be
taken and handed over to the Bishop in Zion who
shall pay the debt out of that which the Lord
shall put into his hands and they of the faith-
-ful who labour in Spiritual things in admin
-istering the gospel and the things of the King
-dom unto the church and unto the world
shall answer the debt unto the Bishop in
Zion thus it cometh out of the church for
acording to the Law every man who cometh
up to Zion must lay all things before the
Bishop in Zion an now verily I say unto
you that every Elder in this part of the
vinyard must give an account of his steward
-ship unto the Bishop in this part of the
vinyard a certifycate from the Judge or
Bishop in this part of the vinyard unto
the Bishop in Zion rendereth every man ac-
-cepted and answereth all things for an inh
-eritance and to be received as a wise Steward
and as a faithful labourer otherwise he shall
nott be accepted of the Bishop in Zion
and now verily I say unto you let every one
who shall give an account unto the Bishop
of the church in this part of vinyard

16 [verso]

²³and listen to the councel of him who has ordained

you from on high who shall speak in your ears

the words of wisdom that salvation may be unto you

in that thing which you have presented before me

saith the Lord God, for verily I say unto you the time

has come, and is now at hand, a{ɵ\nd} behold and lo

it must needs be that there be an organization of

the literary and mercantile establishments of my

church both in this place and in the land of Zion

for a permanent and everlasting establishment

and firm unto my Church to advance the

cause which ye have espoused to the salvation

of man and to the glory of your father who is

in heaven that you may be equal in the bonds

of heavenly kings yea and earthly things also for

the obtaining of heavenly things for if ye are not

equal in earthly things ye cannot be equal in obtain

-ing heavenly things, for if ye will that I give unto you a place

in the celestial world you must prepare yourselves

by doing the things which I have commanded and

required of you and now verily thus saith the Lord

it is expedient that all things be done unto my

glory that ye should who are joined together in

this firm or in other words that my servant

Newel [K.] Whitney and my servant Joseph Smith J[r.]

and my servant Sidney Rigdon sit in council

with the saints who are in Zion otherwise Satan

seeketh to ~~destroy~~ turn there hearts away from th[e]

truth that they become blinded and understand

not ~~not~~ the things which are prepared for them

wherefore a commandment I give unto you

                         a bond or

to²⁴ prepare and organize yourselves by an everlasting

covenant which cannot be broken and he who

breaketh it shall loose his office and standing

ORIGINAL INSCRIPTION
Frederick G. Williams

REVISIONS
Oliver Cowdery
William W. Phelps
Joseph Smith
Frederick G. Williams
Unidentified

23. Manuscript pages 15–30 contain a series of small holes. (See 443n20 herein.)

24. Although "to" appears to be stricken, the ink blot is actually offsetting from the opposite leaf (manuscript page 17).

in the church and shall be delivered over unto the buffet
-tings of Satan untill the day of redemption, behold this
is the preperation wherewith I prepare you and the
foundation and the ensample which I give unto you
whereby you may accomplish the commandment
which are given to you that through my providence
you father notwithstanding the tribulation which
shall discend upon you that the church may stand
independent above all other creatures beneath the
celestial world that you may come up unto the crown
prepared for you and be made rulers over many
kingdoms saith the Lord god, the holy one of Israel
verely, verely I say unto you ye are little children
and ye have not as yet understood how great
blessings the father has put into his own hands
and prepared for you and ye cannot bear
all things now nevertheless be of good cheer for I
will lead you along the kingdom is yours and the
blessings thereof are yours and the riches of eternity
are yours and he who receiveth all things with
thankfulness shall be made glorious and the things
of this world shall be added unto him even an hundred fold yea more
wherefore do the things which I have commanded
you saith your Redeemer even Jesus Christ who
prepareth all things before he cometh and then
he will come even with the church of the first
born and receive you in the cloud and appoint
every man his portion and he that is a faith
-ful and wise steward shall inherit all things Amen

Hiram Portage Co Ohio March 15th 1832
verely verely I say unto you my servant
Frederick G Williams
listen to the voice of him who speaketh to thee
the word of the Lord your God, and hearken

[35]be built begining at the temple lo{◊\t} which is

appointed by the finger of the Lord in the western

boundaries of the State of Missouri and dedicated

Smith Jr
by the hand of Joseph ^and others with whom

the Lord was well pleased verily this is the

word of the Lord that the city New Jerusalem shall be

built by the gathering of the saints begining at

this place even the place of the temple which

Temple shall be reared in this generation for

verily this generation shall not all pass away

untill an house shalt be built unto the Lord

and a cloud shall rest upon it which cloud

shall be even the glory of the Lord which shall

fill the house, and the sons of Moses according

to the holy Priesthood which he received under

the hand of his father in Law Jethro and Jethro

received it under the hand of Caleb and Caleb

received it under the hand of Elihu and

Elihu under the hand of Jeremy and Jeremy

under the hand of Gad, and Gad under the hand of

Esaius, and Esaius {◊◊◊\received} it under the hand of

God, Esaius also lived in the days of Abraham and

was blessed of him which Abraham, received the

priesthood from Melchesideck who received it

through the linage of his Fathers even till

Noah, and from Noah till Enoch through

the linage of there fathers and from Enoch

to Abel, who was slain by the conspiracy of his

brother who received the priesthood by the com-

-mandment of God, by the hand of his father

Adam who was the first man which priesthood

continueth in the church of God, in all genera-

-tions and is without begining of days or end

of years, and the Lord confirmed a Priesthood

ORIGINAL INSCRIPTION
Frederick G. Williams

REVISIONS
Oliver Cowdery
William W. Phelps
Joseph Smith
Frederick G. Williams
Unidentified

35. Manuscript pages 15–30
contain a series of small holes.
(See 443n20 herein.)

also upon Aaron and his seed throughout all their generation
~~of the key~~ which priesthood also continueth and
abideth forever with the priesthood which is after
holiest order of God and this greater priesthood
administereth the gospel and holdeth the key of the
mysteries of the kingdom even the key of the
knowledge of God therefore in the ordinances
thereof the power of Godliness is manifest
and without the ordinances thereof and
the authority of the Priesthood the power
of Godliness is not manifest unto men
in the flesh for without this no man
can see the face of God even the father
and live, now this Moses plainly taught
to the children of Israel in the wilderness
and sought dilligently to sanctify his
people that they might behold the
face of God, but they hardened there
hearts and could not endure his presence
therefore the Lord in his wrath (for his
anger was kindled against them) sware
that they should not enter into his rest
which rest is the fulness of his glory while in
the wilderness, therefore he took Moses out of ~~their~~ midst
and the holy priesthood also, and the lesser
priesthood continued which priesthood holdeth
the key of the ministring of Angels and the
preparetory gospel which gospel is the gospel
of repentance and of baptism and the remision
of sins and the law of Carnal commandment
which the Lord in his wrath ~~were~~ caused to con-
-tinue with the house of Aaron, among the children
of Israel untill John, whom God raised up being
filled with the holy Ghost from his mothers womb

⁴²of there former evil works for they are to be upbraided

_{hearts}
for there evil ~~works~~ of unbelief and your brethren in Zion
                 ^

for there rebellion against you at the time I sent you

and again I say unto you my friends for from

hence forth I shall call you friends it is expedient

that I give unto you this commandment that ye

become even as my friends in days when I was

with them travling to preach this gospel in my

power for I suffered them not to have pures [purse] or

scrip neither two coats behold I send you out to

proove the world and the Labourer is worthy of

his hire and any man that shall go and preach

this gospel of the kingdom and fail not to continue

faithful in all things shall not be weary in

mind neither darkened neither in body limb or

joint and an hare of his head shall not fall

to the ground unnoticed and they shall not go

hungry neither athurst, therefore take no thought

for the morrow for what ye shall eat or what

ye shall drink or wherewith all ye shall be-

clothed (for consider the lillies of the field how they

grow, they toil not neither do they spin and

the kingdoms of the world in all there glory are

not arayed like one of these) for your father

who art in heaven knoweth that you have

need of all these things therefore let the morrow

take thought for the things of itself neither

take ye thought before hand what ye shall

say {~~tre~~\but} treasure up in your mind contin-

ually the words of life and it shall be given

you in the very hour that portion that

shall be meeted unto evry {~~o~~ n\man} therefore let

no man among you (for this commandment

is unto all the faithful who are called of God

ORIGINAL INSCRIPTION
Frederick G. Williams

REVISIONS
Oliver Cowdery
William W. Phelps
Joseph Smith
Frederick G. Williams
Unidentified

42. Manuscript pages 15–30 contain a series of small holes. (See 443n20 herein.)

in the church unto the ministry) therefore let
no man from this hour take purse or scrip,
that goeth forth to proclaim the gospel of the kingdom
behold I send you out to reprove the world of all
their unrighteous deeds and to teach them of a judgment
which is to come and whoso receiveth you there
I will be also for I will go before your face I will
be on your right hand and on your left and my spirit
shall be in your hearts and mine angels round
about you to bear you up whoso receiveth you
receiveth me and the same will feed you and
clothe you and give you money and he who
feedeth you or clothe you or giveth you money
shall in no wise lose his reward and he that
doeth not these things is not my disciple
by this you may know my disciples he that receiveth
you not go away from him alone by yourselves
and cleanse your feet even with water pure
water whether in heat or in cold and bear testimony
of it unto your father which is in heaven
and return not again unto that man and in
whatsoever village or city ye enter do likewise
nevertheless search diligently and spare not and
woe unto that house or that village or city that
rejecteth you or your words or testimony concerning me woe I say again unto that house or
that village or city that rejecteth you or your
words or your testimony of me for I the Almighty
have laid my hand upon the nations to
scourge them for their wickedness and plagues
shall go forth and they shall not be taken from
the earth until I have completed my work
which shall be cut short in righteousness until all
shall know me who remain even from the least

⁴³in the church unto the ministry) therefore let

no man from this hour take purse or scrip

that goeth forth to proclaim this gospel of the kingdom

behold I send you out to reproove the world of all

there unrighteous deeds and to teach them of a judgment

which is to come and whoso receiveth you there

I will be also for I will go before your face I will

                    hand
be on your right ^ and on your lift [left] and my spirit

shall be in your hearts and mine {an\Angels} round

about you to bear you up whoso receiveth you

receiveth me and the same will feed you and

clothe you and give you money and he who

feedeth you or clothe you or giveth you mony

shall in no wise loose his reward and he that

doeth not these things is not my deciple

by this you may know my deciple he that receiveth

you not go away from him alone by yourselves

and clense your feet even with water pure
                    heat
water whether in ^ or in cold and bear testamony

of it unto your fathe[r] which is in heaven

and return not again unto that man and in

whatsoeve[r] village or city ye enter do like wise

nevertheless search diligently and spare not and

wo unto that house or that village or city that

rejecteth you or your words or testamony concer-

{-\ning} me wo I say again unto that house or

that village or city that rejecteth you or you[r]

words or your testamony of {◊\me} for I the Alm[i]ghty

have laid my hand up on the nations to

scourge them for there wickedness and plag[u]es

shall go forth and {it\they} shall not be taken from

the earth untill I have completed my work

which shall be cut short in righteousness untill all

shall know me who remain even from the least

ORIGINAL INSCRIPTION
Frederick G. Williams

REVISIONS
Oliver Cowdery
William W. Phelps
Joseph Smith
Frederick G. Williams
Unidentified

43. Manuscript pages 15–30
contain a series of small holes.
(See 443n20 herein.)

unto the greatest and shall be filled with the knowledge of the Lord and shall see eye to eye and shall lift up their voice and with the voice together sing this new song saying the Lord hath brought again Zion, the Lord hath redeemed his people Israel according to the election of grace which was brought to pass by the faith and covenant of their fathers, the Lord hath redeemed his people, and satan is bound and time is no longer, the Lord hath gathered all things in one, the Lord hath brought down Zion from above, the Lord hath brought up Zion from beneath, the earth hath travailed and brought forth her strength, and truth is established in her bowels and the heavens hath smiled upon her and she is clothed with the glory of her god for he standeth in the midst of his people, Glory, & honor, & power, and might, be ascribed to our God for he is full of mercy, justice, grace and truth, and peace forever and ever Amen ————————

And again verily verily I say unto you it is expedient that every man who goes forth to proclaim mine everlasting gospel that in as much as they have families and receive monies by gift that they should send it unto them or make use of it for there benefit as the Lord shall direct them for thus it seemeth me good and let all those who have not families who receive monies send it up unto the bishop in Zion or unto the Bishop in Ohio that it may be consecrated for the bringing forth of the revelation and the printing thereof and for establishing of Zion and if any man shall give unto any of you a coat or a suit take the old and cast it unto the poor and go your way rejoicing and if any man among you be strong in the spirit let him take with him he that is weak that he may be edified in all

the

⁴⁴unto the greatest and shall be filled with knowledge of the Lord

and shall see eye to eye and shall lift up there voice and with

the voice together sing this new song saying the Lord hath brought

again Zion, the Lord hath redeemed his people Israel according to

the election of grace which was brought to pass by the faith

and covenant of there fathers, the Lord hath redeemed his

people, and Satan is bound and time is no lon-

-ger, the Lord hath gathered all things in one, the

Lord hath brought down Zion from above, the

Lord ha[t]h brought up Zion from beneath, the

earth hath travailed and brought forth her stren-

-gth, and truth is established in he**r** bowels and

the heavens ha{th\ve} smiled upon her and she is

clothed with the glory of her god for he stand{e\s}th

in the midst of his people, Glory, & honor, & power,

and might, be ascribed to our God for he is

full of mercy, justice, grace and truth, and peace

forever and ever Amen——

And again verily verily I Say unto you it is expedient that every

man who goes forth to proclaim mine everlasting gospel that in as

much as they have families and receive monies by gift they *that*

Should Send it unto them or make use of it for there benifit as the

Lord Shall direct them for thus it seemeth me good and

let all those who have not families who receive monies

send it up unto the bishop in Zion or unto the

Bishop in Ohio that it may be consecrated for the

bringing forth of the revelations and the printing

thereof and for establishing ~~of~~ Zion and if any

man shall give unto any of you a coat or a suit

take the old and cast it unto the poor and go

your way rejoicing and if any man among you

be strong in the spirit let him take with him he

that is weak that he may be edified in all

ORIGINAL INSCRIPTION
Frederick G. Williams
Joseph Smith

REVISIONS
Oliver Cowdery
William W. Phelps
Joseph Smith
Frederick G. Williams
Unidentified

44. Manuscript pages 15–30 contain a series of small holes. (See 443n20 herein.)

meekness that he may become strong also therefore
take with you those who are ordained unto the
Lesser Priesthood, and send them before you
to make appointment and to prepare the way
and to fill appointments that you yourselves
are not able to fill behold this is the way that
mine Apostles in ancient days built up my
church unto me therefore let every man stand
in his own office, and labour in his own calling
and let not the head say unto the feet it hath
no need of the feet, for without the feet how
shall the body be able to stand also the body
hath need of every member that all may be edefied
together that the system may be kept perfect and behold
the high priesthood should travel and also the
Elders, and also the lesser priest, but the Deacon
and Teachers should be appointed to watch
over the church to be a standing ministers
unto the church, and the Bishop also, should
travail round about and among all the
churches searching after the poor to administer
to their wants by humbling the rich and the
proud, he should also employ an agent
for to take charge and to do his secular
business as he shall direct, nevertheless let
the Bishop go unto the city of New York and
also to the city of Albany and also to the city of
Boston, and warn the people of those cities
with the sound of the gospel with a loud
voice of the desolation and utter abolishment
which awaits them if they do reject these
things, for if they do reject these things the
hour of their judgment is nigh and their
house shall be left unto them desolate

⁴⁵meekness that he may become strong also therefore

take with you those who are ordained unto the

Lesser Priesthood, and send them before you

to make appointments and to prepare the way

and to fill appointments that you yourselves

are not able to fill behold this is the way that

mine Apostles in ancient days built up my

church unto me therefore let evry man stand

in his own office, and labour in his own calling

and let not the head say unto the feet it hath

no need of the feet, for without the feet how

shall the body be able to stand also the body

hath need of evry member that all may be edefied

together that the system may be kept perfect and behold

the high priest~~hood~~ should travail and also the

Elders, and also the lesser priests, but the Deacons

and Teachers should be appointed to watch

over the church to be ~~a~~ standing minister**s**

Newel ~~K. Whitney in Kirtland~~⁴⁶
unto the church, and the Bishop also, should

travail round about and among all the

churches searching after the poor to administe[r]

to there wants by humbling the rich and the

proud, he should also employ an agent

for to take charge and to do his secular

business as he shall direct, nevertheless let

the Bishop go unto the city of New York and

also to the city of Albany and also to the city of

Boston, and warn the people of those cities

with the sound of the gospel with a loud

voice of the desolation and utter abolishment

which awaits them if they do reject these

things, for if they do reject these things the

hour of there judgement is nigh and there

house shall be lift [left] unto them dessolate

ORIGINAL INSCRIPTION
Frederick G. Williams

REVISIONS
Oliver Cowdery
William W. Phelps
Joseph Smith
Frederick G. Williams
Unidentified

45. Manuscript pages 15–30 contain a series of small holes. (See 443n20 herein.)

46. "in Kirtland" appears to have been written first; "Newel K. Whitney" added later.

let him trust in me and he shall not be confounded and one
hair of his head shall not fall to the ground unnoticed and
verely I say unto you the rest of my servants go ye forth
as your circumstances shall permit in your several
callings unto the great and notable cities and villages
reproving the world in righteousness of all their unri
ghteous and ungodly deeds setting forth clearly and
understandingly the dessolation of Abomination in
the last days for with you saith the Lord almighty
I will rend their kingdom I will not only shake
the earth but the starry heaven shall tremble also
for I the Lord have put forth mine hand to exert
the powers of heaven, ye cannot see it now, yet
a little while, and ye shall see it and know that
I am, and that I will come and reign with my people
I am Alpha & Omega the begining and the end Amen,
                              F, S, William Scribe —

‡ To Go into the covenant
A Revelation explaining the parable of the Wheat & the tears
Verily thus saith the Lord unto you my servants
concerning the parable of the wheat and of the
tears, Behold verily I say that the field was the world
and the Apostles were the sowers of the seed and after
they have fallen asleep the great persecutor of the Church
the apostate, the whore, even Babylon, that maketh
all nationsto drunk of her cup, in whose hearts the
enemy even Satan sitteth to reign, behold he soweth
the tears, wherefore the tears choke the wheat and drive
the church into the wilderness, but behold in the
last days, even now while the Lord is begining to
bring forth the word, and the blade is springing
up and is yet tender, behold verily I say unto
you the angels are crying unto the Lord, day and
night who are ready, and waiting to be sent forth

let him trust in me and he shall not be confounded and an

                  not

h̶ ha{re**ir**} of his head shall fall to the ground unnoticed and

verely I say unto you the rest of my servants go ye forth

as your circumstances shall permit in your several

callings unto the great and notable cities and villages

reprooving the world in righteousness of all there unri

ghteous and undodly [ungodly] deeds setting forth clearly and

understandingly the dessolation of Abomination in

the last days for with you saith the Lord almighty

I will rend these⁴⁷ kingdoms⁴⁸ I will not only shake

the earth but the stary heavens⁴⁹ shall tremble also

for I the Lord have put forth mine hand to ex{h̶o̶r̶\ert}

the powers of heaven, ye cannot see it now, yet

a little while, and ye shall see it and know that

I am, and that I will come and reign with my people

I am Alpha & Omega the begining and the end Amen,

— — — — — — — — — — — F[rederick], G, Williams Scribe — —

ORIGINAL INSCRIPTION
Frederick G. Williams

REVISIONS
Oliver Cowdery
William W. Phelps
Joseph Smith
Frederick G. Williams
Unidentified

47. Or "there".

48. Or "kingdom", with an accidental extra stroke on "m".

49. Or "heaven", with an accidental extra stroke on "n".

50. This mark likely indicates the intent or instruction to publish this revelation in the 1835 Doctrine and Covenants (section 6).

51. This notation corresponds to similar ones on manuscript pages 20 and 111; these notations mark the material that became sections 4, 5, and 6 in the 1835 Doctrine and Covenants.

#⁵⁰ **To go into th[e] covenants**⁵¹

                                      the

♦ A Revelation explaining the parable of the wheet & ^Tears [tares]

Verily thus saith the Lord unto you my servants

concerning the parable of the wheat and of the

tears, Behold verily I say that the field was the world

and the Apostles were the sowers of the seed and after

they have fallen asleep the great persecutor of the Church

the apostate, the whore, even Babylon, that maketh

all nations ⟨to⟩ dr{u̶\⟨i⟩}nk of her cup, in whose hearts the

enemy even Satan sitteth to reign, behold he soweth

the tears, wherefore the tears choke the wheet and drive

the church in to the wilderness, but behold in the

last days, even now while the Lord is begining to

bring forth ⟨t⟩h{i\⟨e⟩}s̶ word, and the blade is springing

up and is yet tender, b{◊\ehold} verily I say unto

you the angels are crying unto the Lord, day and

night who are ready, and waiting to be sent forth

to reap down the fields, but the Lord saith unto
them pluck not up the tears while the blade is yet
tender(for verily your faith is weak,) least you
distroy the wheat also, therefore let the wheat and
the tears grow together untill the harvest is
fully ripe then ye shall first gather out the
wheat from among the tears and after the gathering
of the wheat, behold and lo the tears are bound
in bundles, and the field remaineth to be burned
therefore thus saith the Lord unto you with
whom the priesthood hath continued through
the lineage of your fathers, for ye are lawful
heirs according to the flesh and have been
hid from the world with Christ in God therefore
your life, and the Priesthood hath remained
and must needs remain through you and
your lineage untill the restoration of all things
spoken by the mouth of all the holy Prophets
since the world began, therefore blessed are ye
if ye continue in my goodness, a light unto
the gentiles and through this Priesthood a saviour
unto my people Israel the Lord hath said it
___

Kirtland December 6th AD 1832 given by
Joseph the seer and written by Sidney the
scribe an Councellor, & Transcribed by Frederick
assistant scribe and councellor — — — — —

~~~~~~

A Prophecy given Decm 25th 1832
Verily thus saith the Lord, concerning the wars
that will shortly come to pass begining at the rebellion
of South Carolina which will eventually terminate
in the death and misery of many souls. and the
days will come that war will be poured out
upon all Nations begining at this place for

32 [verso]

to reap down the fields. but the Lord saith unto

them pluck not up the tears [tares] while the blade is yet

tender (for verily your faith is weak) least you

distroy the wheat also, therefore let the wheat and

the tears grow together untill the harvest is

fully ripe then ye shall first gather out the

wheat from among the tears and after the gathering

of the wheat, behold and lo the tears are b{u\ound}

in bund[l]es, and the field remaineth to be burned

therefore thus saith the Lord unto you with

whom the priesthood hath continued through

the line{g\age} of your fathers, for ye are lawful

heirs according to the flesh and have been

hid from the world with christ in God therefore

your life, and the Priesthood hath remained

and must needs remain through you and

your lineage untill the restoration of all things

spoken by the mouth of all the holy Prophets

since the world began, therefore blessed are ye

if ye continue in my goodness, a light unto

the Gentiles and though this Priesthood a saviour

unto my people Israel the Lord hath said it

Kirtland December 6th. A[D] 1832 given by

Joseph the seer and writen by Sidney [Rigdon] the

scribe an[d] Councellor{—\,} & Transcribed by Frederick [G. Williams]

assistent scribe an⟨d⟩ counceller — — — — — — —

◆ A Propecy given Dec^{m.} 25th 1832

Verily thus saith the Lord, concerning the wars

that will shortly come to pass begining at the rebellion

of South Carolina which will eventually terminate

in the death and missery of many souls, and the

days will come that war will be poured out

upon all Nations begining at this place for

ORIGINAL INSCRIPTION
Frederick G. Williams

REVISIONS
Oliver Cowdery
William W. Phelps
Joseph Smith
Frederick G. Williams
Unidentified

behold the Southern States shall be divided against the
Northern States, and the Southern States will call on other
Nations even the Nation of Great Brittain as it is called
and they shall also call upon other Nations in order
to defend themselves against other Nations and thus
war shall be poured out upon all Nations and it shall
come to pass after many days Slaves shall rise up
against their Masters who shall be Martialed and
disciplined for war and it shall come to pass also
that the remnants who are left of the land will
martial themselves also and shall become exceeding
angry and shall vex the Gentiles with a soar vexation
and thus with the sword and by bloodshed the
inhabitants of the earth shall mourn and with
famine and plague, and Earthquake and the
thunder of heaven and the fierce and vivid lightning also shall the inhabitants of the earth be
made to feel the wrath and indignation and
chastning hand of an Almighty God untill the
consumption ~~decribed~~ decreed hath made a full
end of all Nations that the cry of the saints and
of the blood of the saints shall cease to come up
into the ears of the Lord of Sabaoth from the
earth to be avenged of their enimies, wherefore
stand ye in holy places and be not moved
untill the day of the Lord come, for behold
it cometh quickly saith the Lord – Amen
Given by Joseph the Seer written by F. G. Williams

A Revelation given to the first Elders of this
Church of Christ in the last days. Dec 27th 1832
Verily thus saith the Lord unto you, who have
asembled yourselves together, to receive his will
concerning you, behold this is pleasing unto

behold the southern states shall be divided against the

Northern States, and the Southern States will call on other

Nations⁵²
even the Nation of Great Britian as it is called
^

and they shall also call upon other Nations in order

to defend themselves against other Nations and thus

war shall be poured out upon all Nations and it shall

come to pass after many days Slaves shall rise up

against there Masters who shall be Martialed and

di{◊\⟨s⟩}aplined for war and it shall come to pass also

that the remnants who are left of the land will

martial themselves also and shall become exceding

angry and shall vex the Gentiles with a soar vexation

and thus with the sword and by bloodshed the

inhabitants of the earth shall mourn and with

famine and plague, and Earthquake and the

thunder of heaven and the fierce and vivid light-

-ning also shall the inhabitants of the earth be

made to feel the wrath and indignation and

chastning hand of an Almighty God untill the

consumption ~~decribed~~ decreed hath made a full

end of all Nations that the cry of the saints and

of the blood of the saints shall cease to come up

into the ears of the Lord of Saboath from the

earth to be avenged of their enimies, wherefore

stand ye in holy places and be not moved

untill the day of the Lord come, for be hold

it cometh quickly saith the Lord. Amen

Given by Joseph the Seer wr{◊\ittn} by F[rederick] G Williams

---

◆   A Revelation given ᵗᵒ the first Elders of this
                         ^

Church of Christ in the last days Dec 27ᵗʰ 1832⁵³

Verily thus saith the Lord unto you, who have

assembled yourselves together, to receive his will

concerning you, behold this is pleasing unto

ORIGINAL INSCRIPTION
Frederick G. Williams

REVISIONS
Oliver Cowdery
William W. Phelps
Joseph Smith
Frederick G. Williams
Unidentified

52. "Nations" possibly written at the time of original
inscription.

53. Evidence suggests that
this revelation should be dated
27 and 28 December 1832. For
more information about this
dating, see the discussion of
this revelation in the
Documents series.

into your love, and the Angels rejoice over you,
the ~~prayer~~ alms of your prayers have come
up into the ears of the Lord of Sabaoth, and
are recorded in the book of the names of the
sanctified, even ~~they~~ them of the celestial world,
wherefore, I now send upon you another comforter,
even upon you my friends; that it may abide
in your hearts, even the holy spirit of promise
which other comforter, is the same, that I
promised unto my disciples, as is recorded
in the testimony of John. This comforter
is the promise which I give unto you of
eternal life; even the glory of the celestial
kingdom, which glory is that of the church
of the first born; even of God the holiest
of all; through Jesus Christ, his son. he that
ascended upon high, as also he, descended
below all things; in that he comprehended
all things, that he might be in all, and
through all things; the light of truth, ~~which~~
which truth shineth — this is the light of Christ as
also he is in the sun, and the light of
the sun, and the power thereof by which it
was made, as also he is in the moon, & is the
light of the moon, and the power thereof,
by which it was made, as also the light
of the stars, and the power thereof; by which
they were made; and the earth also, ~~and~~
and the power thereof, even the earth upon
which you stand; and the light which
now shineth, which giveth you light,
is through him which enlighteneth your
eyes; which is the same light that quick-
-neth your understandings, which light,

ORIGINAL INSCRIPTION
Frederick G. Williams

REVISIONS
Oliver Cowdery
William W. Phelps
Joseph Smith
Frederick G. Williams
Unidentified

unto your lord, and the Angels rejoice over you,

the ~~prayers~~ alms of your prayers have come

up into the ears of the Lord of sabaoth, and

are recorded in the book of the names of the

sanctified, even ~~they~~ them of the celestial world,

wherefore, I now send upon you another comfortor,

even upon you my friends; that it may abide

in your hearts, even the holy spirit of promise

which other comforter, is the same, that I

promised unto my deciples, as is recorded

in the testamony of John, This comfortor

is the promise which I give unto you of

eternal life; even the glory of the celestial

kingdom, which glory is that of the church

of the first born; even of God. the holiest

of all; through Jesus Christ, his son. he that

assended up on high, as also he, decended

blow all things; in that he comprehended

all things, that he might be in all, and

through all things; the light of truth, ~~therefore~~

which shineth— this is the light of Christ as

also he is in the s{◊\u}n, and the light of

the s{o\u}n, and the power thereof by which it

was made, as also he is in the moon, & is, the

light of the moon, and the power thereof,

by which it was made, as also the light

of the stars, and the power thereof; by which

they were made; and the earth also, ~~and~~

and the power thereof, even the earth upon

which you stand, and the light which

now shineth; which giveth you light,

is through him which enlightneth you{◊\r}

eyes; which is the same light that quick-

-neth your understandings, which light,

proceedeth forth from the presence of God, to fill the immensity of space; the light which is in all things, which giveth life to all things, which is the law by which all things are governed, even the power of God, who sitteth upon his throne; who is in the bosom of eternity, who is in the midst of all things. Now verily I say unto you, that through the redemption, which is made for you, is brought to pass the resurrection from the dead; (and the spirit and the body is the soul of man) and the resurrection from the dead, is the redemption of the soul; and the redemption of the soul, is through him, who quickeneth all things, in whose bosom, it is decreed, that the poor, and the meek of the earth, shall inherit it; therefore it must needs be sanctified, from all unright- eousness, that it may be prepared for the celestial glory; for after it hath filled the measure of its creation, it shall be crowned with glory, even with the presence of God the father, that bodies, who are of the celestial kingdom may possess it, for ever, & ever, for, for this intent was it made, and created, and for this intent, are they sanctified, and they who are not sanctified through the law which I have given unto you, even the law of Christ, must inherit another kingdom even that of a Terestial kingdom, or that of a Celestial Kingdom, for he that is not able to abide the law of a celestial kingdom, cannot abide a celestial glory, and he who cannot abide, the law of a Terestial kingdom, cannot, abide a Terestial glory, he who cannot abide the law of a Telestial Kingdom

procedeth forth from the presence of God; to fill the

emencity of space; the light which is in all things

which giveth {f\life} to all things, which is the law

by which all things are govorned, even the power

of God, who sitteth upon his throne; who is in the

bosom of eternity, who is in the midst of all things

Now verily I say unto you, that through the

redemption, which is made for you; is bro-

-ught to pass the resurection {◊\from} the dead{◊\;}

(and the spirit, and the body is the soul of man)

and the resurection from the dead, is the redemp-

-tion of the soul; and the redemption of the soul,

is through him, who quickneth all things, in

whose bosom, it is decreed, that the poor, and

the meek of the earth, shall inherit it; therefore

it must needs be sanctified, from all unright

-eousness, that it may be prepared for the

celestial glory; for after it hath filled

the measure of its creation, it shall be {◊\crowned}

with ~~the~~ glory, even with the presence of God

the father; that bodies, who are of the celestial

kingdom may posses it, for ever, & ever; for,

for this intent was it made, and created,

and for this inte{ten\nt}, are they sanctified, and

they who are not sanctified, through the law

which I have given unto you; even the law

of Christ, must inherit another kingdom

even that of a Terestrial kingdom, or that of

who

a telestial kingdom, for he ~~that~~ is not

able to abide the law of a celestial kingdom

cannot abide a celestial glory, and he who

o

cannt abide, the law of a Terestrial kingdom

cannot, abide a Terestrial glory, he who

cannot abide {◊\the} law of a Telestial kingdom

ORIGINAL INSCRIPTION
Frederick G. Williams

REVISIONS
Oliver Cowdery
William W. Phelps
Joseph Smith
Frederick G. Williams
Unidentified

cannot abide a Celestial glory; therefore he is
not meet, for a kingdom of glory; therefore
he must abide a kingdom, which is not a
kingdom of glory. And again, verily I say
unto you, the earth abideth the law, of a
celestial kingdom, for it filleth, the measure
of its creation; and transgresseth not the law,
wherefore it shall be sanctified, yea notwithstanding it shall die, it shall be quickened
again, and shall abide the power, by which it
is quickened, and the righteous shall inherit
it; for notwithstanding they die, they also shall
rise again, a spiritual body, they who are of a
celestial spirit, shall receive the same body which
was a natural body, even ye shall, receive your
bodies; and your glory, shall be that glory, by
which your bodies are quickened, ye who are
quickened, by a portion, of the celestial glory,
shall then receive of the same, even a fulness;
and they, who are quickened, by a portion
of the Terestrial glory, shall then, receive of the
same even a fulness; and also they who are quickened
by a portion, of the Telestial glory, shall then
receive of the same, even a fulness, and they
who remain, shall also be quickened, nevertheless
they shall, return again, to there own place, to
enjoy that which they are willing to receive;
because they were not, willing, to enjoy that which
they might have received; for what doth it
profit a man, if a gift, is bestowed, upon him
and he receive not the gift; behold he rejoiceth
not, in that which is given unto him; neither
rejoiceth in him, who is the giver of the gift; and
again, verily I say unto you, that which is

36 [verso]

cannot abide a Telestial glory; therefore he is

not meet, for a kingdom of Glory, therefore

he must abide a kingdom, which is not a

kingdom of glory. And again, verily I say

unto you, the earth abideth the law, of a

celestial kingdom, for it filleth, the measur

of its creation; and transgresseth not the law

wherefore it shall be sanctified, yea not-

withstanding it shall die, it shall be quickened

again, and shall abide the power, by which it

was is⁵⁴ quickened, and the righteous shall inherit

it, for notwithstanding they die, they also shall

rise again, a spiritual body, they who are of a

celestial spirit, shall receive the same body which

was a natural body, even ye shall, receive your

bodies; and your glory, shall be that glory, by

which your bodies, are quickened, ye who are

quickened, by a portion, of the celestial glory,

shall then receive of the same, even a fulness,

and they, who are quickened, by a portion

of the Terestriall glory, shall then, receive of the

same even a fulness; and also they who are quickened

by a portion, of the Telestial glory, shall then

receive of the same, even a fulness, and they

who remain, shall also be quickend, nevertheless

they shall, return again, to there own place, to

enjoy that which they are willing to receive;

because they were not, willing, to enjoy that which

they might have received; for what doth it

poffet [profit] a man, if a gift, is bestowed, upon him

and he receive not the gift, behold he rejoice{th\s}

not, in that which is given unto him, neither

rejoices in him, who is the giver of the gift; and

again, verily I say unto you, that which is

ORIGINAL INSCRIPTION
Frederick G. Williams

REVISIONS
Oliver Cowdery
William W. Phelps
Joseph Smith
Frederick G. Williams
Unidentified

54. Frederick G. Williams
possibly made revisions
throughout this revelation
at the time of original
inscription.

governed by law, is also preserved by law, and perfected, and
sanctified by the same; that which breaketh a law, and abideth
not by law, but seeketh to become a law unto itself, and willeth
to abide in sin; and altogether abideth in sin, cannot be
sanctified by law; neither by mercy, justice, or judgment; therefore
they must remain filthy still. all kingdoms have a law given;
and there are many kingdoms; for there is no space, in the
which there is no kingdom; and there is no kingdom,
in which there is no space, either a greater or lesser kingdom.
and unto every kingdom, is given a law, and unto every law
there are certain bounds also, and conditions. all beings
who abide not, in those conditions, are not justified,
for intelligence, cleaveth unto intelligence, wisdom, receiveth
wisdom; truth embraceth truth, virtue, loveth virtue,
light, cleaveth unto light, mercy hath compassion
on mercy, and claimeth her own; justice continueth
its course and claimeth its own, judgment, goeth
before the face of him, who sitteth upon the throne,
and governeth, and executeth all things; he
comprehendeth all things, and all things, are before
him, and all things, are round about him, and
he is, above all things. and in all things; and is
through all things, and is round about all things,
and all things are by him, and of him, even
God for ever, and ever. And again verily I say unto you,
he hath given a law, unto all things, by which they
moove in their times, and their seasons, and their
courses, are fixed, even the courses of the heavens,
and the earth which, comprehend the earth, and
all the planets, and they give light to each other
in their times, and in their seasons, in their min
-uts in their hours, in their days, in their weeks,
in their months, in their years; all these are
one year with God. but not with man; the

govorned by law, is also preserved by law, and perfected, and

sanctified by the same; that which breaketh a law, and abideth

not by law, but seeketh to become a law unto itself, and willeth

to abide in sin; and altogether abideth in sin, cannot be

sanctified by law; neither ~~of~~ by by[55] mercy, justice, or judgment; therefore

they must remain filthy still, all kingdoms have a law given;

and there are many kingdoms; for there is no space, in the

which there is no kingdoms; and there is no kingdom,

in which there is no space, eather a greater or lesser kingdom,

//[56]and unto evry kingdom, is given a law, and unto evry law

there are certain bounds also, and conditions, all beings

who abide not, in those conditions, are not justified,

for inteligence, cleaveth unto inteligence, wisdom, receiveth

wisdom, truth embraceth truth, virtue, Loveth virtue,

light, Cleaveth unto light, mercy hath compassion

on mercy, and claimeth her own; justice continueth

its course and claimeth its own, judgment, goeth

before the face of him, who sitteth up-on the throne,

and gove[r]neth, and executeth all things, he

comprehendeth all things, and all things, are before

him, and all things, are round about him, and

he is, above all things, and in all things, and is

through all things, and is round about all thing

and all things are by him, and of him, even

God for ever, and ever, A{nde\nd} verily again I say unto you,

he hath given a law, unto all things, by which they

moove in there times, and there seasons, and there

cources, are fixed, even the cour{s\ces} of the heavens,

and the earth which, comprehend the earth, and

all the planets, and they give light to each other

in there times, and in there seasons, in there min

-uits in there hours, in there days, in there week,

in there months, in there years; all these are

one year with God. but not with man; the

ORIGINAL INSCRIPTION
Frederick G. Williams

REVISIONS
Oliver Cowdery
William W. Phelps
Sidney Rigdon
Joseph Smith
Frederick G. Williams
Unidentified

55. Both insertions appear to be in the same ink flow. The first "by" is misshapen.

56. This revelation first appears in print in the 1835 Doctrine and Covenants as section 7, verses 1–38. The ink flow of double slashes throughout this revelation appears to match the ink flow of notations on manuscript pages 20, 31, and 111. The notations on those three pages mark the material that became sections 4, 5, and 6 in the 1835 Doctrine and Covenants, but the meaning of the slashes in this revelation is unknown.

Earth
rolls upon her wings, and the sun giveth his
light by day, and the moon, giveth her light by
night, and the stars also giveth their light
as they roll upon their wings, in their glory
in the midst of the power, of God, unto what shall I
liken these kingdoms, that ye may understand,
behold all their are kingdoms, and any man,
who hath seen any, or the least of these, hath
seen God, moving in his majesty and power; I
say unto you, he hath seen him, nevertheless, he
who came unto his own, was not comprehended,
the light shineth in darkness, and the darkness
comprehendeth it not, nevertheless; the day shall
come, when you shall, comprehend even God,
being quickened in him, and by him, then
shall ye know, that ye have seen me, that I
am, and that I am the true light, that is
in you, and that you are in me, otherwise
ye could not abound, Behold I will liken
these kingdoms, unto a man, having a field,
and he sent forth, his servant, into the
field, to dig in the field, and he said
unto the first, go ye and labour in the
field, and in the first hour, I will come,
unto you, and ye shall behold the joy of
my countenance, and he said, unto the
second, go ye also into the field, and in
the second hour, I will visit you with
the joy of my countenance, and also unto
the third saying, I will visit you, and
unto the fourth; and so on unto the
twelfth, and the lord of the vineyard field
went unto the first, in the first hour, and
tarried with him, all that hour, and he was

38 [verso]
Earth

rolls upon her wings, and the sun giveth h{er\is}

light by day, and the moon, giveth her light by

night, and the stars also giveth there light

as they roll upon, there wings, in there glory

in the midst, of the power, of God, unto what shall I⁵⁷

liken th{◊\ese} kingdoms, that ye may understand,

are
behold ◊all these kingdoms, and any man,

who hath seen, any, or the least of these, ha{ve\th}

seen God, moving in his magesty and power; I

say unto you, he hath seen him, nevertheless, he

who came unto his own, was not comprehended,

the light shineth in darkness, and the darkness

hen
compredeth it not, nevertheless, the day shall

come, when you shall, comprehend even God,

being quickened in him, and by him, then⁵⁸

shall ye know, that ye have seen me, that I

am, and that I am the true light, that is

in you, and that you are in me, otherwise

ye could not abound, Behold I will liken

these⁵⁹ kingdoms, unto a man, having a field,

and he sent forth, his servants, into the

field, to dig in the field, and he said

unto the first, go ye and labour in the

field, and in the first hour, I will come

unto you, and ye shall behold the joy of

my countenance, and he said, unto the

seccond, go ye also into the field, and in

the seccond hour, I will visit you with

the joy of my countenance, and also unto

the third saying, I will visit you, and

unto the fourth; and so on unto the

twelth, and the lord of the ~~vine{◊y\yard}~~⁶⁰ field

went unto the first, in the first hour, and

tarried with him, all that hour, and he was

Original Inscription
Frederick G. Williams

Revisions
Oliver Cowdery
William W. Phelps
Joseph Smith
Frederick G. Williams
Unidentified

57. "I" possibly inserted.
58. Or "thus".
59. Or "there".
60. "◊y" wipe-erased and written over; then whole word stricken.

made glad, with the light of his countenance, of his lord; and then he withdrew from the first, that he might visit the second also, and the third, and the fourth, and so on, unto the twelveth, and this they all received the light of the countenance of their Lord, every man in his hour, and in his time, and in his season, begining at the first, and so on unto the last, and from the last unto the first, and from the first, unto the last, every man in his own order, untill his hour was finished, even according as his lord had commanded him, and he in turn that they all might be glorified that his Lord might be glorified in him; therefore unto this parable will I liken all those kingdoms; and the inhabitants thereof, every kingdom, in it hour, and in its time, and in its season, even according to the decrees which God hath made; and again; and no verily I say unto you, my friends, I leave these sayings with you, for to ponder in your hearts; with this commandment, which I give unto you, that ye shall call upon me while I am near; draw near unto me, and I will draw near unto you, seek me diligent-ly, and ye shall find me, ask, and ye shall receive, knock, and it shall be opened unto you; whatsoever ye ask the father, in my name, it shall be given unto you, that is expedient for you, and if ye ask any thing, that is not expedient for you, it shall turn unto your condemnation, behold, that which you hear, is as the voice, of one crying in the wilderness, in the wilderness; because you cannot see him; my voice, because my voice, is spirit, my spirit is truth, truth abideth, and hath no end, and if it be in you, it shall abound, and if your eye be single to my glory, your whole bodies, shall be filled with light, and there shall bee no darkness in you, and that body, which is filled with light comprehendeth all things; therefore sanctify yourselves that your minds

made glad, with the light of this countenance, of his

lord, and then he withdrew, from the first, that he

might visit the seccond also, and the third, and the fourth,

thus
and so on, u{◊\⟨n⟩}to the twelveth, and they all received, the light of the
                                        ^

countinance, of their Lord, every man, in his hour, and in his

time, and in his season, begining at the first, and so

on unto the last, and from the last unto the first,

and from the first, unto the Last, evry man in his own

order, untill his hour was finished, even according, as his

lord, had commanded him, that his Lord might be glor[i]fied
        and he in him that they all might be glorified
in him{,\;} therefore unto this parable, will I liken all those
            ^

kingdoms; and the inhabitants thereof, evry kingdom, in

its hour, and in its time, and in its season, even

// according to the decree, which God, hath made; and

again; ~~and now~~ verily I say unto you, my friends, ~~I~~ I

leave these sayings, with you, ~~for to,~~ ponder in your

hearts; with this commandment, which I give unto you,

that ye shall call upon me, while I am near, draw near

                                                i
unto me, and I will draw near unto you, seek me dillgen

-tly, and ye shall find me, ask, and ye shall receive,

knock, and it shall be opened unto you; whatsoever ye

ask the father, in my name, it shall be given unto

you, that is expedient for you, and if ye ask any

thing, that is not, expedient for you, it shall turn

unto your ~~own~~ condemption [condemnation], b{~~ut~~\ehold}, that which

you hear, is as the voice, of one crying in the wilderness,

In the wilderness, because you cannot see him; my

voice, because my voice, is spirit, my spirit is

truth, truth abideth, and hath no end, and if it

be in you, it shall abound, and if your eye be

single to my glory, your whole bodies, shall be filled

with light, and there shall be no darkness in you,

and that body, which is filled with light comprehendeth

all things; therefore sanctify yourselves that your minds

ORIGINAL INSCRIPTION
Frederick G. Williams

REVISIONS
Oliver Cowdery
William W. Phelps
Joseph Smith
Frederick G. Williams
Unidentified

become single to God, and The day will come, that you shall
see him, for he will, unveil his face unto you, and it
shall be in his own time, and in his own
way, and according, to his own will; Remember
the great and last promise which I have made unto you, cast away
your idle thoughts, and your excess of laughter,
far from you; tarry ye, tarry ye in this place,
and call a solemn assembly, even of thou, who are
the first Labourers, in this last kingdom, and
let thou, whom they have warned, in there
traveling. call on the Lord and ponder, the warning
in there hearts; which they have received, for
a little season, behold and lo I will take care
of your flocks, and will rain up elders, and
send unto them, behold I will hasten my
work, in its time, and I give unto you,
who are the first Labourers, in this last
kingdom, a commandment, that you assemble
yourselves together, and organize yourselves,
and prepare yourselves, and sanctify yourselv
yea purify your hearts, and clean your
hands, and your feet, before me, that I
may make you clean, that I may testify
unto your father, and your God, and my God,
that you are clean, from the blood of this,
wicked generation, that I may fulfil this
promise, this great and last promise, which
I have made unto you, when I will; also I
give unto you a commandment, that
ye shall continue in prayer, and fasting,
from this time forth; (and I give unto
you a commandment, that you shall
teach one another, the doctrines, of the
kingdom, teach ye diligently, and my

42 [verso]

// time is not yet come, there garments are not

clean from the blood of this generation, abide

ye in the liberty, wherewith ye are made

free, entangle not yourselves in sin, but

lit [let] your hands be clean, untill the lord

come, for not many days hence, and the

earth shall tremble, and real to and

fro as a drunken man, and the sun

shall hide his face, and shall refuse to give

light, and the moon shall be bathed in blood,

and the stars shall become exceding angry

and shall cast themselves down, as a fig,

that falleth from off a fig tree, and after

your testamony, cometh wrath, and—

indignation, upon the people, for after

your testamony cometh the testamony, of

earthquakes, ~~and~~ ^{that} shall cause gronings

in the midst of her, and men, shall fall

upon the ground, and shall not be

able to stand, and also, cometh the

testamony, of the voice of thunderings, and

the voice of lightnings, and the voice

of tempests, and the voice of the waves

of the sea heaving themselves, beyond

there bounds, and all things shall be in

commotion; and surely mens hearts, shall

fail them, for fear shall come up on

all people, and Angels shall fly through

the midst of heaven crying, with a loud

voice, sounding the trump of God, saying

prepare ye, prepare ye, O inhabitants of

the earth, for the judgment of our God

is come, behold and lo, the bridegroom

cometh, go ye out to meet him and

ORIGINAL INSCRIPTION
Frederick G. Williams

REVISIONS
Oliver Cowdery
William W. Phelps
Joseph Smith
Frederick G. Williams
Unidentified

immediately, there shall appear, a great sign in
heaven, and all people, shall see it together, &
another Angel shall sound, his trump, saying
that great Church, the mother of abominations
that made all nations, drink of the wine, of the
earth of her fornication, that persiteth the saints
of God, that shed their blood, her who sitteth upon
many waters, and upon the Islands of the sea
behold she is, the tears of the earth, she is
bound in bundles, her bands are made strong
no man can loose them, therefore she is ready
to be burned and he shall sound his trump
both long and loud, and all nations shall
hear it, and there shall be silence in heaven
for the space, of a half an hour, immediately
after, shall the curtain, of heaven be unfolded
as a scroll is unfolded after it is rolled up
and the face, of the Lord, shall be unveiled
and the saints, that are upon the earth, who are
alive, shall be quickened, and be caught up to meet
him, and they who have slept in their graves,
shall come forth, for their graves shall be
opened, and they also shall be caught up to
meet him in the midst of the pillar of heaven
they are Christs the first fruits, they who shall
descend with him first, and they who are
on the earth, and in their graves, who are
first caught up to meet him, and all this by
the voice, of the sounding of the trump, of the
Angel of God, and after this, another trump
shall sound, which is the second trump
and then cometh, the redemption of those
who are Christs, at his coming, who have received
their part in that prison, which is prepared
for them, that they might receive the gospel

immediately, there shall appear, a great sign in

heaven, and all people, shall see it together, &

another Angel shall sound, his trump, saying

that great Church, the mother of abominations

that made all nations, drink of the wine, of the

{e\wr}arth [wrath] of ~~its~~ **her** fornication, that per{◊\◊}iteth [persecuteth] i the saints

of God, that shed th{e\i}re blood, her who sitteth upon

many waters, and upon the Is[l]ands of the sea

behold she is, the tears [tares] of the earth, she is

bound in bundles, her bands are made strong

no man can loose them, therefore she is ready

to be burned and he shall sound his trump

both long and loud, and all nations shall

hear it, and there shall be silence in heaven

for the space, of a half an hour, & imediately

after, shall the curtain, of heaven be unfolded

as a scroll is unfolded, after it is rolled up

and the face, of the Lord, shall be unveiled

and the saints, that are upon the earth, who are

alive, shall be quickened, and be caught up to meet

him, and they who have slept in[61] there graves,

shall come forth, for there graves shall be

opened, and they also shall be caught up to

meet him in the midst of the pillar of heaven

they are Christs the first fruits, they who shall

decend with him first, and they who are

on the earth, and in there graves, who are

first caught up to {;\meet} him, and all this by

the voice, of the sounding of the trump, of the

Angel of God, and after this, another trump

shall sound, which is the seccond trump

and then cometh, the redemption of those

who are Christs, at his coming, who have receved

there part in that prision, which is prepared

for them, that they m[i]ght receive the gospel

ORIGINAL INSCRIPTION
Frederick G. Williams

REVISIONS
Oliver Cowdery
William W. Phelps
Joseph Smith
Frederick G. Williams
Unidentified

61. There is a small hole through "in", likely made by a pin.

and be judged, according to men in the flesh, and
again, another trump shall sound, which is the third
trump, and then cometh, the spirits of men. who
are to be judged, and are found under condemnation
and these, are the rest of the dead, and they
live not again, untill the thousand years are
ended, neither again, untill, the end of the
earth, and another trump shall sound, which
is the forth trump, saying; there are found
among those. who are to remain, untill that
great, and last day, even the end, who shall
remain filthy still, and another trump shall
sound, which is the fifth trump, which is the fifth
angel, who comitteth the everlasting gospel, flying
through the midst of heaven, unto all Nations, Kindred
Tongues, & people, and this, shall be the sound of
his trump, saying, to all people, both in
heaven, and in earth, and that are under
the earth, for every ear shall hear it; and every
knee, shall bow, and every tongue shall confess, while,
they hear, the sound of the trump, saying fear God.
and give glory to him, who sitteth upon the throne
for ever, and ever, for the hour of his judgment
is come; and again another angel, shall sound,
his trump, which is the sixth Angel, saying, & she
is fallen, who made, all Nations drink, of the wine,
of the wrath, of her fornication; she is fallen, is fallen,
and again, another Angel, shall sound, his trump,
which is the seventh Angel, saying, it is finished,
it is finished, the Lamb of God, hath overcome
and troden the wine press alone, even the wine
of the fierceness, of the wrath, of Almighty God,
then shall the Angels be crowned, & the glory is
might, and the saints shall be _____ with his glory,

46 [verso]
thing

and establish, an house, even an house of prayer

and house of fasting, an house of faith, an house

of Learning, an house of glory, an house of order

an house of God, that your incomings {b\may} be

         that
in the name of the Lord, and your outgoing
       ^

may be in the name of the Lord, that all your

salutations, may be in the name of the Lord,

with uplifted hands, unto the most high, therefore

ceace from all your light speaches, from all laughter

from all your lustful des[i]res, from all your pride

and lightmindness, and from all your wicked

doings, appoint among yourselves, a teacher, and

and lit [let], not all be spokesmen at once, but let

one speak at a time, and lit [let] all listen, unto his

sayings that when all have spoken, that all may

be edified, of all, and that evry man, may have

an equal privelege, see that {I\ye} love one another

ceace to be covetous, learn to impart, one to

another as the gospel requires, ceace to be Idle, cease

          to
to be unclean, ceace find fault, one with another
         ^

ceace to sleep, any longer then is needful, retire to

thy bed early that ye may not be weary, arise

early, that your bodies, and your minds may

be invigorated, and above all things, clothe

yourselves, with the bonds of charity, as with a

        the
mantle, which is bonds of perfectness and peace,
      ^

prey always, that you may not faint until I

come, behold, and lo, I will come quickly and

receive you unto myself Amen; — —

Given by Joseph the seer and written by F[rederick]. G. William[s]

assistan[t] scribe and counceller to ˢ[ai]ᵈ· Joseph — — —

ORIGINAL INSCRIPTION
Frederick G. Williams

REVISIONS
Oliver Cowdery
William W. Phelps
Joseph Smith
Frederick G. Williams
Unidentified

Kirtland January 3d 1833. Revelation given to &c for a pastor &

The order of the house, of God prepared for the presidency, and instruction, in all things, that are expedient for the officers; or in other words, them who are called to the ministry in the church, begining at the high Priests, even down to the deacon, and this shall be the order of the house, he that is appointed, to be a teacher, shall be found standing in his place, which shall be prepared for him, in the house of God, in a place that the congregation, in the house may hear his words correctly and distinctly; not with loud speach; and when he cometh into the house of God (for he should be first in the house, behold this is beautiful, that he may be an example) let him offer himself in prayer upon his knees, before God, in token of the everlasting covenant. and when any shall, come in after him, let the teacher arise, and with uplifted hands to heaven, yea even directly, salute his brother, or brethren, with these words saying, art thou a brother, or brethren, I salute you in the name of the Lord Jesus Christ, in token of the everlasting covenant, in which covenant, I receive you to fellowship, in a determination, that is fixed immovable, and unchangable, to be your friend and brother, through the grace of God, in the bonds of Love, to walk in all the commandments, of God, blameless, in thanksgiving for ever and ever; Amen. and he that cometh in, and is a brother, or brethren shall salute the teacher with uplifted hands to heaven, with this same prayer, and covenant or by saying amen; in token of the same, Behold verily I say unto you, this is a sample, unto you for a salutation, to one another, in the house of God; and ye are called to do this by prayer, and thanksgiving, as the spirit shall give utterance

◆ Kirtland January 3ᵈ· 1833. Revelation given to ~~organize~~ for a patern &c

The order of the house, ~~of God~~ prepared for the presedency,

and instruction, in all things, that ^{are} ~~is~~ expedient for the

officers; or in other words, them who are called to the ministry

in the Church, begining at the high Priests, even down to

the deacon, and this shall be the order of the house, he

that is appointed, to be a teacher, shall be found

standing in his place, which shall be ~~appointed~~ pre-

pared, for him, in the house of God, in a place that

the congregation, in the house may hear his words, correctly

and distinctly; not with loud speach; and he ^{when} cometh

into the house of God, (for he should be first in the

house, behold this is beautiful, that he may be an

example) let him offer himself in prayer upon his

knees, before God, in token of the everlasting covenant,

and when any shall, come in after him, let the teacher

arise, and with uplifted hands to heaven, yea even

directly, salute his brother, or brethren, with these words

saying, art thou a brother, or brethren, I salute you in

the name of the Lord Jesus Christ, in to{ce**ke**}n of the ever-

lasting covenant, in which covenant, I receive you

to fellowship, in a determination, that is fixed

immovable, and unchangable, to be your friend

and brother, through the grace of God, in the bonds

of Love, to walk in all the commandments, of God,

blameless, in thanksgiving for ever, and ever; Amen.

and he that cometh, in, and is a brother, or brethren

shall salute the teacher with uplifted hands to

heaven, with this same prayer, and covenant

or by saying amen; in token of the same, Behold

verily I say unto you, this ^{is} a sample, unto you

for a salutation, to one another, in the house of

God, and ye are called to do this by prayer, and

thanksgiving, as the spirit shall give utterence

ORIGINAL INSCRIPTION
Frederick G. Williams

REVISIONS
Oliver Cowdery
William W. Phelps
Joseph Smith
Frederick G. Williams
Unidentified

in all your doings, in the house of the Lord, that
it may become a sanctury, a tabernacle, of the
holy spirit to you, edefication Amen
Given by Joseph the seer, and written by Frederick
a pisting scribe and counsellor —

―――――――――――――――――――――

Sang by the gift of Tongues & Translated

age after age has rolled away, according to the sad fate
of man, countless millions for ever gone at length the
period of time has come that oft was seen by a prophetic
eye and written too by all holy men Inspired of the Lord
a time which was seen by Enoch of old at a time when
he stood upon the mount which was called the mountain
of God as he gazed upon nature and the corruption of
man and mourned their sad fate and wept
and cried with a loud voice and heaved forth
his sighs Omnipotence Omnipotence O may I
see thee — and with his finger he touched
his eyes and he saw heaven he gazed on
eternity, and sang an Angelic song and
mingled his voice with the heavenly throng
Hosanna Hosanna the sound of the trump around the throne
of God echoed & echoed again and rang and
reechoed until eternity was filled with his
voice he saw yea he saw and he glorified
God the salvation of his people his City
caught up through the gospel of Christ
he saw the begining the ending of men
he saw the time when Adam his father
was made and he saw that he was in
eternity before a grain of dust in the
ballance was weighed he saw that he em
=anated and came down from God he saw
what had passed and then was and is present

48 [verso]

in all your doings, in the house of the Lord, that

it may become a sanctury, a tabernacle, of the

holy spirit to your, edefication Amen

Given by Joseph the seer, and writen by Frederick [G. Williams]

assistant scribe and councellor — — — — —

♦   ⁶⁷Sang by the gift of Tongues & Translated

age after age has rolled away, according to the sad fate

of man. countless millions {of\for} ever gone at length the

period of time has come that oft was seen by a prophetic

eye and writen too by all holy men {of\Inspired} of the Lord

a time which was seen by Enoch of Old at a time when

he stood upon the mount which was called the mountain

of God as he gazed upon nature and the corruption of

~~man~~⁶⁸ of man and mourned their sad fate and wept

and cried with a Loud voice and heaved forth

his sighs Omnipotence Omnipotence o may I

see thee— and with his finger he touched

his eyes and he saw heaven he gazed on

eternity and sang an Angelic song and

mingled his vo{◊◊e\ice} with the heavenly throng
                                the throne
Hozana Hozana the sound of the trump around ͜

of God echoed & echoed again and rang and

reechoed until eternity was filled with his

voice he saw yea he saw and he glorified

God the salvation of his people his city

caught up through the gospel of Christ

he saw the begining the ending of man

he saw the time when Adam his father

was made and he saw that he was in

eternity before a grain of dust in the

ballance was weighed he saw that he em

-enated and came down from God he saw

what had passed and then was and is present

ORIGINAL INSCRIPTION
Frederick G. Williams

REVISIONS
Oliver Cowdery
William W. Phelps
Joseph Smith
Frederick G. Williams
Unidentified

67. No other version of this item exists to provide additional detail about its creation, so its authorship is unknown. This item was never canonized.

68. "man" wipe-erased and then partially stricken.

and to come therefore he saw the Last days the angel
that came down to John and the Angel that now is
now flying having the everlasting Gospel to com
mit ye to men — which in my soul I have received
and from death and bondage from the Devil
I'm freed and am free in the gospel of Christ
and I'm waiting and with patience I'll wait
on the Lord Hosanna loud sound the trump came
eternity to wing hosanna for ever I'm waiting the coming
of Christ a mansion on high a celestial abode a seat
on the right hand of God Angels are coming the holy
Ghost is falling upon the saints and will continue to fall
the saviour is coming ye the Bridegroom prepare
ye prepare ye the cry has gone forth go wait on
the Lord the Angels in glory will soon be descending
go join you in singing the praises of God the trump
loud shall sound the dark vail soon shall rend
heaven shall shake the earth shall tremble and
all nature shall feel the power of God. gaze ye
saints gaze ye upon him, gaze upon Jesus
hosanna loud sound the trump his chariot is
caught up hosanna praise him ye saints they
stand at his feet behold they are weeping they
strike hands with Enoch of Old they inherit a
city as it is written the city of God Sound sound
the trump, they receive a celestial crown hosanna
hosanna the heaven of heavens and the heavens
are filled with the praises of God Amen
Given February 27 — 1833 —

A Revelation for the benefit of the saints &
a word of wisdom for the benefit of the council
of high Priests assembled in Kirtland and Church
and also the saints in Zion to be sent greeting
not by commandment or constraint but

and to come therefore he saw the Last days the Angel

that came down to John and the Angel that ~~now~~ is

now flying having the everlasting Gospel to com

mit {t̶o̶\unto} men— which in my soul I have recivd

and from death and bondage from the Devil

I'm freed an{◊\d} am free in the gospel of Christ

and Im waiting and with patience Ill wait

on the Lord hozana loud sound the trump cause

eternity to wring hozana for ever Im waiting the coming

of Christ a mansion on high a celestial abode a seat

on the right hand of God Angels are coming the holy

Ghost is falling upon the saints and will continue to fall

the saviour is coming yea the Bride groom prepare

ye prepare yea the cry has gone forth go wait on

the Lord the Angels in glory will soon be descending

go join you in singing the praises of God the trump

Loud shall sound the dark vail soon shall rend

heaven shall shake the earth shall tremble and

all nature shall feel the power of God, gaze ye

saints gaze ye upon him, gaze upon Jesus

hozana loud sound the trump his church is

caught up hozana praise him ye saints they

stand at his feet behold they are weeping they

strike hands with Enoch of Old they inherit a

city as it is writen the City of God, Loud sound

the trump, they receive a celestial crown hozana

hozana the heaven of heavens and the heavens

are filled with {his**the**} praises of God Amen
Given Februa[r]y 27— 1833—

ORIGINAL INSCRIPTION
Frederick G. Williams

REVISIONS
Oliver Cowdery
William W. Phelps
Joseph Smith
Frederick G. Williams
Unidentified

♦   A Revelation for the benefit of the saints &c

a word of wisdom for the benefit of the council

of high Priests assembled in Kirtland and Church

and also the saints in Zion to be sent Greeting

not by commandment or constraint but

by revelation and the word of wisdom shewing
forth the order and will of God in the temporal
salvation of all saints in the last days given
for a principle with promise adapted to the
capacity of the weak and the weakest of all saints
who are or can be called saints behold verily
thus saith the Lord unto you in consequence
of evils and designs which do and will exist
in the hearts of conspiring men in the last
days I have warned you and forewarn you
by giving unto you this word of wisdom
by revelation that inasmuch as any man
drinketh wine or strong drink among
you behold it is not good neither meet in
the sight of your father only in assembling
yourselves together to offer up your sacrament
before him and behold this should be wine
yea pure wine of the grape of the vine of
your own make, and again strong drinks
are not for the belly but for the
washing of your bodies, and again Tobacco
is not for the body neither for the belly and
is not good for man, but is an herb for
bruises and all sick cattle to be used with
judgment and skill and again hot drinks
are not for the body or belly and again
verily I say unto you all wholsome herbs God
hath ordained for the constitution nature and use
of men every herb in the season thereof and every
fruit in the season thereof, all these to be
used with prudence and thanksgiving yea
flesh also of beasts and of the fowls of the air
I the Lord hath ordained for the use of man
with thanksgiving nevertheless they are to be

language, through those who are ordained unto this power

by the administration of the comforter shed forth upon

them for the revelation of Jesus Christ. And now verily

I say unto you, I give unto you a commandment, that you

continue in this ministry, and presidency; and when

you have finished the translations of the prophets, you

shall from thenceforth preside over the affairs of the

church, and the school, and from time, to time, as

shall be manifest by the comforter, receive revelations;

to unfold the mysteries of the kingdom, and set in order

the churches; and study, and Learn, and become

acquainted with all good books, and with Languages,

Tongues & people &c. &c. And this shall be your busin-

-ess and mission, in all your lives, to preside ~~over~~

in council, and set in order all the affairs of the

^c
churh; and kingdom. Be[70] not ashamed,[71] neither con-

-founded, but be admonished in all your high mind

-edness, and pride; for it bringeth a snare upon

your souls; set in order your houses, keep slothfulness

uncleanness
and ~~idleness~~ far from you. Now verely I say unto

you, let there be a place provided, as soon as it

is possable, for the family of thy councellor and

scribe, even Frederick; and let mine aged serve-

-nt Joseph [Smith Sr.], continue with his family upon the place

where he now lives, and let it not be sold, until

the mouth of the Lord shall name, and let thy

councellor, even Sidney, remain where he now

resides, until the mouth of the Lord shall name,

and let the Bishop, search diligently to ob-

-tain an agent; and let it be a man, who has

got riches, in store, a man of God, and of strong

faith, that thereby he may be enabled to discharge

evry debt, that the store house of the Lord may not

be brought into disrepute before the eyes of the

ORIGINAL INSCRIPTION
Frederick G. Williams

REVISIONS
Oliver Cowdery
William W. Phelps
Joseph Smith
Frederick G. Williams
Unidentified

70. There is a pinhead impression before "Be". (See 523n78 herein.)

71. There is a pinhole above "ashamed" and another below. (See 521n72 herein.)

people. Search diligently, pray always, and
be believing, and all things shall work together
for your good, if ye walk uprightly, and remember the covenant, wherewith ye have covenanted
one with another. Let your families be small,
especially mine aged servant Joseph; as pertaining to those, who do not belong to your families.
that those things, that are provided for you to
bring to pass my work, are not taken from
you and given to those, that are not worthy;
and thereby you are hindered in accomplishing those things which I have commanded
you; And again, verily I say unto you, it
is my will that my handmaid Vena,
should receive money, to bear her expenses,
and go up unto the Land of Zion, and receive
an inheritance from the hand of the Bishop
that she may settle down in peace inasmuch
as she is faithful, and not be idle in her
days from thenceforth. And behold verily
I say unto you that ye shall write this
commandment, and say unto your brethren
in Zion, in love greeting, that I have called
you also to preside over Zion, in mine own
due time; therefore let them cease wearing
me concerning this matter. Behold I say
unto you, that your brethren in Zion,
begin to repent, and the Angels rejoice over
them; nevertheless I am not well pleased
with many things, and I am not well pleased with
my servant William E. McLelin, neither
with my servant Sidney Gilbert, and the Bishop
also; and others have many things to repent
of: But verily I say unto you that I the Lord
will contend with Zion, and plead with her

people. Search diligently, pray always, and

be believing, and all things shall work together

for your good, if ye walk uprightly, and remem-

-ber the covenant, wherewith ye have covenented

one with another. Let your families be small,

especially mine aged servant Joseph [Smith Sr.]; as pertai-

-ning to those who do not belong to your families.

that those things, that are provided for you to

bring to pass my work, are not taken from

you and given to those, that are not worthy;

and thereby you are hindred in accomplish-

-ing those things which I have commanded

you; And again, verily I say unto you, it

is my will that my handmaid Vien[n]a [Jacques],

should recive[72] money, to bear her expences,

and go up unto the Land[73] of Zion,*[74] and receive

an inheritance from the hand of the Bishop

that she may settle down in peace inasmuch

as she is faithful, and not be idle in her

days from thenceforth. And behold verely

I say unto you that ye shall write this

commandment, and say unto your brethren

in Zion, in Love greeting that I have called

you also to preside over Zion, in mine own

due time; therefore let them cease wearing

me concerning this matter. Behold I say

unto you, that your brethren in Zion,

begin to repent, and the Angels rejoice over

~~you~~ them, nevertheless I am not well pleased
        many things, and I am not well pleased with
with my servant William E McLel[l]in, neither
        ^

with my servant Sidney Gilbert, and the Bishop

also; and others have many things, to repent

of; But verily I say unto you that I the Lord

will contend with Zion, and plead with her

ORIGINAL INSCRIPTION
Frederick G. Williams

REVISIONS
Oliver Cowdery
William W. Phelps
Joseph Smith
Frederick G. Williams
Unidentified

72. There is a pinhole below "recive" on this line and another above "unto" on the next line, both likely caused by pinning a slip of paper to the page. This slip, which is no longer extant, was likely an aid for publishing the 1835 Doctrine and Covenants and was possibly a key to the numbers inserted in the revelation at the bottom of manuscript page 55. Because the text on page 55 was used to prepare the 1835 Doctrine and Covenants but the text on this page was not, the slip was likely initially pinned to page 55 and then moved to this page so the text on page 55 would not be obscured.

73. There is a pinhead impression just after "Land". (See 523n78 herein.)

74. This asterisk refers to two lines of text inserted by Frederick G. Williams at the end of this revelation (see 523n75 herein), indicating where the additional text should be inserted for publication.

strong ones, and chasten her, until she overcomes, and
are clean before me; for she shall not be moved
out of her place, I the Lord have spoken it Amen
Seven by Joseph the seer and written by
Frederick Councellor & Scribe
✱ And the residue of her money I will consecrate unto myself, and reward her in mine own due
time verily I say unto you that it is meet in mine eyes that she should go up unto the land of Zion.

Kirtland 9th of March 1883
A Revelation given concerning Apocrypha
Verily thus saith the Lord unto you concerning
the Apocrypha there are many things contained
therein that are true and it is mostly translated correct—there are many things contained
therein that are not true which are interpolations
by the hands of men—verily I say unto you that
it is not needful that the Apocrypha should
be translated therefore whoso readeth it let him
understand for the Spirit manifesteth truth and
and whoso is enlightened by the Spirit shall
obtain benefit therefrom and whoso receiveth
not the Spirit cannot be benefited; therefore
it is not needful that it should be translated Amen

Kirtland 15th March 1833—
Verily thus saith the Lord I give unto the united firm
organized agreeable to the commandment previously
given a revelation & commandment concerning
my servant Frederick that ye shall receive him into
the firm what I say unto one I say unto all. And
again I say unto you my servant Frederick thou shalt
be a lively member in this firm and inasmuch as you
act faithful in keeping all former commandments
you shall be blessed for ever   Amen —

strong ones, and chasten her, until she overcomes, and

are clean before me; for she shall not be moved

out of her place, I the Lord have spoken it Amen

Geven by Joseph the seer and writen by—

Frederick councellor & Scribe
*And the residue of her money I will consecrate unto myself and reward her in mine own due time verely I say unto you that it is meet in mine eyes that she should go up unto the land ↵ of Zion.[75]

◆   Kirtland 9th of March 1833

A Revelation given concerning Apocrypha

☙[76] [Verily[77] thus saith the Lord unto you concerning

the Apocrypha there are many things contained

therein that are true and it is mostly tran-

-slated correct— there are many things contained

therein that are not true which are interpelations

by the hands of men varely I say unto you that

it is not needful that the Apocrypha should

be translated therefore[78] whoso readeth it let him

understand for the spirit manifesteth truth and

and whoso is enlightened by the spirit shall

obtain benifit therefrom and whoso receiveth

not the spirit cannot be benefited; Therefore

it is not needful that it should be translated. Amen

◆   K⟨i⟩rtland 15th March 1833—

1[79]
Verely thus saith the Lord I give unto the united firm

organized agreeable to the commandment previously

given a revelation & commandment concerning

2
my servant Frederick [G. Williams] that ye shall r[e]ceive him into

3
the firm what I say unto one I say unto all. and

4   you shall
again I say unto you my servant Frederick ~~thou shalt~~

5   you
be a lively member in this firm and inas much as ~~thou~~

ar{t\e} faithful in keeping all former commandments

you
~~thou~~ shal{t\l} be blessed for ever   Amen — — — —
^

ORIGINAL INSCRIPTION
Frederick G. Williams

REVISIONS
Oliver Cowdery
William W. Phelps
Joseph Smith
Frederick G. Williams
Unidentified

75. The asterisk at the beginning of this insertion refers to an asterisk on the previous page, indicating where the additional text should be inserted for publication.

76. "☙" possibly "◊".

77. The printer's mark before "Verily" possibly indicates the intent or instruction to publish this revelation in the 1835 Doctrine and Covenants. The text after the mark matches section 92 of that volume.

78. A pinhole and several scratch marks made by a pin appear after "therefore". This pinhole is in the same position as the one found on the following leaf but is slightly higher than the one found on the leaf containing manuscript pages 59–60. The relative positions of these pinholes indicate that a pin was pushed at an angle through manuscript pages 55–60, scratching manuscript page 59 before being forced through. These pinholes possibly resulted from pinning a slip of paper to manuscript page 55. The pinhead impression on the previous leaf indicates that the pin possibly remained in that position for some time before being removed. Because the text of the revelation on this page would have been obscured by the slip of paper, the slip may have been moved to manuscript page 54 during publication of the 1835 Doctrine and Covenants. (See 521n72 herein.)

79. The numbers inserted in this revelation, all inscribed in red grease pencil, appear above words that were changed to code words for publication in the 1835 Doctrine and Covenants (section 93). A key to these numbers was possibly pinned to this page and then moved to manuscript page 54. (See 521n72 herein.)

Verily thus saith the Lord, it shall come to pass that every soul who forsaketh their sins and cometh unto me and calleth on my name and obeyeth my voice and keepeth all my commandments, shall see my face and know that I am, and that I am the true light that lighteth every man who cometh into the world, and that I am in the Father and the Father in me, and the Father and I are one. The Father because he gave me of his fullness, and the Son because I was in the world and made flesh my tabernacle and dwelt among the sons of men. I was in the world and received of my Father, and the works of him were plainly manifest and I John saw and bare record of the fullness of my glory, and the fullness of John's record is hereafter to be revealed, and he bare record saying "I saw his glory that he was in the beginning before the world was. Therefore in the beginning the word was, for He was the word even the messenger of salvation, the light and the redeemer of the world; the spirit of truth who came into the world because the world was made by him, and in him was the life of men, and the light of men. The worlds were made by him. Men were made by him. All things were made by him and through him and of him. and I John bear record that I beheld his glory, as the glory of the onely begotten of the father full of grace and truth, even the spirit of truth which came and dwelt in flesh, and dwelt among us. And I John saw that he received not of the fullness at the first, but received grace for grace, and he received not of the fullness at first but continued from grace to grace untill he received a fullness, and thus he was called the Son of God because he received not of the fullness at the first. And I John bear record and lo; the heavens were opened and the holy Ghost descended upon him in the form of a dove and set upon him, and there came a voice out of heaven saying, this is my beloved son and I John bare record that he received a fullness of the glory of the Father

tabernacle of God. yea man is the tabernacle of God, even temples

and whatsoever temple is defiled God shall destroy that temple

The glory of God is intelligence, or in other words, light and truth

light and truth forsaketh that evil one. Every spirit of man was

innocent in the beginning, and God haveing redeemed man from

the fall, man became again in their infant state innocent before

God, and that wicked one cometh and taketh away light and truth

through disobedience from the children of men, and because of the

tradition of their fathers.\⁸³ But I have commanded you to bring up

your children in light and truth, but verily I say unto you, my

servant Frederick [G. Williams] you have continued under this condemnation

you have not taught your children light and truth according to

the commandments and that wicked one hath power as yet over

you, and this is the cause of your affliction. And now a comm-

andment I give unto you, and if ye will be delivered you shall

set in order your own house for there are many things that are

not right in your house. Verily I say⁸⁴ unto my servant Sidney [Rigdon]

that in some things he hath not kept the commandments concerning

his children. Therefore firstly set in order thy house. And verily I

say unto ~~you~~ my servant Joseph, or in otherwords, I will call you

friends for ye are my friends and ye shall have an inheritance with

me. I called you servants for the worlds sake. and ye are their

servants for my sake, and now verily I say unto ^you^ Joseph you have

not kept the commandments and must needs stand rebuked before

the lord. Your family must needs repent and forsake some

things. and give more earnest heed unto your sayings or be removed

out of their place. what I say unto one I say unto all. pray al-

ways lest that wicked one have power ^in^ ~~over~~ you, and remove

you out of your place. My servant Newell [Newel K. Whitney] also. the Bishop of

my church hath need to be chastened, and set in order his

family, and see that they are more dilligent and concerned

at home, and pray always or they shall be removed out of

their place. Now I say unto you my friends, let my serv-

ant Sidney go his journey and make haste and also proclaim

Original Inscription
Orson Hyde

Revisions
Oliver Cowdery
Orson Hyde
William W. Phelps
Joseph Smith
Frederick G. Williams
Unidentified

83. The 1835 Doctrine and Covenants (section 82) has a line break after "fa" in "fathers"; this mark was likely intended to correspond to that line break.

84. There is a pinhole below "say". (See 523n78 herein.)

the acceptable year of the Lord and the gospel of salvation as
I shall give him utterance and by your prayer of faith with
one consent. I will uphold him. and let my servants, Joseph
and Fredrick make haste also, and it shall be given them even
according to the prayer of faith, And in as much as you keep
my sayings you shall not be confounded in this world nor in
the world to come — And verily I say unto you that it is my
will that ye should hasten to translate my scriptures and to obtain a knowledge of history and of countries and of Kingdoms
and of laws of God and man, and all this for the salvation of
Zion, Amen

<hr>

Kirtland June 1st 1833

Verily thus saith the Lord unto you whom I love, and whom I love
I also chasten that their sins may be forgiven. for with the chastisement I prepare a way for their deliverance in all things out of
temptation and I have loved you therefore ye must needs be chast-
ned and stand rebuked before my face, for ye have sinned
against me a verry grievous sin in that ye have not considered
the great commandment in all things that I have given unto you
concerning the building of mine house for the preparation wherewith I design to prepare mine Apostles to prune my vineyard
for the last time that I may bring to pass my strange act
that I may pour out my spirit upon all flesh. But behold
verily I say unto you there are many who have been ordained
among you whom I have called but few of them are chosen. they
who are not chosen have sinned a verry grievous sin in that
they are walking in darkness at noon day. and for this cause
I gave unto you a commandment that you should call
your solem assembly that your fastings and your mourn-
ing might come up into the ears of the Lord of sabaoth
which is by interpretation the creator of ~~all things~~ the first day
the beginning and the End. Yea verily I say unto you I gave
unto you a commandment that you should build an house
in the which house I design to endow those whom I have

the acceptable year of the Lord and the gospel of salvation as

I shall give him utterance and by your prayer of faith with

one consent. I will uphold him. and let my servants Joseph

and Frederick make haste also, and it shall be given them even

according to the prayer of faith. And in as much as you keep

my sayings you shall not be confounded in this world nor in

the world to come— And verily I say unto you that it is my

will that ye should hasten to translate my scriptures and to obt-

ain a knowledge of history and of countries and of Kingdoms

and of laws of God and m{en\⟨an⟩}, and all this for the salvation of

Zion. Amen

<hr>

◆   Kirtland June 1ˢᵗ· 1833—

Verily thus saith the Lord unto you whom I love, and whom I love

I also chasten that their sins may be forgiven, for with the chas-

tisement I prepare a way for their deliverance in all things out of

temptation and I have loved you t{◊◊\herefore} ye must needs be chast-

ned and stand rebuked before my face. for ye have sinned

against me a verry grievous sin[85] in that ye have not considered

the great commandment in all things that I have given unto you

concerning the building of mine house for the preparation where-

-with I deign to prepare mine Apostles to prune my vineyard

for the last time that I may bring to pass my strange act

that I may pour out my spirit upon all flesh. But behold

verily I say unto you there are many who have been ordained

among you whom I called but few[86] of them are chosen. they
                    have

who are not chosen have sinned a verry grievous sin in that

they are walking in darkness at noon day, and for this cause

I gave unto you a commandment that you should call

your solem assembly that your fastings and your mourn-

-ing might come up into the ears of the Lord of sabaoth

which is by interpretation the creator of ~~all things~~ the first day

the beginning and the end. Yea verily I say unto you I gave

unto you a commandment that you should build an house

in the which house I design to endow those whom I have

ORIGINAL INSCRIPTION
Orson Hyde

REVISIONS
Oliver Cowdery
Orson Hyde
William W. Phelps
Joseph Smith
Frederick G. Williams
Unidentified

85. A pinhole and a scratch mark made by a pin appear above "sin". (See 523n78 herein.)

86. There are four pinholes in the words "but few" and several pinhead impressions below "called". (See 533n88 herein.)

chosen with power from on high, for this is the promise of the
Father unto you. Therefore, I commanded you to tarry even
as mine Apostles at Jerusalem. Nevertheless my servants sinned
a verry grievous sin and contentions arose in the school of
the prophets, which was verry grievous unto me saith your
Lord, therefore I sent them forth to be chastened. Verily I say
unto you, it is my will that you should build an house. If ye
keep my commandments, ye shall have power to build it. If
ye keep not my commandments the love of the father shall not
continue with you therefore ye shall walk in darkness. now
here is wisdom and the mind of the Lord, Let the house be
built not after the manner of this world, for I give not unto
you that ye shall live after the manner of the world. Therefore
let it be built after the manner which I shall show unto three
of you whom ye shall appoint and ordain unto this power
and the size thereof shall be fifty and five feet in width
and let it be sixty and five feet in length in the inner Court
thereof, and let the lower part of the inner court ~~thereof~~
be dedicated unto me for your sacrament offering and
for your preaching and your fasting and your praying
and the offering up your most holy desires unto me saith
your lord, and let the higher part of the inner Court be
dedicated unto me for the school of mine Apostles saith Son
ah Man, or in otherwords Alphas, or in other words Omegas
even Jesus Christ your lord Amen.

///

Kirtland June 4th 1833

Behold I say unto you here is wisdom whereby ye may
know how to act concerning this matter. for it is expedient
in me that this stake that I have set for the strength of
Zion should be made strong. Therefore let my servant
Shadarach
~~Aaron~~ take charge of the place which is named among you
upon which I design to build mine holy house, and again
let it be divided into lots, according to wisdom for the

in Zion, I the Lord am well pleased that there

should be a school in Zion: and also with
P Pratt
my servant Parley, for he abideth in me;

and inasmuch as he continue to abide

in me he shall continue to preside over
untill I shall give unto him other com{a\mandments};
the school, in the Land of Zion and I
^

will bless him with a multiplicity of

blessings, in expounding all scriptures

and mysteries to the Edefication of the

school, and of the church in Zion: and to

the residue of the school I {◊◊◊\the} Lord am

willing to shew mercy, nevertheless there

are those that must needs be chastened

and their works shall be mad[e] known{,\:} {t\T}he

axe is laid at the root of the tree{s\s}, and

evry trees that bringeth not forth good

fruit, shall be hewn down and cast into
                                      ¶
the fire: I the Lord hath spoken it{,\.} {v\V}erily

I say unto you, all among them who

know their hearts are honest, and are broken,

and their spirits contrite, and are willing

to observe their covenants by sacrifice; yea,

every sacrifice which I the Lord shall

command, they are all accepted of me,

for I the Lord will cause them to bring

forth as a very fruitful[97] tree which

is planted in a goodly land, by a pur{e\e}[98]

stream that yealdeth much precious

fruit{,\.} ¶ Verely I say unto you that it is

my will that an house should be built

unto me in the Land of Zion, like unto

the pattern which I have given you; yea,

let it be built speedely by the tithing

of my people: behold this is the tithing

ORIGINAL INSCRIPTION
Frederick G. Williams

REVISIONS
Oliver Cowdery
William W. Phelps
Joseph Smith
Frederick G. Williams
Unidentified

97. There are several pin-head impressions above "fruitful", indicating that the pin in the previous leaf remained in the same general location for some time. (See 533n88 herein.)

98. "e" likely inserted to clarify the original word, which had a misshapen "e".

and the sacrifice which I the Lord require at the
~~hand of~~ their hands, that there may be an house
built unto me for the salvation of Zion,
for a place of thanksgiving for all saints, and
for a place of instruction for all those who are
called to the work of the ministry, in all their
several callings, and offices: that they may be
perfected in the understanding of their min-
-istry; in theory; in principle, and in doc
-trine, in all things pertaining to the
Kingdom of God, on the earth, the keys
of which kingdom have been conferred
upon you, and inasmuch as my peo
-ple build an house unto me, in the name
of the Lord, and do not suffer any unclean
thing to come into it, that it be not
defiled, my glory shall rest upon it,
yea, and my presence shall be there, for I
will come into it and all the pure in heart
that shall come into it, shall see God,
but if it be defiled I will not come into
it, and my glory shall not be there, for I
will not come into unholy temples. I am
now behold if Zion do these things, she
shall prosper and spread herself and become
very glorious, very great and very terrible,
and the Nations of the earth shall honor
her, and shall say surely Zion is the city of
our God; and surely Zion cannot fall
neither be moved out of her place, for
God is there, and the hand of the Lord is
there, and he hath sworn by the power of
his might to be her salvation and
her high tower: therefore verily thus saith

and the sacrifice which I the Lord require at ~~the~~
~~hand~~ ~~of~~ there hands, that there may be an house
built unto me for the salvation of Zion:
for a place of thanksgiving, for all[99] saints, and
for a place of instruction for all those who ar{e\e}[100]
called to the work of the ministry, in all their
several callings, and offices: that they may be
perfected in the understanding of their min
-istry; in theory; in principle, and in doc
-trine, in all thing pertaining to the
Kingdom of God on the earth; the keys
of which kingdom have been confered
upon you. and inas much as my peo
-ple build an house unto me, in the name
of the Lord, and do not suffer any unclean
thing to come into it, that it be not
defiled, my glory shall rest upon it;
yea, and my presence shall be therefor I
will come into it and all the pure in heart
that shall come into it, shall see God:
but if it be defiled I will not come into
it, and my glory shall not be there, for I
will not come into unholy temples. ¶ and
now behold if Zion do these things, she
shall prosper and spread herself and become
very glorious, very great and very tereble;
and the Nations of the earth shall honor
her, and shall say surely Zion is the city of
our God; and surely Zion cannot fall,
neithe[r] be mooved out of her place, for
God is there, and the hand of the Lord is
there, and he hath sworn by the power of
his might to be her salvation, and
her high tower: therefore verily thus saith

ORIGINAL INSCRIPTION
Frederick G. Williams

REVISIONS
Oliver Cowdery
William W. Phelps
Joseph Smith
Frederick G. Williams
Unidentified

99. Ink blot before "all" possibly a cancellation of an illegible character.

100. "e" likely inserted to clarify the original word, which had a misshapen "e".

the Lord let Zion rejoice for this is Zion the
pure in heart; therefore let Zion rejoice
while all the wicked shall mourn; for
behold and lo, vengence cometh speedily upon
the ungodly, as the whirlwind, and who
shall escape it: the Lords scurge
shall pass over by night and by day; and
the report thereof shall vex all people, yet
it shall not be staid until the Lord
come; for the indignation of the Lord is
kindled against their abominations, and
all their wicked works: nevertheless Zion
shall escape if she observe to do all things
whatsoever I have commanded her, but if
she observe not to do whatsoever I have
commanded her, I will visit her according
to all her works, with sore affliction; with
pestilence; with plague, with sword, with
vengence; with devouring fire nevertheless
let it be read this once in their ears, that
I the Lord have accepted of their offering;
but if she sin no more none of these
things shall come upon her, and I will
bless her with blessings, and multiply
a multiplicity of blessings upon her,
and upon her generations for ever
and ever saith the Lord your God Amen

Kirtland 2d August 1833
And again verely I say unto you my
friends a commandment I give unto
you that ye shall commence a work of laying
out and preparing a beginning and
foundation of the City of the stake of Zion

64 [verso]

the Lord let Zion rejoice, for this Zion, the

pure in heart:[101] therefore let Zion rejoice,

while all the wicked shall mourn: for

behold and lo, vengence cometh speedily upon

the ungodly, as the whirlwind, and who

shall escape it: the Lords scurge shall

shall pass over by night and by day; and

the report thereof shall vex all people, yet

it shall not be staid until the Lord

come: for the indignation of the Lord is

kindled against their abominations, and

all their wicked works: nevertheless {◊◊\Zion}

shall escape if she observe to do all things

whatsoever I have commanded her, but if

she observe not to do whatsoeve[r] I have

commanded her, I will visit her according

to all her works; with sore afflictions; with

pestilence; with plague; with sword; with

vengence; with devouring fire: nevertheless,

let it be read this once in their ears, that

I the Lord have accepted of their offering{:\.}

{b\B}ut if she sin no more none of these

things shall come upon her, and I will

bless her with blessings, and multiply

a multiplicity of blessing upon her,

and upon her generations for ever

and ever, saith the Lord your God. Amen

◆ [102]Kirtland 2^d August 1833

And again verely I say unto {◊\you} my

friends a commandment I give unto

you that ye shall commence a work of laying

out and preparing a begining and

foundation of the city of the stake of Zion

ORIGINAL INSCRIPTION
Frederick G. Williams

REVISIONS
Oliver Cowdery
William W. Phelps
Joseph Smith
Frederick G. Williams
Unidentified

101. Double underlining indicates the intent or instruction to set this text in small caps, which is how it appears in the 1835 Doctrine and Covenants.

102. The first publication reflecting several redactions in this revelation is the 1835 Doctrine and Covenants (section 83).

hou in the land of Kirtland beginning
at my house and behold it must be done
according to the pattern which I have given
unto you and let the first lot on the South
consecrated unto me for the building of an
house for the presidency for the work of the
presidency in obtaining revelations and
for the work of the ministry of the presidency
in all things pertaining to the church and
kingdom verely I say unto you that it
shall be built fifty five by sixty five feet in
the width thereof and in the length thereof
in the inner court and there shall be a
lower court and an higher court according
to the pattern which shall be given unto you
hereafter and it shall be dedicated unto
the Lord from the foundation thereof
according to the order of the Priesthood
according to the pattern which shall be
given unto you hereafter and it shall
be wholly dedicated unto the Lord for
the work of the presidency and ye shall not
suffer any unclean thing to come into it
and my glory shall be there and my presence shall be there but if there shall
come into it any unclean thing my
glory shall not be there and my presence shall not come into it and again
verely I say unto you the second lot on
the South shall be dedicated unto me for
the building of an house unto me
for the work of the printing of the
translation of my scriptures and all
things whatsoever I shall command you

here in the land of Kirtland begining

at my house and behold it must be done

according to the pattern which I have given

unto you and let the first lot on the south ^be^

consecrated unto me for the building of an

house for the presidency for the work of the

presidency in obtaining revelations and

for the work of the ministry of the presidency

in all things pertaining to the Church and

Kingdom verely I say unto you that it

shall be built fifty five by sixty five ^-feet^ in

the width thereof and in the length thereof

in the inner court and there shall be a

lower court and an higher court according

to the pattern which shall be given unto you

hereafter and it shall be dedecated unto

the Lord from the foundation thereof

according to the order of the Priesthood

according to the pattern which shall be

given unto you hereafter and it shall

be wholly dedecated unto the Lord for

the work of the presedency and ye shall not

suffer any unclean thing to come into it

and my glory shall be there and my pres-

ence shall be there but if ther shall

come into it any unclean thing my

glory shall not be there and my pres-

ence shall not come into it and again

verily I say unto you the seccond lot on

the south shall be dedecated unto me for

the building of an house unto me

for the work of the printing of the

translation of my scripturs and all

things whatsoever I shall command you

ORIGINAL INSCRIPTION
Frederick G. Williams

REVISIONS
Oliver Cowdery
William W. Phelps
Joseph Smith
Frederick G. Williams
Unidentified

and it shall be fifty five by sixty five feet
in the width there of and in the length there
of — is the inner court and there shall be a
lower and an higher court and this house
shall be wholly dedecated unto the Lord from
the foundation there of for the work of
the printing in all thing whatsoever I
shall command you to be holy and un-
-defiled according to the pattern in all
things as it shall be given unto you
and on the third lot shall my servant
Hyrum receive his inheritance and
on the first and second lots on the
North shall my servants Reynolds
and Jared receive their inheritance
that they may do the work which I
have appointed unto them to be a
committe to build mine houses
according to the commandment
which I the Lord God have given
unto you and now I give unto you
no more at this time Amen — (them
There two houses are not to be beualt till I give you a command ment concerning

Kirtland 6th of August 1833 —
Verely I say unto you my friends fear not
let your hearts be comforted yea rejoice
ever more and in every thing give thanks
waiting patiently on the Lord for your
prayers have entered into the ears of the
of the Lord of Sabbaoth and are recorded
with this seal and testement the Lord hath
sworn and decreed that they shall be
granted therefor he giveth this promise
unto you with an immutable covenant

66 [verso]

and it shall be fifty five by sixty five feet

in the width therof and in the length there

of— in the inne[r] court and there shall be a[103]

lower {◊◊\and} an higher court and this house

shall be wholly dedecated unto the Lord from

the foundation there of for the work of

the printing in all thing whatsoever I

shall command you to be holy and un-

-defiled according to the pattern in all

things as it shall be given unto you

and on the third lot shall my servant

Hyrum [Smith] receive his inheritance and

on the first and seccond lots on the

North shall my servants Reynolds [Cahoon]

and Jared [Carter] receive their inheritence

that they may do the work which I

have appointed unto them to be a

committe to build mine houses

according to the commandment

which I the Lord God have given

unto you and now I give unto you

no more at this time Amen   (them
These two houses are not to be built till I give you a commandment concerni[n]g

♦   Kirtland {◊\6}th[104] of August 1833—

Verily I say unto you my friends fear not

let your hearts be comforted yea rejoice

ever more and in evry thing give thanks

waiting patiently on the Lord for your

prayers have entered into the ears of the

of the Lord of sabbaoth and are recorded

with this seal and testament the Lord hath

sworn and decreed that they shall be

granted therefore he giveth this promise

unto you with an immutable covenant

ORIGINAL INSCRIPTION
Frederick G. Williams

REVISIONS
Oliver Cowdery
William W. Phelps
Joseph Smith
Frederick G. Williams
Unidentified

103. "a" possibly inserted.
104. "◊" possibly "7" or "9".

that they shall be fulfilled and all things where
with you have been afflicted shall work
together for your good and to my names
glory saith the Lord God and now verily I say
unto you concerning the Laws of the land it is
my will that my people should observe to do
all things whatsoever I command them and that
Law of the land which is constitutional sup-
-ting the principles of freedom in maintaining the
rights and priviledges belonging to all mankind
is justifyable before me therefore I the Lord Justify
you and your Brethren of my Church in
befriending that Law which is the constitut-
-onal Law of the land and as pertaining to law
of man whatsoever is more or less than this cometh of evil
I the Lord your God maketh you free therefore ye are
free indeed and the law also maketh you free
nevertheless when the wicked rule the people do mourn
whereupon honest men and wise men should be sought
for diligently and good men and wise men ye should
observe to uphold otherwise whatsoever is less than these
cometh of evil and again unto you a commandm
-ent that ye shall forsake all evil and cleave unto
all good that ye shall live by every word that proceedeth
forth out of the mouth of God for he will give unto the
faithful line upon line precept upon precept and he
will try you and prove you herewith and whoso layeth
down his life in my cause for my name sake shall
find it again even life eternal therefore be not
afraid of your enemies for I have decreed in my
heart saith the Lord that I will prove you in
all things whether you will abide in my covenant
even unto death that ye may be found worthy
for if ye will not abide in my covenant ye are

[105]that they shall be fulfilled and all things where

-with you have been afflicted shall work

together for your good and to my names

glory saith the Lord ^God^ and now verely I say

unto you concerning the Laws of the land it is

my will that my people {◊\should} observe to do

all things whatsoever {i\I} ^m^comand them and that

Law of the land which is constitutonal supor

=ting the principles of freedom in maintaning ^the^

rights and privealiges belonging to all mankind

is justifyable before me therefore I the ^Lord^ justify

you and your Brotheren of my Chirch in ◊◊[106]

befriending that Law which ^is^ the constituto

=onal Law of the land and as pertaining to law

of man whatsoever is {◊\more} or less then this cometh of evil

I the Lord your God maketh you free therefore ye are

free indeed and the law also maketh you free—

nevertheless when the wicked rule the people mo{r\urn}

wherefore honest men and wise men should be sought

for dilligently and good men and wise men ye should

observe to uphold otherwise whatsoever is less then these

cometh of evil and I give unto you a commandm-

-ent that ye shall forsake all evil and cleave unto

all good that ye shall live by evry word that procedeth

forth out of the mouth of God for he will give unto the

faithful {l◊◊◊\line}[107] ^line^ upon line precept upon precept and {I\he}

will try you and prove you herewith and whoso layeth

down his life in my cause for my name sake shall

find it again even life eternal therefore be not

afraid of your enemies for I have decreed in my

heart saith the Lord that I will prove you in

all things whether you will abide in my covenant

even unto death that ye may be found worthy

for if ye will not abide in my covenant ye are

Original Inscription
Frederick G. Williams
Joseph Smith

Revisions
Oliver Cowdery
William W. Phelps
Joseph Smith
Frederick G. Williams
Unidentified

105. Pinhead impressions on this page correspond to the position of pinholes on manuscript pages 69–70, where a slip of paper was pinned. (See 555n111 herein.)

106. "◊◊" wipe-erased and then stricken.

107. "l◊◊◊" wipe-erased and written over; then whole word stricken.

not worthy of me therefore renounce war and proclaim
peace and seek diligently to turn the hearts of the
children to their fathers and the hearts of the fathers
to the children ~~and the hearts of the fathers to the
children~~, and again the hearts of the Jews unto the
prophets and the prophets unto the Jews lest I come
and smite the whole earth with a curse and all
all flesh be consumed before me let not your
hearts be troubled for in my fathers house is
are many mansions and I have prepared
a place for you and when my father and I am
then ye shall be also behold I the Lord
am not well pleased with many who are
in the church at Kirtland for they do
not forsake their sins and their wicked ways
the pride of their hearts and their covetousness
and all their detestable things and observe
the words of wisdom and eternal Life which
I have given unto them verily I say unto you
that I the Lord will chasten them ~~and~~
and will do whatsoever I list if they do
not repent and observe all things whatsoever
I have said unto them and again I say unto
you if ye observe to do whatsoever I command
you the Lord will turn away all wrath and indignation from you and the gates of hell shall
not prevail against you, now I speak unto
you concerning your families, if men will
smite you or your families once and ye
bear it patiently and revile not against
them neither ~~will~~ seek revenge ye shall be
rewarded but if ye bear it not patiently
it shall be accounted unto ~~you~~ you as being
meted out a just measure unto you and

68 [verso]

¹⁰⁸not worthy of me therefore renounce war and proclaim

peace and seek dilligently to turn the hearts of the

Children to their fathers and the hearts of the father

to the Children ~~and the hearts of the father to the~~

~~Children~~, and again the hearts of the Jews unto the

prophets and the prophets unto the Jews lest I come

and smite the whole earth with a curse ⟨and⟩ ~~all~~

all fles{s\h} be consumed before me let not your

hearts be troubled for in my father['s] house ~~is~~

are many mansions and I have prepared
      you
a place for ‸ and {◊\where} my father and I am

there ye shall be also behold I the Lord

am not well {◊\pleased} with many who are

in the church at Kirtland for they do

not forsake their sins and their wicked ways

the pride of their hearts and their covetiousness

and all their detestable things and {~~the~~\observe}

{◊\the} words of wisdom and eternal Life which

I have given unto them verily I say unto you

that I the Lord will chasten them ~~verily~~

and will do whatsoever I List if they do

not repent and observe all things whatsoever

I have said unto {~~you~~\them} and again I say unto

you if ye {◊◊s\observe} to do whatsoevr I command
      away
you I the Lord will turn all ‸ wrath and indig-

-nation from you and the gates of hell shall

not prevail against you, Now I speak unto

you concerning your families, if men will

smite you or your families once and ye

bear it patiently and revile not against

them neither ~~revile~~ seek revenge ye shall be

rewarded but if ye bear it not patiently
     you
it shall be accounted unto ~~them~~ ‸ as being

meeted out a just measure unto you and

ORIGINAL INSCRIPTION
Frederick G. Williams

REVISIONS
Oliver Cowdery
William W. Phelps
Joseph Smith
Frederick G. Williams
Unidentified

108. Pinhead impressions on this page correspond to the position of pinholes on manuscript pages 69–70, where a slip of paper was pinned. (See 555n111 herein.)

again if your enemies shall smite you a secend
time and you revile not against your enemy &
bear it patiently your reward shall be an hundred
fold and again if he shall smite you a third time
and ye bear it patiently your reward shall be doubled
unto you four fold and these three testimonies shall
stand against your enemy if he repent not and shall
not be blotted out, and now verely I say unto you
if that enemy shall escape my vengence that he
be not brought into Judgment before me then ye
shall see to it that ye warn him in my name
that he come no more upon you neither upon
your families neither your children nor your chil
dren Children unto the third and fourth Gen
eration and then if he shall come upon you
or your Children or your childrens Children
unto the third and forth generation ~
I have deliverd
thine enemy into thine hands and then if thou
reward him according to his works thou art
Justified if he has sought thy life and thy life
is endangered by him, thine enemy is in
thine hands and thou art Justified behold
this is the Law I gave unto my servant
Nephi and thy fathers Joseph and Jacob Isaac
and Abraham and all mine ancient
prophets and Apostles and again this is the
Law that I gave unto mine ancient that they
should not go out unto battle against any
Nation kindred Tongue or people save I the
Lord commanded them and if any Nation
Tongue or people should proclaim war against
them they should first lift a standard of peace
unto that people Nation or tongue and if
that people did not accept the offering of

70 [verso]

¹¹³peace neithr the seccond nor third time they should

bring their testamonies before the Lord then I the

Lord would give unto them a commandment

and justify them in going out to battle against

that Nation Tongue or people and I the Lord

would fight their battles and their childrens battles

Battle
and their children['s] children['s] until they had
                              ^

avenged themselves {of\upon} all their enemies

unto the third and◊ forth generation, behold

this is an ensample unto all people saith

the Lord your God for justification befor me

and again verely I say unto you if after

thine enemy has come upon thee the first time

and he repent and come unto thee praying

thy forgivness thou shalt forgive him and sha{ll\lt}

hold it no more as a testamony against thine

enemy and so on unto the seccond and third

time and as oft as thine enemy repenteth

of the trespass wherewith he has trespassed—

against thee thou shalt forgive him until

seventy times seven and if he trespass against

thee and repent not the first time nevertheless

thou shalt forgive him and if he trespass

against thee seccond time and repent not

never theless thou shalt forgive him and if

he tresspass against thee the third time and

repent not thou shalt also forgive him but

the[e]
if he trespass against ~~him~~ the forth time

thou shalt not forgive him but shall

bring these testamon[i]es before the Lord and they

shall not be blotted out untill he repen{t\ts}

and rewards th{em\ee} four fold in all things

wherewith he has trespased against ~~them~~ [thee] and

~~if~~ and if he do this thou shalt forgive him

ORIGINAL INSCRIPTION
Frederick G. Williams

REVISIONS
Oliver Cowdery
William W. Phelps
Joseph Smith
Frederick G. Williams
Unidentified

113. This page contains a series of pinholes. (See 553n109 herein.)

with all their heart and if he do not this I the Lord
will avenge thee of thine enemy and hundred fold
and upon his children and upon his Children
Children of all them that hate me unto the third and
forth generation but if the Children Shall repent
on the childrens children and turn unto the Lord
their God with all their heart with all their might
mind and strength and restore fourfould for
all their trespasses wherewith they have trespassed
or wherewith their fathers have trespassed or their
fathers fathers then thine indignation Shall be
turned away and vengeance Shall no more
come upon them Saith the Lord your God
and their trespasses shall never be brought any
more as a testimony before the Lord against
them Amen —

Perrysburgh, Chautauque County, New York, Saturday, October 12, 1833.
A Revelation to Joseph and Sidney, given them while on
their journey to Canada, according to direction of the Spirit.

Verily thus saith the Lord unto you my friends, Sidney
and Joseph, your families are well; they are in mine
hands, and I will do with them as seemeth me good; for
in me there is all power. Therefore, follow me and listen
to the counsel which I shall give unto you: Behold, and lo,
I have much people in this place in the regions round about,
and an effectual door shall be opened in the regions round
about in this eastern lands. Therefore, I the Lord have suffered you to come unto this place, for thus it was expedient
in me for the salvation of souls. Therefore, verily I say unto you,
lift up your voices unto this people, speak the thoughts
that I shall put into your hearts, and ye shall not be
confounded before men; for it shall be given you in
the very hour, yea, in the very moment what ye shall say.

with all thine heart and if he do not this I the Lord

will avenge thee of thine enem{ies\y} and [an] hundred fold

and upon his children and upon his childrens

children of all them that hate me unto the third and

forth generation but if the children shall repent

or the childrens children and turn unto the Lord

their God with all their heart with all their might

mind and strenght and restore four fould for

all their trespasses wherewith they have trespassed

or wherewith their fathers have trespassed or their

fathers fathers then thine indignation shall be

turned away and vengence shall no more

come upon them saith the Lord your God

and their trespasses shall neve[r] be brought any

more as a testamony before the Lord against

them Amen———

ORIGINAL INSCRIPTION
Frederick G. Williams
Oliver Cowdery

REVISIONS
Oliver Cowdery
William W. Phelps
Joseph Smith
Frederick G. Williams
Unidentified

114. Frederick G. Williams handwriting ends; Oliver Cowdery begins. The first publication reflecting most redactions in this revelation is the 1835 Doctrine and Covenants (section 94).

115. Oliver Cowdery's revisions throughout this revelation were possibly made after the time of original inscription.

◆ /¹¹⁴Perrysburgh, Chautauque [Cattaraugus] County New York, Saturday, October 12, 1833.¹¹⁵

A Revelation to Joseph and Sidney [Rigdon], given them while on

their journey to Canada, according to direction of the Spirit.

Verily thus saith the Lord unto you my friends, ~~Joseph,~~ Sidney,

and ~~Sidney,~~ Joseph, your families are well; they are in mine

hands, and I will do with them as seemeth me good; for

in me there is all power. Therefore, follow me and ~~give~~ listen

to the counsel which I shall give unto you: Behold, and lo,

I have much people in this place in the regions round about,

and an effectual door shall be opened in the regions round

about in th{e\is} eastern land{s\.} Therefore, I the Lord have suf=

=fered you to come unto this place, for thus it was expedient

in me for the salvation of souls. Therefore, verily I say unto you,

lift up your voices unto this people, speak the thoughts

that I shall put {u\i}nto your hearts, and ye shall not be

confounded before men; for it shall be given you in

the very hour, yea, in the very moment what ye shall say.

But a commandment I give unto you, that ye shall declare whatsoever things ye declare in my name, in solemnity of heart in the spirit of meekness, in all things. And I give unto you this promise, that inasmuch as ye do this the Holy Ghost shall be shed forth in bearing record unto all things whatsoever ye shall say.

And it is expedient in me, that my servant you, Sidney, should be a spokesman unto this people; yea, verily, I will ordain you unto this calling; even to be a spokesman unto my servant Joseph. And I will give unto him power to be mighty in testimony. And I will give unto thee power to be mighty in expounding all scriptures, that thou mayest be a spokesman unto him, and he shall be a revelator unto thee, that thou mayest know the certainty of all things pertaining to the things of my kingdom on the earth. Therefore, continue your journey and let your hearts rejoice, for behold, and lo, I am with you even unto the end.

And now I give unto you a word concerning Zion: Zion shall be redeemed although she is chastened for a little season: Thy brethren, my servants, Orson, Hyde, John Gould, are in my hands, and inasmuch as they keep my commandments they shall be saved.

Therefore, let your hearts be comforted, for all things shall work together for good to them that walk uprightly; and to the sanctification of the church; for I will raise up unto myself a pure people that will serve me in righteousness: And all that call on the name of the Lord and keep his commandments shall be saved; even so, Amen.

But a commandment I give unto you, that ye

shall declare whatsoever things ye declare in my name

in solemnity of heart in the spirit of meekness in all

things. And I give unto you this promise, that in as=

=much as ye do this the Holy Ghost shall be shed forth

in bearing record unto all things whatsoever ye ~~shal~~

shall say.

                                  my servant
And it is expedient in me, that you, Sidney,

should be a spokesman unto this people; yea, verily I will

ordain you unto this calling; even to be a spokesman unto

my servant Joseph. And I will give unto him

power to be mighty in testimony. And I will give

unto thee power to be mighty in expounding all scrip=

=tures,[115] that thou mayest be a spokesman unto him,

and he shall be a revelator unto thee, that thou

mayest know the certainty of all things pertaining to

the things of my kingdom on the earth. Therefore, con=

=tinue your journey and let your hearts rejoice, for

behold, and lo, I am with you even unto the end.

And now I give unto you a word concerning Zion:
                       although
Zion shall be redeemed ~~after~~ she is chastened for a
                                        Hyde
little season: Thy brethren, my servants, Orson, &
   Gould
John, are in my hands, and inasmuch as they

keep my commandments they shall be saved.

    Therefore, let your hearts be comforted, for all

things shall work together for good to them that walk

uprightly; and to the sanctification of the church; for

I will raise up unto myself a pure people that will

serve me in righteousness: And all that call on the

name of the Lord and keep h⟨i⟩s commandments

shall be saved{;\:} even so; Amen.

ORIGINAL INSCRIPTION
Oliver Cowdery

REVISIONS
Oliver Cowdery
William W. Phelps
Joseph Smith
Frederick G. Williams
Unidentified

115. "s" possibly inserted.

Verily I say unto you concerning your brethren who have been afflicted, and persecuted, and cast out from the land of their inheritance, I the Lord have suffered the affliction to come upon them, wherewith they have been afflicted, in consequence of their transgressions; yet I will own them, and they shall be mine in that day when I shall come to make up my jewels. Therefore they must needs be chastened, and tried, even as Abraham, who was commanded to offer up his only son; for all those who will not endure chastening, but deny me, cannot be sanctified. Behold I say unto you, there were jarrings, and contentions, & envyings, and strifes, and lustful and covetous desires among them; Therefore by these things they polluted their inheritances; they were slow to hearken unto the voice of the Lord their God. Therefore the Lord their God is slow to hearken unto their prayers, to answer them in the day of their trouble. In the day of their peace they esteemed lightly my counsel; but in the day of their trouble, of necessity they feel after me. Verily I say unto you, notwithstanding their sins, my bowels are filled with compassion towards them; I will not utterly cast them off, and in the day of wrath I will remember mercy, I have sworn and the decree hath gone forth by a former commandment which I have given unto you, that I would let fall the sword of mine indignation in the behalf of my people. and even as I have said

♦ /[116]Verily I say unto you concerning your breth

-ren who have been afflicted, and persecuted,

and cast out from the Land of their inheriten=

=ces. I the Lord have suffered the affliction to come

upon them, wherewith they have been afflicted,

in consequence of their transgressions; yet, I

will own them and they shall be mine in that

day when I shall come to make up my jewels.

Therefore, they must needs be chastened, and

tried, even as Abraham, who was comman-

-ded to offer up his only son; for all those

who will not endure chastening, but deny me,

cannot be sanctified, Behold I say unto you,

there were jar[r]ings, and contentions, & envyings,

and strifes, and lustful and covetous desires

among them; Therefore, by these things they

poluted their inheritances; they were ~~also~~

slow to hearken unto the voice of the Lord

their God. Therefore the Lord their God

is slow to hearken unto their prayers, to

answer them in the day of their trouble:

In the day of their peace they esteemed

lightly my council; but in the day of their

trouble, of necessity they feel after me.

Verely, I say unto you, notwit{s\hstanding}

their sins, my bowels are filled with compas-

-sion towards[117] them; I will not utterly cast

them off; and in the day of wrath I will

remember mercy, I have sworn and the

decree hath gone forth by a former com-

-mandment which I have given unto

you, that I would let fall the sword

of mine indignation in the behalf

of my people. and even as I have said

ORIGINAL INSCRIPTION
Frederick G. Williams

REVISIONS
Oliver Cowdery
William W. Phelps
Joseph Smith
Frederick G. Williams
Unidentified

116. Oliver Cowdery hand-writing ends; Frederick G. Williams begins. Much of the punctuation in this revelation was possibly inserted at the time of original inscription.

117. "s" wipe-erased and then stricken.

it shall come to pass. Mine indignation is soon to be poured out without measure upon all nations, and this will I do when the cup of their iniquity is full; and in that day, all who are found upon the watch tower, or in other words, all mine Israel shall be saved; and they that have been scattered shall be gathered; and all they who have mourned shall be comforted; and all they who have given their lives for my name, shall be crowned. Therefore, let your hearts be comforted concerning Zion, for all flesh is in mine hands: be still, and know that that I am God. Zion shall not be moved out of her place, Notwithstanding, her children are scattered; they that remain and are pure in heart, shall return and come to their inheritances, they and their children, with songs of everlasting joy, to build up the waste places of Zion; and all these things that the prophets might be fulfilled. And behold, there is none other place appointed than that which I have appointed, neither shall there be any other place appointed than that which I have appointed for the work of the gathering of my saints until the day cometh when there is found no more room for them, ↑then I have other places which I will appoint unto them↑ and they shall be called stakes for the curtains or strength of Zion.

Behold it is my will that all they who call on my name and

it shall come to pass{,\.} {m\M}ine indignation

is soon to be poured without measure upon

all nations, and this will I do when the

cup of their eniquity is full; and in

that day, all who are found upon the

watch tower, or in other words, all mine

Israel shall be saved; and they that have

been scattered shall be gathered; and all

they who have mourned shall be comforted,

and all they who have given their lives

for my name, shall be crowned,

Therefore, let your hearts be comforted

concerning Zion, for all flesh is in

mine hands: be still, and know that

that I am God: Zion shall not be moved

out of her place{,\.} {n\N}otwithstanding, her

children are scattered, they that remain

and are pure in heart, shall return

and come to their inheritances, they and

their children, with songs of everlasting

joy, to build up the waste places of Zion;

and all these things that the prophets might

~~might~~ be fulfilled. {a\A}nd behold, there is

none other place appointed than that

which I have appointed, neither shall there

be any other place appointd th{at\en} that

which I have appointed for the work

of the gathering of my saints until the

day cometh when there is found no

& then I have other places which I will ~~and the{◊\n} I have other places~~ appoint unto=

more room for them ◊[118]and they shall =them[119]

be called stakes for the curtain{s\s}, ~~of Zion~~

or strength of Zion.

{b\Behold} it is my will that all

they who call on my name and

ORIGINAL INSCRIPTION
Frederick G. Williams

REVISIONS
Oliver Cowdery
William W. Phelps
Joseph Smith
Frederick G. Williams
Unidentified

118. "◊" wipe-erased and then stricken.

119. Oliver Cowdery began writing this insertion in the middle of the line but then ran out of space. He struck the insertion and began again at the beginning of the line.

worship me according to mine everlasting
gospel, should gather together and stand in
holy places, and prepare for the revelation
which is to come when the veil of the covering
of my temple in my tabernacle which hideth
the earth shall be taken off and all flesh
shall see me together. And every corruptable
thing, both of men, or of the beasts of the field
or of the fowls of heaven or of the fish
of the sea, that dwell upon all the face
of the earth shall be consumed. And also
that of element shall melt with fervent
heat and all things shall become
new that my knowledge and glory may
dwell upon all the earth and in that
day the enmity of men and the enmity of beasts yea the enmity of all
flesh shall cease from before my face.
And in that day whatsoever any man
shall ask it shall be given unto him
and in that day Satan shall not
have power to tempt any man; and
there shall be no sorrow because there
is no death, In that day an infant
shall not die until he is old, and his life
shall be as the age of a tree; and when he
dies he shall not sleep, (that is to say in the
earth) but shall be changed in the twinkling of an eye, and shall be caught
up, and his rest shall be glorious; yea,
verily, I say unto you, in that day
when the Lord shall come he shall reveal all things, things which have passed
and hidden things which no man knew

worship me according to mine everlasting

gospel, should gather to gether and stand in

holy places and prepare for the revelation

which is to come when the veil of the covering

of my temple in my tabernacle which hideth

the earth shall be taken off[120] and all flesh

shall see me together and evry coruptable

thing, both of man, or of {of\the} beasts of the field

or of the fowls of heaven or of the fish

of the sea, that dwell upon all the face of

of the earth shall be consumed. And also

that of {Ele\element} shall melt with ferva

-nt heat and all things shall become

new that my knowledge and glory may

dwell upon all the earth and in that

day the enmity of man and the en-

-mity of beasts yea the enmity of all

flesh shall cease from before my face.

And in that day whatsoever any man

{ask\shall} ask it shall be given unto him

and in that day shall satan shall not

have power to tempt any man; and

there shall be no sorrow because there

is no death, In that day an infant

shall not _{die} until he is old, and his life

shall be as the age of a tree: and when he

dies he shall not sleep, (that is to say in the

earth,) but shall be changed in the twin-

-kling of an eye, and shall be caught

up; and his rest shall be glorious; yea,

verely, I say unto you, in that day

when the Lord shall come he shall rev-

-eal all things, things which have passed

and hidden things which no man {kno\know}

ORIGINAL INSCRIPTION
Frederick G. Williams

REVISIONS
Oliver Cowdery
William W. Phelps
Joseph Smith
Frederick G. Williams
Unidentified

120. Second "f" possibly inserted.

things of the earth by which it was made and
the purpose and the end thereof; things most
precious; things that are above, and things that
are beneath, things that are in the earth and
upon the earth, and in heaven; And all they that
suffer persecution for my name and endure
in faith, though they are called to lay down their
lives for my sake yet shall they partake of
all this glory wherefore fear not even unto
death for in this world your joy is not full
but in me your joy is full therefore care
not for the body neither for the life of the
body but care for the soul and for the
life of the soul and seek the face of the
Lord always that in patience ye may possess
your souls and ye shall have eternal life
When men are called unto mine everlasting
gospel and covenant with an everlasting cov-
-enant they are accounted as the salt of
the earth and the savor of men; they are
called to be the savor of men; therefore if
that salt of the earth hath lost its savor
behold it is thenceforth good for nothing
only to be cast out and trodden under the
feet of men. Behold here is wisdom
concerning the children of Zion even many
but not all they were found transgressors
therefore they must needs be chastened
he that exalteth himself shall be abased
and he that abaseth himself shall be exalted
And now I will shew unto you a parable
that you may know my will concerning
the redemption of Zion A certain nobleman
had a spot of land very choice and he

and establish her waste places no more to be

thrown down were the churches who call themsel-

-ves after my name willing to {hear\harken} to my

voice and again I say unto you those who

have been scattered by their enemies it is

my will that they should continue to impor

-tune for redress and redemption by the

hand of those who are placed as rulers and

are in authority over you according to the

La{◊\w} and constitution of the people which

I have suffered to be established and should

be maintained for the rights and protection

of all flesh according to just and holy prin-

ciples, that evry man may act in doctrine

and principle pertaining to futurity

according to the moral agency which I

have given unto them that evry man

may be accountable for his own sin{ i\s}n̶¹²⁶

the day of judgment therefor it is not

right that any man should be in bon-

-dage one to another and for this purpose

have I established the constitution of this

Land by the hands of wise men whom

I raised up unto this very purpose and

redeemed the Land by the shedding of

blood, Now unto what shall I liken

the children of Zion I will liken them t̶o̶

unto the parable of the woman and the

unjust judge (for men ought always

to pray and not faint) which saith

there was in a city a judge which

feared not God neither regarded

man and there was a widow in that

city and she came unto him saying

ORIGINAL INSCRIPTION
Frederick G. Williams

REVISIONS
Oliver Cowdery
William W. Phelps
Joseph Smith
Frederick G. Williams
Unidentified

126. "sin in" changed to
"sins".

avenge me of mine adversary and he would
not for a while but afterward he said
within himself though I fear not God nor
regard man yet because this widow
troubleth me I will avenge her lest
by her continual coming she weary
me thus will I liken the children of
Zion let them importune at the feet
of the Judge and if he hear them
not let them importune at the feet of
the Governor and if the Governor hear them
not let them importune at the feet
of the President and if the President
hear them not then will the Lord arise
and come forth out of his hiding place &
in his fury vex the nation and in
his hot displeasure and in his fierce
anger in his time will cut off those
wicked unfaithful and unjust stew
-ards and appoint them their portion
among hypocrits and unbelievers even
in outer darkness where there is weeping
and wailing and gnashing of teeth
pray ye therefore that their ears may be
be opened unto your cries that I may
be merciful unto them that these things
may not come upon them what I have said
unto you must needs be that all men
may be left without excuse that all
men and rulers may hear and know
that which they have never considered
that I may proceed to bring to pass
my act my strange act and perform
my work my strange work that men

avenge me of mine adver[s]ary and he would

not for a while but afterward he said

within himself though I fear not God nor

regard man yet because this widow

troubleth me I will avenge her lest

by her continual coming she weary

me thus will I liken the children of

Zion let them impertune at the feet

of the judge and if he heed them

not let them impertune at the feet of

the Govoner and if the Govoner heed them

not let them importune at the feet

of the President and if the President

heed them not then will the Lord arise

and come forth out of his place &

     hiding

in his fury vex the nation and in

his hot displeasure and in his fierce

 anger

~~ander~~ in his time will cut off these

wicked unfaithful and unjust stew-

-ards and appoint them their portion[127]

among hypocrits and unbelievers even

in outer darkness where there is weeping

and wailing and gnashing of teeth

pray ye therefore that their ears may

be opened {to\unto} your cries that I may

be merciful unto them that these things

 may come

~~come~~ not upon them what I have said

unto you must needs be that all men

may be left without excuse that wise

men and rulers may hear and know

that which {I\⟨they⟩} have never considered

that I may procede to bring to pass

my act my strange act and perform

my work my strange work that men

Original Inscription
Frederick G. Williams

Revisions
Oliver Cowdery
William W. Phelps
Joseph Smith
Frederick G. Williams
Unidentified

127. Possibly "portions".

may desern between the righteous and the
wicked saith your God and again I say
unto you it is contreary to my commandment and my will that my servant
Algenon Sidney Gilbert should sell my
store house which I have appointed unto
my people into the hands of mine en-
mies let not that which I have
appointed be poluted by mine enem-
is by the consent of them who call themselves after my name for this is a very
sore and grievious sin against me and
against my people in consequence of those
things which I have decreed and are
soon to befall the nations therefore it is
my will that my people should
claim and hold claim upon that
which I have appointed unto them
though they should not be permited
to dwell thereon nevertheless I do not
say they shall not dwell thereon for in
as much as they bring forth fruit
and works meet for my Kingdom
they shall dwell thereon they shall
build and another shall not inherit it & they shall plant vineyards
and they shall eat the fruit thereof
even so amen

Revelation to Parley Pratt to go to the wilderness
And now concerning my servant Parley behold
I say unto him that as I live I will that he shall
declare my gospel and learn of me and be

may desern between; the righteous and the

wicked saith your God and again I say

unto you it is conterary to my command-

-ment and my will that my servant

Alge[r]non Sidney Gilbert should sell my

store house which I have appointed unto

my people {u\⟨i⟩}nto the hands of mine en-

-em{e\ies} let not that which I have

appointed be poluted by mine enem-

-ies by the consent of those who call them-

-selves afte[r] my {θ\name} for this is a very

soar and grievous sin against me and

against my people in consequence of those[128]

things which I have decreed and are
      be
soon to fall the nations therefore it is
    ^

my will that my people should

claim and hold claim upon that

which I have appointed unto them

though they should not be permited

to dwell thereon nevertheless I do not

say they shall not dwell thereon for in

as much as they bring forth fruit

and works meet for my kingdom

they shall dwell thereon they shall

build and anothe[r] shall not inher

-it it they shall plant vineyards

and they shall eat the fruit thereof

even so amen

♦   Revelation to Parley [P.] Pratt to go {th\to} th[e] wilderness

And now concerning my servant Parley behold

I say unto him that as I live I will that he shall

declare my gospel and Learn of me and be

ORIGINAL INSCRIPTION
Frederick G. Williams

REVISIONS
Oliver Cowdery
William W. Phelps
Joseph Smith
Frederick G. Williams
Unidentified

128. Possibly "these".

meek and lowly of heart and that which I have
appointed unto him is that he shall go with
my servant Oliver and Peter into the wilderness
among the Lamanites and Ziba also shall go
with them and I myself will go with them and
bee in their midst and I am there advocate with
the Father and nothing shall prevail and they
shall give heed to that which is written and
pretend to no other revelation and they shall
pray always that I may unfold them to their
understanding and they shall give heed
unto these words and trifle not and I will
bless them amen Manchest Oct 1830 —

Revelation given November 1831 Conference Co Ohio
regulating the Presidency of the Church
To the church of Christ in the Land of Zion in addition
to the Church Laws respecting church business verily
I say unto you saith the Lord of host there must
needs be presiding Elders to preside over those who
are of the office of a priest and also teachers over
those who are of the office of a teacher in like manner and also the deacon wherefore from Deacon
to Teacher and from Teacher to Priest and from
Priest to Elder severally as they are appointed according to the Church Articles and Covenants then
cometh the High Priesthood which is the greatest
of all wherefore it must needs be that one be
appointed of the high Priesthood to preside over
the Priesthood and he shall be called President
of the high priesthood of the Church or in
other words the presiding high Priest over the
high priesthood of the Church from the same
cometh the administring of ordinances and blessings

84 [verso]

meek and lowly of heart and that which I have

appointed unto him is that he shall go with

my servant Oliver [Cowdery] and Peter [Whitmer Jr.] into the wilderness

among the Lamanites and Ziba [Peterson] also shall go

with them and I myself will go with them and

be in their midst and I am their advocate with

the Father and nothing shall prevail and they

shall give heed to that which is writen and

pretend to no other revelation and they shall

pray always that I may unfold them to their

understanding and they shall give heed

unto these words and trifle not and I will

bless them amen Manchester Oct 1830—

♦ Revelation given November {ᴓ\1831} Cuyahog[a] Co Ohio

regulating the Presidency of the Church

To the church of Christ in the Land of Zion in addition

to the Church Laws respecting church business verily

I say unto you saith the Lord of hosts there must

needs be presiding Elders to preside over those who

are of the office of a priest and also teachers over

those who are of the office of a teacher in like man-

-ner and also the Deacons wherefore from Deacon

to Teacher and from Teacher to Priest and from

Priest to Elder severally as they are appointed accor-

-ding to the Church Articles and Covenants then

cometh the High Priesthood which is the greatest

of all wherefore it must needs be that one be

appointed[129] of the high Priesthood to preside over

the Priesthood and he shall be called President

of the high priesthood of the Church or in

other words the presiding high Priest over the

high priesthood of the Church from the same

cometh the administring of ordinances and blessings

ORIGINAL INSCRIPTION
Frederick G. Williams

REVISIONS
Oliver Cowdery
William W. Phelps
Joseph Smith
Frederick G. Williams
Unidentified

129. A hole in the manuscript through "appointed" was likely caused by the creation of the horizontal separator on the opposite side of the leaf (manuscript page 83).

upon the church by the laying on of the hands wherefore
the office of a Bishop is not equal unto it for the office
of a Bishop is in administering all temporal things
nevertheless a Bishop must be chosen from the high
priesthood that he may be set apart unto the ministering
of temporal things having a knowledge of them by the
spirit of truth and also to be a judge in Israel to do
the business of the church to sit in judgment upon
transgressors upon testimony as it shall be laid before
him according to the laws by the assistance of his
councillors whom he hath chosen or will choose among
the Elders of the church this shall he be a judge even
a common judge among the inhabitants of Zion until
the borders are enlarged and it becomes necessary to have
other Bishops or judges and inasmuch as there are Bishops
appointed they shall act in the same office, and
again verily I say unto you the most important business of the church and the most difficult cases of the
church inasmuch as there is not satisfaction decision
of the judges it shall be handed over and carried up
unto the court of the church before the President of
the high Priesthood and the President of the court
of the high priesthood shall have power to call
other high Priests even twelve to assist as Councillors
and thus the president of the high priesthood and
his councillors shall have power to decide upon
testimony according to the laws of the church
and after the decision it shall be had in
remembrance no more before the Lord for this
is the highest court of the church of God and
a final decision upon controversies there is not
any person belonging to the church who is exempt from this court of the church and inasmuch as the President of the high priesthood

upon the church by the laying on of the hands wherefore

the office of a Bishop is not equal unto it for the office

of a Bishop is in administring all temporal things

nevertheless a Bishop must be chosen from the high

priesthood that he may be set apart unto the ministering

of temporal things having a knowledge of them by the

spirit of truth and also to be a judge in Israel to do

the business of the church to sin in judgment upon

transgressors upon testamony as it shall be laid before

him according to the Laws by the assistance of his

councellors whom he hath chosen or will choose among

the Elders of the church thus shall he be a judge even

a common judge among the inhabitants of Zion until

the borders are enlarged and it becomes necessary to have

other Bishops or judges and inasmuch as there are Bishops

appointed they shall act in the same office, And

again verily I say unto you the most important busi

-ness of the church and the most difficult cases of the

church inasmuch as there is not satisfaction decission

of the judges it shall be handed over and carried up

unto the court of the church before the President of

the high Priesthood and the President of the court

of the high priesthood shall have power to call

other high priests even twelve to assist as councellors

and thus the president of the high priesthood and

his councillors shall have power to decide upon

testamony according to the laws of the church

and after the decision it shall be had in

remembrance no more before the Lord for this

is the highest court of the church of God and

a final decission upon controverses there is not

any person belonging to the church who is {ᴓ\ex-}

-empt from this court of the church and inas

much as the President of the high priesthood

ORIGINAL INSCRIPTION
Frederick G. Williams

REVISIONS
Oliver Cowdery
William W. Phelps
Joseph Smith
Frederick G. Williams
Unidentified

shall transgress he shall be had in remembrance
before the common court of the church who shall
be assisted by twelve councellors of the high priest
hood and their decision upon his head shall be an
end of controversy concerning him thus none
shall be exempt from the justice and the laws
of God that all things may be done in order and in solemnity before me according to truth and righteousness
Amen. — —

A few more words in addition to the laws of the church
and again verily I say unto the duty of a President
over the office of a deacon is to preside over twelve Deacons
to sit in councel with them and to teach them their duty
edefying one another as it is given according to the
covenants and also the duty of the president over the
office of the Teachers is to preside over twenty four of the
Teachers and to sit in councel with them teaching
them the duties of their office as given in the covenants
also the duty of the president over the priesthood is
to preside over forty eight Priests and to sit in
councel with them and to teach them the duties of
their office as given in the covenants and again
the duty of the President over the office of the Elders is
to preside over Ninety six Elders and to set in councel
with them and to teach them according to the covenants
and again the duty of the President of the office of
the high Priesthood is to preside over the whole
and to be like unto Moses. Behold here is wisdom yea to be a seer a revelator a translator
and a prophet having all the gifts of God which
he bestoweth upon the head of the church wherefore
let every man learn his duty and to act in the office
in which he is appointed in all diligence he that is slothful
shall not be counted worthy to stand and he that learneth not his duty
and sheweth himself not approved shall not be counted worthy to stand even so amen

shall transgress he shall be had in remembrance

before the common court of the church who shall

be assisted by twelve councellors of the high priest-

hood and their decission upon his head shall be an

end of controversy concerning him thus none

shall be exempt from the justice and the laws

of God that all things may be done in order and in sol-

emnity before me according to truth and righteousness

Amen. — — —

 A few more words in addition to the laws of the church

And again verily I say ^{you} unto the duty of a President

over the office of a deacon is to pr{◊◊ide\eside} over twelve Deacons

to sit in council with them and to teach them their duty

edefying one another as it is given according to the

covenants and also the duty of the president over the

office of the Teachers is to preside over twenty four of the

Teachers and to sit in council with them teaching

them the duties of there office as given in the covenants

also the duty of the president over the priesthood is

to preside over forty eight Priests and to sit in

councel with them and to teach them the duties of

their office as given in the covenants. and again

the duty of the President over the office of the Elders is

to preside over Ninety six Elders and to set in council

with them and to teach them according to the covenants

And again the duty of the President of the office of

the high Priesthood is to preside over the whole

and to be like unto Moses. Behold here is wis

-dom yea to be a seer a revelator a translator

and a prophet having all the gifts of God which

he bestoweth upon the heads of the church wherefore

let every man learn his duty and to act in the office

in which he is appointed in all diligence he that is slothful
shall not be counted worthy to stand and he that learneth not his duty
and sheweth himself not approved shall not be counted worthy to stand even so amen

ORIGINAL INSCRIPTION
Frederick G. Williams

REVISIONS
Oliver Cowdery
William W. Phelps
Joseph Smith
Frederick G. Williams
Unidentified

Revelation given in Hiram Portage County Oct 30 1831

Hearken and lo a voice as one sent down from above on
high who is mighty and powerful whose going forth is
unto the ends of the earth yea whose voice is unto all
men prepare ye the way of the Lord and make his paths
strait the keys of the kingdom of God are committed unto
men on the earth and from thence shall the gospel
roll forth unto the ends of the earth as the stone which
is hewed from the mountain without hands shall roll
forth until it has filled the whole earth yea a voice
crying prepare ye the way of the Lord prepare ye the
supper of the Lamb make ready for the coming of the
bridegroom pray unto the Lord call upon his holy
name make known his wonderful works among the people
call upon the Lord that his kingdom may go forth upon
the earth that the inhabitants thereof may receive it
and be prepared for the days to come in the which the
son of man shall come down in heaven clothed in
the brightness of his glory to meet the kingdom of
God which is set upon the earth wherefore may the
kingdom of God go forth that the kingdom of heaven may come that thou O God may be glorified
in heaven so on earth that thine enemies may
be subdued for thine is the honor power and glory
for ever and ever Amen.

Thompson August 20th 1831

Hearken unto me saith the Lord your God and I
will speak unto my servant Edward and give unto
him directions for it must needs be that he receive
directions how to organize this people for it must
needs be that they are organized according to my
laws if otherwise they will be cut off wherefore let my
servant Edward receive the properties of this people

♦   Revelation given in Hiram Portage county Oct 30— 183{ө\1}

Hearken and lo a voice as one sent down from ~~above~~ on

high who is mighty and powerful whose going forth is

unto the ends of the earth yea whose voice is unto all

men prepare ye the way of the Lord and make his paths

strait the keys of the kingdom of God are committed unto

men on the earth and from thence shall the gospel

roll forth unto the ends of the earth as the stone which

is hewed from the mountain without hands shall roll

forth until it has filled the whole earth yea a voice

crying prepare ye the way of the Lord prepare ye the

supper of the Lamb make ready for the coming of the

bridegroom pray unto the Lord call upon his holy

name make known his wonderful works among the people

call upon the Lord that his kingdom may go forth upon

the earth that the inhabitants thereof may receive it

and be prepared for the days to come in the which the

son of man shall come down in heaven clothed in

the brightness of his glory to meet the kingdom of

God which is set upon the earth wherefore may the

kingdom of God go forth that the kingdom of hea-

-ven may come that thou O God may be glorifid

in heaven so on earth that thine enemies may

be subdued for thine is the honor power and glory

for ever and ever Amen.——

♦   Thomp[s]on {August\⟨May⟩}, 20, 1831

Hearken unto me saith the Lord your God and I

will speak unto my servant Edward [Partridge] and give unto

him directions for it must needs be that he receive

directions how to organise this people for it must

needs be that they are organized according to my

laws if otherwise they will be cut off wherefore let my

servant Edward receive the properties of this people

ORIGINAL INSCRIPTION
Frederick G. Williams

REVISIONS
Oliver Cowdery
William W. Phelps
Joseph Smith
Frederick G. Williams
Unidentified

which have covenanted with me to obey the laws which
I have given and let my servant Edward receive the
money as it shall be laid before him according to the
covenant and go and obtain a deed or article of this
land unto himself of him who holdeth it if he harden
not his heart for I have appointed him to receive
these things and then through him the properties of
the Church shall be consecrated unto me Wherefor
let my servant Edward and those whom he
has chosen in whom I am well pleased appoint
unto this people their portion every man alike
according to their families according to their wants
and their needs and let my servant Edward when
he shall appoint a man his portion give unto
him a writing that shall secure unto him his portion
that he shall hold it of the church until he trans-
gresses and is not counted worthy by the voice of
the church according to the Laws to belong to the
church and then all things shall be made sure accor
ding to the Laws of the land and let that which
belongeth to this people be appointed unto this
people and the money which is left unto this people
let there be an agent appointed unto this people to take
the money to provide food and raiment according
to the wants of this people and let every man deal
honestly and be alike among this people and
receive alike that ye may be one even as I have
commanded you and let that which belongeth to
this people not be taken and given unto that of
another church wherefore if another church would
receive money of this church let them pay unto
this church again according as they shall agree and
this shall be done through the Bishop or the agent
which shall be appointed by the voice of the church

which have covenanted with me to obey the Laws which

I have given and let my servant Edward receive the

money as it shall be laid before him according to the

covenant and go and obtain a deed or article of this

land unto himself of him who holdeth it if he harden

not his heart for I have appointed him to receive

these things and thus through him the properties of

the Church shall be consecrated unto me wherefore

let my servant Edward and those whom he

has chosen in whom I am well pleased appoint

unto this people their portion every man alike

according to their families according to their wants

and their needs and let my servant Edward when

he shall appoint a man his portion give unto

him a writing that shall secure unto him his portion

that he shall hold it of the church until he transg-

-ress and is not counted worthy by the voice of

the church according to the Laws to belong to the

church and thus all things shall be made sure accor

-ding to the Laws of the land and let that which

belongeth to this people be appointed unto this

people and the money which is left unto this people

let there be an agent appointed unto this people to take

the money to provide food and raiment according

to the wants of this people and let every man deal

honestly and be alike among this people and

receive alike that ye may be one even as I have

commanded you and let that which belongeth to

this people not be taken and given unto that of

another church wherefore if another church would

receive mony of this church let them pay unto

this church again according as they shall agree and

this shall be done through the Bishop or the agent

which shall be appointed by the voice of the church

ORIGINAL INSCRIPTION
Frederick G. Williams

REVISIONS
Oliver Cowdery
William W. Phelps
Joseph Smith
Frederick G. Williams
Unidentified

and again let the Bishop appoint a storehouse unto
this church and let all things both in money and in
meat which is more than is needful for the wants of this
people be kept in the hands of the Bishop and let him also
reserve unto himself for his own wants and for the wants
of his family as he shall be employed in doing this bu-
-siness and thus I grant unto this people a priveledge
of organising themselves according to my laws and I
consecrate unto them this land for a little season untill
I the Lord shall provide for them otherwise and com-
-mand them to go hence and the hour and the day is
not given unto them wherefore let them act upon this
land as for years and this shall turn unto them for
their good behold this shall be an example unto my
servant Edward in other places in all churches and
whoso is found a faithful and Just and a wise
steward shall enter into the Joy of his lord and shall
inherit eternal life Verily I say unto you I am
Jesus Christ who cometh quickly in an hour you
think not Amen ------------------

Revelation given in independence July th 20
1831 shewing that to be the place of the city of Zion
and the gathering — — — — — — — —
Hearken O ye Elders of my church saith the Lord your
God who have assembled yourselves together according
to my commandments, in this land which is the land of
Missouri which is the land which I have appointed
and consecrated for the gathering of the saints Wherefore
this is the land of promise and the place for the city of
Zion and thus saith the Lord your God if ye will
receive wisdom here is wisdom behold the place which
is now called Independence is the center place

ORIGINAL INSCRIPTION
Frederick G. Williams

REVISIONS
Oliver Cowdery
William W. Phelps
Joseph Smith
Frederick G. Williams
Unidentified

and again let the Bishop appoint a storehouse unto

this church and let all things both in money and in

meat which is more than is needful for the wants of this

people be kept in the hands of the Bishop and let him also

reserve unto himself for his own wants and for the wants

of his family as he shall be employed in doing this bu

-siness and thus I grant unto this people a privelige

of organizing themselves according to my laws and I

consecrate unto them this land for a little season until

I the Lord shall provide for them otherwise and com-

-mand them to go hence and the hour and the day is

not given unto them wherefore let them act upon this

land as for years and this shall turn unto them for

their good behold this shall be an example unto my

servant Edward in other places in all churches and

whoso is found a faithful and just and a wise

steward shall enter into the joy of his lord and shall

inherit eter{l\nal} life Verily I say unto you I am

Jesus Christ who cometh quickly in an hour you

think not Amen — — — — — — — — — — — — — — — — —

♦   Revelation given in independence July the 20—

1831 shewing that to be the place of the city of Zion

and the gathering — — — — — — — — —

Hearken O ye Elders of my church saith the lord your

God who have assembled yourselves together according

to my commandments, in this land which is the land of

Missouri which is the land which I have appointed

and consecrated for the gathering of the sainsts Wherefore

this is the land of promise and the place for the city of

Zion yea and thus saith the Lord your God if ye will

receive wisdom here is wisdom behold the place which

is now called Independence is the center place.

and the spot for the temple is lying westward upon
a lot which is not far from the courthouse wherefor
it is wisdom that the land should be purchased
by the saints and also every tract lying westward
westward even unto the line running directly between
Jew and Gentile and also every tract bordering
by the prairies in asmuch as my disciples are enabled
to buy lands behold this is wisdom that they may
obtain it for an everlasting inheritance and let
my servant Sidney Gilbert stand in the office
which I have appointed him to receive monies
to be an agent unto the church to buy lands
in all the regions round about inasmuch
as can be in righteousness and as wisdom
shall direct and let my servant Edward stand
in the office which I have appointed unto
him to divide unto the saints their inheritance
even as I have commanded and also them
whom he has appointed to assist him And again
verily I say unto you let my servant Sidney
Gilbert plant himself in this place and establish
a store that he may sell goods without fraud
that he may obtain money to buy lands for
the good of the saints and that he may obtain
provisions and whatever things the disciples may
need to plant them in their inheritance and also
let my servant Sidney obtain a license (Behold
here is wisdom and whoso readeth let him under—
stand) that he may send goods also unto the Lam—
anites even by whom I will as clerks employed in
his service and thus the gospel may be preached
unto them.

And again verily I say unto you let my
servant William also be planted in this place

90 [verso]

and the spot for the temple is lying westward upon

a lot which is not far from the courthouse wherefore

it is wisdom that the Land should be purchased

by the saints and also every tract lying ~~directly~~

westward even unto the line runing directly between

Jew and ~~J~~Gentile and also every tract bordering

by the prairies in asmuch as my deciples are enabled

to b{y\uy} lands behold this is wisdom that they may

obtain it for an everlasting inhertance and let

my servant Sidney Gilbert stand in the office

which I have appointed him to receive monies

to be an agent unto the church to buy lands

in all the regions round about inasmuch

as can be in righteousness and as wisdom

shall direct and let my servant Edward [Partridge] stand

in the office which I have appointed unto

him to divid unto the saints their inheritance

even as I have commanded and also them

whom he has appointed to assist him And again

verily I say unto you let my servant Sidney

Gilbert plant himself in this place and establish

a store that he may sell goods without fraud

that he may obtain money to buy lands for

the good of the saints and that he may obtain

provision and whatsoever things the deciples may

need to plant them in their inheritance and also

let my servant Sidney obtain a licence (Behold

here is wisdom and whoso readeth let him under-

-stand) that he may send goods also unto the Lam-

-anites even by whom I will as clerks employed in

his service and then[130] the gospel may be preached

unto them.

  And again verily I say unto you let my

servant William [W. Phelps] also be planted in this place

ORIGINAL INSCRIPTION
Frederick G. Williams

REVISIONS
Oliver Cowdery
William W. Phelps
Joseph Smith
Frederick G. Williams
Unidentified

130. Or "thus".

and be established as a printer unto the church and lo if the world receiveth his writings (Behold this is wisdom) let him obtain whatsoever he can obtain in righteousness for the good of saints and let my servant Oliver assist him even as I have commanded in whatsoever place I shall appoint unto him to copy and to correct and select so that all things may be right before me as it shall be proved by the spirit through him And thus let those of whom I have spoken be planted in the land of Zion as speedily as can be with their families to do those things even as I have spoken

And now concerning the gathering let the Bishop and the agent make preparations for those families which have been commanded to come to this land as soon as possible and plant them in their inheritance and unto the residue of both Elders and members for the directions shall be given hereafter even so Amen — — —

Revelation given May 1831 in Kirtland concerning the farm owned by Frederick and also concerning Joseph & Ezra — — — — — — — —
Hearken unto my words and behold I will make known unto you what ye shall do as it shall be pleasing unto me for verily I say unto you it must needs be that ye let the bargain stand that ye have made concerning those farms until it be so fulfilled behold ye are holden for the one even so likewise thine adversary is holden for the other Wherefore it must needs be that ye pay no more money for the present time until the contract be fulfilled and let mine aged servant Joseph and his family go into the house after thine adversary is gone and let my servant Ezra

and be established as a printer unto the church

and lo if the world receiveth his writings ⟨Behold

this is wisdom⟩ let him obtain whatsoever he can ob-

-tain in righteousness for the good of saints and

let my servant Oliver [Cowdery] assist him even as I have

commanded in whatsoever place I shall appoint unto

him to copy and to correct and select ⟨&c⟩ that all things

may be right before me as it shall be proved by the

spirit through him   and thus let those of whom

I have spoken be planted in the land of Zion as speee

-dely as can be with their families to do these things

even as I have spoken

　　And now concerning the gathering let the

Bishop and the agent make preperations for

those families which have been commanded to

come to this land as soon as possable and plant

them in their inheritance and unto the residue

of both Elders and me{nb\mbers} further directions

shall be given hereafter even so Amen — — — —

♦　　Revelation given May 1831 in Kirtland concer-

-ning the farm owned by Frederick [G. Williams] and also

concrning Joseph [Smith Sr.] & Ezra [Thayer] — — — — — — — — — — — —

Hearken unto my words and behold I will make

known unto you what ye shall do as it shall be

pleasing unto m{y\e} for verily I say unto you i{s\t} must

needs be that ye let the bargain stand that ye have

made concerning those farms until it be so fulfilled behold

ye are holden for the one even so likewise thine a{d\dvisary} is

holden for the other wherefore it must needs be

that ye pay no more money for the present time until

the contract be fulfilled and let mine aged servent

Joseph [Smith Sr.] and his family go into the house after thine

advisary is gone and let my servant Ezra

ORIGINAL INSCRIPTION
Frederick G. Williams

REVISIONS
Oliver Cowdery
William W. Phelps
Joseph Smith
Frederick G. Williams
Unidentified

bound with him and let all the brethren immediately
assemble together to put up an hour for my servant
Ezra and let my servant Frederick's family remove
and let the house be prepared and their wants
be supplied and when my servant Frederick
returns from the west behold and lo he desireth
to take his family in mine own due time unto
the west let that which belongeth unto my
servant Frederick be secured unto him by
deed or bond and thus he willeth that the
brethren reap the good thereof let mine aged
servant Joseph govern the things of the
farm and provide for the families and
let him have help in as much as he standeth
in need let my servant Ezra humble
himself and at the conference meeting he
shall be ordained unto power from on high
and he shall go from thence if he be obedient
unto my commandments and proclaim
my gospel unto the western regions with
my servants that must go forth even unto
the borders by the Lamanites for behold I have
a great work for them to do and it shall be
given unto you to know what ye shall do
at the conference meeting even so amen —
What shall the brethren do with the monies
ye shall go forth and seek diligently among
the brethren and obtain lands and save
the money that it may be consecrated
to purchase lands in the west for an
everlasting inheritance even so Amen

92 [verso]

board with him and let all the brethren immediately

assemble together to put ^up^ an house for my servant

Ezra and let my servant Fredericks family remain[131]

and let the house be prepared and their wants

be supplied and when my Servant Frederick

returns from the west behold and lo he desireth

to take his family in mine own due time unto

the west let that which belongeth unto my

servant Frederick be secured unto him by

deed or bond and thus he willeth that the

brethren reap the good thereof let mine aged

servant Joseph [Smith Sr.] govern the things of the

farm and provide for the families and

let him have healp in as much as he standeth

in need let my servant Ezra humble

himself and at the conference meeting he

shall be ordained unto power from on high

and he shall go from thence if he be obedient

unto my commandments and proclaim

my gospel unto the western regions with

my servants that must go forth even unto

the borders by the Lamanites for behold I have

a great work for them to do and it shall be

given unto you to know what ye shall do

at the conference meeting even so amen.—

    What shall the brethren do with the mon{y\ies}

ye shall go forth and seek dilligently among

the brethren and obtain lands and save

the money that it may be consecrated

to purchace lands in the west for an

everlasting inheritance even so Amen

ORIGINAL INSCRIPTION
Frederick G. Williams

REVISIONS
Oliver Cowdery
William W. Phelps
Joseph Smith
Frederick G. Williams
Unidentified

131. Possibly "remove".

Zion April 30 – 1832

Verily thus saith the Lord in addition to the laws
of the church concerning women and children those
who belong to the church who have lost their husbands
or fathers women have claim for their maintainance
on their husbands
until their husbands are taken and if they are
not found transgressors they shall have fellowship in the church and if they are not faithful
they shall not have fellowship in the church yet
they may remain upon their inheritances according
to the laws of the Land all children have claim
upon their parents for their maintainance until they
are of age and after that they have claim upon the
church or in other words upon the Lords stone house which
should be replenished by the consecrations of their
parents have not wherewith to give them inheritances
and the storehouse shall be kept by the consecrations of the church that widows and orphans
shall be provided for as also the poor — Amen

A Commandment given Febuary 4th 1831 to
choose A Bishop &c — — — — — — —
Hearken and hear oh ye my people saith your Lord
and your God ye whom I delight to bless with the
greatest blessing ye that hear me and ye that hear me
not will I curse that have professed my name with
the heaviest of all cursings; Hearken O ye Elders
of my church whom I have called behold I give unto
you a commandment that ye shall assemble yourselves together to agree upon my word by the prayer
of your faith ye shall receive my law that ye may
know to govern my church and have all things right
before me and I will be your ruler and ye
shall see that my law is kept he that receiveth my law

◆   ¹³²Zion April 30— 1832

Verily thus saith the Lord in addition to the Laws

of the church concerning women and Children those

who belong to the church who have lost their husbands

for their maintainence
or fathers women have claim on their husbands ^

until their husbands are taken and if they are

not found transgressors they shall have fellow-

ship in the church and if they {Oho\are} not faithful

they shall not have fellowship in the church yet

they may remain upon their inheritences according

to the laws of the Land all children have claim

upon there parents for there maintanence until they

are of age and after that they have claim upon the

Lords
church or in other words upon the ^ store house ~~which~~

~~shall be replenished by the consecrations~~ if their

parents have not wherewith to give them inheritencs

and the storehouse shall be kept by the consecrat-

-ions of the church that widows and orphans

shall be provided for as also the poor— Amen

◆   A Commandment given Febury 4th 1831 to

choose A Bishop &c — — — — — — — — — — — — —

Hearken and hear oh ye my people saith your Lord

and your God ye whom I delight to bless with the

greatest blessing ye that hear me and ye that hear me

not will I curse that have prof{f\essed} my name with

the heaviest of all cursings, Hearken O ye Elders

of my church whom I have called be hold I give unto

you a commandment that ye shall assemble your-

-selves together to agree upon my word by the prayer

of your faith ye shall receive my law that ye may

know to govern my church and have all things right

before me and I will be your ruler and ye

shall see that my law is kept he that receiveth my law

ORIGINAL INSCRIPTION
Frederick G. Williams

REVISIONS
Oliver Cowdery
William W. Phelps
Joseph Smith
Frederick G. Williams
Unidentified

132. The first publication
reflecting the redactions in
this revelation is the 1835
Doctrine and Covenants
(section 88).

and doeth it the same is my disciple and he
that saith he receiveth it and doth it not the same
is not my disciple and shall be cast out from
among you for it is not meet that the things
which belong to the children of the kingdom
should be given to them that are not worthy
or to dogs or the pearls to be cast before swine and
again it is meet that my servant Joseph should
have a house built in which to live and translate
And again it is meet that my servant Sidney
should live as seemeth him Good And again
I have called my servant Newel and give
a commandment that he should be appointed by
the voice of the church and ordained a Bishop unto
the church to leave his merchandise and to spend
all his time in the labours of the church to see
to all things as it shall be appointed in my
law in the day that I shall give them And this
because his heart is pure before me for he is
like unto Nathaniel of Old in whom there
is no guile these words are given unto you
and they are pure before me Wherefore be
ye aware how you hold them for they are
to be answered upon your souls in the
day of Judgment even so Amen ———

An explanation of the 14th verse of the 7 chap
of the first corinthians

Now in the days of the Apostles the law of circumcision
was had among all the Jews which believed not
the Gospel of Jesus Christ And it came to pass
that there arose a great contention among the
people concerning the law of circumcision for

and doeth it the same is my deciple and he

that saith he receiveth it and doth it not the same

is not my deciple and shall be cast out from

among you for it is not meet that the things

which belong to the children of the kingdom

should be given to them that are not worthy

or to dogs or the pirls to be cast before swine and

again it is meet that my servant Joseph should

have a house built in which to live and translate

And again it is meet that my servant Sidn[e]y [Rigdon]

should live as seemeth him Good And again

I have called my servant Edward [Partridge] and give

a commandment that he should be appointed by

the voice of the church and ordained a Bishop unto

the church to leave his merchandize and to spend

all his time in the Labours of the church to see

to all things as it shall be appointed in my

law in the day that I shall give them and this

because his heart is pure before me for he is

like unto Nathaniel of Old in whom there

is no guile these words are given unto you

and they are pure before me Wherefore be

ye aware how {ɵ\you} hold them for they are

to be answered upon your souls in the

day of judgment even so Amen. — — — —

◆   An explanation of the 14th verse of the 7 chap.—[133]

    of the first corinthians

    Now in the days of the Apostles the law of circumcision

was had among all the Jews which believed not

the Gospel of Jesus Christ And it came to pass

that there arose a great contention among the

people concerning the law of circumcission for

ORIGINAL INSCRIPTION
Frederick G. Williams

REVISIONS
Oliver Cowdery
William W. Phelps
Joseph Smith
Frederick G. Williams
Unidentified

133. Possibly "chapt" (with no punctuation).

the unbelieving husband was desirous that his chil
dren should be circumcised and become subject to the
law of Moses which law was fulfilled and it came
to pass that their children being brought up in
subjection to the law of Moses and gave heed to
the traditions of their fathers and believed not
the gospel of Christ wherein they became unholy
wherefore for this cause the Apostle wrote unto
the church giving unto them a commandment
not of the Lord but of himself that a believer
should not be united to an unbeliever except
the law of Moses should be done away among them
that their children might remain without circum
cision and that the traditions might be done away
which saith that little children are unholy for it
was had among the Jews but little children
are holy being sanctified through the atonement
of Jesus Christ and this is what their scrip
tures mean

Rev So Wm E. Mc Lelin Oct 1831 —
Behold thus saith the Lord unto you my
servant William blessed are you inasmuch
as you have turned away from your iniquities
and have received my truths saith the Lord your
redeemer the saviour of the world even of as
many as believe on my name. Verily I say
unto you blessed are you for receiving mine everlasting
gospel covenant even the fulness of my gospel sent forth
unto the children of men that they might have life
and be made partakers of the glories which are to
be revealed in the last days as it was written by the
prophets and Apostles in days of old Verily I say
unto you my servant William that you are

the unbelieving husband was desirous that his chil

-dren should be circumcised and become subject to the

law of Moses which law was fulfilled and it came

to pass that the children being brought up in

subjection to the law of Moses and gave heed to

the traditions of their fathers and believed not

the gospel of Christ wherein they became unholy

wherefore for this cause the apostle wrote unto

the church giving unto them a commandment

not of the Lord but of himself that a believer

should not be united to an unbeliever except

the law of Moses should be done away among them

that their children might remain without circum

-cision and that the tradition might be done away

which saith that little children are unholy for it

was had among the Jews but little children

are holy being sanctified through the {◊◊\atonement}

of Jesus Christ and this is what these scrip

tures mean

◆   Rev To Wm E Mᶜ Lel[l]in Oct 1831—

Behold thus saith the Lord unto you my

servant W{m\illiam} b{ss\lessed} are you inasmuch

as you have turned away from your iniquities

and have received my truths saith the Lord your

redeemer the savior of the world even of as

many as believe on my name. Verily I say

unto you blessed are you for receiving mine everlasting

~~gospel~~ covenant even the fulness of my gospel sent forth

unto the children of men that they might have life

and be made partakers of the glories which are to

be revaled in the last days as it was writen by the

prophets and Apostles in days of old Verily I say

unto you my servant William that you are

ORIGINAL INSCRIPTION
Frederick G. Williams

REVISIONS
Oliver Cowdery
William W. Phelps
Joseph Smith
Frederick G. Williams
Unidentified

clear but not all repent therefore of those things
which are not pleasing in my sight saith the Lord
for the Lord will shew them unto you and now
verily I the Lord will shew unto you what I will
concerning you or what is my will concerning
you Behold verily I say unto you that it is my
will that you should proclaim ~~my gospel from~~
land to land and from city to city yea in
those regions round about where it hath not
been proclaimed tarry not many days in this
place go not up unto the Land of Zion as
yet but inasmuch as you can send send
otherwise think not of thy property Go unto
the Eastern lands bear testimony in every place
unto every people and in their synagogues reasoning with the people let my servant Samuel
go with you and forsake him not and give
him thine instruction and he that is faithful
shall be made strong in every place and I
the Lord will go with you lay your hands
upon the sick and they shall recover return
not until I the Lord shall send you
be patient in affliction ask and ye shall
receive Knock and it shall be opened unto
you seek not to be cumbered forsake all
unrighteousness commit not adultery a
temptation with which thou hast been
troubled Keep these sayings true and faithful
and thou shalt magnify thine office and push many
people to Zion with songs of everlasting Joy upon their heads continue in these things even unto the end
and you shall have a crown of eternal
life ~~at~~ the right hand of my father who is full of grace and truth

{8\9}6 [verso]

clean but not all repent therefore of those things

which are not pleasing in my sight saith the Lord

for the Lord will shew them unto you and now

verily I the Lord will shew unto you what I will

concerning you or what is my will concerning

you Behold verily I say unto you that it is my

will that you should proclaim my gospel from

land to land and from city to city yea in

those regions round about where it hath not

been proclaimed tarry not many days in this

place go not up unto the Land of Zion as

yet but inasmuch as you can send send

otherwise think not of thy property go unto

Ɛ͟Eastern lands bear testamony in every place

unto every people and in their sinegogues rea-

-soning with the people let my servant Samuel [Smith]

go with you and forsake him not and give

him thine instructions and he that is faithful

shall be made strong in every place and I

the Lord will go with you lay your hands

upon the sick and they shall recover return

not until I the Lord shall send you

be patient in affliction ask and ye shall

receive knock and it shall be opened unto

you seek not to be cumbered forsake all

unrighteousness commit not Adultry a

temptation with which thou hast been

troubled keep these sayings tru and faithful

and thou shalt magnify thine office and push many

people to Zion with songs of everlasting joy upon their heads con

tinue in these things even unto the end

and you shall have a crown of eternal

life a{n\t}d̶ the right hand of my father

who is full of grace and truth

ORIGINAL INSCRIPTION
Frederick G. Williams

REVISIONS
Oliver Cowdery
William W. Phelps
Joseph Smith
Frederick G. Williams
Unidentified

Verily thus saith the Lord, you, even your
redeemer, even Jesus Christ. Amen—

A Revelation given to William E. McLelin
a true descendant from Joseph that was sold
into Egypt down through the loins of Ephraim
his son – – – – –

⁓⁓⁓⁓⁓⁓⁓⁓⁓⁓⁓⁓⁓⁓⁓⁓⁓

Clay County, Missouri, June 22, 1834.

Verily, I say unto you, who have assembled yourselves together,
that you may learn my will concerning the redemption of mine
afflicted people: Behold, I say unto you, were it not
for the transgressions of my people, speaking concerning the church,
and not individuals, they might have been redeemed, even
now; but, behold, they have not learned to be obedient to the
things which I require at their hands, but are full of all man=
=ner of evil, and do not impart of their substance, as becom=
=eth saints, to the poor and afflicted among them, and are not
united according to the union required by the law of the ~~~~
Celestial
~~~~~~ Kingdom; and Zion cannot be built up unless it
is by the principles of the law of the Celestial Kingdom, other=
=wise I cannot receive her unto myself. And my people
must needs be chastened until they learn obedience, if it
must needs be by the things which they suffer. I speak not
concerning those who are appointed to lead my people,
who are the first elders of my church; for they are not all
under this condemnation; but I speak concerning the
churches abroad: there are many who will say, Where is
their God? Behold, he will deliver in time of trouble,
otherwise we will not go up unto ~~~~~~~ Zion,
and will keep our moneys.

Therefore, in consequence of the transgression of my people,
it is expedient in me that mine elders should wait for a
little season for the redemption of Zion, that they them=
selves

{8\9}7 [recto]

Verily thus saith the Lord your God your

redeemer even Jesus Christ Amen

A Revelation given to W{m\illiam} E McLelin

a true decendant from Joseph that was sold

into Egypt down through the Loins of Ephraim

his son — — — — —

ORIGINAL INSCRIPTION
Frederick G. Williams
Oliver Cowdery

REVISIONS
Oliver Cowdery
William W. Phelps
Joseph Smith
Frederick G. Williams
Unidentified

134. Frederick G. Williams
handwriting ends; Oliver
Cowdery begins. The first
publication reflecting some
redactions in this revelation is
the 1844 Doctrine and
Covenants (section 102).

/[134]Clay County, Missouri, June 22, 1834.

Verily, I say unto you, who have assembled yourselves together

that you may learn my will concerning the redemption of ~~Zion~~

mine afflicted people: Behold, I say unto you, were it not

for the transgressions of my people, speaking concerning the church,

and not individuals, they might have been redeemed, even ~~now~~

now; but, behold, they have not learned to be obedient to the

things which I require at their hands, but are full of all man=

=ner of evil, and do not impart of their substance as becom=

=eth saints, to the poor and afflicted among them, and are not

united according to the union required by the law of the ~~ever=~~
Celestial
~~=lasting~~ Kingdom; and Zion cannot be built up unless it

is by the principles of the law of the Celestial kingdom, other=

=wise I cannot receive her unto myself. And my people

must needs be chastened until they learn obedience, if it

must needs be by the things which they suffer. I speak not

concerning those who are appointed to lead my people,

who are the first elders of my church, for they are not all

under this condemnation; but I speak concerning the

churches abroad: there are many who will say, Where is

their God? Behold, he will deliver in time of trouble,

otherwise we will not go up unto ~~the land of~~ Zion,

and will keep our moneys.

Therefore, in consequence of the transgression⟨s⟩ of my people,

it is expedient in me that mine elders should wait for a

little season for the redemption of Zion, that they them=
=selves

may be prepared, and that my people, may be taught more perfectly, and have experience, and know more perfectly concerning their duty, and the things which I require at their hands: And this cannot be brought to pass until mine elders are endowed with power from on high; for, behold, I have prepared a greater endowment and blessing to be poured out upon them, inasmuch as they are faithful, and continue in humility before me. Therefore, it is expedient in me that mine elders should wait a little season for the redemption of Zion; for behold, I do not require at their hands to fight the battles of Zion; for as I have said in a former commandment, even so I will fulfil: I will fight your battles. Behold, the destroyer I have already sent forth to ~~lay waste and~~ destroy and lay waste mine enemies, and not many years hence they shall not be left to pollute mine heritage, and to blaspheme my name upon the lands which I have consecrated for the gathering together of my saints. Behold, I have commanded my servant Joseph Smith jr to say to the strength of my house, even my warriors, my young men and middleaged, to gether together for the redemption of my people, and throw down the towers of mine enemies, and scatter their watchmen; but the strength of mine house has not hearkened unto my words: but inasmuch as there are those that have hearkened unto my words I have prepared a blessing and an endowment for them, if they continue faithful: I have heard their prayers and will accept their offering. And it is expedient in me that they should be brought thus far for a trial of their faith.

And now, verily I say unto you, a commandment I give unto you, that as many as have come up hither that can stay in the region round about, let them stay, and those who cannot stay, ~~for a little season~~ who have families in the east, let them tarry for a little season, inasmuch as my servant Joseph Smith jr shall appoint unto them; for I will counsel him concerning this matter, and all things whatsoever he shall appoint unto them, shall be fulfilled. And let all my people who dwell in the regions round about be very faithful, and prayerful, and humble before me, and reveal

{8\9}8 [verso]

may be prepared, and that my people may be taught more

perfectly, and have experience, and know more perfectly con=

=cerning their duty and the things which I require at their

hands. And this cannot be brought to pass until mine

elders are endowed with power from on high; for, behold, I

have prepared a greater endowment and blessing to be boured [poured]

out upon them, inasmuch as they are faithful, and ~~contrite~~,
_{continue}

in humility before me. Therefore, it is expedient in me that

mine elders should wait ~~for~~ a little season for the redemption of

Zion; for behold, I do not require at their hands to fight the bat=

=tles of Zion; for as I have said in a former commandment, even so

I will fulfil: I will fight your battles. Behold, the destroyer I have
already
sent forth to ~~lay waste and~~ destroy and lay waste mine enemies, and not

many years hence they shall not be left to pollute mine heritage, and to {◊\blas=}

=pheme my name upon the lands which I have consecrated for the gath=

=ering together of my saints. Behold, I have commanded my servant Joseph _{Smith, jr.} to

say to the strength of my house, even my warriors, my young men and

middleaged, to gether together for the redemption of my people, and

throw down the towers of mine enemies, and scatter their watch=

=men; but the strength of mine house has not hearkened unto

my words: but inasmuch as there are those that have hear=

=kened unto my word I have prepared a blessing and an endow=
if they contin[u]e faithful:
=ment for them, I have heard their prayers and will accept

their offering. And it is expedient in me that they should be

brought thus far for a trial of their faith.

And now, verily I say unto you, a commandment I give unto

you, that as many as have come up hither that can stay in the regions
~~who~~
round about, let them stay, and those who cannot stay, ~~for a~~

~~little season~~ who have families in the east, let them tarry for
Smith, jr.
a little season, inasmuch as my servant Joseph shall appoint

unto them; for I will counsel him concerning this matter, and all

things whatsoever he shall appoint unto them, shall be fulfulled.

And let all may [my] people who dwell in the regions round about be

very faithful, and prayerful, and humble before me, and reveal

Original Inscription
Oliver Cowdery

Revisions
Oliver Cowdery
William W. Phelps
Joseph Smith
Frederick G. Williams
Unidentified

until it is wisdom in me that they should be revealed; but the things which I have revealed unto them, and talk not of judgments, neither boast of faith nor of mighty works, but carefully gather together as much in one region as can be ~~constantly~~ consistantly with the feelings of the people; and behold, I will give unto you favor and grace in their eyes, that you may rest in peace and safety, while you are saying unto the people, Execute judgment and justice for us, according to law, and redress us of our wrongs.

Now behold, I say unto you my friends, in this way you may find favor in the eyes of the people until the army of Israel has become very great, and I will soften the hearts of the people as I did the heart of Pharaoh, from time to time, until my Servant Joseph, Smith, jr. and mine elders, whom he shall appoint, shall have time to gather up the strength of mine house, and to have sent wise men to fulfil that which I have commanded concerning the purchasing of all the lands in Jackson county that can be purchased, and in the ad-=joining counties round about; for it is my will that these lands should be purchased; and after they are purchased, that my saints should possess them according to the law of consecration which I have given. And after these lands are purchased I will hold the armies of Israel guiltless in taking possession of their own lands, which they have previously purchased with their moneys, and of throwing down the towers of mine enemies that may be upon them, and scattering their watchmen and avenging me of mine enemies, unto the third and forth generation of them that hate me. But firstly let my army become very great, and let it be sanctified before me, that it may become fair as the Sun, and clear as the moon, and that her banners may be terrible unto all nations, that the kingdoms of this world may be constrained to acknowledge that the kingdom of Zion is, in, very ~~deed~~ deed, the kingdom of our God and his Christ; therefore, let us become subject unto her laws.

Verily, I say unto you, it is expedient in me that the first elders of my church should receive their endowment from on high in mine house which I have commanded to be built unto my name in the land of Kirtland, and let those commandments which I have given con-=cerning

{8\9}9 [recto]

until it is wisdom in me that they should be ⟨revealed;⟩
not the things which I have revealed unto them, and talk not of

judgments, neither boast of faith nor of mighty works, but carefully gather

together as much in one region as can be ~~constantly~~ consistantly with

the feelings of the people; and behold, I will give unto you favor and

grace in their eyes, that you may rest in peace and safety, while

you are saying unto the people, Execute judgment and justice for us,

according to law, and redress us of our wrongs.

Now behold, I say unto you my friends, in this way you may find

favor in the eyes of the people until the army of Israel has become

very great, and I will soften the hearts of the people as I did the heart

of Pharaoh, from time to time, until my servant Joseph, Smith, jr. and mine

elders, whom he shall appoint, shall have time to gather up the

strength of mine house, and to have sent wise men to fulfil

that which I have commanded concerning the purchasing of all the

lands in Jackson county that can be purchased, and in the ad=

=journing counties round about; for it is my will that these lands

should be purchased; and after they are purchased, that my saints

should possess them according to the law of consecration which

I have given. And after these lands are purchased I will hold

the armies of Israel guiltless in taking possession of their own lands,
which they have previously purchased with their moneys,
and of throwing down the towers of mine enemies that may ~~be~~ be

upon them, and scattering their watchmen and avenging me of

mine enemies, unto the third and forth generation of them that

hate me. But firstly let my army become very great, and let

it be sanctified before me, that it may become fair as the

sun, and clear as the moon, and that her banners may be

terrible unto all nations, that the kingdoms of this world

may be constrained to acknowledge that the kingdom of Zion,

is, in very ~~deed~~ deed, the kingdom of our God and his christ;

therefore, let us become subject unto her laws.

Verily, I say unto you, it is expedient in me that the first elders

of my church should receive their endowment from on high in mine

house which I have commanded to be built unto my name in the

land of Kirtland, and let those commandments which I have given con=
=cerning

ORIGINAL INSCRIPTION
Oliver Cowdery

REVISIONS
Oliver Cowdery
William W. Phelps
Joseph Smith
Frederick G. Williams
Unidentified

Zion, and her law, be executed and fulfilled after her redemption. There has been a day of calling, but the time has come for a day of choosing; and let those be chosen that are worthy: and it shall be manifest unto my servant Joseph by the voice of the Spirit those who are chosen, and they shall be sanctified: and inasmuch as they follow the counsel which they receive, they shall have power after many days to accomplish all things pertaining to Zion.

And again, I say unto you, sue for peace, not only the people that have smitten you, but also to all people; and lift up an ensign of peace, and make a proclamation for peace unto the ends of the earth: and make proposals for peace unto those who have smitten you, according to the voice of the Spirit which is in you; and all things shall work together for your good; therefore be faithful: and behold, and lo, I am with you even unto the end, even so; Amen.

~~~~~~~~~~~~~~~~~~~~~~~~~~~~~~~~~~~~~~

Revelation given April 23 — 1834
appointing to each member of the united firm their Stewardship

Verily I say unto you my friends I give unto you council and a commandment concerning all the properties which belong to the Firm which I commanded to be ~~established~~ organised and established to be a United firm and an everlasting firm for the benefit of my church and for the Salvation of men until I come, with promise immutable and unchangeable that inasmuch as those whom I commanded were faithful they should be blessed with a multiplicity of blessings; but inasmuch ~~as they were not~~ faithful they were nigh unto cursing: therefore inasmuch as some of my servants have not kept the commandment but have broken the covenant by covitousness and with feigned words, I have cursed them with a very sore and grievous curse, for I the Lord have decreed in my

1{9\0}0 [verso]

Zion, and her law, be executed and fulfilled after her redemp

=tion. There has been a day of calling, but the time has come for

a day of choosing; and let those be chosen that are worthy:

and it shall be manifest unto my servant Joseph by the voice

of the Spirit those who are chosen, and they shall be sanctified;

and inasmuch as they follow the counsels which they receive, they

shall have power after many days to accomplish all things pertain=

=ing to Zion.

And again, I say unto you, sue for peace, not only the people

that have smitten you, but also ~~to~~ all people; and lift up an

ensign of peace, and make a proclamation for peace unto the

ends of the earth: and make proposals for peace unto those

who have smitten you, according to the voice of the Spirit which

                                    therefore

is in you; and all things shall work together for your good; ~~and~~ be

faithful: and behold, and lo, I am with you even unto the end,

even so; Amen.

/135 ————————————————————————————————

♦   Revelation given April 23ᵈ— 1834

appointing to each member of the united firm

their Stewardship

Verily I say unto you my friends I give unto

you council and a commandment concerning

all the properties which belong to the Firm which I

commanded to be ~~established~~ organised and establish

-ed to be a united firm and an everlasting firm

for the benefit of my church and for the salvation

of men until I come, with promise immutable

and unchangable that inasmuch as those whom

I commanded were faithful they should be blessed

                        as they were not

with a multiplicity of blessings. but inasmuch ~~as some of~~

faithful they were nigh unto curseing; therefore inasmuch as some of 136

my servants have not kept the commandment but

have broken the covenant by Coviteousness and with

feigned words, I have cursed them with a very soar

and grievous curse, for I the Lord have decreed in my

ORIGINAL INSCRIPTION
Oliver Cowdery
Frederick G. Williams

REVISIONS
Oliver Cowdery
Orson Hyde
William W. Phelps
Joseph Smith
Frederick G. Williams
Unidentified

135. Oliver Cowdery hand-writing ends; Frederick G. Williams begins.

136. Orson Hyde possibly made revisions throughout this revelation when he inscribed the latter portion of the revelation. The ink flow of this revision appears to match that of Orson Hyde's other revisions throughout the revelation, suggesting that he wrote all of them at the same time.

heart that inasmuch as any man belonging to the firm
shall be found a transgressor or in other words shall
break the covenant with which ye are bound, he shall
be cursed in his life and shall be trodden down by whom
I will for I the Lord am not to be mocked in these things
and all this that the innocent among you may not be
condemned with the unjust and that the guilty among
you may not escape because I the Lord have promised
unto you a crown of Glory at my right hand.
Therefore inasmuch as ye are found transgressors
ye cannot escape my wrath in your lives, and
inasmuch as ye are cut off by transgression ye
cannot escape the buffettings of Satan unto the
day of redemption, And I now give unto you
power from this very hour that if any man am
-ong you of the firm is found a transgressor and rep
-enteth not of the evil that ye shall deliver him
over unto the buffettings of Satan and he shall
have no more power to bring evil upon you but
as long as ye hold communion with transgressors
behold they bring evil upon you, It is wisdom
in me, therefore a Commandment I give unto
you that ye shall organize yourselves and
appoint every man his stewardship that every
man may give an account unto me of the stew-
-ardship which is appointed unto him for it is expedi
ent that I the Lord should make every man
accountable as steward over earthly blessings
which I have made and prepared for my creatures.
I the Lord stretched out the heavens and build
-ed the Earth as a very handy work, and all things therein
are mine, and it is my business to provide for my saints
for all things are mine, But it must needs be done in
mine own way, and behold this is the way that I

heart that inasmuch as any man belonging to the firm

shall be found a transgressor or in other words shall

break the covenant with which ye are bound, he shall

be cursed in his life and shall be trodden down by whom

I will for I the Lord am not to be mocked in these things

and all this that the innocent among you may not be

condemned with the unjust and that the guilty among

you may not escape because I the Lord have promised

unto you a crown of glory at my right hand.

Therefore inasmuch as ye are found transgressors

{◊◊\ye} cannot escape my wrath in your lives, and

inasmuch as ye are cut off by transgresion ye

cannot escape the buffittings of Satan unto the

day of redemption, And I now give unto you

power from this very hour that if any man am-

-ong you of the firm is found a transgressor and rep

-enteth not of the evil that ye shall deliver him

over unto the buffittings of satan and he shall

have no more power to bring evil upon you but

as {if\long} as ye hold communion with transgressors

behold they bring evil upon you, It is wisdom

in me, therefore a commandment I give unto

you that ye shall organize yourselves and

appoint every man his stewardship that eve[r]y

man may give an account unto me of the stewar-

-dship which is appointed unto him for it is expedi

ent that I the Lord should make every man

accountable as steward over earthly blessings

which I have made and prepared for my cre[a]tur[e]s.

I the Lord streached out the heavens and /[137]build

=ed the Earth as a very handy work, and all things therein

are mine, and it is my business to provide for my saints;

for all things are mine; But it must needs be done in

mine own way, and behold this is the way that I

ORIGINAL INSCRIPTION
Frederick G. Williams
Orson Hyde

REVISIONS
Oliver Cowdery
William W. Phelps
Joseph Smith
Frederick G. Williams
Unidentified

137. Frederick G. Williams
handwriting ends; Orson
Hyde begins.

the Lord hath decreed to provide for my Saints, that the poor shall be exalted in that the rich are made low; for the earth is full and there is enough and to spare; yea, I have prepared all things, and have given unto the children of men to be agents unto themselves. Therefore, if any man shall take of the abundance which I have made and impart not his portion according to the law of my Gospel unto the poor and the needy, he shall with Dives in hell lift up his eyes being in torments.

And now, verily I say unto you concerning the properties of the Firm. Let my servant Sidney have appointed unto him the place where he now resides, and the lot of the Tannery for his stewardship for his support while he is labouring in my vineyard, even as I will, when I shall command him; and let all things be done according to counsell of the Firm, and united consent or voice of the Firm which dwells in the land of Kirtland. And this stewardship and blessing, I the Lord confer upon my servant Sidney for a blessing upon him and upon his seed after him and I will multiply blessings upon him and upon his seed after him inasmuch as he shall be humble before me.

And again, let my servant Martin have appointed unto him for his stewardship the lot of land which my servant John obtained in exchange for his farm, for him and his seed after him; and inasmuch as he is faithful I will multiply a multiplicity of blessings upon him and his seed after him. And let my servant Martin devote his moneys for the printing of my word according as my servant Joseph shall direct.

And again, let my servant Frederick have the place upon which he now dwells; and let my servant Oliver have the lot which is set off joining the house which is to be for the printing office, which is lot number one, and also the lot upon which his father resides; and let my servants Frederick and Oliver have the printing office and all things that pertain unto it; and this shall be their stewardships which shall be appointed unto them; and inasmuch as they are faithful

1{9\0}2 [verso]

the Lord hath decreed to provide for my saints, that

the poor shall be exalted in that the rich are made

low; for the earth is full and there is enough and to

spare; yea, I have prepared all things, and have given unto

the children of men to be agents unto themselves: Therefore,

if any man shall take of the abundance which I have made

and impart not his portion according to the law of my

Gospel unto the poor and the needy, he shall with Dives
in hell¹³⁸
lift up his ey{s\es} being in torment.

And now, verily I say unto you concerning the properties of

the Firm; let my servant Sidney [Rigdon] have appointed unto him, the

place where he now resides, and the lot of the Tannery for his

stewardship for his support while he is labouring in my vineyard,

even as I will, when I shall command him; and let all things be

done according to coun{cl\sel} of the Firm, and united consent or

voice of the Fir{ɵ\m} which dwells in the land of Kirtland. And

this stewardship and blessing, I the Lord confer upon my servant

Sidney for a blessing upon him and upon his seed after
and I will multiply blessings upon him and upon his seed after ~~him~~
him inasmuch as he shall be humble before me.

And again, let my servant martin [Harris] have appointed unto

him for his stewardship the lot of land which my servant

John [Johnson] obtained in exchange for his farm, for him and his seed

after him; and inasmuch as he is faithful I will multiply a mul-

tiplicity of blessings upon him and his seed after him. And let

my servant Martin devote his moneys for the printing of my

word according as my servant Joseph shall direct.

And again, let my servant Frederick [G. Williams] have the place upon

which he now dwells; and let my servant Oliver [Cowdery] have the lot

which is set off joining the house which is to be for the

printing office, which is lot number one, and also the lot

upon which his father resides; and let my servants Frederick

and Oliver have the printing office and all things that

pertain unto it; and this shall be their stewardships which

shall be appointed unto them; and inasmuch as they are faithful,

Original Inscription
Orson Hyde

Revisions
Oliver Cowdery
Orson Hyde
William W. Phelps
Joseph Smith
Frederick G. Williams
Unidentified

138. Orson Hyde's revisions throughout this revelation are possibly in the same ink flow as the original text, which would indicate that he made them at the time of original inscription.

behold I will bless them, and multiply blessings upon them, and this is the beginning of the stewardships which I have appointed unto them, for them and their seed after them; and inasmuch as they are faithful I will multiply blessings upon them and their seed after them even a multiplicity of blessings.

And again, let my servant John have the house in which he lives, and the farm, all, save the ground which has been reserved for the building of my houses which pertains to that farm, and those lots which have been named for my servant Oliver, and inasmuch as he is faithful I will multiply blessings upon him. And it is my will that he should sell the lots that are laid off for the building up of the city of my saints, inasmuch as it shall be made known to him by the voice of the spirit, and according to the counsel of the Firm, and by the voice of the Firm, and this is the beginning of the stewardships which I have appointed unto him for a blessing unto him and his seed after him; and inasmuch as he is faithful I will multiply a multiplicity of blessings upon him.

And again, let my servant Newel have appointed unto him, the house and lot where he now resides, and the lot & building on which the store stands, and the lot also which is on the corner south of the store, and also the lot on which the Ashery is situated. And all this I have appointed unto my servant Newel for his stewardships, for a blessing upon him and upon his seed after him for the benefit of the mercantile establishment of my Firm which I have established for my Stake in the land of Kirtland. Yea, verily, this is the stewardship which I have appointed unto my servant Newel, even this whole mercantile establishment, him and his agent, and his seed after him; and inasmuch as he is faithful in keeping the commandments which I have given unto him, I will multiply blessings upon him and his seed after him, even a multiplicity of blessings.

And again, let my servant Joseph have appointed

behold I will bless them, and multiply blessings upon them, and

this is the beginning of the stewardships which I have appointed

unto them, for them and their seed after them; and inasmuch

as they are faithful I will multiply blessings upon them and

their seed after them even a multiplicity of blessings.

And again, let my servant John have the house in which

he lives, and the farm, all, save the ground which has been

reserved for the bu{l\ilding} of my houses which pertains to that

farm, and those lots which have been named for my servant

Oliver, and inasmuch as he is faithful I will multiply blessings

upon him. And it is my will that he should sell the lots that

are laid off for the building up of the city of my saints,

inasmuch as it shall be made known to him by the voice of the

spirit, and according to the counsel of the Firm, and by the

voice of the Firm, and this is the beginning of the stewardships

for a blessing unto him

which I have appointed unto him and his seed after him; and

inasmuch as he is faithful I will multiply a multiplicity

of blessings upon him.

And again, let my servant Newel [K. Whitney] have appointed unto

him, the house and lot where he now resides, and the lot &

building on which the store stands, and the lot also which is on

the corner south of the store, and also the lot on which the

Ashery is situated, and all this I have appointed unto my

servant Newel for his stewardships, for a blessing upon

him and upon his seed after him for the benefit of the mer=

cantile establishment of my Firm which I have established

for my stake in the land of Kirtland. Yea, verily, this is

the stewardships which I have appointed unto my servant

Newel, even this whole mercantile establishment, him and

his agent, and his seed after him; and inasmuch as he is

faithful in keeping the commandments which I have given

unto him, I will multiply blessings upon him and his

seed after him, even a multiplicity of blessings.

And again, let my servant Joseph have appoint{d\ed}

Original Inscription
Orson Hyde

Revisions
Oliver Cowdery
Orson Hyde
William W. Phelps
Joseph Smith
Frederick G. Williams
Unidentified

unto him the lot which is laid off for the building of
my houses, which is forty rods ~~wide~~ long and twelve
wide; and also the farm upon which his father now
resides; and this is the beginning of the Stewardships
which I have appointed unto him, for a blessing upon
him and upon his father, for his support. for behold I have reserved an inheritance for his father Therefore, he
shall be reckoned in the house of my servant Joseph; &
I will multiply blessings upon the house of my servant
Joseph inasmuch as he is faithful, even a multiplicity
of blessings.

And now a commandment I give unto you concerning
Zion, that you shall no longer be bound as a United
Firm to your brethren of Zion, only on this wise: After
you are organized, you shall be called The United Firm
of the Stake of Zion, the city of Kirtland among yourselves.
And your brethren, after they are organized, shall be called
The United Firm of the city of Zion; and they shall be
organized in their own names, and in their own name;
and they shall do their business in their own name and
in their own names; and you shall do your business in
your own name and in your own names. And this I
have commanded to be done for your salvation, as also
for their salvation in consequence of their being driven
out, and that which is to come. The covenant being
broken through transgression, by covetousness and
feigned words, therefore, you are dissolved as a United
Firm with your brethren, that you are not bound
only up to this hour unto them, only on this wise,
as I said, by loan, as shall be agreed by this Firm in
counsels as your circumstances will admit, and the voice
of the council direct.

And again, a commandment I give unto you concerning
your stewardships which I have appointed unto you. Behold
all these properties are mine, or else, your faith is vain,

1{9\0}4 [verso]

unto him the lot which is laid off for the building of

my houses, which is forty rods ~~wide~~ long and twelve

wide; and also the farm upon which his father now

resides; and this is the beginning of the stewardships

which I have appointed unto him, for a blessing upon

for behold I have reserved an inheritance for his father

him and upon his father, for his support. Therefore, he

shall be reckoned in the house of my servant Joseph; &

I will multiply blessings upon the house of my servant

Joseph inasmuch as he is faithful, even a multiplicity

of blessings.

And now a commandment I give unto you concerning

Zion, that you shall no longer be bound as a United

Firm to your brethren of Zion, only on this wise: After

you are organized, you shall be called, The United Firm

of the Stake of Zion, the city of Kirtland among yourselvs.

And your brethren, after they are organized, shall be called

The United Firm of the city of Zion; and they shall be

organized in their own names, and in their own name;

and they shall do their business in their own name and

in their own names; and you shall do your business in

your own name and in your own names. And this I

have commanded to be done for your salvation, as also

for their salvation in consequence of their being driven

out, and that which is to come. The covenant being

broken through transgressions, by covetousness and

feigned words, therefore, you are d{s\issolved} as a United

Firm with your brethren, that you are not bound

only up to this hour unto them, only on this wise,

as I said, by loan, as shall be agreed by this Firm in

counsel as your circumstances will admit, and the voice

of the council direct.

And again, a commandment I give unto you concerning

your Stewardships which I have appointed unto you. Behold

all these properties are mine, or else, your faith is vain

ORIGINAL INSCRIPTION
Orson Hyde

REVISIONS
Oliver Cowdery
Orson Hyde
William W. Phelps
Joseph Smith
Frederick G. Williams
Unidentified

and ye are found hypocrits, and the covenants which you have made unto me are broken; and if these properties are mine, then ye are stewards, otherwise ye are no stewards: But, verily, I say unto you I have appointed unto you to be stewards over mine house, even stewards indeed, and for this purpose have I commanded you to organize yourselves, even to print my word, the fullness of my scriptures, the revelations which I have given unto you, and which I shall hereafter, from time to time, give unto you, for the purpose of building up my church and kingdom on the earth, and to prepare my people for the time of my comeing which is nigh at hand. Therefore, a commandments I give unto you, that ye shall take the books of Mormon and also the copy-right, and also the copy-right which shall be secured of the articles and covenants, in which covenants all my commandments which it is my will should be printed, shall be printed, as it shall be made known unto you; and also the copy-right of the New translation of the scriptures; and this I say that others may not take the blessings away from you which I have conferred upon you. And ye shall prepare for yourselves a place for a treasury and consecrate it unto my name, and ye shall appoint one among you to keep the treasury; and he shall be ordained unto this blessing: And there shall be a seal upon the treasury, and all these sacred things shall be delivered into the treasury, and no man among you shall call it his own or any part of it, for it shall belong to you all with one accord, and I give it unto you from this very hour; and now see to it, that ye go to and make use of the stewardships which I have appointed unto you, exclusive of these sacred things, for the purpose of printing these sacred things, according as I have said; and the avails of these sacred things shall be had in the treasury, and a seal shall be upon it, & it shall not be used or taken out of the treasury by

and ye are found hypocrites, and the covenants which
you have made unto me are broken; and if these properties
are mine, then ye are stewards, otherwise ye are no stewards:
But, verily, I say unto you I have appointed unto you to
be stewards over mine house, even stewards indeed, and for
this purpose have I commanded you to organize yourselves,
even to print my word, the fullness of my Scriptures, the
revelations which I have given unto you, and which I shall
hereafter, from time to time, give unto you, for the purpose
of building up my church and kingdom on the Earth, and
to prepare my people for the time of my comeing which is
nigh at hand. Therefore, a commandment I give unto you,
that ye shall take the books of Mormon and also the copy=
right, and also the copy=right which shall be secured of the
Articles and covenants, in which covenants all my comm=
andments which it is my will should be printed, shall be
printed, as it shall be made known unto you; and also
the copy=right of the New translation of the scriptures; and
this I say that others may not take the blessings away from
you which I have conferred upon you. And ye shall pre=
pare for yourselves a place for a treasury and consecrate
it unto my name, and ye shall appoint one among you to keep
the treasury; and he shall be ordained unto this blessing:
and there shall be a seal upon the treasury, and all these
sacred things shall be delivered into the treasury, and no
man among you shall call it his own or any part of it;
for it shall belong to you all with one accord, and I give
it unto you from this very hour; and now see to it, that
ye go to and make use of the stewardships which I have
appointed unto you, exclusive of these sacred things,
for the purpose of printing these sacred things, according
as I have said; and the avails of these sacred things shall
be had in the treasury, and a seal shall be upon it, &
it shall not be used or taken out of the treasury by

ORIGINAL INSCRIPTION
Orson Hyde

REVISIONS
Oliver Cowdery
William W. Phelps
Joseph Smith
Frederick G. Williams
Unidentified

any one, neither shall the seal be loosed which shall be
placed upon it only by the voice of the Firm, or by
commandment. And thus shall ye preserve all the avails of
these sacred things in the treasury for sacred and holy
purposes. And this shall be called the sacred Treasury of
the Lord. And a seal shall be kept upon it, that it may
be holy and consecrated unto the Lord.

And again, there shall be another treasury prepared, &
a treasurer appointed to keep the treasury and a seal shall
be placed upon it, and all moneys that you receive
in your stewardships by improveing upon the properties which
I have appointed unto you, in houses or in lands or in cattle,
and in all things save it be the holy and sacred writings
which I have reserved unto myself for holy and sacred
purposes, shall be cast into the treasury as fast as you
receive moneys, by hundreds, or by fifties, or by twenty, or
by tens, or by fives, or in otherwords. if any man among you
obtain five dollars, let him cast it into the treasury, or if he
obtain ten or twenty or fifty or a hundred let him do likewise,
and let not any man among you say that it is his own,
for it shall not be called his nor any part of it; and there shall
not any part of it be used or taken out of the treasury only
by the voice and common consent of the Firm. And this
shall be the voice and common consent of the Firm: That any
man among you say unto the treasurer, I have need of this to
help me in my stewardship, if it be five dollars, or if it be
ten dollars, or twenty, or fifty or a hundred, the treasurer shall
give unto him the sum which he requires to help him in
his stewardship, until he be found a transgressor, and
it is manifest before the council of the Firm plainly
that he is an unfaithful and an unwise steward: But so
long as he is in full fellowship and is faithful and
wise in his stewardship, this shall be his token unto the
treasurer, that the treasurer shall not withhold; but in

1{9\0}6 [verso]

any one, neither shall the seal be loosed which shall be

placed upon it only by the voice of the Firm, or by

commandment. And thus shall ye preserve all the avails of

these sacred things in the treasury for sacred and holy

purposes, and this shall be called the sacred Treasury of

the Lord, and a seal shall be kept upon it, that it may

be holy and consecrated unto the Lord.

And again, there shall be another treasury prepared, &

a treasurer appointed to keep the treasury and a seal shall

be placed upon it, and all moneys that you receive

in your stewardships by improveing upon the properties which

I have appointed unto you, in houses or in lands or in cattle,

and in all things save it be the holy and sacred writings

which I have reserved unto myself for holy and sacred

purposes, shall be cast into the treasury as fast as you

receive moneys, by hundreds, or by fifties, or by twenties, or

by tens, or by fives, or in otherwords, if any man among you

obtain five dollars, let him cast it into the treasury, or if he

obtain ten or twenty or fifty or a hundred let him do likewise;

and let not any man among you say that it is his own;

for it shall not be called his nor any part of it; and there shall

not any part of it be used or taken out of the treasury only

by the voice and common consent of the Firm. And this

shall be the voice and common consent of the Firm: That any

man among you say unto the treasurer, I have need of this to

help me in my stewardship, if it be five dollars, or if it be

ten dollars, or twenty, or fifty or a hundred, The treasurer shall

give unto him the sum which he requires to help him in

his stewardship, until he be found a transgressor, and

it is manifest before the council of the Firm plainly

that he is an unfaithful and an unwise steward; But so

long as he is in full fellowship and is faithful and

wise in his stewardship, this shall be his token unto the

treasurer, that the treasure{d\r} shall not withold; but in

ORIGINAL INSCRIPTION
Orson Hyde

REVISIONS
Oliver Cowdery
William W. Phelps
Joseph Smith
Frederick G. Williams
Unidentified

case of transgression the Treasurer shall be subject unto the council and voice of the Firm; and in case the Treasurer is found an unfaithful and an unwise steward, he shall be subject to the council and voice of the Firm and shall be removed out of his place and another shall be appointed in his stead.

And again, verily I say unto you concerning your debts, Behold it is my will that you should pay all your debts; and it is my will that you should humble yourselves before me and obtain this blessing by your dilligence, and humility and the prayer of faith; and inasmuch as you are dilligent and humble and exercise the prayer of faith behold I will soften the hearts of those to whom you are indebted until I shall send means unto you for your deliverance. Therefore, write speedily unto New York, and write according to that which shall be dictated by my spirit, and I will soften the hearts of those to whom you are in debt, that it shall be taken away out of their minds to bring afflictions upon you. And inasmuch as ye are humble and faithful, and call on my name, behold I will give you the victory; I give unto you a promise that you shall be delivered this once out of your bondage. Inasmuch as you obtain a chance to loan money by hundreds or by thousands, even until you shall loan enough to deliver yourselves from bondage, it is your privilege, & pledge the properties which I have put into your hands this once by giving your names by common consent or otherwise as it shall seem good unto you, I give unto you the privilege this once, and behold if you proceed to do the things which I have laid before you, according to my commandment, all these things are mine, and ye are my stewards, and the master will not suffer his house to be broken up; even so Amen.

Recorded by O. Hyde 18 Augt. 1834 upon this Book

case of transgression the Treasurer shall be subject unto

the council and voice of the Firm; and in case the Treasurer

is found an unfaithful and an unwise steward, he shall

be subject to the counsel and voice of the Firm and

shall be removed out of his place and another shall be

appointed in his stead.

   And again, verily I say unto you concerning your debts,

Behold it is my will that you should pay all your debts;

and it is my will that you should humble yourselves before

me and obtain this blessing by your dilligence, and humility

and the prayer of faith; and inasmuch as you are dilliget [diligent]

and humble and exercise the prayer of faith behold I

will soften the hearts of those to whom you are in debt

until I shall send means unto you for your deliverance.

Therefore, write speedily unto New York, and write according

to that which shall be dictated by my spirit, and I will

soften the hearts of those to whom you are in debt,

that it shall be taken away out of y̶o̶u̶r̶ ^their^ minds to bring

afflictions upon you. And inasmuch as ye are humble

and faithful, and call on my name, behold I will

give you the victory; I give unto you a promise that you

shall be deliverd this once out of your bondage. Inas=

much as you obtain a chance to loan money by hund[r]eds

or by thousands, even until you shall loan enough to

deliver yourselves from bondage, it is your privilege, &

pledge the properties which I have put into your hands

this once by giveing your names by common consent

or otherwise as it shall seem good unto you, I give unto

you the privilege this once, and behold if you proceed

to do the things which I have laid before you, according

to my commandment, all these things are mine, and

ye are my s{◊rv\tew}a{nts\rds},[139] and the master will not suffer

his house to be broken up; even so Amen.

   <u>Recorded by O[rson]</u>. <u>Hyde 18 Augt. 1834 upon this Book</u>[140]

ORIGINAL INSCRIPTION
Orson Hyde

REVISIONS
Oliver Cowdery
Orson Hyde
William W. Phelps
Joseph Smith
Frederick G. Williams
Unidentified

   139. "s◊rvants" changed to "stewards".

   140. This is the first of four consecutive items that Orson Hyde copied into Revelation Book 2. Textual analysis indicates that he copied them from a notebook of revelations he had previously created with the assistance of Orson Pratt. (See Hyde and Pratt, Notebook, [19]–[43].)

Kirtland February 24 1834.

Verily I say unto you my friends, behold I will give unto you a revelation and commandments that you may know how to act in the discharge of your duties concerning the salvation and redemption of your brethren who have been scattered from the land of Zion: Being driven and smitten by the hands of mine enemies on whom I will pour out of my wrath without measure in mine own time; for I have suffered them thus far that they might fill up the measure of their iniquities, that their cup might be full; and that those who call themselves after my name might be chastened for a little season with a sore and grievous chastisement because they did not hearken altogether unto the precepts and commandments which I gave unto them. But verily I say unto you that I have decreed a decree which my people shall realize in asmuch as they hearken from this hour unto the council which I the Lord their God shall give unto them. Behold they shall, for I have decreed it, begin to prevail against mine enemies from this very hour; and by hearkning to observe all the words which I the Lord their God shall speak unto them, they shall never cease to prevail untill the kingdoms of the world are subdued under my feet and the earth is given unto the saints to possess it forever and ever. But inasmuch as they keep not my commandments & hearken not to observe all my words, the kingdoms of the world shall prevail against them; for they were set to be a light unto the world and to be the saviors of men, and inasmuch as they are not the saviors of men, they are as salt that has lost its savor and is thenceforth good for nothing but to be cast out and to be trodden under the feet of men. But verily I say unto you, I have decreed that your brethren who have been scattered shall return to the lands of their inheritances and build up the waste places of Zion.

1{9\0}8 [verso]

♦ ¹⁴¹Kirtland February. {◊◊\24}¹⁴² 1834.

Verily I say unto you my friends, behold I will give unto

you a revelation and commandment that you may know

how to act in the discharge of your duties concerning the

salvation and redemption of your brethren who have

been scattered from the land of Zion: Being driven and

smitten by the hands of mine enemies on whom I will

pour out of my wrath without measure in mine own

time; for I have suffered them thus far that they

might fill up the measure of their iniquities, that their

cup might be full; and that those who call themselves

after my name might be chastened for a little season

with a sore and grievous chastisement because they did

not hearken altogether unto the precepts and commandments

which I gave unto them. But verily I say unto you that

I have decreed a decree which my people shall realize in=

asmuch as they hearken from this hour unto the council

which I the Lord their God shall give unto them. Behold

they shall, for I have decreed it, begin to prevail against

mine enemies from this very hour; and by hearkening to

observe all the words which I the Lord their God shall

speak unto them, they shall never cease to prevail untill

the Kingdoms of the world are subdued under my feet and

the earth is given unto the saints to possess it forever and

ever. But inasmuch as they keep not my commandments &

hearken not to observe all my words, the Kingdoms of the world

shall prevail against them; for they were set to be a light

unto the world and to be the savio{rs\urs} of men, and inasmuch

as they are not the saviors of men, they are as salt that

has lost its savor and is thence forth good for nothing

but to be cast out and to be trodden under the feet of

I have decreed

men. But verily I say unto you, that your brethren
^

who have been scattered shall return to the lands of their

inheritances and build up the waste places of Zion,

ORIGINAL INSCRIPTION
Orson Hyde

REVISIONS
Oliver Cowdery
Orson Hyde
William W. Phelps
Joseph Smith
Frederick G. Williams
Unidentified

141. Diagonal use mark in graphite through entire page. Although similar use marks were made as part of other record-keeping efforts in Nauvoo, there is no clear correlation between this manuscript version and the first publication of this revelation in the 1844 Doctrine and Covenants (section 101).

142. "◊◊" possibly "19" revised to "10" and then wipe-erased; then written over by "24", with "4" apparently rewritten over a misshapen "4".

for after much tribulation, as I have said unto you in a former commandment, cometh the blessing. Behold this is the blessing which I have promised after your tribulations, and the tribulations of your brethren; your redemption and the redemption of your brethren, even their restoration to the land of Zion, to be established no more to be thrown down. Nevertheless if they shall pollute their inheritances they shall be thrown down; for I will not spare them if they shall pollute their inheritances. Behold I say unto you that the redemption of Zion must needs come by power; Therefore I will raise up unto my people a man who shall lead them like as Moses led the children of Israel; for ye are the children of Israel and of the seed of Abraham, and ye must needs be led out of bondage by power and with a stretched out arm; and as your fathers were led at the first even so shall the redemption of Zion be. Therefore, let not your hearts faint, for I say not unto you as I said unto your fathers, mine angel shall go up before you, but not my presence; but I say unto you mine angel shall go up before you and also my presence and in time ye shall possess the goodly land.

Verily, Verily, I say unto you that my servant Joseph (Smith Jr is the man to whom I likened the servant to whom the Lord of the vineyard spake in the parable which I have given unto you. Therefore, let my servant Joseph Smith Jr say unto the strength of my house, my young men, and the middle aged, gather ye together unto the land of Zion, upon the lands which I have bought with moneys that have been consecrated unto me. And let all the churches send up wise men with their moneys and purchase lands even as I have commanded them. And inasmuch as mine enemies come against you to drive you from my goodly land which I have consecrated to be the land of Zion, even from your own lands after these testimonies which ye have brought before me

¹⁴³for after much tribulation, as I have said unto you in a

former commandment, cometh the blessing: Behold this is the

blessing which I ~~have~~ promised after your tribulations, and

the tribulations of your brethren, your redemption and

the redemption of your brethren, even their restoration

to the land of Zion, to be established no more to be thrown

down: Nevertheless if they shall pollute their inheritances

they shall be thrown down; for I will not spare them if

they shall pollute their inheritances. Behold I say unto you

that the redemption of Zion must needs come by power;

Therefore I will raise up unto my people a man who shall

lead them like as {mos\Moses} led the children of Israel;

for ye are the children of Israel and of the seed of

Abraham, and ye must needs be led out of bondage by

power and with a streched out arm; and as your fathers

were led at the first even so shall the redemption of Zion

be, Therefore, let not your hearts faint, for I say not unto

you as I said unto your fathers, mine angel shall go up

before you, but not my presence; but I say unto you mine

angel shall go up before you and also my presence and

in time ye shall possess the goodly land.

⟨Smith Jr⟩
Verily, Verily, I say unto you that my servant Joseph‸

is the man to whom I likened the servant to whom the Lord

of the vineyard spake¹⁴⁴ in the parable which I have given unto

Smith Jr
you: Therefore, let my servant Joseph‸ say unto the strengt[h]

of my house, my young men, and the middle aged,

ye
gather‸ together unto the land of Zion, upon the lands which

I have bought with moneys that have been consecrated unto

me; And let all the churches send up wise men with their

commanded
moneys and purchase lands even as I have ~~told~~‸ them:

And inasmuch as mine enemies come against you to drive

yo{◊◊\u} from my goodly land which I have consecrated to

be the land of Zion, even from your own lands ~~after~~

after these testimonies which ye have brought before me

ORIGINAL INSCRIPTION
Orson Hyde

REVISIONS
Oliver Cowdery
Orson Hyde
William W. Phelps
Joseph Smith
Frederick G. Williams
Unidentified

143. Diagonal use mark in graphite through entire page. (See 633n141 herein.)

144. Or "spoke".

against them ye shall curse them, and whomsoever
ye curse I will curse, and ye shall avenge me of mine
enemies; and my presence shall be with you even in avenging
me of mine enemies unto the third and fourth generation
of them that hate me. Let no man be afraid to lay down
his life for my sake, for whoso layeth down his life for
my sake shall find it again: and whoso is not willing to
lay down his life for my sake is not my disciple.

It is my will that my servant Sidney ^Rigdon should lift up
his voice in the congregation in the eastern countries in
preparing the church to keep the commandments which I
have given unto them concerning the restoration and
redemption of Zion. It is my will that my servant
Parley ^Pratt and my servant Lyman ^Wight should not return to
the land of their brethren until they have obtained com-
panies to go up unto the land of Zion, by tens, or by twenties
or by fifties or by a hundred until they have obtained
unto the number of five hundred of the strength of my
house. Behold this is my will. Ask and ye shall receive.
But men do not always do my will; therefore, if ye cannot
obtain five hundred, seek dilligently that peradventure ye may
obtain three ^hundred; and if ye cannot obtain three hundred
seek dilligently that peradventure ye may obtain one
hundred: But verily I say unto you a commandment
I give unto you that you shall not go up unto the
land of Zion until you have obtained a hundred of the
strength of my house to go up with you unto the land
of Zion. Therefore, as I said unto you, ask and you
shall receive. Pray earnestly that peradventure my
servant Joseph may go up with you and preside in
the midst of my people and organize my Kingdom
upon the consecrated land and establish the children
of Zion upon the laws and commandments which
have been given and which shall be given unto you.

110 [verso]

¹⁴⁵against them ye shall curse them, and whomsoever

ye curse I will curse, and ye shall avenge me of mine

enemies; and my presence shall be with you even in avenging

me of mine enemies unto the third and fourth generation

of them that hate me. Let no man be afraid to lay down

his life for my sake, for whoso layeth down his life for

my sake shall find it again: and whoso is not willing to

lay down his life for my sake is not my disciple.

         Rigdon

  It is my will that my servant Sidney should lift up

his voice in the congregations in the Eastern countries in

prepareing the churchs to keep the commandments which I

have given unto them concerning the restoration and

redemption of Zion. It is my will that my servant

  P Pratt   Wight

Parley and my servant Lyman should not return to

the land of their b{◊\⟨r⟩}ethren until they have obtained com=

panies to go up unto the land of Zion, by tens, or by twenties

or by fifties or by a hundred until they have obtained

unto the number of five hundred of the strength of my

house. Behold this is my will. Ask and ye shall receive:

But men do not always do my will; therefore, if ye cannot

obtain five hundred, seek dilligently that peradventure ye may

     hundred

obtain three; and if ye cannot obtain three hundred

seek dilligently that peradventure ~~that~~ ye may obtain one

hundred: But verily I say unto you a commandment

I give unto you that you shall not go up unto the

land of Zion until you have obtained a hundred of the

strength of my house to go up with you unto the land

of Zion. Therefore, as I said unto you, ask and you

shall receive. Pray earnestly that peradventure my

servant Joseph may go up with you and preside in

the midst of my people and organize my Kingdom

upon the consecrated land and establish the children

of Zion upon the laws and commandments which

have been given and which shall be given unto you.

ORIGINAL INSCRIPTION
Orson Hyde

REVISIONS
Oliver Cowdery
William W. Phelps
Joseph Smith
Frederick G. Williams
Unidentified

145. Diagonal use mark in graphite through entire page. (See 633n141 herein.)

All victory and glory is brought to pass unto you thro' your dilligence, faithfulness and prayers of faith. Let my servant Parley journey with my servant Joseph, let my servant Lyman journey with my servant Sidney, Let my servant Hyrum journey with my servant Frederick; Let my servant Orson Hyde journey with my servant Orson Pratt whithersoever my servant Joseph shall counsel them, in obtaining the fulfilment of these commandments which I have given unto you and have the residue in my hands: even so Amen. Recorded on this book by
O. Hyde 18. Augt 1834.

~~~~~~~~~~~~~~~~~~~~~~~~~~~~~~~~~~~~~

Kirtland, 28 April, 1834.

Verily thus saith the Lord concerning the division and settlements of the United Firm: Let there be reserved three thousand Dollars for the right and claim of the Firm in Kirtland for inheritances in due time, even when the Lord will: and with this claim, to be had in rememberance when the Lord shall reveal it for a right of inheritance, ye are made free from the Firm of Zion; and the Firm in Zion is made free from the Firm in Kirtland: Thus saith the Lord. Amen.
Recorded on this book by O. Hyde 27 Augt. 1834.

───────────────────────

To go into the covents,   Kirtland 17 Feby 1834.

This day a general council of twenty four high priests assembled at the house of Joseph Smith jr by revelation, and proceeded to organize the High Council of the church of Christ which was to consist of twelve high priests and one or three presidents as the case might require. This high council was appointed by revelation for the purpose of settling important difficulties which might arise in the Church which could not be settled by the church

[146]All victory and glory is brought to pass unto you thro'

your dilligence, faithfulness and prayers of faith. Let my

servant Parley journey with my servant Joseph, let my

servant Lyman journey with my servant Sidney, Let my

servant Hyrum [Smith] journey with my servant Frederick [G. Williams]; Let

my servant Orson Hyde journey with my servant Orson

                                    shall
Pratt whithersoever my servant Joseph counsel them, in
                                    ^

obtaining the fulfilment of these commandments which

I have given unto you and leave the residue in my

hands: even so Amen. Recorded on this book by

   O. Hyde 18 Augt 1834.——[147]

 ♦ Kirtland, 28 April, 1834.—

  Verily thus saith the Lord concerning the division and

settlement of the United Firm: Let there be reserved three Thou-

sand Dollars for the right and claim of the Firm in Kirtland

for inheritances in due time, even when the Lord will; and

with this claim, to be had in rememberance when the Lord

shall reveal it for a right of inheritance, ye are made

free from the Firm of Zion; and the Firm in Zion is made

free from the Firm in Kirtland: Thus saith the Lord. Amen.

  Recorded on this book by O[rson]. Hyde 27 Augt. 1834.[148]

♦ **To go into the coven**[an]**ts,**[149] Kirtland 17,— Feb.y 1834.—

#[150] This day a general council of twenty four high

priests assembled at the house of Joseph Smith Jr.

by revelation, and proceeded to organize the High

council of the church of christ which was to

consist of twelve high priests and one or three

presidents as the case might require. This high

council was appointed by revelation for the purpose

of settleing important difficulties which might arise in

the church which could not be settled by the church

ORIGINAL INSCRIPTION
Orson Hyde

REVISIONS
Oliver Cowdery
William W. Phelps
Joseph Smith
Frederick G. Williams
Unidentified

146. Diagonal use mark in graphite from top of page to end of this revelation. (See 633n141 herein.)

147. This is the second of four consecutive items that Orson Hyde copied into Revelation Book 2. Textual analysis indicates that he copied them from a notebook of revelations he had previously created with the assistance of Orson Pratt. (See Hyde and Pratt, Notebook, [7]–[18].)

148. This is the third of four consecutive items that Orson Hyde copied into Revelation Book 2. Textual analysis indicates that he copied them from a notebook of revelations he had previously created with the assistance of Orson Pratt. (See Hyde and Pratt, Notebook, [44].)

149. This notation corresponds to similar ones on manuscript pages 20 and 31; these notations mark the material that became sections 4, 5, and 6 in the 1835 Doctrine and Covenants.

150. This mark likely indicates the intent or instruction to publish this item in the 1835 Doctrine and Covenants, the first publication that reflects the redactions in this item (section 5).

or the Bishop's council to the satisfaction of the
parties. Joseph Smith Jun. Sidney Rigdon and Frederick
G Williams, were acknowledged Presidents by the voice of
the council; and Joseph Smith Sen. John Smith,
Joseph Coe, John Johnson, Martin Harris, John S
Carter, Jared Carter, Oliver Cowdery, Saml. H
Smith, Orson Hyde, Sylvester Smith and Luke Johnson
High priests, were chosen to be a standing council
for the Church by the unanimous voice of the council.
The above named counsellors were then asked whither
they accepted their appointments, and whether they would act
in that office according to the law of heaven, to which
they all answered that they accepted their several appointments,
and would fill their offices according to the grace of
God bestowed upon them. The number composing the council
who voted in the name and for the church in appointing
the above named counsellors, were forty three, as follows,
Nine High Priests, Seventeen Elders, four priests and thirteen
members.——

Voted, that the high council cannot have power
to act without seven of the above named counsellors
or their regularly appointed successors, are present. These
seven shall have power to appoint other high priest,
whom they may consider worthy and capable to act
in the place of absent counsellors. Voted, that whenever
any vacancy shall occur by the death, removal from office
for transgression, or removal from the bounds of this church
government of any one of the above named counsellors,
it shall be filled by the nomination of the President or
Presidents and sanctioned by the voice of a general
council of High Priests convened for that purpose to act in the name
of the church. The president of the church who is
also the president of the council, is appointed by the
voice of the Same revelation, and acknowledged in his ad-

or the Bishop's council to the satisfaction of the

parties. Joseph Smith Jur., Sidney Rigdon and Frederick

G Williams, were acknowledged Presidents by the voice of

the council; and Joseph Smith Sen. John Smith,

Joseph Coe, John Johnson, Martin Harris, John S

Carter, Jared Carter, Oliver Cowdery, Saml. H

Smith, Orson Hyde, Sylvester Smith and Luke Johnson

high priests, were chosen to be a standing council

for the church by the unanimous voice of the council.

The above named counsellors were then asked whether

they accepted their appointments and whether they would act

in that office according to the law of heaven, to which

they all answered that they accepted their several appointme[n]ts,

and would fill their offices according to the grace of

God bestowed upon them. The number composeing the council

who voted in the name and for the church in appointing

the above named counsellors, were forty Three, as follows;

Nine High Priests, Seventeen Elders, four priests, and thirteen

members.—

Voted, that the high council cannot have power

to act without seven of the above named counsellors

or their regularly appointed successors, are present. These

seven shall have power to appoint other high priests

whom they may consider worthy and capable to act

in the place of absent counsellors. Voted, that whenever

any vacancy shall occur by the death, removal from office

for transgression, or removal from the bounds of this church

goverment of any one of the above named counsellors,

it shall be filled by the nomination of the President or

Presidents and sanctioned by the voice of a general

for that purpose
council of High Priests convened ^ to act in the name

of the church. The president of the church who is

also the president of the council, is appointed by ~~the~~

revelation,
~~voice of the Savior~~ ^ and acknowledged in his ad-

ORIGINAL INSCRIPTION
Orson Hyde

REVISIONS
Oliver Cowdery
Orson Hyde
William W. Phelps
Joseph Smith
Frederick G. Williams
Unidentified

ministration by the voice of the church; and it is according to the dignity of his office that he should preside over the high council of the church; and it is his privilege to be assisted by two other presidents, appointed after the same manner that he himself was appointed; and in case of the absence of one or both of those who are appointed to assist him, he has power to preside over the council without an assistant, and in case that he himself is absent, the other presidents have power to preside in his stead, both or either of them.

Whenever a high council of the church of Christ is regularly organized according to the foregoing pattern, it shall be the duty of the twelve counsellors to cast lots, by numbers, and thereby ascertain who of the twelve shall speak first; commencing with No. 1. and so in succession to No. 12.—

Whenever this council convenes to act upon any case, the twelve counsellors shall consider whether it is a difficult one or not; if it is not, two only of the counsellors shall speak upon it according to the form above written: But if it is thought to be difficult, four shall be appointed, and if more difficult, six: But in no case, shall more than six be appointed to speak. The accused in all cases has a right to one half of the council to prevent insult or injustice; and the counsellors appointed to speak before the council, are to present the case after the evidence is examined, in its true light, before the council, and every man is to speak according to equity and justice. Those counsellors who draw even numbers, that is, 2, 4, 6, 8, 10 and 12 are the individuals who are to stand up in the behalf of the accused and prevent insult or injustice. In all cases the accuser and the accused shall have a privilege of speaking for themselves before the council after the evidences are heard and the counsellors who are appointed to speak on the case, have finished their

ministration by the voice of the church; and it is

according to the dignity of his office that he should preside

over the high council of the church; and it is his privil=

ege to be assisted by two other presidents appointed after

the same manner that he himself was appointed; and in

case of the abscence of one or both of those who are

appointed to assist him, he has power to preside over the

council without an assistant, and in case that he himself

is absent, the other presidints have power to preside in his

stead, both or either of them.

Whenever a high council of the church of Christ is regu=

larly organized according to the foregoing pattern, it shall

be the duty of the twelve counsellors to cast lots by numbers

and thereby ascertain who of the twelve shall speak first;

commenceing with No. 1. and so in succession to No. 12.—

Whenever this council convenes to act upon any case, the

twelve counsellors shall consider whether it is a difficult

one or not; if it is not, two only of the counsellors shall

speak upon it according to the form above written: But if

it is thought to be difficult, four shall be appointed, and

if more difficult, six: But in no case, shall more than

six be appointed to speak. The accused in all cases has

a right to one half of the council to prevent insult or

injustice; and the counsellors appointed to speak before

the council, are to present the case after the evidence is

examined, in its true light, before the council, and every man

is to speak according to equity and justice. Those counsellors

who draw even numbers, that is, 2, 4, 6, 8,[151] 10 and 12 are

the individuals who are to stand up in the behalf of the

accused and prevent insult or injustice. In all cases

the accuser and the accused shall have a privilege of

speaking for themselves before the council after the evi=

dences are heard and the counsellors who are appo=

=inted to speak on the case, have finished their

ORIGINAL INSCRIPTION
Orson Hyde

REVISIONS
Oliver Cowdery
William W. Phelps
Joseph Smith
Frederick G. Williams
Unidentified

151. There is a pinhead impression above "8", indicating that the pin in the following leaf remained in the same general location for some time. (See 647n154 herein.)

remarks. After the evidence are heard, the counsellors, accusers, and the accused, have spoken, the president shall give a decision according to the understanding which he shall have of the case, and call upon the twelve counsellors to sanction the same by their vote. But should the remaining counsellors who have not spoken, or any one of them, after hearing the evidence and pleadings impartially, discover an error in the decision of the president, they can manifest it and the case shall have a re-hearing; and if after a careful rehearing any additional light is thrown upon the case, the decision shall be altered accordingly. But in case no additional light is given, the first decision shall stand, the majority of the council having power to determine the same.

In cases of difficulty respecting doctrine or principle, (if there is not a sufficiency written to make the case clear to the minds of the council) the President may inquire and obtain the mind of the Lord by revelation. The high priests when abroad have power to call and organize a council after the manner aforesaid of the foregoing to settle difficulties when the parties or either of them shall request it and the said council of high priests shall have power to appoint one of their own number to preside over such council for the time being. It shall be the duty of said council to transmit, immediately, a copy of their proceedings with a full statement of the testimony accompanying their decision to the high council at the seat of the government of the church. Should the parties or either of them be dissatisfied with the decision of said council they may appeal to the high council of the seat of the ~~government of~~ of the church and have a re-hearing which case shall there be conducted according to the former pattern written as though no such decision had been made. ————

remarks. After the evidences are heard, the counsellors, accuser

and the accused, have spoken, the president shall give

a decision according to the understanding which he shall

have of the case, and call upon the twelve counsellors

to sanction the same by their ~~voices~~ vote: But should the

remaining counsellors who have not spoken, or any one

of them, after hearing the evidences and pleadings

impartially, discover an error in the decision of the

president, they can manifest it and the case shall

have a re=hearing; and if after a careful rehearing

any additional light is thrown upon the case, the decision

shall be altered accordingly: But in case no additional

light is given, the first decision shall stand, the majority

of the council haveing powir to determine the same.

 In cases of difficulty respecting doctrine or

principle, (if there is not a sufficiency written to make

the case clear to the minds of the council) the President

may inquire and obtain the mind of the Lord by revelatio[n].

The high priests when abroad have power to call and

organize a council after the manner ~~aforesaid~~ of the foregoing

to settle difficulties when the parties or either of them shall

request it and the said council of high priests shall have

power to appoint one of their own number to preside over

such council for the time being. It shall be the duty of

said council to transmit, immediately, a copy of their pro=

ceedings with a full statement of the testimony accompanying

their decision to the high council at the seat of the

goverment of the[152] church. Should the parties or either

of them be dissatisfied with the decision of said council

they may appeal to the high council {at\of} the seat of the

first Presidency

~~general goverment~~ of the church and have a re=

hearing which case shall there be conducted accor=

ding to the former pattern written as though no

such decision had been made.——

ORIGINAL INSCRIPTION
Orson Hyde

REVISIONS
Oliver Cowdery
William W. Phelps
Joseph Smith
Frederick G. Williams
Unidentified

 152. There is a pinhead
impression above "the", indicating that the pin in the following leaf remained in the
same general location for some
time. (See 647n154 herein.)

This council of high priests abroad is only to be
called on the most difficult cases of church matters;
and no common or ordinary case is to be sufficient
to call such councils. The traveling or located high priests
abroad have the power to say whether it is necessary
to call such a council or not.

*Resolved, that the president or presidents at the seat
of ~~general Church government~~ The first Presidency of the Church shall have power to determine
whether any such case as may be appealed is justly entitled
to a re-hearing after examining the appeal and the
evidence and statements accompanying it.

The twelve counsellors then proceeded to cast lots, or
ballot to ascertain who should speak first; and the following
was the result, namely,

Oliver Cowdery	drew	No.	1
Joseph Coe	"	"	2
Samuel H Smith	"	"	3
Luke Johnson	"	"	4
John S Carter	"	"	5
Sylvester Smith	"	"	6
John Johnson	"	"	7
Orson Hyde	"	"	8
Jared Carter	"	"	9
Joseph Smith Sen	"	"	10
John Smith	"	"	11
Martin Harris	"	"	12

The Council then adjourned to meet on wednesday
the 19th Inst. at 10 O'clk A. M.

Orson Hyde, } Clerks.
Oliver Cowdery,

This council of high priests abroad is only to be

called on the most difficult cases of church matters;

and no common or ordinary case is to be sufficient

to call such councils. The traveling or located high priests

abroad have the power to say whether it is necessary

to call such a council or not.

*153Resolved, that the president or presidents {at\of} the seat
the first Presidency of the Ch[u]rch
of ~~general church goverment~~ shall have power to determine
            ^

whether any such case as may be appealed is justly entitled

to a re-hearing after examining the appeal and the

evidences and statements accompanying it.

The twelve counsellors then proceeded to cast lots or

ballot to ascertain who should speak first; and the following

was the result, namely, Oliver Cowdery   Drew   No.   1

Joseph Coe	"	"	2
Samuel H Smith	"	"	3
Luke Johnson	"	"	4
John S Carter	"	"	5
Sylvester Smith	"	"	6
John Johnson	"	"	7
Orson Hyde	"	"	8
Jared Carter	"	"	9
Joseph Smith Sen	"	"	10
John Smith	"	"	11
Martin Harris	"	"	12.

154The council then adjournd to meet on wednesday

the 19th. Inst. at 10 O'cl'k A.M.

Orson Hyde,
Oliver Cowdery,   } Clerks.155

ORIGINAL INSCRIPTION
Orson Hyde

REVISIONS
Oliver Cowdery
William W. Phelps
Joseph Smith
Frederick G. Williams
Unidentified

153. At this point in the 1835 Doctrine and Covenants, there is a seven-line verse not found in Revelation Book 2. The asterisk likely indicates where this new material was to be inserted for publication.

154. In the following sentence there are several differences between this version and the version in the 1835 Doctrine and Covenants. A slip of paper was likely pinned above "Orson" two lines below, where two pinholes appear. The slip possibly contained these changes or the seven-line verse mentioned above. (See Doctrine and Covenants 5, 1835 ed. [D&C 102].)

155. This is the fourth of four consecutive items that Orson Hyde copied into Revelation Book 2. Textual analysis indicates that he copied them from a notebook of revelations he had previously created with the assistance of Orson Pratt. (See Hyde and Pratt, Notebook, [45]–[55].)

Kirtland, November 25, 1834.

It is my will that my servant Warren ^A. Cowdery^ should ~~be ap~~ the ap=
=pointed and ordained a presiding High Priest over my Church
in the land of Freedom and the regions round about; and should
preach my everlasting gospel, and lift up his voice and warn
the people, not only in his own place, but in the adjoining Counties, and devote his whole time in this high
and holy calling which I now give unto him; seeking
dilligently the kingdom of heaven and its righteousness,
and all things necessary shall be added thereunto; for
the laborer is worthy of his hire.

And again, verily I say unto you, the coming of
the Lord draweth nigh, and it overtaketh the
world as a thief in the night: therefore, gird up your
loins, that ye may be the children of the light, ~~and~~
and that day shall not overtake you as a thief.

And again, verily I say unto you, there was joy
in heaven when my servant Warren bowed to my
sceptre and separated himself from the crafts of men.
Therefore, blessed is my servant Warren, for I will
have mercy on him, and notwithstanding the vanity of
his heart, I will lift him up, ~~and~~ inasmuch as he will
humble himself before me; ^and^ I will give ^unto^ him grace and as-
=surance wherewith he may stand; and if he continues to be
a faithful witness, and a light unto the Church, I have pre-
=pared a crown for him in the mansion of my Father: even
so. Amen.

120 [verso]

which I have given you, the gates

of hell shall not prevail against you;

for my grace is sufficient for you:

and ye shall be lifted up at the

Last day. {a\A}nd I Jesus Christ, your

Lord and your God, have spoken it

unto you, that I might bring about

my righteous purposes unto the children

of men. Amen—— /¹⁶² [*162 pages blank*]

ORIGINAL INSCRIPTION
Frederick G. Williams

REVISIONS
Oliver Cowdery
William W. Phelps
Joseph Smith
Frederick G. Williams
Unidentified

162. Frederick G. Williams handwriting ends.

Material facts

left out of the history of the church
are noted here that they may be brought
in, in their place.

1 — The Conference minutes in Book
E, from page 1 to 33 are to be revised
and after the facts are collected, entered
into the general history.

× 2ᵈ The Conference minutes in Book
× C from page 1 to #17 do do &c
not found

Singular Phenomenon seen by W. Partridge
in 1832 See his Journal & note

× Memory — Hyrum Smith & Reynolds Cahoon commenced digging
the trench for the walls of the Lords house on the 6
of June, and accomplished the same by their own
× hands, — see — Orders of exercises of laying the
corner stones — on the 23ᵈ July, 1833,

~~E in the Book, from Nov 29ᵗʰ 1832 to Oct 4ᵗʰ 1833~~

× A page 76. Kirtland Nov 23ᵈ 1833
× F March 13ᵗʰ 1833, page 48"
× " June 21" " " 4.9,
× A Nov- 23 " " 76

Joseph Smith said in 1831 that the
~~Lord~~ had decided that the doctors
should not heal people; that medicine would
have no effect. The Gentiles should use
medicine, and had use for it.

XXXXXXXXXXXXXXXX

Dec 20" "Evening and Morning Star" 269, page 441 extract
Jan 20, Every " " " 270 do do extract
× 0624. Book C page 41 Conference of highpriests
× C page 48"." Council April 4 1834 Kirtland
not found
Nov. 20. 1833 A recommend to Geo Wᵐ Akin marked
"W."

[inside back cover and 6 pages blank][163]

[1] [recto]

♦

/[164]**Material** facts

left out of the history of the church

are noted here that they may be brought

in. in their place

☞ 1—The Conference minutes {f⟨◊⟩\in} Book

E, from page 1 to 33 are to be reveiled[165]

and after the facts are collected, {i\⟨e⟩}ntered

into the general history.

X 2[d] The conference minutes {f⟨◊⟩\in} Book

X C from page 1 to ~~14~~ 17 d[itt]o do &c

Singular Phenamena Sean by Br [Edward] Partridge

not found in 1832 S{◊\ee} his Journal ¶ note

X /[166]Memory— Hyrum Smith, & Reynold{◊\s} Cahoon commenced digging

the trench for the walls of the Lords house on the 6

of June. and accomplished the same by their own

X hands,— [see]— order of exercises of laying the

corner stones on the 23[d] July. 1833.

{◊\F}X~~small Book, from Nov 29~~[th]~~, 1832 To Oct 4~~[th]~~ 1833.~~

X A pag 76. Kirtland Nov 23[d] 1833

X F March 13[th.] 1833. page 48,,

X " June 21,, " " 49,

X A Nov— 23 " " 76

/[167]Joseph Smith said in 1831 that the

{Doctors\⟨Lord⟩} ◊had decided that the Doctors
    not
should heal people; that medicine would
    ^

have no effect. The gentiles studied

medicine, and had use for it.

~~Thomas Shaws Letter 1833—~~[168]

/[169]Dec 20 "Evening and Morning Star." 269. page,   ext[r]act
   X[170]
Jan 20. Even[in]g " " " 270 D[itt]o   Extract

entered on page 441.

X /[171]Feb 24. Book C pag 41 conference of high priests

X /[172]C page 48[th.] council April 4, 183{3\4} Kirtland

not found. /[173]Nov. 20. 1833 A recommend to Geo W. Pitkin markd

"W."

ORIGINAL INSCRIPTION
William W. Phelps
Willard Richards

REVISIONS
Willard Richards
Unidentified

163. When compiling JS's history in 1843, Willard Richards and William W. Phelps turned Revelation Book 2 upside down and used three blank leaves at the back for notations about their history-writing effort. The title on the back cover reflects this usage: "Facts left out | Re[g]istered | herei[n]". The final blank page bears offsetting from the opposite inscribed side (first page of historical material) and has an adhesive wafer on the inside edge.

164. William W. Phelps handwriting begins.

165. Possibly "revewd".

166. William W. Phelps handwriting ends; Willard Richards begins.

167. Willard Richards handwriting ends; William W. Phelps begins.

168. Dash included in cancellation.

169. William W. Phelps handwriting ends; Willard Richards begins.

170. A vertical line through the inserted X indicates that the X applies to the lines immediately above and below.

171. Willard Richards handwriting ends; William W. Phelps begins.

172. William W. Phelps handwriting ends; Willard Richards begins.

173. Willard Richards handwriting ends; William W. Phelps begins.

X April 4th 1834, C. = Conference on Geo. F. James

X December 28 1834. — C. 81. Council

X Thomas Shows Letter for Heart to visit America 316 p
    Messenger & Advocate   April 21, 1835

1836.
Jan 5 Doct Piexotto's Letter to Warren Parrish and
    answer — January 11. 1836. D. p 127, 8, 9, 130 —
1835 May 2 — R T. page 5. C

+ D. p. 153. Feb 8th 1836. Council

Jan 13. 1836. Rules to Govern the Lords house Jan 13. 1836. Book C. 231

1836. Apr 15th E. page 68. —

1837 Feb Joseph Hyrum Olevn went to Monkague on return
    Mob collected at Heartar, B. Young, Wm Smith went funk
    took Joseph out of the Stage & carried him to Kirtley

1837. May Grandmire Newell complain Joseph thisted his
    Some Life.........................

1836. 25 July — E. 69, 70. minutes conference.

1836. January 13th & 15th C. 231. Rules and Regulations of the Lords House

1837 Sept 27th O. Granger Letter of attorney from Joseph & Sidney

1838 Jan 15th Marvellous scene. Pompet Branch.

1838 April 10th Between 9 & 10 hundred had been baptized
    in England. — 77 ordained — viz Elder Priets Teachers & Deacons,
    And about 20 Branches had been established

1838 May, about 23 a bundle of straw and a fire
    Brand in it found in the house of the Lord in Kirtland
    put in through the window.

1838. Last of May or first June O. Cowdery, John & David Whitmer Lyman E.
    Johnson, Run away to Clay County, See G. 47.

1838. January 12. Revelation Kirtland — G. 51.
    "   "   "   "   G. 52
    "   "   "   "   G. 53.

1837 Octo 3 William Store   295 Alice Hodson

1838 Oct 25 Letter Book   1819 O. Hyde man

1838. Aug 16 to 20. Joseph went the 3 forks of grand River, with Rigdon
    Hyrum & Babbit. to see the country. with Anson Call —
    mob tried to intercept him on his return. —

[2] [verso]

X /[174]April 4th 1834, C.= Conferenc[e] on Geo F. James

X December 28 1834,— C. 81. Council

X ⟨Thomas⟩ Shaws Letter for [John] Hewit[t] to visit Americ[a] 316 p

Messenger & advocate April 21, 1835

⟨1836.⟩
Jan 5 Doct Piexotto [Daniel Peixotto]'s Letter to Warren Parrish and

answer— January 11. 1836. D. p 127, 8, 9, 130—
1835 May 2— RT page 5.
X D. p. 153. Feb 8th 1836. Council

⟨Jan 13. 1836,,⟩ Rules to Govern the Lords house Jan 13. 1836 Book C. 231

~~1836.~~ ~~Nov 15th.~~ E. page 68—

1837 Feb Joseph Hyrum [Smith], Oliver [Cowdery] went to M{◊◊◊\ichagin} on return

mob collected at ~~Mentor~~. B[righam]. Young. Wm Smith went frum K

took Joseph out of the stage & carr[i]ed him to Kirtland

1837. May Grandison Newell complaind Joseph thretnd his

life
same
1836. 25 July— E. 69, 70, minutes conference,

1836. Janua[r]y {◊\13}.th & 15th C, 231, Rules and Regulations of the Lord House

1837 Sept 27th O[liver]. Grangers Letter of atteny [attorney] from Joseph & Sidney [Rigdon]

1838 Jan 15th Marvellous scene. Pomfret Branch,,

1838 April 10th. {◊◊◊◊\Between} 9. & 10 hundred had been baptizd

in England.— 77 ordaind— viz. Elder Prie[s]ts Teacher & Deacons,

and about 20 Bran[c]hes had been established

1838 May . about 23 a bundle of straw and a fire

Brand in it found in the house of the Lord in Kirtland

put in through the window.

1838 ~~Last of May~~ or first June O. Cowdry. John & David Wh[i]tm[e]r, Lym[a]n E.

Johnson, Run[175] away to Clay Co[u]nty, See G, 47,

6
1838. January 12. Revelation Kirtland— G, 51,

"   "   "   "   G. 52

"   "   "   "   G. 53,

1838 {Sept\Octr} {2\3} ~~Millenial Star~~   ~~295 Alice~~ Hodson

1838 Oct 25   Letter Book   18, 19 O[rson] Hyde Mail

1838. Aug 16 to 20.   Joseph was att the 3 forks of grand River, with Rigdon

Hyrum & [Almon] Babbit[t], to see the country. with Anson Call.—

mob tried to intercept him on his ret[u]rn.—

ORIGINAL INSCRIPTION
Willard Richards

REVISIONS
Willard Richards
Unidentified

174. William W. Phelps handwriting ends; Willard Richards begins.

175. Or "Ran".

1838 September 8th Letter to Col Price

1838 About Oct 12, Mob left Dewitt for Davies, took
Amasa Lyman prisoner. rode him an the commue
4 days

"   Oct 3v. Joseph had advised the brethren at Haun's
Mills to go to Far West Haun was 1 of the committee
Hiram Comstock said to Davis Lewis I am the man
that shot your Brother.

~~1838 18 Dec. D H Redfield chairman~~

1838 July 8. Revelation. Duty of F G Williams & W W Phelps

1837 April 3 & 5. High council 72, 73.

"   3v & 31. Oct. C. C. Rich was fired upon by Bogart. when bearing a flag

"   2d Nov 66

1838 Sept 30 Sunday Thomas Webster was cut off at
Preston pub[l]ishing Hyde & Kimballs prophey, of april

1841. Feb 9. James Kelly was Elected Predt of ctenaua
University, J & S. 320.

1841 - 24 + 25 december J & S. 666

[3] [recto]

1838   September 8ᵗʰ Letter to Col [Sterling] Price

1838   Ab[o]ut Oct 12, mob left Dewitt for Davies[s], took

        Amasa Lym[a]n prisoner, rode him on the Cannon

        4 days

   "   Oct 30. Joseph had advised the brthrn at Haun's

        Mills to go to Far West Haunes was 1 o{n\f} the committee

        Hiram Comstock said to David ~~Lewi~~ Lewis I am the man

        that shot your Brother.

~~1838   18 Dec. DH Redfields[176] Memorial~~

1838   July 8. Revelation, Duty of F[rederick] G. Williams, W[illiam],W, Phelps

1837   April 3 & 5. High council 72.73.

   "   30 or 31. Oct. C[harles]. C. Rich was fired upon by [Samuel] Bogart. when bearing a ᶠˡᵃᵍ

   "   2ᵈ Nov CC

18.38   Sept 30 Sunday Thomas Webster was cut off at

        Preston [England] fullfilling [Orson] Hyde & [Heber C.] Kimballs prophecy, of april

1841.   Feb 9. James Kelly was Elected Presdnt of Nauvoo

        Univers[i]ty. (T&S. 320.

1841— 21 & 25 december T&S. 666 [*page [4] blank*]

ORIGINAL INSCRIPTION
Willard Richards

REVISIONS
Willard Richards
Unidentified

176. David Harvey Redfield.

Left out in the History

1838 " Oct 25 Letter Book 18-19 Marsh & Hyde letter

"   "   24 Documents 57. 58. 59. Marsh & Wyle

"   2 Nov. Charles Charles C. Rich. Statement. N. to Iowa

1838 Nov 28. Documents of Mo 87. certificate

1838 Oct 25 - C.C. Rich. statements Brethren flee north part
                                                    exert. him
                                                    notho. penn.

"   Dec ___ D.H. Redfields Book. Names of witnesses given by
              Mr Phelps to Legislature of Mo. Capt Bogart Reed Peck
              W.W. Phelps, Hervey Stanly, J. Hunt &

[5] [recto]

Left out of the History

1838 " Oct 25 Letter Book 18–19 [Thomas B.] Marsh & Hydes lettre

"   " 24 Documnts. 57. 58 59. Marsh & Hyde

"   2 Nov.   Charles Charles C. Rich. Stateme[n]t. N. to Iowa

1838 Nov 23.   Docume[n]ts of Mo 87. certificate
                                              crookd Rivr
1838 Oct 25— C.C. Rich, statements Brethrn fled north[177] from

"   Dec 28— DH. Redfilds Book. Names of witnesses given by

        Mr Phelps to Legislatur of Mo. Capt Bogart Reed Peck

        W,{P\W}, Phe[l]ps, Harvey Stanl[e]y, J. Hunt.[178] &

ORIGINAL INSCRIPTION
Willard Richards

REVISIONS
Willard Richards
Unidentified

177. The text on this line up to this point was originally written in graphite and then retraced in ink.

178. Possibly James Hunt.

APPENDIX 2: THOMAS BULLOCK, NOTES FOR JS HISTORY, CIRCA SPRING 1845

Source Note

Thomas Bullock, Notes for JS History, [Nauvoo, IL], [ca. spring 1845]; handwriting of Thomas Bullock; two pages; inserted into Revelation Book 2; Revelations Collection, CHL.

This document consists of a single ruled leaf measuring 8⅛ x 6⅞ inches (21 x 17 cm). The top and one side have a rough edge, as though the leaf was torn from a larger sheet or book. The paper has twenty-four horizontal lines on each side in faded blue-green ink. One side of the paper has two hand-drawn vertical lines and the other side has one, all three of which are in black ink that later turned brown. Other writing on the leaf is in black ink and in black ink that later turned brown.

Historical Introduction

Thomas Bullock began working as a scribe for JS in November 1843, but he likely did not begin working on JS's multivolume manuscript history with Willard Richards until December 1844. Eventually Bullock wrote nearly seven hundred pages of the JS history, first in Nauvoo, Illinois, and then in Salt Lake City. He wrote the historical notes on this loose document while working on the JS history in Nauvoo. The document was inserted into Revelation Book 2 at an unknown time, thereby becoming associated with the manuscript book though not physically part of it. The notes are similar to historical notes written by Willard Richards and William W. Phelps on three leaves at the back of Revelation Book 2 (pages 659–665 herein), but the Bullock notes are included here as an appendix, not as part of the manuscript book, because they are not written on leaves of the book itself.

A note on one side of the document reads "these pages not yet recorded". Six separate manuscript documents are then listed with specific page numbers and dates, presumably identifying certain information that had not been recorded in the history. The purpose of the opposite side of the document is less certain. Dates of 1838 and 1839 appear alongside references to documents and events. The tear along the top and side cuts off some text, perhaps indicating that preserving text on this side was not important.

Thomas Bullock may have created this document over an extended period of time to facilitate incorporating information into the JS history as it was being written. However, the document's physical characteristics, including the handwriting, suggest that Bullock wrote it as part of a single process, analyzing portions of the history that had already been written. Because dates on the document do not extend past 1839, Bullock likely created it after he finished the 1839 portion of the history on 15 March 1845 but before he wrote much more of the history.[1] By the time the church records, including the JS history, were boxed up in early 1846 to be shipped west, Bullock had written the history through 1 March 1843.

---

1. Bullock, Journal, 15 Mar. 1845.

These pages not yet recorded

Record of the apostles pages 5. 6. 7. 8. 9
        (May 1835)

Record Letter D page 5. ~~23 to 26~~ 63. 127 — 157
      (1835)   Jan.⁵ 5   Feb. 19
           1836   1836

Record of the Conference Minutes page 1. to 40. — 66. — 69.
       1831 to 1833   Nov.ʳ 5   July 25
           1834   1837

Record Letter E page 64. to 108.
       (1838)

Book of Revelations — and Facts to be registered
(1832 to 1834)

Record C. page ~~14~~ ~~16. 17. 18. 81. 84. 85.~~   209. 210. 211.   219.   231. 232. 233.
               June 10./36   May 11   Jan.ʸ 13. 1836
                   1837

               240. 241.   245. 246.   253 to 256
               Sept.ʳ 10/37   Sept.ʳ 23   Oct.ʳ 27
                   1837   1837

/¹Record of the Apostles pages 5.6.7.8.9
          (May 1835)

Record Letter D page 5. ~~23 to 26.~~ 63. 127 — 157
      (1835)   Jany 5 Feb 19
               1836   1836

Record of the Conference Minutes page 1. to 40. — 66. — 69.
                1831 to 1833   Nov. 5 July 25
                       1834   1837

Record Letter G page 64. to 108.
      (1838)

Book of Revelations — and Facts to be registered
  (1832 to 1834)

Record C. page ~~1—H²~~ ~~14.~~ ~~41.~~ ~~48.~~ ~~81.~~ ~~84.~~ ~~85.~~ 209.210.211. 219.   231.232.233.
  ~~1832-&-33~~ ~~March 19 1833~~ ~~Feb 24/34~~ ~~April 4/34~~ ~~Decd 28/34~~ ₃ 1835 ~~March 16~~ June 10./36 May 11 Jan.ʸ 13.1836
                                                  1837
                                  240.241.   245.246. 253 to 256
                                  Sept.ᵐ 10/37 Sept.ʳ 23 Oct.ʳ 27
                                          1837   1837

these pages not yet recorded (left margin, rotated)

[*end of recto*]

ORIGINAL INSCRIPTION
Thomas Bullock

REVISIONS
Unidentified

1. Thomas Bullock hand-writing begins.

2. Or "1–4.6" or "111".

3. This information is also crossed out with an X.

May 4 6	Minutes of Conference } see letter book d⁰ —— d⁰ ——
June 4	Joseph's Bill of Damage in Missouri
Aug⁹ 19	An appeal to the American People
November 1ˢᵗ 6	an appeal to the American People Agreement between Mormons and Mob at Diahman
1839	Minute book. J. Smith's escape from Prison Facts relative to the Expulsion of the L.D.S. from Missouri by J.P. Petition to Congress for redress W. Richards Journal — Journal in

May 4   Minutes of Conference

6   d[itt]°.— d[itt]°.—   } see letter book

ORIGINAL INSCRIPTION
Thomas Bullock

REVISIONS
Unidentified

4. A line connects the end of "November" with "1ˢᵗ", indicating that this entry falls in November as well.

June 4   Joseph's Bill of Damage in Missouri

Augʳ. 19   An Appeal to the American People

1ˢᵗ ⁴ an appeal to the American People

November 6 Agreement between Mormons and Mob at Diahman [Adam-ondi-Ahman]

1839 Minute book. J. Smith's escape from Prison

Facts relative to the Expulsion of the L.°D.S. from Missouri by J[ohn]. P. [Greene]
Petition to Congress for redress   W[illard]. Richards Journal— Journal in
                                [end of verso]

November	4	JS returned to Kirtland from journey to Mount Pleasant.
	25	JS notified by Orson Hyde and John Gould that Latter-day Saints had been expelled from Jackson County earlier in month, Kirtland.
December		Fifteenth issue of *The Evening and the Morning Star* published, Kirtland, marking first issue published following destruction of printing office in Missouri.

1834

ca. January		Four revelations printed as broadsides, Kirtland.
February	17	JS organized first high council, Kirtland.
April	19	JS and others blessed Oliver Cowdery and Sidney Rigdon to continue selecting and arranging revelations for publication, Norton, Ohio.
	23	Revelation appointing Oliver Cowdery and Frederick G. Williams to oversee printing office, directing that copyrights be secured for Bible revision and future publication of revelations, and mandating establishment of treasury to house sacred writings before publication, Kirtland.
May	5	JS departed Kirtland for Missouri at head of Camp of Israel expedition (later known as Zion's Camp) to restore Mormons to Missouri land. Oliver Cowdery and Sidney Rigdon remained in Kirtland.
ca. May		Frederick G. Williams appointed to keep record of expedition to Missouri; record later lost.
June	22	Revelation in Washington Township, Clay County, indicating that redemption of Zion must "wait for a little season" until elders were "endowed with power from on high" in Kirtland temple.
July	3	High council organized for church in Missouri with David Whitmer appointed president and William W. Phelps and John Whitmer appointed assistants, Liberty, Clay County.
	late	JS returned to Kirtland from expedition to Missouri.
September	24	Kirtland high council appointed JS, Oliver Cowdery, Sidney Rigdon, and Frederick G. Williams to arrange and publish revelations.
October		First issue of *LDS Messenger and Advocate* published, Kirtland; Oliver Cowdery appointed as editor.
December	5	JS appointed Oliver Cowdery an assistant president of the church, Kirtland.

1835

January		First issue of *Evening and Morning Star* (an edited reprint of *The Evening and the Morning Star*) published, Kirtland.
	14	Copyright for Doctrine and Covenants secured, Ohio.
February		First issue of political newspaper *Northern Times* published on Mormon press, Kirtland.
	14	Three Witnesses to the Book of Mormon selected Quorum of the Twelve Apostles, Kirtland.
		JS organized Quorum of the Seventy, Kirtland.
May	16	John Whitmer and William W. Phelps arrived in Kirtland from Clay County to participate in dedication of Kirtland temple.
	late	John Whitmer replaced Oliver Cowdery as editor of *LDS Messenger and Advocate,* Kirtland; William W. Phelps began assisting with editorial duties.
ca. June		First lecture that became part of "Lectures on Faith" in 1835 Doctrine and Covenants published as broadside, Kirtland.
July	early	JS purchased Egyptian mummies and papyri associated with later book of Abraham translation, Kirtland.

August	17	Church conference approved publication of Doctrine and Covenants, Kirtland.
September	mid	Doctrine and Covenants became available for purchase, Kirtland.
	16	Samuel Smith and David Whitmer assigned "to act in the name of and for the literary firm," Kirtland.
	22	JS began second Kirtland journal, a record of more than six months of activity.
Fall		JS worked periodically on book of Abraham translation, Kirtland.

Scribal Directory

The following biographical sketches provide information about the scribes who penned or revised documents in Revelation Books 1 and 2. Other people who are mentioned by name in this volume or who inscribed material not associated with the original purpose of the manuscript books are not identified in this directory. These entries identify scribes by complete name (correctly spelled), birth and death dates, and additional information, such as parentage and birthplace, migrations and places of residence, dates of marriage and names of spouses, occupation and denominational affiliation, religious and civic positions, and place of death. The entries emphasize the years 1828–1835, with particular emphasis on scribal work and assignments. Because unverified and sometimes incorrect data has been recirculated for decades, professional genealogists on the staff of the Joseph Smith Papers Project have utilized original sources to ensure accuracy.

In these sketches, "LDS church" refers to the church established by JS in 1830 and later known as the Church of Jesus Christ of Latter-day Saints. Locations that are noted include city or town, county, and state, when identified, for the first mention of a locale in each sketch. The entries in this directory provide, of necessity, only a bare skeleton of a person's life. Readers wishing to conduct further research may consult the documented biographical directory posted on the Joseph Smith Papers website.

Following the entry for each scribe who penned substantial sections of the manuscript is a description of his most problematic handwriting characteristics. Ambiguous or unusual habits of the scribes are explained to help readers understand how certain characteristics have been transcribed. These descriptions refer to specific lines in the manuscript books that contain examples of these handwriting characteristics. The line numbering starts with the first line of text, not with the page number, and the page numbers refer to original manuscript page numbers, not page numbers in the present volume. No such description is included for scribes who simply made editorial corrections.

Cowdery, Oliver (3 Oct. 1806–3 Mar. 1850), teacher, justice of the peace, lawyer, newspaper editor; born at Wells, Rutland Co., Vermont. Son of William Cowdery and Rebecca Fuller. Raised Congregationalist. Moved to western New York and clerked at a store, ca. 1825–1828. Taught term as local schoolmaster at Manchester, Ontario Co., New York, 1828–1829. Assisted JS as principal scribe in translation of Book of Mormon, 1829. Baptized, 1829. With JS, received Aaronic and Melchizedek priesthoods, 1829. One of the Three Witnesses of the Book of Mormon, June 1829. Helped oversee printing of Book of Mormon by E. B. Grandin, 1829–1830. Among six original members of church, 6 Apr. 1830. Frequently acted as scribe for meetings, and assisted JS as scribe in revision of Bible, 1830. Led small group of missionaries through Ohio and to Missouri on mission to unorganized Indian Territory, 1830–1831. Returned to Ohio and frequently acted as scribe for meetings, 1831. With John Whitmer, left Ohio to take revelations to Missouri for publication, Nov. 1831. Assisted William W. Phelps in setting up and conducting church's printing operations at Jackson Co., Missouri, 1832–1833, which included printing revelations in *The Evening and the Morning Star* and Book of Commandments. Married Elizabeth Ann Whitmer, 1832, in Jackson Co. Member of United Firm, Literary Firm, and Kirtland, Geauga Co., Ohio, high council, 1832–1837. Edited Kirtland continuation of *The Evening and the Morning Star,* 1833–1834, and directed Kirtland republication and revision of these volumes under modified title *Evening and Morning Star,* 1835–1836. Edited *LDS Messenger and Advocate,* 1834–1835, 1836–1837, and *Northern Times,* 1835. Appointed assistant president of church, 5 Dec. 1834. Appointed church recorder, 1835. Assisted in publishing Doctrine and Covenants, 1835, and second edition of Book of Mormon, 1837. Elected justice of the peace in Kirtland, 1837. Moved to Far West, Caldwell Co., Missouri, 1837. Excommunicated, 1838. Briefly

Scribes of manuscript revelation books. Seven men copied Joseph Smith's revelations into Revelation Books 1 and 2 or revised the copied revelations to prepare them for publication. An unknown number of unidentified scribes also helped prepare the revelations for publication. This page, clockwise from top left: Oliver Cowdery, Orson Hyde, William W. Phelps. Opposite page, clockwise from top left: Sidney Rigdon, Joseph Smith, John Whitmer, Frederick G. Williams. (Smith image courtesy Community of Christ Library-Archives, Independence, MO. Williams image courtesy Church History Museum, Salt Lake City. All others: Church History Library, Salt Lake City.)

practiced law at Kirtland and then moved to Tiffin, Seneca Co., Ohio, where he continued law practice and held political offices, 1840–1847. Helped incorporate and for a time attended Methodist Protestant Church at Tiffin. Moved to Elkhorn, Walworth Co., Wisconsin, 1847–1848. Ran unsuccessfully for Wisconsin State Assembly, 1848. Coeditor of *Walworth County Democrat,* 1848. Requested and received readmission to LDS church, Kanesville, Pottawattamie Co., Iowa, 1848. Died at Richmond, Ray Co., Missouri.

Handwriting characteristics: The shape of Cowdery's *s* often indicates whether it is uppercase or lowercase (see "Servant," line 24, and "servant," line 25, p. 113, Revelation Book 1). Comparing the size of the letter to surrounding letters also helps distinguish the two (see "Synagogues," line 10, and "spirit," line 8, p. 113, Revelation Book 1). The difference between *C* and *c* is also determined by comparing the size of the letter to surrounding letters (see "Comforter," line 15, and "confounded," line 19, p. 169, Revelation Book 1).

Hyde, Orson (8 Jan. 1805–28 Nov. 1878), clerk, storekeeper, schoolteacher, editor, businessman, lawyer; born at Oxford, New Haven Co., Connecticut. Son of Nathan Hyde and Sally Thorpe. Joined Methodist church, ca. 1827. Later affiliated with Reformed Baptists (later Disciples of Christ or Campbellites). Baptized into LDS church by Sidney Rigdon, 2 Oct. 1831, at Kirtland, Geauga Co., Ohio. Baptized many during proselytizing mission with Samuel Smith to eastern states, 1832. Appointed clerk to First Presidency, 1833. Member of Kirtland high council, 1834. Participated in Zion's Camp expedition to Missouri, 1834. Married to Marinda Nancy Johnson by Sidney Rigdon, 4 Sept. 1834, at Kirtland. Member of Quorum of the Twelve, 1835; served as clerk. Served mission to western New York and Upper Canada, 1836. Served mission to England with Heber C. Kimball, 1837–1838. Sided with dissenters against JS, 1838. Lived at Howard Co., Missouri, winter 1838–1839. Restored to church and to Quorum of the Twelve at Commerce (later Nauvoo), Hancock Co., Illinois, 27 June 1839. Served mission to Palestine to dedicate land for gathering of Israel, 1840–1842. Member of Nauvoo City Council, 1843–1844. Participated in plural marriage during JS's lifetime. Departed Nauvoo during exodus to the West, mid-May 1846. Served mission to Great Britain, 1846–1847. Presided over Latter-day Saints in Iowa before migrating to Utah Territory. Published *Frontier Guardian* at Kanesville, Pottawattamie Co., Iowa, 1849–1852. Migrated to Utah Territory, 1852. Elected to Utah territorial legislature, 27 Nov. 1852. Presided over church in Carson Co., Utah Territory, 1855–1856. Moved to Sanpete Co., Utah Territory, 1860; presiding ecclesiastical authority there, 1860–1877. Died at Spring City, Sanpete Co.

Handwriting characteristics: Hyde does not always break a word at the end of the line but rather forces the word in by writing small and illegibly. If counting the strokes of such words accounts for the correct number of letters in the word, the words are transcribed as if Hyde used all the correct letters (see "because," line 18, p. 56, and "temples," line 1, p. 58, Revelation Book 2). His *o* and *a* are at times indistinguishable, as are his *r* and *e* (see "continue," line 10, p. 60, and "obtained," line 15, p. 110, Revelation Book 2; see "there," line 24, p. 59, and "Behold," line 19, p. 110, Revelation Book 2). The transcripts render these ambiguous characters according to scribal intent.

Phelps, William Wines (17 Feb. 1792–7 Mar. 1872), newspaper editor; born at Hanover, Morris Co., New Jersey. Son of Enon Phelps and Mehitabel Goldsmith. Married Sally Waterman, 1815. Founding member of Anti-Masonic Party in New York, ca. 1828. Edited Anti-Masonic newspapers, *Lake Light* at Trumansburg, Thompkins Co., New York, and *Ontario Phoenix* at Canandaigua, Ontario Co., New York. Obtained copy of Book of Mormon, 1830. Met JS, 24 Dec. 1830, at Peter Whitmer Sr. farm, Fayette, Seneca Co., New York. Migrated to Kirtland, Geauga Co., Ohio, 1831. Baptized and ordained an elder by JS, 16 June 1831, at Kirtland. Appointed church printer by revelation, 20 July 1831. Moved to Jackson Co., Missouri, Oct. 1831. Became editor of *The Evening and the Morning Star* and *Upper Missouri Advertiser,* published 1832–1833 at Independence, Jackson Co. Published Book of Commandments, but most copies destroyed by mob action when printing office destroyed, 20 July 1833. Exiled from Jackson Co. to Clay Co., Missouri, Nov. 1833. Appointed counselor/assistant president to David Whitmer (president of church in Missouri), 3 July 1834. Appointed to return to Kirtland to assist with printing. Helped compile Doctrine and Covenants and first Latter-day Saint hymnal, 1835, at Kirtland. Prolific writer of hymns. Acted as scribe for JS in translation of book of Abraham. Returned from Kirtland to Clay Co., where he resumed duties with Missouri presidency, 1836. Excommunicated, 10 Mar. 1838. Reconciled with church, July 1840; joined

Latter-day Saints at Nauvoo, Hancock Co., Illinois, 1841. Assisted in writing JS's multivolume manuscript history, 1843. Acted as clerk to JS and assisted John Taylor in editing *Times and Seasons* and *Nauvoo Neighbor.* Migrated to Salt Lake Valley, 1848. Admitted to Utah territorial bar, 1851. Member of territorial legislative assembly, 1851–1857. Died at Salt Lake City, Salt Lake Co., Utah Territory.

Rigdon, Sidney (19 Feb. 1793–14 July 1876), tanner, farmer, minister; born at St. Clair, Allegheny Co., Pennsylvania. Son of William Rigdon and Nancy Gallaher. In 1817, joined United Baptists. Preached at Warren, Trumbull Co., Ohio, and vicinity, 1819–1821. Married Phoebe Brook, 12 June 1820, at Warren. Minister of First Baptist Church of Pittsburgh, Allegheny Co., 1821–1824. Later joined Reformed Baptist (later Disciples of Christ or Campbellite) movement and was influential preacher. Introduced to Mormonism by his former proselyte to Reformed Baptist faith, Parley P. Pratt, who was en route with Oliver Cowdery and others on mission to unorganized Indian Territory. Baptized into LDS church, Nov. 1830, by Oliver Cowdery. Acted as scribe for JS in revision of Bible, 1830–1832. Accompanied JS to Upper Canada on proselytizing mission and helped keep JS's diary during trip, 1833. A counselor/assistant president in church presidency, 1832–1844. Arrived at Far West, Caldwell Co., Missouri, from Kirtland, Geauga Co., Ohio, 4 Apr. 1838. With JS in jail at Liberty, Clay Co., Missouri, Nov. 1838–Feb. 1839. After release, found refuge at Quincy, Adams Co., Illinois. Accompanied JS to Washington DC to seek redress for Missouri grievances, 1839–1840. Member of Nauvoo City Council; postmaster of Nauvoo, Hancock Co., Illinois. Claimed right to lead church after death of JS; excommunicated, 1844. Moved to Pittsburgh to lead schismatic Church of Jesus Christ of Latter Day Saints, 1844; name of church changed to Church of Christ, 1845. Located near Greencastle, Antrim Township, Franklin Co., Pennsylvania, 1845. Removed to Friendship, Allegany Co., New York, where he died.

Smith, Joseph (23 Dec. 1805–27 June 1844); for biographical information, see General Introduction: Joseph Smith and His Papers, in *JSP,* J1:xv–xli, and Timeline of Joseph Smith's Life, p. xvi herein.

Handwriting characteristics: JS's handwriting is similar to that of Frederick G. Williams. His *J* and *j* are indistinguishable; modern usage prevails when the difference in unclear (see "Jr," line 34, p. 1, "judge," line 25, p. 14, and "justifyable," line 11, p. 67, Revelation Book 2).

Whitmer, John (27 Aug. 1802–11 July 1878), farmer, stock raiser, newspaper editor; born in Pennsylvania. Son of Peter Whitmer Sr. and Mary Musselman. Member of German Reformed Church, Fayette, Seneca Co., New York. Evidently baptized by Oliver Cowdery, June 1829, in Seneca Lake, Seneca Co. Acted as scribe during translation of Book of Mormon at Whitmer home, June 1829. One of the Eight Witnesses of the Book of Mormon, June 1829. Ordained an elder by 9 June 1830. Copied revelations as scribe to JS, beginning July 1830. Acted as scribe for JS in revision of Bible. Sent by JS to Kirtland, Geauga Co., Ohio, ca. Dec. 1830. Appointed church historian, ca. 8 Mar. 1831. Wrote a church history covering 1831–1838. Ordained a high priest, 3 June 1831, at Kirtland. With Oliver Cowdery, left Ohio to take revelations to Missouri for publication, Nov. 1831. Member of Whitmer branch at Kaw Township, Jackson Co., Missouri. Married to Sarah Maria Jackson by William W. Phelps, 10 Feb. 1833, at Kaw Township. Forced to remove from Jackson Co. to Clay Co., Missouri, Nov. 1833. Appointed an assistant to his brother David Whitmer in Missouri church presidency, 3 July 1834. Editor of *LDS Messenger and Advocate,* Kirtland, 1835–1836. Lived in Clay Co., 1836. Helped establish Latter-day Saints at Far West, Caldwell Co., Missouri. Excommunicated, 10 Mar. 1838, at Far West. Left Far West for Richmond, Ray Co., Missouri, June 1838. Returned to Far West after departure of Latter-day Saints. In Sept. 1847, met with his brother David Whitmer and William E. McLellin at Far West in an attempt to reconstitute Church of Christ under presidency of David Whitmer. Died at the site of Far West. Buried at Kingston, Caldwell Co.

Handwriting characteristics: Whitmer's *a* and *o* are usually indistinguishable; modern usage prevails when the difference is unclear (see "spoken," line 2, p. 27, and "command," line 21, p. 33, Revelation Book 1). At times his *s* and *r* are also indistinguishable (see "treasures," line 22, p. 107, and "creatures," line 6, p. 146, Revelation Book 1). The difference between *S* and *s* is usually determined by comparing the size of the letter to surrounding letters (see "should," line 3, "Servent," line 4, and "Sidney," line 4, p. 62, Revelation Book 1). The difference between *C* and *c* is usually determined by the shape of the letter (see "Church," line 4, "Christ," line 5, and "continue," line 11, p. 104, Revelation Book 1). Occasionally, Whitmer writes what looks like a backward comma. This mark sometimes functions as a comma or a period but other times is simply a random mark. When the mark serves as punctuation, it has been transcribed; when it is random, it has not been included in the transcripts.

Williams, Frederick Granger (28 Oct. 1787–10 Oct. 1842), farmer, ship's pilot, teacher, physician, justice of the peace; born at Suffield, Hartford Co., Connecticut. Son of William Wheeler Williams and Ruth Granger. Practiced Thomsonian botanical system of medicine as physician. Married Rebecca Swain, Dec. 1815. Lived at Warrensville, Cuyahoga Co., Ohio, by 1816. Worshipped with Sidney Rigdon's Reformed Baptist (later Disciples of Christ or Campbellite) congregation. Baptized into LDS church, confirmed, and ordained an elder, Nov. 1830, at Kirtland, Geauga Co., Ohio, by missionaries under leadership of Oliver Cowdery who were en route to Missouri and unorganized Indian Territory. Accompanied Cowdery to Missouri frontier on mission. Appointed clerk and scribe to JS, 20 July 1832, although acted as scribe for JS as early as Feb.–Mar. 1832. Assistant president/counselor in presidency of church, 1833–1837. Consecrated by deed to JS roughly 142 prime acres in Kirtland, 1834. Inscribed Revelation Book 2; parts of JS History, ca. summer 1832; JS, Journal, 1832–1834; JS Letterbook 1; Minute Book 1; numerous revelations; and JS History, 1834–1836. Participated in Zion's Camp expedition to Missouri, 1834. Editor of *Northern Times* and member of publications committee that printed Doctrine and Covenants and Emma Smith's *A Collection of Sacred Hymns, for the Church of the Latter Day Saints* under auspices of firm F. G. Williams & Co., 1835–1836. Helped organize and was a trustee of School of the Prophets. Elected justice of the peace, Kirtland, 1837. Officer in Kirtland Safety Society, 1837. Removed from church presidency, 7 Nov. 1837. Moved to Far West, Caldwell Co., Missouri, late 1837. An 8 July 1838 JS revelation directed Williams to be ordained an elder and preach abroad. Rebaptized into LDS church by 5 Aug. 1838. Excommunicated, 17 Mar. 1839, at Quincy, Adams Co., Illinois. Restored to fellowship at Commerce (later Nauvoo), Hancock Co., Illinois, 8 Apr. 1840. Died at Quincy.

Handwriting characteristics: Williams's handwriting is similar to JS's. Some words, such as those ending in *er,* are not finished (see "fathe," line 5, p. 4, and "neithe," line 8, p. 5, Revelation Book 2). However, small strokes written for letters are transcribed as if they were letters (see "neither," line 27, p. 27, "over," line 1, p. 34, and "the," line 1, p. 35, Revelation Book 2). The *s* ending certain words is sometimes written only as a slight mark but is rendered herein as a complete *s* (see "things," line 15, p. 11, and "priests," lines 30 and 32, p. 5, Revelation Book 2). The long □ often used in nineteenth-century handwriting to represent the first *s* of a double *s* is sometimes used as a single *s* (see "Jesus," line 36, p. 6, and "Joseph," line 3, p. 18, Revelation Book 2). No attempt has been made to typo-graphically represent these letters. Williams's *J* and *j* are indistinguishable (see "Jesus," line 14, p. 5, "just," line 16, p. 5, and "Jews," line 3, p. 23, Revelation Book 2), as are, at times, his *J* and *I* (compare "I," line 4, and "I," line 14, p. 52, Revelation Book 2, with "Jews," line 28, and "Joseph," line 31, p. 52, Revelation Book 2). Modern usage prevails in such cases. His *C* and *c* are often very similar, usually distinguishable only by a tail at the bottom of the *C* that spirals back on itself before forming the next letter (compare "church," line 9, and "Church," line 11, p. 16, Revelation Book 2, with "Counceller," line 25, and "counceller," line 26, p. 32, Revelation Book 2).

Works Cited

This list of sources serves as a comprehensive guide to all sources cited in this volume (documentation supporting the reference material in the back of this volume may be found at the Joseph Smith Papers website, josephsmithpapers.org). Annotation has been documented with original sources where possible and practical. In entries for manuscript sources, dates identify when the manuscript was created, which is not necessarily the time period the manuscript covers.

Some sources cited in this volume are referred to on first and subsequent occurrences by a conventional shortened citation. For convenience, some documents are referred to by editorial titles rather than by their original titles or by the titles given in the catalogs of their current repositories, in which case the list of works cited provides the editorial title followed by full bibliographic information.

Scriptural References

The annotation within volumes of *The Joseph Smith Papers* includes numerous references to works accepted as scripture by The Church of Jesus Christ of Latter-day Saints. The principal citations of Mormon scripture appearing in annotation are to JS-era published or manuscript versions. However, for reader convenience, these citations also include a bracketed reference to the current and widely available Latter-day Saint scriptural canon. All versions of scripture cited in this volume, early or modern, are identified in the list of works cited.

The church's current scriptural canon consists of the King James (or Authorized) Version of the Bible (KJV), plus three other volumes: the Book of Mormon, the Doctrine and Covenants, and the Pearl of Great Price. The following paragraphs provide more detailed information about uniquely Mormon scriptures and how they are cited in the *Papers*.

Book of Mormon. The first edition of the Book of Mormon was printed for JS in 1830. He oversaw the publication of subsequent editions in 1837 and 1840. The Book of Mormon, like the Bible, consists of a number of shorter books. However, *Papers* volumes cite early editions of the Book of Mormon by page numbers because these editions were not divided into numbered verses. The bracketed references to the modern (1981) Latter-day Saint edition of this work identify the book name with modern chapter and verse.

Doctrine and Covenants. JS authorized publication of early revelations beginning in 1832 in *The Evening and the Morning Star,* the church's first newspaper, and initiated the publication of a compilation of revelations, which first appeared in 1833 under the title Book of Commandments. Revised and expanded versions of this compilation were published in 1835 and 1844 under the title Doctrine and Covenants. Since JS's time, The Church of Jesus Christ of Latter-day Saints has continued to issue revised and expanded versions of the Doctrine and Covenants, as has the Community of Christ (formerly the Reorganized Church of Jesus Christ of Latter Day Saints). The bracketed references to the modern (1981) Latter-day Saint edition of the Doctrine and Covenants, which cite by section number and verse, use the abbreviation D&C in the place of Doctrine and Covenants. A table titled Correspondence of Items in Revelation Books 1 and 2 with Selected Published Versions, which appears after the list of works cited (page 690 herein), can help readers refer from the manuscript copy of each revelation or other item found in this volume to certain published versions of that same item. For more information about the format of Doctrine and Covenants citations, see the Editorial Method (pages xxxv–xxxvi herein).

Joseph Smith Bible revision. Beginning in June 1830, JS systematically reviewed the text of the KJV and made revisions and additions to it. JS largely completed the work in 1833, but only a few excerpts were published in his lifetime. The Reorganized Church of Jesus Christ of Latter Day Saints published the entire work in 1867 under the title Holy Scriptures and included excerpts from the writings of Moses in two sections of its Doctrine and Covenants. The Church of Jesus Christ of Latter-day Saints, which today officially refers to JS's Bible revisions as the Joseph Smith Translation, has never published the entire work, but two excerpts are canonized in the Pearl of Great Price and many other excerpts are included in the footnotes and appendix of the modern (1979) Latter-day Saint edition of the KJV. In the *Papers,* references to JS's Bible revision are cited to the original manuscripts, with a bracketed reference given where possible to the relevant book, chapter, and verse of the Joseph Smith Translation.

Pearl of Great Price. The Pearl of Great Price, a collection of miscellaneous shorter writings that originated with JS, was first published in 1851 and was canonized by The Church of Jesus Christ of Latter-day Saints in 1880. The modern (1981) edition of this work consists of the following: selections from the book of Moses, an extract from JS's Bible revision manuscripts; the book of Abraham, writings translated from papyri JS and others acquired in 1835 and first published in the *Times and Seasons* in 1842; Joseph Smith—Matthew, another extract from JS's Bible revision manuscripts; Joseph Smith—History, a selection from the history JS began working on in 1838; and the Articles of Faith, a statement of beliefs included in a JS letter to Chicago newspaper editor John Wentworth and published in the *Times and Seasons* in 1842. Except in the case of Joseph Smith—History, citations in the *Papers* to early versions of each of these works also include a bracketed reference to the corresponding chapter and verse in the modern Latter-day Saint canon. The Pearl of Great Price is not part of the canon of the Community of Christ. References to the history JS began work on in 1838 are cited to the original manuscript of that history (see entry on "JS History" in the list of works cited).

Abbreviations for Frequently Cited Repositories

CCLA   Community of Christ Library-Archives, Independence, Missouri

CHL   Church History Library, The Church of Jesus Christ of Latter-day Saints, Salt Lake City

——————— ℰↄ ———————

Abzug, Robert H. *Cosmos Crumbling: American Reform and the Religious Imagination.* New York: Oxford University Press, 1994.

A Book of Commandments, for the Government of the Church of Christ, Organized according to Law, on the 6th of April, 1830. Zion [Independence], MO: W. W. Phelps, 1833.

Book of Doctrine and Covenants: Carefully Selected from the Revelations of God, and Given in the Order of Their Dates. Independence, MO: Herald Publishing House, 2004.

The Book of Mormon: An Account Written by the Hand of Mormon, upon Plates Taken from the Plates of Nephi. Palmyra, NY: E. B. Grandin, 1830. The copy used for this volume is available at CHL.

The Book of Mormon: Another Testament of Jesus Christ. Salt Lake City: The Church of Jesus Christ of Latter-day Saints, 1981.

Bullock, Thomas. Journal, Feb. 1844–Aug. 1845. In Historian's Office, Journal, 1844–1997. CHL.

Bushman, Richard Lyman. *Believing History: Latter-day Saint Essays.* Edited by Reid L. Neilson and Jed Woodworth. New York: Columbia University Press, 2004.

———. *Joseph Smith: Rough Stone Rolling.* With the assistance of Jed Woodworth. New York: Knopf, 2005.

Coltrin, Zebedee. Diary, Mar. 1833–Feb. 1834. Zebedee Coltrin, Diaries, 1832–1834. CHL.

Copyright for Book of Mormon, 11 June 1829. Copyright Registration Forms, 1829–1870. Copyright Office, Library of Congress, Washington DC. Retained copy at CHL.

Cowdery, Oliver. Revelation, ca. June 1829. CHL.

———. Letterbook, 1833–1838. Henry E. Huntington Library, San Marino, CA.

D&C. See *Doctrine and Covenants of the Church of Jesus Christ of Latter-day Saints* (1981).

Deseret News. Salt Lake City. 1850–.

De Vinne, Theodore Low. *The Printers' Price List: A Manual for the Use of Clerks and Book-Keepers in Job Printing Offices*. New York: Francis Hart, 1871. As excerpted in Richard-Gabriel Rummonds, *Nineteenth-Century Printing Practices and the Iron Handpress*, 2 vols. (New Castle, DE: Oak Knoll Press, 2004).

Doctrine and Covenants, 2004 Community of Christ edition. See *Book of Doctrine and Covenants.*

Doctrine and Covenants of the Church of the Latter Day Saints: Carefully Selected from the Revelations of God. Compiled by Joseph Smith, Oliver Cowdery, Sidney Rigdon, and Frederick G. Williams. Kirtland, OH: F. G. Williams, 1835.

The Doctrine and Covenants of the Church of Jesus Christ of Latter Day Saints; Carefully Selected from the Revelations of God. Compiled by Joseph Smith. 2nd ed. Nauvoo, IL: John Taylor, 1844.

The Doctrine and Covenants of the Church of Jesus Christ of Latter-day Saints: Containing Revelations Given to Joseph Smith, the Prophet, with Some Additions by His Successors in the Presidency of the Church. Salt Lake City: The Church of Jesus Christ of Latter-day Saints, 1981.

Ensign of Liberty. Kirtland, OH. Mar. 1847–Aug. 1849.

Evening and Morning Star. Edited reprint of *The Evening and the Morning Star.* Kirtland, OH. Jan. 1835–Oct. 1836.

The Evening and the Morning Star. Independence, MO, June 1832–July 1833; Kirtland, OH, Dec. 1833–Sept. 1834.

F. G. Williams and Company. Account Book, 1833–1835. CHL.

Givens, Terryl L. *By the Hand of Mormon: The American Scripture That Launched a New World Religion.* Oxford: Oxford University Press, 2002.

Hatch, Nathan O. *The Democratization of American Christianity.* New Haven: Yale University Press, 1989.

Historian's Office. Catalogs and Inventories, 1846–1904. CHL.

Holifield, E. Brooks. *Theology in America: Christian Thought from the Age of the Puritans to the Civil War.* New Haven: Yale University Press, 2003.

Hyde, Orson, and Parley P. Pratt. Notebook of Revelations, 1834. Revelations Collection, 1831–ca. 1844, 1847, 1861, ca. 1876. CHL.

"Inventory of President Joseph Fielding Smith's Safe," 23 May 1970. CHL.

Jessee, Dean C. "The Original Book of Mormon Manuscript." *BYU Studies* 10 (Spring 1970): 259–278.

JS. In addition to the entries that immediately follow, see entry under "Smith, Joseph."

JS History / Smith, Joseph, et al. History, 1839–1856. Vols. A-1–F-1 (originals), A-2–E-2 (early security copies). CHL. The history for the period after 5 Aug. 1838 was composed after the death of Joseph Smith. Also available as *History of the Church of Jesus Christ of Latter-day Saints, Period 1: History of Joseph Smith, the Prophet, by Himself,* edited by B. H. Roberts, 6 vols. (Salt Lake City: Deseret News, 1902–1912).

JS History, ca. summer 1832 / Smith, Joseph. "A History of the Life of Joseph Smith Jr," ca. summer 1832. In Joseph Smith, "Letterbook A," 1832–1835, 1–[6] (earliest numbering). Joseph Smith Collection. CHL. Also available in Dean C. Jessee, ed., *The Papers of Joseph Smith* (Salt Lake City: Deseret Book, 1989), 1:1–10.

JS Letterbook 1 / Smith, Joseph. "Letter Book A," 1832–1835. Joseph Smith Collection. CHL.

JS Letterbook 2 / Smith, Joseph. "Copies of Letters, &c. &c.," 1839–1843. Joseph Smith Collection, CHL.

JSP, J1 / Jessee, Dean C., Mark Ashurst-McGee, and Richard L. Jensen, eds. *Journals, Volume 1: 1832–1839.* Vol. 1 of the Journals series of *The Joseph Smith Papers,* edited by Dean C. Jessee, Ronald K. Esplin, and Richard Lyman Bushman. Salt Lake City: Church Historian's Press, 2008.

Juster, Susan. *Doomsayers: Anglo-American Prophecy in the Age of Revolution.* Philadelphia: University of Pennsylvania Press, 2003.

Kirschner, Ann. "'Tending to Edify, Astonish, and Instruct': Published Narratives of Spiritual Dreams and Visions in the Early Republic." *Early American Studies* 1, no. 1 (2003): 199–229.

Latter Day Saints' Messenger and Advocate. Kirtland, OH. Oct. 1834–Sept. 1837.

McLellin, William E. Journal, 18 July–20 Nov. 1831. William E. McLellin, Papers, 1831–1836, 1877–1878. CHL. Also available as Jan Shipps and John W. Welch, eds., *The Journals of William E. McLellin, 1831–1836* (Provo, UT: BYU Studies; Urbana: University of Illinois Press, 1994).

———. Letter, Independence, MO, to Joseph Smith III, [Plano, IL], July 1872. Letters and Documents Copied from Originals in the Office of the Church Historian, Reorganized Church, no date. Typescript. CHL. Original at CCLA.

Minute Book 1 / "Conference A," 1832–1837. CHL. Also available as Fred C. Collier and William S. Harwell, eds., *Kirtland Council Minute Book* (Salt Lake City: Collier's Publishing, 1996).

Minute Book 2 / "The Conference Minutes and Record Book of Christ's Church of Latter Day Saints," 1838–ca. 1839, 1842, 1844. CHL. Also available as Donald Q. Cannon and Lyndon W. Cook, eds., *Far West Record: Minutes of the Church of Jesus Christ of Latter-day Saints, 1830–1844* (Salt Lake City: Deseret Book, 1983).

"Minutes of First Presidency, March 1898 to September 1907, Record No. 1." CCLA.

Missouri Republican. St. Louis. 1822–1919.

Painesville Republican. Painesville, OH. 1836–1841.

Pratt, Parley P. *The Autobiography of Parley Parker Pratt, One of the Twelve Apostles of the Church of Jesus Christ of Latter-Day Saints, Embracing His Life, Ministry and Travels, with Extracts, in Prose and Verse, from His Miscellaneous Writings.* Edited by Parley P. Pratt Jr. New York: Russell Brothers, 1874.

Quorum of the Twelve Apostles, Record / Quorum of the Twelve Apostles. "A Record of the Transactions of the Twelve Apostles of the Church of the Latter Day Saints from the Time of Their Call to the Apostleship Which Was on the 14th Day of Feby. AD 1835," Feb.–Aug. 1835. In Patriarchal Blessings, 1833–, vol. 2. CHL.

Revelations Collection, 1831–ca. 1844, 1847, 1861, ca. 1876. CHL.

Roberts, Brigham H. "History of the Mormon Church." *Americana* 1 (Dec. 1909): 1016–1025. Also available in B. H. Roberts, *A Comprehensive History of the Church of Jesus Christ of Latter-day Saints: Century I* (Salt Lake City: Deseret News, 1930), 1:157–166.

Skousen, Royal, ed. *The Original Manuscript of the Book of Mormon: Typographical Facsimile of the Extant Text.* Provo, UT: Foundation for Ancient Research and Mormon Studies, Brigham Young University, 2001.

———, ed. *The Printer's Manuscript of the Book of Mormon: Typographical Facsimile of the Entire Text in Two Parts.* Part 1, *Copyright, 1830 Preface, 1 Nephi 1:0–Alma 17:26.* Provo, UT: Foundation for Ancient Research and Mormon Studies, Brigham Young University, 2001.

Smith, Joseph. In addition to the entry that follows, see entries under "JS."

Smith, Joseph. Collection, 1827–1846. CHL.

Smith, Joseph Fielding. Letter, Salt Lake City, UT, to John R. Haldeman, Independence, MO, 24 May 1907. Joseph Fielding Smith, Papers, 1893–1973. CHL.

Smith, Lucy Mack. History, 1844–1845. 18 books. CHL. Also available in Lavina Fielding Anderson, ed., *Lucy's Book: A Critical Edition of Lucy Mack Smith's Family Memoir* (Salt Lake City: Signature Books, 2001).

———. History, 1845. CHL.

Smith, Walter W. Letter, Independence, MO, to R. L. Fulk, Ogden, UT, 13 Dec. 1919. Subject Folder Collection, Book of Commandments. CCLA.

———. Letter, Independence, MO, to S. A. Burgess, Independence, MO, 15 Apr. 1926. J. F. Curtis, Papers. CCLA.

———. Letter, Independence, MO, to the RLDS First Presidency, Independence, MO, 14 Sept. 1925. Whitmer Papers. CCLA.

Stein, Stephen J. "America's Bibles: Canon, Commentary, and Community." *Church History* 64, no. 2 (1995): 169–184.

Times and Seasons. Commerce/Nauvoo, IL. Nov. 1839–Feb. 1846.

Utah Christian Advocate. Salt Lake City. Jan. 1884–Nov. 1887.

Van Dam, Cornelis. *The Urim and Thummim: A Means of Revelation in Ancient Israel.* Winona Lake, IN: Eisenbrauns, 1997.

Verily, I say unto you, concerning your brethren who have been afflicted. [Kirtland, OH: ca. Jan. 1834]. Copy at CHL.

Wadsworth, Nathaniel Hinckley. "Copyright Laws and the 1830 Book of Mormon." *BYU Studies* 45, no. 3 (2006): 77–99.

Wallace, Anthony F. C. *The Death and Rebirth of the Seneca*. New York: Knopf, 1970.

Correspondence of Items in Revelation Books 1 and 2 with Selected Published Versions

The following table is intended to help readers refer from the manuscript copy of each revelation or other item found in Revelation Books 1 and 2 to published versions of that same item. This table does not account for substantive revisions made to revelations or other items after they were first copied into the manuscript books; significant revisions will be identified in the appropriate volumes of the Documents series. Nor does this table provide a comprehensive list of all JS revelations and similar items; it lists only the items that were copied into the manuscript books published in this volume. A table titled Corresponding Section Numbers in Editions of the Doctrine and Covenants, found on page 497 of the first volume of the Journals series, provides cross-reference information for additional JS revelations and other similar items not listed in the following table.

The first column in the table gives the standard date of each item, based on careful study of original sources. The "standard date" is the date a revelation was originally dictated or recorded. If that date is ambiguous or unknown, the standard date is the best approximation of the date, based on existing evidence. The standard date provides a way to identify each item and situate it chronologically with other documents, but it cannot be assumed that every date corresponds to the day an item was first dictated or recorded. In some cases, an item was recorded without a date notation. It is also possible that a few items were first dictated on a date other than the date surviving manuscripts bear, including the manuscripts published in this volume. The dates found in this table were assigned based on all available evidence, including later attempts by JS and his contemporaries to recover date, place, and circumstances.

Where surviving sources provide conflicting information about dating, editorial judgment has been exercised to select the most likely date (occasionally only an approximate month), based on the most reliable sources. In cases in which two or more items bear the same date, they have been listed in the order in which they most likely originated, and a letter of the alphabet has been appended, providing each item a unique editorial title (for example, Oct. 1830–A or Oct. 1830–B). Information on dating issues will accompany publication of these items in the Documents series.

The second and third columns indicate the manuscript page numbers for each item in Revelation Books 1 and 2. Some items appear in both manuscript books. Because Revelation Book 1 is missing several leaves, it is impossible to give inclusive page ranges for some items. In such cases, the beginning page number can be determined from an index written in the original manuscript book, and this number is marked with an asterisk (*).

The fourth column shows the date an item was published in *The Evening and the Morning Star,* the church's first newspaper. The date given is the date of the issue in which the item was published as a separate document (either completely or in extracted form), not the date of any issue in which the item may simply have been quoted in editorial matter. The remaining five columns provide the number of the chapter (in the case of the Book of Commandments) or section (in the case of editions of the Doctrine and Covenants) in which the item was published in one or more of five different canonical editions, the first three of which were initiated by JS. Full bibliographic information about these five editions and *The Evening and the Morning Star* is given in the list of works cited. See also the Scriptural References section in the introduction to the Works Cited for more information about the origins of the Doctrine and Covenants and other Mormon scriptures.

Information in this table is presented in the order of the dates in the first column, which is not necessarily the same order as the contents of this volume. For a list of the contents of this volume in order, see Detailed Contents of Revelation Books (page xi herein).

Key to column titles

RB1:   Revelation Book 1
RB2:   Revelation Book 2
Star: *The Evening and the Morning Star*
1833:   Book of Commandments
1835:   Doctrine and Covenants, 1835 edition, part 2
1844:   Doctrine and Covenants, 1844 edition, part 2
1981:   Doctrine and Covenants, 1981 edition, The Church of Jesus Christ of Latter-day Saints
2004:   Doctrine and Covenants, 2004 edition, Community of Christ

| | | | | JS-Era Canon | | | | |
Date	RB1	RB2	Star	1833	1835	1844	1981	2004
July 1828	1–2			2	30	30	3	2
Feb. 1829	2–3			3	31	31	4	4
Mar. 1829	3*			4	32	32	5	5
Apr. 1829–A	5*			5	8	8	6	6
ca. Apr. 1829	8–12			9	36	36	10	3
Apr. 1829–B	12–13			7	34	34	8	8
Apr. 1829–C	13–14			6	33	33	7	7
Apr. 1829–D	14–15			8	35	35	9	9
May 1829–A[1]	15*			10	37	37	11	10
June 1829–A	17*			12	39	39	14	12
June 1829–B	18*			15	43	43	18	16
June 1829–C	20*			13	40	40	15	13
June 1829–D	21*			14	41	41	16	14
ca. June 1829	21–25							
June 1829–E	25*	119–120			42	42	17	15
Mar. 1830	25–28			16	44	44	19	18
6 Apr. 1830	28–29			22	46	46	21	19
Apr. 1830–A	29			17	45:1	45:1	23:1–2	21:1
Apr. 1830–B	29			18	45:2	45:2	23:3	21:2
Apr. 1830–C	29–30			19	45:3	45:3	23:4	21:3
Apr. 1830–D	30			20	45:4	45:4	23:5	21:4
Apr. 1830–E	30			21	45:5	45:5	23:6–7	21:5
ca. early 1830	30–31							
10 Apr. 1830	52–58		June 1832, June 1833	24	2	2	20	17
16 Apr. 1830	32		June 1832	23	47	47	22	20
July 1830–A	32–34			25	9	9	24	23
July 1830–B	34			27	49	49	26	25
July 1830–C	34–35			26	48	48	25	24
ca. Aug. 1830	35–36		Mar. 1833	28	50	50	27	26
Sept. 1830–A	36–40		Sept. 1832	29	10	10	29	28
Sept. 1830–B	40–41			30	51	51	28	27
Sept. 1830–C	42			31	52:1	52:1	30:1–4	29:1
Sept. 1830–D	42			32	52:2	52:2	30:5–8	29:2

1. This table does not include a revelation dated May 1829–B [D&C 12] because it was not copied into Revelation Book 1 or 2.

CORRESPONDENCE OF ITEMS IN REVELATION BOOKS 1 AND 2

Date	RB1	RB2	*Star*	JS-Era Canon				
				1833	1835	1844	1981	2004
Sept. 1830–E	43			33	52:3	52:3	30:9–11	29:3
Sept. 1830–F	43–44			34	53	53	31	30
Oct. 1830–A		83–84			54	54	32	31
Oct. 1830–B	44–45			35	55	55	33	32
4 Nov. 1830	45–46			36	56	56	34	33
ca. Dec. 1830	60–61	94–95; 117			73	74	74	74
7 Dec. 1830	46–48			37	11	11	35	34
9 Dec. 1830	48–49			38	57	57	36	35
30 Dec. 1830	49			39	58	58	37	37
2 Jan. 1831	49–52		Jan. 1833	40	12	12	38	38
5 Jan. 1831	58–60			41	59	59	39	39
6 Jan. 1831	60			42	60	60	40	40
4 Feb. 1831	61–62	93–94		43	61	61	41	41
9 Feb. 1831	62–67		July 1832	44	13:1–19	13:1–19	42:1–73	42:1–19
Feb. 1831–A	67–70		Oct. 1832	45	14	14	43	43
Feb. 1831–B	70–71			46	62	62	44	44
23 Feb. 1831	67²	117–118	July 1832	47:21–24	13:20	13:20	42:74–77	42:20
ca. 7 Mar. 1831	71–76		June 1832	48	15	15	45	45
ca. 8 Mar. 1831–A	76–78		Aug. 1832	49	16	16	46	46
ca. 8 Mar. 1831–B	79–80	12–13		50	63	63	47	47
10 Mar. 1831	79			51	64	64	48	48
7 May 1831	80–82		Nov. 1832	52	65	65	49	49
9 May 1831	82–85		Aug. 1832	53	17	17	50	50
15 May 1831	85	91–92						
20 May 1831	86–87	87–89			23	23	51	51
6 June 1831	87–89			54	66	66	52	52
8 June 1831	89–90			55	66³	67	53	53
10 June 1831	90–91			56	67	68	54	54
14 June 1831	91			57	68	69	55	55
15 June 1831	91–93			58	69	70	56	56
20 July 1831	93–94	89–91			27	27	57	57
1 Aug. 1831	94–98			59	18	18	58	58
7 Aug. 1831	98–100		July 1832	60	19	19	59	59
8 Aug. 1831	100–101			61	70	71	60	60
12 Aug. 1831	101–103		Dec. 1832	62	71	72	61	61
13 Aug. 1831	104			63	72	73	62	62
30 Aug. 1831	104–108		Feb. 1833	64	20	20	63	63
11 Sept. 1831	108–111			65	21	21	64	64
29 Oct. 1831	111–112	95–97			74	75	66	66
30 Oct. 1831	112	87	Sept. 1832		24	24	65	65
ca. 1 Nov. 1831	121							
1 Nov. 1831–A	113–114		Oct. 1832		22	22	68	68

2. A portion of this revelation is found on a slip of paper attached to manuscript page 67.

3. The second of two sections numbered 66. Numbering remains one off for subsequent sections within the 1835 edition.

CORRESPONDENCE OF ITEMS IN REVELATION BOOKS 1 AND 2

Date	RB1	RB2	Star	JS-Era Canon				
				1833	1835	1844	1981	2004
1 Nov. 1831–B	125–127		Mar. 1833	1	1	1	1	1
2 Nov. 1831	114–115				25	25	67	67
3 Nov. 1831	116–121; 1–[6] (appendix)		May 1833		100	108	133	108
11 Nov. 1831–A	122				28	28	69	69
11 Nov. 1831–B	122–123	84–86			3 (partial)[4]	3 (partial)[5]	107 (partial)[6]	104 (partial)[7]
12 Nov. 1831	124–125				26	26	70	70
1 Dec. 1831	134[a]	11–12			90	91	71	71
4 Dec. 1831	132–134[a]	13–15[8]	Dec. 1832		89	90	72	72
10 Jan. 1832	146–147				29	29	73	73
25 Jan. 1832	129–132				87	88	75	75
16 Feb. 1832	135[a]–139	1–10	July 1832		91	92	76	76
27 Feb. 1832		10						
ca. Mar. 1832	141–144						77	
ca. Mar. 1832	144							
1 Mar. 1832	145–146	15–17			75	76	78	77
7 Mar. 1832	147	18–19			77	78	80	79
12 Mar. 1832	147	12			76	77	79	78
15 Mar. 1832	139–140	17–18			79	80	81	80
20 Mar. 1832	148	19						
26 Apr. 1832	128–129				86	87	82	81
30 Apr. 1832	132	93	Jan. 1833		88	89	83	82
29 Aug. 1832	148	19–20			78	79	99	96
22 and 23 Sept. 1832	149–156	20–31			4	4	84	83
6 Dec. 1832	177	31–32			6	6	86	84
25 Dec. 1832	157; 202–203	32–33					87	
27 and 28 Dec. 1832	158–166	33–46	Feb. 1833		7:1–38	7:1–38	88:1–126	85:1–38
3 Jan. 1833	166–167	47–48	Mar. 1833		7:39–46	7:39–46	88:127–141	85:39–46
27 Feb. 1833		48–49						
27 Feb. 1833	167–168	49–51			80	81	89	86
8 Mar. 1833	168–170	51–55			84	85	90	87
9 Mar. 1833		55			92	93	91	88
15 Mar. 1833		55			93	94	92	89
6 May 1833	178–181	56–59			82	83	93	90
1 June 1833	181–182	59–60			95	96	95	92
4 June 1833	182–183	60–61			96	97	96	93
2 Aug. 1833–A	171–172	61–64			81	82	97	94
2 Aug. 1833–B	172–173	64–66			83	84	94	91

4. Verses 31–33, 35–42, 44.

5. Verses 31–33, 35–42, 44.

6. Verses 59–69, 71–72, 74–75, 78–87, 89, 91–92, 99–100.

7. Verses 31–33, 35–42, 44.

8. This revelation was divided into two parts in Revelation Book 2. The second part begins with verse 3 in all editions except the 1981 edition, where it begins with verse 9.

Date	RB1	RB2	*Star*	JS-Era Canon				
				1833	1835	1844	1981	2004
6 Aug. 1833	173–177	66–71			85	86	98	95
12 Oct. 1833		71–72			94	95	100	97
16 and 17 Dec. 1833	183–189	73–83			97	98	101	98
17 Feb. 1834	202 (heading only)	111–115			5	5	102	99
24 Feb. 1834	189–192	108–111				101	103	100
23 Apr. 1834	192–198	100–107			98	99	104	101
28 Apr. 1834	198	111						
22 June 1834	199–201	97–100				102	105	102
25 Nov. 1834		116			99	100	106	103

The Use of Revelation Books 1 and 2 in Preparing the Revelations for Publication

Although Revelation Books 1 and 2 appear to have been used initially as the record copies of revelations, they soon served as copy texts from which to set type for publication. The books contain clear signs of use by printers in Independence, Missouri, and Kirtland, Ohio, to prepare the revelations for publication in *The Evening and the Morning Star,* the Book of Commandments, and the 1835 Doctrine and Covenants. Examining the manuscript books page by page sheds light on the changes made in individual items, but examining all the items together reveals patterns that suggest how these items were prepared for publication.

In lieu of an index, the following three tables present relevant information about the relationship between Revelation Books 1 and 2 and the aforementioned publications. The tables allow comparison of the manuscript books with these early publications and identify important editorial marks made in preparation for each publication. Because nineteenth-century printing standards called for a clean copy to be made from a corrected manuscript before typesetting took place, the presence of editing marks on either manuscript book does not conclusively indicate that the marked pages were used as copy for the actual typesetting.[1] However, the editing marks clearly indicate that these pages were used at some point to prepare the items for publication.

A comprehensive index of the revelations' content and historical context will be available in the Documents series of *The Joseph Smith Papers.*

Table 1: Relationship between Items in Revelation Book 1 and *The Evening and the Morning Star*

Printing of the revelations began in June 1832 in the church's first newspaper, *The Evening and the Morning Star.* Two months earlier, a committee overseeing the publication of the revelations appointed William W. Phelps, Oliver Cowdery, and John Whitmer to review the revelations and "select for printing such as shall be deemed by them proper, as dictated by the Spirit & make all necessary verbal corrections."[2] Nineteen of the twenty-two items in Revelation Book 1 that were published in *The Evening and the Morning Star* contain editing marks that are first reflected in that publication. All the items published in the newspaper also appear in Revelation Book 1, with the exception of a portion of one revelation.[3] Five revelations are marked with double slashes that likely identify portions of the text that were to be published. Five items have inked or etched marks that correspond to line breaks in the newspaper.[4] These are referred to in the table as "end-of-line marks," and they likely indicate that the manuscript page itself, rather than a clean copy, was used to typeset the page.

The items in table 1 are listed in order of publication in *The Evening and the Morning Star,* allowing analysis of how Revelation Book 1 was used to prepare items for publication therein. For example, certain editing marks, such as end-of-line marks, appear more often in items that were printed in the

---

1. This accepted standard was captured by De Vinne, *The Printers' Price List,* 402, as excerpted in Rummonds, *Nineteenth-Century Printing Practices,* 2:822–823.

2. Minute Book 2, 30 Apr. 1832; see also p. xxvi herein.

3. The October 1832 issue of *The Evening and the Morning Star* contains the portion of Revelation, 23 Feb. 1831 [D&C 42:78–93, 74–77] that would become verses 78–93, which is not found in Revelation Book 1.

4. Marks etched into manuscript pages were likely made with a bodkin or a printer's awl.

newspaper's earlier issues. Four revelations in Revelation Book 1, printed toward the end of the *Star*'s publication in Missouri, contain no redactions made for that publication. The absence of such marks in these revelations suggests that other sources may have been used for later printing.

The first column lists the issue in which each item was published as a separate document (in either complete or extracted form) in *The Evening and the Morning Star,* not any issue in which the item may simply have been quoted in editorial matter.[5] Where more than one item was published within the same issue of the *Star,* the items are listed in the order they appeared therein. The second column provides the standard date for each item (see page 690 herein for more information) and a bracketed "D&C" reference to the section number in which the item appears in the 1981 Latter-day Saint edition of the Doctrine and Covenants.

The third column indicates the manuscript page numbers of the entire item in Revelation Book 1, and the fourth column notes editing marks in Revelation Book 1 that likely relate to publication in *The Evening and the Morning Star.* For more information about the meaning of such marks, please see the pages where they appear within the present volume—especially the sidenotes, where the marks are explained in detail. "Standard revisions" signifies that an item was revised by one or more of the following methods: adding punctuation; noting capitalization; changing spelling; revising grammar; or inserting, deleting, or substituting words or phrases. If this column is empty, no editing marks appear in Revelation Book 1 that likely relate to publication in the *Star.*

Key to column titles

Star: *The Evening and the Morning Star*

Date: Date of item, followed by section number in Doctrine and Covenants, 1981 edition, The Church of Jesus Christ of Latter-day Saints

RB1: Revelation Book 1

Editing Marks: Editing marks in Revelation Book 1 that likely relate to publication in *The Evening and the Morning Star*

STAR	DATE	RB1	EDITING MARKS
June 1832	10 Apr. 1830 [D&C 20]	52–58	standard revisions; end-of-line mark
June 1832	16 Apr. 1830 [D&C 22]	32	standard revisions; brackets
June 1832	ca. 7 Mar. 1831 [D&C 45]	71–76	standard revisions; end-of-line mark; double slashes
July 1832	9 and 23 Feb. 1831 [D&C 42][6]	62–67[7]	standard revisions; end-of-line marks
July 1832	7 Aug. 1831 [D&C 59]	98–100	standard revisions
July 1832	16 Feb. 1832 [D&C 76]	135[a]–139	standard revisions; end-of-line marks
Aug. 1832	ca. 8 Mar. 1831–A [D&C 46]	76–78	standard revisions; double slashes
Aug. 1832	9 May 1831 [D&C 50]	82–85	standard revisions; double slashes
Sept. 1832	Sept. 1830–A [D&C 29]	36–40	standard revisions
Sept. 1832	30 Oct. 1831 [D&C 65]	112	standard revisions; double slashes
Oct. 1832	23 Feb. 1831 [D&C 42:78–93]		

---

5. The revelations herein that were printed in extracted form are Revelation, 9 and 23 Feb. 1831, pp. 95–107 [D&C 42:11–72, 78–93, 74–77]; Revelation, Feb. 1831–A, pp. 109–113 [D&C 43:15–35]; Revelation, ca. 7 Mar. 1831, pp. 115–125 [D&C 45:1–67, 71]; Revelation, 30 Aug. 1831, pp. 181–189 [D&C 63:1–64]; Revelation, 27 and 28 Dec. 1832, pp. 307–309 [D&C 88:117–126]; and Revelation, 3 Jan. 1833, pp. 309–311 [D&C 88:127–137].

6. Excerpts from these two revelations were combined and printed together in this issue of the *The Evening and the Morning Star.*

7. The portion of Revelation, 23 Feb. 1831 [D&C 42:78–93, 74–77] that would become verses 74–77 is found on a slip of paper attached to manuscript page 67.

Star	Date	RB1	Editing Marks
Oct. 1832	Feb. 1831–A [D&C 43]	67–70	standard revisions; double slashes
Oct. 1832	1 Nov. 1831–A [D&C 68]	113–114	standard revisions
Nov. 1832	7 May 1831 [D&C 49]	80–82	standard revisions
Dec. 1832	12 Aug. 1831 [D&C 61]	101–103	standard revisions
Dec. 1832	4 Dec. 1831 [D&C 72]	132–134[a]	standard revisions; brackets
Jan. 1833	2 Jan. 1831 [D&C 38]	49–52	standard revisions
Jan. 1833	30 Apr. 1832 [D&C 83]	132	
Feb. 1833	27 and 28 Dec. 1832 [D&C 88:1–126]	158–166	
Feb. 1833	30 Aug. 1831 [D&C 63]	104–108	standard revisions; end-of-line mark
Mar. 1833	ca. Aug. 1830 [D&C 27]	35–36	standard revisions
Mar. 1833	1 Nov. 1831–B [D&C 1]	125–127	
Mar. 1833	3 Jan. 1833 [D&C 88:127–141]	166–167	
May 1833	3 Nov. 1831 [D&C 133]	116–121	standard revisions; brackets[8]
June 1833	10 Apr. 1830 [D&C 20][9]	52–58	standard revisions

Table 2: Relationship between Items in Revelation Book 1 and the Book of Commandments

Most revelations recorded in Revelation Book 1 before mid-September 1831 were published in the Book of Commandments.[10] At least nine additional revelations in the manuscript book were likely intended for inclusion in the Book of Commandments, but they were not printed because destruction of the printing office in July 1833 interrupted publication efforts. These nine revelations contain verse numbers and other editorial additions that appear to have been inserted in preparation for publication. Of the items that appear in both the Book of Commandments and the extant portions of Revelation Book 1, all but five contain redactions to the manuscript text.[11]

The Book of Commandments comprises five printed signatures, or gatherings, three of which are identified in Revelation Book 1 with an editing mark called a "take mark," which brackets the last word or words on the manuscript page that correspond to the last page of the printed gathering.[12] Six items in Revelation Book 1 bear notations indicating they should not be printed.[13] None of these items were printed in *The Evening and the Morning Star* and only one was printed in the Book of

---

8. While these brackets appear to have been inserted for publication of this item in the Book of Commandments, it is possible they were put in place for publication in *The Evening and the Morning Star.*

9. Articles and covenants, 10 Apr. 1830, pp. 75–87 herein [D&C 20], appeared in two different issues of *The Evening and the Morning Star.* Most redactions in this item are first reflected in the June 1832 issue, but some redactions are first reflected in chapter 24 of the Book of Commandments or the June 1833 issue of the *Star.*

10. Revelation, May 1829–B [D&C 12] and a portion of Revelation, 23 Feb. 1831 [D&C 42:78–93, 74–77] appear in the Book of Commandments but not in Revelation Book 1.

11. The five items herein that do not contain redactions are Revelation, ca. Aug. 1830, pp. 41–43 [D&C 27]; Revelation, 23 Feb. 1831, p. 107 [D&C 42:78–93, 74–77]; Revelation, 7 May 1831, pp. 133–137 [D&C 49]; Revelation, 7 Aug. 1831, pp. 169–173 [D&C 59]; and Revelation, 1 Nov. 1831–B, pp. 223–227 [D&C 1].

12. These marks appear on manuscript pages 39, 90, and 111. Manuscript pages 12 and 68 are also the last pages of their respective gatherings. It is unknown if such a mark appears on manuscript page 12 because the page is missing from the manuscript book, but no mark is visible on manuscript page 68.

13. See the following herein: Explanation of scripture, ca. Dec. 1830, pp. 91–93 [D&C 74]; Revelation, 15 May 1831, p. 143; Revelation, 20 May 1831, pp. 145–147 [D&C 51]; Revelation, 20 July 1831, pp. 159–161 [D&C 57]; Revelation, 8 Aug. 1831, pp. 173–175 [D&C 60]; and Revelation, 26 Apr. 1832, pp. 229–231 [D&C 82].

Commandments, but in the latter case the notation on the manuscript is stricken, suggesting that the instruction not to print was reversed.[14] The instruction not to publish the other items was later revised, and all but one of these six items appear in the 1835 Doctrine and Covenants.[15]

To facilitate analysis of how items were prepared for publication in the Book of Commandments, the items in table 2 are listed in order of publication therein. It appears, for example, that those preparing the Book of Commandments for publication at times used printed copies of the revelations, if they existed, rather than working directly from Revelation Book 1. This is suggested by the lack of versification or other editing marks in some items that were published in *The Evening and the Morning Star* before being published in the Book of Commandments.

The first column of table 2 lists the number of the chapter in which each item was published in the Book of Commandments. If an item was not printed but contains redactions made in preparation for publication, "NP" for "not printed" appears in this column. The second column provides the standard date for each item (see page 690 herein for more information) and a bracketed "D&C" reference to the section number in which the item appears in the 1981 Latter-day Saint edition of the Doctrine and Covenants.

The third column provides the date each item was published (in either complete or extracted form) in *The Evening and the Morning Star,* and the fourth indicates the manuscript page numbers of these items in Revelation Book 1. A single asterisk (*) appears when both the beginning and ending page of an item are identifiable, but some portion of the item is missing from the volume. Where missing leaves make it impossible to give an inclusive page range for an item, two asterisks (**) appear in this column. In such cases, the beginning page number was determined from the index John Whitmer wrote at the end of the manuscript book.

The fifth column notes editing marks in Revelation Book 1 that likely relate to publication of the Book of Commandments. For more information about the meaning of such marks, please see the pages where they appear within the present volume—especially the sidenotes, where the marks are explained in detail. "Standard revisions" signifies that an item was revised by one or more of the following methods: adding punctuation; noting capitalization; changing spelling; revising grammar; or inserting, deleting, or substituting words or phrases. If this column is empty, no editing marks appear in Revelation Book 1 that likely relate to publication in the Book of Commandments. The leaves missing from Revelation Book 1 also likely contained changes made for this publication.

Key to column titles

1833:   Book of Commandments; "NP" indicates the revelation was not printed therein
Date: Date of item, followed by section number in Doctrine and Covenants, 1981 edition, The Church of Jesus Christ of Latter-day Saints
Star: *The Evening and the Morning Star*
RB1:   Revelation Book 1
Editing Marks: Editing marks in Revelation Book 1 that likely relate to publication in the Book of Commandments

1833	Date	*Star*	RB1	Editing Marks
1	1 Nov. 1831–B [D&C 1]	Mar. 1833	125–127	
2	July 1828 [D&C 3]		1–2	standard revisions
3	Feb. 1829 [D&C 4]		2–3*	added date
4	Mar. 1829 [D&C 5]		3**	
5	Apr. 1829–A [D&C 6]		5**	
6	Apr. 1829–C [D&C 7]		13–14	standard revisions; added date

---

14. Revelation, 8 Aug. 1831, pp. 173–175 herein [D&C 60], was printed as chapter 61 of the Book of Commandments.

15. The revelation not printed in the 1835 Doctrine and Covenants is Revelation, 15 May 1831, p. 143 herein.

1833	Date	*Star*	RB1	Editing Marks
7	Apr. 1829–B [D&C 8]		12–13	standard revisions; added date
8	Apr. 1829–D [D&C 9]		14–15*	standard revisions; added date
9	ca. Apr. 1829 [D&C 10]		8–12*	standard revisions; versification
10	May 1829–A [D&C 11]		15**	
11	May 1829–B [D&C 12]			
12	June 1829–A [D&C 14]		17**	
13	June 1829–C [D&C 15]		20**	
14	June 1829–D [D&C 16]		21**	
15	June 1829–B [D&C 18]		18**	
16	Mar. 1830 [D&C 19]		25–28*	standard revisions; versification
17	Apr. 1830–A [D&C 23:1–2]		29	standard revisions; added date
18	Apr. 1830–B [D&C 23:3]		29	standard revisions; versification
19	Apr. 1830–C [D&C 23:4]		29–30	standard revisions; versification
20	Apr. 1830–D [D&C 23:5]		30	standard revisions; versification
21	Apr. 1830–E [D&C 23:6–7]		30	standard revisions; versification
22	6 Apr. 1830 [D&C 21]		28–29	standard revisions; corrected date
23	16 Apr. 1830 [D&C 22]	June 1832	32	standard revisions
24	10 Apr. 1830 [D&C 20]	June 1832, June 1833	52–58	standard revisions[16]
25	July 1830–A [D&C 24]		32–34	standard revisions; added date
26	July 1830–C [D&C 25]		34–35	standard revisions
27	July 1830–B [D&C 26]		34	standard revisions; versification
28	ca. Aug. 1830 [D&C 27]	Mar. 1833	35–36	
29	Sept. 1830–A [D&C 29]	Sept. 1832	36–40	standard revisions; added date; take mark
30	Sept. 1830–B [D&C 28]		40–41	standard revisions
31	Sept. 1830–C [D&C 30:1–4]		42	standard revisions; versification
32	Sept. 1830–D [D&C 30:5–8]		42	standard revisions; versification
33	Sept. 1830–E [D&C 30:9–11]		43	standard revisions; versification; added date
34	Sept. 1830–F [D&C 31]		43–44	standard revisions; versification
35	Oct. 1830–B [D&C 33]		44–45	standard revisions; versification; added date
36	4 Nov. 1830 [D&C 34]		45–46	standard revisions; versification
37	7 Dec. 1830 [D&C 35]		46–48	standard revisions; versification
38	9 Dec. 1830 [D&C 36]		48–49	standard revisions; versification
39	30 Dec. 1830 [D&C 37]		49	standard revisions; versification
40	2 Jan. 1831 [D&C 38]	Jan. 1833	49–52	standard revisions; versification
41	5 Jan. 1831 [D&C 39]		58–60	standard revisions
42	6 Jan. 1831 [D&C 40]		60	standard revisions; versification
43	4 Feb. 1831 [D&C 41]		61–62	standard revisions; versification
44	9 Feb. 1831 [D&C 42:1–72]	July 1832	62–67	standard revisions; versification
45	Feb. 1831–A [D&C 43]	Oct. 1832	67–70	standard revisions
46	Feb. 1831–B [D&C 44]		70–71	standard revisions

16. Because of the proximity of printing dates, it is unclear whether some redactions in this item were made first for publication in the Book of Commandments (chapter 24) or in the June 1833 issue of *The Evening and the Morning Star.*

1833	Date	Star	RB1	Editing Marks
47	23 Feb. 1831 [D&C 42:78–93, 74–77]	Oct. 1832	67[17]	
48	ca. 7 Mar. 1831 [D&C 45]	June 1832	71–76	standard revisions
49	ca. 8 Mar. 1831–A [D&C 46]	Aug. 1832	76–78	standard revisions; corrected date; "Compared thus far by J & O"
50	ca. 8 Mar. 1831–B [D&C 47]		79–80	standard revisions; versification
51	10 Mar. 1831 [D&C 48]		79	standard revisions
52	7 May 1831 [D&C 49]	Nov. 1832	80–82	
53	9 May 1831 [D&C 50]	Aug. 1832	82–85	standard revisions
54	6 June 1831 [D&C 52]		87–89	standard revisions; versification
55	8 June 1831 [D&C 53]		89–90	standard revisions; versification
56	10 June 1831 [D&C 54]		90–91	standard revisions; versification; take mark
57	14 June 1831 [D&C 55]		91	standard revisions; versification
58	15 June 1831 [D&C 56]		91–93	standard revisions; versification
59	1 Aug. 1831 [D&C 58]		94–98	standard revisions; versification
60	7 Aug. 1831 [D&C 59]	July 1832	98–100	
61	8 Aug. 1831 [D&C 60]		100–101	standard revisions; versification; "~~Not to be printed now~~"
62	12 Aug. 1831 [D&C 61]	Dec. 1832	101–103	standard revisions
63	13 Aug. 1831 [D&C 62]		104	standard revisions; versification
64	30 Aug. 1831 [D&C 63]	Feb. 1833	104–108	standard revisions; versification
65[18]	11 Sept. 1831 [D&C 64]		108–111	standard revisions; versification; take mark
NP	29 Oct. 1831 [D&C 66]		111–112	standard revisions; versification
NP	1 Nov. 1831–A [D&C 68]	Oct. 1832	113–114	standard revisions[19]
NP	2 Nov. 1831 [D&C 67]		114–115	standard revisions; versification
NP	3 Nov. 1831 [D&C 133]	May 1833	116–121	standard revisions; versification; brackets
NP	11 Nov. 1831–A [D&C 69]		122	standard revisions; versification
NP	11 Nov. 1831–B [D&C 107 (partial)]		122–123	standard revisions; versification; corrected date
NP	12 Nov. 1831 [D&C 70]		124–125	standard revisions; versification
NP	1 Dec. 1831 [D&C 71]		134[a]	standard revisions; versification
NP	25 Jan. 1832 [D&C 75]		129–132	standard revisions; versification

---

17. The portion of Revelation, 23 Feb. 1831 [D&C 42:78–93, 74–77] that would become verses 74–77 is found on a slip of paper attached to manuscript page 67.

18. Because printing was disrupted, this revelation was not printed in full.

19. The small introduction not printed in the October 1832 issue of *The Evening and the Morning Star* appears to have been punctuated by William W. Phelps in preparation for publication in the Book of Commandments.

Table 3: Relationship between Items in Revelation Books 1 and 2 and the 1835 Doctrine and Covenants

Those preparing the revelations for publication in the 1835 Doctrine and Covenants initially had access to Revelation Book 2, *The Evening and the Morning Star,* and the Book of Commandments. Revelation Book 1 became a supplemental source for the publication effort after John Whitmer returned to Kirtland in the middle of May 1835, evidently bringing the manuscript book with him. In addition to preparing the Doctrine and Covenants for publication at this time, church leaders were also editing and reprinting all issues of *The Evening and the Morning Star* under the title *Evening and Morning Star.* Editorial changes made in revelations for this reprint are often reflected in the 1835 Doctrine and Covenants as well.

As Oliver Cowdery and others worked on the 1835 Doctrine and Covenants, they likely used *The Evening and the Morning Star* and the Book of Commandments to prepare items that had been previously published, while using the manuscript books to prepare the unpublished items. For example, the items that constitute sections 45–53 and 55–72 of the 1835 Doctrine and Covenants had previously been published in the Book of Commandments. In Revelation Books 1 and 2, these items do not have editing marks made for the 1835 publication, suggesting the Book of Commandments was likely used to prepare them for publication. In contrast, the items that constitute sections 73–77 of the 1835 Doctrine and Covenants had not been published previously, and in Revelation Book 1 all of these items have editing marks made for the 1835 publication.

Editing marks made in Revelation Books 1 and 2 for the 1835 publication are similar. Both manuscript books contain notations made in red grease pencil, which was used to arrange and edit items in the manuscript books. Such grease pencil marks appear not only in these books but also in a copy of the Book of Commandments that was owned by Oliver Cowdery, where many chapters are marked for inclusion in the 1835 publication.[20] Small holes also appear in both manuscript books, suggesting that slips of paper were pinned into the books. Extant slips include editorial corrections, and other slips likely contained editorial corrections or additional material.

Other distinctive editing marks were used as well. Two revelations in Revelation Book 2 that did not appear in any JS-era publication are each crossed out with a large X.[21] Brackets were used intermittently through Revelation Books 1 and 2 to indicate which revelations (or which portions of them) were to be prepared for the 1835 Doctrine and Covenants or earlier publications.

In table 3, the first column lists the number of the section in which each item was published in the 1835 Doctrine and Covenants. The second column provides the standard date for each item (see page 690 herein for more information) and a bracketed "D&C" reference to the section number in which the item appears in the 1981 Latter-day Saint edition of the Doctrine and Covenants. The third column provides the date each item was published (in either complete or extracted form) in *The Evening and the Morning Star,* and the fourth lists the number of the chapter in which each item was published in the Book of Commandments.

The fifth and seventh columns identify the manuscript page numbers of these items in Revelation Books 1 and 2. A single asterisk (*) appears when both the beginning and ending pages of an item are identifiable, but some portion of the item is missing from the volume. Where missing leaves make it impossible to give an inclusive page range for an item, two asterisks (**) appear in the fifth column. In such cases, the beginning page number was determined from the index John Whitmer wrote at the end of Revelation Book 1.

The sixth and eighth columns note editing marks in Revelation Books 1 and 2 that likely relate to publication of the 1835 Doctrine and Covenants. For more information about the meaning of such marks, please see the pages where they appear within the present volume—especially the sidenotes, where the marks are explained in detail. "Standard revisions" signifies that an item was revised by one or more of the following methods: adding punctuation; noting capitalization; changing spelling; revising grammar; or inserting, deleting, or substituting words or phrases. If these columns are

---

20. The Book of Commandments once owned by Oliver Cowdery is located at CHL.

21. See the following herein: Revelation, 27 Feb. 1832, p. 433; and Revelation, 20 Mar. 1832, p. 451.

empty, no editing marks appear in Revelation Books 1 or 2 that likely relate to publication in the 1835 Doctrine and Covenants. The leaves missing from Revelation Book 1 also possibly contained changes made for this publication.

Key to column titles

1835:	Doctrine and Covenants, 1835 edition, part 2
Date:	Date of item, followed by section number in Doctrine and Covenants, 1981 edition, The Church of Jesus Christ of Latter-day Saints
Star:	*The Evening and the Morning Star*
1833:	Book of Commandments
RB1:	Revelation Book 1
RB1 Editing Marks:	Editing marks in Revelation Book 1 that likely relate to publication in the 1835 Doctrine and Covenants
RB2:	Revelation Book 2
RB2 Editing Marks:	Editing marks in Revelation Book 2 that likely relate to publication in the 1835 Doctrine and Covenants

1835	Date	*Star*	1833	RB1	RB1 Editing Marks	RB2	RB2 Editing Marks
1	1 Nov. 1831–B [D&C 1]	Mar. 1833	1	125–127			
2	10 Apr. 1830 [D&C 20]	June 1832, June 1833	24	52–58			
3	11 Nov. 1831–B [D&C 107]			122–123		84–86	
4	22 and 23 Sept. 1832 [D&C 84]			149–156		20–31	standard revisions; small holes;[22] "To go into th[e] covenents"
5	17 Feb. 1834 [D&C 102]			202 (heading only)		111–115	standard revisions; pinholes; "To go into the coven[an]ts"
6	6 Dec. 1832 [D&C 86]			177		31–32	"To go into th[e] covenants"
7	27 and 28 Dec. 1832 and 3 Jan. 1833 [D&C 88]	Feb. 1833, Mar. 1833		158–167		33–48	standard revisions; double slashes; small holes
8	Apr. 1829–A [D&C 6]		5	5**			
9	July 1830–A [D&C 24]		25	32–34			
10	Sept. 1830–A [D&C 29]	Sept. 1832	29	36–40			
11	7 Dec. 1830 [D&C 35]		37	46–48			
12	2 Jan. 1831 [D&C 38]	Jan. 1833	40	49–52			
13	9 and 23 Feb. 1831 [D&C 42][23]	July 1832, Oct. 1832	44, 47	62–67[24]		117–118	
14	Feb. 1831–A [D&C 43]	Oct. 1832	45	67–70			
15	ca. 7 Mar. 1831 [D&C 45]	June 1832	48	71–76	"Compared thus far by J & O"		
16	ca. 8 Mar. 1831–A [D&C 46]	Aug. 1832	49	76–78			
17	9 May 1831 [D&C 50]	Aug. 1832	53	82–85	standard revisions		
18	1 Aug. 1831 [D&C 58]		59	94–98	standard revisions		
19	7 Aug. 1831 [D&C 59]	July 1832	60	98–100			

22. Such holes were likely made by pins used to attach slips of paper to the manuscript books but may also have been made by needles, awls, or other instruments.

23. Excerpts from these two revelations were combined and printed together in the July 1832 issue of *The Evening and the Morning Star*. The portion of Revelation, 23 Feb. 1831 [D&C 42:78–93, 74–77] that would become verses 78–93 was printed in the October 1832 issue of the *Star*.

24. The portion of Revelation, 23 Feb. 1831 [D&C 42:78–93, 74–77] that would become verses 74–77 is found on a slip of paper attached to manuscript page 67.

1835	Date	*Star*	1833	RB1	RB1 Editing Marks	RB2	RB2 Editing Marks
20	30 Aug. 1831 [D&C 63]	Feb. 1833	64	104–108	standard revisions		
21	11 Sept. 1831 [D&C 64]		65	108–111	standard revisions		
22	1 Nov. 1831–A [D&C 68]	Oct. 1832		113–114	standard revisions; asterisk; "No 1"		
23	20 May 1831 [D&C 51]			86–87	standard revisions; pinholes; brackets; "Not printed"[25]	87–89	
24	30 Oct. 1831 [D&C 65]	Sept. 1832		112	standard revisions; "No 3"	87	
25	2 Nov. 1831 [D&C 67]			114–115	standard revisions; "No 4"		
26	12 Nov. 1831 [D&C 70]			124–125	standard revisions; "No 5"		
27	20 July 1831 [D&C 57]			93–94	standard revisions; "No 6"; "Not to be printed at present"	89–91	
28	11 Nov. 1831–A [D&C 69]			122	standard revisions; "No 7"		
29	10 Jan. 1832 [D&C 73]			146–147	"No 8"; "Compared [Read]"		
30	July 1828 [D&C 3]		2	1–2			
31	Feb. 1829 [D&C 4]		3	2–3*			
32	Mar. 1829 [D&C 5]		4	3**			
33	Apr. 1829–C [D&C 7]		6	13–14			
34	Apr. 1829–B [D&C 8]		7	12–13			
35	Apr. 1829–D [D&C 9]		8	14–15*			
36	ca. Apr. 1829 [D&C 10]		9	8–12*			
37	May 1829–A [D&C 11]		10	15**			
38	May 1829–B [D&C 12]		11				
39	June 1829–A [D&C 14]		12	17**			
40	June 1829–C [D&C 15]		13	20**			
41	June 1829–D [D&C 16]		14	21**			
42	June 1829–E [D&C 17]			25**		119–120	
43	June 1829–B [D&C 18]		15	18**			
44	Mar. 1830 [D&C 19]		16	25–28*			
45	Apr. 1830–A; Apr. 1830–B; Apr. 1830–C; Apr. 1830–D; Apr. 1830–E [D&C 23]		17–21	29–30			
46	6 Apr. 1830 [D&C 21]		22	28–29			
47	16 Apr. 1830 [D&C 22]	June 1832	23	32			
48	July 1830–C [D&C 25]		26	34–35			
49	July 1830–B [D&C 26]		27	34			
50	ca. Aug. 1830 [D&C 27]	Mar. 1833	28	35–36			
51	Sept. 1830–B [D&C 28]		30	40–41			
52	Sept. 1830–C; Sept. 1830–D; Sept. 1830–E [D&C 30]		31–33	42–43			
53	Sept. 1830–F [D&C 31]		34	43–44			
54	Oct. 1830–A [D&C 32]					83–84	
55	Oct. 1830–B [D&C 33]		35	44–45			

25. While the five notations indicating the instruction not to publish were not made for the 1835 publication, they are included in this chart to show the reversal of all but one of the original six notations. (See Revelation, 15 May 1831, p. 143 herein.)

1835	DATE	STAR	1833	RB1	RB1 EDITING MARKS	RB2	RB2 EDITING MARKS
56	4 Nov. 1830 [D&C 34]		36	45–46			
57	9 Dec. 1830 [D&C 36]		38	48–49			
58	30 Dec. 1830 [D&C 37]		39	49			
59	5 Jan. 1831 [D&C 39]		41	58–60			
60	6 Jan. 1831 [D&C 40]		42	60			
61	4 Feb. 1831 [D&C 41]		43	61–62		93–94	
62	Feb. 1831–B [D&C 44]		46	70–71			
63	ca. 8 Mar. 1831–B [D&C 47]		50	79–80		12–13	
64	10 Mar. 1831 [D&C 48]		51	79			
65	7 May 1831 [D&C 49]	Nov. 1832	52	80–82			
66	6 June 1831 [D&C 52]		54	87–89			
66[26]	8 June 1831 [D&C 53]		55	89–90			
67	10 June 1831 [D&C 54]		56	90–91			
68	14 June 1831 [D&C 55]		57	91			
69	15 June 1831 [D&C 56]		58	91–93			
70	8 Aug. 1831 [D&C 60]		61	100–101	"Not to be printed now"		
71	12 Aug. 1831 [D&C 61]	Dec. 1832	62	101–103			
72	13 Aug. 1831 [D&C 62]		63	104			
73	ca. Dec. 1830 [D&C 74]			60–61	"Not to be printed"; standard revisions; versification; "For the covenants"	94–95; 117	
74	29 Oct. 1831 [D&C 66]			111–112	standard revisions	95–97	
75	1 Mar. 1832 [D&C 78]			145–146	standard revisions; small holes; code words	15–17	small holes
76	12 Mar. 1832 [D&C 79]			147	standard revisions	12	
77	7 Mar. 1832 [D&C 80]			147	standard revisions	18–19	small holes
78	29 Aug. 1832 [D&C 99]			148		19–20	small holes
79	15 Mar. 1832 [D&C 81]			139–140	red grease pencil[27]	17–18	small holes
80	27 Feb. 1833 [D&C 89]			167–168		49–51	
81	2 Aug. 1833–A [D&C 97]			171–172		61–64	standard revisions; versification; red grease pencil
82	6 May 1833 [D&C 93]			178–181		56–59	pinholes
83	2 Aug. 1833–B [D&C 94]			172–173		64–66	standard revisions
84	8 Mar. 1833 [D&C 90]			168–170	standard revisions; versification	51–55	pinholes
85	6 Aug. 1833 [D&C 98]			173–177		66–71	pinholes
86	26 Apr. 1832 [D&C 82]			128–129	standard revisions; pinholes; asterisk; red grease pencil; large X; "Not to be published now"		
87	25 Jan. 1832 [D&C 75]			129–132	standard revisions; versification; red grease pencil; "Section LXXXVII"		
88	30 Apr. 1832 [D&C 83]	Jan. 1833		132	red grease pencil; large X	93	standard revisions

26. The second of two sections numbered 66. Numbering remains one off for subsequent sections within the 1835 edition.

27. The single redaction made with red grease pencil changes "Jesse Gause" to "Frederick G. Williams." For all other changes that appear in this section of the 1835 Doctrine and Covenants, no corresponding redactions appear in Revelation Book 1.

1835	Date	*Star*	1833	RB1	RB1 Editing Marks	RB2	RB2 Editing Marks
89	4 Dec. 1831 [D&C 72]	Dec. 1832		132–134[a]	red grease pencil; large X	13–15	small holes
90	1 Dec. 1831 [D&C 71]			134[a]		11–12	
91	16 Feb. 1832 [D&C 76]	July 1832		135[a]–139		1–10	
92	9 Mar. 1833 [D&C 91]					55	brackets
93	15 Mar. 1833 [D&C 92]					55	standard revisions; code words
94	12 Oct. 1833 [D&C 100]					71–72	standard revisions
95	1 June 1833 [D&C 95]			181–182		59–60	
96	4 June 1833 [D&C 96]			182–183		60–61	standard revisions; pinholes; code words
97	16 and 17 Dec. 1833 [D&C 101]			183–189		73–83	
98	23 Apr. 1834 [D&C 104]			192–198	standard revisions; code words; red grease pencil	100–107	
99	25 Nov. 1834 [D&C 106]					116	pinholes
100	3 Nov. 1831 [D&C 133]	May 1833		116–121			

Acknowledgments

The Joseph Smith Papers Project is made possible by the help and cooperation of hundreds of people. Though we here primarily identify the individuals and institutions who have contributed to this volume, we are mindful of our ever-increasing debt to our many colleagues and friends who are assisting with later volumes or more general undertakings.

Administrators and officials of The Church of Jesus Christ of Latter-day Saints, Salt Lake City, and Brigham Young University, Provo, Utah, have provided support and resources that have facilitated this work. We give special acknowledgment to management and staff at the Church History Library, Salt Lake City, where the bulk of the Joseph Smith papers are housed. We also express deep appreciation to officials of the Community of Christ, Independence, Missouri, who made the four loose leaves from Revelation Book 1 available from their archives. In addition to the Church History Library and the Community of Christ Library-Archives, other repositories have provided valuable material and assistance, including L. Tom Perry Special Collections, Harold B. Lee Library, Brigham Young University; and the Family History Library, The Church of Jesus Christ of Latter-day Saints, Salt Lake City.

We express special thanks to Community of Christ historian Mark Scherer and archivist Ronald E. Romig for helping coordinate the photographing of the four loose leaves of Revelation Book 1. Chris McAfee and Russell C. Fuhriman of the Church History Library's conservation lab provided necessary work in conserving the fragile pages of Revelation Book 1, including the loose leaves. Glenn N. Rowe, of the Church History Department, The Church of Jesus Christ of Latter-day Saints, provided important transcription work and careful custodianship of the documents.

The Joseph Smith Papers Project relies on the skills and dedication of employees of the Church History Department; faculty, researchers, and editors at Brigham Young University; retired scholars and other volunteers; and independent researchers and editors. Among those who contributed to the development of this volume are Linda Hunter Adams, Mark Ashurst-McGee, Ronald O. Barney, Brian P. Barton, Noel R. Barton, Alexander L. Baugh, Kathryn Burnside, Jeffrey G. Cannon, Lee Ann Clanton, Jared P. Collette, Justin Collings, Lia Suttner Collings, Joseph F. Darowski, Kay Darowski, Karen Lynn Davidson, Patrick C. Dunshee, William G. Hartley, Kay Hausheer, Maurice G. Hausheer, Sharalyn D. Howcroft, Elizabeth L. Jensen, Emily W. Jensen, Carol H. Jones, Christopher C. Jones, Viola Knecht, Mary-Celeste Lewis, Mark I. Macdonald, Andrea Maxfield, Kaitlin W. Merkley, Steven Motteshard, Helen Jo Murphy, Benjamin E. Park, Martha Parker, Max Parkin, Elizabeth Pinborough, Ryan W. Saltzgiver, Heather Seferovich, Alex D. Smith, Kelli M. Smith, Anna Staley, Elizabeth Stubbs, Grant Underwood, Norman E. Waite, Kathryn Jensen Wall, F. Michael Watson, Lorin Welker, Vivian Wellman, David J. Whittaker, and Ellen Yates. We also wish to thank Jed Woodworth, a former Joseph Smith Papers editor, whose significant contributions to *Journals, Volume 1* we neglected to mention in the acknowledgments of that volume.

Employees of several other departments at church headquarters in Salt Lake City provided invaluable assistance. Welden C. Andersen, of the Audiovisual Department, shot the textual photographs in this volume. Charles M. Baird, Materials Management Department, prepared the photographs for publication with assistance from Stephen L. Chamberlain, of the same department. The quality and quantity of the textual photographs published herein attest to the expertise of these three gentlemen and to the generosity of their respective managers in allowing us to use so much of their time. Among the skilled professionals in the Curriculum Department who advised us on editorial or design matters are Neil E. Brown, Susan Hainsworth, Daniel B. Hogan, Scott M. Mooy, Andrew D. Olsen, and Scott Welty. We benefited from the wisdom of Craig K. Sedgwick and his colleagues at the church's Salt Lake Printing Center, a division of the Materials Management Department. Clark D. Christensen, Information and Communications Systems Department, provided technical support.

We are grateful for the expertise of Gene A. Ware, Brigham Young University, who applied multispectral imaging techniques to assist with the recovery of badly faded text. Management and staff at Deseret Book Company, Salt Lake City, expertly and patiently assisted with the design, typesetting, printing, and distribution of this volume. In particular, we thank Sheri L. Dew, Cory H. Maxwell, Anne Sheffield, Richard Erickson, Suzanne Brady, Laurie C. Cook, Gail Halladay, Sophie Barth, Vicki Parry, and Lani Rush. We thank Scott Eggers, of Scott Eggers Design, Salt Lake City, for designing the dust jacket and cover. Curt Bench, owner of Benchmark Books, Salt Lake City; Jared Smith, an assistant editor with Gibbs Smith Publisher, Layton, Utah; and Doug Maxwell, director of Print Services at Brigham Young University, shared helpful insights on the design of the volume.

In addition to generous support from the Church History Library and Brigham Young University, our institutional sponsors, the project has been blessed by generous funding by Larry H. and Gail Miller. Larry passed away before this volume was completed, but we are grateful he was able to read and express enthusiasm about earlier drafts. His boundless energy and his vision for what this project could be will always inspire us. We thank the Miller family for their continuing support and friendship.

Finally, we express gratitude to our families, who have stood by us during the long process of preparing this volume.

FACSIMILE EDITION OF MANUSCRIPT REVELATION BOOKS

Art direction by Richard Erickson
Cover and jacket designed by Scott Eggers
Interior designed by Richard Erickson
Typeset by Laurie C. Cook and Riley M. Lorimer
Printed and bound by Worzalla Publishing Company, Stevens Point, Wisconsin

Composed in Adobe Garamond Pro
Printed on 80# Lustro Dull White
Bound in Rainbow Brillianta

Distributed by Deseret Book Company, Salt Lake City, Utah